Santa's Price Guide to Contemporary Christmas Collectibles

Santa's Price Guide to

Contemporary Christmas Collectibles

by Beth Dees

krause publications

700 East State Street, Iola, WI 54990-0001
www.krause.com

Photo Credits: pp. 240 - Stephanie Mann; Photographs are used with the permission of the companies whose products they represent:

June McKenna Collectibles, Inc.
Santa's Crystal Valley
Pipka Collectibles

The Boyds Collection
The Bearstone Collection
The Folkstone Collection
The Dollstone Collection
The Shoe Box Bears

Byers' Choice Ltd.
The Carolers Figurines

Old World Christmas
Annalee Mobilitee Dolls, Inc.

Possible Dreams
Crinkle Claus
The Clothtique Santa Collection

Hallmark Cards Inc.

Kurt S. Adler Collectibles
Polonaise Collection

Steinbach Nutcrackers
Christopher Radko
Prizm/Figi Collectibles
Lynn Haney
Lynn West
Margaret Furlong
Vaillancourt Folk Art

Library of Congress Cataloging-in-Publication Data: 82-84065
ISBN: 0-87341-528-0

Acknowledgements

Glenda Dees, my mother, deserves much credit for this book. A lover of all things Christmas and co-owner of a year-round Christmas shop, she encouraged, suggested, informed and spent hours helping me. Her business partner, Elizabeth Bishop, came up with the book idea while talking with Dan Alexander, publisher of Books Americana, which Krause Publications later purchased.

Special thanks to Suzanne and Michael Belofsky with ***MSdataBase Solutions Inc.*** who received so many of my calls for help. Michael created a directory file on his computer in my honor. I appreciate the patient and gentle guidance of my editor at Krause, Elizabeth Noll. John Jones provided friendship and editing skills. Terri Cowie helped with the initial stages of the book. Thanks go to Ellen Gordon with ***The Collection Connection,*** Melanie and Brad Benshaw with ***Radko's Glitter Newsletter,*** and to The Collector's Society of America for sharing price guide information with me. Peter and Jeanne George provided background information about Department 56 in their book ***"Collecting Department 56*."*** Merna Dudley at Krause was kind enough to share ornaments from her Hallmark Keepsake Ornament collection to be photographed.

My thanks go to the artists/designers/owners and company representatives who took their time to gather and send critical information and photographs. I am grateful to my friends who provided words of encouragement throughout the process. Others who provided either information or support were: my father, Joe Dees; Arlene Wagner, director for the Steinbach Nutcracker Museum; Pam Danziger with ***Business Collectibles Newsletter,*** Tom Smith, Mickey Frabott, Billie Ayers, Marilyn Bassett, Helen Reid, Sylvie Wilkerson and Allegra, and David Hackett.

* Regrettably, an agreement with Department 56 was reached after the final stages of production on this publication. Information about Department 56 is not included in this guide. However, the company is mentioned throughout this publication with great respect and gratitude.

Contents

Acknowledgments 5
Introduction 7

Section One: Common Questions & Answers About Collecting
Looking, Finding, Buying, Selling 10

Section Two: For Your Information
How your computer can help 15
Keeping up with your collectibles 15
How to use this price guide 16

Section Three: Designer Background
Artists/Designers/Companies - biographies, features and information
Individual tips on care and display

Annalee Mobilitee Dolls 17
Boyds Bears 21
– Folkstones, Dollstones and Bearstones 23
Byers' Choice 25
– Carolers 25
Christopher Radko 29
Figi Collectibles (Santa's Crystal Valley) 65
Hallmark 70
– Keepsake Ornaments 70
June McKenna 73
Lynn Haney 79
Lynn West 83
Margaret Furlong 87
Old World Christmas 91
– Ornaments 91
Pipka Santas 95
Polonaise 98
Possible Dreams 101
– Clothtique 101
– Crinkle Claus 102
Steinbach Nutcrackers 105
Vaillancourt Folk Art 109

Section Four: Resource Listing
Publications 220
Organizations 222

Glossary 223
Index 225
About the Author 226

Introduction

Missing the beauty and wonder of the subject, Scrooge would grumble "Bah Humbug" in the face of anyone about to spend money on a Christmas collectible. However, he would undoubtedly turn around and discretely invest in a copy of *Santa's Price Guide to Contemporary Christmas Collectibles.* The shrewd old soul would appreciate the value of possessing such a wealth of information about premier Christmas collectibles available today.

Scrooge might be motivated to begin collecting for the investment. Your motives may go well beyond investment potentials. You might collect for the eye and soul appeal of Christmas collectibles. You may enjoy the search or the excitement of the find. Or, you may simply want to enjoy them now and save them for the future.

Whether you collect for love, money–or both–*Santa's Price Guide to Contemporary Christmas Collectibles* will assist you in becoming a better collector. This guide is selective, rather than definitive. It includes nineteen contemporary Christmas collectible lines. Popularity of these lines have been proven by increasing in value and demand. Some of the collectibles, such as Annalee Mobilitee Dolls and Steinbach Nutcrackers, have been around for dozens of years. Others, like Santa's Crystal Valley figurines and Pipka's Santas are relatively new. This book is an example of what Santa himself would collect--if he had the time of course.

THIS BOOK IS USEFUL TO:

- **Find the secondary market price for a piece.**
- **Learn the story behind a collectible.**
- **Get an overview of collecting.**
- **Get a good look at some of the top Christmas collectible lines.**

In Santa's List:

- A comprehensive price guide for nineteen of the most popular contemporary Christmas collectible lines listing more than 12,000 items.
- Detailed information on nineteen of the most desired Christmas collectible lines in the country.
- Each section offers a history list of current, plus retired pieces, background on the artist and/or company behind the collectible, photographs, and special tips on care and display.
- Learn how to make it easier, and more profitable, to keep up with your collection.
- Discover new ways to display your Christmas collectibles--for the holiday season or year round.
- Find easy definitions for terms every collector needs to know.
- Discover what collector's clubs can do for you and where to find them.
- Go online with your computer and find scores of current prices, collector's clubs and other collectible information sources.

Santa's Price Guide secondary market prices are meant to be used as general guidelines when buying, selling and insuring your collection. The secondary market is ever changing. Look at several resources to help determine the most realistic price. If your source for information on secondary market prices also sells the collectibles themselves, consider whether this will affect its objectivity. Know that some secondary market prices remain stable for years, while others fluctuate quickly; even the season or a geographical region may affect the price. The information in this book is a compilation of research from collectors, dealers, numerous publications and other computer databases. Where possible, the artists, owners or manufacturers have helped to ensure accuracy by reviewing the basic information about the collectibles.

Price Guide Key

Order Number - Some companies use order numbers as the primary means of identifying each piece. Others, such as June McKenna Collectibles or early Annalee Mobilitee Dolls, rely instead on the name or title of a piece.

Title - Name given to specific collectible.

Type Number - Numbers used as a means of identifying a specific piece.

Theme - The subject matter of a specific collectible.

Retired - Refers to a collectible that is no longer in circulation. This may be show by the term "Yes," meaning the collectible has been retired. Some listings state the year it was retired.

Introduction Year - The year the collectible first appeared on the retail market.

Issue Price/Original Retail - The original manufacturer price of a collectible when it first appears on the retail market.

Secondary Market Price - A guide reflecting the average price a mint condition collectible would bring on the secondary market.

PLEASE NOTE:

This book includes a listing of each collectible line, including current and retired pieces. Price guides for individual collectibles begin on page 114. Collectibles are listed alphabetically by manufacturer and alphabetically by theme.

Section 1: Common Questions & Answers About Collecting

Q - What is a Christmas collectible?

A - Truth is, the definition isn't black or white. Some consider those sequin-covered Styrofoam balls, made as a child, to be a collectible. Others consider a priceless, collection of early 1900s, European, papier-mâché Santas, which have become family heirlooms to be collectibles. To yet another, a Christmas collectible is J.D. Nichols Toy Shop from ***Department 56's Dickens' Village Series®****. Generally speaking, a collectible can be anything someone accumulates as a hobby.*

For the purposes of this book a collectible is defined as an item that has market value. More than likely, a collectible is appreciated for its beauty, detail, appeal and craftsmanship. Many collectibles are new. However, more often they tend to be old and not necessarily antiques.

Unlike the average pack rat who collects everything, a collector is someone on a mission, looking for a specific item or items that will bring pleasure and/or profit. Collectors can be picky, or more attractively stated, selective about what they collect. Christmas collectors are even more discriminating!

Collecting probably began in the Stone Ages. Cave men and women, with big knees and hair on their shoulders, may have agreed that some stones were more precious than others. They most likely took them home and proudly displayed their "treasures" around the fire. Thousands of years later, we continue the "treasure hunt." Today an estimated twenty two million collectors have "caught the fever" of year-round Christmas collecting. Christmas is number one among theme collectors.

"Christmas is a natural for collecting," said Pam Danziger, president of ***Unity Marketing****. Unity Marketing reports on the giftware and collectibles industry. "Nearly every family has a collection of holiday ornaments and decorations, but serious collectors take Christmas to an entirely new level. While the typical household might purchase two-to-three special ornaments each year, a collector will buy six-to-twelve new ornaments and spend three-to-five times as much on their Christmas collection."*

Hallmark™*, the world's largest maker of Christmas ornaments, introduced their first ornaments in 1973. Hallmark is the leader in the industry, continuously expanding the large lines. In 1997 alone, they added more than two hundred new ornaments.*

Q - What's the difference between collectible and collectable?

A - Just a different letter in the spelling. "Collectible" is the most commonly used, but both spellings are correct.

The different letters do make all the difference if shopping, selling or researching Christmas collectibles online with the computer. Using the keyword "collectible" will produce different search results from "collectable." Try both.

Q - Who determines what becomes a collectible?

A - The market or more specifically, you, determine what becomes a collectible.

Many designers and manufacturers declare their creations to be collectibles. Although they can only declare a collectible as such, they certainly do create the opportunity for an item to become a collectible.

In part, the old supply and demand theory from economics class applies. If no one wants it, no one buys it. Regardless of the hype surrounding the item, it will never be a collectible. For example: If Company A makes 10,000 porcelain angel ornaments but only one hundred collectors buy it (the first year it is on the shelves), it probably won't be a collectible. On the other hand, take the five original ***Wayside Houses, Department '56*** *introduced in 1977. The immediate demand for them created a market need for further production. However, more were not produced immediately and the continuing demand made them a collectible.*

Q -What's hot?

A - Christmas is the number one theme among collectors today. While the attraction for the more traditional subjects of Christmas, like Santas, angels and nativities remain strong, collectors love affair with this festive, religious holiday has expanded. St. Nicholas now competes for collector's attention with Barbie™, Mickey Mouse™, and Star Trek™ spaceships. These mass media ornaments reflect what is popular in our culture today. Collectors often choose these ornaments realizing that they will be symbolic reminders of the past.

Some complain of the commercial influence of licensed properties, yet they continue to flood the Christmas collectibles market. Licensed properties are items or images which specified companies have the legal rights to use. For example, Santa Claus himself is not a licensed property, but the famous image of Santa drinking a Coca-Cola™ is. Barbie, Star Trek and sports figures like Super Bowl-winning quarterback Troy Aikman and basketball great, Larry Byrd are all considered licensed properties and have become popular themes in Christmas ornaments.

The collectors' desire for nostalgia and a return to the simple life, shows up in the strong demand for the Department 56 houses. If anything, collector's attraction to angels have strengthened within the past few years as the country has seen a renewed interest in these lovely symbols of spirituality. In addition, detailed Santa's continue to do well as these "big elves" remind collectors of the fun of Christmas!

Q - Why Christmas collectibles?

A - Some people collect for fun; others see collecting as an absorbing passion. There is no right or wrong reason to collect.

To better focus on collecting, consider the following questions:

- *Am I interested in Christmas Collectibles as a possible investment? Do I enjoy the challenge of following the market and keeping up with trends?*
- *Do I already own Santas, angels or collectibles with which to start a collection? Am I curious about their worth, their origin and how they were produced?*
- *Would I like to start a family tradition of collecting? Am I interested in building a collection of heirlooms to be passed down through the generations?*
- *Do I enjoy searching for interesting items?*
- *Am I interested in collecting because I already like a particular collectible?*

Q - What is the best collectible to purchase?

A - Oft-repeated advice to collectors, "buy what you like." This makes sense for more than the obvious reason. If a collectible's value doesn't appreciate the way you had hoped, you will still be in possession of something you enjoy.

Q - Is it necessary to look before you buy?

A - The answer is YES! Find out everything you can before you break out the checkbook. As with car-buying, it pays to study the market before buying collectibles. Attend antique/collectibles shows and read books or magazines about the lines in which you are interested. If a computer is available, go on-line and find news groups, collector groups or related web sites.

Q - How do I find collectibles?

A - There are several ways to find collectibles. Some collectors enjoy searching far and wide. They find items when they travel, go to collectible shows, browse garage sales or peruse antique stores.

Other collectors prefer a less involved search and seek the assistance of one dealer or retailer. A close connection is created by bringing in a dealer's personal interest and can make collecting easier. He/she, can "keep an eye out" for special pieces. The supplier should be reputable and willing to provide good service. If you have found a dealer, but he/she won't take the time to answer your questions about collectibles, keep looking.

Q - What are dealerships and how can they help me?

A - Dealerships are retail stores. They are selected by collectibles manufacturers or artists to represent products and/or creations.

*Dealerships may be rated by a manufacturer or artist. Rating levels are based on the quality of dealership displays, extent of involvement with special promotional events and the variety and size of the carried line. For example, a "Gold Key" dealership for **Department 56**, is expected to carry the complete line of **Department 56** items. A "Silver Key" dealership is expected to carry most, but not necessarily all, of the line.*

Q - What can you expect from a dealership?

A - A good dealership will help you to stay current with a collection. This means keeping records on what pieces you have purchased. It is a good idea to keep a copy of the basic information. A good dealer will provide applicable magazine articles, newsletters, brochures and any appropriate information about your collection. In addition, you should be informed of special promotional events, such as artist's signings.

Because starting a collection can be intimidating, a valuable dealer is one who will take time to answer all of your questions and make you feel comfortable with the collection. A good dealer will promptly inform you when pieces are introduced and retired.

Let a dealer know that you are dedicated to collecting a particular line. This will influence the dealer to contact you about purchasing opportunities.

Some serious collectors will give personal credit card information to their dealer to keep on file. The dealer can then promptly purchase any new or special requests for the collector.

Q - Can I collect by mail or through an on-line computer service?

A - This approach is fast-gaining popularity. Whether a purchase is made through a collectibles exchange, store, club or from an individual, ask about a money-back guarantee. This allows the option of returning the item if necessary.

Q - Collector's Clubs: What can they do for me?

A - Joining a collector's club gives you a jump start to collecting. Manufacturers often supply a club application card with a collectible, making it easy for you to join. Collector's club organizers and their members can answer questions. Club benefits include discounts; sometimes a free collectible item and often collectibles made exclusively for its members.

The Markets: Primary and Secondary

Q - What is the primary market?

A - The primary market price is the original retail store price of a collectible when it first appears on the market.

Q - What is the secondary market?

A - Think of the secondary market as a "re-sell" market. The secondary market is also referred to as the aftermarket. This means the collectible is no longer available through its original "primary" source; the manufacturer or artist. Collectors then look for the item on the secondary market; from another collector, through collectible exchanges or secondary market dealers located throughout the country.

The primary market is fairly routine in terms of pricing. Retailers usually follow the suggested manufacturer retail price.

The secondary market is an entirely different ballgame. Do your homework if you are interested in buying or selling through the secondary market. Educate yourself by reading collectible magazines and books, joining collector clubs and searching for information online. Before jumping in to buy or sell, learn about a collectible line and track it's progress. June McKenna of June McKenna Collectibles advises collectors, "...the keys to success are education, patience, rational thinking and advice from the experts."

It is the collectors who significantly affect secondary prices. Secondary market prices can vary tremendously. One theory goes like this: Collectors, who are trying to acquire a complete set of a chosen line, pay attention to any pieces that go out of production and are retired. For example, each year in early November, ***Department 56*** *runs a full-page ad in the* ***USA Today*** *newspaper announcing which pieces are retiring. Phones ring, lines form at store fronts and collectors scurry to obtain these retired pieces before they disappear. The collectible not available goes on collectors "most wanted" list. The economics of supply and demand kick in at this time. When collectors want or "demand" a particular collectible, and there aren't enough to go around, its perceived value rises. However, after collectors who possess the "wanted" pieces begin to sell, availability increases, the price may again drop.*

Despite the usual ups and downs in secondary market prices, the general rule of thumb predicts that the price of an item will double after one year of retirement. The price typically triples after two years of retirement.

Q - How can I find out what my collection is worth?

A - Flip through several price guides at a bookstore or go online through the computer. In addition, ask the artist or manufacturer, collector club members and dealerships. "Don't put all of your eggs in one basket," is my advice. Look to more than one source to find information.

***Books/price guides** - It is common practice in the industry, for some publishers of secondary market collectible information, to sell or broker books and price guides. Although this makes sense due to common interest, investment and knowledge of the collectibles, it may create a conflict of interest. Some collectors prefer getting price guide information from a source that will not benefit and/or suffer from the printed price information.*

***Artists/manufacturers** - There is a sharp difference of opinion, among artists and manufacturers, as to who distributes secondary market price information. Some artists/companies are adamant about not disclosing secondary market prices. Others, like June McKenna, will print current secondary market prices in their catalogs.*

***Periodic publications, magazines** - These often provide the most current information.*

***Newsletters** - Many newsletters focus on a particular line. For example, the **Village Exchange** focuses on the **Department 56** villages. Other newsletters, such as Glitter include information on several lines, including Christopher Radko®, Polonaise® and other glass ornaments.*

***Computer** - There are several excellent software programs available with complete, built in price guides. This makes life, and collecting, easy. When selecting a computer software collectors program, consider how often it is updated and the related expenses. This is a worthy investment for many collectors because, with few key strokes, the value of an entire collection can be updated.*

***Word of mouth or word of e-mail** - Ask and ye shall find out! It's an interesting phenomenon that people love to answer other people's questions. Be aware that not everyone is an expert. Taking an informal, random survey works well. For example, go to a collectors' club on-line and ask, "What is my **Santa's Workshop** in **Department '56's North Pole Village** worth?" You may get all the answers you can handle.*

Q - Do I need to know what my collection is worth?

A - Yes. It is advantageous to know this for insurance purposes or in the event of selling. Look for price guides and compare information. For example, several sources of information on **Department 56's** lines are:

Greenbook	**Collector's Value Guide**
Willage Mania	**Dickens' Exchange Newsletter**

Q - How can I buy and sell?

A - You can sell by describing what you would like to buy or sell through on-line services. Or, place advertisements in local newspapers or appropriate magazines.

You might also consider going through a broker to buy or sell. Brokers commission a percentage of the sale and are generally very knowledgeable of the market, ensuring a good price. A broker will place the ads, make appropriate contacts and make sure you receive your money.

Section Two: Some Things You Should Know

How your computer can help

The Internet is set up with various search engines. These engines do the hard work of researching your subject in a deep sea of information.

Go to a search engine such as "Yahoo" or "Excite" and type in the word or words describing the collectible. Various online services contain a "keyword." Type in some of the topics to find a jumping off place. The number of web sites for collectible lines are numerous, if not infinite!

Online is a great place to meet other collectors, ask questions or chat about what you love to collect. Various web sites give you the "nitty-gritty" on very current secondary prices. Web sites are good places to shop for hard-to-find collectibles and to find out who is selling what items. As technology improves more of these web sites offer pictures with refined quality.

Keep in mind that online services have a dozen ways to describe the same thing. For example, you can find the **Department 56 Dicken's Village** by entering the words: "Dicken's Village," "Department 56" and "Collecting Villages."

Be aware, some web sites are here today and gone the next. New web sites appear frequently so it pays to check the same topic from time to time.

Following is a beginner's list of on-line topics:

Search - Word
Collectibles **Collectables** (the different spelling gives different search results) **Hobbies** (then go to porcelain and glass)

Keeping Up With Your Collectibles

It is important to keep records of your treasures. Stay organized and be aware of what your collection is worth, how much you have spent, and for what amount the collection needs to be insured.

There are wonderful tools available to help. If you find it tedious to update your insurance and inventory lists every year, consider a collectibles computer software program. Make sure the computer and software are compatible and up-to-date.

Rather than spend long hours keying in a price guide, for approximately $15 you can purchase a diskette or CD ROM, then easily transfer information into your collection files. Startup software generally costs $50 and usually includes two to three price guides.

Find out how often the program is updated with prices, new pieces and retirement information. Twice a year is average. If you start on such a system, you will need to keep it current by purchasing updates. Consider these updates a part of the investment. Also, inquire about available support services before you order software.

There are more than one hundred listings on the market for collectible price guides. These are advertised in collectible software programs and in collectible magazines. Some collectibles computer programs, such as **Collectibles Database For Collectors**, by **MSdataBase Solutions Inc.** provide hundreds of exceptional graphics. The graphics assist in the identification of a piece. *See Resource Listing on page 220.*

Using a computer or not, it is still necessary to keep track of collectibles. A set of 3 x 5 index cards will do the trick.

Basic List Categories:
Name of Collectible:
Year of Induction: Year of Retirement:
Issue Price: $ Purchase Price: $
Current Value: $ Date of Purchase:
Where Purchased: (include name of the dealer, address & phone)
3" X 5" Card

If desired, go into more detail and describe the color, material and manufacturer's print mark (if available). It is fun to add a few notes and comments about who accompanied you on a search expedition or any unusual or memorable events.

How to use this price guide

This price guide includes a listing of each collectible line. Basic information is included in each guide. Unique characteristics are noted at the beginning of each guide.

Collectibles are listed alphabetically by company or artist, chronologically by the year of introduction and then alphabetically by the name of the piece.

Price Guide - Order of Reference
1. Company Order Number (where applicable)
2. Item Title or Name
3. Type
4. Theme
5. Retirement Year
6. Introduction Year
7. Issue Price/Original Retail Price
8. Secondary Market Price

Abbreviations
CL - Closed
OP - Open
Ret - Retired
NA - Not available

SECTION THREE: DESIGNER BACKGROUND

This section provides background information on the designer, history and origination of a collectible line.

ANNALEE DOLLS™

About Annalee Davis Thorndike - artist/owner

Growing up in an artistic family, in Concord, New Hampshire, Annalee Davis Thorndike liked puppets. She and her friends made them, built theaters and created magical stories to bring them to life. Throughout her lifetime, Annalee wove her enthusiasm and magic into the thousands of dolls she designed and created.

Annalee and Chip Thorndike

After she graduated from high school in 1933, Thorndike turned to dollmaking to help the family income. She sold her first dolls through **The League of New Hampshire Craftsmen** and to small shops in the Boston area.

In 1941 she married the son of a prominent Boston surgeon, Charles "Chip" Thorndike and the newlyweds bought a farm. The Harvard-educated

1970 Mr. & Mrs. Santa on Ski Bob

Chip followed his free-spirit and was bent to become a gentleman chicken farmer and tinkerer. It was Thorndike's husband who came up with the wire frame design that enables her dolls to be pose-able. Because of lower labor costs, the poultry business literally went South. So, the couple invested their energies in Thorndike's fledging home-based doll business.

While working and raising two sons, Chuck and Townsend, the Thorndikes got a "big break" when New Hampshire's Department of Vacation Travel and Development commissioned her for a project. Thorndike was asked to create one hundred and fifty dolls depicting the state's recreational opportunities. A display of dolls skiing, fishing, sledding and pursuing other pleasant New Hampshire pastimes greeted visitors to the state's tourist information office in New York City. A number of major New York and Boston department stores soon requested dolls for window displays. When the orders started flowing, the Thorndikes hired several neighbors to help. The Thorndike's big farmhouse began to look like a factory and is known today as the "Factory in the Woods."

The Thorndikes continue to share their success with others. From the artist's proof dolls offered at the annual auction, they donate the sales. They also offer a percentage of total sales from "special cause" dolls to go to charitable organizations. Some of their favorite causes are education, conservation and health. Thorndike has designed dolls, such as the California Mud Slide Mouse, to draw attention to particular situations or events and to help raise donations.

12" Tree Top Angel

Thorndike says a nine-to-five job never appealed to her; and she has never had one. Even at 82, Thorndike has no problem showing up for a full day's "work."

"It's not work if you love what you're doing," says the woman with the wizened and whimsical smile, strikingly similar to that on her dolls.

FYI

- Thorndike made her first dolls in 1933.
- At the annual Annalee Doll Society Auction Weekend, several proofs are sold along with some of her early and one-of-kind dolls. Also the current year's Thorndike Doll Society's exclusive "Great American Era Series" is made available to attendees.
- Current Thorndike dolls cost from $5 to $184.
- Hundreds of Thorndike's Dolls vary in subject matter from human figures to flowers.

1967 7" Mr. Santa Mouse

Best Care

- Beware of sunshine as it is the main culprit in fading any of the one hundred thirty different fabrics used in Annalee Dolls.
- Artificial light can also cause fabrics to fade.
- Be selective in the positioning of your dolls.

Display Tips

Because of the pose-ability of Annalee Dolls, they are fun to display in many different positions. They can sit on the branches of the Christmas tree, hang on the side of stacked gifts and recline in the inside circle of a wreath. The presence of these dolls also add color and joy to the top of a mantel, door-frame and in a windowsill.

Elves and people figures can also be encouraged to hug each other or the entire collection can easily be encouraged to hold hands.

Secondary Market Sizzler

At the 1996 Annalee Doll Society Auction Weekend a 18" circa 1955, special order female doll, wearing a long camel hair-like dress coat, sold for $6,500. *Note: There is no name for these early dolls. They were identified by the garments in which they were dressed.*

Collectors' Club - Annalee Doll Society established in 1983

Membership includes:

- a gift of a 7" logo doll, membership pin and card
- opportunities to buy from the exclusive-to-members **Great American Eras Doll Series**
- a subscription to **The Collector**, the Society's quarterly magazine
- opportunities to take part in members-only auctions

Contact

Annalee Doll Society
P.O. Box 1137
Meredith, NH 03253-1137
tel. 800-43-Dolls

1989 18" Reindeer with 10" Elves

1989 18" Mr. Santa with Stocking

1990 7" Mouse with Presents

7" Mr. & Mrs. Santa Exchanging Gifts

Go and Behold - Annalee Doll Museum

Visit the Annalee Doll Museum in New Hampshire. Admission is free. Some of her rare and older dolls are among the five hundred dolls on display. Note: Closed during winter months.

Annalee Doll Museum
50 Reservoir Road
Meredith, NH 03253

Contact

Annalee Dolls
P.O. Box 708
Meredity, New Hampshire 03253-070850
tel. 800-258-4647

The Boyd's™ Collection

About G.M. Lowenthal - artist/designer/owner

Gary M. Lowenthal is Boyd's chief designer, chief executive officer and self-proclaimed "Head Bean." Lowenthal is to be credited, he might say "blamed," for the bear madness he has created with his Christmas collectible lines.

Gary Lowenthal: Owner/Artist

Santa's Flight Plan

Lowenthal was born in New York City in 1949. After growing up, he went upstate to Alfred University and earned an undergraduate degree. He continued his education and earned a master of science degree in biology. Describing himself as a true child of the sixties, he joined the U.S. Peace Corps, and "split" for the Fiji Islands in the South Pacific.

Edmund with Wreath

The BOYDS COLLECTION LTD.®

The Boyd's Collection Logo

Jingle Moose

Nicholai with Tree

Windy with Book

Chilly & Son with Dove

After his contribution to world peace, he returned to the "Big Apple." Now he was not only making a contribution to the world of business, but also to his bank account.

He embarked on a seven year career in purchasing, design and merchandising at Bloomingdales the "mother-of-all-upscale department stores." Lowenthal reaped great benefits from exposure to top clothing designers. Assessing his knowledge and experience, he decided to change career directions and moved to Boyds, Maryland, a village north of Washington D.C.

In 1979, with the help of Justine "Tina" Unger, he opened **The Boyds Collection Ltd.** It was an out-of-the-way antique shop on a street of ten Victorian houses. They soon discovered their love for antiques outweighed their means to purchase antiques. The two then decided to shift their focus to antique reproductions because they had the look and feel of an antique without the authentic price tag. In addition to designing and selling a line of replica "antique" duck decoys, Lowenthal also created the **Gnome Homes**, a village of miniature ceramic houses.

Seraphina with Jacob and Rachel

As the retail venture prospered over the next decade, they began wholesaling. In 1987 Lowenthal and Unger moved their business to a warehouse in a small town outside of Gettysburg, Pennsylvania. Lowenthal began designing wool teddy bears that were well received. In 1992, he interpreted the distinct personalities of his plush creations, cast them into acrylic resin, and thus created the **Bearstones**. Today there are more than three hundred different styles of collectible teddy bears, hares, tabbies and pooches.

His success continuing, in 1993, Lowenthal introduced **The Folkstone Collection** which features whimsical folk art figurines of santas, snowmen, angels, and of course, hares. In 1996 Lowenthal introduced **The Dollstone Collection** with figurines depicting the dress and innocence of earlier times. **The Shoe Box Bears** are jointed resin bears which came on-stage in 1996. Lowenthal has mentioned the possibility of a new series called the **Poochstones**.

The start-up team of Lowenthal and Unger has expanded to about one hundred workers. All are located at the Boyd's shipping warehouse and office in Adams County, Pennsylvania.

Lowenthal claims that some things haven't changed. "We're a lot bigger than when we were a 'mom and pop' shop, but for better or worse, we still run it like a 'mom and pop' shop, just bigger. We're still a little disorganized and a little off-center, slightly eccentric—just like our bears," he said.

Robin … Snowbird Lover

The Boyd's Collection Identification Marks

Lowenthal continues his contribution to world peace. The beauty, and sometimes humor, in his **Bearstone, Folkstone** and **Dollstone** figurines bring a smile to the hearts of many.

About The Boyds Collection Ltd.

Look in the face of a Boyd's figurine and "feel" the philosophy behind **The Boyds Collection**. Elegant and goofy; sweet and savvy; goodness with an occasional touch of grumpiness. Collectors seem to "go wild" for the cold cast figurines. They oftentimes can personally identify with one of the three hundred represented personalities. For whatever reason, the demand has pushed **Boyds Bears & Friends** to the top of the Christmas collectibles list.

FYI

- Each **Bearstone, Folkstone and Dollstone** is hand-cast, hand-painted, individually numbered, gift-boxed and includes a certificate of authenticity signed by the designer Gary Lowenthal.
- The **Bearstones** tend to be short and round in comparison with **The Folkstones** which are tall and thin, created in the American tradition of pencil figures. In 1996, the first in a series of wee fairies, gnomes and elves were introduced.
- More than a dozen of the resin **Bearstones** have been nominated for and have won the TOBY and Golden Teddy awards.
- The **Dollstones** are produced in editions of 4,800.
- The **Bearstones** and **Folkstones** run to editions of 3,600 pieces.
- Each piece is stamped on the bottom with a tiny doll shoe for the **Dollstones**, a bear paw for the **Bearstones** and a star for the **Folkstones**.
- Average retail price is $17.
- New pieces are issued every six months.

Best Care

- A soft makeup brush or new paint brush easily removes dust.
- A can of compressed air or a small electronics vacuum works as well for dust removal.
- Cat's aren't the only creatures who don't care for baths! Boyds Bears don't like water at all, please dust only.

Display Tips

In keeping with the antiquated appearance of the Boyds pieces, create a display including one or several of the following: Shaker boxes, old books, antiques, lace, dried flowers or old photographs.

Secondary Market Sizzler

Grenville … With Green Scarf originally sold for $11. Today a first edition on the secondary market sells for approximately $400.

Boyds Bears & Friends Collectors Club - established 1996

FoB Department
P. O. Box 1387
Gettysburg, PA 17325

Membership includes:

- a one year subscription to the humorous, insightful and informative Boyd's Bear Retail Inquirer Newsletter. The newsletter includes a classified ads section informing members where to buy, sell and trade pieces.
- a Bearstone pin
- a membership card
- a directory of dealers
- a product list and special purchase opportunities

Contact

Somein' Ta Say (Customer Service)
P.O. Box 4386
Gettysburg, PA 17325
tel. 717-633-7080
fax. 717-633-6597

Byers Choice™

About Byers' Choice

For Joyce Byers, Byers Choice started in the 1960's as a kitchen table hobby. She enjoyed creating caroling figures, from hanger wire and tissue, for Christmas gifts.

The Byers' Choice Ltd. Logo

The idea for the Carolers bloomed through a combination of events and discoveries. First, while visiting an antique shop, she was enamored with the way a set of porcelain figurines perfectly captured the spirit of 19th century England. Shortly after, she saw a reflection of the true Christmas spirit in a set of papier-mâché choir figures. The proverbial light bulb went off in her head, 'Why not create caroling figures with the feeling of 19th-century England *and* Christmas?'

Today Byers' Choice employs one hundred eighty people, all of whom help make the half million Carolers sold each year. Despite financial success,

Grandparents, Father and Children Carolers

Joyce Byers' husband Bob expressed that money has never been the bottom line. He once told *Philadelphia Enterprise Magazine*, "I've frequently wondered; "What is it that has created all the success that we've had?" It's not because of any strategic planning...or brilliant management...making more money is of absolutely no consequence to us, and hasn't been for years. We've just more or less said, "Whatever the Lord wants to happen—we'll leave it in his hands."

Byers' Choice is not typical of most companies.

(Left to Right) Black Peter and Saint Nicholas

Promoting the Carolers as a collectible is not the main objective. Jeff Byers, one of two sons of the company founders said, "Although we are glad our Carolers are beloved by collectors, in our experience we have seen where a collectible line will get caught up in the market, with the numbers, supply and demand, pricing...to the point it becomes rather controlled and even manipulated. Because we value and respect *every* customer. . .we are a little leery of having our line of Carolers defined, and possibly limited, as a collectible."

This isn't a new philosophy at Byers' Choice. In 1995, the family ended a program which offered an exclusive series to the collectors. They discovered the

Singing Dogs

program was being abused by some retailers and collectors. In some instances, the Byers have declined advice to retire particular items in order to increase value. In fairness to some of their collectors, Byers try to make it easy to get a piece for a collection.

With actions as proof, Byers cares for their customers, community and employees. In 1986 Bob and Joyce Byers founded a program to annually donate twenty percent of the company's annual before-tax profits. Profits benefit such charities and non-profit organizations as the Salvation Army® and Meals-on-Wheels™ programs. Outgrowing space for a second time, the Byers built a wonderful workplace for their employees. Included are the makings of a plush hotel with ornate wallpapers, original paintings and fine furnishings. A convenient covered awning spans the space between the plant and the employee's parking lot. In addition a large sculpture of playing children adorn meticulously manicured grounds at the plant's entrance.

The Creation of Byers Carolers - Making Faces

Step One - People Watchin'

Some may think people-watching is an idle past time, but not Joyce Byers. She watches people in search of new faces for the Carolers collection. "My favorite places (for people-watching) are ... the theater and the airport. However, I'm not trying to capture any face in particular, rather I like to give each face a personality of its own," she said.

Starting with a handful of oil-based clay, Byers roughly forms a dozen faces before getting serious about refining and reshaping each head, pinching a

Caroling Children With Skates

Bob Crachet and TIny Tim

sharper nose and/or massaging a cheek. After sharpening the details, a plaster mold is made of the head. Latex is poured into the corrected mold, which then hardens into the master form used to make other plastic molds.

Next, artisans press special clay into these molds.

The Bird Feeder

They carefully remove the head then smooth and shape the features, such as the nostrils. This individual handling accounts for the unique features of each face.

After the clay dries, flesh tones are painted, then the tiny details of eyes and lips are created. The Caroler then comes to life!

One key artist commented that the eyebrows were difficult to paint as the lines had to be quite thin, spaced evenly and precisely curved. The heads are then returned to the artisans for the creation of a body and wardrobe.

Canine and Feline Carolers

In 1986, Byers gave each of the employees a lump of clay and announced a "best singing dog contest." That's how Lucy, the illustrious hound, became the first of a menagerie to join the Carolers. Several cats also caterwaul along with this group.

FYI

- These collectibles are made individually after an order is placed. They are not mass produced.
- The first Carolers, made in the 1960s, looked different from today's. The facial features were less detailed and less colorful.
- Each step of the creating process, from painting the faces to fitting the clothes, is done by hand. Each figure is a slight variation on the signature theme of the "O" shaped mouth, high cheekbones and arched eyebrows.
- Byers' Choice tries to discourage retailers and collectors from changing or adding to the accessories held by the Carolers. This tends to cause problems and disappointment for collectors who end up with a Caroler different from the original design.
- **Traditional** and **Victorian Carolers** all have a matching partner.
- All **Traditional** and **Victorian Carolers** are stamped on the bottom with the creation year. The artisan who dresses a particular figure also signs, and numbers each caroler. For example, "25/100" means it is the twenty-fifth figure, from one hundred total, made of that design.
- With the exception of a few second-edition pieces, all have been retired in the **Dickens** and the **Nutcracker** series.
- In 1989, Byers' Choice introduced a one hundred and seventeen page edition of *Charles Dickens' "A Christmas Carol."* Color photographs of the Carolers accompanied the copy. Although sold out

for several years, this book may still be available from some retailers or on the secondary market.
- The whimsical, old-fashioned figures are still made using hanger wire and tissue paper.
- Retail prices range from $20 to $100.

Best Care

- Carolers store best standing. The sturdy custom-designed gift boxes, available at your Caroler dealer, work well. Or, use partitioned boxes from a local package store.
- Crush paper and place it under skirts to help hold the shape. Avoid wrapping the entire figure in paper because it tends to crush the fabric.
- Use your fingers to gently manipulate a felt hat brim back into shape.
- An iron, set on gentle, will remove wrinkles from large hat brims and long coats. A hand-held steam iron works great for removing wrinkles from skirts, jackets or paper scrolls.
- Does the paper scroll held by the Caroler look limp? Roll the ends around a pencil to curl.
- If you live in an area of high humidity, remove accessories such as lanterns/bells and store separately. Dampness may rust Caroler accessories.
- Cedar is not recommended to repel mice and moths as it can dissolve the face paints.
- When displaying your Carolers, avoid bright sunlight. Sun will fade clothing and face paint. If the cheek color requires "touch up," apply powder blush with a cotton swab. Perk up lip color with a natural shade of nail polish.
- Hair spray will settle the frazzled hairdo of a Caroler.
- Use a nail file to smooth small chips on the base. Touch up with a dark green, felt tip marker.

Display Tips

- Sprigs of live or artificial greenery and a couple of brass candlesticks create a simple and effective backdrop for Carolers.
- While a glass display case can give an fresh look to a Carolers display, the folks at Byers Choice Limited feel that it detracts from the warm, earthy appeal of the figures.
- The size of the Carolers are perfect for display in traditional places such as mantle pieces, sideboards and in bay windows.

- Artificial snow scattered or cotton batting smoothed over the bases can bring additional attention to a display of Carolers.

Secondary Market Sizzler

The popular **Apple Lady** produced in 1991, for the **Cries of London** series, sold in a New England auction for $1,000. It originally sold for $80.

Collectors' Club and Newsletter

Early each year, three newsletters and a complete chronological listing of the Carolers, new and retired, are mailed to retailers and members. Request these by fax, mail or phone. An official collectors' club does not exist.

Go and Behold - The Gallery

Visitors may enter the Caroler's showplace The Gallery, which opened in 1994.

In a cozy 19th century English parlor, festively decorated for Christmas, live more than four hundred Carolers. Those who populate The Gallery live, work, play and of course sing. Three original Carolers are on display in a special glass case.

The Gallery is open to the public Monday through Saturday 10 a.m. to 4 p.m. Closed on major holidays.

Contact

Byers Choice does not sell directly to customers but will gladly provide information about a retailer nearest you.

Byers' Choice Ltd.
4355 County Line Roads
Chalfont, PA 18914
tel. 215-822-6700

Christopher Radko™ Collectibles

About Christopher Radko - artist/designer/owner

A Christmas catastrophe inspired Christopher Radko's to design Christmas ornaments. Just weeks before the Christmas of 1983, his family's fourteen foot Balsam fell after the tree stand buckled. The tree was laden with 2,000 antique ornaments. Radko remembers feeling not only guilty, because he purchased the tree stand, but also heartbroken about the shattered ornaments. These ornaments linked four generations of family Christmas celebrations. That year, dried flowers decorated the tree, replacing the European ornaments.

Realizing these treasures could never be replaced, Radko attempted to make amends for the catastrophe. "The next year I found a glass blower in Poland willing to remake some of our lost treasures ... provided I created the designs for him. I brought some samples home and the next thing I knew, collectors everywhere wanted them," Radko said of the experience.

At 38, Christopher Radko is as gleaming and colorful as his thousands of ornament designs. He may think himself a Christmas elf, believing his purpose is to add more magic to Christmas. The son of doctors, Radko grew up in Scarsdale, New York and worked for a talent agency before venturing into ornament design.

"I realized I could be making more money and having more fun if I went into business designing ornaments," he said. As a successful artist and entrepreneur he admittedly still thinks of returning to the show business arena. "I could easily see myself either producing a film, buying a script, or supporting people who make movies," he told *Collector's Mart Magazine.*

Radko also designs holiday dinnerware, scarves, ties, wrapping paper, gift bags and other holiday related items including Christmas cards and a home fragrance collection. Radko hopes to keep the title to which he is often referred; "The King of Christmas."

Radko is also designing special, fine glass ornaments for Warner Brothers™ and the Walt Disney™ Company. Each of these lines have been expanded in both 1996 and 1997 and many will be limited editions.

Saturated with a shining style, Radko and his company of twelve years have received considerable media attention. In 1995 he was interviewed on *The Today Show* by Katie Couric, and has been mentioned in such publications as *The New York Times, USA Today,* and the *Ladies' Home Journal.*

Radko shares his success by designing two charity ornaments each year. More than half a million in profits from these ornaments benefit research efforts for AIDS and Pediatric Cancer. The 1997 AIDS ornament is called **A Caring Clown** and the design for Pediatric Cancer is **Kitty Cares**.

Radko has adopted an orphanage in Poland which he visits several times a year. He provides many essentials for the sixty five children residents. In addition, he has furnished such amenities as a satellite dish and a group trip to summer camp.

As the Christopher Radko story continues to unwind, there is a happy ending to the Christmas tree catastrophe chapter. At the Radko family Christmas celebrations, two trees stand; one for the antique ornaments collected since "the crash," and another to showcase Christopher's creations.

The Creation of Christopher Radko Ornaments

First, an artisan carves a plastic or clay replica of the design and, using the "lost-wax" technique forms a casting mold. The wax design is buried in fine, packed sand. Then, to "lose" the wax, molten pewter is poured over it. The melted wax is replaced with the pewter which hardens into the "mother mold."

Clear Pyrex® glass is heated and carefully blown into the mold. The original shape is adapted immed-iately, but is allowed to cure overnight.

Next, a technique called "silvering" is performed. This is a method whereby liquid silver is poured or injected into the glass shape and allowed to dry for one day. The silver shines

Finials

Nutcracker Suite II

Veronique Magnifique

Three Little Jigs

Holy Family

through the glass producing a luminance, mirror finish.

Two layers of mat lacquer are then applied. One day drying time is required for each layer.

After the lacquer has dried, the tiny, delicate details, such as eyelashes and belt buckles are painted. The ornament is then coated in glitter and diamond dust.

Finally, a metal crown and the Christopher Radko tag is applied.

FYI

- Christopher Radko is generally recognized as having revived this country's interest in artistic glass Christmas ornaments.
- The 1997 Christopher Radko collection includes seven hundred and fifty designs, bringing the total collection to nearly 4,000.
- Over 3,000 retail outlets throughout the United States sell Radko, including Bloomingdale's, Neiman Marcus, Marshall Field and Saks Fifth Avenue.
- Ornament prices range from $15 to $90.
- Radko collectors include: Barbra Streisand, Katherine Hepburn, Dolly Parton, Bruce Springsteen, Elton John, Liza Minelli and Mikhail Barishnikov.
- There are many themes within Radko's lines; religious, classically traditional, whimsical and others which defy categorization.
- Many of Radko's ornaments are inspired by old world European designs. Some are new designs while others are new coloration's of old designs.
- More than one thousand craftspeople in Poland, Germany, Italy and the Czech Republic contribute their talents to Radko's creations.

Best Care

- If dusting is necessary, use a soft cloth or a feather duster. Never use liquid of any kind. Some of the

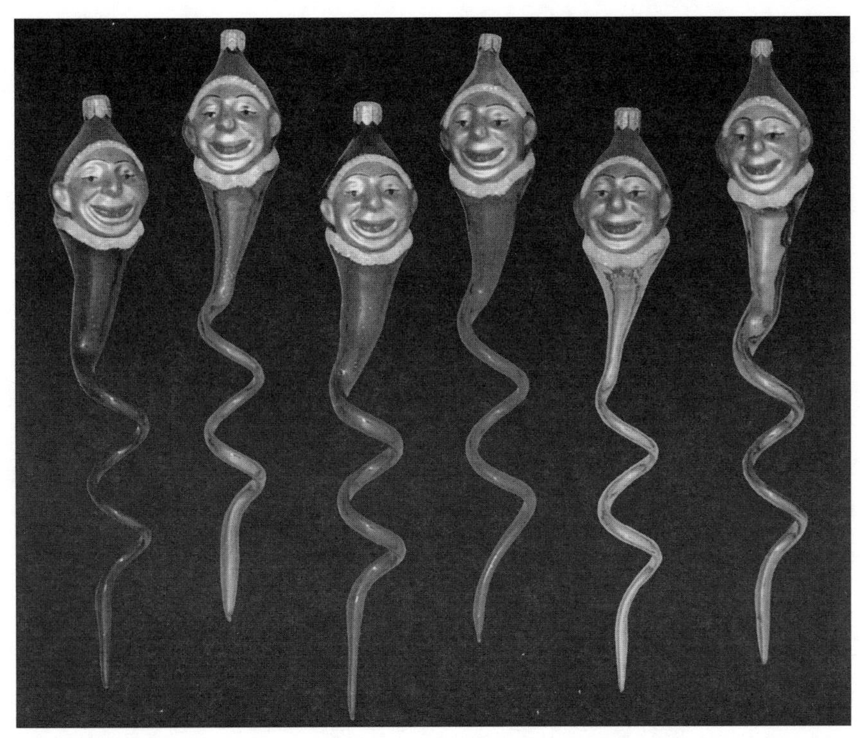

Clown Snakes

paints are water-soluble and will dissolve.

- The best way to store the delicate ornaments is in a three-layered partitioned cardboard box. These boxes are often found in the storage item department at major department stores. Radko recommends wrapping each ornament in Bounty™ microwave paper towels as they are acid-free and will not damage the colors. Place each wrapped ornament in a plastic bag and place carefully in the storage box.

A Winter Bear's Heart

Display Tips

- Some individuals believe 'less is more,' but Radko's decorating style is more is more beautiful. To accomplish a full, opulent appearance, consider using a small tree and limit the space between the ornaments.
- Consider staying with a single theme, color or shape when thinking of new ways to display your Radko collectibles. For example, all red ornaments on a tree or only fruits and vegetables in a garland can make an emphatic, attractive decoration statement.
- The luscious colors and shine of Radko ornaments can be shown off to their natural advantage by carefully placing several on a simple platter or in a vase, to be used as a centerpiece or on a foyer table.

Secondary Market Sizzler

The 1993 **Partridge in a Pear Tree** ornament from the **Twelve Days of Christmas** series originally sold for $35. Currently it's sale price is between $650 and $1,000. Also strong on the secondary market is **Leader of the Band**. Selling originally in 1994 for $25, it now sells for approximately $360.

Starlight Family of Collector's Club - established in 1993

Christopher Radko's Starlight Collector's Club has more than 20,000 members throughout the United States.

Membership includes:

- a one year subscription to the official newsletter ***Starlight***
- a gift
- a handsome folio for newsletter storage
- Radko brochures and information
- an exclusive pin
- a membership card
- an ornament button
- a current catalog
- a redemption certificate entitling the right to purchase the current year's members-only ornament

Contact

Christopher Radko Collectibles
P.O. Box 238
Dobbs Ferry, NY 10522
tel. 1-800-71-RADKO

(Left To Right) Twilight Santa, Pere Noel, Winter Fantasy, Edwardian Santa, Pere Noel

Magic Sleigh Ride

Ernst The Toy Elf

Life-Size Father Christma

(Left)Rocking Reindeer (Right) Harpberry Fair

Angel Babies Santa

Lance

Sarah Rose Angel On Swing

Old Tyme Santa With Toys

ꞓart Wreath

Cross Angels And (Center)1993 Limited Edition Star Of Bethlehem

ʼadonna Of The Cross

Sunflower Angel

Oh Sweetest Heart

Possible Dreams

Pet Project Clothtique Collection

A New Suit For Santa
Clothtique Collection

Nicholas Clothtique Collection

Lighted Crinkle Castle Crinkle Claus Collecti

(Left) Netherlands Santa
Crinkle Claus Collection

English Santa
Crinkle Claus Collection

(Left To Right) Raggey Ann, Candle And Holder, Gramophone, Clown Head

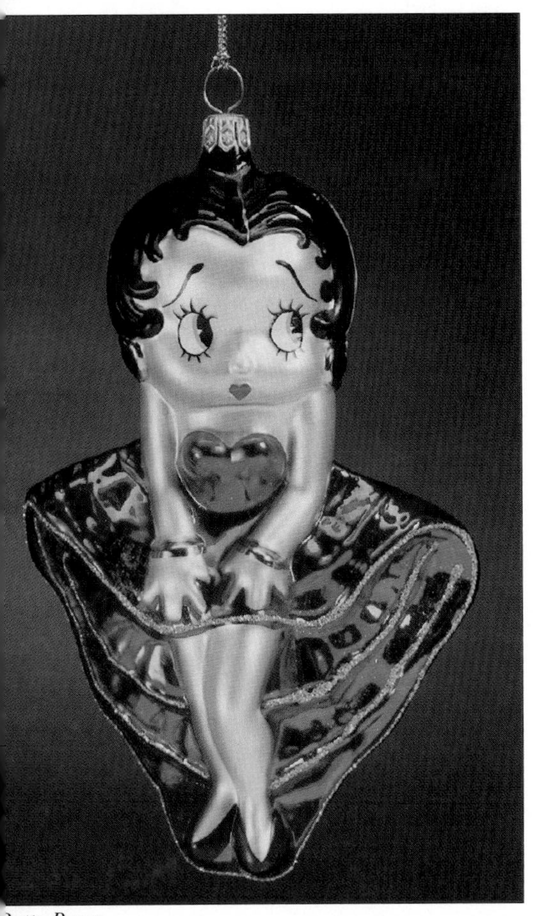

Betty Boop

Cinderella's Pumpkin Coach

Top Selling 1995 Santa: Star Catcher Santa

Five Of First Six Pipka Santas: (Left to Right) Czechoslovakian Santa, Starcoat Santa, Russian Santa, Midnight Visitor, Santa's Ark

(Right) Gardening Angel

Pipka's
memories
of
Christmas

Puppies For Christmas" Santa

30" Old World Mrs. Santa

997 Santas: (Left to Right)
'olish Father Christmas,
:ussian Santa, Where's
:udolph?, Norwegian
ılenisse, St. Nicholas,
anta's Spotted Grey

1983 5" Santa With Gift

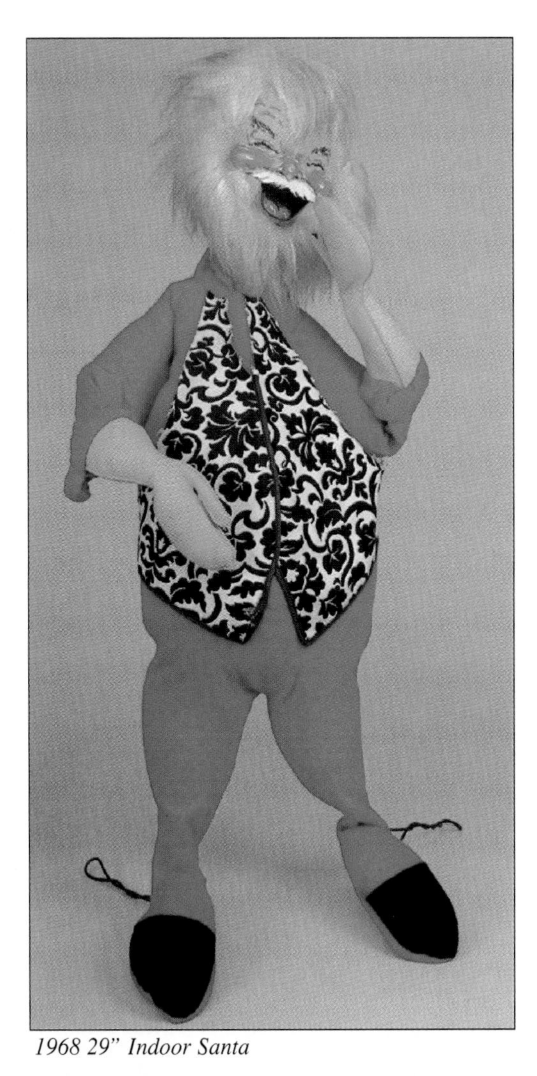

1968 29" Indoor Santa

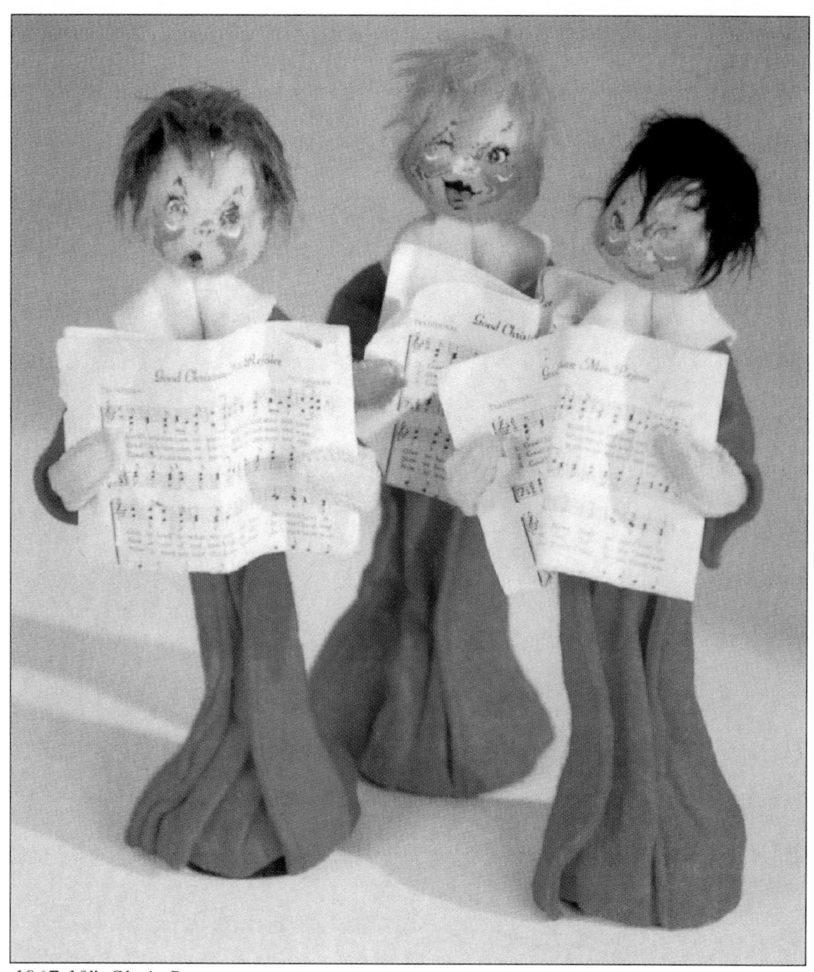

1967 10" Choir Boys

1967 7" Mr. & Mrs. Santa In Wicker Love Seat

Boyds Bears

Fixit...Santa's Faerie

Edmund With Wreath from the Bearstone Collection

ringle And Company

(Left To Right on Ground) Adult Female Caroler, Little Boy Caroler, Grandparent Carolers, Little Drummer Boy, Victorian Girl and Adult Male (On The Stairs) Choir Director and Adult Victorian Carolers...And Two Caroling Dogs.

Mrs. Claus In Velvet

Treetop Angel

(Clockwise from top) Christy—All God's Children, Making His Rounds, A Celebration Of Angels

(Front Row, Left To Right) Native American BARBIE, NFL Buffalo Bill, NFL Kansas City Chiefs, Nolan Ryan (Middle Row, Left To Right) Holiday BARBIE, NFL New York Jets, STAR TREK—30 Years (Back Row, Left To Right) Gone With The Wind, LaVerne, Citor and Hugo, Quasimodo, Esmeralda and Djali, It's A Wonderful Life—Anniversary Edition.

IT'S A WONDERFUL LIFE
HK1
Ryan's 5,714 career strike-outs is easily the best in baseball history. With his "Ryan Express," the right-handed flamethrower led his league in strikeouts 11 times in 27 seasons. His seven no-hitters is also a major league record, as is his career strikeout ratio of 9.55 per nine innings.
NOLAN RYAN
We're #1

Christmas Magic

Yippy Yi Yo

Holiday Skaters

Bearly Awake

Fruit Wreath

Palace Playground

Journey To Crystal Valley

Capture The Spirit

ok Of Legends

Santa's Crystal Valley

1989 Traditional Santa

1987 Kris Kringle

1992 Christmas Gathering

1987 Christmas Eve

(Left To Right)1930s Santa, Father Christmas, St. Nicholas

Grandfather Frost

Ebenenzer Scrooge

Santa with Angel

Father Christmas with Moon and Star

Snow Angel

Figi™ Collectibles

About Steve Kehrli - artist/ceo

Not every chief executive officer would trek to the North Pole, as did Figi's, to make a point. In August 1996, Chairman J. Todd Figi left the San Diego climate and went to the land of ice. He spent three days traveling by land, sea and air to reach The North Pole. Figi avowed that he was "searching for the whereabouts of Santa's Crystal Valley."

Steve Kehrli: Artist for Santas Crystal Valley

A photograph of a smiling Figi, standing on an iceberg with the Arctic Ocean in the background was published in the official collector's newsletter *The Valley News.* It is stated in the newsletter that Figi would not comment on his avowed search results. However, it is known that he did find, as the photograph proves, fifteen story icebergs. It is said that he also discovered whales, seals, walruses and the polar bears.

In about the time it takes an ice cube to melt in August, **Santa's Crystal Valley's** illuminated sculptures became one of the country's top Christmas collectibles.

The Daring Rescue

Introduced in 1995, the line of eleven sculptures sold out of production capacity in the first nine days of market release. The unique combination of ice-like acrylic and brightly painted North Pole characters quickly captured the attention of collectors.

Founding the company in 1969, J. Todd Figi wanted his company to be recognized as being innovative. Figi's business evolved from a small company that designed and manufactured framed graphics and wall art. The company become a leader in the gift industry, making a variety of products ranging from lamps and stamp dispensers to theme collectible lines.

Figi contends to be the first to develop the use of resin in a product line. When he first approached his designers with the idea of Christmas collectibles, they didn't know how to start and cited the many companies already producing Christmas lines.

Figi challenged his team to be innovative. Team member, Steve Kehrli said, "My personal challenge was to create a truly original collectible, something the world has never seen."

Kehrli is a resident of Canyon Country, California. With a history of being unique in his approach, he took a varied and circuitous route to arrive at illuminated sculptures.

"When I was in junior high I did an exact replica

In The Spirit

CV-23 Christmas Blessing

Wings of Love

Bearly Finished

A Cuddly Masterpiece

Beary Best Friend

Magic Touch

Holiday Anticipation

of my father's dump truck. It won some award...which in turn gave me the confidence to sculpt [the painting of] The Last Supper," said Kehrli.

At age eighteen, Kehrli embarked upon a professional career. He experimented with a wide range of subjects and techniques. Subjects ranged from a bas-relief of Salvador Dali's "Christ of the Saint of the Cross" to three-dimensional sculpting of circus clowns.

Kehrli said that it took a lot of thinking time and work to conceive the idea for **Santa's Crystal Valley**. Santa's Crystal Valley was one of thirty to forty holiday theme ideas that he presented to senior vice-president of the design department. Collectors have been delighted with this top choice.

About Santa's Crystal Valley

The story(book) behind the legend is a little book. A twenty four page, 5 x 7 book to be exact. The storybook *The Legend of Santa's Crystal Valley®* answers many of the burning questions which children and adults have about Santa. Such questions include, "Where do the toys come from?" and "Where are they made?" All questions are answered within a tale about a humble toy maker's fantastic adventure into a hidden valley of crystal.

Welcome Home

All Aboard!

The Legend of Santa's Crystal Valley features full-color illustrations, a brief artist biography and a list of the collectible items. Space is provided for collectors to write in purchase dates.

FYI

- Santa's Crystal Valley is a line of illuminated collectible sculptures.
- Designs portray whimsical vignettes of Santa and his elves at work as well as scenes from the Crystal Valley.
- Each Santa's Crystal Valley sculpture is personalized with a backstamp.
- In 1995 and 1996, Santa's Crystal Valley was nominated for the Collector Editions' Annual Awards Of Excellence
- Certain sculptures are issued only in limited editions.
- In 1995, eleven sculptures were introduced. Two of these have been retired.
- In 1996, nine pieces were introduced. The first piece **Star Bright** was retired.
- In 1997 ten pieces were introduced and **Capture The Spirit** was retired.

Best Care

- It may only be necessary to dust with a soft cloth.
- If a collectible requires cleaning, wipe with a soft rag that has been soaked in a mild detergent, diluted with water. Rinse in the same manner.

Display Tips

- Create a completely different look for a collectible by using colored cellophane. Cut cellophane to fit the base of the figure and set the collectible on top of it. The colors will reflect into the cracks and crevices.
- Set pieces on or near mirrors to enhance the "icy" appearance.
- Clear construction blocks make great 'ice' bases for collectible. These are available at tile stores.
- Crumple clear plastic wrap and place near collectible, creating even more 'ice'.

Secondary Market Sizzler

Because this line is so current, at the time of publication, there is not any secondary market information available.

Collectors' Club

A collectors club has not been established.

Contact

Figi Collectibles
P.O. Box 85515
San Diego, CA 92186
tel. 800-678-FIGI

Santa's Junior Express

Hallmark®

About Hallmark

Hallmark, the world's largest manufacturer of greeting cards, began producing eighteen Hallmark Keepsake Ornaments in 1973. Before this time, the standard decorations for the family's Christmas tree were colored glass balls.

Hallmark claims over half of all households, collecting Christmas ornaments today, collect Hallmark Keepsake Ornaments.

In 1993 alone, Hallmark introduced more than two hundred fifty new collectibles. The 19,000 employees and nineteen Hallmark Keepsake Ornament studio artists combine talent, labor, and skill to produce an entirely new ornament line every year. The previous years' line is retired.

A dozen colorful home-made looking yarn figures, including Santa, two styles of **Betsey Clark** and four other styles of glass balls made up the first year's offering.

Since then Santa has come a long way in a hundred different forms at Hallmark. One of Hallmark's longest-running Keepsake Ornaments, **Here Comes Santa**, has been around since 1979. In it, Santa and his toys show up each year using a different method of transportation.

In another long-running series in 1996, Hallmark came out with the sixteenth and last of the **Rocking Horse Collector Series.** Linda Sickman, who created the designs, said that ending the series was like saying good-bye to an old friend. "I think the rocking horse symbolizes little girls' dreams to own horses," said Sickman.

In 1996 Hallmark came out with ***Holiday BARBIE*** ™ who is the fourth in the ***Holiday BARBIE*** **Ornament Collector's Series**. It is among the most popular in Hallmark's lines. This line generally debuts in November.

STAR TREK® has been on television for over thirty years and Hallmark ornaments add to the credibility of the popular science fiction series. One of the more animated ornaments, **The U.S.S. Enterprise** craft is suspended above a stand and the **Galileo Shuttlecraft** has a button to press, activating the voice of Captain James T. Kirk.

Other licensed property holiday-themed ornaments include the **PEZ**® **Snowman** and the famous Santa swigging Coca-Cola® on an ornament called **Welcome Guest**.

One of the most beloved Christmas movies *It's a Wonderful Life*, is captured in an anniversary edition with characters George Bailey and his family standing next to the Christmas tree.

From "Here Comes Santa" Collection: (Clockwise from top) 1989, 1984, 1991, 1987, 1988.

(Left to Right) Baby's First Christmas, Rocking Horse, 1959 Cadillac De Ville

(Left to Right) Mother Goose: Humpty Dumpty 1993, Nostalgic Houses and Shops 1986, Hark! It's Herald 1992, Church, Hark! It's Herald 1989, Santa and Toys, Feliz Navidad 1985, Hark! It's Herald 1990, Nostalgic Houses and Shops 1984, Dolls of the World: Native American Barbie 1996.

Pansy (Left) and Come All Ye Faithful

In 1976, Hallmark introduced movement with **Twirl-Abouts** which have a three-dimensional figure in the center of each ornament that rotates on a brass pin. In the same year, Hallmark introduced **Baby's First Christmas**. The ornament has become the most popular captioned ornament in Hallmark's Keepsake Ornament lines. After movement, came music in 1989 with **Baby's First Christmas** ornament capable of producing a tune. In 1992 came speech. Designs such as **Santa's Answering Machine** and **Shuttlecraft Galileo** literally had something to say to collectors.

FYI

- Keepsake Ornaments are the most collected Christmas collectible in the country.
- Sixty percent of the ornaments are priced under $10. In 1978, seventy percent were under $3.50.
- Hallmark introduced more than 250 new collectible designs in 1977 alone.
- Hallmark considers all of its ornaments to be limited editions. Current ornaments are marked with the year made
- All lines are available at retail for only one season.
- Hallmark has twenty-six ongoing series on topics ranging from *Gone with the Wind* to *Star Wars*.
- Ten new series appeared in 1997.
- The collectible series ornaments, which began in 1982, have a tree-shaped symbol with a number inside, showing the ornaments sequence in the series.

COLLECTOR'S CLUB - established in 1987

Membership benefits include:

- opportunities to buy club-exclusive membership ornaments and exclusive club-edition ornaments
- four issues of the *Collector's Courier* newsletter
- the annual *Dream Book catalog of Keepsake Ornaments*
- a personalized membership card.

Contact:

Hallmark Keepsake Collector's Club
P.O. Box 419034
Kansas City, MO 64141-6034
tel. 800-425-5627

Website

http://www/hallmark/com
Official Hallmark Website

Cinderella–1995, Lionel 700E Hudson Steam Locomotive, Freedom 7

June McKenna Collectibles™

About June McKenna - artist/owner

One day in the late 1970's, June McKenna, and her oldest son Scott, made a brontosaurus for his third grade science project. The two combined their best efforts, and with cornstarch and salt, sculpted a dinosaur. Little did they know that this would mark the beginning of a professional career for McKenna. This science project led to the creation of the June McKenna Santa figurines which are now among the country's top Christmas collectibles.

June McKenna: Owner/Artist

Named for the month of her birth, June McKenna fell in love with art after attending several high school drawing classes.

In the early years of her marriage, her main focus was on raising her boys, Scott and Joey. However, McKenna still found time to paint quilts, mailboxes, wooden figures, different types of dolls and even detergent bottle covers.

She began selling her creations at local craft fairs and McKenna's family provided more than just moral support. Her husband Dan, cut wooden shapes, her sons assisted with the painting and her in-laws made doll accessories.

After the "Dino" experiment, McKenna used her new skills and came up with an original technique for creating figurines. She first molded them from wood resin and carved thirteen folk art figurines; including several storybook characters and an African-American doll named "Mammie."

The McKenna's business continued to grow. In 1982, Dan, an electrician, joined their new business, J & M Collectibles, on a full-time basis. June discontinued the original thirteen designs and introduced nineteen new figurines. Included in these new designs was the first Santa called **Father Christmas**, for which she is now famous.

McKenna enjoys carving her creations late at night. After the family has gone to bed she gets comfortable on the couch and carves, occasionally watching television.

June McKenna Collectibles™ Logo

About June McKenna Collectibles

Father Christmas, the first June McKenna Santa was unlimited in production, so several are un-numbered.

Only 4,000 of the second **Father Christmas** were created. By 1985 it sold out and was retired. Each year June McKenna introduces a new limited Santa figurine and calls it the **4,000 Series**.

1987 Mr. Santa

1988 Jolly Ole Santa

1987 Mrs. Santa

1990 Noel

In the early 1980's McKenna introduced her first flatback ornaments. These were thinner than those made today and oval wooden display bases were required for display. Today June McKenna's ornaments stand without a wooden base. The bases are no longer sold and are also considered a collectors item.

"The eyes have it," as they give the distinctive look for which June McKenna figures are known. Large pupils with long vertical highlights are considered her unique signature. June McKenna Collectibles are notorious for outstanding detail, quality hand-painting and historical accuracy. In 1986 she was asked by the **Williamsburg Foundation** to carve a Santa typical of early Colonial Williamsburg.

June McKenna is best known for her Santas but also creates angels, fairy tale characters, African-American folk art, colonial times and country settings.

Even June McKenna Collectibles catalogs have become collectibles, especially her first three. The collector's guides and information packets, which goes out to every member, are certainly impressive. Her distinguished **Father Christmas** logo is embossed on the front of a black fine-grain, leather three-ring binder. The catalogs contain dozens of full page, full-color photographs of June McKenna's collectibles. A detailed and complete history of the company is included as well as a secondary market price guide. The book provides several blank printed record forms to assist in tracking pieces.

FYI - Company History Highlights

- **Late 1970's** June McKenna created her first project at her kitchen table. Folk art figurines were numbered one to thirteen and signed with initials "**J McK.**"
- **Early 1980's** A new line of folk art designs and her first Santa were introduced. These were numbered fourteen through thirty-three. McKenna began bringing home awards and income from the arts and crafts shows in the Richmond, Virginia area.
- **1982** The first flatback ornament, called **Santa with Toys** was created
- **1984** The McKennas' business, **J & M Collectibles**™, grew beyond their kitchen table and they purchased and renovated an antiquated fire station in nearby Doswell, Virginia. Unfortunately and ironically, a fire destroyed their fire station which was filled with inventory about to be shipped. Fortunately, the molds were located at their home. Disheartened yet determined, the McKennas quickly rebuilt. With this renewal came the new business name **June McKenna Collectibles, Inc**.
- **1984-1985** June McKenna introduced the first set of Christmas carolers.
- **1986** marked the beginning of the **Registered Edition Santa** collection.
- **1987** The company was moved to its current location in Ashland, Virginia. A new limited edition line of larger Santas, some standing at seventeen inches, was introduced.
- **1988** June McKenna began limited editions of her **Nativity Series**.
- **1989** The **Personal Appearance Santa Collection** was introduced. These Santas are replicas of the sold-out **4,000 Series**. They are only available for purchase at "June McKenna" personal appearances. These pieces are signed and dated for collectors.
- **1991** marked the addition of **Bedtime Stories** to the line. This piece depicts Santa sitting on his chair surrounded by children from various cultures. **Bedtime Stories** reflects McKenna's vision of a peaceful and united world.
- **1992** McKenna designed **Little Guardian Angel** in commemoration of the ten year anniversary of the company. This is the first three-dimensional angel McKenna has carved, symbolizing peace, harmony and tranquility. Circulation of this piece was limited to the number of pieces ordered and produced during 1992. She ascertains that this piece reflects her feelings about the major geopolitical changes of the time, such as the lowering of The Berlin Wall. "It was certainly a time when the world could use a guardian angel," she said.
- **1997** Today the company employs approximately fifty people and is located in a 12,000 square foot, two-story building.
- With each limited or registered edition purchased you will be given a 3 x 5 registration card to be filled in and mailed to June McKenna. Name and address information is entered into the June McKenna Collectors Registry. The collector is then sent a certificate of authenticity and added to the *Visions Newsletter* mailing list. This certificate authenticates a registered original.

Best Care

- Dust with a soft bristle brush such as a soft camel or sable artist's brush. Carefully work brush downward into crevices. Blow away dust as you go and clean the brush frequently. If additional

1989 Last Gentle Nudge

1993 The Patriot Santa

1992 Little Guardian Angel

1991 Santa's Hot Air Balloon

1989 Santa's Wardrobe

cleaning is necessary, use a brush soaked with a mixture of water and a mild soap detergent. Follow with a brush soaked in plain water. Pat dry with a soft cloth.

- Avoid packing in newsprint as the ink may transfer onto the collectible.
- June McKenna offers a repair service for a nominal fee. Contact the business office for details.

1990 Night Before Christmas

Display Tips

- The fine detail of a June McKenna collectible shows well when displayed against natural wood finishes.
- Use a mirror behind the collectible to display more of the entire figurine.
- These collectibles are relatively fragile. Care should be taken to display them out of the way of children and pets.

Secondary Market Sizzler

The 1983 Limited Edition of Father Christmas originally sold for $120. At the 1996 June McKenna Festival auction the collectible sold for $2,400.

Collector's Club - June McKenna Collectors' Society established in 1995

Membership includes:

- a subscription to *Visions Newsletter*
- an exclusive membership gift figurine
- a personalized membership certificate and membership card
- a current retail price list

The *Collector's Guide Book* is available at June McKenna retail stores and may be purchased for $50.

Contact

June McKenna Collectibles
P.O. Box 1540
Ashland, VA 23005
tel. 804-798-2024

Web Site

http:\\www.jmckenna.com
Official June McKenna Collectibles Website

Lynn Haney Santas™

About Lynn Haney - artist/owner

Lynn Haney didn't begin with a blueprint plan for success, he just followed his passion. "I'm a great believer in providence," said Lynn. "It seems one opportunity has led to the next."

In the early 1970's Haney studied and learned to teach art, with an emphasis on sculpture and fabrics, at Texas Technical University. After earning a master's degree, he began teaching Junior High students. He left the classroom six years later to enter the business world as a salesman.

In 1987 he began creating his own world, combining business, art and Santas. "I did know I wanted to do my own designs, work at my own pace, make my own decisions," said Haney.

Specializing in Christmas and Santas, Haney brings his artistic eye to all aspects of life. "I'm conscious of the aesthetics of everything around me--whether it's furniture, accessories or apparel."

"I try to pay attention to what I like and to what others around me like. For example, I know there is a lot of interest in old world ornaments so this year I'm incorporating them into several of my new designs,"

Haney confesses that he doesn't sketch out his ideas. "I like the feel of sculpting the faces and playing with the fabrics when I'm creating. Everybody assumes I draw them first, but I'm a very three-dimensional person. I do a lot of planning in my mind," he said. "I have a collage board where I may put up a couple of pieces of fabric and lay some braid there too, then come back in a couple of days and see what I think about it."

Lynn Haney: Artist/Owner

When asked where he gets his ideas for new pieces he responded, "Everywhere. We might go on a trip to New York and stop in a museum. A particular collection may inspire me to create something. Or sometimes I will find just one element that will be the start for a new piece and everything will evolve from it." An example of this was an occasion when he found a small well-crafted, hand-tooled leather saddle at a show. "That led directly to my making a cowboy Santa," he said.

Mountain Man

Haney is exceptionally pleased with his **Holy Family** series. "As a Christian, it is important to me because it more specifically reflects my personal beliefs," he said.

Haney has known his wife, Sue, since the fifth grade. They have been married for twenty-six years and have twenty-three-year-old twin daughters, Julie and Jill. Their studio is in Lubbock, Texas.

The Creation of the Lynn Haney Santas

- Haney spends between thirty to forty hours creating each new Santa design. He sculpts the head, designs the costumes, drafts the costume patterns, chooses trims and accessories and plans the Santa's beard and wig.

- The head, and on some designs the hands, are sculpted in clay.
- All details of the original design are finished and a latex rubber mold is created.
- Pecan shells are ground into a fine flour and mixed with a liquid polymer resin. This mixture is then poured into the molds. Haney chose the popular pecan resin because it allows for the creation of fine detail and easily absorbs paint.
- The cast face is removed from the mold after the pieces have dried.
- A new costume design is given to professional seamstresses to cut, trim and finish each pattern. The Hungarian costumes used in many of Haney's designs are authentic. More than four hundred women in Hungarian villages cut, appliqué and assemble the costumes.
- The costumes are then sent across the Atlantic to Haney's studios. Approximately two dozen people then add the finishing touches.
- At the studio, wool from around the world is used to create the Santa beards and wigs.
- Using birch tree bark, the Minnesota Ojibwe Indians hand craft the accessory. The bark is harvested by the tribes, as they have done for centuries, without damaging the trees.

(Clockwise from Top) Santa of Christmas Past, Vineyard Santa, Christmas Fantasy

Fireside Santa

Santa of Christmas Cottage

(Top to Bottom) Melchior, Kaspar, Balthasar

(Clockwise from Top) Rocky Mountain Santa (Red Coat), Rocky Mountain Santa (White Coat), Starry Night Santa

(Clockwise from Top) Santa of Toy Hamlet, Homestead Santa, Let It Snow-Let It Snow-Let It Snow

(Clockwise from Top) Santa of Deer Valley (White and Red) Santa of Deer Valley (Black and Red) Santa of Northwest Journey

FYI

- Each costume and face is an original design and signed by the artist.
- The Lynn Haney Collection consists of open edition pieces and limited edition pieces. Open edition pieces are retired at his discretion.
- Haney's Limited Editions range between seventy five to1,200 pieces.
- **The Holy Family of Joseph, Mary and Baby Jesus** are the1997 Limited Edition pieces.
- An official collectors' newsletter began publication in 1997.

Best Care

- Haney suggests using plastic bags to help keep dust and dirt off the Santas. He recommends allowing enough space for air to circulate around the piece.
- Avoid storing the Santas in extreme heat, dampness or in an area of rapid temperature changes.
- Moths can cause considerable damage to the costumes. Haney cautions against using moth balls as the strong odor absorbs into the fabric. Cedar chips are recommended for protection.

(Left to Right) Mrs. Gumdrop, Mr. Gumdrop, Snow Country Santa

Display Tips

- Allow the old to accentuate the new by displaying a Lynn Haney Santa on an antique plant stand.
- Arrange a mirror behind the Santa to give a better view of the bag of goodies typically carried by these figures.
- Place a Santa, or more than one Lynn Haney collectible on a large, lazy wooden Susan in the middle of a dining room table. This enables observers to gently turn the base and view the collectible without handling.

Collectors' Club

There is not an official collector's club at this time.

Contact

Lynn Haney Collection
3515 34th Street
Lubbock, Texas 79410
tel. 806-788-1271
fax. 806-788-1275

Lynn West Collections™

About Lynn West - artist

When Lynn West was eleven years old she took the words of a Walt Disney™ tune to heart. Expecting her dreams to come true, she would look out her bedroom window in Lakewood, California and "wish upon a star."

Almost fifty now, the internationally-acclaimed designer believes most of her dreams have come true. One such example is the success of her limited edition Santa figurines. The designs have become one of the country's premier Christmas collectibles.

West credits her parents with providing a safe, loving environment and giving her confidence to explore ideas. Her father roused her childhood imagination by reading fairytales and whispering stories as he tucked her into bed. Her seventy-year-old mother is active in West's business. In many aspects, her mother assisted in starting West's business. "Mother taught me to sew. Together we made my clothes and my dolls' clothes when I was a child. She is still the wind beneath my wings," West said.

Her grandmother helped by crocheting the wings for West's early fairies' and her sister was also involved with the business. "We've always been an entrepreneurial family," West said.

Artist/Owner: Lynn West

Winter's Angels

As a child, her parents arranged for West to take art lessons. At the age of nine she sold her first oil painting. In the early 1970's West was busy caring for her household, two young children and her husband. When time allowed, she would visit the popular Eschbach's Florist in nearby Laguna Beach, California. She daydreamed over the Christmas displays. "Crowds paid to see the forest of wonderfully decorated trees. Everything was so balanced, comfortable to look at … just wonderful," West said. "This place was a great inspiration to me."

The opportunity then presented itself for her to meet owner Jack Eschbach, and his friend Kitty Coleman. Coleman designed and organized the handmade ornaments for the Eschbach trees. "Jack Eschbach was my idol and became a mentor," said West.

Lynn West Collections™ Logo

Rocking Horse Elf

West joined creative forces with Coleman and several other women. They opened **St. Nicholas**, a Christmas store in San Juan Capistrano. Their items were top-sellers. West describes her time working with the group as "a strong growth period."

Eschbach later introduced West to the inventors and founding owners, Pat and Alen Ripynski, of the Armor All® Corporation. For investment purposes, the Ripynski's were always seeking new businesses. Impressed with the West creation **Professor Grizzlin**, the couple offered to buy her company. She accepted their offer, was placed on salary and driving a company car.

"That was another dream come true," Lynn said. **Lasting Endearments**, the new company, allowed her to created with top quality materials. She comfortably chose gorgeous, expensive fabrics and added such details as multi-colored, gold-embossed tags.

The Ripynski's sold the company after five years. West eventually opted to begin her own business, called **Lynn West Designs**. Simultaneously, two former co-workers started their own companies which were interrelated; a marketing company; called **To Be Announced**, owned by Kim Brennan and Amaranth Productions, owned by Michela Engle. The latter produced Santas, elves and fairies, designed by West, from 1988 to 1996.

In 1989 West also began producing her own line of limited edition Santas called **Lynn West Collections**. Limited to only several hundred pieces, each design is realistically elaborate and constructed by West. She views her rekindling of Christmas magic, which we sometimes lose with age, as her gift to the world.

In January 1997, West began to focusing all of her energies on her own company and no longer designs for **Amaranth Productions**. Despite a demanding workload filling orders, "ideas for new projects keep flowing," she said. She is toying with the idea of creating a new line of fabric-covered ornaments.

Burgundy Rose Fairy

Yuletide Large Fairy

Reindeer Fairy

(Left to Right) Courtly Faeries: Douglas, Tyrone and Errol

For West the fairytale continues and wishes do come true.

FYI

- Santas range from fourteen inches to life-size. Introduced in 1996, her four-foot Santas have become so popular that it is somtimes difficult to support requests.
- West intentionally limits her editions by producing a minimum of fifteen of a design or a maximum of two hundred. She accepts commissions for one-of-a-kind pieces.
- West hires cottage workers to help prepare the costumes, accessories and other parts of her Santas. Each piece is finished at her home workshop in LaQuinta, California.
- Every Lynn West Collectible is personally signed and numbered.
- Lynn West Collectibles are limited in years and the number produced.
- Each collectible includes a personalized registration tag to be sent to the company. The company then sends a certificate of authenticity which increased the value. The collector's name is added to a mailing list and will receive updated information.

(Left to Right) Break Tim Elves: Half Note, Rocky, Rump-Papa-Pum and Skeeter

Crystal Angel

Best Care

- "Letting dust settle and stay isn't good," West said. She adds that the figurines are not extremely delicate and can be easily cleaned. Use a can of compressed air or clean with a soft artist's paint brush.
- Store figurines in a material that breaths. Avoid plastic.

Up On The Rooftop

Swan Sleigh Fairy

- Avoid wrapping figurines in used newsprint as the ink may transfer onto the collectible.

Display Tips

- Although a glass display case will protect Lynn West creations, the artist expressed that she feels they look better out in the open.
- Lynn West Santas and other figurines are wonderful on the mantle or near the fireplace.
- Most designs are complete with accessories and details. Many owners feel that these art pieces are best displayed without distractions, such as greenery.

Secondary Market Sizzler

Lynn West's special edition **Father Christmas**, from the Lasting Endearments selection, originally sold for $1,800. It has sold on the secondary market for $8,000.

Collectors' Club

There is not an official collector's club for Lynn West collectors. However, secondary market information is still available by calling 800-251-3530.

Contact

Lynn West Designs
10 LaQuinta
Irvine, CA 92612-2928
tel. 714-854-0973
fax. 714-854-8382

Margaret Furlong™ Designs

About Margaret Furlong - artist/owner

The name Margaret Furlong equals the word "success."

The artist with softly-curled auburn hair and bird-egg blue eyes speaks frankly about the many challenges she has faced along the way. "I consider the disappointments and mistakes...as the stepping stones to success," she said in a December '92 *Collector's Mart Magazine* article.

Proving her point, she has 1,000 pink angels packed away in boxes. Margaret Furlong is known for her love of white. White was the intended color for her first large batch of angels. However, they came out of the kiln pink. Although scarcely noticeable, they were pink and she was disappointed. She decided against distributing the slightly pink items on the market. She refused to throw them away, packed them in boxes and has since moved them twice.

"Almost sixteen years ago, I had an idea to create a business which might support my desire to make art," said Furlong. "A vital part of this dream would be closely related to my pottery and painting background, since these were the only things I knew and the only things I really wanted to do.

"I was then established in a studio, an old carriage house in Lincoln, Nebraska doing "snowscapes." Using large thin slabs of porcelain doctored with nylon fibers, I draped these torn-edged cloths of porcelain over forms to create snow-covered furrow, hills and haystacks. After firings, I would arrange these largely unglazed forms like a stack of slightly disarrayed papers and raise them to supposedly ethereal heights on boxes of clear plex."

"Also, I was working on a commission using shells as a subject matter. The shell forms which I had cast for this project were strewn all over my studio. It wasn't long before I combined several shell forms, a molded face, a textured coil and tapered trumpet into a shell angel, my first design for the gift trade."

Messiah Angel 1994 Limited Edition/5th and Final Design in "Joyeux Noel" Series

Shell Tassle 5"/Introduced in 1994

At the University of Nebraska, Furlong studied, and eventually taught, sculpture and pottery. With the original love of the openness of abstract sculpture, her artwork has evolved into today's ornaments of fine details and realistic designs of nature.

In 1979, working on a shell motif for a commissioned set of plates, she instead found herself designing an angel. "This angel design in white-on-white unglazed porcelain satisfied my more purist sculptural tendencies and yet had a sweetness which I felt would have appeal in the marketplace," she said. "...my first year was a rather slow, laborious involvement in production techniques, mold making, a limited marketing plan through museum gift shops, and doing all production myself.

"With what I naively thought to be the hardest part behind me, I entered into year two of launching a business, a year of dramatic changes. The first was my marriage to Jerry Alexander and an immediate move to Seattle, Washington. With a transplanted studio, this time in a not-romantic basement garage of suburban condo, I started all over.

"With advice from my husband, a businessman, I set up a new marketing plan. Within a few months I had sales representatives in the major markets all over the United States. Now besides production, there were sample kits, product catalogs, package designs for the whole product line, a system for the hiring and training of production artists and on and on.

Tree Top Star

"The third year of business presented a new set of problems to solve with yet another move. So with the added baggage of kilns, studio equipment and several large boxes of pink angels we moved to where we are now, Salem, Oregon."

Other design ideas have blossomed from her garden of white flowers. She was inspired by the birth of her now fourteen-year-old daughter, Caitlin. Furlong expressed that it was her strongly held Christian beliefs that moved her to weave in spiritual elements when designing her ornaments.

Her first angel appeared in 1979 and combined several shell forms, a molded face, a textured coil and a tapered trumpet. Each design is created by making a clay model which is cast into a master mold. Furlong currently designs approximately sixty new pieces a year.

Furlong has a staff of ninety people to who assist in molding, crafting, firing and packaging of the pieces. They work in the Carriage House Studio, a 19,000 square foot antiquated brick warehouse which has been restored outside and remodeled inside.

The Carriage House Studio is open for tours. One wall holds the inscription of words by poet Henry Wadsworth Longfellow; "Silently, one by one in the infinite meadows of heaven blossomed the lovely stars, the forget-me-nots of the angels."

Conveniently, Fulong is able to design at her home, which is only five minutes away. She expressed that, while her days of designing can be long, most days she can adjust her schedule to her daughter's, allowing more time together.

FYI

- Margaret Furlong is recognized for her white porcelain angels.
- The first shell ornament, the **Trumpeter Angel**, was introduced in1980.
- Prices range from $5 to $45.
- Subjects include angels, shells and hearts.
- Other product designs include wreaths, picture frames, jewelry and note cards.
- The ornament line includes close to one hundred designs with an average introduction of six new designs yearly.
- The1995 **Faith Angel** limited edition pieces sold out within ten days of introduction.

1982 Star Angels

Best Care

- Margaret Furlong collectibles are among the easiest to care for and clean. To clean, wash in a mild detergent that has been diluted with water.
- Store Furlong collectibles in the original, specially designed boxes. A Christmas store owner who has carried these fine porcelain ornaments for many years, said as compared with other collectible lines, very few of the Furlong ornaments have ever arrived at her shop broken. She attributes this to the well designed box.

Display Tips

- Simplicity is behind the beauty of Margaret Furlong's designs. Sometimes just a bit of holly or other greenery will enhance, without overshadowing, the designs.
- Ornaments hang easily on tree limbs and in wreaths or garland.
- Display on the small clear plastic stand which is included with each collectible.
- Arrange ornaments on a wall. Use tiny, thin nails to hang the ornaments. Nail heads will require painting.

Morning Star 3"/Introduced in 1980

"Each year the stark canvas of winter, nurtured by the sun and rain and helped by our caring hands, slowly awakens. The silent seed of seasons past take form leaf by leaf, petal by petal to bloom into a masterpiece of vibrant colors and rich texture. The seasons constantly shift, but with purpose, and in these changes we find God's enduring promise of new beginnings."

—Margaret Furlong

Hallelujah Angel 1986 5" Limited Edition/2nd and Final Design in "Joyeux Noel" Series

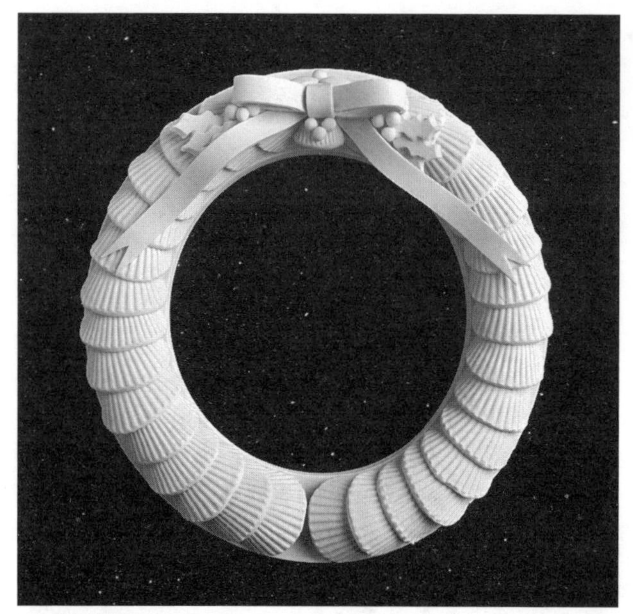

Shell Wreath

Secondary Market Sizzler

The **Hallelujah Angel** issued in 1986 originally sold for $45 and now sells for about $500.

Contact

Margaret Furlong Designs
210 State Street
Salem, Oregon 97301
tel. 800-255-3114

1980 Trumpeter Angels

Old World Christmas®

About Elizabeth M. Merck - artist/designer/owner

E.M. Merck, preferably called "Beth," is a premier designer for and owner of Old World Christmas. Beth leans on her strong background in German cultural traditions, art and history when designing ornaments and her popular line of nutcrackers. At least once a year she returns to Germany to spend time in the workshops.

"Years ago the craftsmen worked quickly because they were paid by the piece." However, detail being important to Beth, she said, "We work very differently, meticulously painting real features on ornament faces, instead of just a line for the mouth or two dots for the eyes."

Collectors often express to Beth that Old World Ornaments arouse childhood memories. "I am delighted by how many people remember these ornaments from their childhood. Even particular forms, such as the birds, or certain Santas," she said.

Although taking great pride in her Old World Christmas's ornaments and nutcrackers, Beth considers her children, Jonathan and Katherine, her best accomplishments.

Origination of Old Word Christmas Ornaments

About twenty years ago, Tim and Beth Merck traveled to Europe as newlyweds and spent hours ambling through many antique shops. Because of Beth's childhood memories of and desire for beautiful German heirloom ornaments on her grandmother's Christmas tree, and the necessity to supply their antique dealership with inventory, they returned to Germany many times to find suppliers of quality glass ornaments.

E.M. "Beth" Merck

Special Event Santa

Mr. and Mrs. Snowman

A friendship grew and a partnership with Klaus Mueller-Blech and his father, a thirteenth century glass blower and owner of Inge-Glas™ workshop. The Blech's purchased thousands of antique ornament molds through the years.

To fill a void in the market for high quality glass ornaments, Old World Christmas was founded in 1981 in Spokane, Washington. Today, as one of the country's largest distributors of glass ornaments, Old World Christmas has long-term contracts with various German companies for sole distributorship.

The Most Popular Old World Christmas Ornament is ... a pickle!

The tradition of the Christmas pickle began generations ago in Germany. As early as the 1800s, the children knew to look for the special ornament on Christmas morning. The first child observant enough to find the pickle, hidden deep in the branches, received a special present.

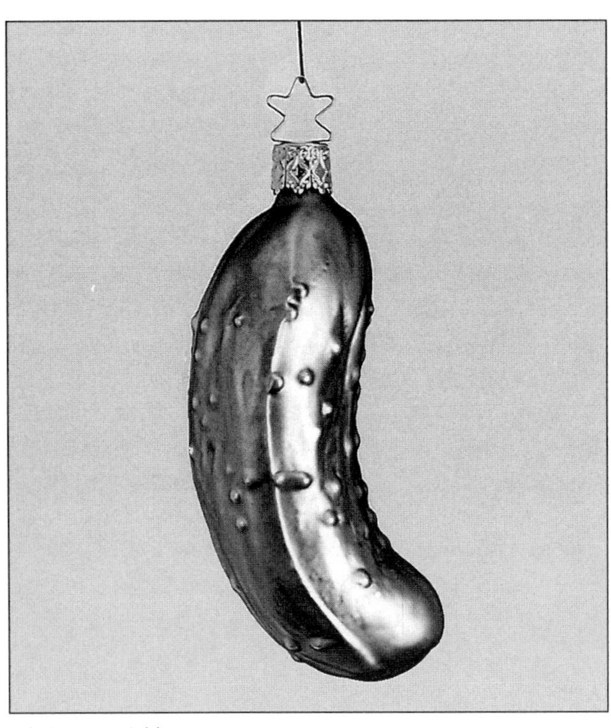

Christmas Pickle

Lauscha's connection to Old World Christmas

In the 1590s many Germans were persecuted for their Protestant faith. At this time, many glassblowers left their homes in southwestern Germany and ventured to mountains of Thuringia in central German. The small village of Lauscha was chosen due to the abundance of required glassblowing materials; limestone, sand and wood. Lauscha became known throughout Europe as a supplier of drinking glasses, beads, marbles and other glass products.

(Left to Right) Woodland Musician and Santa in Chimney

Gasworks, built in 1867, assumed a steady, consistent flame which was far superior to the wood fires formerly used by glassblowers. It was soon discovered that molds could be made much thinner. The technique of blowing a bubble of glass into cookie molds was developed. Shaped ornaments, such as apples, pears and pine cones, began showing up on Christmas trees throughout Europe. Lauscha is the home for many current Old World Christmas glass ornaments. The ornaments are made in cottages scattered throughout the village.

On the second Sunday of each month, master glassblowers meet at the Inge-Glas™ workshop to collect their assignments and gather and required molds. Two weeks later the ornaments are returned and ready to be silvered and painted in the Inge-Glas™ workshop. After completion, they are shipped to America.

FYI

- Using a century old art form, each Old World Christmas ornament is mouth-blown into an antique porcelain mold. The inside is washed with a liquid silver and the outside is hand-painted with brightly colored lacquers.
- The star-shaped ornament hangar on every Old World Christmas ornaments is a registered trade-mark and making it easily recognized as such. The trademark was introduced in 1985.

Christmas Eve

Elegant Santa Face

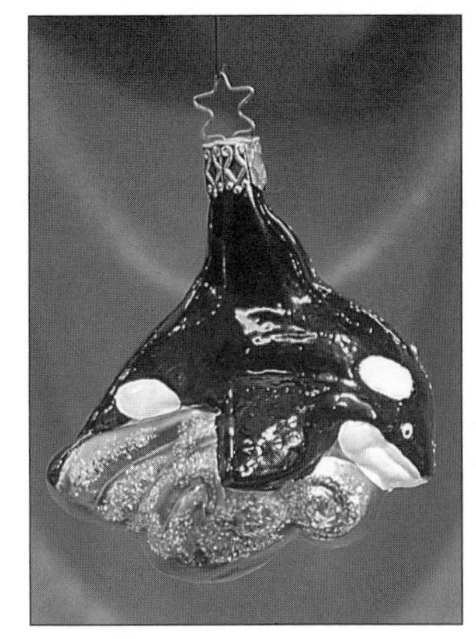
Orca Whale

Large Gingerbread House

Oma's Coffee Pot

Hearty Santa

Fruit Centerpiece

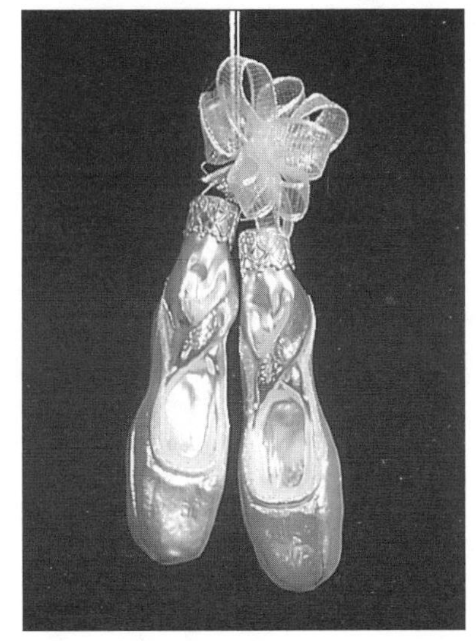
Pair of Ballet Slippers

Bunny in Basket

- Old World Christmas stakes claims to the introduction of the slip-on light bulb glass covers. The replications are fashioned after turn-of-the-century Christmas lights. The actual light bulbs were originally painted and shaped.
- Old World Christmas carries the popular Christmas line of nutcrackers by E.M. Merck Collection.
- Ornaments, nutcrackers and other Old World Christmas lines are sold by more than 14,000 retail locations nationwide.

Shiny Red Apple

Best Care

- Wrap the ornaments loosely in tissue paper and pack in sturdy boxes. Store in a secure place where temperatures do not reach extremes.
- Strong sunlight and fluorescent light can fade the brightly colored lacquer paints.
- As needed, dust with an artist's soft paintbrush or cosmetic brush.
- Never wash with water as it affects the durability of the lacquer.

Display Tip

For a colorful and fun centerpiece, fill a glass bowl with Old World Christmas fruits and vegetables.

Secondary Market Sizzler

The first issue of the 1985 **Santa Nightlight** sold for $25. It has sold on the secondary market for $3,000.

Collectors Club - Old World Collectors Club established in 1992

Membership includes:

- exclusively purchase Old World Christmas ornaments
- receive a subscription to the club newsletter
- receive free ornaments
- receive a 120-page, full-color guide

The collectors' club magazine, *The Old World Star Gazette*, is a quarterly publication. It provides members with updated information on new/retired items and general information on the history and traditions surrounding the collectibles. Call 800-965-7669 for information.

Contact

Old World Christmas Collector's Club
P.O. Box 8000 - Dept. C
Spokane, WA 99203-0030

Pipka™ Collectibles

About Pipka Ulvilden - artist

Over twenty years ago, amidst a personal crisis, Pipka Ulvilden (pronounced O' vil din) was inspired to create the **Old World Santas**. Today, her creations are revered by Christmas collectors.

"I was recently divorced," Ulvilden told *Figurines & Collectibles Magazine*, "with two kids and a house payment and wondering what to do." In 1972 Ulvilden's mother, while in Germany on a trip back to their homeland, sent a large brown paper package with paints, brushes and books on the Bavarian folk art "Bauernmalerei" or peasant painting.

"I used the supplies as a way to relax and get in touch with my feelings," Pipka told *Collector Editions Magazine*. "At first my work looked like a kindergarten child did it. But after painting sixteen hours a day for months on end, I eventually found my niche . . . I loved art so much that I decided this was how I would make a living and support my family."

Ulvilden studied and painted flowers and gained enough confidence to enter her artwork in the Renaissance Festival, Minnesota's most recognized art fair. Encouraged by the enthusiastic reception and requests for her work she continued her venture. She began painting furniture and accessories and sold them to homes, inns and restaurants throughout Minnesota and Wisconsin.

Pipka Ulvilden: Artist/Writer/Teacher

Storytime Santa

Ulvilden was again inspired during a heavy snowstorm. It was at this time she designed her first Father Christmas image. Snowbound in her cottage, she spent the quiet day designing a Russian Santa for her mother.

She was and is still enamored with the stories, myths and traditions surrounding Father Christmas. In her travels she continues to research the subject.

Ulvilden was five years old when, just after World War II, she traveled on a ship to America. In 1949, with her family, she left behind her home in Germany.

In exchange for a U.S. Army sponsorship, her father, an English speaking Czechoslovakian army physician, agreed to establish a practice in a small community in North Dakota. Ulvilden formed new friendships in America and each year traveled to Germany to visit old friends and family.

As a child, Ulvilden enjoyed drawing. She loved the "Old Masters'" paintings portrayed in her parent's books. As she grew up, she continued to draw and considers herself blessed.

In addition to her successful collectible lines, she owns a store in Bay, Wisconsin. Ulvilden expresses her passion for European folk art by designing Santas, teaching art and writing. She sells art supplies and folk art by various artists.

Ukranian Santa

Aussie Santa and Boomer

Pipka Earth Angels (Left to Right) Guardian Angel, Angel of Roses, Messenger Angel

Good News Santa

Despite success, she perceives her mistakes as having taught the best lessons. Ulvilden tells her students, "If you don't like your project; keep it, study it and decide where and how you would improve it."

About Prizm™ - sole distributor for Pipka

It was all in the timing. In 1992 Gary Meidinger was an accountant and Michele Johnson was a graphic artist for TLC, a greeting card company. Ulvilden's assistant contacted TLC, after noticing an advertisement. Meidinger and Johnson had a strong interest in the growing collectibles industry and were immediately attracted to Ulvilden's art.

Based on Ulvilden's Old World Santas, plans were drawn with TLC for a seventy two piece product line. This dream dimmed when TLC's parent company, McCall's Pattern™ Company, announced the closing of TLC.

Facing relocation or possible unemployment, Meidinger and Johnson met with Ulvilden and took the bold steps of forming Prizm. Prizm would produce, market and distribute her work.

Her flat artwork went overseas to a talented Taiwanese master sculptor, who interpreted them into three-dimensional figurines. Pipka was proud of the results. The initial shipment of the first six Pipka Santas went out March 23, 1995.

FYI

- The 10" and 11" figurines are made of cold-cast resin.
- Pipka artwork is the foundation and sole product of Prizm Inc.
- Prizm Inc.markets and distributes **Pipka's Old World Santas** and **Angels.**
- A maximum of six Pipka Santas or Earth Angels are introduced yearly.
- Santa editions are limited to 3,600.
- Angel editions are limited to 5,400.
- Approximately 1,000 retailers throughout the United States carry Pipka Collectibles.
- In 1997, six **Memories of Christmas Santas**, six smaller Santas and three **Earth Angels** were introduced.

Best Care

- Keep out of direct sunlight to prevent fading.
- Dusting with a dry cloth. The use of chemical cleaners and water can cause damage.
- Keep original packaging for storage and transporting.

Pipka Earth Angels (Left to Right) Angel of Hearts, Gardening Angel, The Cottage Angel

Display Tips

- Bring out the exquisite details of Pipka Santa ornaments by displaying in a cabinet with mirrored back panels. For a dramatic affect, direct a spotlight on the faces.
- Place **Good News Santa** on or near a real bible. (This figure carries a bible.)
- Display **Gingerbread Santa** as a kitchen table centerpiece and have a plate of real cookies nearby, ready for visitors.
- Prizm Inc. has a book available which includes all Pipka designs ever created. The book includes sections on display ideas, history and more.

Secondary Market Sizzler

The average secondary market price for **Midnight Visitor** is approximately $200. According to a company spokesman, the Pipka figure, which initially sold for $85, recently sold for $1,450.

Collectors' Club - not established at this time.

Contact

Pipka Collectibles
P.O. Box 1106
Manhattan, KS 66505
tel. 888-427-4752
fax. 913-776-6550

Polonaise™ Ornaments

About Kurt S. Adler - owner

Having served in the U.S. Army in WWII, Kurt S. Adler traveled back to Europe. He returned in search of beautiful, unique home decorating items to resell to Americans.

Adler returned to America and worked diligently to maintain his European contacts. At the same time, he was creating his own designs.

Adler traveled around the country to various department stores. He presented to store buyers the dozens of samples in his cases. He was successful in his persistence in promoting a worthy product. His work began connecting with the demand for his items.

The Kurt S. Adler corporation began to grow and today professes to be the world's leading resource for European glass ornaments.

The Komozja line is considered the crown jewel of KSA's contemporary collectibles lines.

The creation of Polonaise ornaments

Using a welding flame, master artisans heat a simple glass tube. The tube is placed into a mold and the craftsman blows into it, inflating the soft glass liquid to fill every crevice.

After cooling, which takes only minutes, the form is reheated in the flame. The re-heating process creates a smooth surface.

Suggestive of a lollipop due to the long glass stems, the ornaments are dipped in a silver solution and are set on racks to dry. After drying the ornament is then dipped into a varnish bath.

Using German Kaiser paint, which is considered the world's top quality paint, artists finalize ornament production by painting delicate details and dusting with gold sparkles.

FYI

- Winner of the 1995 **Best Glass Ornament Collection** and 1996 winner in the Collectors' Choice Awards.

Cherubim Boxed Set

Garden of Mary Boxed Set

- With the age-old tradition of the European master glassblowers, each Polonaise ornament is handcrafted and hand-painted in Poland.
- Kurt S. Adler acquires decorative items and ornaments from more than two hundred contacts. These contacts are maintained throughout the world.
- Polonaise means a Polish costume or a Polish dance.

Best Care

- "Because the glass ornaments are very fragile, actually the less you do to them the better," said a Polonaise spokesman.
- If necessary, use a soft artist's brush to dust. Do not use water. The earlier designs were decorated with water-based paint. Even a drop of water can destroy the finish.

(Left to Right) The Great Egyptian Pyramid, The Egyptian Cat, Egyptian Princess and The Sphinx

Display Tips

- Wire display stands which display one, two or more ornaments work well. These are available at Christmas and other gift-ware stores. The stands show the intricate design details of the Polonaise collectibles.
- In one corner of a room, tack a wide swathe of fabric in an unstructured, loose design, from the ceiling. Use invisible fishing line or other monofilament to hang a collection of ornaments against this colorful backdrop.

Secondary Market Sizzler

Cinderella's Slipper, in the gold tones, has sold on the secondary market for $2,000. The initial cost of this collectible was $20.

Industry Standings Maintained by Kurt S. Adler

- First to design, develop, import and distribute ornaments crafted of high quality materials including glass, wood, ceramics, Capiz shell (a byproduct of mother-of-pearl) resin and high-quality plastics.
- World's leading resource for authentic European glass ornaments.
- Largest team of first-class, exclusive in-house designers.
- First to create African-American Santas and Santas set in unique and whimsical settings.
- The first company to introduce high quality snowglobes, or water domes, in the mid 1950s.

Collectors' Club - Polonaise Collector's Guild established 1997

After a half century of "first introductions," Kurt S. Adler is particularly proud of its line of old world glass ornaments called Polonaise.

Membership includes:

- a member's only ornament
- an illustrated video of ornament production
- a collector's pin
- membership certificate
- a portfolio of new, current and retired pieces

Contact

Kurt S. Adler
1107 Broadway
New York, NY 10010
tel. 800-243-9627

POSSIBLE DREAMS®

About Warren Stanley - artist/co-founder

It 1983, Warren Stanley and Leonard Miller founded Possible Dreams. Stanley used his talent designing Santas for the **Clothtique Santas** and acquired designs from America's top artists for the **American Artist Collection.**

Stanley was in Europe on a buying trip when he became intrigued with a centuries-old method of stiffening cloth. A businessman with an artistic flair, he mused on the possibilities of putting a new twist on the old technique.

Returning to America he conferred with his top designers and they began experimenting. The goal was to create costumes for the porcelain and resin figurines already produced by Possible Dreams. The first seven Santas in the Possible Dreams **Clothique** line successfully portrayed a rich realism.

Clothique Collection: Winter Wanderer

Top contributing artists

Tom Browning
Judith Ann Griffith
Mary Monteiro
David Wenzel
Joyce Cleveland
Judi Vaillancourt

About Tom Browning - A Possible Dream's Artist

The term "struggling artist" does not apply to Tom Browing, one of Possible Dreams premier designers. At age ten he knew what he wanted to be. He has progressed to a 48-year-old nationally known artist who is filled with talent and good fortune.

"I feel very lucky," he told an interviewer for *Santa Fe's Focus Magazine.* "Getting into painting full time was an easy transition for me...it got to the point where I began selling my work so I quit my job because it was the logical thing to do ... I know it doesn't often happen that way and sometimes people struggle for years...I'm just lucky."

Browning acknowledges that his quiet personality in portrayed in his creations, be it an oil painting or a Santa design for Possible Dreams. The subject of his designs changes through the years; wildlife, landscapes, still life and figure work. "I'm a little more romantic now," he admits.

Browning credits his parents and his fourth grade teacher for encouraging his interest in drawing. "On Saturday mornings I'd tune into a "learn-to-draw" program on television and follow the instructions. I was a great fan of Disney," he said.

Browning spends eight to ten hours a day, in front of a canvas, at his studio located in Eugene, Oregon.

Designers and craftsmen at the Possible Dream company in Foxboro, Massachusetts interpret Browning's paintings to create the Possible Dream Santas.

FYI

- **The Crinkle Claus Collection** are cold cast sculptured Santas with a unique puckered and wrinkled surface.
- **The Clothtique Santas** are figurines created using a blend of stiffened cloth, porcelain and resin.
- In 1996, for the first time in the company's history, President and designer Warren Stanley attached his signature to the exclusive **Clothtique Signature Series**. The series has a limited run of 6,000 pieces.
- **The American Artist Collection** is made up of **Clothtique Santas**. The collection was inspired by the artwork of great American illustrators.
- The packaging for Possible Dream items is beautifully designed. The boxes are sturdy and provide protection during shipping and storage.
- Possible Dreams donates a percentage from each sale of individual **Clothtique Santas** to **The**

Crinkle Claus Collection: Italian Santa

Starlight Foundation. The Starlight Foundation is a charity which works to brighten the lives of seriously ill children.

Best Care for a Clothtique

- Water and **Clothtique Santas** don't mix! A dry, soft paintbrush or shaving brush works well to clear out dust from crevices or folds.
- Use a soft cloth to dust the larger areas of the figure.
- Strong sunlight and artificial light, when placed closely to a **Clothtique** figure, can fade colors.

Display Tips

- Display Clothtiques and Crinkle Claus collectibles on antique furniture or wood with a patina-like finish.
- Indirect lighting creates a dramatic affect.
- Coordinate the main colors on the collectible with accessories or other items. For example, use coordinating flowers, ribbons, wrapping materials or fabric.

Clothique Collection: Fresh From the Oven

Clothique Collection: Kriss Kringle/USA Circa 1840

Crinkle Claus Collection: Kelly Crinkle

Clothique Collection: Three Alarm Santa

Crinkle Claus Collection: (Left to Right) Santa Windmill and Santa Castle

Crinkle Claus Collection: Crinkle Soccer Player

Secondary Market Sizzler

Bestsellers in the Possible Dreams collections include **Giving Thanks**, #15045 in the Clothtique line and **Starburst Krinkle**, #65903 in the Crinkle Clause line.

Collectors' Club - Santa Claus Network

Membership includes:

- a gift
- opportunities to purchase exclusive members-only designs
- a newsletter
- collector's guide book
- a membership card

Contact

Possible Dreams
Six Perry Drive
Foxboro, Massachusetts 02035
tel. 800-782-8837
fax. 508-543-4255
e-mail. POSSDREAMSS@AOL.COM

Steinbach Nutcrackers®

About the Steinbachs

The name Steinbach is synonymous with collectible nutcrackers. For nearly two hundred years, six generations of Steinbachs have created hand-turned, hand-painted, high-quality creations from wood.

Originally from Austria, the family dates to the late 1200's. Erwin Steinbach, a famous architect, was the master builder for the "Muenster" or Dome of Strasbourg. This large church still stands as a testament to quality and beauty.

The Steinbach factory began in 1832 with a single timber yard and a sawmill powered by a stream. When the Erzegebirge region's main industry of mining dwindled, the families turned to carving wood into such items as staffs, spindles, plates, toys and other household particulars. They eventually began making music boxes and other fine wood products.

In 1949 the Steinbachs started making nutcrackers. Since then approximately six hundred personality types have been created. More than a million nutcrackers have been produced.

Chimney Sweep

Owners: Karla Steinbach with Father, Christian Steinbach

The Steinbach factory is located in Hohenhamein, West Germany. After the Berlin Wall came down in 1989, another factory was built in East Germany.

In 1991 the U.S.-based company, Kurt S. Adler, introduced one of the first limited edition **Steinbach Nutcrackers** called **Merlin the Magician**.

Owner and President Herr Christian Steinbach celebrated his 75th birthday in 1996. He was honored with a special nutcracker in his honor. Steinbach is man known for his strong work ethic as well as his poetical thoughts. Enthusiastically he continues to travel with his daughter, Karla, to collectible shows, markets and promotional events around the world.

As a sixth generation member, Karla Steinbach is overseeing factory operations. For many years father and daughter exercised authority over product development and the manufacturing of limited edition nutcrackers.

Karla is the company vice-president and mother of two. Steinbach says her two children are learning the business. "They come to the factory after school and they already know the machines, the types of wood and the people who work there."

Nutcrackers: Why the big teeth?

The dictionary defines a nutcracker as "an instrument for cracking nuts." However, nutcracker collectors know the expanded meaning has to do with ballet, German history, big teeth and master woodcarvers.

In German folklore, nutcrackers are symbolic of good luck, power and strength. They were often given as protective keepsakes for the home and family. According to Herr Christian Steinbach, president of Steinbach Nutcrackers, the guardian nutcrackers "show their teeth to all the bad things of the world." Karla Steinbach believes in the powers of nutcrackers. "To give a nutcracker to a small child is to give protection to him or her," she said.

Presidents Series: (Left to Right) George Washington, Thomas Jefferson, Abraham Lincoln, Theodore Roosevelt

The history of nutcrackers relates to the early dining customs of Germans. It was common in social circles, after a meal, to crack hazelnuts and soft-shelled pecans and consume them with wine and sweets. A funny or unusual nutcracker often became a conversation piece.

Interest in nutcrackers boomed in the late 1700's after the novel, *The Nutcracker and the King of Mice* was written by Amadeus Hoffman. The book was also the inspiration for Peter Tchaikovsky's ever-popular *Nutcracker Suite* ballet.

Tales of Sherwood Forest: (Left to Right) Friar Tuck and Robin Hood

The Creation of a Steinbach Nutcracker

Creating a Steinbach Nutcracker requires more than the artistic application of a knife to a block of wood. It may require one hundred thirty different procedures to complete one nutcracker. Nutcrackers are "born" from such European woods as aged Beech, Maple, Birch, Linden and Pine.

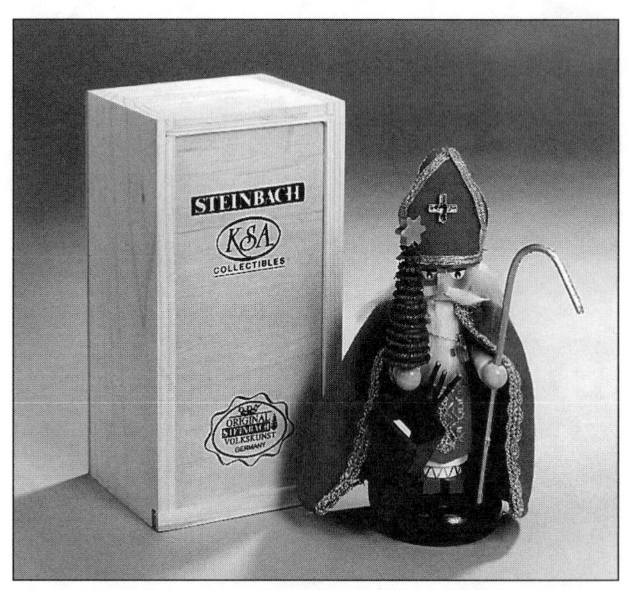

St. Nicholas Mini Nutcracker

"You have to know a thing or two about wood to work with it, because it is a living material with its own rules," -- Herr Christian Steinbach

Major production steps:

1. **Cutting** - Curing and drying the wood may take longer than three years. To achieve the lighter yellow color, the woods are taken from forests far from lakes and rivers which tend to grow trees of darker, red or black wood.
2. **Shaping** - A high-speed milling cutter shapes such large pieces as the legs, jaws, arms and torso.
3. **Customizing** - Because all wood is different, each rough-shaped block is placed on a machine that is hand-turned so the highly skilled operator can customize the piece. "If you lay ten pieces of, say an arm, on a table side by side, each would look slightly different," explained Karla Steinbach.
4. **Lathe Work** - The introduction of the lathe in the fifteenth century propelled the art of woodworking forward. Many more nutcrackers could be produced with this machine that steadied the wood, while turning it rapidly against a cutting/shaping edge.
5. **Polishing and Drilling** - Power drills and polishing wheels are used to help smooth the wood and piece the sections together.
6. **Priming and Spraying** - Craftspeople spray on the primer or base coat of paint.
7. **Carving** - No machine can take the place of handwork. Using knives, experienced wood carvers add finishing touches.
8. **Painting** - Each nutcracker is hand-painted with infamous bright, glossy colors.

The term "environmentally conscious" was not prevalent when the Steinbachs began replanting trees to replenish those cut down to create nutcrackers. Today, five trees, for every one used, is planted. "We are now using wood from trees my grandparents planted and we must continue that cycle," said Vice President Karla Steinbach. The Steinbachs profess a deep understanding and appreciation of nature's cycles and the need to look to the future.

Best Care

- Dry is best for nutcrackers.
- Avoid storing in a cellar or basement for extended periods of time. Moisture can damage collectibles.
- Nutcrackers are easy-care collectibles. Simply dust with a soft cloth.
- Pay attention to individual care of the fabrics used in various costumes. For example, hats made of felt may fade if displayed in sunlight for an extended period of time.

Display Tips

- Build elaborate shelving to display collection, or
- simply set them on a fireplace mantle, high shelf or by a door enterance.

Secondary Market Sizzler

One of the first limited edition nutcrackers in this country, **Merlin the Magician** recently sold for $4,000 on the secondary market. Original sale price was $185.

Collectors' Club - Steinbach Collectors' Club established 1996

Membership kit includes:

- a miniature Steinbach Nutcracker
- a binder of historical information on the nutcrackers

Moses

- a collector's log to help with inventory
- a dealership list
- a Steinbach Club lapel pin
- a member's certificate
- a full-color current brochure
- a subscription to the club's quarterly newsletter

Go and Behold - The Nutcracker Museum

The Nutcracker Museum, located in Leavenworth, Washington, houses one of the world's largest collection of nutcrackers. One of the oldest **Town Criers**, which was made in 1569, was recently added to the collection.

More than 3,500 varieties of nutcrackers, from antique to current and nut-size to life-size, are on display at the museum. Display times for May - October are 2 p.m. to 5 p.m. and on weekends only November - April or by appointment. A small admission fee is required.

Contact

Kurt S. Adler - Steinbach Nutcrackers
1107 Broadway, New York, NY 10010
tel. 800-243-9627

Vaillancourt™ Folk Art

About the Vaillancourts

The typical fourteen year old girl does not take up the hobby of refinishing antique furniture. Fortunately, the interest came naturally to Judi Vaillancourt. While her friends were interested in the trend of the times, she was fascinated with old homes. Even in the seventies, with the emphasis on modern art and abstract forms, Vaillancourt was more interested in finding classic antiques for restoration.

Vaillancourt developed an appreciation for tradition and Americana which permeates her personal and professional life today. She shares her interests with her husband, Gary Vaillancourt. The two met at high school dance and after graduation both pursued their studies. Judi studying art at The Boston Massachusetts College of Art and Gary attended sales and marketing courses.

The Vaillancourts reside in an antique-filled seventeenth-century home in eastern Massachusetts. They operate **Vaillancourt Folk Art** (VFA) which is considered the country's top producer of collectible chalkware. Within their colonial farmhouse is the company art gallery filled with works by top folk artists in the country.

The Vaillancourt business began at home in 1984. They had collected antique chocolate molds and began experimenting with various substances with which to fill them. They eventually chose chalkware.

Vaillancourt was invited to display a sample of her new work at a local art fair. She took home twenty orders. Demand increased when *Country Sampler Magazine* featured her first exhibit of chalkware. Her husband poured the molds at night after he came home from his job as president of a computer software firm. The demand for Vaillancourt's work increased rapidly and within two years six assistants were hired. By 1986 the husband and wife team joined forces on a full-time basis.

What about the Belsnickels?

Germans immigrating to the New World brought with them the tradition of the Belsnickel.

Elves aren't the only Christmas helpers. In German folklore, Belsnickel was a helper to Father Christmas, but he wasn't as sweet as the elves. Belsnickel brought switches to punish naughty children.

Nordic

Quite popular in Europe and America at the turn of the century, the Belsnickel was well-represented in the chocolate mold industry. Because of the lead content, the use of such molds in chocolate making was abandoned in the 1960's. The Vaillancourts began buying the molds on the antique market and to date own approximately 2,000 molds. See page 111.

What is chalkware?

Made of chalk as the name implies, the material was first used to make ornaments and figurines in the mid-1800s to the early 1990s. Chalkware was less expensive than the English ceramics and came to be called "the poor man's Staffordshire."

The Creation of Vaillancourt Folk Art Chalkware

Thirty people, including Gary Vaillancourt's mother and father, help produce nearly two hundred designs for Vaillancourt Folk Art.

1. Artisans pour the plaster-like "chalk" in an antique mold made of two halves held together by clips.
2. The mix sets in roughly half an hour.
3. Removing the clips, the artisan carefully pries open the mold to remove the figure or ornament.
4. Another artisan applies the first coat of oil-based paint to the item.
5. Detail painters then go to work adding the unique features. They base their work on a master copy created by Vaillancourt.

Belsnickels

6. An antiquating solution is applied, then rubbed to fill indentations in the robes, beards and other details.
7. This substance creates a slightly crackled finished when baked under a heat lamp for twenty minutes.
8. Each piece is signed, numbered and dated.

FYI

- The original chocolate Belsnickels carried gold Dresden ornament trees or actual feather sprigs in their arms. Vaillancourt Folk Art follows this design tradition by including real twig switches or real goose feather sprigs in many cases.
- On occasion Vaillancourt Folk Art has designed custom pieces for retailers such as Bloomingdales™ Gorham™ and *Country Home Magazine.* The name of the retailer is marked on the bottom.
- All Vaillancourt Folk Art collectibles are numbered and classified as open numbers.
- For easy identification, the item number is stamped on the bottom of all chalkware made after 1988.
- Vaillancourt Folk Art collectors should always send in, either to their retailer or to Vaillancourt Folk Art, the certificate of authenticity they receive when buying a VFA item. This ensures being added to a master list that keeps track of each collector's inventory, on the mailing list for the newsletter, and notifications of special VFA events.
- Vaillancourt Folk Art produces a line of classical Christmas dinnerware, chalkware chess sets, a Noah's Ark set and colonial wall clocks.
- The American Museum of Folk Art recognizes Vaillancourt chalkware for its fine detail and quality.
- The biannual newsletter *Traditions* focuses on the historical aspect of Vaillancourt Folk Art's chalkware and has information on special events such as their annual collectors weekend, usually held early Spring.

Best Care

- Keep Vaillancourt Folk Art collectibles dust free. Dust with a soft, dry cloth.
- When storing, avoid extreme temperatures.

Wink

Santa

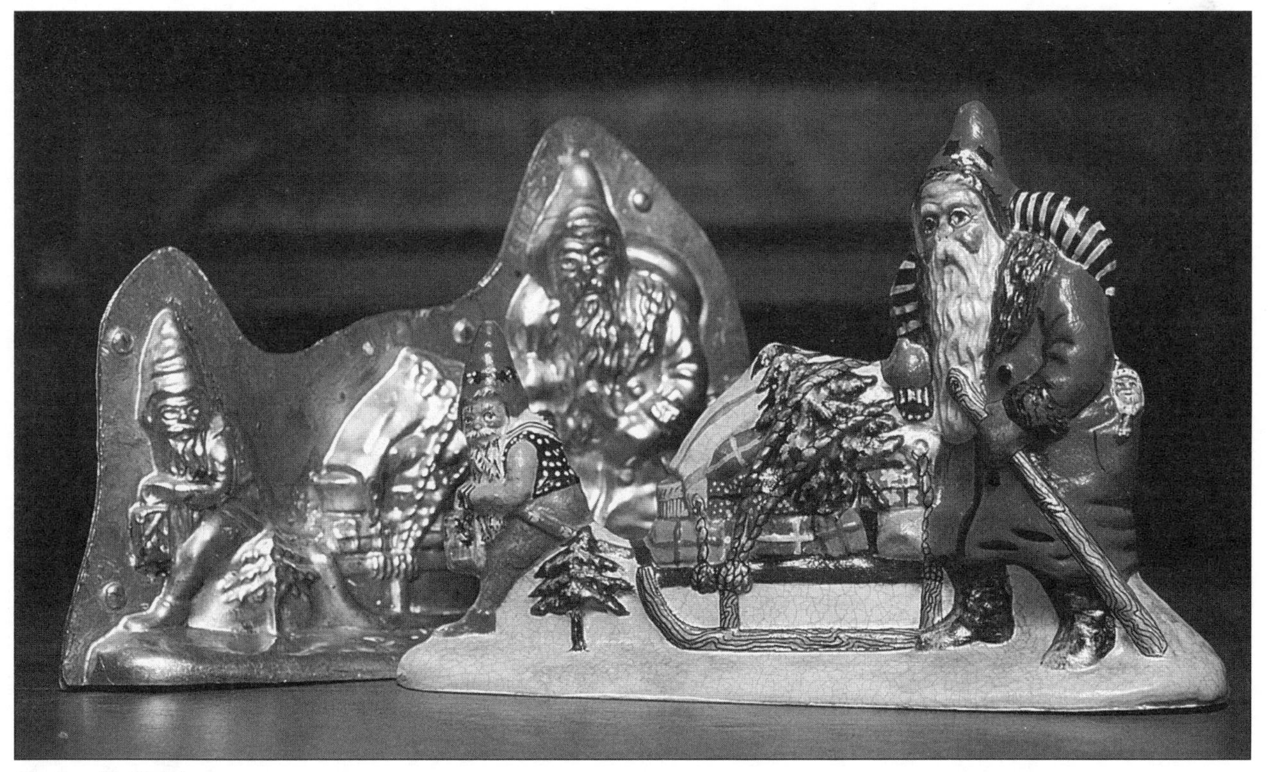

Santa with Sleigh

Display Tips

- Because of their 'antiquated' appearance, the aesthetics of these collectibles standout beautifully when displayed against antique wood or other weathered materials.
- The Vaillancourt's feel that the ornaments display best in antique cabinets or wood hutches.

Secondary Market Sizzler

The 1990 **Starlight Santa**, which originally sold for $95, has sold for $1,950 on the secondary market.

Vaillancourt Snowmen

Collectors' Club

An official collector's club does not exist, however there is a newsletter called *Traditions* which began in 1995.

Contact

Vaillancourt Folk Art
145 Armsby Road
Sutton, MA 01590
tel. 508-865-9183

Order No.	Title	Type	Theme	Retired	Intro. Year	Retial Price	Secondary Price
ANNALEE MOBILITEE DOLLS							
001	7 IN. SANTA W/SLEIGH	ANNALEE DOLLS	AN - SANTAS	83	83	$14.95	$275.00
002	7 IN. MOUSE ON CHEESE	ANNALEE DOLLS	AN - ANIMALS	93	92	$25.95	$225.00
003	10 IN. CHRISTMAS MUSHROOM W/2 - 7 IN. GNOMES	ANNALEE DOLLS	AN - ASSORTED DOLLS	70	70	$9.95	$650.00
004	10 IN. CHRISTMAS PANDA W/TOY BAG	ANNALEE DOLLS	AN - ANIMALS	86	85	$17.95	$300.00
005	10 IN. KITTEN ON SLED	ANNALEE DOLLS	AN - ANIMALS	91	90	$35.95	$350.00
006	10 IN. SKIER	ANNALEE DOLLS	AN - ASSORTED DOLLS	88	87	$34.95	$475.00
007	18 IN. SNOWMAN W/BIRD	ANNALEE DOLLS	AN - ASSORTED DOLLS	79	78	$15.95	$350.00
008	18 IN. INDOOR SANTA	ANNALEE DOLLS	AN - SANTAS	68	68	$7.45	$375.00
009	5 IN. BUCK ON FLEXIBLE FLYER SLED	ANNALEE DOLLS	AN - ANIMALS	94	87	$21.95	$300.00
010	10 IN. CAROLLER	ANNALEE DOLLS	AN - CAROLLERS	76	76	$5.50	$400.00
011	18 IN. MRS. INDOOR SANTA	ANNALEE DOLLS	AN - SANTAS	68	68	$7.45	$350.00
012	18 IN. REINDEER W/CHRISTMAS SADDLEBAGS	ANNALEE DOLLS	AN - ANIMALS	79	79	$20.95	$275.00
013	12 IN. MRS. SANTA MOUSE W/MUFF	ANNALEE DOLLS	AN - SANTAS	88	88	$31.95	$350.00
014	18 IN. PS KID W/STOCKING	ANNALEE DOLLS	AN - ASSORTED DOLLS	77	77		$425.00
015	18 IN. SANTA W/VEST, CARDHOLDER SACK	ANNALEE DOLLS	AN - SANTAS	88	71	$7.95	$325.00
016	18 IN. SLEDDING BOY	ANNALEE DOLLS	AN - ASSORTED DOLLS	84	81		$400.00
017	10 IN. BEAN NOSE SANTA	ANNALEE DOLLS	AN - SANTAS	NA	94	$119.50	
018	CHRISTMAS LOGO W/COOKIE	DOLL SOCIETY	AN - LOGO KIDS	86	85		$675.00
019	CHRISTMAS MORNING LOGO	DOLL SOCIETY	AN - LOGO KIDS	90	89		$150.00
020	DRESS UP SANTA LOGO	DOLL SOCIETY	AN - LOGO KIDS	95	94		
021	3 IN. REINDEER HEAD	ANNALEE DOLLS	AN - ANIMALS	76	71	$1.00	$200.00
022	5 IN. WEE SKIS	ANNALEE DOLLS	AN - ASSORTED DOLLS	NA	60	$3.95	$325.00
023	7 IN. AIRPLANE PILOT MOUSE	ANNALEE DOLLS	AN - ANIMALS	81	78	$3.95	$425.00
144	7 IN. ANGEL IN A BLANKET	ANNALEE DOLLS	AN - ANGELS	64	64	$2.45	
024	7 IN. ANGEL ON A STAR	ANNALEE DOLLS	AN - ANGELS	84	84	$32.95	$475.00
026	7 IN. M/M INDOOR SANTA	ANNALEE DOLLS	AN - SANTAS	66	66	$5.95	$450.00
025	7 IN. ANGEL W/MUSICAL INSTRUMENT ON MUSIC BOX	ANNALEE DOLLS	AN - ANGELS	83	83	$29.95	$425.00
027	7 IN. M/M SANTA ON SKI BOB	ANNALEE DOLLS	AN - SANTAS	70	70	$5.95	$600.00
028	7 IN. M/M SANTA W/BASKET	ANNALEE DOLLS	AN - SANTAS	83	83	$25.95	$300.00
029	7 IN. M/M SANTA W/POT BELLY STOVE	ANNALEE DOLLS	AN - SANTAS	80	80	$2.09	$320.00
030	7 IN. M/M TUCKERED SANTA W/HOT WATER BOTTLE	ANNALEE DOLLS	AN - SANTAS	71	70	$6.45	$195.00
031	7 IN. MR. A.M. MOUSE	ANNALEE DOLLS	AN - ANIMALS	83	82	$11.95	$145.00
032	7 IN. MR. HOLLY MOUSE	ANNALEE DOLLS	AN - ANIMALS	70	70	$3.95	$225.00
033	7 IN. MR. SANTA MOUSE	ANNALEE DOLLS	AN - ANIMALS	79	77	$6.00	$295.00
034	7 IN. MRS. HOLLY MOUSE	ANNALEE DOLLS	AN - ANIMALS	76	67	$3.95	$245.00
035	7 IN. MRS. SANTA W/FUR-TRIMMED CAPE	ANNALEE DOLLS	AN - SANTAS	73	67	$2.95	$440.00
036	7 IN. NAUGHTY ANGEL	ANNALEE DOLLS	AN - ANGELS	71	71	$10.95	$265.00
037	7 IN. NEEDLEWORK MOUSE	ANNALEE DOLLS	AN - ANIMALS	78	76	$6.95	$395.00
038	7 IN. NUDE ANGEL BATH PUFF	ANNALEE DOLLS	AN - ANGELS	65	64	$3.95	$265.00
039	7 IN. TUCKERED MR. & MRS. SANTA WATER BOTTLE	ANNALEE DOLLS	AN - SANTAS	69	67	$5.95	$395.00
040	7 IN. WORKSHOP MOUSE	ANNALEE DOLLS	AN - ANIMALS	92	92	$21.95	$270.00
041	10 IN. CHOIR BOY (SET/3)	ANNALEE DOLLS	AN - ASSORTED DOLLS	67	67	$2.95	$725.00
042	10 IN. CHRISTMAS GIRL	ANNALEE DOLLS	AN - ASSORTED DOLLS	57	50		$2,345.00
043	10 IN. CHRISTMAS MUSHROOM W/07 IN. MOUSE	ANNALEE DOLLS	AN - ANIMALS	70	70	$7.95	$400.00
044	10 IN. ELF	ANNALEE DOLLS	AN - ASSORTED DOLLS	66	60		$400.00
045	10 IN. ELF	ANNALEE DOLLS	AN - ASSORTED DOLLS	NA	50		$895.00
046	10 IN. ELF	ANNALEE DOLLS	AN - ASSORTED DOLLS	63	63		$350.00
047	10 IN. ELF W/CAP	ANNALEE DOLLS	AN - ASSORTED DOLLS	54	54		$1,125.00
048	10 IN. ELF W/PLANTER	ANNALEE DOLLS	AN - ASSORTED DOLLS	78	78	$6.95	$275.00
049	10 IN. ELF W/SKIS AND POLES	ANNALEE DOLLS	AN - ASSORTED DOLLS	71	67	$2.95	$650.00
050	10 IN. FALL ELF	ANNALEE DOLLS	AN - ASSORTED DOLLS	88	88	$13.95	$125.00
051	10 IN. HOLLY ELF	ANNALEE DOLLS	AN - ASSORTED DOLLS	57	57		$1,600.00
052	10 IN. JACK FROST ELF	ANNALEE DOLLS	AN - ASSORTED DOLLS	77	77	$6.00	$225.00
053	10 IN. JACK FROST ELF W/10 IN. SNOWFLAKE	ANNALEE DOLLS	AN - ASSORTED DOLLS	82	82	$13.50	$145.00
054	10 IN. JACK FROST ELF W/05 IN. SNOWFLAKE	ANNALEE DOLLS	AN - ASSORTED DOLLS	81	81	$31.95	$315.00
055	10 IN. MONK (RED ROBE)	ANNALEE DOLLS	AN - ASSORTED DOLLS	65	64	$2.95	$795.00
056	10 IN. MONK W/CHRISTMAS TREE PLANTING	ANNALEE DOLLS	AN - ASSORTED DOLLS	67	65	$2.95	$445.00
057	10 IN. MONK W/JUG	ANNALEE DOLLS	AN - ASSORTED DOLLS	69	67	$2.95	$380.00
058	10 IN. MONK W/SKIS AND POLES	ANNALEE DOLLS	AN - ASSORTED DOLLS	72	70	$3.95	$345.00
059	10 IN. MUSHROOM W/07 IN. SANTA	ANNALEE DOLLS	AN - SANTAS	71	70	$7.95	$245.00
060	10 IN. NUN (GREEN)	ANNALEE DOLLS	AN - ASSORTED DOLLS	67	67	$42.95	$790.00
061	10 IN. NUN W/BASKET	ANNALEE DOLLS	AN - ASSORTED DOLLS	67	67	$2.95	$590.00
062	10 IN. REINDEER	ANNALEE DOLLS	AN - ANIMALS	65	65	$4.95	$415.00
063	10 IN. REINDEER W/ 7 IN. SANTA	ANNALEE DOLLS	AN - ANIMALS	76	75	$10.50	$390.00
064	10 IN. ROBIN HOOD ELF	ANNALEE DOLLS	AN - ASSORTED DOLLS	65	64	$2.50	$490.00
066	10 IN. SKI ELF	ANNALEE DOLLS	AN - ASSORTED DOLLS	71	71	$3.95	$270.00
067	10 IN. SKI ELF	ANNALEE DOLLS	AN - ASSORTED DOLLS	87	87	$19.95	$345.00
068	10 IN. SKIER (CROSS COUNTRY)	ANNALEE DOLLS	AN - ASSORTED DOLLS	85	85	$33.50	$220.00
070	10 IN. VICTORY SKI DOLL	ANNALEE DOLLS	AN - ASSORTED DOLLS	91	91	$49.50	$325.00
071	10 IN. WOMAN	ANNALEE DOLLS	AN - ASSORTED DOLLS	56	56		$2,595.00
072	10 IN. WOMAN IN RED	ANNALEE DOLLS	AN - ASSORTED DOLLS	59	59	$5.75	$2,190.00
073	10 IN. WOMAN'S HEAD	ANNALEE DOLLS	AN - ASSORTED DOLLS	59	59		$490.00
074	10 IN. WOOD SPRITE	ANNALEE DOLLS	AN - ASSORTED DOLLS	67	59		$750.00
075	10 IN. WORKSHOP ELF	ANNALEE DOLLS	AN - ASSORTED DOLLS	66	66		$415.00
076	12 IN. ANGEL	ANNALEE DOLLS	AN - ANGELS	79	76	$10.95	$345.00
077	12 IN. BABY IN GREEN	ANNALEE DOLLS	AN - ASSORTED DOLLS	60	60		$545.00
078	12 IN. CHRISTMAS BONNET LADY MOUSE	ANNALEE DOLLS	AN - ANIMALS	65	65	$9.95	$395.00
079	12 IN. MR. SANTA W/TOY BAG	ANNALEE DOLLS	AN - SANTAS	71	70	$10.95	$520.00
080	12 IN. MRS. SANTA W/MUFF	ANNALEE DOLLS	AN - SANTAS	67	65	$9.95	$545.00
081	12 IN. NIGHT SHIRT BOY MOUSE	ANNALEE DOLLS	AN - ANIMALS	76	69	$9.95	$545.00
082	12 IN. SANTA	ANNALEE DOLLS	AN - SANTAS	57	57		$920.00
083	12 IN. SANTA (BEAN NOSE)	ANNALEE DOLLS	AN - SANTAS	57	54	$19.95	$9,990.00
084	12 IN. SANTA DUCK	ANNALEE DOLLS	AN - ANIMALS	91	90	$49.95	$295.00
085	12 IN. SANTA MONKEY	ANNALEE DOLLS	AN - ANIMALS	81	81	$23.95	$590.00
086	15 IN. CHRISTMAS DRAGON	ANNALEE DOLLS	AN - ANIMALS	90	90	$49.95	$400.00
088	18 IN. ANGEL W/INSTRUMENT	ANNALEE DOLLS	AN - ANGELS	90	90	$51.95	$320.00
089	CHRISTMAS PANDA	ANNALEE DOLLS	AN - ANIMALS	73	73	$10.50	$590.00
090	18 IN. MARTHA CRACHET	ANNALEE DOLLS	AN - DICKENS	74	74	$11.95	$420.00
091	18 IN. MONK W/JUG	ANNALEE DOLLS	AN - ASSORTED DOLLS	82	82	$26.45	$520.00
092	18 IN. MR. & MRS. FIRESIDE COUPLE	ANNALEE DOLLS	AN - ASSORTED DOLLS	70	70	$7.45	$300.00
093	18 IN. MRS. SANTA W/BOUDOIR CAP & APRON	ANNALEE DOLLS	AN - SANTAS	68	68	$7.45	$250.00

Order No.	Title	Type	Theme	Retired	Intro. Year	Retail Price	Secondary Price
094	18 IN. MRS. SANTA W/HOT WATER BOTTLE	ANNALEE DOLLS	AN - SANTAS	68	68	$7.45	$515.00
098	18 IN. PJ KID	ANNALEE DOLLS	AN - ASSORTED DOLLS	64	64	$6.95	$490.00
099	18 IN. SANTA FROG W/TOY BAG	ANNALEE DOLLS	AN - ANIMALS	80	80	$24.95	$440.00
100	18 IN. SANTA FUR KID	ANNALEE DOLLS	AN - ASSORTED DOLLS	72	71	$7.45	$250.00
101	18 IN. SANTA KID	ANNALEE DOLLS	AN - ASSORTED DOLLS	65	64	$6.95	$425.00
102	18 IN. SANTA PLAYING W/ELECTRIC TRAIN	ANNALEE DOLLS	AN - SANTAS	90	90	$119.00	$345.00
103	18 IN. SPECIAL MRS. SANTA (SPECIAL ORDER)	ANNALEE DOLLS	AN - SANTAS	87	87		$395.00
104	18 IN. WORKSHOP SANTA (SPECIAL ORDER)	ANNALEE DOLLS	AN - SANTAS	87	87		$445.00
105	22 IN. CHRISTMAS GIRAFFE W/10 IN. ELF	ANNALEE DOLLS	AN - ANIMALS	82	81	$36.95	$495.00
106	22 IN. CHRISTMAS STOCKING	ANNALEE DOLLS	AN - ASSORTED DOLLS	75	74	$4.95	$145.00
107	22 IN. HOLLY HOBBY	ANNALEE DOLLS	AN - ASSORTED DOLLS	73	73		$990.00
108	26 IN. ELF	ANNALEE DOLLS	AN - ASSORTED DOLLS	56	54	$9.95	$545.00
109	26 IN. FRIAR	ANNALEE DOLLS	AN - ASSORTED DOLLS	63	63	$14.95	$2,490.00
110	26 IN. WOMAN	ANNALEE DOLLS	AN - ASSORTED DOLLS	55	55		$6,490.00
111	29 IN. CAROLLER MOUSE	ANNALEE DOLLS	AN - ANIMALS	78	78	$49.95	$470.00
112	29 IN. FUR TRIM SANTA	ANNALEE DOLLS	AN - SANTAS	79	60		$990.00
113	29 IN. MR. SANTA MOUSE W/SACK	ANNALEE DOLLS	AN - ANIMALS	77	77	$49.94	$790.00
114	29 IN. MRS. INDOOR SANTA	ANNALEE DOLLS	AN - SANTAS	68	68	$16.95	$475.00
115	29 IN. MRS. SANTA MOUSE W/MUFF	ANNALEE DOLLS	AN - ANIMALS	77	77	$49.95	$800.00
116	29 IN. MRS. SANTA W/WIRED CARDHOLDER SKIRT	ANNALEE DOLLS	AN - SANTAS	72	72	$18.95	$245.00
117	29 IN. MRS. SNOW WOMAN W/CARDHOLDER SKIRT	ANNALEE DOLLS	AN - ASSORTED DOLLS	72	72	$19.95	$690.00
118	30 IN. SANTA IN CHAIR W/2 18 IN. KIDS	ANNALEE DOLLS	AN - SANTAS	84	84	$169.96	$1,100.00
119	30 IN. SNOWGIRL W/MUFF	ANNALEE DOLLS	AN - ASSORTED DOLLS	84	84	$79.50	$995.00
120	48 IN. MRS. SANTA	ANNALEE DOLLS	AN - SANTAS	78	78	$150.00	$1,425.00
121	48 IN. SANTA	ANNALEE DOLLS	AN - SANTAS	78	78	$150.00	$1,425.00
122	48 IN. VELOUR SANTA	ANNALEE DOLLS	AN - SANTAS	88	86	$269.96	$750.00
127	3 IN. ELF	ANNALEE DOLLS	AN - ASSORTED DOLLS	89	87	$12.95	$325.00
125	SNOWMAN KID	ANNALEE DOLLS	AN - ASSORTED DOLLS	71	71	$3.95	$345.00
128	3 IN. SKIER	ANNALEE DOLLS	AN - ASSORTED DOLLS	NA	92	$14.45	$170.00
129	7 IN. ANGEL W/PAPER WINGS	ANNALEE DOLLS	AN - ANGELS	66	60		$390.00
130	7 IN. BABY ANGEL	ANNALEE DOLLS	AN - ANGELS	50	50	$2.45	$1,645.00
131	7 IN. BABY ANGEL (YELLOW FEATHER HAIR)	ANNALEE DOLLS	AN - ANGELS	62	60		$345.00
132	7 IN. BABY ANGEL FLYING W/HALO	ANNALEE DOLLS	AN - ANGELS	64	64	$2.45	$445.00
133	7 IN. BABY ANGEL ON CLOUD	ANNALEE DOLLS	AN - ANGELS	63	62	$2.45	$600.00
134	7 IN. BABY ANGEL W/STAR	ANNALEE DOLLS	AN - ANGELS	62	62	$2.00	$215.00
135	7 IN. BABY IN BASSINET	ANNALEE DOLLS	AN - ASSORTED DOLLS	83	80	$13.95	$270.00
136	7 IN. BABY IN CHRISTMAS BAG	ANNALEE DOLLS	AN - ASSORTED DOLLS	68	68	$2.95	$345.00
137	7 IN. BABY IN SANTA'S HAT	ANNALEE DOLLS	AN - ASSORTED DOLLS	69	68	$2.95	$495.00
138	7 IN. BALLOONING SANTA	ANNALEE DOLLS	AN - SANTAS	83	80	$49.95	$345.00
139	7 IN. BLACK SANTA W/OVERSIZED BAY	ANNALEE DOLLS	AN - SANTAS	75	74	$5.45	$550.00
140	7 IN. CHRISTMAS BABY ON HAT BOX	ANNALEE DOLLS	AN - ASSORTED DOLLS	71	70	$2.95	$350.00
143	7 IN. CHRISTMAS MOUSE IN SANTA'S MITTEN	ANNALEE DOLLS	AN - ANIMALS	77	75	$7.95	$175.00
141	7 IN. CHRISTMAS DUMB BUNNY	ANNALEE DOLLS	AN - ANIMALS	65	65	$3.95	$770.00
142	7 IN. CHRISTMAS MOUSE IN SANTA MITTEN	ANNALEE DOLLS	AN - ANIMALS	76	75	$5.45	$370.00
5433	10 IN. WISEMAN BEARING FRANKINCENSE	ANNALEE DOLLS	AN - NATIVITY			$45.00	
5432	10 IN. JOSEPH	ANNALEE DOLLS	AN - NATIVITY			$45.00	
5434	10 IN. WISEMAN BEARING GOLD	ANNALEE DOLLS	AN - NATIVITY			$45.00	
5435	10 IN. WISEMAN BEARING MYRRH	ANNALEE DOLLS	AN - NATIVITY			$45.00	
5436	10 IN. PEASANT	ANNALEE DOLLS	AN - NATIVITY		97	$37.00	
5437	12 IN. CAMEL	ANNALEE DOLLS	AN - NATIVITY		97	$42.00	
5438	8 IN. DONKEY	ANNALEE DOLLS	AN - NATIVITY		97	$33.00	
5481	12 IN. WORKSHOP SANTA/COLLECTOR EDITION	ANNALEE DOLLS	AN - SANTAS				
5488	12 IN. MRS. SANTA QUILTING	ANNALEE DOLLS	AN - SANTAS		97	$55.00	
5498	12 IN. CHRISTMAS EVE SANTA	ANNALEE DOLLS	AN - SANTAS		96	$0.00	
5499	12 IN. CHRISTMAS EVE MRS. SANTA	ANNALEE DOLLS	AN - SANTAS			$0.00	
5503	18 IN. MUSICAL SANTA	ANNALEE DOLLS	AN - SANTAS		97	$67.50	
5505	18 IN. GIFT LIST SANTA	ANNALEE DOLLS	AN - SANTAS		96		
5628	18 IN. TUCKERED SANTA W/PJ KID	ANNALEE DOLLS	AN - SANTAS		96		
5629	18 IN. TUCKERED MRS. SANTA W/PJ KID	ANNALEE DOLLS	AN - SANTAS		96		
5635	18 IN. CATCH OF THE DAY SANTA	ANNALEE DOLLS	AN - SANTAS		97	$95.00	
5642	18 IN. MRS. SANTA W/DOVE	ANNALEE DOLLS	AN - SANTAS		97		
6218	30 IN. FINISHING TOUCH SANTA	ANNALEE DOLLS	AN - SANTAS		97	$150.00	
6216	30 IN. MRS. SANTA LAST MINUTE WRAPPING	ANNALEE DOLLS	AN - SANTAS		97	$150.00	
6021	30 IN. MRS. SANTA & SQUEAK	ANNALEE DOLLS	AN - SANTAS			$184.00	
6211	30 IN. DECK THE HALLS SANTA	ANNALEE DOLLS	AN - SANTAS		97	$180.00	
6266	FATHER CHRISTMAS	ANNALEE DOLLS	AN - SANTAS		97	$156.00	
6426	5 IN. SPOTTED FAWN	ANNALEE DOLLS	AN - ANIMALS		94	$14.95	
6428	10 IN. WHITE TAIL DOE	ANNALEE DOLLS	AN - ANIMALS		94	$21.95	
6430	10 IN. DEAR FRIENDS	ANNALEE DOLLS	AN - ANIMALS		97	$40.00	
6432	10 IN. WHITE TAIL BUCK	ANNALEE DOLLS	AN - ANIMALS			$24.00	
6435	10 IN. CAROLLING REINDEER	ANNALEE DOLLS	AN - ANIMALS		96	$25.00	
6600	18 IN. REINDEER WITH SANTA BAGS	ANNALEE DOLLS	AN - ANIMALS				
6700	36 IN. REINDEER	ANNALEE DOLLS	AN - ANIMALS				
7109	7 IN. CATCH A STAR ANGEL	ANNALEE DOLLS	AN - ANGELS		97	$29.50	
7116	7 IN. NAUGHTY ANGEL	ANNALEE DOLLS	AN - ANGELS			$29.50	
7172	30 IN. HERALDING ANGEL	ANNALEE DOLLS	AN - ANGELS		97	$165.00	
7174	5 IN. MISTLETOE ANGEL	ANNALEE DOLLS	AN - ANGELS				
7176	5 IN. HOLLY BERRY ANGEL	ANNALEE DOLLS	AN - ANGELS			$26.00	
7200	7 IN. DRUMMER BOY	ANNALEE DOLLS	AN - ASSORTED DOLLS				
7225	12 IN. DRUMMER BOY	ANNALEE DOLLS	AN - ASSORTED DOLLS				
7234	7 IN. ICE FISHING BOY	ANNALEE DOLLS	AN - ASSORTED DOLLS		97	$45.00	
7264	10 IN. OLD TYME CAROLLING MAN	ANNALEE DOLLS	AN - CAROLLERS			$39.00	
7265	10 IN. OLD TYME CAROLLING WOMAN	ANNALEE DOLLS	AN - CAROLLERS		96	$39.00	
7277	10 IN. ANGELICA TREE TOPPER	ANNALEE DOLLS	AN - ASSORTED DOLLS		97	$47.00	
7340	5 IN. CHRISTMAS ELF/RED	ANNALEE DOLLS	AN - ASSORTED DOLLS		94	$13.95	
7341	5 IN. CHRISTMAS ELF/GREEN	ANNALEE DOLLS	AN - ASSORTED DOLLS		94	$13.95	
7345	5 IN. FROSTY ELF	ANNALEE DOLLS	AN - ASSORTED DOLLS		94		
7354	10 IN. FROSTY ELF	ANNALEE DOLLS	AN - ASSORTED DOLLS				
7368	5 IN. UNGNOME TAILOR	ANNALEE DOLLS	AN - ASSORTED DOLLS		97	$40.00	
7421	4 IN. PUPPY PRESENT	ANNALEE DOLLS	AN - ANIMALS		96	$19.00	
7432	5 IN. CHRISTMAS MONKEY	ANNALEE DOLLS	AN - ANIMALS		97	$23.00	
7448	22 IN. CHRISTMAS ELF/RED	ANNALEE DOLLS	AN - ASSORTED DOLLS				
7449	22 IN. CHRISTMAS ELF/GREEN	ANNALEE DOLLS	AN - ASSORTED DOLLS		95	$35.95	

Order No.	Title	Type	Theme	Retired	Intro. Year	Retial Price	Secondary Price
7451	30 IN. CHRISTMAS ELF/RED	ANNALEE DOLLS	AN - ASSORTED DOLLS			$68.50	
7473	10 IN. JESTER AND FRIEND	ANNALEE DOLLS	AN - ASSORTED DOLLS		96		
7477	22 IN. JUST-A-JESTER	ANNALEE DOLLS	AN - ASSORTED DOLLS		96		
7503	7 IN. CAROLLING SNOWMAN	ANNALEE DOLLS	AN - ASSORTED DOLLS		96	$29.50	
7504	7 IN. CAROLLING SNOWWOMAN	ANNALEE DOLLS	AN - ASSORTED DOLLS		96	$28.00	
7509	7 IN. MAKIN' FRIENDS SNOWMAN	ANNALEE DOLLS	AN - ASSORTED DOLLS		96	$28.00	
7512	10 IN. COUNTRY SNOWMAN	ANNALEE DOLLS	AN - ASSORTED DOLLS		97	$37.50	
7513	10 IN. COUNTRY SNOWWOMAN	ANNALEE DOLLS	AN - ASSORTED DOLLS		97	$37.50	
7525	18 IN. MR. SNOWMAN	ANNALEE DOLLS	AN - ASSORTED DOLLS				
7550	22 IN. PEEK-A-BOO MOUSE STOCKING	ANNALEE DOLLS	AN - ANIMALS				
7700	3 IN. MATCHBOX MICE	ANNALEE DOLLS	AN - ANIMALS			$34.00	
7706	7 IN. HEAVENLY ANGEL MOUSE (TREE TOP)	ANNALEE DOLLS	AN - ANIMALS		97	$35.00	
7713	7 IN. STRINGING GARLAND MOUSE	ANNALEE DOLLS	AN - ANIMALS		97	$21.00	
7719	7 IN. SLEIGH RIDE MICE	ANNALEE DOLLS	AN - ANIMALS		97	$75.00	
7720	7 IN. SLEDDING MOUSE	ANNALEE DOLLS	AN - ANIMALS		97	$28.50	
7722	7 IN. SKATING GIRL MOUSE	ANNALEE DOLLS	AN - ANIMALS				
7722	7 IN. ANGEL MOUSE	ANNALEE DOLLS	AN - ANIMALS			$23.50	
7746	7 IN. SANTA MOUSE CENTERPIECE	ANNALEE DOLLS	AN - ANIMALS			$29.00	
7747	7 IN. TUCKERED BOY MOUSE	ANNALEE DOLLS	AN - ANIMALS		91	$23.00	
7749	7 IN. TUCKERED GIRL MOUSE	ANNALEE DOLLS	AN - ANIMALS		91	$23.00	
7751	7 IN. LETTER TO SANTA MOUSE	ANNALEE DOLLS	AN - ANIMALS			$29.00	
7755	7 IN. HOSTESS MOUSE	ANNALEE DOLLS	AN - ANIMALS			$25.00	
7842	4 IN. SANTA CLAWS CAT	ANNALEE DOLLS	AN - ANIMALS		97	$21.00	
7903	3 IN. MOUSE IN SANTA'S HAT ORNAMENT	ANNALEE DOLLS	AN - ANIMALS		96	$18.00	
7906	3 IN. MONK W/CASK	ANNALEE DOLLS	AN - ASSORTED DOLLS		97	$26.00	
7907	7 IN. MONK W/CASK	ANNALEE DOLLS	AN - ASSORTED DOLLS		97	$35.00	
7908	18 IN. VINEYARD MONK	ANNALEE DOLLS	AN - ASSORTED DOLLS		97	$60.00	
7928	3 IN. SWEET SURPRISE MOUSE	ANNALEE DOLLS	AN - ANIMALS		97	$22.50	
8032	3 IN. SLEIGH RIDE SANTA	ANNALEE DOLLS	AN - SANTAS		96		
8055	10 IN. CAROLLING GIRL BEAR	ANNALEE DOLLS	AN - ANIMALS		96	$42.00	
8061	10 IN. CAROLLING BOY BEAR	ANNALEE DOLLS	AN - ANIMALS		96	$42.00	
8200	7 IN. HAPPY NEW YEAR KID	ANNALEE DOLLS	AN - ASSORTED DOLLS		97	$29.00	
5002	7 IN. MR. & MRS. SANTA EXC. GIFTS	ANNALEE DOLLS	AN - SANTAS		96		
5046	7 IN. HEARTH & HOME SANTA	ANNALEE DOLLS	AN - SANTAS		97	$39.00	
5105	7 IN. HOLIDAY BASKET COUPLE	ANNALEE DOLLS	AN - ASSORTED DOLLS				
5108	7 IN. SANTA'S TOUCH	ANNALEE DOLLS	AN - SANTAS			$37.00	
5231	7 IN. TRIM TIME SANTA	ANNALEE DOLLS	AN - SANTAS		96		
5233	7 IN. SNOW FUN FOR SANTA	ANNALEE DOLLS	AN - SANTAS		97	$32.00	
5360	7 IN. SHOPPING SANTA	ANNALEE DOLLS	AN - SANTAS		96		
5363	7 IN. SHOPPING MRS. SANTA	ANNALEE DOLLS	AN - SANTAS		96		
5364	7 IN. SLEIGH RIDE SANTA COUPLE	ANNALEE DOLLS	AN - SANTAS		96		
5389	10 IN. MYSTICAL SANTA/COLLECTOR EDITION	ANNALEE DOLLS	AN - SANTAS		97	$43.00	
5390	10 IN. TRUE BLUE SANTA	ANNALEE DOLLS	AN - SANTAS		97	$63.00	
5391	10 IN.PUPPIES FOR CHRISTMAS SANTA COLLECTOR ED.	ANNALEE DOLLS	AN - SANTAS		96		
5394	10 IN. HOOK, LINE & SANTA/COLLECTOR EDITION	ANNALEE DOLLS	AN - SANTAS		96		
5424	5 IN. LAMB	ANNALEE DOLLS	AN - NATIVITY		97	$17.00	
5431	10 IN. MARY HOLDING BABY JESUS	ANNALEE DOLLS	AN - NATIVITY			$45.00	
088A	BOB CRATCHET W/TINY TIM	ANNALEE DOLLS	AN - DICKENS	74	74	$11.95	$420.00
2841	NOEL THE CAROUSEL HORSE	ANNALEE DOLLS	AN - ANIMALS			$68.00	
5393	10 IN. WANDERING SAINT NICHOLAS/COLLECTOR EDITION	ANNALEE DOLLS	AN - SANTAS	96	96	$49.00	
5392	10 IN. WOODLAND SANTA AND REINDEER/COLLECTOR ED.	ANNALEE DOLLS	AN - SANTAS	YES	96		
6255	30 IN. FATHER CHRISTMAS	ANNALEE DOLLS	AN - SANTAS		97	$156.00	
7233	7 IN. SNOWBALL FIGHT KID	ANNALEE DOLLS	AN - ASSORTED DOLLS				
7232	7 IN. PJ KID ON ROCKING HORSE	ANNALEE DOLLS	AN - ASSORTED DOLLS		95	$29.95	
5005	7 IN. FREE STANDING SANTA	ANNALEE DOLLS	AN - SANTAS				
5045	7 IN. CHEF SANTA	ANNALEE DOLLS	AN - SANTAS				
5245	7 IN. SANTA CENTERPIECE	ANNALEE DOLLS	AN - SANTAS	YES			
5200	7 IN. MOON BEAM SANTA MOBILE	ANNALEE DOLLS	AN - SANTAS		96		
6510	10 IN. SANTA HUGGING REINDEER	ANNALEE DOLLS	AN - SANTAS				
5242	7 IN. SKIING SANTA	ANNALEE DOLLS	AN - SANTAS				
5496	12 IN. CAROLLING MRS. SANTA	ANNALEE DOLLS	AN - SANTAS		96		
5497	12 IN. CAROLLING SANTA	ANNALEE DOLLS	AN - SANTAS		96		
5521	18 IN. MRS. SANTA HANGING CRANBERRIES AND POPCORN	ANNALEE DOLLS	AN - SANTAS		96		
5504	18 IN. HO HO HO SANTA	ANNALEE DOLLS	AN - SANTAS				
5503	18 IN. MUSICAL CAROLLING SANTA	ANNALEE DOLLS	AN - SANTAS		96		
5505	18 IN. GIFT LIST SANTA	ANNALEE DOLLS	AN - SANTAS		97		
5628	18 IN. TUCKERED SANTA W/PJ KID	ANNALEE DOLLS	AN - SANTAS		97		
5629	18 IN. TUCKERED MRS. SANTA W/PJ KID	ANNALEE DOLLS	AN - SANTAS		97		
5642	18 IN. MRS. SANTA W/DOVE	ANNALEE DOLLS	AN - SANTAS		96		
7473	10 IN. JESTER AND FRIEND	ANNALEE DOLLS	AN - ASSORTED DOLLS		97		
6015	30 IN. MRS. SANTA WITH CARDHOLDER APRON	ANNALEE DOLLS	AN - SANTAS		94	$119.95	
6212	30 IN. SHOPPING MRS. SANTA	ANNALEE DOLLS	AN - SANTAS		96		
6011	30 IN. SUNDAY MORNING SANTA	ANNALEE DOLLS	AN - SANTAS		96		
6211	30 IN. DECK THE HALLS SANTA	ANNALEE DOLLS	AN - SANTAS		96	$169.50	
5152	7 IN. OLD WORLD MRS. SANTA	ANNALEE DOLLS	AN - SANTAS	YES	96	$32.00	
5153	7 IN. OLD WORLD SANTA	ANNALEE DOLLS	AN - SANTAS	YES	96	$40.00	
5450	12 IN. OLD WORLD SAINT NICHOLAS	ANNALEE DOLLS	AN - SANTAS	YES			
7276	10 IN. OLD WORLD TREE TOP ANGEL	ANNALEE DOLLS	AN - ANGELS	YES	96	$47.00	
5652	18 IN. OLD WORLD SANTA	ANNALEE DOLLS	AN - SANTAS	YES	96	$76.00	
5653	18 IN. OLD WORLD MRS. SANTA HUGGING LAMB	ANNALEE DOLLS	AN - SANTAS	YES	96	$84.00	
6252	30 IN. OLD WORLD SANTA	ANNALEE DOLLS	AN - SANTAS	YES	96	$160.00	
6253	30 IN. OLD WORLD MRS. SANTA	ANNALEE DOLLS	AN - SANTAS	YES	96	$152.00	
6751	36 IN. OLD WORLD REINDEER	ANNALEE DOLLS	AN - ANIMALS		96	$146.00	
7711	7 IN. HOLLY GIRL MOUSE	ANNALEE DOLLS	AN - ANIMALS	YES	95		
7902	3 IN. MIDNIGHT SNACK MOUSE ORNAMENT	ANNALEE DOLLS	AN - ANIMALS	96	96	$18.00	
7736	7 IN. CHRISTMAS PARTY GIRL MOUSE	ANNALEE DOLLS	AN - ANIMALS	YES			
7729	7 IN. DOWN THROUGH THE CHIMNEY MOUSE	ANNALEE DOLLS	AN - ANIMALS			$34.95	
7749	7 IN. TUCKERED GIRL MOUSE	ANNALEE DOLLS	AN - ANIMALS		96		
7747	7 IN. TUCKERED BOY MOUSE	ANNALEE DOLLS	AN - ANIMALS		96		
7755	7 IN. HOSTESS MOUSE	ANNALEE DOLLS	AN - ANIMALS		96		
7751	7 IN. LETTER TO SANTA MOUSE	ANNALEE DOLLS	AN - ANIMALS		96		
7740	7 IN. SNOWBALL MOUSE	ANNALEE DOLLS	AN - ANIMALS				
7754	7 IN. CAROLLING MOUSE	ANNALEE DOLLS	AN - ANIMALS		92		

Order No.	Title	Type	Theme	Retired	Intro. Year	Retail Price	Secondary Price
8205	7 IN. NEW YEAR'S MOUSE	ANNALEE DOLLS	AN - ANIMALS		96	$20.00	
7358	10 IN. CHRISTMAS ELF/GREEN	ANNALEE DOLLS	AN - ASSORTED DOLLS				
7357	10 IN. CHRISTMAS ELF/RED	ANNALEE DOLLS	AN - ASSORTED DOLLS				
7341	5 IN. CHRISTMAS ELF/GREEN	ANNALEE DOLLS	AN - ASSORTED DOLLS				
7340	5 IN. CHRISTMAS ELF/RED	ANNALEE DOLLS	AN - ASSORTED DOLLS			$15.50	
7345	5 IN. FROSTY ELF	ANNALEE DOLLS	AN - ASSORTED DOLLS				
7356	5 IN. WORKSHOP ELF	ANNALEE DOLLS	AN - ASSORTED DOLLS		94	$13.95	
7346	5 IN. ELF CENTER PIECE	ANNALEE DOLLS	AN - ASSORTED DOLLS		96	$27.00	
7451	30 IN. CHRISTMAS ELF/RED	ANNALEE DOLLS	AN - ASSORTED DOLLS			$67.00	
5455	10 IN. GHOST OF CHRISTMAS PAST	ANNALEE DOLLS	AN - DICKENS	YES	96	$39.50	
5456	10 IN. GHOST OF CHRISTMAS PRESENT	ANNALEE DOLLS	AN - DICKENS	YES	96	$56.00	
5458	12 IN. SCROOGE'S BED	ANNALEE DOLLS	AN - DICKENS	YES	96	$44.00	
5467	10 IN. MR. SCROOGE	ANNALEE DOLLS	AN - DICKENS	YES	96	$37.50	
5457	10 IN. GHOST OF CHRISTMAS FUTURE	ANNALEE DOLLS	AN - DICKENS	YES	96	$29.50	
8034	3 IN. CAROLLING GIRL	ANNALEE DOLLS	AN - CAROLLERS		96	$18.00	
8036	3 IN. CAROLLING BOY	ANNALEE DOLLS	AN - CAROLLERS		96	$18.00	
7425	5 IN. CHRISTMAS LAMB/BLACK	ANNALEE DOLLS	AN - NATIVITY				
7424	5 IN. CHRISTMAS LAMB/WHITE	ANNALEE DOLLS	AN - NATIVITY		92		
9162	10 IN. CRECHE	ANNALEE DOLLS	AN - NATIVITY				
7110	7 IN. ANGEL MAKING MUSIC	ANNALEE DOLLS	AN - ANGELS				
7274	10 IN. TREE TOP ANGEL	ANNALEE DOLLS	AN - ANGELS		94	$29.95	
7177	5 IN. ANGEL CENTER PIECE	ANNALEE DOLLS	AN - ANGELS		96	$31.00	
7113	7 IN. FLYING ANGEL	ANNALEE DOLLS	AN - ANGELS		94	$23.95	
7505	7 IN. SNOWMAN WITH BROOM	ANNALEE DOLLS	AN - ASSORTED DOLLS				
7527	18 IN. PUTTING ON THE RITZ SNOWMAN	ANNALEE DOLLS	AN - ASSORTED DOLLS		96	$64.50	
6605	18 IN. SANTA HUGGING REINDEER	ANNALEE DOLLS	AN - ANIMALS				
5396	10 IN. COLLECTOR MRS. NASHVILLE SANTA	ANNALEE DOLLS	AN - SANTAS		95	$44.95	
5397	10 IN. COLLECTOR MR. NASHVILLE SANTA	ANNALEE DOLLS	AN - SANTAS		95	$44.95	
5398	10 IN. COLLECTOR MR. SANTA WITH WEE HELPERS	ANNALEE DOLLS	AN - SANTAS		95	$74.95	
5410	10 IN. COLLECTOR ST. NICHOLAS	ANNALEE DOLLS	AN - SANTAS		95	$44.95	
5395	10 IN. COLLECTOR OLD SALTY SANTA	ANNALEE DOLLS	AN - SANTAS		95	$49.95	
5003	7 IN. MR. SANTA WITH USEABLE GIFT	ANNALEE DOLLS	AN - SANTAS		95	$27.95	
5006	7 IN. MRS. OUTDOOR SANTA	ANNALEE DOLLS	AN - SANTAS		94	$22.50	
5239	7 IN. MR. & MRS. INDOOR SANTA WITH TREE	ANNALEE DOLLS	AN - SANTAS		95	$69.95	
5001	7 IN. MRS. SANTA WITH PRESENTS	ANNALEE DOLLS	AN - SANTAS		95	$30.95	
5241	7 IN. MR. INDOOR SANTA WITH LIGHTS	ANNALEE DOLLS	AN - SANTAS		95	$31.95	
5235	7 IN. MR. INDOOR SANTA FREE STANDING	ANNALEE DOLLS	AN - SANTAS		95	$19.95	
5243	7 IN. MR. SANTA WITH SNOWSHOES AND TREE	ANNALEE DOLLS	AN - SANTAS		94	$29.95	
5230	7 IN. VELOUR SANTA IN SLEIGH	ANNALEE DOLLS	AN - SANTAS		95	$37.95	
6510	10 IN. SANTA HUGGING REINDEER	ANNALEE DOLLS	AN - SANTAS				
5030	7 IN. VELOUR SANTA WITH NORTH POLE	ANNALEE DOLLS	AN - SANTAS		95	$35.95	
5494	12 IN. MRS. INDOOR SANTA WITH GARLAND	ANNALEE DOLLS	AN - SANTAS				
5493	12 IN. MR. OUTDOOR SANTA IN CHIMNEY	ANNALEE DOLLS	AN - SANTAS				
5495	12 IN. MR. INDOOR SANTA WITH TREE TOP SANTA	ANNALEE DOLLS	AN - SANTAS		95	$49.95	
5491	12 IN. MRS. SANTA WITH CARDHOLDER APRON	ANNALEE DOLLS	AN - SANTAS		94	$39.95	
5632	18 IN. CHEF SANTA	ANNALEE DOLLS	AN - SANTAS				
5603	18 IN. MR. INDOOR SANTA WITH LIGHTS	ANNALEE DOLLS	AN - SANTAS		94	$56.95	
5637	18 IN. MRS. INDOOR SANTA WITH GARLAND	ANNALEE DOLLS	AN - SANTAS		95	$54.95	
5639	18 IN. MR. INDOOR SANTA WITH TREE TOP STAR	ANNALEE DOLLS	AN - SANTAS		95	$59.95	
5551	18 IN. MRS. SANTA WITH CARDHOLDER APRON	ANNALEE DOLLS	AN - SANTAS		95		
5510	18 IN. MR. SANTA WITH CARDHOLDER SACK	ANNALEE DOLLS	AN - SANTAS		94	$54.95	
6605	18 IN. REINDEER WITH 18 IN. SANTA	ANNALEE DOLLS	AN - ANIMALS		95	$89.95	
5504	18 IN. MR. OUTDOOR SANTA ON STAND	ANNALEE DOLLS	AN - SANTAS		94	$45.95	
5505	18 IN GIFT LIST SANTA	ANNALEE DOLLS	AN - SANTAS		95	$49.95	
9905	18 IN. MUSICAL GIFT LIST SANTA	ANNALEE DOLLS	AN - SANTAS		95	$61.95	
5642	18 IN. MRS. SANTA W/DOVE	ANNALEE DOLLS	AN - SANTAS		95		
5642	18 IN. MUSICAL MRS. SANTA W/DOVE	ANNALEE DOLLS	AN - SANTAS		95		
5643	18 IN. MR. OUTDOOR SANTA ON TOBOGGAN	ANNALEE DOLLS	AN - SANTAS				
6010	30 IN. MR. SANTA WITH CARDHOLDER SACK	ANNALEE DOLLS	AN - SANTAS		94	$119.95	
6050	30 IN. MRS. SANTA WITH CARDHOLDER APRON	ANNALEE DOLLS	AN - SANTAS				
6224	30 IN. MR. OUTDOOR SANTA WITH NORTHPOLE	ANNALEE DOLLS	AN - SANTAS				
6226	30 IN. MR. OUTDOOR SANTA WITH TOY SACK	ANNALEE DOLLS	AN - SANTAS		92		
7251	10 IN. OLD WORLD CAROLLER MAN	ANNALEE DOLLS	AN - CAROLLERS		94	$27.95	
7252	10 IN. OLD WORLD CAROLLER WOMAN	ANNALEE DOLLS	AN - CAROLLERS		94	$27.95	
4650	5 IN. OLD WORLD CAROLLER BOY	ANNALEE DOLLS	AN - CAROLLERS		94	$19.95	
4651	5 IN. OLD WORLD CAROLLER GIRL	ANNALEE DOLLS	AN - CAROLLERS		94	$19.95	
5150	7 IN. MR. OLD WORLD SANTA	ANNALEE DOLLS	AN - ASSORTED DOLLS		94	$27.95	
5151	7 IN. MRS. OLD WORLD SANTA	ANNALEE DOLLS	AN - ASSORTED DOLLS		94	$27.95	
6650	18 IN. OLD WORLD REINDEER WITH BELLS	ANNALEE DOLLS	AN - ANIMALS		94	$59.95	
5651	18 IN. MRS. OLD WORLD SANTA	ANNALEE DOLLS	AN - SANTAS		94	$49.95	
5650	18 IN. MR. OLD WORLD SANTA WITH STAFF	ANNALEE DOLLS	AN - SANTAS		94	$51.95	
5450	12 IN. OLD WORLD SAINT NICHOLAS	ANNALEE DOLLS	AN - SANTAS		95	$54.50	
6250	30 IN. MR. OLD WORLD SANTA	ANNALEE DOLLS	AN - SANTAS		94	$124.95	
6251	30 IN. MRS. OLD WORLD SANTA	ANNALEE DOLLS	AN - SANTAS		94	$124.95	
7111	7 IN. ANGEL WITH HARP	ANNALEE DOLLS	AN - ANGELS		95	$26.95	
7106	7 IN. ANGEL WITH BLACK HAIR	ANNALEE DOLLS	AN - ANGELS				
7106	7 IN. ANGEL WITH BROWN HAIR	ANNALEE DOLLS	AN - ANGELS				
7116	7 IN. NAUGHTY ANGEL WITH BLACK EYE	ANNALEE DOLLS	AN - ANGELS		95	$25.95	
7113	7 IN. FLYING ANGEL	ANNALEE DOLLS	AN - ANGELS		95	$25.95	
7173	5 IN. ANGEL WITH 18 CHRISTMAS MOON	ANNALEE DOLLS	AN - ANGELS		95	$44.95	
7174	5 IN. ANGEL WITH MISTLETOE	ANNALEE DOLLS	AN - ANGELS		95	$16.50	
7736	7 IN. CHRISTMAS PARTY GIRL MOUSE	ANNALEE DOLLS	AN - ANIMALS		95	$18.95	
7726	7 IN. WHITE MOUSE ON TOBOGGAN	ANNALEE DOLLS	AN - ANIMALS				
7724	7 IN. ANGEL MOUSE	ANNALEE DOLLS	AN - ANIMALS				
8204	7 IN. MOUSE IN CHAMPAGNE GLASS	ANNALEE DOLLS	AN - ANIMALS				
7723	7 IN. WHITE MOUSE IN SLIPPER	ANNALEE DOLLS	AN - ANIMALS				
7730	7 IN. MOUSE IN VELOUR HAT	ANNALEE DOLLS	AN - ANIMALS				
7427	10 IN. KITTEN WITH ORNAMENT	ANNALEE DOLLS	AN - ANIMALS				
7070	7 IN. JOSEPH CHILD	ANNALEE DOLLS	AN - NATIVITY		95	$28.95	
7071	7 IN. MARY CHILD WITH DOLL	ANNALEE DOLLS	AN - NATIVITY		95	$28.95	
7426	7 IN. CHRISTMAS DOVE	ANNALEE DOLLS	AN - NATIVITY				
7072	7 IN. SHEPHERD CHILD WITH LAMB	ANNALEE DOLLS	AN - NATIVITY		95	$39.95	
7175	5 IN. BABY JESUS IN MANGER	ANNALEE DOLLS	AN - NATIVITY				

Order No.	Title	Type	Theme	Retired	Intro. Year	Retial Price	Secondary Price
6434	10 IN REINDEER WITH SANTA HAT AND BELL	ANNALEE DOLLS	AN - ANIMALS				
7342	5 IN. WHITE CHRISTMAS ELF	ANNALEE DOLLS	AN - ASSORTED DOLLS		94	$13.95	
7359	10 IN. WHITE CHRISTMAS ELF	ANNALEE DOLLS	AN - ASSORTED DOLLS				
7508	7 IN. SNOWMAN ON TOBOGGAN	ANNALEE DOLLS	AN - ASSORTED DOLLS				
7506	7 IN. SNOW WOMAN	ANNALEE DOLLS	AN - ASSORTED DOLLS				
7507	7 IN. RITZ SNOWMAN	ANNALEE DOLLS	AN - ASSORTED DOLLS				
7410	18 IN. SNOWY OWL	ANNALEE DOLLS	AN - ANIMALS				
7412	10 IN. SNOWY OWL	ANNALEE DOLLS	AN - ANIMALS		90		
7406	24 IN. CHRISTMAS SWAN		AN - ANIMALS				
7408	5 IN. BABY CHRISTMAS SWAN		AN - ANIMALS				
7416	12 IN. SANTA DUCK		AN - ANIMALS				
7418	15 IN. CHRISTMAS DRAGON		AN - ANIMALS				
7414	10 IN. SANTA PIG		AN - ANIMALS		90		
8052	10 IN. BEAR WITH SNOWBALL, KNIT HAT WITH SCARF		AN - ANIMALS				
8054	10 IN. BEAR IN VELOUR SANTA SUIT		AN - ANIMALS				
8056	10 IN. BEAR IN NIGHTSHIRT WITH CANDLE		AN - ANIMALS				
8058	10 IN. ESKIMO BEAR		AN - ANIMALS				
8070	5 IN. DUCK ON FLEXBILE FLYER SLED		AN - ANIMALS				
8062	10 IN. KITTEN ON SLED		AN - ANIMALS				
8064	10 IN. KITTEN WITH KNIT MITTENS		AN - ANIMALS				
8068	10 IN. 2 BUNNIES ON FLEXIBLE FLYER SLED		AN - ANIMALS				
7414	10 IN. SANTA PIG		AN - ANIMALS		90		
9920	36 IN. REINDEER (ANIMATED)		AN - ANIMALS				
9914	18 IN. SANTA SLEIGH AND REINDEER (ANIMATED)		AN - ANIMALS				
7742	7 IN. MOUSE WITH TENNIS RAQUET SNOWSHOES		AN - ANIMALS		90		
7744	7 IN. MOUSE IN BOX		AN - ANIMALS		90		
7762	12 IN. CAROLLER MOUSE		AN - ANIMALS				
7730	7 IN. MOUSE IN VELOUR HAT		AN - ANIMALS				
7735	7 IN. MOUSE WITH PRESENT		AN - ANIMALS				
7705	7 IN. CAROLLER MOUSE		AN - ANIMALS				
7712	7 IN. MOUSE WITH CANDY CANE		AN - ANIMALS				
7714	7 IN. MOUSE WITH STOCKING		AN - ANIMALS				
7720	7 IN. SLEDDING MOUSE		AN - ANIMALS				
7740	7 IN. MOUSE WITH SNOWBALL		AN - ANIMALS				
7172	30 IN. ANGEL		AN - ANGELS		90		
7170	18 IN. ANGEL WITH INSTRUMENT		AN - ANGELS		90		
7564	10 IN. CHRISTMAS FAIRIE (FLYING)		AN - ANGELS				
7140	7 IN. FLYING ANGEL WITH MISTLETOE		AN - ANGELS				
7165	12 IN. TREETOP ANGEL		AN - ANGELS				
7110	7 IN. ANGEL WITH INSTRUMENT		AN - ANGELS				
7168	7 IN. ANGEL ON SLED WITH CLOUD		AN - ANGELS		90		
5210	7 IN. VELOUR SANTA		AN - SANTAS				
5215	7 IN. VELOUR MRS. SANTA		AN - SANTAS				
5100	7 IN. MR. AND MRS. TUCKERED SANTA		AN - SANTAS				
6510	10 IN. REINDEER WITH 7 IN. VELOUR SANTA		AN - SANTAS				
5001	7 IN. MRS. SANTA WITH PRESENTS		AN - SANTAS				
5110	7 IN. SANTA WITH SLEIGH AND 1 REINDEER		AN - SANTAS				
5225	7 IN. SANTA WITH GIFT LIST AND TOY BAG		AN - SANTAS				
5003	7 IN. SANTA WITH PRESENTS		AN - SANTAS				
5460	10 IN. SCROOGE		AN - DICKENS				
5464	10 IN. JACOB MARLEY		AN - DICKENS		90		
5462	10 IN. BOB CRATCHET AND 5 IN. TINY TIM		AN - DICKENS				
5702	18 IN. MORNING KID WITH TRAIN		AN - ASSORTED DOLLS		90		
5708	18 IN. CHOIR GIRL		AN - ASSORTED DOLLS		90		
5704	18 IN. WINTER DRESS UP BOY		AN - ASSORTED DOLLS		90		
5706	18 IN. GIRL ON SLED		AN - ASSORTED DOLLS		90		
5424	5 IN. LAMB		AN - NATIVITY				
5422	10 IN. SHEPHERD BOY WITH LAMB		AN - NATIVITY		90		
9162	CRECHE FOR NATIVITY		AN - NATIVITY		90		
5420	10 IN. NATIVITY SET WITH GLASS DOME		AN - NATIVITY				
5428	10 IN. WISE MAN W/CAMEL		AN - NATIVITY				
5426	10 IN. 2 WISE MEN		AN - NATIVITY		90		
5482	12 IN. VELOUR SANTA WITH NORTH POLE		AN - SANTAS				
5486	12 IN. SANTA WITH STOCKING		AN - SANTAS				
5480	12 IN. VELOUR SANTA WITH TOY BAG		AN - SANTAS				
7505	7 IN. SNOWMAN		AN - SNOWPEOPLE				
7260	7 IN. GIRL CAROLLER		AN - CAROLLER				
7262	7 IN. BOY CAROLLER		AN - CAROLLER				
7355	10 IN. CHRISTMAS ELF		AN - ASSORTED DOLLS				
7560	10 IN. TOY SOLDIER		AN - ASSORTED DOLLS				
7562	18 IN. TOY SOLDIER		AN - ASSORTED DOLLS				
7355	10 IN. CHRISTMAS ELF		AN - ASSORTED DOLLS				
5516	18 IN. SANTA PLAYING WITH ELECTRIC TRAIN		AN - SANTAS		90		
5514	18 IN. DAY-AFTER-CHRISTMAS SANTA		AN - SANTAS		90		
5602	SANTA TRIMMING LIGHTED TREE		AN - SANTAS				
5600	MR. AND MRS. SANTA WITH BASKET		AN - SANTAS				
5505	SANTA WITH GIFT LIST AND TOYBAG		AN - SANTAS				
5615	18 IN. VELOUR SANTA		AN - SANTAS				
5620	18 IN. VELOUR MRS. SANTA		AN - SANTAS				
5512	18 IN. MRS. SANTA WITH TRAY		AN - SANTAS		90		
5630	18 IN. SANTA WITH STOCKING		AN - SANTAS				
6600	18 IN. REINDEER WITH SADDLEBAGS		AN - ANIMALS				
5625	18 IN. WORKSHOP SANTA		AN - SANTAS				
5638	18 IN. MRS. SANTA WITH PRESENTS		AN - SANTAS				
5636	18 IN. MR AND MRS. TUCKERED		AN - SANTAS				
7448	22 IN. CHRISTMAS ELF		AN - ASSORTED DOLLS				
7640	12 IN. P.J. KID BROWN HAIR		AN - ASSORTED DOLLS		90		
7642	12 IN. P.J. KID RED HAIR		AN - ASSORTED DOLLS		90		
7644	12 IN. P.J. KID BLONDE HAIR		AN - ASSORTED DOLLS		90		
7658	18 IN. P.J. KID IN 2' STOCKING		AN - ASSORTED DOLLS				
7655	18 IN. P.J. KID		AN - ASSORTED DOLLS				
7672	18 IN. P.J. KID HANGING STOCKING		AN - ASSORTED DOLLS				
6210	30 IN. VELOUR SANTA		AN - SANTAS				

Order No.	Title	Type	Theme	Retired	Intro. Year	Retail Price	Secondary Price
6215	30 IN. VELOUR MRS. SANTA		AN - SANTAS				
6205	30 IN. MR. AND MRS. TUCKERED W/2-KIDS		AN - SANTAS				
6222	30 IN. MRS. SANTA WITH TRAY		AN - SANTAS				
5410	10 IN. ST. NICHOLAS		AN - SANTAS		94	$43.95	
5414	10 IN. MAUI SANTA/LIMITED 1 YR.		AN - SANTAS		90		
5412	10 IN. MRS. SANTA W/TRAY AND TURKEY		AN - SANTAS				
5408	10 IN. SANTA PLAYING WITH TRAIN		AN - SANTAS				
5400	10 IN. SANTA IN ROCKING CHAIR W/CHILD		AN - SANTAS				
5407	10 IN. COLLECTOR SUMMER SANTA/LIMITED 1 YR.		AN - SANTAS		91		
5403	10 IN. COLLECTOR SANTA ON ROCKING HORSE		AN - SANTAS		91		
5401	10 IN. COLLECTOR SANTA FEEDING REINDEER		AN - SANTAS		91		
5405	10 IN. COLLECTOR SANTA WITH REINDEER GOLFING		AN - SANTAS		91		
5232	7 IN. SANTA BRINGING HOME CHRISTMAS TREE		AN - SANTAS		91		
5234	7 IN. SANTA WITH MAILBAG AND LETTERS		AN - SANTAS		91		
5238	7 IN. SANTA IN SLEIGH		AN - SANTAS		91		
5240	7 IN. SANTA IN TUB WITH RUBBER DUCKIE		AN - SANTAS		91		
5236	7 IN. MRS. SANTA HANGING BANNER		AN - SANTAS		91		
5003	7 IN. SANTA WITH PRESENTS		AN - SANTAS				
5430	10 IN. NATIVITY ANGEL		AN - NATIVITY		91		
5487	12 IN. TUCKERED COUPLE		AN - SANTAS		91		
5483	12 IN. VELOUR MRS. SANTA		AN - SANTAS		91		
5489	12 IN. BASKET COUPLE		AN - SANTAS		91		
5485	12 IN. SANTA WITH POT-BELLY STOVE		AN - SANTAS		91		
5640	18 IN. SANTA WITH CARDHOLDER MAILBAG		AN - SANTAS		91		
5466	10 IN. MARTHA CRATCHET		AN - DICKENS		91		
7267	10 IN. MAN SKATER		AN - ASSORTED DOLLS		91		
7269	10 IN. WOMAN SKATER		AN - ASSORTED DOLLS		91		
7270	10 IN. GIRL WITH BASKET		AN - ASSORTED DOLLS		91		
5710	18 IN. CHOIR BOY		AN - ASSORTED DOLLS		91		
7367	7 IN. CHRISTMAS GNOME		AN - ASSORTED DOLLS		91		
6219	30 IN. SANTA WITH LIGHTED TREE		AN - SANTAS		91		
6221	30 IN. MRS. SANTA WITH CARDHOLDER BASKET		AN - ASSORTED DOLLS		91		
7300	18 IN. GINGERBREAD BOY		AN - ASSORTED DOLLS				
7365	10 IN. TINSEL ELF		AN - ASSORTED DOLLS				
7403	12 IN. CHRISTMAS SWAN		AN - ASSORTED DOLLS		91		
8057	10 IN. HUSKY W/5 PUPPY IN SLED		AN - ASSORTED DOLLS		91		
7420	5 IN. CHRISTMAS DRAGON		AN - ASSORTED DOLLS				
8074	10 IN. SKATING BUNNY		AN - ASSORTED DOLLS		91		
7752	7 IN. MOUSE W/MAILBAG AND LETTERS		AN - ANIMALS		91		
7750	7 IN. WORKSHOP MOUSE		AN - ANIMALS		91		
5236	7 IN. MRS. SANTA HANGING SIGN		AN - SANTAS				
5032	7 IN. MRS. SANTA W/ POINSETTIA		AN - SANTAS		92		
5234	7 IN. SANTA W/MAILBAG AND LETTERS		AN - SANTAS				
5040	7 IN. MRS. SANTA CANDLEHODER		AN - SANTAS				
5042	7 IN. SANTA CANDLEHOLDER		AN - SANTAS				
5035	7 IN. SANTA IN CHIMNEY		AN - SANTAS				
5225	7 IN. SANTA W/GIFT LIST AND TOYBAG		AN - SANTAS				
5200	7 IN. SANTA ON 18 IN. MOON		AN - SANTAS		92		
7008	10 IN. SNOWQUEEN		AN - ANGELS		92		
7171	7 IN. ANGEL ON MOON		AN - ANGELS		92		
5416	10 IN. SANTA AT WORKBENCH		AN - SANTAS		92		
5418	10 IN. TENNIS SANTA		AN - SANTAS		92		
5415	10 IN. FISHING SANTA IN BOAT W/MRS. CLAUS		AN - SANTAS		92		
5417	10 IN. SAVING SANTA		AN - SANTAS		92		
5490	12 IN. MRS. SANTA W/POINSETTIA		AN - SANTAS		92		
5492	12 IN. CHEF SANTA		AN - SANTAS		92		
5470	10 IN. CHRISTMAS EVE BOB CRATCHET AT DESK		AN - DICKENS		92		
6602	18 IN. REINDEER W/NORTH POLE		AN - ANIMALS		92		
5520	18 IN. MRS. SANTA WITH POINSETTIA		AN - SANTAS		92		
5518	18 IN. SANTA W/BANNER		AN - SANTAS		92		
7295	10 IN. GINGERBREAD BOY		AN - ASSORTED DOLLS		91		
7422	7 IN. SANTA SKUNK		AN - ANIMALS		92		
7510	12 IN. SNOWMAN		AN - SNOWPEOPLE		92		
7555	32 IN. STOCKING W/10 IN. ELF		AN - ASSORTED DOLLS				
7756	7 IN. MOUSE ON CHEESE		AN - ANIMALS		92		
7754	7 IN. CAROLLER MOUSE W/BIG HAT AND TREE		AN - ANIMALS		92		
7758	7 IN. MOUSE WITH NORTH POLE		AN - ANIMALS		92		
8059	10 IN. MRS. BEAR IN NIGHTSHIRT W/CANDLE		AN - ANIMALS		92		
5003	7 IN. SANTA W/USEABLE GIFTBOX		AN - SANTAS		94	$24.95	
5035	7 IN. SANTA IN CHIMNEY		AN - SANTAS				
5241	7 IN. SANTA W/LIGHTS		AN - SANTAS		93		
5242	7 IN. SANTA SKIING		AN - SANTAS		93		
5238	7 IN. SANTA IN SLEIGH		AN - SANTAS		93		
5409	10 IN. SKATING SANTA		AN - SANTAS		93		
5411	10 IN. MRS. SKATING SANTA		AN - SANTAS		93		
5421	10 IN. GARDENING SUMMER SANTA		AN - SANTAS		93		
5419	10 IN SANTA W/FIREPLACE AND CHILD		AN - SANTAS		93		
5413	10 IN. TOBOGGAN SANTA		AN - SANTAS		93		
5493	12 IN. SANTA IN CHIMNEY		AN - SANTAS		93		
7106	7 IN. ANGEL BLACK HAIR		AN - ANGELS		93		
7175	5 IN. BABY JESUS IN MANGER		AN - NATIVITY		93		
7108	7 IN. ANGEL BLONDE HAIR		AN - ANGELS		93		
7107	7 IN. ANGEL BROWN HAIR		AN - ANGELS		93		
7273	10 IN. SNOWQUEEN TREETOP		AN - ANGELS		93		
7140	7 IN. FLYING ANGEL WITH MISTLETOE		AN - ANGELS				
7724	7 IN. ANGEL MOUSE		AN - ANIMALS		93		
7723	7 IN. WHITE MOUSE IN SLIPPER		AN - ANIMALS		93		
7726	7 IN. WHITE MOUSE ON TOBOGGAN		AN - ANIMALS		93		
7721	7 IN. WHITE MOUSE W/PRESENT		AN - ANIMALS		93		
7722	7 IN. WHITE SKATING MOUSE		AN - ANIMALS		93		
7550	22 IN. STOCKING W/MOUSE IN TOE		AN - ANIMALS				
7630	12 IN. P.J. GIRL		AN - ASSORTED DOLLS				
7635	12 IN. P.J. BOY		AN - ASSORTED DOLLS				

Order No.	Title	Type	Theme	Retired	Intro. Year	Retial Price	Secondary Price
7674	12 IN. SANTA'S POSTMAN W/MAILBAG		AN - SANTAS				
5643	18 IN. SANTA ON TOBOGGAN		AN - SANTAS		93		
5641	18 IN. SANTA W/LIGHTS		AN - SANTAS		93		
5644	18 IN. SANTA IN SLEIGH		AN - SANTAS		93		
5642	18 IN. MRS. OUTDOOR SANTA		AN - SANTAS		93		
5468	10 IN. CHRISTMAS EVE SCROOGE		AN - DICKENS				
5476	18 IN. MAN SKATER		AN - ASSORTED DOLLS		93		
7477	18 IN. WOMAN SKATER		AN - ASSORTED DOLLS		93		
6815	7 IN. VICTORIAN MRS. SANTA		AN - ASSORTED DOLLS		93		
6810	7 IN. VICTORIAN SANTA		AN - ASSORTED DOLLS		93		
6819	7 IN. VICTORIAN SANTA IN SLEIGH		AN - ASSORTED DOLLS		93		
6855	18 IN. VICTORIAN MRS. SANTA		AN - ASSORTED DOLLS		93		
6850	18 IN. VICTORIAN SANTA		AN - ASSORTED DOLLS		93		
7506	7 IN. SNOWMAN		AN - SNOWPEOPLE		93		
7507	7 IN. RITZ SNOWMAN		AN - SNOWPEOPLE				
7425	5 IN. BLACK CHRISTMAS LAMB		AN - ANIMALS				
7430	10 IN. SKATING PENGUIN		AN - ANIMALS		93		
7426	SMALL CHRISTMAS DOVE		AN - ANIMALS		93		
8070	5 IN. DUCK ON FLEXIBLE FLYER SLED		AN - ANIMALS				
7424	5 IN. WHITE CHRISTMAS LAMB		AN - ANIMALS		93		
7428	CHRISTMAS CHICKEN		AN - ANIMALS		93		
7427	10 IN. KITTEN W/ORNAMENT		AN - ANIMALS		93		
7366	14 IN. WREATH W/10 IN. WINTER ELF		AN - ASSORTED DOLLS		93		
7508	7 IN. SNOWMAN ON TOBOGGAN		AN - SNOWPEOPLE		93		
8051	10 IN. SANTA'S HELPER BEAR		AN - ANIMALS		93		
8053	10 IN. ANGEL BEAR		AN - ANIMALS		93		
6228	30 IN. SANTA WITH BANNER		AN - SANTAS				
7248	7 IN. CHOIR GIRL		AN - ASSORTED DOLLS		93		
7249	7 IN. CHOIR BOY		AN - ASSORTED DOLLS		93		
7230	7 IN. BOY BUILDING SNOWMAN		AN - ASSORTED DOLLS				
5238	7 IN. SANTA IN SLEIGH		AN - SANTAS				
5244	7 IN. SANTA W/TREE AND SLED		AN - SANTAS		94	$28.95	
5399	10 IN. MRS SANTA LAST MINUTE MENDING		AN - SANTAS				
5352	10 IN. OLD WORLD SKATERS ON MUSIC BOX		AN - SANTAS		94	$119.95	
9907	18 IN. MUSICAL MRS. SANTA		AN - SANTAS		94	$59.95	
5603	18 IN. INDOOR SANTA W/LIGHTS		AN - SANTAS		94		
5350	10 IN. OLD WORLD SANTA W/SKIS		AN - SANTAS		94	$49.95	
4550	5 IN. OLD WORLD SANTA W/9 IN. WREATH		AN - SANTAS		94	$32.95	
7247	7 IN. CHOIR BOY WITH BLACK EYE		AN - SANTAS		94	$26.95	
7431	10 IN. WINDOW SHOPPER OSTRICH		AN - ANIMALS		94	$37.95	
7427	10 IN. KITTEN W/ORNAMENT		AN - ANIMALS				
7536	30 IN. SNOWMAN		AN - SNOWPEOPLE		94	$119.95	
7231	7 IN. GIRL BUILDING SNOWMAN		AN - ASSORTED DOLLS		94	$23.95	
BOYD'S COLLECTION							
2002	NEVILLE...THE BEDTIME BEAR/Limited	BB - BEARSTONES	THE BASICS	96	93	$13.50	$115.00
2003-03	ARTHUR...WITH RED SCARF	BB - BEARSTONES	THE BASICS	94	93	$14.20	$52.00
2003-03	ARTHUR...WITH RED SCARF/First Edition	BB - BEARSTONES	THE BASICS	94	93	$14.20	$100.00
2003-04	GRENVILLE...WITH GREEN SCARF	BB - BEARSTONES	THE BASICS	93	93	$10.50	
2003-04	GRENVILLE...WITH GREEN SCARF/First Edition	BB - BEARSTONES	THE BASICS	93	93	$10.50	$375.00
2003-08	GRENVILLE...WITH RED SCARF	BB - BEARSTONES	THE BASICS	95	93	$10.50	$45.00
2003-08	GRENVILLE...WITH RED SCARF/First Edition	BB - BEARSTONES	THE BASICS	95	93	$10.50	$120.00
2008	FATHER CHRISBEAR WITH SON	BB - BEARSTONES	THE BASICS	93	93	$14.50	$150.00
2008	FATHER CHRISBEAR WITH SON/First Edition	BB - BEARSTONES	THE BASICS	93	93	$14.50	$300.00
2029-10	JULIETTE ANGEL BEAR	BB - BEARSTONES	VICTORIANS	95	94	$12.00	$28.00
2029-10	JULIETTE ANGEL BEAR/First Edition	BB - BEARSTONES	VICTORIANS	95	94	$12.00	$84.00
2029-11	CLARENCE ANGEL BEAR	BB - BEARSTONES	THE BASICS	95	94	$12.00	$32.00
2029-11	CLARENCE ANGEL BEAR/First Edition	BB - BEARSTONES	THE BASICS	95	94	$12.00	$84.00
2030	GRENVILLE THE SANTABEAR	BB - BEARSTONES	HOME FOR THE HOLIDAYS	96	94	$13.50	$17.00
2030	GRENVILLE THE SANTABEAR/First Edition	BB - BEARSTONES	HOME FOR THE HOLIDAYS	96	94	$13.50	$450.00
2099	GRENVILLE & NEVILLLE...THE SIGN	BB - BEARSTONES	THE BASICS		93	$15.00	$15.00
2099	GRENVILLE & NEVILLLE...THE SIGN/First Edition	BB - BEARSTONES	THE BASICS		93	$15.00	$55.00
2228	MANITOBA MOOSEMEN	BB - BEARSTONES	SPECIAL EDITIONS		96	$18.00	$18.00
2228	MANITOBA MOOSEMEN/First Edition	BB - BEARSTONES	SPECIAL EDITIONS		96	$18.00	$18.00
2230	CELESTE THE ANGEL RABBIT	BB - BEARSTONES	VICTORIANS		94	$15.50	$16.00
2230	CELESTE THE ANGEL RABBIT/First Edition	BB - BEARSTONES	VICTORIANS		94	$15.50	$250.00
2235	KRINGLE & BAILY WITH LIST	BB - BEARSTONES	HOME FOR THE HOLIDAYS		94	$13.50	$13.50
2235	KRINGLE & BAILY WITH LIST/First Edition	BB - BEARSTONES	HOME FOR THE HOLIDAYS		94	$13.50	$80.00
2236	ELGIN THE ELF BEAR	BB - BEARSTONES	HOME FOR THE HOLIDAYS		94	$13.50	$14.00
2236	ELGIN THE ELF BEAR/First Edition	BB - BEARSTONES	HOME FOR THE HOLIDAYS		94	$13.50	$80.00
2237	COOKIE THE SANTA CAT	BB - BEARSTONES	HOME FOR THE HOLIDAYS	95	94	$14.50	$30.00
2237	COOKIE THE SANTA CAT/First Edition	BB - BEARSTONES	HOME FOR THE HOLIDAYS	95	94	$14.50	$70.00
2238	MAYNARD THE SANTA MOOSE	BB - BEARSTONES	HOME FOR THE HOLIDAYS		94	$14.50	$15.50
2238	MAYNARD THE SANTA MOOSE/First Edition	BB - BEARSTONES	HOME FOR THE HOLIDAYS		94	$14.50	$60.00
2239	BESSIE THE SANTA COW	BB - BEARSTONES	HOME FOR THE HOLIDAYS	96	94	$15.00	$18.00
2239	BESSIE THE SANTA COW/First Edition	BB - BEARSTONES	HOME FOR THE HOLIDAYS	96	94	$15.00	$65.00
2240	EDMUND & BAILEY/GATHER HOLLY	BB - BEARSTONES	HOME FOR THE HOLIDAYS		94	$23.00	$23.00
2240	EDMUND & BAILEY/GATHER HOLLY/First Edition	BB - BEARSTONES	HOME FOR THE HOLIDAYS		94	$23.00	$100.00
2241	ELLIOT & THE TREE	BB - BEARSTONES	HOME FOR THE HOLIDAYS		94	$15.50	$16.00
2241	ELLIOT & THE TREE/First Edition	BB - BEARSTONES	HOME FOR THE HOLIDAYS		94	$15.50	$135.00
2242	ELLIOT & SNOWBEARY	BB - BEARSTONES	HOME FOR THE HOLIDAYS		94	$14.50	$14.50
2242	ELLIOT & SNOWBEARY/First Edition	BB - BEARSTONES	HOME FOR THE HOLIDAYS		94	$14.50	$60.00
2243	MANHEIM AND ECOMOOSE	BB - BEARSTONES	HOME FOR THE HOLIDAYS		94	$14.50	$15.00
2243	MANHEIM AND ECOMOOSE/First Edition	BB - BEARSTONES	HOME FOR THE HOLIDAYS		94	$14.50	$62.00
2265	GRENVILLE...THE STORYTELLER/Limited Edition	BB - BEARSTONES	LIMITED EDITIONS	95	95	$47.00	$60.00
2265	GRENVILLE...THE STORYTELLER/Limited Edition/First Edition	BB - BEARSTONES	LIMITED EDITIONS	95	95	$47.00	$125.00
2266	ANGELICA...THE GUARDIAN	BB - BEARSTONES	THE BASICS		95	$17.50	$18.00
2266	ANGELICA...THE GUARDIAN/First Edition	BB - BEARSTONES	THE BASICS		95	$17.50	$45.00
2267	SIMONE & BAILEY/HELPING HAND	BB - BEARSTONES	THE BASICS		95	$25.00	$25.50
2267	SIMONE & BAILEY/HELPING HAND/First Edition	BB - BEARSTONES	THE BASICS		95	$25.00	$52.50
2273	JUSTINA...MESSAGE BEARER	BB - BEARSTONES	HEART TO HEART		96	$15.00	$22.00
2002	NEVILLE...THE BEDTIME BEAR/Limited	BB - BEARSTONES	THE BASICS	96	93	$13.50	$17.50

Order No.	Title	Type	Theme	Retired	Intro. Year	Retail Price	Secondary Price
2273	JUSTINA...MESSAGE BEARER/First Edition	BB - BEARSTONES	HEART TO HEART		96	$15.00	$78.00
2283	KRINGLE AND COMPANY	BB - BEARSTONES	HEAD TO HEART		96	$17.00	$17.50
2283	KRINGLE AND COMPANY/First Edition	BB - BEARSTONES	HEAD TO HEART		96	$17.00	$25.00
2401	NEVILLE...AS JOSEPH	BB - BEARSTONES	HOLIDAY PAGEANT		95	$14.00	$25.00
2401	NEVILLE...AS JOSEPH	BB - BEARSTONES	HOLIDAY PAGEANT		94	$14.00	$40.00
2401	NEVILLE...AS JOSEPH	BB - BEARSTONES	HOLIDAY PAGEANT		95	$14.00	$25.00
2401	NEVILLE...AS JOSEPH	BB - BEARSTONES	HOLIDAY PAGEANT		96	$14.00	$17.00
2402	THERESA...AS MARY	BB - BEARSTONES	HOLIDAY PAGEANT		94	$14.00	$14.50
2402	THERESA...AS MARY	BB - BEARSTONES	HOLIDAY PAGEANT		95	$14.00	$30.00
2402	THERESA...AS MARY	BB - BEARSTONES	HOLIDAY PAGEANT		96	$14.00	$25.00
2402	THERESA...AS MARY	BB - BEARSTONES	HOLIDAY PAGEANT		95	$14.00	$18.00
2403	BALDWIN...AS THE CHILD	BB - BEARSTONES	HOLIDAY PAGEANT		95	$14.00	$14.50
2403	BALDWIN...AS THE CHILD	BB - BEARSTONES	HOLIDAY PAGEANT		94	$14.00	$30.00
2403	BALDWIN...AS THE CHILD	BB - BEARSTONES	HOLIDAY PAGEANT		95	$14.00	$20.00
2403	BALDWIN...AS THE CHILD	BB - BEARSTONES	HOLIDAY PAGEANT		96	$14.00	$17.00
2404	WILSON AS MELCHOIR	BB - BEARSTONES	HOLIDAY PAGAENT		96	$16.00	$15.50
2404	WILSON AS MELCHOIR	BB - BEARSTONES	HOLIDAY PAGAENT		95	$16.00	$30.00
2404	WILSON AS MELCHOIR	BB - BEARSTONES	HOLIDAY PAGAENT		96	$16.00	$16.00
2405	HEATH AS CASPAR	BB - BEARSTONES	HOLIDAY PAGAENT		96	$16.00	$15.50
2405	HEATH AS CASPAR	BB - BEARSTONES	HOLIDAY PAGAENT		95	$16.00	$30.00
2405	HEATH AS CASPAR	BB - BEARSTONES	HOLIDAY PAGAENT		96	$16.00	$15.50
2406	RALEIGH AS BALTHASAR	BB - BEARSTONES	HOLIDAY PAGAENT		96	$16.00	$15.50
2406	RALEIGH AS BALTHASAR	BB - BEARSTONES	HOLIDAY PAGAENT		95	$16.00	$30.00
2406	RALEIGH AS BALTHASAR	BB - BEARSTONES	HOLIDAY PAGAENT		96	$16.00	$15.50
2407	THATCHER & EDEN AS THE CAMEL	BB - BEARSTONES	HOLIDAY PAGAENT		96	$17.00	$17.50
2407	THATCHER & EDEN AS THE CAMEL	BB - BEARSTONES	HOLIDAY PAGAENT		95	$17.00	$30.00
2407	THATCHER & EDEN AS THE CAMEL	BB - BEARSTONES	HOLIDAY PAGAENT		96	$17.00	$17.50
2425	SCHOOL PAGEANT...THE STAGE	BB - BEARSTONES	HOLIDAY PAGEANT		95	$33.50	$34.00
2425	SCHOOL PAGEANT...THE STAGE	BB - BEARSTONES	HOLIDAY PAGEANT		94	$33.50	$45.00
2425	SCHOOL PAGEANT...THE STAGE	BB - BEARSTONES	HOLIDAY PAGEANT		95	$33.50	$45.00
2425	SCHOOL PAGEANT...THE STAGE	BB - BEARSTONES	HOLIDAY PAGEANT		96	$33.50	$34.00
2500	FAITH/First Edition	BB - BEARSTONES	REJOICE ORNAMENTS	96	94	$9.00	$12.50
2500	FAITH	BB - BEARSTONES	REJOICE ORNAMENTS	96	94	$9.00	$12.50
2501	HOPE/First Edition	BB - BEARSTONES	REJOICE ORNAMENTS	96	94	$9.00	$12.50
2501	HOPE	BB - BEARSTONES	REJOICE ORNAMENTS	96	94	$9.00	$12.50
2502	CHARITY/First Edition	BB - BEARSTONES	REJOICE ORNAMENTS	96	94	$9.00	$12.50
2502	CHARITY	BB - BEARSTONES	REJOICE ORNAMENTS	96	94	$9.00	$12.50
2505	EDMUND-BELIEVE/Limited/First Edition	BB - BEARSTONES	SANTAS COMIN ORNAMENTS		95	$9.00	$9.50
2505	EDMUND-BELIEVE/Limited	BB - BEARSTONES	SANTAS COMIN ORNAMENTS		95	$9.00	$9.50
2506	MANHEIM/First Edition	BB - BEARSTONES	SANTAS COMIN ORNAMENTS		95	$9.00	$9.50
2506	MANHEIM	BB - BEARSTONES	SANTAS COMIN ORNAMENTS		95	$9.00	$9.50
2507	ELLIOT WITH TREE/First Edition	BB - BEARSTONES	SANTAS COMIN ORNAMENTS		95	$9.00	$9.50
2507	ELLIOT WITH TREE	BB - BEARSTONES	SANTAS COMIN ORNAMENTS		95	$9.00	$9.50
2550	NICHOLAI WITH TREE/First Edition	BB - FOLKSTONES	HO-HO-HO ORNAMENTS		95	$9.00	$12.00
2550	NICHOLAI WITH TREE	BB - FOLKSTONES	HO-HO-HO ORNAMENTS		95	$9.00	$9.00
2551	NICHOLAI THE GIFTGIVER/First Edition	BB - FOLKSTONES	HO-HO-HO ORNAMENTS		95	$9.00	$9.50
2551	NICHOLAI THE GIFTGIVER	BB - FOLKSTONES	HO-HO-HO ORNAMENTS		95	$9.00	$9.50
2552	SLIKNICK IN THE CHIMNEY/First Edition	BB - FOLKSTONES	HO-HO-HO ORNAMENTS		95	$9.00	$9.50
2552	SLIKNICK IN THE CHIMNEY	BB - FOLKSTONES	HO-HO-HO ORNAMENTS		95	$9.00	$9.50
2553	FATHER CHRISTMAS/First Edition	BB - FOLKSTONES	HO-HO-HO ORNAMENTS		95	$9.00	$9.50
2553	FATHER CHRISTMAS	BB - FOLKSTONES	HO-HO-HO ORNAMENTS		95	$9.00	$9.50
2560	OLAF...LET IT SNOW/First Edition	BB - FOLKSTONES	LET IT SNOW ORNAMENTS		95	$9.00	$9.50
2560	OLAF...LET IT SNOW	BB - FOLKSTONES	LET IT SNOW ORNAMENTS		95	$9.00	$9.50
2561	JEAN CLAUSE & JACQUE...SKIERS/First Edition	BB - FOLKSTONES	LET IT SNOW ORNAMENTS		95	$9.00	$9.50
2561	JEAN CLAUSE & JACQUE...SKIERS	BB - FOLKSTONES	LET IT SNOW ORNAMENTS		95	$9.00	$9.50
2562	JINGLES THE SNOWMAN W/WREATH/First Edition	BB - FOLKSTONES	LET IT SNOW ORNAMENTS		95	$9.00	$9.50
2562	JINGLES THE SNOWMAN W/WREATH	BB - FOLKSTONES	LET IT SNOW ORNAMENTS		95	$9.00	$9.50
2563	WINDY WITH TREE/First Edition	BB - FOLKSTONES	SNOWMAN ORNAMENTS		96	$10.00	$10.00
2563	WINDY WITH TREE	BB - FOLKSTONES	SNOWMAN ORNAMENTS		96	$10.00	$10.00
2564	CHILLY WITH WREATH/First Edition	BB - FOLKSTONES	SNOWMAN ORNAMENTS		96	$10.00	$10.00
2564	CHILLY WITH WREATH	BB - FOLKSTONES	SNOWMAN ORNAMENTS		96	$10.00	$10.00
2565	WILLIE WITH BROOM/First Edition	BB - FOLKSTONES	SNOWMAN ORNAMENTS		96	$10.00	$10.00
2565	WILLIE WITH BROOM	BB - FOLKSTONES	SNOWMAN ORNAMENTS		96	$10.00	$10.00
25700	EDMUND WITH WREATH/First Edition	BB - BEARSTONES	DECK THE HALLS ORNAMENTS		96	$10.00	$10.00
25700	EDMUND WITH WREATH	BB - BEARSTONES	DECK THE HALLS ORNAMENTS		96	$10.00	$10.00
25701	CLAIR WITH GINGERBREAD MAN/First Edition	BB - BEARSTONES	DECK THE HALLS ORNAMENTS		96	$10.00	$10.00
25701	CLAIR WITH GINGERBREAD MAN	BB - BEARSTONES	DECK THE HALLS ORNAMENTS		96	$10.00	$10.00
2600	NICHOLAS/First Edition	BB - BEARWEAR		95	94	$4.00	$4.50
2600	NICHOLAS	BB - BEARWEAR		95	94	$4.00	$4.50
26002	ELLIOT WITH TREE/First Edition	BB - BEARWEAR			96	$4.50	$4.50
26002	ELLIOT WITH TREE	BB - BEARWEAR			96	$4.50	$4.50
26003	EDMUND AND BAILEY...CAROLING/First Edition	BB - BEARWEAR			96	$4.50	$4.50
26003	EDMUND AND BAILEY...CAROLING	BB - BEARWEAR			96	$4.50	$4.50
26004	EDMUND SANTA BEAR...BELIEVE/First Edition	BB - BEARWEAR			96	$4.50	$4.50
26004	EDMUND SANTA BEAR...BELIEVE	BB - BEARWEAR			96	$4.50	$4.50
2603	MURGATROYD THE CHRISMOOSE/First Edition	BB - BEARWEAR		95	94	$4.00	$4.50
2603	MURGATROYD THE CHRISMOOSE	BB - BEARWEAR		95	94	$4.00	$4.50
2604	BESSIE'S CHRIS-MOOSESE/First Edition	BB - BEARWEAR		95	94	$4.00	$4.50
2604	BESSIE'S CHRIS-MOOSESE	BB - BEARWEAR		95	94	$4.00	$4.50
2605	ANGELICA'S FLIGHT/First Edition	BB - BEARWEAR		95	95	$4.00	$4.50
2605	ANGELICA'S FLIGHT	BB - BEARWEAR		95	95	$4.00	$4.50
2606	ELLIOT'S WREATH/First Edition	BB - BEARWEAR		95	95	$4.00	$4.50
2606	ELLIOT'S WREATH	BB - BEARWEAR		95	95	$4.00	$4.50
2607	SANTA CAT/First Edition	BB - BEARWEAR		95	94	$4.00	$4.50
2607	SANTA CAT	BB - BEARWEAR		95	94	$4.00	$4.50
2609	WILSON'S FLIGHT/First Edition	BB - BEARWEAR		95	94	$4.00	$4.50
2609	WILSON'S FLIGHT	BB - BEARWEAR		95	94	$4.00	$4.50
2616	ALICE'S FLIGHT/First Edition	BB - BEARWEAR		96	95	$4.00	$4.50
2616	ALICE'S FLIGHT	BB - BEARWEAR		96	95	$4.00	$4.50
2625	FLORENCE WINGSIT/First Edition	BB - FOLKWEAR		95	95	$4.00	$4.50
2625	FLORENCE WINGSIT	BB - FOLKWEAR		95	95	$4.00	$4.50
26300	NICHOLAI WITH TREE/First Edition	BB - FOLKWEAR			96	$5.00	$4.50
26300	NICHOLAI WITH TREE	BB - FOLKWEAR			96	$5.00	$4.50

Order No.	Title	Type	Theme	Retired	Intro. Year	Retial Price	Secondary Price
26301	SLICK NICK ON THE CHIMNEY/First Edition	BB - FOLKWEAR			96	$5.00	$5.00
26301	SLICK NICK ON THE CHIMNEY	BB - FOLKWEAR			96	$5.00	$5.00
26302	JINGLES WITH WREATH/First Edition	BB - FOLKWEAR			96	$5.00	$5.00
26302	JINGLES WITH WREATH	BB - FOLKWEAR			96	$5.00	$5.00
26303	ASHLEY THE ANGEL/First Edition	BB - FOLKWEAR			96	$5.00	$5.00
26303	ASHLEY THE ANGEL	BB - FOLKWEAR			96	$5.00	$5.00
2631	ELGIN THE ELF BEAR/First Edition	BB - BEARWEAR		95	95	$4.00	$4.50
2631	ELGIN THE ELF BEAR	BB - BEARWEAR		95	95	$4.00	$4.50
2636	ELLIOT BEAR/JINGLE BELL WREATH/First Edition	BB - BEARWEAR		95	95	$4.00	$4.50
2636	ELLIOT BEAR/JINGLE BELL WREATH	BB - BEARWEAR		95	95	$4.00	$4.50
2638	BEATRICE'S WREATH/First Edition	BB - FOLKWEAR		95	95	$4.00	$4.50
2638	BEATRICE'S WREATH	BB - FOLKWEAR		95	95	$4.00	$4.50
2642	ELLIOT AND THE LIGHTS/First Edition	BB - BEARWEAR		95	95	$4.00	$4.50
2642	ELLIOT AND THE LIGHTS	BB - BEARWEAR		95	95	$4.00	$4.50
2647	MINERVA'S FLIGHT/First Edition	BB - FOLKWEAR		95	95	$4.00	$4.50
2647	MINERVA'S FLIGHT	BB - FOLKWEAR		95	95	$4.00	$4.50
2648	NICHOLAI...W/DOVE/First Edition	BB - FOLKWEAR		95	95	$4.00	$4.50
2648	NICHOLAI...W/DOVE	BB - FOLKWEAR		95	95	$4.00	$4.50
2649	NICHOLAS...W/TREE/First Edition	BB - FOLKWEAR		95	95	$4.00	$4.50
2649	NICHOLAS...W/TREE	BB - FOLKWEAR		95	95	$4.00	$4.50
2650	NA-NICK OF THE NORTH/First Edition	BB - FOLKWEAR		95	95	$4.00	$4.50
2650	NA-NICK OF THE NORTH	BB - FOLKWEAR		95	95	$4.00	$4.50
2651	JEAN CLAUSE THE SKIER/First Edition	BB - FOLKWEAR		95	95	$4.00	$4.50
2651	JEAN CLAUSE THE SKIER	BB - FOLKWEAR		95	95	$4.00	$4.50
2652	WINDY THE SNOWMAN/First Edition	BB - FOLKWEAR		95	95	$4.00	$4.50
2652	WINDY THE SNOWMAN	BB - FOLKWEAR		95	95	$4.00	$4.50
2653	SIEGFRIED THE SANTA MOOSE/First Edition	BB - FOLKWEAR		95	95	$4.00	$4.50
2653	SIEGFRIED THE SANTA MOOSE	BB - FOLKWEAR		95	95	$4.00	$4.50
2658	MINERVA WITH DAFFODILS/First Edition	BB - FOLKWEAR			96	$5.00	$4.50
2658	MINERVA WITH DAFFODILS	BB - FOLKWEAR			96	$5.00	$5.00
2662	JULIETTE WITH ROSE/First Edition	BB - BEARWEAR			96	$4.50	$5.00
2662	JULIETTE WITH ROSE	BB - BEARWEAR			96	$4.50	$4.50
2669	RALPH ANGELPOOCH/First Edition	BB - FOLKWEAR			96	$5.00	$4.50
2669	RALPH ANGELPOOCH	BB - FOLKWEAR			96	$5.00	$5.00
2671	ARIEL THE GUARDIAN/First Edition	BB - FOLKWEAR			96	$5.00	$5.00
2671	ARIEL THE GUARDIAN	BB - FOLKWEAR			96	$5.00	$5.00
2674	OCEANIA/First Edition	BB - FOLKWEAR			96	$5.00	$5.00
2674	OCEANIA	BB - FOLKWEAR			96	$5.00	$5.00
2679	SIMONE IN HEART WREATH/First Edition	BB - BEARWEAR			96	$4.50	$4.50
2679	SIMONE IN HEART WREATH	BB - BEARWEAR			96	$4.50	$4.50
2700	GRENVILLE THE SANTABEAR/First Edition	BB - BEARSTONES	WATERGLOBES		94	$34.00	$38.00
2700	GRENVILLE THE SANTABEAR	BB - BEARSTONES	WATERGLOBES		94	$34.00	$50.00
2702	ANGELICA...THE GUARDIAN/First Edition	BB - BEARSTONES	WATERGLOBES		95	$36.00	$37.00
2702	ANGELICA...THE GUARDIAN	BB - BEARSTONES	WATERGLOBES		95	$36.00	$37.00
2703	SANTA'S FLIGHT PLAN/First Edition	BB - FOLKSTONES	WATERGLOBES	96	95	$38.00	$43.00
2703	SANTA'S FLIGHT PLAN	BB - FOLKSTONES	WATERGLOBES	96	95	$38.00	$52.00
2704	ELLIOT & THE TREE/First Edition	BB - BEARSTONES	WATERGLOBES		95	$34.00	$35.00
2704	ELLIOT & THE TREE	BB - BEARSTONES	WATERGLOBES		95	$34.00	$35.00
2705	SIMONE/BAILEY..HELPING HANDS/First Edition	BB - BEARSTONES	WATERGLOBES		96	$34.00	$35.00
2705	SIMONE/BAILEY..HELPING HANDS	BB - BEARSTONES	WATERGLOBES		96	$34.00	$35.00
2710	SNOWMAN SKIERS/First Edition	BB - FOLKSTONES	WATERGLOBES		95	$38.00	$38.00
2710	SNOWMAN SKIERS	BB - FOLKSTONES	WATERGLOBES		95	$38.00	$38.00
2720	MEGAN/ELLIOT-CHRISTMAS CAROL/First Edition	BB - DOLLSTONES	WATERGLOBES		96	$45.00	$30.00
2720	MEGAN/ELLIOT-CHRISTMAS CAROL	BB - DOLLSTONES	WATERGLOBES		96	$45.00	$30.00
2771	ELGIN & ELLIOT THE ELVES/First Edition	BB - BEARSTONES	VOTIVES		96	$25.00	$25.50
2771	ELGIN & ELLIOT THE ELVES	BB - BEARSTONES	VOTIVES		96	$25.00	$25.50
2772	EDMUND THE ELF BEAR/First Edition	BB - BEARSTONES	VOTIVES		96	$25.00	$25.50
2772	EDMUND THE ELF BEAR	BB - BEARSTONES	VOTIVES		96	$25.00	$25.50
2800	NICHOLAI WITH TREE/First Edition	BB - FOLKSTONES	NORTHWOODS		94	$16.00	$16.50
2800	NICHOLAI WITH TREE	BB - FOLKSTONES	NORTHWOODS		94	$16.00	$54.00
2801	NIKI WITH CANDLE/First Edition	BB - FOLKSTONES	NORTHWOODS		94	$16.00	$16.50
2801	NIKI WITH CANDLE	BB - FOLKSTONES	NORTHWOODS		94	$16.00	$54.00
2802	NICHOLAS W/BOOK OF LIST/First Edition	BB - FOLKSTONES	HOLIDAYS	96	94	$16.00	$28.00
2802	NICHOLAS W/BOOK OF LIST	BB - FOLKSTONES	HOLIDAYS	96	94	$16.00	$62.00
2803	SLIKNICK THE CHIMNEY SWEEP/First Edition	BB - FOLKSTONES	NORTHWOODS		95	$17.00	$17.00
2803	SLIKNICK THE CHIMNEY SWEEP	BB - FOLKSTONES	NORTHWOODS		95	$17.00	$25.00
2804	NA-NICK OF THE NORTH/First Edition	BB - FOLKSTONES	NORTHWOODS		95	$17.00	$17.50
2804	NA-NICK OF THE NORTH	BB - FOLKSTONES	NORTHWOODS		95	$17.00	$28.00
2805	NO-NO NICK...BAD BOY SANTA/First Edition	BB - FOLKSTONES	NORTHERN LIGHTS		96	$18.00	$18.00
2805	NO-NO NICK...BAD BOY SANTA	BB - FOLKSTONES	NORTHERN LIGHTS		96	$18.00	$28.00
2806	NICK NOAH...SANTA WITH ARK/First Edition	BB - FOLKSTONES	NORTHERN LIGHTS		96	$18.00	$18.00
2806	NICK NOAH...SANTA WITH ARK	BB - FOLKSTONES	NORTHERN LIGHTS		96	$18.00	$28.00
2807	NANICK & SIEGFRIED...THE PLAN/Limited Edition/First Edition	BB - FOLKSTONES	LIMITED EDITIONS		96	$18.00	$45.00
2807	NANICK & SIEGFRIED...THE PLAN/Limited Edition	BB - FOLKSTONES	LIMITED EDITIONS		96	$18.00	$55.00
2810	WINDY WITH BOOK/First Edition	BB - FOLKSTONES	HOLIDAYS	96	94	$16.00	$24.00
2810	WINDY WITH BOOK	BB - FOLKSTONES	HOLIDAYS	96	94	$16.00	$55.00
2811	CHILLY & SON WITH DOVE/First Edition	BB - FOLKSTONES	NORTHWOODS		94	$16.00	$16.50
2811	CHILLY & SON WITH DOVE	BB - FOLKSTONES	NORTHWOODS		94	$16.00	$55.00
2812	JINGLES & SON WITH WREATH/First Edition	BB - FOLKSTONES	HOLIDAYS	96	94	$16.00	$28.00
2812	JINGLES & SON WITH WREATH	BB - FOLKSTONES	HOLIDAYS	96	94	$16.00	$45.00
2814	NORTHBOUND WILLIE/First Edition	BB - FOLKSTONES	NORTHWOODS		95	$16.00	$16.50
2814	NORTHBOUND WILLIE	BB - FOLKSTONES	NORTHWOODS		95	$16.00	$35.00
2815	JEAN CLAUDE & JACQUES...SKIERS/First Edition	BB - FOLKSTONES	NORTHWOODS		95	$16.00	$16.50
2815	JEAN CLAUDE & JACQUES...SKIERS	BB - FOLKSTONES	NORTHWOODS		95	$16.00	$35.00
2816	ROBIN...THE SNOWBIRD LOVER/First Edition	BB - FOLKSTONES	NORTHERN LIGHTS		96	$18.00	$18.00
2816	ROBIN...THE SNOWBIRD LOVER	BB - FOLKSTONES	NORTHERN LIGHTS		96	$18.00	$23.00
2817	NANNY...THE SNOWMOM/First Edition	BB - FOLKSTONES	NORTHERN LIGHTS		96	$18.00	$18.00
2817	NANNY...THE SNOWMOM	BB - FOLKSTONES	NORTHERN LIGHTS		96	$18.00	$22.00
2820	ANGEL OF FREEDOM/First Edition	BB - FOLKSTONES	ANGELS	96	94	$15.00	$27.00
2820	ANGEL OF FREEDOM	BB - FOLKSTONES	ANGELS	96	94	$15.00	$55.00
28201	COSMOS...GARDENING ANGEL/First Edition	BB - FOLKSTONES	ANGELS		96	$18.00	$18.50
28201	COSMOS...GARDENING ANGEL	BB - FOLKSTONES	ANGELS		96	$18.00	$23.00
28202	ATHENIA...WEDDING ANGEL/First Edition	BB - FOLKSTONES	ANGELS		96	$18.00	$18.50

Order No.	Title	Type	Theme	Retired	Intro. Year	Retail Price	Secondary Price
28202	ATHENIA...WEDDING ANGEL/First Edition	BB - FOLKSTONES	ANGELS		96	$18.00	$23.00
28203	ILLUMINA...ANGEL OF LIGHT	BB - FOLKSTONES	NORTHERN LIGHTS		96	$18.00	$18.50
28203	ILLUMINA...ANGEL OF LIGHT/First Edition	BB - FOLKSTONES	NORTHERN LIGHTS		96	$18.00	$23.00
28203-06	ETHEREAL...ANGEL OF LIGHT	BB - FOLKSTONES	ANGELS		96	$18.00	$18.50
28203-06	ETHEREAL...ANGEL OF LIGHT/First Edition	BB - FOLKSTONES	ANGELS		96	$18.00	$23.00
28204	SERENITY...THE MOTHERS ANGEL	BB - FOLKSTONES	ANGELS		96	$18.00	$18.50
28204	SERENITY...THE MOTHERS ANGEL/First Edition	BB - FOLKSTONES	ANGELS		96	$18.00	$23.00
2821	ANGEL OF LOVE	BB - FOLKSTONES	ANGELS	96	94	$15.00	$26.00
2821	ANGEL OF LOVE/First Edition	BB - FOLKSTONES	ANGELS	96	94	$15.00	$55.00
2822	ANGEL OF PEACE	BB - FOLKSTONES	ANGELS		94	$15.00	$15.50
2822	ANGEL OF PEACE/First Edition	BB - FOLKSTONES	ANGELS		94	$15.00	$55.00
2823	OCEANIA-OCEAN ANGEL	BB - FOLKSTONES	ANGELS		94	$15.00	$15.50
2823	OCEANIA-OCEAN ANGEL/First Edition	BB - FOLKSTONES	ANGELS		94	$15.00	$50.00
2824	FLORENCE-KITCHEN ANGEL	BB - FOLKSTONES	ANGELS	96	95	$18.00	$23.00
2824	FLORENCE-KITCHEN ANGEL/First Edition	BB - FOLKSTONES	ANGELS	96	95	$18.00	$47.50
2826	MINERVA-BASEBALL ANGEL	BB - FOLKSTONES	ANGELS	97	95	$18.00	$23.00
2826	MINERVA-BASEBALL ANGEL/First Edition	BB - FOLKSTONES	ANGELS	97	95	$18.00	$42.50
2827	LIZZIE-SHOPPING ANGEL	BB - FOLKSTONES	ANGELS		95	$18.00	$18.50
2827	LIZZIE-SHOPPING ANGEL/First Edition	BB - FOLKSTONES	ANGELS		95	$18.00	$40.00
2828	SERAPHINA W/JACOB & RACHAEL	BB - FOLKSTONES	ANGELS		95	$19.00	$19.00
2828	SERAPHINA W/JACOB & RACHAEL/First Edition	BB - FOLKSTONES	ANGELS		95	$19.00	$35.00
2829	ABIGAIL...PEACEABLE KINGDOM	BB - FOLKSTONES	ANGELS		95	$18.00	$18.50
2829	ABIGAIL...PEACEABLE KINGDOM/First Edition	BB - FOLKSTONES	ANGELS		95	$18.00	$35.00
2830	JINGLE MOOSE	BB - FOLKSTONES	HOLIDAYS	96	94	$16.00	$24.00
2830	JINGLE MOOSE/First Edition	BB - FOLKSTONES	HOLIDAYS	96	94	$16.00	$62.00
2836	BEATRICE...THE GIFTGIVER	BB - FOLKSTONES	HAPPY HOLIDAY		95	$17.00	$18.00
2836	BEATRICE...THE GIFTGIVER/First Edition	BB - FOLKSTONES	HAPPY HOLIDAY		95	$17.00	$40.00
3000	SANTA'S FLIGHT PLAN	BB - FOLKSTONES	SANTA AND FRIENDS	97	94	$31.00	$43.00
3000	SANTA'S FLIGHT PLAN/First Edition	BB - FOLKSTONES	SANTA AND FRIENDS	97	94	$31.00	$77.50
3001	NICK ON ICE	BB - FOLKSTONES	SANTA AND FRIENDS	97	94	$31.00	$43.00
3001	NICK ON ICE/First Edition	BB - FOLKSTONES	SANTA AND FRIENDS	97	94	$31.00	$77.50
3002	SANTA'S CHALLENGE	BB - FOLKSTONES	SANTA AND FRIENDS	97	94	$31.00	$40.00
3002	SANTA'S CHALLENGE/First Edition	BB - FOLKSTONES	SANTA AND FRIENDS	97	94	$31.00	$77.50
3003	26TH FOR DECEMBER	BB - FOLKSTONES	SANTA AND FRIENDS	97	96	$32.50	$50.00
3003	26TH FOR DECEMBER/First Edition	BB - FOLKSTONES	SANTA AND FRIENDS	97	96	$32.50	$65.00
3502	VICTORIAN LADIES	BB - DOLLSTONES	THE BASICS		96	$19.00	$19.00
3502	VICTORIAN LADIES/First Edition	BB - DOLLSTONES	THE BASICS		96	$19.00	$64.00
3502	VICTORIAN LADIES/QVC Premium	BB - DOLLSTONES	THE BASICS		96	$19.00	$110.00
3504	CHRISTMAS CAROL	BB - DOLLSTONES	FALL COLLECTION		96	$19.00	$19.00
3504	CHRISTMAS CAROL/First Edition	BB - DOLLSTONES	FALL COLLECTION		96	$19.00	$83.00
3504	CHRISTMAS CAROL/QVC Premium	BB - DOLLSTONES	FALL COLLECTION		96	$19.00	$215.00
3512	COURTNEY W/PHOEBE..OVER THE RIVER & THRU WOODS	BB - DOLLSTONES	FALL COLLECTION		96	$24.00	$24.00
3512	COURTNEY W/PHOEBE..OVER THE RIVER & THRU WOODS/1st Edition	BB - DOLLSTONES	FALL COLLECTION		96	$24.00	$50.00
3600	FIXIT...SANTA'S FAIRIE	BB - WEE FOLKSTONES	FAIRIES		96	$17.00	
28205	CONSTANCE & FELICITY	BB - FOLKSTONES	SPECIAL EDITIONS	97	97	$36.00	
28240	MERCY...ANGEL OF NURSES	BB - FOLKSTONES	ANGELS		97	$18.00	
28241	MS. PATIENCE...ANGEL OF TEACHERS	BB - FOLKSTONES	ANGELS		97	$18.00	
3004	SANTA'S HOBBY	BB - FOLKSTONES	SANTA AND FRIENDS		97	$34.00	
36302	IMMACULATA FAERIEBURG	BB - FOLKSTONES	FAIRIES		97	$17.00	
36100	ANGELINA SMIDGE	BB - WEE FOLKSTONES	FAIRIES		97	$15.00	
36102	DENTINATA FAERIEFLOSS	BB - FOLKSTONES	FAIRIES		97	$15.00	
36101	INFINITI FAERIELOVE	BB - FOLKSTONES	FAIRIES		97	$15.00	
36300	ELECTRA ANGELBYTE	BB - FOLKSTONES	FAIRIES		97	$17.00	
36301	ESTUDIOUS CRAM AERIEBAUM	BB - FOLKSTONES	FAIRIES		97	$17.00	
2838	ZIGGY...THE DUFFER	BB - FOLKSTONES	HOLIDAYS		97	$18.00	
227705	LOUELLA & HEDDA...THE SECRET/Limited	BB - BEARSTONES	THE BASICS		97	$18.00	
25702	WILSON/First Edition	BB - BEARSTONES	DECK THE HALLS ORNAMENTS		96	$10.00	$9.50
25702	WILSON	BB - BEARSTONES	DECK THE HALLS ORNAMENTS		96	$10.00	$9.50
2411	ARIEL & CLARENCE..PAIR OF ANGELS/First Edition	BB - BEARSTONES	HOLIDAY PAGAENT		95	$17.00	$30.00
2411	ARIEL & CLARENCE..PAIR OF ANGELS	BB - BEARSTONES	HOLIDAY PAGAENT		96	$17.00	$17.50
2411	ARIEL & CLARENCE..PAIR OF ANGELS	BB - BEARSTONES	HOLIDAY PAGAENT		96	$17.00	$17.50

BYER'S CHOICE

Order No.	Title	Type	Theme	Retired	Intro. Year	Retail Price	Secondary Price
14	ADULT CAROLER(1ST EDITION)	BC - CAROLERS	BC - VICTORIAN CAROLERS	82	82	$32.00	$375.00
15	ADULT CAROLER (DRESSED ALIKE)(2ND EDITION)	BC - CAROLERS	BC - VICTORIAN CAROLERS	83	82	$46.00	$350.00
18	CHILD CAROLER (2ND EDITION)	BC - CAROLERS	BC - VICTORIAN CAROLERS	83	83	$33.00	$45.00
6	SINGING DOGS	BC - CAROLERS	BC - CAROLERS		86	$13.00	$14.00
13	GRANDPARENTS	BC - CAROLERS	BC - TRADITIONAL CAROLERS		86	$35.00	$40.00
4	CHILDREN WITH SKATES	BC - CAROLERS	BC - CAROLERS		88	$40.00	$45.00
5	SINGING CATS	BC - CAROLERS	BC - CAROLERS		88	$38.00	$15.00
20	GRANDPARENT CAROLERS	BC - CAROLERS	BC - VICTORIAN CAROLERS		88	$40.00	$45.00
156	SLED WITH DOG	BC - CAROLERS	BC - TODDLERS		91	$30.00	
1	CAT IN HAT	BC - CAROLERS	BC - ACCESSORIES	95	95	$10.00	$10.00
157	SHOVEL	BC - CAROLERS	BC - TODDLERS	93	92	$17.00	
158	SLED W/WHITE TODDLER	BC - CAROLERS	BC - TODDLERS	93	92	$17.00	
159	SNOWBALL	BC - CAROLERS	BC - TODDLERS	94	92	$17.00	
22	DUTCH BOY	BC - CAROLERS	BC - CHILDREN OF THE WORLD	92	92	$50.00	$280.00
23	DUTCH GIRL	BC - CAROLERS	BC - CHILDREN OF THE WORLD	92	92	$50.00	$280.00
21	BAVARIAN BOY	BC - CAROLERS	BC - CHILDREN OF THE WORLD	93	93	$50.00	$225.00
24	IRISH GIRL	BC - CAROLERS	BC - CHILDREN OF THE WORLD	94	94	$50.00	$175.00
160	TOYMAKER	BC - CAROLERS	BC - STORE EXCLUSIVES	88	88	$59.00	
26	LADY WITH APPLES/RED STOCKINGS	BC - CAROLERS	BC - CRIES OF LONDON	91	91	$80.00	$995.00
28	BAKER	BC - CAROLERS	BC - CRIES OF LONDON	92	92	$62.00	$175.00
29	CHESTNUT ROASTER	BC - CAROLERS	BC - CRIES OF LONDON	92	93	$64.00	$250.00
32	FLOWER VENDOR	BC - CAROLERS	BC - CRIES OF LONDON	94	94	$64.00	$170.00
31	DOLLMAKER	BC - CAROLERS	BC - CRIES OF LONDON	95	95	$64.00	$83.00
34	GIRL HOLDING DOLL	BC - CAROLERS	BC - CHILDREN OF THE WORLD	95	95	$48.00	$60.00
47	SCROOGE (1ST EDITION)	BC - CAROLERS	BC - DICKENS SERIES	83	83	$36.00	$1,300.00
43	MRS. CRATCHET (1ST EDITION)	BC - CAROLERS	BC - DICKENS SERIES	84	84	$38.00	$1,100.00
48	SCROOGE (2ND EDITION)	BC - CAROLERS	BC - DICKENS SERIES		84	$38.00	$45.00
41	MR. FEZZIWIG (1ST EDITION)	BC - CAROLERS	BC - DICKENS SERIES	85	85	$43.00	$700.00
44	MRS. CRACHIT (2ND EDITION)	BC - CAROLERS	BC - DICKENS SERIES		85	$39.00	$45.00

Order No.	Title	Type	Theme	Retired	Intro. Year	Retial Price	Secondary Price
45	MRS. FEZZIWIG (1ST EDITION)	BC - CAROLERS	BC - DICKENS SERIES	85	85	$43.00	$700.00
39	MARLEY'S GHOST (1ST EDITION)	BC - CAROLERS	BC - DICKENS SERIES	86	86	$40.00	$325.00
43	MR. FEZZIWIG (2ND EDITION)	BC - CAROLERS	BC - DICKENS SERIES	90	86	$43.00	$600.00
46	MRS. FEZZIWIG (2ND EDITION)	BC - CAROLERS	BC - DICKENS SERIES	90	86	$43.00	$400.00
40	MARLEY'S GHOST(2ND EDITION)	BC - CAROLERS	BC - DICKENS SERIES	92	87	$42.00	$275.00
51	SPIRIT OF CHRISTMAS PAST (1ST EDITION)	BC - CAROLERS	BC - DICKENS SERIES	87	87	$42.00	
46	SPIRIT OF CHRISTMAS PAST (2ND EDITION)	BC - CAROLERS	BC - DICKENS SERIES	91	88	$46.00	$350.00
53	SPIRIT OF CHRISTMAS PRESENT (1ST EDITION)	BC - CAROLERS	BC - DICKENS SERIES	88	88	$44.00	$350.00
49	SPIRIT OF CHRISTMAS FUTURE (1ST EDITION)	BC - CAROLERS	BC - DICKENS SERIES	89	89	$46.00	$325.00
54	SPIRIT OF CHRISTMAS PRESENT (2ND EDITION)	BC - CAROLERS	BC - DICKENS SERIES	89	89	$48.00	$300.00
35	BOB CRACHIT & TINY TIM(1ST EDITION)	BC - CAROLERS	BC - DICKENS SERIES	90	90	$84.00	$115.00
37	HAPPY SCROOGE (1ST EDITION)	BC - CAROLERS	BC - DICKENS SERIES	91	91	$50.00	$225.00
61	LADY	BC - CAROLERS	BC - DISPLAY	81	81		$2,000.00
50	SPIRIT OF CHRISTMAS FUTURE (2ND EDITION)	BC - CAROLERS	BC - DICKENS SERIES	91	90	$48.00	$275.00
36	BOB CRATCHIT & TINY TIM (2ND EDITION)	BC - CAROLERS	BC - DICKENS SERIES		91	$86.00	$250.00
62	MAN	BC - CAROLERS	BC - DISPLAY	81	81		$2,000.00
59	DRUMMER BOY (1ST VERSION)	BC - CAROLERS	BC - DISPLAY	83	82	$96.00	$1,000.00
64	DISPLAY SANTA	BC - CAROLERS	BC - DISPLAY	83	82	$96.00	$580.00
57	CAROLERS	BC - CAROLERS	BC - DISPLAY	83	83	$200.00	$480.00
67	WORKING SANTA	BC - CAROLERS	BC - DISPLAY	85	84	$260.00	$480.00
58	CHILDREN	BC - CAROLERS	BC - DISPLAY	87	85	$140.00	$1,300.00
60	DRUMMER BOY (2ND VERSION)	BC - CAROLERS	BC - DISPLAY	86	85	$160.00	$500.00
63	OLD WORLD SANTA	BC - CAROLERS	BC - DISPLAY	85	85	$160.00	$480.00
56	ADULTS	BC - CAROLERS	BC - DISPLAY	87	86	$170.00	$480.00
68	MECHANICAL BOY W/DRUM	BC - CAROLERS	BC - DISPLAY	87	87		$700.00
69	MECHANICAL GIRL W/BELL	BC - CAROLERS	BC - DISPLAY	87	87		$700.00
65	SANTA-BAYBERRY	BC - CAROLERS	BC - DISPLAY	90	90	$250.00	$475.00
66	SANTA-RED	BC - CAROLERS	BC - DISPLAY	90	90	$250.00	$450.00
40	MARLEY'S GHOST(2ND EDITION)	BC - CAROLERS	BC - DICKENS SERIES	92	87	$42.00	$210.00
38	HAPPY SCROOGE (2ND EDITION)	BC - CAROLERS	BC - DICKENS SERIES	92	92	$50.00	$170.00
2	DOG WITH HAT	BC - CAROLERS	BC - ACCESSORIES	96	96	$18.50	$19.00
3	DOG WITH SAUSAGES	BC - CAROLERS	BC - ACCESSORIES	95	95	$18.00	$19.00
7	TEENAGERS	BC - CAROLERS	BC - TRADITIONAL CAROLERS		96	$46.00	$50.00
8	TEENAGERS	BC - CAROLERS	BC - VICTORIAN CAROLERS		96	$49.00	$48.00
9	ADULT (1976-1980)	BC - CAROLERS	BC - TRADITIONAL CAROLERS	80	76		$475.00
11	ADULT (UNDATED)	BC - CAROLERS	BC - TRADITIONAL CAROLERS			$45.00	$600.00
12	COLONIAL LADY (W/HANDS)	BC - CAROLERS	BC - TRADITIONAL CAROLERS	78	78		$1,500.00
16	ADULT CAROLER(ASSORTED)(2ND EDITION)	BC - CAROLERS	BC - VICTORIAN CAROLERS		83	$35.00	$75.00
17	CHILD CAROLER (1ST EDITION)	BC - CAROLERS	BC - VICTORIAN CAROLERS	82	82	$32.00	$350.00
19	CHILD CAROLER (ASSORTED)(2ND EDITION)	BC - CAROLERS	BC - VICTORIAN CAROLERS		83	$33.00	$46.00
25	SAINT LUCIA	BC - CAROLERS	BC - CHILDREN OF THE WORLD	94	96	$52.00	$52.00
27	LADY WITH APPLES/RED & WHITE STOCKINGS	BC - CAROLERS	BC - CRIES OF LONDON	91	91	$80.00	$1,100.00
30	CHILDREN BUYING GINGERBREAD	BC - CAROLERS	BC - CRIES OF LONDON	96	96	$46.00	$46.00
33	GINGERBREAD VENDOR	BC - CAROLERS	BC - CRIES OF LONDON	96	96	$75.00	$70.00
70	BOY WITH MANDOLIN	BC - CAROLERS	BC - MUSICIANS	91	91	$48.00	$250.00
71	HORN PLAYER	BC - CAROLERS	BC - MUSICIANS	85	85	$38.00	$650.00
72	HORN PLAYER/CHUBBY FACE	BC - CAROLERS	BC - MUSICIANS	85	85	$37.00	$700.00
74	MUSICIAN WITH CLARINET	BC - CAROLERS	BC - MUSICIANS	89	89	$44.00	$550.00
73	MUSICIAN WITH ACCORDIAN	BC - CAROLERS	BC - MUSICIANS	91	91	$48.00	$250.00
75	MUSICIAN WITH FRENCH HORN	BC - CAROLERS	BC - MUSICIANS	92	92	$92.00	$200.00
76	MUSICIAN WITH MANDOLIN	BC - CAROLERS	BC - MUSICIANS	90	90	$46.00	$250.00
77	VICTORIAN GIRL WITH VIOLIN	BC - CAROLERS	BC - MUSICIANS	86	86	$39.00	$285.00
78	VIOLIN PLAYER MAN (1ST EDITION)	BC - CAROLERS	BC - MUSICIANS	83	83	$38.00	$1,500.00
79	VIOLIN PLAYER MAN (2ND EDITION)	BC - CAROLERS	BC - MUSICIANS	84	84	$38.00	$1,500.00
80	ANGEL GABRIEL	BC - CAROLERS	BC - NATIVITY	91	89	$37.00	$175.00
81	ANGEL/GREAT STAR (BLONDE)	BC - CAROLERS	BC - NATIVITY	91	87	$40.00	$287.00
82	ANGEL/GREAT STAR (BRUNETTE)	BC - CAROLERS	BC - NATIVITY	91	87	$40.00	$225.00
83	ANGEL/GREAT STAR (RED HEAD)	BC - CAROLERS	BC - NATIVITY	91	87	$40.00	$225.00
84	BLACK ANGEL	BC - CAROLERS	BC - NATIVITY	87	84	$36.00	$290.00
85	HOLY FAMILY WITH STABLE	BC - CAROLERS	BC - NATIVITY	91	90	$119.00	$90.00
86	KING BALTHASAR	BC - CAROLERS	BC - NATIVITY	91	89	$40.00	$90.00
76	KING CASPAR	BC - CAROLERS	BC - NATIVITY	91	89	$40.00	$90.00
87	KING MELCHIOR	BC - CAROLERS	BC - NATIVITY	91	89	$40.00	$90.00
89	SHEPHERDS	BC - CAROLERS	BC - NATIVITY	91	88	$37.00	$90.00
90	DROSSELMEIER W/MUSIC BOX (1ST EDITION)	BC - CAROLERS	BC - THE NUTCRACKER	96	96	$83.00	$83.00
91	FRITZ (1ST EDITION)	BC - CAROLERS	BC - THE NUTCRACKER	94	94	$56.00	$150.00
92	FRITZ (2ND EDITION)	BC - CAROLERS	BC - THE NUTCRACKER		95	$57.00	$57.00
93	LOUISE PLAYING PIANO (1ST EDITION_	BC - CAROLERS	BC - THE NUTCRACKER	95	95	$82.00	$115.00
94	LOUISE PLAYING PIANO (2ND EDITION)	BC - CAROLERS	BC - THE NUTCRACKER	96	96	$83.00	$83.00
95	MARIE (1ST EDITION)	BC - CAROLERS	BC - THE NUTCRACKER	83	83	$52.00	$80.00
96	MARIE (2ND EDITION)	BC - CAROLERS	BC - THE NUTCRACKER		94	$53.00	$53.00
97	GIRL WITH WAR CRY	BC - CAROLERS	BC - SALVATION ARMY		95	$55.00	$22.00
98	MAN WITH BASS DRUM	BC - CAROLERS	BC - SALVATION ARMY		95	$60.00	$60.00
99	MAN WITH CORNET	BC - CAROLERS	BC - SALVATION ARMY		93	$54.00	$154.00
100	WOMAN WITH KETTLE	BC - CAROLERS	BC - SALVATION ARMY		92	$64.00	$64.00
101	WOMAN WITH KETTLE(1ST EDITION)	BC - CAROLERS	BC - SALVATION ARMY	92	92	$64.00	$174.00
102	WOMAN WITH TAMBOURINE	BC - CAROLERS	BC - SALVATION ARMY	95	93	$58.00	$90.00
103	FATHER CHRISTMAS	BC - CAROLERS	BC - SANTAS	92	91	$48.00	$170.00
104	KNECHT RUPRECHT (BLACK PETER)	BC - CAROLERS	BC - SANTAS	89	88	$38.00	$165.00
105	KNICKERBOCKER SANTA	BC - CAROLERS	BC - SANTAS		96	$58.00	$58.00
106	MRS. CLAUS	BC - CAROLERS	BC - SANTAS	91	84	$36.00	$300.00
107	MRS. CLAUS (2ND EDITION)	BC - CAROLERS	BC - SANTAS	93	92	$50.00	
108	MRS. CLAUS ON ROCKER	BC - CAROLERS	BC - SANTAS	86	86	$73.00	$600.00
109	MRS. CLAUS' NEEDLEWORK	BC - CAROLERS	BC - SANTAS	95	95	$70.00	$150.00
110	OLD BEFANA	BC - CAROLERS	BC - SANTAS		94	$53.00	$53.00
111	OLD WORLD SANTA	BC - CAROLERS	BC - SANTAS	86	78	$33.00	$400.00
112	RUSSIAN SANTA	BC - CAROLERS	BC - SANTAS	89	89	$85.00	$170.00
113	SAINT NICHOLAS	BC - CAROLERS	BC - SANTAS	92	88	$44.00	$180.00
114	SANTA IN SLEIGH (1ST EDITION)	BC - CAROLERS	BC - SANTAS	83	82	$46.00	
115	SANTA IN SLEIGH (2ND EDITION)	BC - CAROLERS	BC - SANTAS	85	84	$70.00	$750.00
116	SKATING SANTA	BC - CAROLERS	BC - SANTAS	93	93	$60.00	$115.00
117	VELVET MRS. CLAUS	BC - CAROLERS	BC - SANTAS		87	$44.00	$44.00
118	VELVET SANTA	BC - CAROLERS	BC - SANTAS	93	78		$295.00

Order No.	Title	Type	Theme	Retired	Intro. Year	Retail Price	Secondary Price
119	VELVET SANTA WITH STOCKING (2ND EDITION)	BC - CAROLERS	BC - SANTAS		94	$47.00	$50.00
120	VICTORIAN SANTA	BC - CAROLERS	BC - SANTAS	89	86	$39.00	$275.00
121	WEIHNACHTSMANN/GERMAN SANTA	BC - CAROLERS	BC - SANTAS	90	90	$56.00	$170.00
122	WORKING SANTA	BC - CAROLERS	BC - SANTAS	96	92	$52.00	$53.00
123	WORKING SANTA (1ST YEAR ISSUE)	BC - CAROLERS	BC - SANTAS	92	92	$52.00	$200.00
124	WORKING SANTA (1ST YEAR ISSUE)	BC - CAROLERS	BC - SANTAS	91	83	$38.00	$200.00
127	BOY SKATER ON LOG	BC - CAROLERS	BC - SKATERS	93	93	$55.00	$115.00
125	ADULT SKATERS	BC - CAROLERS	BC - SKATERS	94	91	$50.00	$115.00
126	ADULT SKATERS (1991 EDITION)	BC - CAROLERS	BC - SKATERS	91	91	$50.00	$123.00
129	CHILDREN SKATERS (2ND EDITION)	BC - CAROLERS	BC - SKATERS		92	$50.00	$145.00
128	CHILDREN SKATERS	BC - CAROLERS	BC - SKATERS		92	$50.00	$50.00
130	GRANDPARENT SKATERS	BC - CAROLERS	BC - SKATERS	93	93	$60.00	$100.00
131	GRANDPARENT SKATERS (1993 EDITION)	BC - CAROLERS	BC - SKATERS	93	93	$50.00	$148.00
132	MAN HOLDING SKATES	BC - CAROLERS	BC - SKATERS		95	$52.00	$52.00
133	WOMAN HOLDING SKATES	BC - CAROLERS	BC - SKATERS		95	$52.00	$52.00
134	ACTRESS	BC - CAROLERS	BC - SPECIAL CHARACTERS	96	96	$52.00	
135	ADULT MALE ICABOD	BC - CAROLERS	BC - SPECIAL CHARACTERS	79	79	$32.00	$2,500.00
136	ANGEL TREE TOP	BC - CAROLERS	BC - SPECIAL CHARACTERS	88	88		$350.00
137	BABY IN BASKET	BC - CAROLERS	BC - SPECIAL CHARACTERS	94	94	$7.50	$30.00
138	BLACK BOY W/SKATES	BC - CAROLERS	BC - SPECIAL CHARACTERS		89		$425.00
139	BLACK DRUMMER BOY	BC - CAROLERS	BC - SPECIAL CHARACTERS		89		$525.00
140	BLACK GIRL W/SKATES	BC - CAROLERS	BC - SPECIAL CHARACTERS		89		$425.00
141	BOY ON ROCKING HORSE	BC - CAROLERS	BC - SPECIAL CHARACTERS	83	83	$85.00	$2,500.00
142	BOY ON SLED	BC - CAROLERS	BC - SPECIAL CHARACTERS	87	87	$50.00	$350.00
143	BOY WITH APPLE	BC - CAROLERS	BC - SPECIAL CHARACTERS	91	91	$41.00	$230.00
144	BOY WITH GOOSE	BC - CAROLERS	BC - SPECIAL CHARACTERS	95	94	$49.50	$75.00
145	BOY WITH LAMB	BC - CAROLERS	BC - SPECIAL CHARACTERS		96	$52.00	$52.00
146	BOY WITH SKIS	BC - CAROLERS	BC - SPECIAL CHARACTERS		95	$49.50	$50.00
147	BOY WITH TREE	BC - CAROLERS	BC - SPECIAL CHARACTERS	94	91	$49.00	$50.00
148	BUTCHER	BC - CAROLERS	BC - SPECIAL CHARACTERS	95	95	$54.00	$130.00
149	CAROLER WITH LAMP	BC - CAROLERS	BC - SPECIAL CHARACTERS	87	87	$40.00	$650.00
150	CHIMNEY SWEEP-ADULT	BC - CAROLERS	BC - SPECIAL CHARACTERS	84	84	$36.00	$1,350.00
151	CHIMNEY SWEEP-CHILD	BC - CAROLERS	BC - SPECIAL CHARACTERS	94	91	$50.00	$100.00
152	CHOIR CHILDREN/BOY AND GIRL SET	BC - CAROLERS	BC - SPECIAL CHARACTERS	86	82	$32.00	$650.00
153	CHOIR DIRECTOR,LADY/MUSIC STAND	BC - CAROLERS	BC - SPECIAL CHARACTERS	95	93	$56.00	$60.00
154	CONDUCTOR	BC - CAROLERS	BC - SPECIAL CHARACTERS	92	82	$32.00	$100.00
155	CONSTABLE	BC - CAROLERS	BC - SPECIAL CHARACTERS	96	94	$53.00	$53.00
156A	COUPLE IN SLEIGH	BC - CAROLERS	BC - SPECIAL CHARACTERS	95	95	$110.00	$184.00
157A	DRUMMER BOY	BC - CAROLERS	BC - SPECIAL CHARACTERS	92	82	$34.00	$145.00
158A	GIRL HOLDING HOLLY BASKET	BC - CAROLERS	BC - SPECIAL CHARACTERS		96	$52.00	$52.00
159A	GIRL WITH APPLE	BC - CAROLERS	BC - SPECIAL CHARACTERS	91	91	$41.00	$175.00
160A	GIRL WITH APPLE/COIN PURSE	BC - CAROLERS	BC - SPECIAL CHARACTERS	91	91	$41.00	$450.00
161	GIRL WITH HOOP	BC - CAROLERS	BC - SPECIAL CHARACTERS	90	89	$44.00	$170.00
162	GIRL WITH SKIS	BC - CAROLERS	BC - SPECIAL CHARACTERS		95	$49.50	$50.00
163	ICABOD	BC - CAROLERS	BC - SPECIAL CHARACTERS	82	82	$32.00	$1,200.00
164	LAMPLIGHTER	BC - CAROLERS	BC - SPECIAL CHARACTERS	96	93	$48.00	$50.00
165	LAMPLIGHTER (1ST ISSUE)	BC - CAROLERS	BC - SPECIAL CHARACTERS	93	93	$48.00	$70.00
166	NANNY	BC - CAROLERS	BC - SPECIAL CHARACTERS		94	$66.00	$67.00
167	NEWSBOY WITH BIKE	BC - CAROLERS	BC - SPECIAL CHARACTERS	92	89	$78.00	$200.00
168	PAJAMA CHILDREN/PAINTED FLANNEL	BC - CAROLERS	BC - SPECIAL CHARACTERS	89	85	$35.00	$250.00
169	PAJAMA CHILDREN/RED FLANNEL	BC - CAROLERS	BC - SPECIAL CHARACTERS	89	85	$35.00	$250.00
170	PARSON	BC - CAROLERS	BC - SPECIAL CHARACTERS	93	90	$44.00	$125.00
171	POSTMAN	BC - CAROLERS	BC - SPECIAL CHARACTERS	93	90	$45.00	$160.00
172	SANDWICH BOARD MAN/RED BOARD	BC - CAROLERS	BC - SPECIAL CHARACTERS	94	94	$52.00	$100.00
173	SANDWICH BOARD MAN/WHITE BOARD	BC - CAROLERS	BC - SPECIAL CHARACTERS	96	94	$52.00	$52.00
174	SHOPPER-MAN	BC - CAROLERS	BC - SPECIAL CHARACTERS	95	95	$56.00	$77.50
175	SHOPPER-WOMAN	BC - CAROLERS	BC - SPECIAL CHARACTERS	95	95	$56.00	$77.50
176	SHOPPERS/GRANDPARENTS	BC - CAROLERS	BC - SPECIAL CHARACTERS		96	$56.00	$50.00
177	TREETOP ANGEL	BC - CAROLERS	BC - SPECIAL CHARACTERS	96	94	$50.00	$177.00
178	VICTORIAN GIRL ON ROCKING HORSE/BLONDE	BC - CAROLERS	BC - SPECIAL CHARACTERS	91	90	$70.00	$175.00
179	VICTORIAN GIRL ON ROCKING HORSE/BRUNETTE	BC - CAROLERS	BC - SPECIAL CHARACTERS	91	90	$70.00	$200.00
180	VICTORIAN MOTHER WITH TODDLER/GREEN	BC - CAROLERS	BC - SPECIAL CHARACTERS	93	92	$60.00	$175.00
181	VICTORIAN MOTHER WITH TODDLER/BLUE	BC - CAROLERS	BC - SPECIAL CHARACTERS	93	93	$61.00	$175.00
182	VICTORIAN MOTHER WITH TODDLER/WHITE	BC - CAROLERS	BC - SPECIAL CHARACTERS	93	92	$60.00	$125.00
183	RUSSIAN SANTA	BC - CAROLERS	BC - SANTAS	91	91	$100.00	$700.00
184	CHERUB ANGLE/BLUE	BC - CAROLERS	BC - STORE EXCLUSIVES	87	86		$325.00
185	CHERUB ANGLE/CREAM	BC - CAROLERS	BC - STORE EXCLUSIVES	87	86		$400.00
186	CHERUB ANGLE/PINK	BC - CAROLERS	BC - STORE EXCLUSIVES	87	86		$325.00
187	CHERUB ANGLE/ROSE	BC - CAROLERS	BC - STORE EXCLUSIVES	87	87		$325.00
188	MAN WITH GOOSE	BC - CAROLERS	BC - STORE EXCLUSIVES	88	88	$60.00	$285.00
189	SANTA IN ROCKING CHAIR WITH BOY	BC - CAROLERS	BC - STORE EXCLUSIVES	87	87	$130.00	$1,000.00
190	SANTA IN ROCKING CHAIR WITH GIRL	BC - CAROLERS	BC - STORE EXCLUSIVES	87	87	$130.00	$1,000.00
191	VICTORIAN FAMILY OF FOUR	BC - CAROLERS	BC - STORE EXCLUSIVES		90		$385.00
192	SKATING GIRL/BOY	BC - CAROLERS	BC - STORE EXCLUSIVES	YES	93		$445.00
193	MAN W/LOG CARRIER	BC - CAROLERS	BC - STORE EXCLUSIVES		94		$140.00
194	FAMILY OF FOUR/SWEATERS	BC - CAROLERS	BC - STORE EXCLUSIVES	YES	94		$525.00
195	SANTA IN SLEIGH	BC - CAROLERS	BC - STORE EXCLUSIVES	95	95	$88.00	$160.00
196	PENNY CHILDREN (BOY/GIRL)	BC - CAROLERS	BC - STORE EXCLUSIVES	93	93	$42.00	$475.00
197	COLONIAL LADY S/N	BC - CAROLERS	BC - STORE EXCLUSIVES	88	88	$49.00	$550.00
198	COLONIAL LAMPLIGHTER S/N	BC - CAROLERS	BC - STORE EXCLUSIVES	86	86	$46.00	$825.00
199	COLONIAL WATCHMAN S/N	BC - CAROLERS	BC - STORE EXCLUSIVES	87	87	$49.00	$750.00
200	VICTORIAN LAMPLIGHTER	BC - CAROLERS	BC - STORE EXCLUSIVES		NA		$125.00
201	SKIER BOY	BC - CAROLERS	BC - STORE EXCLUSIVES	87	87	$40.00	$300.00
202	SKIER GIRL	BC - CAROLERS	BC - STORE EXCLUSIVES	87	87	$40.00	$300.00
203	SUGARIN KIDS (WOODSTOCK)	BC - CAROLERS	BC - STORE EXCLUSIVES	91	91	$41.00	$295.00
204	WOODSTOCK LADY	BC - CAROLERS	BC - STORE EXCLUSIVES	88	88	$41.00	$350.00
205	WOODSTOCK MAN	BC - CAROLERS	BC - STORE EXCLUSIVES	88	88	$41.00	$350.00
206	BOOK NIGHT BEFORE CHRISTMAS	BC - CAROLERS	BC - TODDLERS		96	$20.00	$20.00
207	DOLL NIGHT BEFORE CHRISTMAS	BC - CAROLERS	BC - TODDLERS		96	$20.00	$20.00
208	GINGERBREAD BOY	BC - CAROLERS	BC - TODDLERS	94	93	$18.50	$20.00
209	PACKAGE	BC - CAROLERS	BC - TODDLERS	93	93	$18.50	$30.00
210	SKIS (SNOWSUIT)	BC - CAROLERS	BC - TODDLERS	96	94	$19.00	$30.00
211	SLED/BLACK TODDLER	BC - CAROLERS	BC - TODDLERS	94	94	$19.00	$20.00

Order No.	Title	Type	Theme	Retired	Intro. Year	Retial Price	Secondary Price
212	SLED/WHITE TODDLER (2ND EDITION)	BC - CAROLERS	BC - TODDLERS	96	95	$19.00	$20.00
213	SNOWFLAKE	BC - CAROLERS	BC - TODDLERS	94	94	$18.00	$18.00
214	TEDDY BEAR	BC - CAROLERS	BC - TODDLERS	93	93	$18.50	$35.00
215	TODDLER WITH WAGON	BC - CAROLERS	BC - TODDLERS	96	95	$19.50	$20.00
216	TREE	BC - CAROLERS	BC - TODDLERS	96	94	$18.00	$18.00
217	TRICYCLE (SNOWSUIT)	BC - CAROLERS	BC - TODDLERS	96	96	$20.00	$20.00
218	VICTORIAN BOY TODDLER	BC - CAROLERS	BC - TODDLERS	95	95	$19.50	$19.50
219	VICTORIAN GIRLTODDLER	BC - CAROLERS	BC - TODDLERS	95	95	$19.50	$19.50
220	MOUSE KING	BC - CAROLERS	BC - THE NUTCRACKER		97	$70.00	
221	SANTA FEEDING REINDEER	BC - CAROLERS	BC - SANTAS		97	$64.50	
222	SHOPPING/MRS. CLAUS	BC - CAROLERS	BC - SANTAS		97	$59.50	
223	BOY WITH FLAG	BC - CAROLERS	BC - SALVATION ARMY		97	$57.00	
224	MILK MAID	BC - CAROLERS	BC - CRIES OF LONDON		97	$67.00	
225	TODDLER W/SKIS (SWEATER)	BC - CAROLERS	BC - TODDLERS		97	$21.50	
226	TODDLER W/TRICYCLE(SWEATER)	BC - CAROLERS	BC - TODDLERS		97	$21.50	
227	TODDLER IN SLEIGH	BC - CAROLERS	BC - TODDLERS		97	$27.50	
228	TODDLER ON ROCKING HORSE	BC - CAROLERS	BC - TODDLERS		97	$27.50	
229	TODDLER HOLDING MERRY CHRISTMAS	BC - CAROLERS	BC - TODDLERS		97	$20.00	
231	DOG WITH LOLLIPOP	BC - CAROLERS	BC - ACCESSORIES		97	$18.50	
233	VICTORIAN ADULT SHOPPERS	BC - CAROLERS	BC - VICTORIAN CAROLERS		97	$61.00	
234	MAN FEEDING BIRDS/ON BENCH	BC - CAROLERS	BC - SPECIAL CHARACTERS		97	$83.00	
232	CAT W/MILK	BC - CAROLERS	BC - ACCESSORIES		97	$18.50	
235	ONE MAN BAND	BC - CAROLERS	BC - SPECIAL CHARACTERS		97	$69.50	
236	GARDENER	BC - CAROLERS	BC - SPECIAL CHARACTERS		97	$69.50	
237	WOMAN WITH GINGERBREAD HOUSE	BC - CAROLERS	BC - SPECIAL CHARACTERS		97	$60.00	
239	CHILDREN WITH TREATS	BC - CAROLERS	BC - SPECIAL CHARACTERS		97	$58.00	
240	MEXICAN CHILDREN	BC - CAROLERS	BC - CHILDREN OF THE WORLD		97	$50.00	
241	DROSSEIMEIER W/MUSIC BOX (2ND EDITION)	BC - CAROLERS	BC - THE NUTCRACKER		97	$83.00	
159	SNOWBALL	BC - CAROLERS	BC - TODDLERS	94	92	$17.00	
	BACKDROP	BC - CAROLERS	BC - ACCESSORIES	93			
	CAT IN A HAT	BC - CAROLERS	BC - ACCESSORIES	95			
	CHRISTMAS TREE WITH LIGHTS	BC - CAROLERS	BC - ACCESSORIES				
	DECORATED LAMP POST	BC - CAROLERS	BC - ACCESSORIES				
	DISPLAY SNOW	BC - CAROLERS	BC - ACCESSORIES				
	DOG WITH HAT	BC - CAROLERS	BC - ACCESSORIES				
	DOOR	BC - CAROLERS	BC - ACCESSORIES	93			
	LAMP BULB	BC - CAROLERS	BC - ACCESSORIES				
	MAILBOX	BC - CAROLERS	BC - ACCESSORIES	94			
	MUSIC	BC - CAROLERS	BC - ACCESSORIES	94			
	PARK BENCH	BC - CAROLERS	BC - ACCESSORIES				
	SLED WITH GIFTS	BC - CAROLERS	BC - ACCESSORIES				
	SNOWMAN/THREE SNOWBALLS	BC - CAROLERS	BC - ACCESSORIES	95			
	SNOWMAN/TWO SNOWBALLS	BC - CAROLERS	BC - ACCESSORIES				
	STREET CLOCK	BC - CAROLERS	BC - ACCESSORIES				
	TOY SHOP	BC - CAROLERS	BC - ACCESSORIES				
	WAGON WITH GIFTS	BC - CAROLERS	BC - ACCESSORIES				
	CHRISTOPHER RADKO						
86-001-0	Pleated Flask	CR - BLOWN GLASS - POLAND	ORNAMENT	YES	1986	$5.00	$5.00
86-002-0	Twisted Flask	CR - BLOWN GLASS - POLAND	ORNAMENT	YES	1986	$5.00	$5.00
86-003-0	Parasol Up	CR - BLOWN GLASS - POLAND	ORNAMENT	YES	1986	$8.00	$8.00
86-004-0	Parasol Down	CR - BLOWN GLASS - POLAND	ORNAMENT	YES	1986	$8.00	$8.00
86-005-0	Candy Cane	CR - BLOWN GLASS - POLAND	ORNAMENT		1986	$4.00	$4.00
86-005-1	Santa's Cane	CR - BLOWN GLASS - POLAND	ORNAMENT		1986	$7.00	$90.00
87-010-0	Scarlett's Wedding Dress	CR - BLOWN GLASS - POLAND	ORNAMENT		1987	$14.00	$14.00
87-010-1	Golden Scarlett	CR - BLOWN GLASS - POLAND	ORNAMENT		1987	$32.00	$32.00
87-010-2	Ruby Scarlett	CR - BLOWN GLASS - POLAND	ORNAMENT		1987	$32.00	$32.00
87-012-0	Blue Floral	CR - BLOWN GLASS - POLAND	ORNAMENT	YES	1987	$15.00	$15.00
87-013-0	Art Nouveau	CR - BLOWN GLASS - POLAND	ORNAMENT	YES	1987	$10.00	$10.00
87-014-0	Neopolitan Angels	CR - BLOWN GLASS - POLAND	ORNAMENT	YES	1987	$13.00	$65.00
87-014-1	Neopolitan Angel	CR - BLOWN GLASS - POLAND	ORNAMENT	YES	1987	$15.00	$15.00
87-014-2	Neopolitan Angel	CR - BLOWN GLASS - POLAND	ORNAMENT	YES	1987	$27.00	$150.00
87-015-0A	Deco Floral II	CR - BLOWN GLASS - POLAND	ORNAMENT		1987	$14.00	$14.00
87-015-0	Deco Floral	CR - BLOWN GLASS - POLAND	ORNAMENT		1987	$14.00	$120.00
87-016-0	Fifties Swirl	CR - BLOWN GLASS - POLAND	ORNAMENT	YES	1987	$5.00	$5.00
87-017-0	Japanese Maple	CR - BLOWN GLASS - POLAND	ORNAMENT	YES	1987	$5.00	$5.00
87-018-0	Memphis Abstract	CR - BLOWN GLASS - POLAND	ORNAMENT	YES	1987	$13.00	$125.00
87-019-0	Fifties Design	CR - BLOWN GLASS - POLAND	ORNAMENT	YES	1987	$5.00	$5.00
87-020-0	Mondrian	CR - BLOWN GLASS - POLAND	ORNAMENT	YES	1987	$14.00	$14.00
87-021-0	Celestial	CR - BLOWN GLASS - POLAND	ORNAMENT		1987	$13.00	$13.00
87-021-1	Celestial	CR - BLOWN GLASS - POLAND	ORNAMENT		1987	$15.00	$15.00
87-026-0	Theatricats	CR - BLOWN GLASS - POLAND	ORNAMENT	YES	1987	$13.00	$13.00
87-028-0	Dream Alice	CR - BLOWN GLASS - POLAND	ORNAMENT	YES	1987	$13.00	$13.00
86-006-0	Long Icicles	CR - BLOWN GLASS - POLAND	ORNAMENT		1986	$7.00	$90.00
86-007-0	Silent Bells	CR - BLOWN GLASS - POLAND	ORNAMENT	YES	1986	$5.00	$300.00
86-008-0	Silent Bells	CR - BLOWN GLASS - POLAND	ORNAMENT	YES	1986	$6.00	$6.00
86-009-0	Snow Bells	CR - BLOWN GLASS - POLAND	ORNAMENT	YES	1986	$6.00	$6.00
86-010-0	Snow Comets	CR - BLOWN GLASS - POLAND	ORNAMENT	YES	1986	$15.00	$15.00
86-011-0	Mushrooms	CR - BLOWN GLASS - POLAND	ORNAMENT	YES	1986	$7.00	$7.00
86-012-0	Snow Balloon	CR - BLOWN GLASS - POLAND	ORNAMENT	YES	1986	$15.00	$15.00
86-014-0	Patriotic Spire	CR - BLOWN GLASS - POLAND	ORNAMENT	YES	1986	$10.00	$10.00
86-015-0	Clown Reflector Spire	CR - BLOWN GLASS - POLAND	ORNAMENT	YES	1986	$12.00	$12.00
86-016-0	Jewel Reflector Spire	CR - BLOWN GLASS - POLAND	ORNAMENT	YES	1986	$12.00	$12.00
86-016-1	Jewel Reflector Spire	CR - BLOWN GLASS - POLAND	ORNAMENT	YES	1986	$12.00	$12.00
86-017-0	Emerald City	CR - BLOWN GLASS - POLAND	ORNAMENT		1986	$5.00	$78.00
86-018-0	Pepper Horn	CR - BLOWN GLASS - POLAND	ORNAMENT	YES	1986	$5.00	$5.00
86-019-0	Little Parachutes	CR - BLOWN GLASS - POLAND	ORNAMENT	YES	1986	$3.00	$3.00
86-021-0	Sphere	CR - BLOWN GLASS - POLAND	ORNAMENT	YES	1986	$5.00	$5.00
86-022-0	Flask	CR - BLOWN GLASS - POLAND	ORNAMENT	YES	1986	$3.00	$3.00
86-023-0	Saturn	CR - BLOWN GLASS - POLAND	ORNAMENT	YES	1986	$5.00	$5.00
86-023-1	Saturn	CR - BLOWN GLASS - POLAND	ORNAMENT	YES	1986	$5.00	$5.00
86-024-0	Parachute	CR - BLOWN GLASS - POLAND	ORNAMENT	YES	1986	$5.00	$5.00

Order No.	Title	Type	Theme	Retired	Intro. Year	Retail Price	Secondary Price
87-069-0	Long Peppers	CR - BLOWN GLASS - POLAND	ORNAMENT	YES	1987	$5.00	$5.00
87-070-0	Satin Orb	CR - BLOWN GLASS - POLAND	ORNAMENT	YES	1987	$5.00	$5.00
87-071-0	Circus Balloon	CR - BLOWN GLASS - POLAND	ORNAMENT	YES	1987	$8.00	$8.00
87-072-0	Jester Scepter	CR - BLOWN GLASS - POLAND	ORNAMENT	YES	1987	$14.00	$14.00
87-074-0	Granny's Reflector	CR - BLOWN GLASS - POLAND	ORNAMENT	YES	1987	$16.00	$16.00
87-074-1	Granny's Reflector	CR - BLOWN GLASS - POLAND	ORNAMENT	YES	1987	$18.00	$18.00
87-076-0	Jestor Reflector	CR - BLOWN GLASS - POLAND	ORNAMENT	YES	1987	$16.00	$16.00
87-077-0	Twin Laurel Sphere	CR - BLOWN GLASS - POLAND	ORNAMENT	YES	1987	$20.00	$20.00
87-079-0	Double Royal Star Reflector	CR - BLOWN GLASS - POLAND	ORNAMENT	YES	1987	$20.00	$20.00
87-079-1	Double Royal Star	CR - BLOWN GLASS - POLAND	ORNAMENT	YES	1987	$20.00	$20.00
87-080-0	Twin Finial	CR - BLOWN GLASS - POLAND	ORNAMENT	YES	1987	$20.00	$100.00
87-080-1	Twin Finial	CR - BLOWN GLASS - POLAND	ORNAMENT	YES	1987	$24.00	$24.00
88-001-0	Crescent Moon Santa	CR - BLOWN GLASS - POLAND	ORNAMENT	YES	1988	$15.00	$15.00
88-002-0	Cardinal Christmas	CR - BLOWN GLASS - POLAND	ORNAMENT	YES	1988	$16.00	$16.00
88-009-0	Squiggles	CR - BLOWN GLASS - POLAND	ORNAMENT	YES	1988	$15.00	$15.00
88-011-0	Circle of Santas 8811	CR - BLOWN GLASS - POLAND	ORNAMENT	YES	1988	$15.00	$140.00
88-011-1	Circle of Santas	CR - BLOWN GLASS - POLAND	ORNAMENT	YES	1988	$22.00	$22.00
88-014-0A	Lilac Sparkle II	CR - BLOWN GLASS - POLAND	ORNAMENT	YES	1988	$15.00	$15.00
88-014-0	Lilac Sparkle	CR - BLOWN GLASS - POLAND	ORNAMENT	YES	1988	$15.00	$140.00
88-017-0	Simply Cartier	CR - BLOWN GLASS - POLAND	ORNAMENT	YES	1988	$15.00	$125.00
88-017-1	French Regency	CR - BLOWN GLASS - POLAND	ORNAMENT		1988	$18.00	$18.00
88-018-0	Royal Crest Oval	CR - BLOWN GLASS - POLAND	ORNAMENT	YES	1988	$15.00	$15.00
88-020-0	Small St. Nickcicle	CR - BLOWN GLASS - POLAND	ORNAMENT	YES	1988	$8.00	$8.00
88-021-0	Holiday Stripes	CR - BLOWN GLASS - POLAND	ORNAMENT	YES	1988	$6.00	$6.00
88-024-0	Buds in Bloom 8874	CR - BLOWN GLASS - POLAND	ORNAMENT	YES	1988	$16.00	$125.00
88-026-0	Harlequin	CR - BLOWN GLASS - POLAND	ORNAMENT		1988	$16.00	$16.00
88-026-3	Pastel Harlequin	CR - BLOWN GLASS - POLAND	ORNAMENT		1988	$32.00	$32.00
88-028-0	Celestial Sherbet 884	CR - BLOWN GLASS - POLAND	ORNAMENT	YES	1988	$15.00	$15.00
88-030-0	Apple Grove	CR - BLOWN GLASS - POLAND	ORNAMENT		1988	$15.00	$15.00
88-031-0	Pear	CR - BLOWN GLASS - POLAND	ORNAMENT		1988	$15.00	$300.00
88-033-0	Black Fish	CR - BLOWN GLASS - POLAND	ORNAMENT	YES	1988	$15.00	$15.00
88-034-0	Pink Face	CR - BLOWN GLASS - POLAND	ORNAMENT	YES	1988	$15.00	$15.00
88-035-0	Poinsettia & Pine	CR - BLOWN GLASS - POLAND	ORNAMENT	YES	1988	$8.00	$8.00
88-037-0	Vienna 1900	CR - BLOWN GLASS - POLAND	ORNAMENT	YES	1988	$16.00	$16.00
88-039-0A	Pear Branch	CR - BLOWN GLASS - POLAND	ORNAMENT	YES	1988	$15.00	$15.00
88-039-0	Cornucopia 8839	CR - BLOWN GLASS - POLAND	ORNAMENT	YES	1988	$15.00	$360.00
88-041-0	Roman Grid	CR - BLOWN GLASS - POLAND	ORNAMENT	YES	1988	$15.00	$15.00
88-043-0	Shiny Brite	CR - BLOWN GLASS - POLAND	ORNAMENT	YES	1988	$5.00	$5.00
88-043-1	Shiny Brite	CR - BLOWN GLASS - POLAND	ORNAMENT	YES	1988	$6.00	$36.00
88-044-0	Ripples on Oval	CR - BLOWN GLASS - POLAND	ORNAMENT	YES	1988	$5.00	$85.00
88-045-0	Baroque Tapestry	CR - BLOWN GLASS - POLAND	ORNAMENT		1988	$16.00	$16.00
88-050-0	Christmas Fanfare 8850	CR - BLOWN GLASS - POLAND	ORNAMENT	YES	1988	$15.00	$120.00
88-052-0	Merry Maiden	CR - BLOWN GLASS - POLAND	ORNAMENT	YES	1988	$15.00	$15.00
88-052-1	Merry Christmas Maiden	CR - BLOWN GLASS - POLAND	ORNAMENT	YES	1988	$26.00	$50.00
88-053-0	Country Flowers	CR - BLOWN GLASS - POLAND	ORNAMENT	YES	1988	$15.00	$15.00
88-054-0	Contemporary Sphere	CR - BLOWN GLASS - POLAND	ORNAMENT	YES	1988	$11.00	$11.00
88-055-0	Hollywood Glitter	CR - BLOWN GLASS - POLAND	ORNAMENT	YES	1988	$15.00	$15.00
88-058-0	Weather Balloon	CR - BLOWN GLASS - POLAND	ORNAMENT	YES	1988	$24.00	$24.00
88-058-1	Weather Balloon	CR - BLOWN GLASS - POLAND	ORNAMENT	YES	1988	$25.00	$25.00
88-059-0	Jules Verne Balloon	CR - BLOWN GLASS - POLAND	ORNAMENT	YES	1988	$24.00	$24.00
88-060-0	Royal Diadem	CR - BLOWN GLASS - POLAND	ORNAMENT	YES	1988	$24.00	$135.00
88-061-0	Herald Trumpets	CR - BLOWN GLASS - POLAND	ORNAMENT	YES	1988	$10.00	$10.00
88-062-0	Mushroom Winter	CR - BLOWN GLASS - POLAND	ORNAMENT	YES	1988	$10.00	$226.00
88-063-0	Blue Rainbow	CR - BLOWN GLASS - POLAND	ORNAMENT	YES	1988	$16.00	$120.00
88-064-0	Tree on Ball	CR - BLOWN GLASS - POLAND	ORNAMENT	YES	1988	$9.00	$95.00
88-065-0	Holiday Popper	CR - BLOWN GLASS - POLAND	ORNAMENT	YES	1988	$10.00	$10.00
88-066-0	Santa's Pipe	CR - BLOWN GLASS - POLAND	ORNAMENT	YES	1988	$8.00	$8.00
88-067-0	Kat Koncert	CR - BLOWN GLASS - POLAND	ORNAMENT	YES	1988	$15.00	$15.00
88-067-1	Papa's Jamboree	CR - BLOWN GLASS - POLAND	ORNAMENT	1994	1988	$29.00	$50.00
88-068-0	Circus Blue	CR - BLOWN GLASS - POLAND	ORNAMENT	YES	1988	$8.00	$8.00
88-070-0	Royal Rooster	CR - BLOWN GLASS - POLAND	ORNAMENT	1993	1988	$15.00	$15.00
88-071-0A	Flask Double Top	CR - BLOWN GLASS - POLAND	ORNAMENT	YES	1988	$8.00	$8.00
88-071-0	Exclamation Flask	CR - BLOWN GLASS - POLAND	ORNAMENT	YES	1988	$8.00	$8.00
88-072-0	Oz Balloon	CR - BLOWN GLASS - POLAND	ORNAMENT		1988	$18.00	$75.00
88-072-1	Circus Star Balloon	CR - BLOWN GLASS - POLAND	ORNAMENT	YES	1988	$28.00	$60.00
88-072-2	Circus Star Balloon	CR - BLOWN GLASS - POLAND	ORNAMENT		1988	$29.00	$29.00
88-073-0	Bird House 8873	CR - BLOWN GLASS - POLAND	ORNAMENT	YES	1988	$9.00	$73.00
88-074-0	Crown Jewels	CR - BLOWN GLASS - POLAND	ORNAMENT	YES	1988	$15.00	$175.00
88-074-2	Crown Jewels	CR - BLOWN GLASS - POLAND	ORNAMENT	1993	1988	$22.00	$100.00
88-075-0	Circus Spikes	CR - BLOWN GLASS - POLAND	ORNAMENT	YES	1988	$9.00	$9.00
88-076-0	Pastel Finial	CR - BLOWN GLASS - POLAND	ORNAMENT		1988	$10.00	$10.00
88-077-0	Striped Balloon	CR - BLOWN GLASS - POLAND	ORNAMENT	YES	1988	$15.00	$75.00
88-078-0	Spin Top	CR - BLOWN GLASS - POLAND	ORNAMENT	YES	1988	$8.00	$60.00
88-079-0	Anchor	CR - BLOWN GLASS - POLAND	ORNAMENT		1988	$10.00	$10.00
88-080-0	Royal Star Tree Top	CR - BLOWN GLASS - POLAND	ORNAMENT	YES	1988	$25.00	$25.00
88-101-4	Medium Nautilus	CR - BLOWN GLASS - POLAND	ORNAMENT		1988	$18.00	$18.00
88-101-0	Medium Nautilus	CR - BLOWN GLASS - POLAND	ORNAMENT		1988	$6.00	$6.00
88-101-1	Medium Nautilus	CR - BLOWN GLASS - POLAND	ORNAMENT		1988	$7.00	$7.00
88-101-2	Medium Nautilus	CR - BLOWN GLASS - POLAND	ORNAMENT		1988	$12.00	$12.00
88-102-0	Large Nautilus	CR - BLOWN GLASS - POLAND	ORNAMENT		1988	$8.00	$8.00
88-102-1	Jumbo Nautilus	CR - BLOWN GLASS - POLAND	ORNAMENT		1988	$26.00	$26.00
89-001-0	Snow Santa	CR - BLOWN GLASS - POLAND	ORNAMENT	YES	1989	$16.00	$16.00
89-012-0	Spanish Rose	CR - BLOWN GLASS - POLAND	ORNAMENT	YES	1989	$17.00	$17.00
89-015-0	Santa Circus	CR - BLOWN GLASS - POLAND	ORNAMENT	YES	1989	$16.00	$16.00
89-017-0	Silver Frost	CR - BLOWN GLASS - POLAND	ORNAMENT	YES	1989	$17.00	$17.00
89-019-0	Winter Landscape	CR - BLOWN GLASS - POLAND	ORNAMENT	YES	1989	$17.00	$220.00
89-020-0	Hi-Fi Pink	CR - BLOWN GLASS - POLAND	ORNAMENT	YES	1989	$17.00	$17.00
89-021-0	Song Birds	CR - BLOWN GLASS - POLAND	ORNAMENT	YES	1989	$18.00	$200.00
89-022-0	Pastel Harlequin	CR - BLOWN GLASS - POLAND	ORNAMENT	YES	1989	$17.00	$17.00
89-023-0	Gilded Birds	CR - BLOWN GLASS - POLAND	ORNAMENT	YES	1989	$18.00	$150.00
89-025-0	Snowfall	CR - BLOWN GLASS - POLAND	ORNAMENT	YES	1989	$17.00	$17.00
89-029-0	Gothic Window	CR - BLOWN GLASS - POLAND	ORNAMENT	YES	1989	$17.00	$17.00
89-030-0	Fleurs De Provence	CR - BLOWN GLASS - POLAND	ORNAMENT	YES	1989	$17.00	$120.00

Order No.	Title	Type	Theme	Retired	Intro. Year	Retial Price	Secondary Price
86-025-0	Russian Tear	CR - BLOWN GLASS - POLAND	ORNAMENT	YES	1986	$8.00	$8.00
86-026-0	Silver Eyes	CR - BLOWN GLASS - POLAND	ORNAMENT	YES	1986	$4.00	$4.00
86-027-0	Satin Reflector	CR - BLOWN GLASS - POLAND	ORNAMENT	YES	1986	$7.00	$7.00
86-028-0	Shiny Top	CR - BLOWN GLASS - POLAND	ORNAMENT	YES	1986	$4.00	$4.00
86-029-0	Baby Rattle	CR - BLOWN GLASS - POLAND	ORNAMENT	YES	1986	$7.00	$7.00
86-030-0	Nautical	CR - BLOWN GLASS - POLAND	ORNAMENT	YES	1986	$6.00	$6.00
86-031-0	Flask	CR - BLOWN GLASS - POLAND	ORNAMENT	YES	1986	$12.00	$12.00
86-033-0	Barbell	CR - BLOWN GLASS - POLAND	ORNAMENT	YES	1986	$12.00	$12.00
86-034-0	Holiday Scepter	CR - BLOWN GLASS - POLAND	ORNAMENT	YES	1986	$12.00	$12.00
86-035-0	Blue Scepter	CR - BLOWN GLASS - POLAND	ORNAMENT	YES	1986	$12.00	$12.00
86-036-0	Diamonds	CR - BLOWN GLASS - POLAND	ORNAMENT	YES	1986	$12.00	$12.00
86-037-0	Checkers	CR - BLOWN GLASS - POLAND	ORNAMENT	YES	1986	$12.00	$12.00
86-038-0	Santa Sleigh	CR - BLOWN GLASS - POLAND	ORNAMENT	YES	1986	$12.00	$12.00
86-039-0	Howdy Santa	CR - BLOWN GLASS - POLAND	ORNAMENT	YES	1986	$12.00	$12.00
86-040-0	Alpine Flowers	CR - BLOWN GLASS - POLAND	ORNAMENT		1986	$12.00	$120.00
86-040-1	Golden Alpine	CR - BLOWN GLASS - POLAND	ORNAMENT		1993	$27.00	$48.00
86-040-2	Alpine Blush	CR - BLOWN GLASS - POLAND	ORNAMENT		1986	$32.00	$32.00
86-041-0	Deep Sea	CR - BLOWN GLASS - POLAND	ORNAMENT		1986	$12.00	$12.00
86-041-1	Deep Sea	CR - BLOWN GLASS - POLAND	ORNAMENT		1989	$29.00	$48.00
86-041-2	Deep Sea	CR - BLOWN GLASS - POLAND	ORNAMENT	1995	1986	$32.00	$32.00
86-042-0	Butterfly	CR - BLOWN GLASS - POLAND	ORNAMENT	YES	1986	$12.00	$12.00
86-043-0	Floral Print	CR - BLOWN GLASS - POLAND	ORNAMENT	YES	1986	$10.00	$10.00
86-044-0	Three Ribbon Oval	CR - BLOWN GLASS - POLAND	ORNAMENT	YES	1986	$12.00	$150.00
86-045-0	Diamond Band Oval	CR - BLOWN GLASS - POLAND	ORNAMENT	YES	1986	$12.00	$12.00
86-046-0	Snowman Oval	CR - BLOWN GLASS - POLAND	ORNAMENT	YES	1986	$12.00	$12.00
86-047-0	Fleur de Lis Oval	CR - BLOWN GLASS - POLAND	ORNAMENT	YES	1986	$12.00	$12.00
86-048-0	Big Top	CR - BLOWN GLASS - POLAND	ORNAMENT	YES	1986	$15.00	$15.00
86-048-1	Big Top	CR - BLOWN GLASS - POLAND	ORNAMENT	YES	1986	$15.00	$15.00
86-049-0	Midas Touch	CR - BLOWN GLASS - POLAND	ORNAMENT	YES	1986	$15.00	$150.00
86-049-1	Midas Touch	CR - BLOWN GLASS - POLAND	ORNAMENT	1993	1986	$28.00	$160.00
86-101-0	Ripe Harvest	CR - BLOWN GLASS - POLAND	ORNAMENT	YES	1986	$15.00	$15.00
86-102-0	Ripe Harvest II	CR - BLOWN GLASS - POLAND	ORNAMENT	YES	1986	$15.00	$15.00
86-103-0	Mimbres I	CR - BLOWN GLASS - POLAND	ORNAMENT	YES	1986	$15.00	$15.00
86-104-0	Mimbres II	CR - BLOWN GLASS - POLAND	ORNAMENT	YES	1986	$15.00	$15.00
86-105-0	Tropics	CR - BLOWN GLASS - POLAND	ORNAMENT	YES	1986	$10.00	$10.00
86-106-0	Tiger/Zebra	CR - BLOWN GLASS - POLAND	ORNAMENT	YES	1986	$15.00	$15.00
86-107-0	Astral	CR - BLOWN GLASS - POLAND	ORNAMENT	YES	1986	$15.00	$15.00
86-108-0	Winter I	CR - BLOWN GLASS - POLAND	ORNAMENT	YES	1986	$15.00	$15.00
86-109-0	Winter II	CR - BLOWN GLASS - POLAND	ORNAMENT	YES	1986	$15.00	$15.00
86-110-0	Siberian Sleighride	CR - BLOWN GLASS - POLAND	ORNAMENT	YES	1986	$15.00	$100.00
86-110-1	Siberian Sleighride	CR - BLOWN GLASS - POLAND	ORNAMENT	YES	1986	$27.00	$27.00
86-112-0	Three Wise Swans	CR - BLOWN GLASS - POLAND	ORNAMENT	YES	1986	$15.00	$15.00
86-112-1	The Wise Swans	CR - BLOWN GLASS - POLAND	ORNAMENT	1994	1989	$29.00	$29.00
86-113-0	Pinocchio Ball	CR - BLOWN GLASS - POLAND	ORNAMENT	YES	1986	$15.00	$15.00
86-114-0	Woodsman	CR - BLOWN GLASS - POLAND	ORNAMENT	YES	1986	$15.00	$15.00
86-115-0	Roses	CR - BLOWN GLASS - POLAND	ORNAMENT	YES	1986	$15.00	$15.00
86-116-0	Strawberries	CR - BLOWN GLASS - POLAND	ORNAMENT	YES	1986	$15.00	$15.00
86-117-0	Berries & Nuts	CR - BLOWN GLASS - POLAND	ORNAMENT	YES	1986	$15.00	$15.00
86-119-0	Cherry Blossoms	CR - BLOWN GLASS - POLAND	ORNAMENT	YES	1986	$15.00	$15.00
86-120-0	Violets	CR - BLOWN GLASS - POLAND	ORNAMENT	YES	1986	$15.00	$15.00
86-121-0	Spring Flowers	CR - BLOWN GLASS - POLAND	ORNAMENT	YES	1986	$15.00	$15.00
86-122-0	Fantasy Blooms	CR - BLOWN GLASS - POLAND	ORNAMENT		1986	$15.00	$15.00
87-005-0	American Southwest	CR - BLOWN GLASS - POLAND	ORNAMENT	YES	1987	$15.00	$250.00
87-006-0	Stained Glass	CR - BLOWN GLASS - POLAND	ORNAMENT	YES	1987	$14.00	$120.00
87-007-0	Babylon	CR - BLOWN GLASS - POLAND	ORNAMENT	YES	1987	$15.00	$15.00
87-008-0	Isis	CR - BLOWN GLASS - POLAND	ORNAMENT	YES	1987	$14.00	$14.00
87-009-0	Royal Porcelain	CR - BLOWN GLASS - POLAND	ORNAMENT		1987	$14.00	$14.00
87-010-0A	Gilded Leaves	CR - BLOWN GLASS - POLAND	ORNAMENT	YES	1987	$14.00	$14.00
87-029-0	Split Sterling	CR - BLOWN GLASS - POLAND	ORNAMENT	YES	1987	$8.00	$8.00
87-030-0	Ebony Split	CR - BLOWN GLASS - POLAND	ORNAMENT	YES	1987	$9.00	$9.00
87-033-0	Striped Oval	CR - BLOWN GLASS - POLAND	ORNAMENT		1987	$7.00	$7.00
87-034-0	Faberge	CR - BLOWN GLASS - POLAND	ORNAMENT		1987	$7.00	$7.00
87-034-1	Faberge	CR - BLOWN GLASS - POLAND	ORNAMENT	YES	1987	$7.00	$65.00
87-034-2	Faberge	CR - BLOWN GLASS - POLAND	ORNAMENT		1987	$32.00	$32.00
87-035-0	Future Streamlined Small	CR - BLOWN GLASS - POLAND	ORNAMENT		1987	$10.00	$10.00
87-036-0	Future Streamlined Medium	CR - BLOWN GLASS - POLAND	ORNAMENT		1987	$12.00	$12.00
87-037-0	Future Streamlined Large	CR - BLOWN GLASS - POLAND	ORNAMENT		1987	$16.00	$16.00
87-038-0	Serpents	CR - BLOWN GLASS - POLAND	ORNAMENT		1987	$6.00	$6.00
87-038-1	Serpents of Paradise	CR - BLOWN GLASS - POLAND	ORNAMENT		1987	$13.00	$13.00
87-039-0	Small Tops	CR - BLOWN GLASS - POLAND	ORNAMENT	YES	1987	$4.00	$4.00
87-041-0	Victorian Parasol	CR - BLOWN GLASS - POLAND	ORNAMENT	YES	1987	$6.00	$6.00
87-042-0	Zeppelins	CR - BLOWN GLASS - POLAND	ORNAMENT	YES	1987	$7.00	$7.00
87-043-0	Liberty Balloon	CR - BLOWN GLASS - POLAND	ORNAMENT	YES	1987	$9.00	$9.00
87-044-0	Baby Balloon	CR - BLOWN GLASS - POLAND	ORNAMENT	YES	1987	$4.00	$4.00
87-046-0	Trumpet Bells	CR - BLOWN GLASS - POLAND	ORNAMENT	YES	1987	$5.00	$5.00
87-047-0	Samovar	CR - BLOWN GLASS - POLAND	ORNAMENT	YES	1987	$6.00	$300.00
87-048-0	Malaga	CR - BLOWN GLASS - POLAND	ORNAMENT	YES	1987	$5.00	$5.00
87-049-0	Venetian Tile Birds	CR - BLOWN GLASS - POLAND	ORNAMENT	YES	1987	$9.00	$9.00
87-050-0	Four Tier Pandant	CR - BLOWN GLASS - POLAND	ORNAMENT	YES	1987	$7.00	$7.00
87-052-0	Grecian Column	CR - BLOWN GLASS - POLAND	ORNAMENT	YES	1987	$8.00	$8.00
87-052-1	Grecian Column	CR - BLOWN GLASS - POLAND	ORNAMENT	YES	1987	$9.00	$9.00
87-053-0	Silver Bells	CR - BLOWN GLASS - POLAND	ORNAMENT	YES	1987	$5.00	$5.00
87-055-0	Dumbells	CR - BLOWN GLASS - POLAND	ORNAMENT	YES	1987	$4.00	$4.00
87-058-0	Satin Scepter	CR - BLOWN GLASS - POLAND	ORNAMENT	YES	1987	$7.00	$7.00
87-059-0	Victorian Basket	CR - BLOWN GLASS - POLAND	ORNAMENT	YES	1987	$6.00	$6.00
87-060-0	Iridescence	CR - BLOWN GLASS - POLAND	ORNAMENT	YES	1987	$5.00	$5.00
87-061-0	Roman Lamp	CR - BLOWN GLASS - POLAND	ORNAMENT	YES	1987	$7.00	$7.00
87-062-0	Star Lamp	CR - BLOWN GLASS - POLAND	ORNAMENT	YES	1987	$7.00	$7.00
87-063-0	Victorian Lamp	CR - BLOWN GLASS - POLAND	ORNAMENT	YES	1987	$7.00	$120.00
87-064-0	At the Market	CR - BLOWN GLASS - POLAND	ORNAMENT	YES	1987	$4.00	$4.00
87-066-0	Pinecone Lamps	CR - BLOWN GLASS - POLAND	ORNAMENT	YES	1987	$7.00	$7.00
87-067-0	Echo Sphere	CR - BLOWN GLASS - POLAND	ORNAMENT	YES	1987	$12.00	$12.00
87-068-0	Echo Sphere	CR - BLOWN GLASS - POLAND	ORNAMENT	YES	1987	$12.00	$12.00

Order No.	Title	Type	Theme	Retired	Intro. Year	Retail Price	Secondary Price
89-031-0A	Swan Lake	CR - BLOWN GLASS - POLAND	ORNAMENT	YES	1989	$17.00	$17.00
89-031-0	Swan Lake	CR - BLOWN GLASS - POLAND	ORNAMENT	YES	1989	$17.00	$17.00
89-032-0	Circle of Santas	CR - BLOWN GLASS - POLAND	ORNAMENT		1989	$17.00	$17.00
89-032-1	Circle of Santas	CR - BLOWN GLASS - POLAND	ORNAMENT		1989	$27.00	$50.00
89-032-2	Circle of Santas	CR - BLOWN GLASS - POLAND	ORNAMENT	1995	1989	$27.00	$27.00
89-032-3	Circle of Santas	CR - BLOWN GLASS - POLAND	ORNAMENT		1989	$32.00	$32.00
89-033-0	Ribbons	CR - BLOWN GLASS - POLAND	ORNAMENT	YES	1989	$16.00	$16.00
89-037-0	Mondrian	CR - BLOWN GLASS - POLAND	ORNAMENT	YES	1989	$17.00	$17.00
89-039-0	Star Brite	CR - BLOWN GLASS - POLAND	ORNAMENT	YES	1989	$17.00	$17.00
89-040-0	Carmen Miranda	CR - BLOWN GLASS - POLAND	ORNAMENT	YES	1989	$17.00	$17.00
89-041-0	Jester	CR - BLOWN GLASS - POLAND	ORNAMENT	YES	1989	$17.00	$120.00
89-042-0	Bloomsbury Bells	CR - BLOWN GLASS - POLAND	ORNAMENT	YES	1989	$18.00	$18.00
89-044-0	Tiffany	CR - BLOWN GLASS - POLAND	ORNAMENT	YES	1989	$17.00	$700.00
89-044-1	Tiffany	CR - BLOWN GLASS - POLAND	ORNAMENT	YES	1989	$19.00	$19.00
89-044-2	Tiffany	CR - BLOWN GLASS - POLAND	ORNAMENT		1989	$22.00	$22.00
89-045-0	Lotus Blossom	CR - BLOWN GLASS - POLAND	ORNAMENT	YES	1989	$17.00	$17.00
89-046-0	Black Lace	CR - BLOWN GLASS - POLAND	ORNAMENT	YES	1989	$17.00	$17.00
89-047-0	The Ivy	CR - BLOWN GLASS - POLAND	ORNAMENT	YES	1989	$17.00	$72.00
89-048-0	Divine	CR - BLOWN GLASS - POLAND	ORNAMENT	YES	1989	$17.00	$17.00
89-049-0	The Holly	CR - BLOWN GLASS - POLAND	ORNAMENT	YES	1989	$17.00	$90.00
89-050-0	Archangel	CR - BLOWN GLASS - POLAND	ORNAMENT	YES	1989	$18.00	$18.00
89-051-0	Vineyard	CR - BLOWN GLASS - POLAND	ORNAMENT	YES	1989	$17.00	$125.00
89-052-0	Patchwork	CR - BLOWN GLASS - POLAND	ORNAMENT	YES	1989	$17.00	$125.00
89-053-0	Harvest	CR - BLOWN GLASS - POLAND	ORNAMENT	YES	1989	$18.00	$18.00
89-054-0	Seahorse	CR - BLOWN GLASS - POLAND	ORNAMENT		1989	$10.00	$100.00
89-054-1	Seahorse	CR - BLOWN GLASS - POLAND	ORNAMENT		1989	$15.00	$100.00
89-054-3	Seahorse	CR - BLOWN GLASS - POLAND	ORNAMENT		1992	$20.00	$20.00
89-055-0	Silent Movie	CR - BLOWN GLASS - POLAND	ORNAMENT		1989	$9.00	$65.00
89-055-1	Silent Movie	CR - BLOWN GLASS - POLAND	ORNAMENT		1989	$9.00	$35.00
89-056-0	Father Christmas	CR - BLOWN GLASS - POLAND	ORNAMENT	YES	1989	$6.00	$6.00
89-056-1	Starlight Santa	CR - BLOWN GLASS - POLAND	ORNAMENT	YES	1989	$12.00	$12.00
89-057-0	Kim Ono	CR - BLOWN GLASS - POLAND	ORNAMENT	YES	1989	$4.00	$60.00
89-057-1	Geisha Girls	CR - BLOWN GLASS - POLAND	ORNAMENT	1993	1989	$12.00	$12.00
89-058-0	Joey Clown	CR - BLOWN GLASS - POLAND	ORNAMENT	YES	1989	$9.00	$80.00
89-058-1	Joey Clown	CR - BLOWN GLASS - POLAND	ORNAMENT	YES	1989	$15.00	$50.00
89-058-2	Stardust Joey	CR - BLOWN GLASS - POLAND	ORNAMENT	YES	1989	$16.00	$55.00
89-059-0	Smiling Sun	CR - BLOWN GLASS - POLAND	ORNAMENT		1989	$7.00	$45.00
89-059-1	Cheerful Sun	CR - BLOWN GLASS - POLAND	ORNAMENT		1989	$9.00	$50.00
89-059-3	Blue Moon	CR - BLOWN GLASS - POLAND	ORNAMENT	1995	1989	$24.00	$24.00
89-060-0	Clown Snake	CR - BLOWN GLASS - POLAND	ORNAMENT		1989	$9.00	$9.00
89-060-1	Clown Snake	CR - BLOWN GLASS - POLAND	ORNAMENT		1989	$15.00	$15.00
89-060-2	Clown Snake	CR - BLOWN GLASS - POLAND	ORNAMENT		1989	$18.00	$18.00
89-060-4	Clown Snakes	CR - BLOWN GLASS - POLAND	ORNAMENT		1989	$22.00	$22.00
89-060-5	Clown Snakes	CR - BLOWN GLASS - POLAND	ORNAMENT		1989	$22.00	$22.00
89-060-6	Clown Snakes	CR - BLOWN GLASS - POLAND	ORNAMENT		1989	$26.00	$26.00
89-060-3	Clown Snakes	CR - BLOWN GLASS - POLAND	ORNAMENT		1989	$22.00	$22.00
89-061-0	Shy Rabbit	CR - BLOWN GLASS - POLAND	ORNAMENT		1989	$7.00	$53.00
89-061-3	A Shy Rabbit's Heart	CR - BLOWN GLASS - POLAND	AIDS FUNDRAISER	1993	1989	$15.00	$60.00
89-061-2	Shy Rabbit	CR - BLOWN GLASS - POLAND	ORNAMENT		1989	$14.00	$60.00
89-062-0	Elf on Ball	CR - BLOWN GLASS - POLAND	ORNAMENT	YES	1989	$10.00	$85.00
89-063-0	Walrus	CR - BLOWN GLASS - POLAND	ORNAMENT		1989	$8.00	$110.00
89-064-0	Kite Face	CR - BLOWN GLASS - POLAND	ORNAMENT	YES	1989	$9.00	$50.00
89-065-0	Fisher Frog	CR - BLOWN GLASS - POLAND	ORNAMENT	YES	1989	$7.00	$40.00
89-066-0	Shy Kitten	CR - BLOWN GLASS - POLAND	ORNAMENT		1989	$7.00	$60.00
89-066-1	Shy Kitten	CR - BLOWN GLASS - POLAND	ORNAMENT		1989	$14.00	$45.00
89-066-2	Shy Kitten	CR - BLOWN GLASS - POLAND	ORNAMENT	1995	1989	$22.00	$22.00
89-068-0	Parachute	CR - BLOWN GLASS - POLAND	ORNAMENT	YES	1989	$7.00	$85.00
89-069-0	Grecian Urn	CR - BLOWN GLASS - POLAND	ORNAMENT	YES	1989	$9.00	$35.00
89-070-0	Tiny Umbrella	CR - BLOWN GLASS - POLAND	ORNAMENT	YES	1989	$7.00	$7.00
89-076-0	Small Reflector	CR - BLOWN GLASS - POLAND	ORNAMENT		1989	$8.00	$8.00
89-078-0	Jungle Scene	CR - BLOWN GLASS - POLAND	ORNAMENT	YES	1989	$6.00	$6.00
89-079-0	Family Choir	CR - BLOWN GLASS - POLAND	ORNAMENT	YES	1989	$16.00	$16.00
89-081-0	Papyrus	CR - BLOWN GLASS - POLAND	ORNAMENT	YES	1989	$16.00	$16.00
89-082-0	Port of Amsterdam	CR - BLOWN GLASS - POLAND	ORNAMENT	YES	1989	$16.00	$16.00
89-084-0	Large Tree	CR - BLOWN GLASS - POLAND	ORNAMENT		1989	$27.00	$27.00
89-086-0	Fluted Column	CR - BLOWN GLASS - POLAND	ORNAMENT		1989	$10.00	$10.00
89-088-0	Drop Reflector	CR - BLOWN GLASS - POLAND	ORNAMENT	YES	1989	$23.00	$90.00
89-089-0	Peppermint Stripe	CR - BLOWN GLASS - POLAND	ORNAMENT	YES	1989	$29.00	$29.00
89-090-0	Circus Balloon	CR - BLOWN GLASS - POLAND	ORNAMENT	YES	1989	$18.00	$18.00
89-091-0	Triple Finial Drop	CR - BLOWN GLASS - POLAND	ORNAMENT	YES	1989	$25.00	$25.00
89-095-0	Poppy	CR - BLOWN GLASS - POLAND	ORNAMENT	YES	1989	$7.00	$7.00
89-096-0	Shadow Santa	CR - BLOWN GLASS - POLAND	ORNAMENT	YES	1989	$7.00	$7.00
89-097-0	Friendly Visitor	CR - BLOWN GLASS - POLAND	ORNAMENT		1989	$11.00	$11.00
89-098-0	Tipsy Santa	CR - BLOWN GLASS - POLAND	ORNAMENT	YES	1989	$7.00	$7.00
89-103-0	King Arthur	CR - BLOWN GLASS - POLAND	ORNAMENT	YES	1989	$12.00	$45.00
89-103-1	King Arthur/Blue	CR - BLOWN GLASS - POLAND	ORNAMENT	YES	1989	$19.00	$45.00
89-104-0	His Boy Elroy	CR - BLOWN GLASS - POLAND	ORNAMENT		1989	$8.00	$120.00
89-105-0	H.M. Scepter	CR - BLOWN GLASS - POLAND	ORNAMENT	YES	1989	$25.00	$144.00
89-106-0	Faberge Tree Finial	CR - BLOWN GLASS - POLAND	ORNAMENT		1989	$36.00	$36.00
89-106-1	Faberge Finial	CR - BLOWN GLASS - POLAND	ORNAMENT		1989	$64.00	$64.00
89-107-0	Harlequin Finial	CR - BLOWN GLASS - POLAND	ORNAMENT		1989	$42.00	$42.00
89-108-0	Royal Star Finial	CR - BLOWN GLASS - POLAND	ORNAMENT	YES	1989	$42.00	$42.00
89-109-0	Alpine Flowers Finial	CR - BLOWN GLASS - POLAND	ORNAMENT		1989	$36.00	$36.00
90-003-0	Poinsettia	CR - BLOWN GLASS - POLAND	ORNAMENT	YES	1990	$18.00	$110.00
90-005-0	Ruby Sparkle	CR - BLOWN GLASS - POLAND	ORNAMENT	YES	1990	$17.00	$17.00
90-006-0	Songbirds	CR - BLOWN GLASS - POLAND	ORNAMENT	YES	1990	$19.00	$19.00
90-007-0	Olympiad	CR - BLOWN GLASS - POLAND	ORNAMENT	YES	1990	$18.00	$85.00
90-010-0	Pair of Cardinals	CR - BLOWN GLASS - POLAND	ORNAMENT	YES	1990	$18.00	$18.00
90-013-0	Polish Folk Dancers	CR - BLOWN GLASS - POLAND	ORNAMENT		1990	$19.00	$150.00
90-015-0	Hearts & Flowers	CR - BLOWN GLASS - POLAND	ORNAMENT		1990	$19.00	$75.00
90-015-1	Hearts & Flowers	CR - BLOWN GLASS - POLAND	ORNAMENT	1995	1990	$32.00	$32.00
90-023-0	Yarn Flight	CR - BLOWN GLASS - POLAND	ORNAMENT	YES	1990	$17.00	$125.00
90-024-0	Early Winter	CR - BLOWN GLASS - POLAND	ORNAMENT	YES	1990	$10.00	$42.00

Order No.	Title	Type	Theme	Retired	Intro. Year	Retial Price	Secondary Price
90-026-0	Polish Folk Art	CR - BLOWN GLASS - POLAND	ORNAMENT	YES	1990	$18.00	$44.00
90-026-0B	Polish Folk Art	CR - BLOWN GLASS - POLAND	ORNAMENT	YES	1990	$18.00	$18.00
90-026-0A	Polish Folk Art	CR - BLOWN GLASS - POLAND	ORNAMENT	YES	1990	$18.00	$18.00
90-026-1	Mission Ball	CR - BLOWN GLASS - POLAND	ORNAMENT		1990	$27.00	$27.00
90-026-2	Mission Ball	CR - BLOWN GLASS - POLAND	ORNAMENT		1990	$32.00	$32.00
90-027-0	Atomic Age	CR - BLOWN GLASS - POLAND	ORNAMENT	YES	1990	$18.00	$18.00
90-031-0	Comet Reflector	CR - BLOWN GLASS - POLAND	ORNAMENT	YES	1990	$16.00	$16.00
90-034-0	Viola	CR - BLOWN GLASS - POLAND	ORNAMENT	YES	1990	$5.00	$5.00
90-035-0	Munchkin	CR - BLOWN GLASS - POLAND	ORNAMENT	YES	1990	$7.00	$40.00
90-035-1	Munchkin	CR - BLOWN GLASS - POLAND	ORNAMENT	YES	1990	$8.00	$16.00
90-035-2	Circus Lady	CR - BLOWN GLASS - POLAND	ORNAMENT	YES	1990	$12.00	$12.00
90-036-0	Nativity	CR - BLOWN GLASS - POLAND	ORNAMENT	YES	1990	$6.00	$60.00
90-037-0	Praying Angel	CR - BLOWN GLASS - POLAND	ORNAMENT	YES	1990	$5.00	$5.00
90-038-0	Calla Lilly	CR - BLOWN GLASS - POLAND	ORNAMENT		1990	$7.00	$50.00
90-039-0	Pudgy Clown	CR - BLOWN GLASS - POLAND	ORNAMENT	YES	1990	$7.00	$60.00
90-039-1	Binky the Clown	CR - BLOWN GLASS - POLAND	ORNAMENT	YES	1990	$12.00	$12.00
90-040-0	Dublin Pipe	CR - BLOWN GLASS - POLAND	ORNAMENT	YES	1990	$14.00	$50.00
90-041-0	Swami	CR - BLOWN GLASS - POLAND	ORNAMENT	1994	1990	$8.00	$8.00
90-042-0	Tabby	CR - BLOWN GLASS - POLAND	ORNAMENT	YES	1990	$7.00	$7.00
90-043-0	Pierre Le Berry	CR - BLOWN GLASS - POLAND	ORNAMENT	YES	1990	$10.00	$75.00
90-043-1	Pierre Le Berry	CR - BLOWN GLASS - POLAND	ORNAMENT	YES	1990	$14.00	$14.00
90-043-2	Pierre Winterbury	CR - BLOWN GLASS - POLAND	ORNAMENT	YES	1990	$17.00	$55.00
90-043-3	Jacques Le Berry	CR - BLOWN GLASS - POLAND	ORNAMENT	1993	1990	$17.00	$17.00
90-044-0	Google Eyes	CR - BLOWN GLASS - POLAND	ORNAMENT		1990	$9.00	$85.00
90-045-0	Snowman on Ball	CR - BLOWN GLASS - POLAND	ORNAMENT	YES	1990	$14.00	$14.00
90-046-0	Angel on Harp	CR - BLOWN GLASS - POLAND	ORNAMENT	YES	1990	$9.00	$70.00
90-047-0	Lullabye	CR - BLOWN GLASS - POLAND	ORNAMENT	YES	1990	$9.00	$52.00
90-052-0	Mother Goose	CR - BLOWN GLASS - POLAND	ORNAMENT		1990	$10.00	$55.00
90-052-1	Mother Goose	CR - BLOWN GLASS - POLAND	ORNAMENT		1990	$11.00	$35.00
90-052-2	Christmas Goose	CR - BLOWN GLASS - POLAND	ORNAMENT	1995	1990	$15.00	$15.00
90-053-0	Golden Puppy	CR - BLOWN GLASS - POLAND	ORNAMENT	YES	1990	$8.00	$92.50
90-054-0	Gypsy Queen	CR - BLOWN GLASS - POLAND	ORNAMENT	YES	1990	$12.00	$35.00
90-054-1	Diva	CR - BLOWN GLASS - POLAND	ORNAMENT	YES	1990	$17.00	$17.00
90-056-0	Crowned Prince	CR - BLOWN GLASS - POLAND	ORNAMENT	YES	1990	$14.00	$45.00
90-056-1	Prince on Ball	CR - BLOWN GLASS - POLAND	ORNAMENT	YES	1990	$15.00	$15.00
90-057-0	Tuxedo	CR - BLOWN GLASS - POLAND	ORNAMENT	YES	1990	$8.00	$750.00
90-058-0	Frog Under Balloon	CR - BLOWN GLASS - POLAND	ORNAMENT		1990	$14.00	$65.00
90-062-0	Frosty	CR - BLOWN GLASS - POLAND	ORNAMENT		1990	$14.00	$14.00
90-063-0	Classic Column	CR - BLOWN GLASS - POLAND	ORNAMENT	YES	1990	$8.00	$8.00
90-066-0	Conch Shell	CR - BLOWN GLASS - POLAND	ORNAMENT		1990	$9.00	$9.00
90-066-1	Conch Shell	CR - BLOWN GLASS - POLAND	ORNAMENT		1990	$11.00	$11.00
90-068-0	Bolero	CR - BLOWN GLASS - POLAND	ORNAMENT	YES	1990	$8.00	$8.00
90-069-0	Eagle Medallion	CR - BLOWN GLASS - POLAND	ORNAMENT	YES	1990	$9.00	$85.00
90-070-0	Sunburst Fish	CR - BLOWN GLASS - POLAND	ORNAMENT		1990	$13.00	$25.00
90-070-1	Sunburst Fish	CR - BLOWN GLASS - POLAND	ORNAMENT		1990	$15.00	$15.00
90-070-2	Tropical Fish	CR - BLOWN GLASS - POLAND	ORNAMENT		1990	$17.00	$17.00
90-070-3	Tropical Fish	CR - BLOWN GLASS - POLAND	ORNAMENT		1990	$17.00	$17.00
90-070-4	Tropical Fish	CR - BLOWN GLASS - POLAND	ORNAMENT		1990	$19.00	$19.00
90-070-5	Tropical Fish	CR - BLOWN GLASS - POLAND	ORNAMENT		1990	$24.00	$24.00
90-071-0	Roly Poly Santa	CR - BLOWN GLASS - POLAND	ORNAMENT		1990	$13.00	$72.00
90-071-1	Roly Poly Santa	CR - BLOWN GLASS - POLAND	ORNAMENT		1990	$18.00	$18.00
90-071-2	Roly Poly Santa	CR - BLOWN GLASS - POLAND	ORNAMENT		1990	$18.00	$18.00
90-071-4	Heritage Santa	CR - BLOWN GLASS - POLAND	ORNAMENT		1990	$24.00	$24.00
90-071-3	Roly Poly Santa	CR - BLOWN GLASS - POLAND	ORNAMENT	1995	1990	$24.00	$24.00
90-072-0	Bathing Baby	CR - BLOWN GLASS - POLAND	ORNAMENT	YES	1990	$11.00	$48.00
90-073-0	Snow Ball Tree	CR - BLOWN GLASS - POLAND	ORNAMENT	YES	1990	$17.00	$50.00
90-075-0	Country Church	CR - BLOWN GLASS - POLAND	ORNAMENT	YES	1990	$12.00	$12.00
90-076-0	Proud Peacock	CR - BLOWN GLASS - POLAND	ORNAMENT		1990	$18.00	$50.00
90-076-1	Proud Peacock	CR - BLOWN GLASS - POLAND	ORNAMENT		1990	$23.00	$23.00
90-076-2	Celestial Peacock	CR - BLOWN GLASS - POLAND	ORNAMENT		1990	$28.00	$28.00
90-076-3	Celestial Peacock	CR - BLOWN GLASS - POLAND	ORNAMENT	1995	1990	$34.00	$34.00
90-079-0	Happy Gnome	CR - BLOWN GLASS - POLAND	ORNAMENT	YES	1990	$8.00	$40.00
90-079-1	Happy Elf	CR - BLOWN GLASS - POLAND	ORNAMENT		1991	$10.00	$80.00
90-082-0	Santa on Ball	CR - BLOWN GLASS - POLAND	ORNAMENT	YES	1990	$16.00	$16.00
90-084-0	Boy Clown on Reflector	CR - BLOWN GLASS - POLAND	ORNAMENT	YES	1990	$18.00	$18.00
90-084-1	Her Majesty	CR - BLOWN GLASS - POLAND	ORNAMENT	YES	1990	$21.00	$21.00
90-085-0	Trumpet Player	CR - BLOWN GLASS - POLAND	ORNAMENT	YES	1990	$18.00	$99.00
90-085-1	Candy Trumpet Men	CR - BLOWN GLASS - POLAND	ORNAMENT	YES	1990	$27.00	$75.00
90-086-0	Elephant on Ball	CR - BLOWN GLASS - POLAND	ORNAMENT		1990	$20.00	$150.00
90-086-1	Elephant on Ball	CR - BLOWN GLASS - POLAND	ORNAMENT		1990	$23.00	$160.00
90-086-2	Jumbo	CR - BLOWN GLASS - POLAND	ORNAMENT		1990	$31.00	$31.00
90-086-3	Center Ring	CR - BLOWN GLASS - POLAND	ORNAMENT		1990	$31.00	$31.00
90-086-4	Center Ring	CR - BLOWN GLASS - POLAND	ORNAMENT		1990	$44.00	$44.00
90-087-0	Ballooning Santa	CR - BLOWN GLASS - POLAND	ORNAMENT	YES	1990	$20.00	$150.00
90-088-0	Rainbow Umbrella	CR - BLOWN GLASS - POLAND	ORNAMENT	YES	1990	$14.00	$60.00
90-090-0	Summer Parasol	CR - BLOWN GLASS - POLAND	ORNAMENT	YES	1990	$7.00	$7.00
90-091-0	Garden Urn	CR - BLOWN GLASS - POLAND	ORNAMENT	YES	1990	$8.00	$8.00
90-096-0	Maracca	CR - BLOWN GLASS - POLAND	ORNAMENT	YES	1990	$8.00	$8.00
90-098-0	Rose Lamp	CR - BLOWN GLASS - POLAND	ORNAMENT	YES	1990	$14.00	$120.00
90-101-0	Jumbo Tree on Ball	CR - BLOWN GLASS - POLAND	ORNAMENT	YES	1990	$30.00	$30.00
90-103-0	Byzantium	CR - BLOWN GLASS - POLAND	ORNAMENT	YES	1990	$10.00	$10.00
91-001-0	Shy Elf	CR - BLOWN GLASS - POLAND	ORNAMENT	YES	1991	$10.00	$55.00
91-003-0	Harvest	CR - BLOWN GLASS - POLAND	ORNAMENT		1991	$14.00	$14.00
91-003-1	Harvest	CR - BLOWN GLASS - POLAND	ORNAMENT	1995	1991	$22.00	$24.00
91-005-0	Tiger	CR - BLOWN GLASS - POLAND	ORNAMENT		1991	$15.00	$35.00
91-005-1	White Tiger	CR - BLOWN GLASS - POLAND	ORNAMENT		1991	$26.00	$26.00
91-005-2	Tiger	CR - BLOWN GLASS - POLAND	ORNAMENT	1996	1991	$28.00	$28.00
91-009-0	Smitty	CR - BLOWN GLASS - POLAND	ORNAMENT		1991	$15.00	$75.00
91-010-0	Irish Laddie	CR - BLOWN GLASS - POLAND	ORNAMENT		1991	$12.00	$52.00
91-011-0	Fu Manchu	CR - BLOWN GLASS - POLAND	ORNAMENT	YES	1991	$15.00	$75.00
91-012-0	Chimney Santa	CR - BLOWN GLASS - POLAND	ORNAMENT	YES	1991	$15.00	$65.00
91-012-2	Down the Chimney	CR - BLOWN GLASS - POLAND	ORNAMENT		1991	$16.00	$16.00
91-012-3	Down the Chimney	CR - BLOWN GLASS - POLAND	ORNAMENT	1995	1991	$24.00	$24.00

Order No.	Title	Type	Theme	Retired	Intro. Year	Retail Price	Secondary Price
91-013-0	Snowman Reflector	CR - BLOWN GLASS - POLAND	ORNAMENT	YES	1991	$16.00	$16.00
91-015-0	Shirley	CR - BLOWN GLASS - POLAND	ORNAMENT	YES	1991	$16.00	$90.00
91-016-0	Cosette	CR - BLOWN GLASS - POLAND	ORNAMENT	YES	1991	$16.00	$80.00
91-017-0	Rainbow Trout	CR - BLOWN GLASS - POLAND	ORNAMENT		1991	$15.00	$15.00
91-017-1	Rainbow Trout	CR - BLOWN GLASS - POLAND	ORNAMENT	1995	1991	$22.00	$22.00
91-018-0	Alter Boy	CR - BLOWN GLASS - POLAND	ORNAMENT	YES	1991	$16.00	$37.00
91-020-0	Evening Santa	CR - BLOWN GLASS - POLAND	ORNAMENT	1993	1991	$15.00	$90.00
91-021-0	Prince Umbrella	CR - BLOWN GLASS - POLAND	ORNAMENT		1991	$15.00	$115.00
91-022-0	Bishop	CR - BLOWN GLASS - POLAND	ORNAMENT	1993	1991	$15.00	$42.00
91-023-0	Puss in Boots	CR - BLOWN GLASS - POLAND	ORNAMENT		1991	$11.00	$35.00
91-023-1	Puss in Boots	CR - BLOWN GLASS - POLAND	ORNAMENT		1991	$15.00	$15.00
91-023-2	Puss in Boots	CR - BLOWN GLASS - POLAND	ORNAMENT	1995	1991	$19.00	$19.00
91-024-0	Patrick's Bunny	CR - BLOWN GLASS - POLAND	ORNAMENT		1991	$11.00	$45.00
91-024-1	Patrick's Bunny	CR - BLOWN GLASS - POLAND	ORNAMENT		1991	$18.00	$18.00
91-024-2	Patrick's Bunny	CR - BLOWN GLASS - POLAND	ORNAMENT	1995	1991	$24.00	$24.00
91-025-0	Madeleine's Puppy	CR - BLOWN GLASS - POLAND	ORNAMENT		1991	$11.00	$55.00
91-025-1	Madeleine's Puppy	CR - BLOWN GLASS - POLAND	ORNAMENT		1991	$18.00	$35.00
91-025-2	Madeleine's Puppy	CR - BLOWN GLASS - POLAND	ORNAMENT	1995	1991	$24.00	$24.00
91-026-0	Froggy Child	CR - BLOWN GLASS - POLAND	ORNAMENT		1991	$9.00	$9.00
91-026-1	Froggy Child	CR - BLOWN GLASS - POLAND	ORNAMENT		1991	$14.00	$14.00
91-027-0	Dutch Boy	CR - BLOWN GLASS - POLAND	ORNAMENT	YES	1991	$11.00	$60.00
91-028-0	Dutch Girl	CR - BLOWN GLASS - POLAND	ORNAMENT	YES	1991	$11.00	$60.00
91-029-0	Aladdin	CR - BLOWN GLASS - POLAND	ORNAMENT		1991	$14.00	$14.00
91-029-1	Aladdin	CR - BLOWN GLASS - POLAND	ORNAMENT		1992	$20.00	$36.00
91-029-2	Aladdin	CR - BLOWN GLASS - POLAND	ORNAMENT		1991	$20.00	$20.00
91-029-3	Aladdin	CR - BLOWN GLASS - POLAND	ORNAMENT	1995	1991	$28.00	$28.00
91-030-0	Timepiece	CR - BLOWN GLASS - POLAND	ORNAMENT	YES	1991	$8.00	$8.00
91-031-0	Lion's Head	CR - BLOWN GLASS - POLAND	ORNAMENT	1996	1991	$16.00	$35.00
91-032-0	Roly Poly Clown	CR - BLOWN GLASS - POLAND	ORNAMENT		1991	$14.00	$45.00
91-032-1	Roly Poly Clown	CR - BLOWN GLASS - POLAND	ORNAMENT		1992	$18.00	$45.00
91-032-2	Roly Poly Clown	CR - BLOWN GLASS - POLAND	ORNAMENT		1991	$18.00	$45.00
91-032-3	Roly Poly Clown	CR - BLOWN GLASS - POLAND	ORNAMENT	1995	1991	$22.00	$22.00
91-033-0	Clown Drum	CR - BLOWN GLASS - POLAND	ORNAMENT	YES	1991	$14.00	$78.00
91-034-0	Dawn & Dusk	CR - BLOWN GLASS - POLAND	ORNAMENT	1995	1991	$14.00	$14.00
91-035-0	Hatching Duck	CR - BLOWN GLASS - POLAND	ORNAMENT		1991	$14.00	$45.00
91-038-0	Woodland Santa	CR - BLOWN GLASS - POLAND	ORNAMENT	YES	1991	$14.00	$65.00
91-038-1	Poinsettia Santa	CR - BLOWN GLASS - POLAND	ORNAMENT	1996	1991	$20.00	$55.00
91-040-0	Fruit in Balloon	CR - BLOWN GLASS - POLAND	ORNAMENT	YES	1991	$22.00	$175.00
91-040-1	Fruit in Balloon	CR - BLOWN GLASS - POLAND	ORNAMENT	YES	1991	$28.00	$28.00
91-041-0	Aztec Bird	CR - BLOWN GLASS - POLAND	ORNAMENT	YES	1991	$20.00	$75.00
91-042-0	Apache	CR - BLOWN GLASS - POLAND	ORNAMENT	1993	1991	$9.00	$45.00
91-043-0	Sally Ann	CR - BLOWN GLASS - POLAND	ORNAMENT	YES	1991	$8.00	$45.00
91-050-0	Bowery Kid	CR - BLOWN GLASS - POLAND	ORNAMENT	YES	1991	$15.00	$60.00
91-052-0	Sleepytime Santa	CR - BLOWN GLASS - POLAND	ORNAMENT		1991	$15.00	$160.00
91-052-1	Sleepytime Santa	CR - BLOWN GLASS - POLAND	ORNAMENT		1991	$18.00	$35.00
91-052-2	Sleepytime Santa	CR - BLOWN GLASS - POLAND	ORNAMENT		1991	$20.00	$35.00
91-052-3	Sleepytime Santa	CR - BLOWN GLASS - POLAND	ORNAMENT	1995	1991	$24.00	$24.00
91-054-0	Pipe Smoking Monkey	CR - BLOWN GLASS - POLAND	ORNAMENT	YES	1991	$11.00	$70.00
91-055-0	Santa Bootie	CR - BLOWN GLASS - POLAND	ORNAMENT	YES	1991	$10.00	$45.00
91-055-1	Santa Bootie	CR - BLOWN GLASS - POLAND	ORNAMENT	YES	1992	$16.00	$35.00
91-055-2	Santa Bootie	CR - BLOWN GLASS - POLAND	ORNAMENT	1993	1991	$16.00	$75.00
91-056-0	Barnum Clown	CR - BLOWN GLASS - POLAND	ORNAMENT		1991	$15.00	$85.00
91-059-0	Pear Face	CR - BLOWN GLASS - POLAND	ORNAMENT	YES	1991	$15.00	$75.00
91-061-0	Tropical Flower	CR - BLOWN GLASS - POLAND	ORNAMENT		1991	$14.00	$14.00
91-062-0	Comet	CR - BLOWN GLASS - POLAND	ORNAMENT	YES	1991	$9.00	$70.00
91-063-0	Tulip Fairy	CR - BLOWN GLASS - POLAND	ORNAMENT	YES	1991	$16.00	$70.00
91-063-1	Tulip Fairy	CR - BLOWN GLASS - POLAND	ORNAMENT	YES	1991	$18.00	$18.00
91-065-0	Anchor America	CR - BLOWN GLASS - POLAND	ORNAMENT	YES	1991	$22.00	$62.00
91-067-0	Sunshine	CR - BLOWN GLASS - POLAND	ORNAMENT		1991	$22.00	$32.00
91-067-1	Mediterranean Sunshine	CR - BLOWN GLASS - POLAND	ORNAMENT		1991	$27.00	$35.00
91-067-2	Mediterranean Sunshine	CR - BLOWN GLASS - POLAND	ORNAMENT	1995	1991	$29.00	$29.00
91-070-0	Pink Elephants	CR - BLOWN GLASS - POLAND	ORNAMENT	YES	1991	$22.00	$125.00
91-070-1	Elephants On Parade	CR - BLOWN GLASS - POLAND	ORNAMENT	YES	1991	$26.00	$26.00
91-073-0	Silver Bells	CR - BLOWN GLASS - POLAND	ORNAMENT	YES	1991	$21.00	$21.00
91-074-0	Peruvian	CR - BLOWN GLASS - POLAND	ORNAMENT	YES	1991	$22.00	$230.00
91-075-0E	Forever Lucy	CR - BLOWN GLASS - POLAND	EVENT PIECE	1995	1991	$32.00	$75.00
91-075-0	Lucy's Favorite	CR - BLOWN GLASS - POLAND	ORNAMENT		1991	$21.00	$21.00
91-075-1	Lucy's Favorite	CR - BLOWN GLASS - POLAND	ORNAMENT		1991	$26.00	$26.00
91-075-2	Blue Lucy	CR - BLOWN GLASS - POLAND	ORNAMENT		1991	$28.00	$28.00
91-076-0	Aspen	CR - BLOWN GLASS - POLAND	ORNAMENT	YES	1991	$21.00	$100.00
91-081-0	Rosebud	CR - BLOWN GLASS - POLAND	ORNAMENT	YES	1991	$22.00	$22.00
91-082-0	Edwardian Lace	CR - BLOWN GLASS - POLAND	ORNAMENT	YES	1991	$22.00	$100.00
91-083-0	Florentine	CR - BLOWN GLASS - POLAND	ORNAMENT		1991	$22.00	$42.00
91-084-0	Cottage Garden	CR - BLOWN GLASS - POLAND	ORNAMENT	YES	1991	$21.00	$21.00
91-087-0	Villandry	CR - BLOWN GLASS - POLAND	ORNAMENT	YES	1991	$21.00	$164.00
91-088-0	Her Purse	CR - BLOWN GLASS - POLAND	ORNAMENT		1991	$10.00	$60.00
91-088-1	Her Purse	CR - BLOWN GLASS - POLAND	ORNAMENT		1991	$20.00	$20.00
91-088-2	Her Purse	CR - BLOWN GLASS - POLAND	ORNAMENT	1995	1991	$24.00	$24.00
91-089-0	Dapper Shoe	CR - BLOWN GLASS - POLAND	ORNAMENT	YES	1991	$10.00	$48.00
91-089-1	Her Slipper	CR - BLOWN GLASS - POLAND	ORNAMENT	YES	1991	$17.00	$17.00
91-090-0	Flower Child	CR - BLOWN GLASS - POLAND	ORNAMENT	YES	1991	$13.00	$60.00
91-092-0	Rainbow Bird	CR - BLOWN GLASS - POLAND	ORNAMENT	YES	1991	$16.00	$32.00
91-093-0	Pipe Man	CR - BLOWN GLASS - POLAND	ORNAMENT	YES	1991	$20.00	$70.00
91-093-1	Talking Pipe	CR - BLOWN GLASS - POLAND	ORNAMENT	YES	1992	$26.00	$93.00
91-093-2	Talking Pipe	CR - BLOWN GLASS - POLAND	ORNAMENT	YES	1991	$26.00	$60.00
91-096-0	Raspberry & Lime	CR - BLOWN GLASS - POLAND	ORNAMENT	YES	1991	$12.00	$45.00
91-097-0	Black Forest Cone	CR - BLOWN GLASS - POLAND	ORNAMENT	YES	1991	$8.00	$36.00
91-098-0	Einstein Kite	CR - BLOWN GLASS - POLAND	ORNAMENT	1994	1991	$20.00	$98.00
91-098-1	Einstein Kite	CR - BLOWN GLASS - POLAND	ORNAMENT		1991	$28.00	$28.00
91-099-0	Melon Slice	CR - BLOWN GLASS - POLAND	ORNAMENT		1991	$18.00	$29.00
91-102-0	Winking St. Nick	CR - BLOWN GLASS - POLAND	ORNAMENT	YES	1991	$16.00	$50.00
91-103-0	Madonna & Child	CR - BLOWN GLASS - POLAND	ORNAMENT		1991	$15.00	$60.00
91-103-1	Madonna & Child	CR - BLOWN GLASS - POLAND	ORNAMENT	1996	1991	$18.00	$18.00

Order No.	Title	Type	Theme	Retired	Intro. Year	Retial Price	Secondary Price
91-104-0	Chance Encounter	CR - BLOWN GLASS - POLAND	ORNAMENT	YES	1991	$14.00	$37.00
91-105-0	Rainbow Cone	CR - BLOWN GLASS - POLAND	ORNAMENT	YES	1991	$10.00	$44.00
91-105-1	Fantasy Cone	CR - BLOWN GLASS - POLAND	ORNAMENT	1994	1991	$18.00	$30.00
91-106-0	Cowboy Santa	CR - BLOWN GLASS - POLAND	ORNAMENT		1991	$16.00	$75.00
91-106-1	Cowboy Santa	CR - BLOWN GLASS - POLAND	ORNAMENT		1991	$24.00	$24.00
91-106-2	Cowboy Santa	CR - BLOWN GLASS - POLAND	ORNAMENT	1995	1991	$32.00	$60.00
91-107-0	Sitting Bull	CR - BLOWN GLASS - POLAND	ORNAMENT	YES	1991	$16.00	$95.00
91-109-0	Cardinal Richelieu	CR - BLOWN GLASS - POLAND	ORNAMENT	YES	1991	$16.00	$96.00
91-111-0	Jemima's Child	CR - BLOWN GLASS - POLAND	ORNAMENT		1991	$16.00	$75.00
91-112-0	Russian Santa	CR - BLOWN GLASS - POLAND	RUSSIAN SANTA		1991	$22.00	$90.00
91-112-1	Santa In Winter White	CR - BLOWN GLASS - POLAND	RUSSIAN SANTA	1996	1991	$28.00	$150.00
91-112-2	Santa In Winter White	CR - BLOWN GLASS - POLAND	RUSSIAN SANTA		1991	$28.00	$60.00
91-112-3	Blue Velvet	CR - BLOWN GLASS - POLAND	RUSSIAN SANTA	1996	1991	$34.00	$34.00
91-112-4	Coral Santa	CR - BLOWN GLASS - POLAND	RUSSIAN SANTA		1991	$32.00	$32.00
91-113-0	Grapefruit Tree	CR - BLOWN GLASS - POLAND	ORNAMENT	YES	1991	$23.00	$200.00
91-114-0	Trigger	CR - BLOWN GLASS - POLAND	ORNAMENT		1991	$15.00	$15.00
91-117-0	Polish Dancers	CR - BLOWN GLASS - POLAND	ORNAMENT	YES	1991	$21.00	$21.00
91-120-0	Galaxy	CR - BLOWN GLASS - POLAND	ORNAMENT	YES	1991	$22.00	$64.00
91-121-0	Red Lace	CR - BLOWN GLASS - POLAND	ORNAMENT	YES	1991	$22.00	$22.00
91-122-0	Ship to Shore	CR - BLOWN GLASS - POLAND	ORNAMENT	YES	1991	$21.00	$21.00
91-123-0A	Carnival	CR - BLOWN GLASS - POLAND	ORNAMENT	YES	1991	$20.00	$20.00
91-123-0B	Carnival	CR - BLOWN GLASS - POLAND	ORNAMENT	YES	1991	$20.00	$20.00
91-123-0	Carnival	CR - BLOWN GLASS - POLAND	ORNAMENT	YES	1991	$20.00	$20.00
91-124-0	By the Nile	CR - BLOWN GLASS - POLAND	ORNAMENT	YES	1991	$22.00	$80.00
91-126-0	Fanfare	CR - BLOWN GLASS - POLAND	ORNAMENT	YES	1991	$22.00	$96.00
91-126-1	Ziegfield Follier	CR - BLOWN GLASS - POLAND	ORNAMENT	YES	1991	$27.00	$27.00
91-127-0	Vienna 1901	CR - BLOWN GLASS - POLAND	ORNAMENT	YES	1991	$22.00	$150.00
91-128-0	Christmas Trim	CR - BLOWN GLASS - POLAND	ORNAMENT	1993	1991	$22.00	$22.00
91-128-1	Star of Wonder	CR - BLOWN GLASS - POLAND	ORNAMENT	YES	1991	$27.00	$27.00
91-129-0	Red Star	CR - BLOWN GLASS - POLAND	ORNAMENT	YES	1991	$22.00	$50.00
91-132-0	Carousel Stripes	CR - BLOWN GLASS - POLAND	ORNAMENT	YES	1991	$21.00	$21.00
91-134-0	Deco Sparkle	CR - BLOWN GLASS - POLAND	ORNAMENT	YES	1991	$21.00	$95.00
91-134-1	Deco Sparkle	CR - BLOWN GLASS - POLAND	ORNAMENT	YES	1991	$26.00	$26.00
91-135-0	Elf Reflector	CR - BLOWN GLASS - POLAND	ORNAMENT		1991	$23.00	$45.00
91-135-1	Elf Reflector	CR - BLOWN GLASS - POLAND	ORNAMENT		1991	$28.00	$28.00
91-137-0	All Weather Santa	CR - BLOWN GLASS - POLAND	ORNAMENT	YES	1991	$32.00	$240.00
91-139-0	Star Quilt	CR - BLOWN GLASS - POLAND	ORNAMENT	YES	1991	$22.00	$90.00
91-140-0	Country Quilt	CR - BLOWN GLASS - POLAND	ORNAMENT	YES	1991	$21.00	$21.00
91-141-0	Aztec	CR - BLOWN GLASS - POLAND	ORNAMENT	YES	1991	$22.00	$88.00
91-142-0	Butterfly Bouquet	CR - BLOWN GLASS - POLAND	ORNAMENT	YES	1991	$22.00	$22.00
91-144-0	Astro Top	CR - BLOWN GLASS - POLAND	ORNAMENT	YES	1991	$12.00	$12.00
91-148-0	Silver Icicle	CR - BLOWN GLASS - POLAND	ORNAMENT	YES	1991	$10.00	$10.00
91-150-0	Hemisphere Finial	CR - BLOWN GLASS - POLAND	FINIAL	YES	1991	$60.00	$60.00
91-151-0	Forest Santa Reflector	CR - BLOWN GLASS - POLAND	ORNAMENT	YES	1991	$35.00	$35.00
91-153-0	The Holly Finial	CR - BLOWN GLASS - POLAND	FINIAL	YES	1991	$54.00	$54.00
91-153-2	Holly Ribbons Finial	CR - BLOWN GLASS - POLAND	FINIAL		1991	$90.00	$90.00
91-154-0	Circle of Santas Finial	CR - BLOWN GLASS - POLAND	FINIAL		1991	$53.00	$53.00
91-158-0	Hearts & Flowers Finial	CR - BLOWN GLASS - POLAND	FINIAL		1991	$53.00	$225.00
91-159-0	Midas Touch Finial	CR - BLOWN GLASS - POLAND	FINIAL	1993	1991	$56.00	$56.00
91-160-0	Poinsettia Finial	CR - BLOWN GLASS - POLAND	FINIAL	YES	1991	$53.00	$53.00
91-094-0	Ms. Maus	CR - BLOWN GLASS - POLAND	ORNAMENT	1991	1991	$14.00	$180.00
92-038-0	Little Eskimo	CR - BLOWN GLASS - POLAND	ORNAMENT	YES	1991	$14.00	$30.00
92-038-1	Little Eskimo	CR - BLOWN GLASS - POLAND	ORNAMENT	YES	1991	$14.00	$30.00
92-046-0	Virgin Mary	CR - BLOWN GLASS - POLAND	ORNAMENT	YES	1992	$10.00	$40.00
92-051-0	Kewpie	CR - BLOWN GLASS - POLAND	ORNAMENT	1994	1992	$18.00	$35.00
92-051-1	Heritage Kewpie	CR - BLOWN GLASS - POLAND	ORNAMENT	1995	1992	$22.00	$22.00
92-053-0	Little League	CR - BLOWN GLASS - POLAND	ORNAMENT	YES	1992	$20.00	$55.00
92-055-0	Wacko's Brother Doofus	CR - BLOWN GLASS - POLAND	ORNAMENT	YES	1992	$20.00	$125.00
92-055-1	Wacko's Brother Doofus	CR - BLOWN GLASS - POLAND	ORNAMENT	1994	1992	$27.00	$27.00
92-059-0	Mr. & Mrs. Claus	CR - BLOWN GLASS - POLAND	ORNAMENT	YES	1992	$18.00	$150.00
92-060-0	Palace Guard	CR - BLOWN GLASS - POLAND	ORNAMENT		1992	$17.00	$17.00
92-060-1	Palace Guard	CR - BLOWN GLASS - POLAND	ORNAMENT		1992	$24.00	$24.00
92-061-0	Sloopy Snowman	CR - BLOWN GLASS - POLAND	ORNAMENT	1993	1992	$20.00	$20.00
92-065-0	Blue Santa	CR - BLOWN GLASS - POLAND	ORNAMENT		1992	$18.00	$18.00
92-067-0	Littlest Snowman	CR - BLOWN GLASS - POLAND	ORNAMENT		1992	$14.00	$24.00
92-067-1	Littlest Snowman	CR - BLOWN GLASS - POLAND	ORNAMENT		1992	$18.00	$18.00
92-069-0	Barbie's Mom	CR - BLOWN GLASS - POLAND	ORNAMENT		1992	$18.00	$115.00
92-071-0	Seafaring Santa	CR - BLOWN GLASS - POLAND	ORNAMENT		1992	$18.00	$25.00
92-071-1	Seafaring Santa	CR - BLOWN GLASS - POLAND	ORNAMENT	1995	1992	$28.00	$28.00
92-074-0	Harlequin Tier Drop	CR - BLOWN GLASS - POLAND	ORNAMENT	YES	1992	$36.00	$55.00
92-075-0	Merlin Santa	CR - BLOWN GLASS - POLAND	ORNAMENT		1992	$32.00	$75.00
92-075-1	Merlin Santa	CR - BLOWN GLASS - POLAND	ORNAMENT		1992	$34.00	$34.00
92-075-2	Merlin Santa	CR - BLOWN GLASS - POLAND	ORNAMENT	1995	1992	$34.00	$34.00
92-076-0	Downhill Racer	CR - BLOWN GLASS - POLAND	ORNAMENT	1993	1992	$34.00	$115.00
92-077-0	Royal Septer	CR - BLOWN GLASS - POLAND	ORNAMENT	YES	1992	$36.00	$36.00
92-078-0	Santa's Helper	CR - BLOWN GLASS - POLAND	ORNAMENT	YES	1992	$17.00	$35.00
92-082-0	Winter Kiss	CR - BLOWN GLASS - POLAND	ORNAMENT	YES	1992	$18.00	$83.00
92-087-0	Mushroom Elf	CR - BLOWN GLASS - POLAND	ORNAMENT	YES	1992	$18.00	$58.00
92-087-1	Mushroom Elf	CR - BLOWN GLASS - POLAND	ORNAMENT	YES	1992	$18.00	$50.00
92-095-0	Folk Art Set	CR - BLOWN GLASS - POLAND	ORNAMENT	YES	1992	$10.00	$12.00
92-101-0	Winter Tree	CR - BLOWN GLASS - POLAND	ORNAMENT		1992	$28.00	$28.00
92-101-1	Winter Tree	CR - BLOWN GLASS - POLAND	ORNAMENT		1992	$29.00	$29.00
92-102-0	Two Sided Santa Reflector	CR - BLOWN GLASS - POLAND	ORNAMENT	YES	1992	$28.00	$100.00
92-103-0	Forest Friends	CR - BLOWN GLASS - POLAND	ORNAMENT	YES	1992	$14.00	$15.00
92-105-0	Alpine Village	CR - BLOWN GLASS - POLAND	ORNAMENT	1993	1992	$24.00	$100.00
92-107-0	St. Nickcicle	CR - BLOWN GLASS - POLAND	ORNAMENT		1992	$26.00	$60.00
92-107-1	St. Nickcicle	CR - BLOWN GLASS - POLAND	ORNAMENT		1992	$28.00	$28.00
92-107-2	St. Nickcicle	CR - BLOWN GLASS - POLAND	ORNAMENT	1995	1992	$32.00	$32.00
92-108-0	Primary Colors	CR - BLOWN GLASS - POLAND	ORNAMENT	YES	1992	$30.00	$150.00
92-115-0	Dolly Madison	CR - BLOWN GLASS - POLAND	ORNAMENT	YES	1992	$17.00	$55.00
92-121-0	French Country	CR - BLOWN GLASS - POLAND	ORNAMENT	1994	1992	$26.00	$60.00
92-122-0A	Victorian Angel Balloon	CR - BLOWN GLASS - GERMANY	ORNAMENT	YES	1992	$68.00	$68.00
92-122-0	Victorian Santa Balloon	CR - BLOWN GLASS - GERMANY	ORNAMENT	YES	1992	$68.00	$550.00

Order No.	Title	Type	Theme	Retired	Intro. Year	Retail Price	Secondary Price
92-123-0	Christmas Cardinals	CR - BLOWN GLASS - POLAND	ORNAMENT	YES	1992	$26.00	$80.00
92-124-0	Delft Design	CR - BLOWN GLASS - POLAND	ORNAMENT	YES	1992	$27.00	$150.00
92-127-0	Ice Poppies	CR - BLOWN GLASS - POLAND	ORNAMENT	YES	1992	$26.00	$50.00
92-134-0	Sputniks	CR - BLOWN GLASS - POLAND	ORNAMENT	YES	1992	$26.00	$105.00
92-142-0	Southern Colonial	CR - BLOWN GLASS - POLAND	ORNAMENT		1992	$27.00	$36.00
92-142-1	Southern Colonial	CR - BLOWN GLASS - POLAND	ORNAMENT		1992	$32.00	$32.00
92-143-0	Christmas Rose	CR - BLOWN GLASS - POLAND	ORNAMENT	YES	1992	$26.00	$48.00
92-146-0	Russian Jewel Hearts	CR - BLOWN GLASS - POLAND	ORNAMENT		1992	$27.00	$100.00
92-146-1	Russian Jewel Hearts	CR - BLOWN GLASS - POLAND	ORNAMENT	1996	1992	$32.00	$32.00
92-149-0	King of Prussia	CR - BLOWN GLASS - POLAND	ORNAMENT	YES	1992	$27.00	$75.00
92-150-0	Scallop Shell	CR - BLOWN GLASS - POLAND	ORNAMENT	YES	1992	$27.00	$27.00
92-151-0	Jester Ball	CR - BLOWN GLASS - POLAND	ORNAMENT	YES	1992	$26.00	$26.00
92-156-0	Winter Wonderland	CR - BLOWN GLASS - POLAND	ORNAMENT	YES	1992	$26.00	$75.00
92-157-0	Diamond Balloon	CR - BLOWN GLASS - POLAND	ORNAMENT		1992	$27.00	$50.00
92-157-1	Diamond Balloon	CR - BLOWN GLASS - POLAND	ORNAMENT	1995	1992	$32.00	$55.00
92-158-0	Pink Lace Tiffany	CR - BLOWN GLASS - POLAND	ORNAMENT	YES	1992	$28.00	$125.00
92-159-0	Tiffany Cabaret	CR - BLOWN GLASS - POLAND	ORNAMENT	1993	1992	$28.00	$28.00
92-160-0	Tiffany Chevron	CR - BLOWN GLASS - POLAND	ORNAMENT	YES	1992	$28.00	$180.00
92-161-0	Tiffany Bright Harlequin	CR - BLOWN GLASS - POLAND	ORNAMENT	YES	1992	$28.00	$76.00
92-162-0	Tiffany Alpine Flowers	CR - BLOWN GLASS - POLAND	ORNAMENT	YES	1992	$28.00	$35.00
92-163-0	Tiffany Pastel Harlequin	CR - BLOWN GLASS - POLAND	ORNAMENT	YES	1992	$28.00	$28.00
92-164-0	Just Like Grandma's	CR - BLOWN GLASS - POLAND	ORNAMENT	YES	1992	$10.00	$180.00
92-166-0	Kitty Rattle	CR - BLOWN GLASS - POLAND	ORNAMENT	1993	1992	$18.00	$73.00
92-167-0	Honey Bear	CR - BLOWN GLASS - POLAND	ORNAMENT		1992	$14.00	$45.00
92-169-0	Country Scene	CR - BLOWN GLASS - POLAND	ORNAMENT	1993	1992	$12.00	$60.00
92-170-0	Norwegian Princess	CR - BLOWN GLASS - POLAND	ORNAMENT	YES	1992	$15.00	$60.00
92-171-0	Snake Prince	CR - BLOWN GLASS - POLAND	ORNAMENT	1994	1992	$19.00	$40.00
92-172-0	Village Carolers	CR - BLOWN GLASS - POLAND	ORNAMENT	YES	1992	$17.00	$35.00
92-172-1	Star Children	CR - BLOWN GLASS - POLAND	ORNAMENT	1993	1992	$17.00	$35.00
92-173-0	Floral Cascade Finial	CR - BLOWN GLASS - POLAND	FINIAL	YES	1992	$68.00	$85.00
92-176-0	Country Star Quilt	CR - BLOWN GLASS - POLAND	ORNAMENT	YES	1992	$12.00	$70.00
92-178-0	Thunderbolt	CR - BLOWN GLASS - GERMANY	ORNAMENT	YES	1992	$60.00	$65.00
92-179-0	Chimney Sweep Bell	CR - BLOWN GLASS - GERMANY	ORNAMENT	1993	1992	$27.00	$75.00
92-181-0	Elephant Reflector	CR - BLOWN GLASS - GERMANY	ORNAMENT	YES	1992	$17.00	$50.00
92-183-0	Faith, Hope & Love	CR - BLOWN GLASS - GERMANY	ORNAMENT	YES	1992	$12.00	$35.00
92-184-0	Polar Bear	CR - BLOWN GLASS - GERMANY	ORNAMENT	1993	1992	$16.00	$40.00
92-185-0	Benjamin's Nutcrackers	CR - BLOWN GLASS - GERMANY	ORNAMENT	1993	1992	$58.00	$145.00
92-186-0	Eveningstar Santa	CR - BLOWN GLASS - GERMANY	ORNAMENT	1993	1992	$60.00	$175.00
92-187-0	Majestic Reflector	CR - BLOWN GLASS - GERMANY	ORNAMENT	1993	1992	$70.00	$175.00
92-188-0	Gabriel's Trumpets	CR - BLOWN GLASS - CZECH REP.	ORNAMENT	YES	1992	$20.00	$22.00
92-189-0	Crescent Moons	CR - BLOWN GLASS - POLAND	ORNAMENT		1992	$26.00	$50.00
92-189-1	Crescent Moons	CR - BLOWN GLASS - POLAND	ORNAMENT	1995	1992	$32.00	$32.00
92-190-0	Versailles Finial	CR - BLOWN GLASS - GERMANY	FINIAL	YES	1992	$80.00	$80.00
92-191-1	Down the Chimney	CR - BLOWN GLASS - POLAND	ORNAMENT	YES	1992	$17.00	$25.00
92-194-A	Old Salem Quilt Series	CR - BLOWN GLASS - POLAND	ORNAMENT	1993	1992	$28.00	$60.00
92-194-B	Old Salem Quilt Series	CR - BLOWN GLASS - POLAND	ORNAMENT	1993	1992	$28.00	$60.00
92-194-0	Quilted Hearts	CR - BLOWN GLASS - POLAND	ORNAMENT	YES	1992	$28.00	$75.00
92-198-0	Scarlett's Wedding Dress	CR - BLOWN GLASS - POLAND	FINIAL		1992	$70.00	$70.00
92-198-1	Ruby Scarlett Finial	CR - BLOWN GLASS - POLAND	FINIAL		1992	$90.00	$90.00
92-201-0	Flutter Bys	CR - BLOWN GLASS - CZECH REP.	ORNAMENT	1993	1992	$11.00	$35.00
92-202-0	Christmas Trim	CR - BLOWN GLASS - CZECH REP.	GARLAND	YES	1992	$16.00	$50.00
92-203-0	Circus Garland	CR - BLOWN GLASS - CZECH REP.	GARLAND	1993	1992	$30.00	$65.00
92-204-0	Sterling Silver	CR - BLOWN GLASS - CZECH REP.	GARLAND	YES	1992	$12.00	$50.00
92-205-0	Federal Garland	CR - BLOWN GLASS - CZECH REP.	GARLAND		1992	$36.00	$36.00
92-206-0	Ice Berries	CR - BLOWN GLASS - CZECH REP.	ORNAMENT	1993	1992	$36.00	$75.00
92-207-0	Ruby Beads	CR - BLOWN GLASS - CZECH REP.	GARLAND	YES	1992	$15.00	$40.00
92-208-0	Gold Link Chain	CR - BLOWN GLASS - CZECH REP.	GARLAND	1993	1992	$16.00	$50.00
92-209-0	Snow Flakes	CR - BLOWN GLASS - CZECH REP.	ORNAMENT	1993	1992	$10.00	$40.00
92-210-0	Glass Sleigh	CR - BLOWN GLASS - CZECH REP.	ORNAMENT	YES	1992	$14.00	$15.00
92-211-0	Starburst Tree Topper	CR - BLOWN GLASS - CZECH REP.	ORNAMENT	YES	1992	$20.00	$25.00
92-211-1	Starburst Tree Topper	CR - BLOWN GLASS - CZECH REP.	ORNAMENT	1994	1992	$26.00	$26.00
92-212-0	Christmas Spider	CR - BLOWN GLASS - CZECH REP.	ORNAMENT		1992	$22.00	$22.00
92-212-1	Christmas Spider	CR - BLOWN GLASS - CZECH REP.	ORNAMENT		1992	$32.00	$32.00
92-213-0	Northstars	CR - BLOWN GLASS - CZECH REP.	ORNAMENT	1993	1992	$12.00	$15.00
92-214-0	Starbursts	CR - BLOWN GLASS - CZECH REP.	ORNAMENT	1993	1992	$12.00	$65.00
92-215-0	Sail Away	CR - BLOWN GLASS - CZECH REP.	ORNAMENT	YES	1992	$22.00	$35.00
92-216-0	Locomotive Garland	CR - BLOWN GLASS - CZECH REP.	GARLAND	1993	1992	$60.00	$120.00
92-217-0	Wedding Bells	CR - BLOWN GLASS - GERMANY	ORNAMENT	YES	1992	$40.00	$220.00
92-218-0A	Harold Lloyd Reflectors	CR - BLOWN GLASS - GERMANY	ORNAMENT	YES	1992	$70.00	$70.00
92-218-0	Harold Lloyd Reflectors	CR - BLOWN GLASS - GERMANY	ORNAMENT	YES	1992	$70.00	$300.00
92-220-0	Santa Claus Garland	CR - BLOWN GLASS - GERMANY	GARLAND	YES	1992	$66.00	$100.00
92-220-1	St. Nicholas Garland	CR - BLOWN GLASS - GERMANY	GARLAND		1992	$64.00	$64.00
92-221-0	Trumpet Angel Garland	CR - BLOWN GLASS - GERMANY	GARLAND	YES	1992	$66.00	$100.00
92-221-1	Heavenly Chords	CR - BLOWN GLASS - GERMANY	GARLAND	1993	1992	$64.00	$100.00
92-222-0	Pink Passion	CR - BLOWN GLASS - CZECH REP.	GARLAND	YES	1992	$18.00	$45.00
92-223-0	Sorbet	CR - BLOWN GLASS - CZECH REP.	GARLAND	YES	1992	$22.00	$50.00
92-223-1	Sorbet	CR - BLOWN GLASS - CZECH REP.	GARLAND	1993	1992	$22.00	$50.00
92-224-0	Pine Cone	CR - BLOWN GLASS - CZECH REP.	GARLAND	YES	1992	$50.00	$60.00
92-226-0	Ice Capade	CR - BLOWN GLASS - CZECH REP.	GARLAND	YES	1992	$42.00	$50.00
92-227-0	Extravagance	CR - BLOWN GLASS - CZECH REP.	GARLAND		1992	$64.00	$64.00
92-227-2	Extravagance	CR - BLOWN GLASS - CZECH REP.	GARLAND	1995	1992	$68.00	$68.00
92-228-0	Candy Stripes	CR - BLOWN GLASS - CZECH REP.	GARLAND	YES	1992	$45.00	$45.00
92-239-0	To Grandmother's House We Go	CR - BLOWN GLASS - POLAND	ORNAMENT	YES	1992	$20.00	$50.00
92-240-0	Cinderella's Bluebirds	CR - BLOWN GLASS - POLAND	ORNAMENT	1993	1992	$26.00	$55.00
92-241-0	Ice Pear	CR - BLOWN GLASS - POLAND	ORNAMENT	YES	1992	$20.00	$50.00
93-052-0	Silver Bells	CR - BLOWN GLASS - CZECH REP.	GARLAND	1993	1993	$27.00	$27.00
93-053-0	Jewel Tones	CR - BLOWN GLASS - CZECH REP.	GARLAND	YES	1993	$29.00	$29.00
93-053-1	Jewel Tones	CR - BLOWN GLASS - CZECH REP.	GARLAND		1993	$56.00	$56.00
93-054-0	Fly Away Home	CR - BLOWN GLASS - CZECH REP.	GARLAND	1993	1993	$33.00	$33.00
93-055-0	Dynasty	CR - BLOWN GLASS - GERMANY	GARLAND		1993	$49.00	$49.00
93-055-1	Dynasty	CR - BLOWN GLASS - GERMANY	GARLAND		1993	$64.00	$64.00
93-055-2	Dynasty	CR - BLOWN GLASS - GERMANY	GARLAND	1995	1993	$60.00	$60.00
93-056-0	Balloon Parade	CR - BLOWN GLASS - CZECH REP.	GARLAND		1993	$38.00	$38.00

Order No.	Title	Type	Theme	Retired	Intro. Year	Retial Price	Secondary Price
93-056-1	Balloon Parade	CR - BLOWN GLASS - CZECH REP.	GARLAND		1993	$66.00	$66.00
93-056-2	Balloon Parade	CR - BLOWN GLASS - CZECH REP.	GARLAND	1995	1993	$70.00	$70.00
93-058-0	Winter Wonderland	CR - BLOWN GLASS - POLAND	GARLAND		1993	$58.00	$58.00
93-058-1	Winter Wonderland	CR - BLOWN GLASS - POLAND	GARLAND		1993	$66.00	$66.00
93-058-2	Winter Wonderland	CR - BLOWN GLASS - POLAND	GARLAND		1993	$68.00	$68.00
93-059-0	Pisces	CR - BLOWN GLASS - CZECH REP.	GARLAND		1993	$37.00	$37.00
93-059-1	Pisces	CR - BLOWN GLASS - CZECH REP.	GARLAND		1993	$76.00	$76.00
93-060-0	Deco Trees	CR - BLOWN GLASS - CZECH REP.	GARLAND	1993	1993	$42.00	$42.00
93-061-0	Jingle Bells	CR - BLOWN GLASS - GERMANY	GARLAND		1993	$64.00	$64.00
93-061-1	Jingle Bells	CR - BLOWN GLASS - GERMANY	GARLAND		1993	$64.00	$64.00
93-061-2	Jingle Bells	CR - BLOWN GLASS - GERMANY	GARLAND	1995	1993	$68.00	$68.00
93-064-0	Nuts & Berries	CR - BLOWN GLASS - CZECH REP.	GARLAND		1993	$58.00	$58.00
93-064-1	Nuts & Berries	CR - BLOWN GLASS - CZECH REP.	GARLAND		1993	$66.00	$66.00
93-064-2	Nuts & Berries	CR - BLOWN GLASS - CZECH REP.	GARLAND		1993	$80.00	$80.00
93-065-0	Starry Night	CR - BLOWN GLASS - GERMANY	GARLAND	1993	1993	$49.00	$49.00
93-067-0	Vintage	CR - BLOWN GLASS - CZECH REP.	GARLAND	1993	1993	$49.00	$49.00
93-068-0	Fantasy I	CR - BLOWN GLASS - CZECH REP.	GARLAND	1993	1993	$48.00	$48.00
93-069-0	South Sea Sparkle	CR - BLOWN GLASS - POLAND	GARLAND	1993	1993	$48.00	$60.00
93-071-0	Precious Jewels	CR - BLOWN GLASS - CZECH REP.	GARLAND		1993	$28.00	$28.00
93-071-1	Precious Jewels	CR - BLOWN GLASS - CZECH REP.	GARLAND	1995	1993	$42.00	$42.00
93-072-0	Eskimo Elves	CR - BLOWN GLASS - CZECH REP.	GARLAND		1993	$40.00	$40.00
93-072-1	Eskimo Elves	CR - BLOWN GLASS - CZECH REP.	GARLAND		1993	$66.00	$66.00
93-074-0	Celestial Garland	CR - BLOWN GLASS - CZECH REP.	GARLAND	1993	1993	$30.00	$30.00
93-075-0	Sparkle Tones	CR - BLOWN GLASS - CZECH REP.	GARLAND		1993	$42.00	$42.00
93-075-1	Sparkle Tones	CR - BLOWN GLASS - CZECH REP.	GARLAND		1993	$66.00	$66.00
93-075-2	Sparkle Tones	CR - BLOWN GLASS - CZECH REP.	GARLAND	1995	1993	$66.00	$66.00
93-076-0	Santa Hearts	CR - BLOWN GLASS - POLAND	GARLAND		1993	$58.00	$58.00
93-076-1	Santa Hearts	CR - BLOWN GLASS - POLAND	GARLAND		1993	$66.00	$66.00
93-076-2	Santa Hearts	CR - BLOWN GLASS - POLAND	GARLAND	1995	1993	$68.00	$68.00
93-077-0	Hooters	CR - BLOWN GLASS - CZECH REP.	GARLAND		1993	$53.00	$53.00
93-079-0	Bishops Cross	CR - BLOWN GLASS - CZECH REP.	GARLAND	1994	1993	$49.00	$60.00
93-080-0	Bubble Gum	CR - BLOWN GLASS - CZECH REP.	GARLAND		1993	$20.00	$20.00
93-080-1	Bubble Gum	CR - BLOWN GLASS - CZECH REP.	GARLAND	1995	1993	$40.00	$40.00
93-080-2	Bubble Gum	CR - BLOWN GLASS - CZECH REP.	GARLAND		1993	$43.00	$43.00
93-081-0	Carnival	CR - BLOWN GLASS - CZECH REP.	GARLAND		1993	$27.00	$27.00
93-081-1	Carnival	CR - BLOWN GLASS - CZECH REP.	GARLAND		1993	$32.00	$32.00
93-082-0	Mushroom Cone	CR - BLOWN GLASS - POLAND	GARLAND	1993	1993	$42.00	$42.00
93-083-0	Clowning Around	CR - BLOWN GLASS - CZECH REP.	GARLAND	YES	1993	$43.00	$68.00
93-083-1	Clowning Around	CR - BLOWN GLASS - CZECH REP.	GARLAND	1995	1993	$68.00	$68.00
93-085-0	Jack N Jill	CR - BLOWN GLASS - CZECH REP.	GARLAND	1993	1993	$41.00	$150.00
93-086-0	Alpine Wings	CR - BLOWN GLASS - POLAND	GARLAND	1993	1993	$58.00	$108.00
93-088-0	Fantasy II	CR - BLOWN GLASS - CZECH REP.	GARLAND	1994	1993	$41.00	$41.00
93-089-0	Snow Bears	CR - BLOWN GLASS - CZECH REP.	GARLAND		1993	$46.00	$46.00
93-091-0	Special Delivery	CR - BLOWN GLASS - GERMANY	ORNAMENT		1993	$17.00	$17.00
93-091-1	Special Delivery	CR - BLOWN GLASS - GERMANY	ORNAMENT		1993	$18.00	$18.00
93-091-2	Special Delivery	CR - BLOWN GLASS - GERMANY	ORNAMENT		1993	$22.00	$22.00
93-092-0	President Taft	CR - BLOWN GLASS - GERMANY	ORNAMENT		1993	$15.00	$15.00
93-092-1	Don't Hold Your Breath	CR - BLOWN GLASS - GERMANY	ORNAMENT	1995	1993	$22.00	$22.00
93-094-0	Tweeter	CR - BLOWN GLASS - CZECH REP.	ORNAMENT	1993	1993	$4.00	$18.00
93-095-0	Waddles	CR - BLOWN GLASS - CZECH REP.	ORNAMENT	1993	1993	$4.00	$30.00
93-096-0	It's A Small World	CR - BLOWN GLASS - GERMANY	ORNAMENT		1993	$17.00	$17.00
93-096-1	It's A Small World	CR - BLOWN GLASS - GERMANY	ORNAMENT		1993	$24.00	$24.00
93-097-0	Monkey Man	CR - BLOWN GLASS - POLAND	ORNAMENT	1993	1993	$16.00	$115.00
93-098-0	Snowday Santa	CR - BLOWN GLASS - GERMANY	ORNAMENT	1993	1993	$20.00	$60.00
93-099-0	Ski Baby	CR - BLOWN GLASS - GERMANY	ORNAMENT		1993	$21.00	$34.00
93-099-2	Ski Baby	CR - BLOWN GLASS - GERMANY	ORNAMENT		1993	$24.00	$24.00
93-100-0	Hansel & Gretel	CR - BLOWN GLASS - GERMANY	ORNAMENT	YES	1993	$24.00	$24.00
93-100-1	Hansel & Gretel	CR - BLOWN GLASS - GERMANY	ORNAMENT	1994	1993	$29.00	$35.00
93-101-0	Piggly Wiggly	CR - BLOWN GLASS - GERMANY	ORNAMENT	1994	1993	$11.00	$30.00
93-102-0	Injun Joe	CR - BLOWN GLASS - GERMANY	ORNAMENT		1993	$20.00	$20.00
93-102-1	Injun Joe	CR - BLOWN GLASS - GERMANY	ORNAMENT		1993	$23.00	$23.00
93-102-2	Injun Joe	CR - BLOWN GLASS - GERMANY	ORNAMENT		1993	$24.00	$24.00
93-103-0	Sunny Side Up	CR - BLOWN GLASS - GERMANY	ORNAMENT	1993	1993	$22.00	$45.00
93-104-0	Radio Monkey	CR - BLOWN GLASS - GERMANY	ORNAMENT	YES	1993	$17.00	$17.00
93-104-1	Radio Monkey	CR - BLOWN GLASS - GERMANY	ORNAMENT	1994	1993	$19.00	$19.00
93-106-0	Mooning Over You	CR - BLOWN GLASS - GERMANY	ORNAMENT		1993	$17.00	$17.00
93-106-2	Mooning Over You	CR - BLOWN GLASS - GERMANY	ORNAMENT		1993	$24.00	$24.00
93-108-0	Beyond The Stars	CR - BLOWN GLASS - GERMANY	ORNAMENT	1993	1993	$19.00	$45.00
93-112-0	Santa Baby	CR - BLOWN GLASS - POLAND	ORNAMENT		1993	$18.00	$18.00
93-114-0	Blue Top	CR - BLOWN GLASS - POLAND	ORNAMENT	1993	1993	$16.00	$35.00
93-116-0	Glory On High	CR - BLOWN GLASS - POLAND	ORNAMENT	1993	1993	$17.00	$17.00
93-118-0	Candle Light	CR - BLOWN GLASS - GERMANY	CLIP-ON ORNAMENT		1993	$16.00	$16.00
93-118-1	Candle Light	CR - BLOWN GLASS - GERMANY	CLIP-ON ORNAMENT		1993	$19.00	$19.00
93-118-2	Candle Light	CR - BLOWN GLASS - GERMANY	ORNAMENT		1993	$21.00	$21.00
93-120-0	Silent Night	CR - BLOWN GLASS - GERMANY	ORNAMENT	YES	1993	$18.00	$48.00
93-120-1	Silent Night	CR - BLOWN GLASS - GERMANY	ORNAMENT	1994	1993	$27.00	$27.00
93-123-0	Wings and a Prayer	CR - BLOWN GLASS - GERMANY	ORNAMENT		1993	$12.00	$12.00
93-123-1	Pretty In Pink	CR - BLOWN GLASS - GERMANY	ORNAMENT		1993	$18.00	$18.00
93-123-2	Wings and a Prayer	CR - BLOWN GLASS - GERMANY	CLIP-ON ORNAMENT		1993	$22.00	$22.00
93-123-3	Wings and a Prayer	CR - BLOWN GLASS - GERMANY	CLIP-ON ORNAMENT		1993	$22.00	$22.00
93-127-0	Santa In Space	CR - BLOWN GLASS - GERMANY	ORNAMENT		1993	$39.00	$180.00
93-124-0	Guardian Angel	CR - BLOWN GLASS - GERMANY	ORNAMENT		1993	$32.00	$32.00
93-124-1	Guardian Angel	CR - BLOWN GLASS - GERMANY	ORNAMENT		1993	$50.00	$50.00
93-124-2	Guardian Angel	CR - BLOWN GLASS - GERMANY	STARLIGHT/RISING STAR EXCL.		1993	$84.00	$120.00
93-125-0	Elf Bell	CR - BLOWN GLASS - GERMANY	ORNAMENT		1993	$18.00	$18.00
93-125-1	Elf Bell	CR - BLOWN GLASS - GERMANY	ORNAMENT		1993	$22.00	$22.00
93-125-2	Elf Bell	CR - BLOWN GLASS - GERMANY	ORNAMENT	1995	1993	$22.00	$22.00
93-126-0	Monkey Business	CR - BLOWN GLASS - GERMANY	ORNAMENT	1993	1993	$15.00	$15.00
93-127-1	Santa In Space	CR - BLOWN GLASS - GERMANY	ORNAMENT		1993	$44.00	$44.00
93-127-2	Santa In Space	CR - BLOWN GLASS - GERMANY	ORNAMENT		1993	$48.00	$48.00
93-128-1A	Moon Dust	CR - BLOWN GLASS - GERMANY	ORNAMENT	1994	1993	$18.00	$18.00
93-128-0	Moon Dust	CR - BLOWN GLASS - GERMANY	ORNAMENT	YES	1993	$15.00	$45.00
93-132-0	Angel Of Peace	CR - BLOWN GLASS - GERMANY	ORNAMENT	1993	1993	$17.00	$48.00

Order No.	Title	Type	Theme	Retired	Intro. Year	Retail Price	Secondary Price
93-133-0	Sailing Sun	CR - BLOWN GLASS - POLAND	ORNAMENT		1993	$42.00	$42.00
93-135-0	Joey B. Clown	CR - BLOWN GLASS - GERMANY	ORNAMENT	1993	1993	$26.00	$65.00
93-136-0A	Forest Bells	CR - BLOWN GLASS - GERMANY	ORNAMENT		1993	$25.00	$25.00
93-136-1A	Forest Bells	CR - BLOWN GLASS - GERMANY	ORNAMENT		1993	$28.00	$28.00
93-136-0	Forest Bells	CR - BLOWN GLASS - GERMANY	ORNAMENT		1993	$25.00	$25.00
93-136-1	Forest Bells	CR - BLOWN GLASS - GERMANY	ORNAMENT		1993	$28.00	$28.00
93-136-2	Forest Bells	CR - BLOWN GLASS - GERMANY	ORNAMENT		1993	$32.00	$32.00
93-136-2A	Forest Bells	CR - BLOWN GLASS - GERMANY	ORNAMENT		1993	$32.00	$32.00
93-137-0	Holiday Inn	CR - BLOWN GLASS - GERMANY	ORNAMENT		1993	$21.00	$21.00
93-138-0	Far Out Santa	CR - BLOWN GLASS - POLAND	ORNAMENT		1993	$39.00	$64.00
93-138-1	Far Out Santa	CR - BLOWN GLASS - POLAND	ORNAMENT		1993	$48.00	$48.00
93-140-0	Saraband	CR - BLOWN GLASS - POLAND	ORNAMENT	1993	1993	$28.00	$190.00
93-142-0	Pinecone Santa	CR - BLOWN GLASS - GERMANY	ORNAMENT		1993	$24.00	$24.00
93-142-1	Pinecone Santa	CR - BLOWN GLASS - GERMANY	ORNAMENT		1993	$30.00	$36.00
93-142-2	Pinecone Santa	CR - BLOWN GLASS - GERMANY	ORNAMENT		1993	$36.00	$36.00
93-143-0	Fantasia	CR - BLOWN GLASS - POLAND	ORNAMENT	1993	1993	$24.00	$24.00
93-144-0	Holiday Sparkle	CR - BLOWN GLASS - POLAND	ORNAMENT		1993	$27.00	$27.00
93-146-0	Pennsylvania Dutch	CR - BLOWN GLASS - POLAND	ORNAMENT	1993	1993	$27.00	$32.00
93-147-0	Deco Snow Fall	CR - BLOWN GLASS - POLAND	ORNAMENT	1993	1993	$27.00	$43.00
93-148-0	Rambling Rose	CR - BLOWN GLASS - POLAND	ORNAMENT	1993	1993	$27.00	$50.00
93-149-0	1939 World's Fair	CR - BLOWN GLASS - POLAND	ORNAMENT	1993	1993	$27.00	$75.00
93-150-0	Pineapple Quilt	CR - BLOWN GLASS - POLAND	ORNAMENT	1993	1993	$27.00	$65.00
93-151-0	Remembrance	CR - BLOWN GLASS - POLAND	ORNAMENT	1993	1993	$27.00	$50.00
93-152-0	French Rose	CR - BLOWN GLASS - POLAND	ORNAMENT	1993	1993	$27.00	$30.00
93-154-0	Rainbow Reflector	CR - BLOWN GLASS - POLAND	ORNAMENT	1993	1993	$27.00	$45.00
93-155-0	Snowman By Candlelight	CR - BLOWN GLASS - POLAND	ORNAMENT	1994	1993	$26.50	$27.00
93-157-0	Serenade Pink	CR - BLOWN GLASS - POLAND	ORNAMENT	1993	1993	$27.00	$68.00
93-158-0	Gold Fish	CR - BLOWN GLASS - POLAND	ORNAMENT	1993	1993	$26.00	$44.00
93-161-0	French Regency Balloon	CR - BLOWN GLASS - POLAND	ORNAMENT		1993	$29.00	$29.00
93-164-0A	Winter Birds	CR - BLOWN GLASS - POLAND	ORNAMENT	1993	1993	$27.00	$40.00
93-164-0	Winter Birds	CR - BLOWN GLASS - POLAND	ORNAMENT	1993	1993	$27.00	$42.00
93-166-0	Copenhagen	CR - BLOWN GLASS - POLAND	ORNAMENT	1993	1993	$27.00	$80.00
93-167-2	Cool Scotch Pine	CR - BLOWN GLASS - POLAND	ORNAMENT	1995	1993	$32.00	$32.00
93-172-0	Anassazi	CR - BLOWN GLASS - POLAND	ORNAMENT	1993	1993	$27.00	$375.00
93-175-0	Star Fire	CR - BLOWN GLASS - POLAND	ORNAMENT		1993	$27.00	$27.00
93-175-1	Star Fire	CR - BLOWN GLASS - GERMANY	ORNAMENT	1995	1993	$32.00	$55.00
93-176-0	Versailles Balloon	CR - BLOWN GLASS - POLAND	ORNAMENT		1993	$29.00	$29.00
93-179-0	Allegro	CR - BLOWN GLASS - POLAND	ORNAMENT	1994	1993	$27.00	$72.00
93-180-0	Little Doggie	CR - BLOWN GLASS - GERMANY	ORNAMENT	1993	1993	$7.00	$25.00
93-181-0	Will	CR - BLOWN GLASS - GERMANY	ORNAMENT	YES	1993	$23.00	$23.00
93-181-1	Will	CR - BLOWN GLASS - GERMANY	ORNAMENT	1994	1993	$25.00	$25.00
93-182-0A	Rising Stars	CR - BLOWN GLASS - GERMANY	ORNAMENT		1993	$9.50	$13.00
93-182-0	Rising Stars	CR - BLOWN GLASS - GERMANY	ORNAMENT		1993	$9.50	$13.00
93-182-1	Rising Stars	CR - BLOWN GLASS - GERMANY	ORNAMENT	1996	1993	$13.00	$13.00
93-184-0	Cool Cat	CR - BLOWN GLASS - GERMANY	ORNAMENT		1993	$21.00	$42.00
93-185-0	Sugar Plum	CR - BLOWN GLASS - GERMANY	ORNAMENT		1993	$7.00	$7.00
93-186-0	Pixie Santa	CR - BLOWN GLASS - GERMANY	ORNAMENT	YES	1993	$16.00	$42.00
93-186-1	Pixie Santa	CR - BLOWN GLASS - GERMANY	ORNAMENT	YES	1993	$20.00	$20.00
93-187-0	Little Slugger	CR - BLOWN GLASS - GERMANY	ORNAMENT	1994	1993	$22.00	$30.00
93-188-0	Letter to Santa	CR - BLOWN GLASS - GERMANY	ORNAMENT	1994	1993	$22.00	$50.00
93-189-0	Accordion Elf	CR - BLOWN GLASS - GERMANY	ORNAMENT	YES	1993	$21.00	$55.00
93-189-1	Accordion Elf	CR - BLOWN GLASS - GERMANY	ORNAMENT	YES	1993	$22.00	$22.00
93-191-0	Goofy Garden	CR - BLOWN GLASS - GERMANY	ORNAMENT	1993	1993	$15.00	$150.00
93-198-0	Victorian Santa Reflector	CR - BLOWN GLASS - GERMANY	ORNAMENT	1993	1993	$28.00	$75.00
93-200-0	Just Like Grandma's	CR - BLOWN GLASS - GERMANY	ORNAMENT	1993	1993	$8.00	$28.00
93-202-0	Sweetheart	CR - BLOWN GLASS - POLAND	ORNAMENT	1993	1993	$16.00	$25.00
93-203-0	Devotion	CR - BLOWN GLASS - GERMANY	ORNAMENT	1993	1993	$17.00	$32.00
93-205-0	Country Flowers	CR - BLOWN GLASS - POLAND	ORNAMENT	1993	1993	$16.00	$35.00
93-206-0	Rainy Day Friend	CR - BLOWN GLASS - POLAND	ORNAMENT	1993	1993	$22.00	$70.00
93-211-0	Daniel Star	CR - BLOWN GLASS - GERMANY	ORNAMENT		1993	$26.00	$26.00
93-211-1	Daniel Star	CR - BLOWN GLASS - GERMANY	ORNAMENT		1993	$29.00	$29.00
93-211-2	Daniel Star	CR - BLOWN GLASS - GERMANY	ORNAMENT	1995	1993	$32.00	$32.00
93-212-0	Mushroom Santa	CR - BLOWN GLASS - POLAND	ORNAMENT		1993	$28.00	$28.00
93-213-0	Jewel Box	CR - BLOWN GLASS - POLAND	ORNAMENT	1993	1993	$12.00	$12.00
93-214-0	Twister	CR - BLOWN GLASS - POLAND	ORNAMENT	1993	1993	$17.00	$55.00
93-217-0	Thomas Nast Santa	CR - BLOWN GLASS - GERMANY	ORNAMENT		1993	$23.00	$42.00
93-217-1	Thomas Nast Santa	CR - BLOWN GLASS - GERMANY	ORNAMENT	1995	1993	$26.00	$26.00
93-219-0	Del Monte	CR - BLOWN GLASS - GERMANY	ORNAMENT		1993	$24.00	$24.00
93-219-1	Del Monte	CR - BLOWN GLASS - GERMANY	ORNAMENT		1993	$44.00	$44.00
93-221-0	Tutti Frutti	CR - BLOWN GLASS - ITALY	ITALIAN FIGURAL		1993	$26.00	$26.00
93-221-1	Tutti Frutti	CR - BLOWN GLASS - ITALY	ITALIAN FIGURAL	1996	1993	$28.00	$43.00
93-221-2	Tutti Frutti	CR - BLOWN GLASS - ITALY	ITALIAN FIGURAL		1993	$36.00	$36.00
93-222-0	One Small Leap	CR - BLOWN GLASS - ITALY	ITALIAN FIGURAL		1993	$26.00	$78.00
93-223-0	Wally	CR - BLOWN GLASS - ITALY	ITALIAN FIGURAL		1993	$26.00	$34.00
93-223-1	Wally	CR - BLOWN GLASS - ITALY	ITALIAN FIGURAL		1993	$34.00	$150.00
93-224-0	Centurian	CR - BLOWN GLASS - ITALY	ITALIAN FIGURAL	1993	1993	$26.00	$150.00
93-225-0	Nellie	CR - BLOWN GLASS - ITALY	ITALIAN FIGURAL	1993	1993	$28.00	$100.00
93-226-0	Teenage Mermaid	CR - BLOWN GLASS - ITALY	ITALIAN FIGURAL		1993	$28.00	$48.00
93-226-1	Teenage Mermaid	CR - BLOWN GLASS - ITALY	ITALIAN FIGURAL		1993	$48.00	$48.00
93-227-0	Siegfred	CR - BLOWN GLASS - ITALY	ITALIAN FIGURAL		1993	$25.00	$60.00
93-227-1	Siegfred	CR - BLOWN GLASS - ITALY	ITALIAN FIGURAL		1993	$26.00	$34.00
93-227-2	Siegfred	CR - BLOWN GLASS - ITALY	ITALIAN FIGURAL		1993	$25.00	$35.00
93-228-0	Bowzer	CR - BLOWN GLASS - ITALY	ITALIAN FIGURAL	1993	1993	$24.00	$300.00
93-229-0	Light In The Window	CR - BLOWN GLASS - ITALY	ORNAMENT		1993	$25.00	$27.00
93-229-1	Light In The Window	CR - BLOWN GLASS - ITALY	ORNAMENT		1993	$28.00	$28.00
93-232-1	Dancing Harlequin	CR - BLOWN GLASS - ITALY	ITALIAN FIGURAL		1993	$44.00	$60.00
93-230-0	V.I.P.	CR - BLOWN GLASS - ITALY	ITALIAN FIGURAL	1993	1993	$23.00	$130.00
93-235-1	Fly Boy	CR - BLOWN GLASS - ITALY	ITALIAN FIGURAL		1993	$60.00	$60.00
93-231-0	Grecian Urn	CR - BLOWN GLASS - ITALY	ORNAMENT	1993	1993	$23.00	$45.00
93-236-0A	Stocking Stuffers	CR - BLOWN GLASS - ITALY	ORNAMENT	1993	1993	$16.00	$19.00
93-232-0	Dancing Harlequin	CR - BLOWN GLASS - ITALY	ITALIAN FIGURAL	1993	1993	$36.00	$60.00
93-237-0	Aladdin's Lamp	CR - BLOWN GLASS - ITALY	ORNAMENT	1994	1993	$20.00	$50.00
93-232-2	Dancing Harlequin	CR - BLOWN GLASS - ITALY	ITALIAN FIGURAL	1995	1993	$60.00	$60.00

Order No.	Title	Type	Theme	Retired	Intro. Year	Retial Price	Secondary Price
93-233-0	Twinkle Toes	CR - BLOWN GLASS - ITALY	ITALIAN FIGURAL	YES	1993	$28.00	$52.00
93-233-1	Twinkle Toes	CR - BLOWN GLASS - ITALY	ITALIAN FIGURAL	YES	1993	$38.00	$52.00
93-233-2	Twinkle Toes	CR - BLOWN GLASS - ITALY	ITALIAN FIGURAL	1996	1993	$48.00	$52.00
93-234-0	English Kitchen	CR - BLOWN GLASS - ITALY	ORNAMENT	YES	1993	$26.00	$43.00
93-235-0	Fly Boy	CR - BLOWN GLASS - ITALY	ITALIAN FIGURAL		1993	$33.00	$60.00
93-239-0	Bedtime Buddy	CR - BLOWN GLASS - ITALY	ITALIAN FIGURAL	1993	1993	$29.00	$100.00
93-236-0	Stocking Stuffers	CR - BLOWN GLASS - ITALY	ORNAMENT	1993	1993	$16.00	$16.00
93-238-0	Sailor Man	CR - BLOWN GLASS - ITALY	ITALIAN FIGURAL	1993	1993	$22.00	$22.00
93-240-0	Maxine	CR - BLOWN GLASS - ITALY	ITALIAN FIGURAL		1993	$20.00	$72.00
93-240-1	Maxine	CR - BLOWN GLASS - ITALY	ITALIAN FIGURAL		1993	$32.00	$28.00
93-241-1	Two Eggs Are Better Than One	CR - BLOWN GLASS - ITALY	ITALIAN FIGURAL		1993	$24.00	$24.00
93-241-0	Eggman	CR - BLOWN GLASS - ITALY	ITALIAN FIGURAL		1993	$22.50	$55.00
93-241-2	Two Eggs Are Better Than One	CR - BLOWN GLASS - ITALY	ITALIAN FIGURAL		1993	$31.00	$31.00
93-242-0	Skating Bettinas	CR - BLOWN GLASS - ITALY	ITALIAN FIGURAL		1993	$29.00	$85.00
93-242-1	Skating Bettinas	CR - BLOWN GLASS - ITALY	ITALIAN FIGURAL		1993	$36.00	$36.00
93-242-2	Skating Bettinas	CR - BLOWN GLASS - ITALY	ITALIAN FIGURAL		1993	$48.00	$48.00
93-243-0	Crystal Fountain	CR - BLOWN GLASS - ITALY	ITALIAN FIGURAL		1993	$34.00	$75.00
93-244-0	Tea & Sympathy	CR - BLOWN GLASS - ITALY	ITALIAN FIGURAL		1993	$20.00	$34.00
93-244-1	Tea & Sympathy	CR - BLOWN GLASS - ITALY	ITALIAN FIGURAL		1993	$35.00	$34.00
93-245-0	Kissing Cousins	CR - BLOWN GLASS - ITALY	ITALIAN FIGURAL		1993	$30.00	$250.00
93-245-1	Kissing Cousins	CR - BLOWN GLASS - ITALY	ITALIAN FIGURAL		1993	$28.00	$28.00
93-245-2	Kissing Cousins	CR - BLOWN GLASS - ITALY	ITALIAN FIGURAL		1993	$56.00	$56.00
93-246-0	Auld Lang Syne	CR - BLOWN GLASS - ITALY	ORNAMENT	1993	1993	$15.00	$50.00
93-247-0	Snow Dance	CR - BLOWN GLASS - ITALY	ITALIAN FIGURAL		1993	$29.00	$63.00
93-248-0	Pinocchio	CR - BLOWN GLASS - ITALY	ITALIAN FIGURAL		1993	$26.00	$47.00
93-248-1	Pinocchio	CR - BLOWN GLASS - ITALY	ITALIAN FIGURAL	1995	1993	$30.00	$50.00
93-249-0	Circus Seal	CR - BLOWN GLASS - ITALY	ITALIAN FIGURAL	1993	1993	$32.00	$70.00
93-250-0	Forest Friends	CR - BLOWN GLASS - ITALY	ITALIAN FIGURAL	1993	1993	$28.00	$32.00
93-251-0	Lamp Light	CR - BLOWN GLASS - ITALY	ITALIAN FIGURAL	1993	1993	$24.00	$24.00
93-252-0	Gerard	CR - BLOWN GLASS - ITALY	ITALIAN FIGURAL	1996	1993	$26.00	$36.00
93-253-0	Emperor's Pet	CR - BLOWN GLASS - ITALY	ITALIAN FIGURAL	1993	1993	$22.00	$140.00
93-254-0	Tinkle Tree	CR - BLOWN GLASS - GERMANY	ORNAMENT	1994	1993	$16.00	$35.00
93-255-0	Flora Dora	CR - BLOWN GLASS - GERMANY	ORNAMENT		1993	$25.00	$25.00
93-255-1	Wednesday	CR - BLOWN GLASS - GERMANY	ORNAMENT	1994	1993	$42.00	$42.00
93-256-0	Angel Light	CR - BLOWN GLASS - GERMANY	ORNAMENT	1993	1993	$16.00	$16.00
93-257-0	Faberge Egg	CR - BLOWN GLASS - GERMANY	ORNAMENT	1993	1993	$18.00	$35.00
93-258-0	Pagoda	CR - BLOWN GLASS - GERMANY	ORNAMENT	1993	1993	$8.00	$12.00
93-259-0	Time Piece	CR - BLOWN GLASS - GERMANY	ORNAMENT		1993	$17.00	$17.00
93-260-0	Grandpa Bear	CR - BLOWN GLASS - GERMANY	ORNAMENT	1993	1993	$13.00	$22.00
93-263-0	Prince Albert	CR - BLOWN GLASS - GERMANY	ORNAMENT	1993	1993	$23.00	$64.00
93-266-0	Northwind	CR - BLOWN GLASS - POLAND	ORNAMENT		1993	$17.00	$60.00
93-268-0A	Bells Are Ringing	CR - BLOWN GLASS - GERMANY	ORNAMENT		1993	$18.00	$18.00
93-268-0B	Bells Are Ringing	CR - BLOWN GLASS - GERMANY	ORNAMENT		1993	$18.00	$18.00
93-268-1A	Bells Are Ringing	CR - BLOWN GLASS - GERMANY	ORNAMENT		1993	$22.00	$22.00
93-268-1B	Bells Are Ringing	CR - BLOWN GLASS - GERMANY	ORNAMENT		1993	$22.00	$22.00
93-268-0	Bells Are Ringing	CR - BLOWN GLASS - GERMANY	ORNAMENT		1993	$18.00	$18.00
93-268-1	Bells Are Ringing	CR - BLOWN GLASS - GERMANY	ORNAMENT		1993	$22.00	$22.00
93-277-0	Rainbow Shark	CR - BLOWN GLASS - GERMANY	ORNAMENT		1993	$18.00	$70.00
93-271-0	Celeste	CR - BLOWN GLASS - GERMANY	ORNAMENT	1993	1993	$26.00	$120.00
93-272-0	Wacko	CR - BLOWN GLASS - POLAND	ORNAMENT	1994	1993	$24.00	$24.00
93-273-0	Tannenbaum	CR - BLOWN GLASS - GERMANY	ORNAMENT		1993	$24.00	$34.00
93-277-1	Rainbow Shark	CR - BLOWN GLASS - GERMANY	ORNAMENT		1993	$26.00	$24.00
93-278-0A	Candied Citrus	CR - BLOWN GLASS - GERMANY	ORNAMENT		1993	$9.00	$13.00
93-316-0	Fiesta Ball	CR - BLOWN GLASS - POLAND	ORNAMENT	1993	1993	$27.00	$66.00
93-278-0	Candied Citrus	CR - BLOWN GLASS - GERMANY	ORNAMENT		1993	$9.00	$13.00
93-279-0	Emerald Wizard	CR - BLOWN GLASS - POLAND	ORNAMENT	1993	1993	$18.00	$60.00
93-281-0	Eskimo Kitty	CR - BLOWN GLASS - POLAND	ORNAMENT	1993	1993	$15.00	$40.00
93-282-0	Fleurice	CR - BLOWN GLASS - GERMANY	ORNAMENT	1993	1993	$24.00	$24.00
93-283-0	Crocus Blossom	CR - BLOWN GLASS - GERMANY	ORNAMENT	1993	1993	$16.00	$16.00
93-284-0	Ice Bear	CR - BLOWN GLASS - GERMANY	ORNAMENT		1993	$18.00	$50.00
93-284-1	Polar Bear	CR - BLOWN GLASS - GERMANY	ORNAMENT		1993	$18.00	$19.00
93-284-2	Ice Bears	CR - BLOWN GLASS - GERMANY	ORNAMENT		1993	$19.00	$19.00
93-285-0	By Jiminy	CR - BLOWN GLASS - GERMANY	ORNAMENT	1993	1993	$17.00	$60.00
93-288-0	Spintop Santa	CR - BLOWN GLASS - GERMANY	ORNAMENT		1993	$23.00	$23.00
93-288-1	Spintop Santa	CR - BLOWN GLASS - GERMANY	ORNAMENT		1993	$38.00	$38.00
93-290-0	Monterey	CR - BLOWN GLASS - POLAND	ORNAMENT	1993	1993	$15.00	$80.00
93-291-0	Bell House Boy	CR - BLOWN GLASS - GERMANY	ORNAMENT	1993	1993	$21.00	$27.00
93-292-0	Georgian Santa	CR - BLOWN GLASS - GERMANY	ORNAMENT		1993	$30.00	$34.00
93-292-1	Georgian Santa	CR - BLOWN GLASS - GERMANY	ORNAMENT		1993	$46.00	$34.00
93-295-0	Church Bell	CR - BLOWN GLASS - GERMANY	ORNAMENT		1993	$24.00	$24.00
93-343-0	Cathedral Bells	CR - BLOWN GLASS - GERMANY	ORNAMENT	1993	1993	$8.00	$8.00
93-295-1	Church Bell	CR - BLOWN GLASS - GERMANY	ORNAMENT	1995	1993	$26.00	$32.00
93-296-0	Beauregard	CR - BLOWN GLASS - GERMANY	ORNAMENT		1993	$24.00	$24.00
93-296-1	Beauregard	CR - BLOWN GLASS - GERMANY	ORNAMENT		1993	$28.00	$28.00
93-296-2	Beauregard	CR - BLOWN GLASS - GERMANY	ORNAMENT		1993	$26.00	$26.00
93-299-0	Crowned Passion	CR - BLOWN GLASS - GERMANY	ORNAMENT	1993	1993	$23.00	$45.00
93-302-0	Jumbo Spintops	CR - BLOWN GLASS - POLAND	ORNAMENT		1993	$27.00	$36.00
93-302-1	Jumbo Spintops	CR - BLOWN GLASS - POLAND	ORNAMENT		1993	$36.00	$36.00
93-303-0	Carnival Rides	CR - BLOWN GLASS - CZECH REP.	ORNAMENT	1993	1993	$18.00	$80.00
93-304-0	Deer Drop	CR - BLOWN GLASS - POLAND	ORNAMENT	1993	1993	$34.00	$34.00
93-305-0A	Palais Royale	CR - BLOWN GLASS - CZECH REP.	ORNAMENT		1993	$16.00	$16.00
93-305-0	Palais Royale	CR - BLOWN GLASS - CZECH REP.	ORNAMENT	1994	1993	$16.00	$16.00
93-306-0	Grand Monarch	CR - BLOWN GLASS - CZECH REP.	ORNAMENT		1993	$16.00	$16.00
93-306-1	Grand Monarch	CR - BLOWN GLASS - CZECH REP.	ORNAMENT	1995	1993	$32.00	$32.00
93-308-0	Crystal Rainbow	CR - BLOWN GLASS - POLAND	ORNAMENT	1993	1993	$30.00	$225.00
93-349-0	Time Will Tell	CR - BLOWN GLASS - GERMANY	ORNAMENT		1993	$22.00	$22.00
93-317-0	North Woods	CR - BLOWN GLASS - POLAND	ORNAMENT	1993	1993	$27.00	$50.00
93-320-0	Santa Tree	CR - BLOWN GLASS - POLAND	ORNAMENT	YES	1993	$66.00	$250.00
93-322-0	Celestial Peacock Finial	CR - BLOWN GLASS - POLAND	FINIAL		1993	$69.00	$223.00
93-323-0	Rose Pointe Finial	CR - BLOWN GLASS - POLAND	FINIAL	1993	1993	$34.00	$27.00
93-329-0	Santa's Helper	CR - BLOWN GLASS - POLAND	ORNAMENT		1993	$17.00	$17.00
93-330-0	St. Nick's Pipe	CR - BLOWN GLASS - CZECH REP.	ORNAMENT	1994	1993	$5.00	$38.00
93-332-0	Class Clown	CR - BLOWN GLASS - GERMANY	ORNAMENT		1993	$21.00	$48.00

Order No.	Title	Type	Theme	Retired	Intro. Year	Retail Price	Secondary Price
93-333-0	Jack Frost	CR - BLOWN GLASS - POLAND	ORNAMENT		1993	$23.00	$34.00
93-333-1	Jack Frost	CR - BLOWN GLASS - POLAND	ORNAMENT		1993	$24.00	$24.00
93-333-2	Jack Frost	CR - BLOWN GLASS - POLAND	ORNAMENT	1995	1993	$24.00	$24.00
93-334-0	Tiffany Bells	CR - BLOWN GLASS - CZECH REP.	ORNAMENT		1993	$9.00	$9.00
93-335-0	Bavarian Santa	CR - BLOWN GLASS - GERMANY	ORNAMENT		1993	$23.00	$37.00
93-335-1	Bavarian Santa	CR - BLOWN GLASS - GERMANY	ORNAMENT		1993	$32.00	$32.00
93-337-0	Action Pack	CR - BLOWN GLASS - CZECH REP.	ORNAMENT		1993	$11.00	$11.00
93-337-1	Action Pack	CR - BLOWN GLASS - CZECH REP.	ORNAMENT		1993	$13.00	$13.00
93-337-2	Action Pack	CR - BLOWN GLASS - CZECH REP.	ORNAMENT		1993	$13.00	$13.00
93-338-0	Texas Star	CR - BLOWN GLASS - CZECH REP.	ORNAMENT	1993	1993	$8.00	$8.00
93-340-0	Starshine	CR - BLOWN GLASS - CZECH REP.	ORNAMENT	1993	1993	$10.00	$10.00
93-341-0	Enchanted Garden	CR - BLOWN GLASS - CZECH REP.	ORNAMENT	1993	1993	$6.00	$10.00
93-342-0	Christmas Stars	CR - BLOWN GLASS - CZECH REP.	ORNAMENT		1993	$14.00	$28.00
93-353-0	U-Boat	CR - BLOWN GLASS - GERMANY	ORNAMENT	1993	1993	$16.00	$51.00
93-344-0	Pompadour	CR - BLOWN GLASS - GERMANY	ORNAMENT	1993	1993	$9.00	$9.00
93-345-0	Sporty	CR - BLOWN GLASS - GERMANY	ORNAMENT	YES	1993	$20.00	$20.00
93-345-1	Sporty	CR - BLOWN GLASS - GERMANY	ORNAMENT	1994	1993	$24.00	$24.00
93-346-0	Lucky Shoe	CR - BLOWN GLASS - GERMANY	ORNAMENT	1993	1993	$16.00	$16.00
93-382-1	Jubilee Finial	CR - BLOWN GLASS - CZECH REP.	FINIAL	1994	1993	$44.00	$44.00
93-358-0	Circus Star	CR - BLOWN GLASS - GERMANY	ORNAMENT		1993	$24.00	$24.00
93-358-1	Circus Star	CR - BLOWN GLASS - GERMANY	ORNAMENT		1993	$34.00	$34.00
93-360-0	Black Forest Clock	CR - BLOWN GLASS - GERMANY	ORNAMENT		1993	$20.00	$20.00
93-361-0	Little Boy Blue	CR - BLOWN GLASS - GERMANY	ORNAMENT	1993	1993	$26.00	$35.00
93-363-0	Confucius	CR - BLOWN GLASS - POLAND	ORNAMENT	1993	1993	$19.00	$47.00
93-365-0	First Snow	CR - BLOWN GLASS - CZECH REP.	ORNAMENT		1993	$10.00	$17.00
93-365-1	First Snow	CR - BLOWN GLASS - CZECH REP.	ORNAMENT		1993	$15.00	$17.00
93-365-2	First Snow	CR - BLOWN GLASS - CZECH REP.	ORNAMENT		1993	$17.00	$17.00
93-366-0	Rainbow Snow	CR - BLOWN GLASS - CZECH REP.	ORNAMENT		1993	$10.00	$16.00
93-366-1	Rainbow Snow	CR - BLOWN GLASS - CZECH REP.	ORNAMENT		1993	$15.00	$16.00
93-366-2	Rainbow Snow	CR - BLOWN GLASS - CZECH REP.	ORNAMENT		1993	$16.00	$16.00
93-367-0A	Goofy Fruits	CR - BLOWN GLASS - GERMANY	ORNAMENT		1993	$14.00	$14.00
93-367-0B	Goofy Fruits	CR - BLOWN GLASS - GERMANY	ORNAMENT		1993	$14.00	$14.00
93-367-0C	Goofy Fruits	CR - BLOWN GLASS - GERMANY	ORNAMENT		1993	$14.00	$14.00
93-367-0	Goofy Fruits	CR - BLOWN GLASS - GERMANY	ORNAMENT		1993	$14.00	$14.00
93-368-0	Sugar Shack	CR - BLOWN GLASS - POLAND	ORNAMENT		1993	$22.00	$24.00
93-368-1	Sugar Shack	CR - BLOWN GLASS - POLAND	ORNAMENT		1993	$24.00	$24.00
93-369-0	Cloud Nine	CR - BLOWN GLASS - GERMANY	ORNAMENT		1993	$25.00	$25.00
93-369-1	Cloud Nine	CR - BLOWN GLASS - GERMANY	ORNAMENT	1995	1993	$42.00	$42.00
93-371-0	Gypsy Girl	CR - BLOWN GLASS - POLAND	ORNAMENT	1993	1993	$16.00	$25.00
93-376-0	Pineapple Slice	CR - BLOWN GLASS - GERMANY	ORNAMENT	1994	1993	$14.00	$14.00
93-377-0	Star Ribbons	CR - BLOWN GLASS - GERMANY	ORNAMENT		1993	$16.00	$16.00
93-377-1	Star Ribbons	CR - BLOWN GLASS - GERMANY	ORNAMENT	YES	1993	$22.00	$22.00
93-379-0	Away In The Manger	CR - BLOWN GLASS - GERMANY	ORNAMENT		1993	$24.00	$24.00
93-379-1	Away In The Manger	CR - BLOWN GLASS - GERMANY	ORNAMENT	1995	1993	$28.00	$28.00
93-380-0	Nesting Stork Finial	CR - BLOWN GLASS - CZECH REP.	FINIAL	1994	1993	$50.00	$50.00
93-380-1	Nesting Stork Finial	CR - BLOWN GLASS - CZECH REP.	FINIAL	YES	1993	$64.00	$64.00
93-381-0	Crescendo Finial	CR - BLOWN GLASS - CZECH REP.	FINIAL		1993	$50.00	$50.00
93-403-0	Siberian Sleighride	CR - BLOWN GLASS - POLAND	ORNAMENT	1996	1993	$27.00	$32.00
93-381-1	Golden Crescendo Finial	CR - BLOWN GLASS - CZECH REP.	FINIAL	1994	1994	$82.00	$120.00
93-382-0	Jubilee Finial	CR - BLOWN GLASS - CZECH REP.	FINIAL	YES	1993	$30.00	$30.00
93-384-0	Mountain Christmas	CR - BLOWN GLASS - GERMANY	ORNAMENT		1993	$26.00	$26.00
93-406-1	Gilded Cage	CR - BLOWN GLASS - POLAND	ORNAMENT		1993	$52.00	$52.00
93-384-1	Mountain Christmas	CR - BLOWN GLASS - GERMANY	ORNAMENT		1993	$29.00	$29.00
93-384-2	Mountain Christmas	CR - BLOWN GLASS - GERMANY	ORNAMENT	1995	1993	$28.00	$28.00
93-388-0	Cathedral Cross	CR - BLOWN GLASS - CZECH REP.	ORNAMENT	1994	1993	$13.00	$13.00
93-389-0	Purse	CR - BLOWN GLASS - CZECH REP.	ORNAMENT	1993	1993	$16.00	$16.00
93-390-0	Star Bell Set	CR - BLOWN GLASS - CZECH REP.	ORNAMENT	1993	1993	$11.00	$11.00
93-392-0	Quartet	CR - BLOWN GLASS - CZECH REP.	ORNAMENT	1993	1993	$4.00	$9.00
93-393-0	Spider And The Fly	CR - BLOWN GLASS - CZECH REP.	ORNAMENT	1993	1993	$7.00	$12.00
93-394-0	Christmas Express	CR - BLOWN GLASS - CZECH REP.	GARLAND		1993	$58.00	$175.00
93-394-1	Christmas Express	CR - BLOWN GLASS - CZECH REP.	GARLAND		1993	$72.00	$80.00
93-394-2	Christmas Express	CR - BLOWN GLASS - CZECH REP.	GARLAND		1993	$80.00	$80.00
93-395-0	Santa Star	CR - BLOWN GLASS - POLAND	GARLAND		1993	$58.00	$68.00
93-395-1	Santa By Starlight	CR - BLOWN GLASS - POLAND	GARLAND		1993	$60.00	$68.00
93-395-2	Santa By Starlight	CR - BLOWN GLASS - POLAND	GARLAND		1993	$68.00	$68.00
93-397-0	Crescent Moons Finial	CR - BLOWN GLASS - POLAND	FINIAL		1993	$69.00	$69.00
93-398-0	Siberian Sleighride Finial	CR - BLOWN GLASS - POLAND	FINIAL		1993	$72.00	$72.00
93-399-0	Russian Jewel Hearts Finial	CR - BLOWN GLASS - POLAND	FINIAL		1993	$80.00	$90.00
93-399-1	Russian Jewel Hearts Finial	CR - BLOWN GLASS - POLAND	FINIAL		1993	$90.00	$90.00
93-421-0	Epiphany	CR - BLOWN GLASS - POLAND	ORNAMENT	1994	1993	$29.00	$82.00
93-405-0	Ice Star Santa	CR - BLOWN GLASS - POLAND	ORNAMENT	1993	1993	$38.00	$350.00
93-406-0	Gilded Cage	CR - BLOWN GLASS - POLAND	ORNAMENT		1993	$44.00	$75.00
93-407-0	Anchor Santa	CR - BLOWN GLASS - POLAND	ORNAMENT		1993	$32.00	$72.00
93-407-2	Anchor Santa	CR - BLOWN GLASS - POLAND	ORNAMENT	1995	1993	$36.00	$36.00
93-408-0	Classic Christmas	CR - BLOWN GLASS - POLAND	ORNAMENT	1994	1993	$29.00	$29.00
91-153-1	Holly Ribbons Finial	CR - BLOWN GLASS - POLAND	FINIAL		1993	$69.00	$69.00
93-412-0	Celestial Finial	CR - BLOWN GLASS - POLAND	ORNAMENT		1993	$69.00	$69.00
89-049-1	Holly Ribbons	CR - BLOWN GLASS - POLAND	ORNAMENT		1993	$27.00	$27.00
89-049-2	Holly Ribbons	CR - BLOWN GLASS - POLAND	ORNAMENT		1989	$32.00	$32.00
93-155-0A	Snowman By Candlelight	CR - BLOWN GLASS - POLAND	ORNAMENT	1994	1993	$26.50	$54.00
93-422-0	Holiday Spice	CR - BLOWN GLASS - POLAND	ORNAMENT	1993	1993	$24.00	$34.00
93-423-0	Moon Jump	CR - BLOWN GLASS - POLAND	ORNAMENT	1993	1993	$29.00	$50.00
93-449-0	King's Ransom	CR - BLOWN GLASS - POLAND	GARLAND		1993	$49.00	$49.00
93-SP1	Angels We Have Heard On High	CR - BLOWN GLASS - GERMANY	STARLIGHT MEMBERS ONLY	1994	1993	$50.00	$475.00
93-SP2	Partridge In A Pear Tree	CR - BLOWN GLASS - POLAND	12 DAYS OF CHRISTMAS SERIES	1994	1993	$33.00	$900.00
94-017-0	Waldo	CR - BLOWN GLASS - GERMANY	ORNAMENT		1994	$22.00	$22.00
94-017-1	Waldo	CR - BLOWN GLASS - GERMANY	ORNAMENT	1995	1995	$18.00	$18.00
94-018-0	King Of Kings	CR - BLOWN GLASS - GERMANY	ORNAMENT		1994	$22.00	$32.00
94-018-1	King Of Kings	CR - BLOWN GLASS - GERMANY	ORNAMENT	1995	1994	$22.00	$22.00
94-019-0	Grape Buzz	CR - BLOWN GLASS - GERMANY	ORNAMENT	1995	1994	$19.00	$19.00
94-021-0	Mittens For Kittens	CR - BLOWN GLASS - GERMANY	ORNAMENT	1994	1994	$22.00	$22.00
94-023-0	Harvest Moon	CR - BLOWN GLASS - GERMANY	ORNAMENT	1994	1994	$19.00	$19.00
94-024-0	Red Cap	CR - BLOWN GLASS - GERMANY	ORNAMENT		1994	$19.00	$19.00

Order No.	Title	Type	Theme	Retired	Intro. Year	Retial Price	Secondary Price
94-024-1	Red Cap	CR - BLOWN GLASS - GERMANY	ORNAMENT		1994	$22.00	$22.00
94-025-0	Rajah	CR - BLOWN GLASS - GERMANY	CLIP-ON ORNAMENT		1994	$19.00	$22.00
94-025-1	Rajah	CR - BLOWN GLASS - GERMANY	CLIP-ON ORNAMENT		1994	$22.00	$22.00
94-027-1	Holy Family	CR - BLOWN GLASS - GERMANY	ORNAMENT		1994	$21.00	$21.00
94-029-0	School's Out	CR - BLOWN GLASS - GERMANY	ORNAMENT		1994	$19.00	$19.00
94-029-1	School's Out	CR - BLOWN GLASS - GERMANY	ORNAMENT	1995	1994	$26.00	$26.00
94-030-0	Spring Chick	CR - BLOWN GLASS - GERMANY	ORNAMENT		1994	$27.00	$27.00
94-030-1	Spring Chick	CR - BLOWN GLASS - GERMANY	ORNAMENT		1994	$28.00	$28.00
94-031-0	Rose Cone	CR - BLOWN GLASS - GERMANY	ORNAMENT	1995	1994	$25.00	$25.00
94-031-1	Rose Cone	CR - BLOWN GLASS - GERMANY	ORNAMENT		1994	$25.00	$25.00
94-033-0	Shooting The Moon	CR - BLOWN GLASS - GERMANY	ORNAMENT		1994	$28.00	$28.00
94-033-1	Shooting The Moon	CR - BLOWN GLASS - GERMANY	ORNAMENT		1994	$28.00	$28.00
94-036-0	Tiny Tunes	CR - BLOWN GLASS - GERMANY	ORNAMENT		1994	$22.00	$22.00
94-036-1	Tiny Tunes	CR - BLOWN GLASS - GERMANY	ORNAMENT	1995	1994	$26.00	$26.00
94-037-0	Mr. Smedley Drysdale	CR - BLOWN GLASS - GERMANY	ORNAMENT	1994	1994	$44.00	$200.00
94-038-0	Dutch Maiden	CR - BLOWN GLASS - GERMANY	ORNAMENT		1994	$44.00	$44.00
94-038-1	Dutch Maiden	CR - BLOWN GLASS - GERMANY	ORNAMENT		1994	$44.00	$44.00
94-039-0	Squirrelling Away	CR - BLOWN GLASS - GERMANY	ORNAMENT		1994	$26.00	$26.00
94-039-1	Squirrelling Away	CR - BLOWN GLASS - GERMANY	ORNAMENT	1995	1994	$28.00	$28.00
94-040-0	Owl Reflector	CR - BLOWN GLASS - GERMANY	ORNAMENT		1994	$54.00	$64.00
94-040-1	Owl Reflector	CR - BLOWN GLASS - GERMANY	ORNAMENT	1995	1994	$74.00	$74.00
94-041-0	Season's Greetings	CR - BLOWN GLASS - GERMANY	ORNAMENT		1994	$42.00	$42.00
94-041-1	Season's Greetings	CR - BLOWN GLASS - GERMANY	ORNAMENT	1995	1994	$45.00	$45.00
94-042-0	Heavens Above Finial	CR - BLOWN GLASS - GERMANY	FINIAL		1994	$76.00	$76.00
94-043-0	Rub A Dub Dub	CR - BLOWN GLASS - POLAND	ORNAMENT	1995	1994	$19.00	$19.00
94-044-0	Queen's Hare	CR - BLOWN GLASS - POLAND	ORNAMENT	1996	1994	$22.00	$22.00
94-045-0	Masquerade	CR - BLOWN GLASS - POLAND	ORNAMENT	1994	1994	$16.00	$20.00
94-075-1	Radiant Birth	CR - BLOWN GLASS - GERMANY	STARLIGHT/RISING STAR EXCL.		1994	$86.00	$86.00
94-046-0	Humpty Dumpty	CR - BLOWN GLASS - POLAND	ORNAMENT		1994	$19.00	$19.00
94-046-1	Humpty Dumpty	CR - BLOWN GLASS - POLAND	ORNAMENT		1994	$22.00	$22.00
94-047-0	Little Orphan	CR - BLOWN GLASS - POLAND	ORNAMENT	1994	1994	$18.00	$18.00
94-076-0	Mandolin Angel	CR - BLOWN GLASS - GERMANY	ORNAMENT		1994	$46.00	$46.00
94-048-0	Andy Gump	CR - BLOWN GLASS - POLAND	ORNAMENT	1994	1994	$18.00	$35.00
94-049-0	Tiny Ted	CR - BLOWN GLASS - POLAND	ORNAMENT		1994	$15.00	$15.00
94-050-0	Fido	CR - BLOWN GLASS - POLAND	ORNAMENT	1994	1994	$20.00	$20.00
94-051-0	Jockey Pipe	CR - BLOWN GLASS - POLAND	ORNAMENT	1994	1994	$36.00	$145.00
94-052-0	Smiley	CR - BLOWN GLASS - POLAND	ORNAMENT	1994	1994	$16.00	$40.00
94-076-1	Mandolin Angel	CR - BLOWN GLASS - GERMANY	ORNAMENT		1994	$48.00	$48.00
94-053-0	Terrance	CR - BLOWN GLASS - POLAND	ORNAMENT	1994	1994	$16.00	$30.00
94-078-1	Time To Spare	CR - BLOWN GLASS - GERMANY	ORNAMENT	1995	1994	$32.00	$32.00
94-055-0	English Santa	CR - BLOWN GLASS - POLAND	ORNAMENT		1994	$26.00	$26.00
94-055-1	English Santa	CR - BLOWN GLASS - POLAND	ORNAMENT	1995	1994	$26.00	$26.00
94-056-0	Bag Of Goodies	CR - BLOWN GLASS - POLAND	ORNAMENT		1994	$26.00	$50.00
94-056-1	Bag Of Goodies	CR - BLOWN GLASS - POLAND	ORNAMENT		1994	$30.00	$30.00
94-057-0	Vaudeville Sam	CR - BLOWN GLASS - POLAND	ORNAMENT	1994	1994	$18.00	$18.00
94-058-0	Roly Poly Angel	CR - BLOWN GLASS - POLAND	ORNAMENT		1994	$22.00	$22.00
94-058-1	Roly Poly Angel	CR - BLOWN GLASS - POLAND	ORNAMENT	1995	1994	$22.00	$22.00
94-059-0	Sweet Pear	CR - BLOWN GLASS - POLAND	ORNAMENT	1994	1994	$24.00	$48.00
94-060-0	Moon Ride	CR - BLOWN GLASS - POLAND	ORNAMENT		1994	$28.00	$28.00
94-060-1	Moon Ride	CR - BLOWN GLASS - POLAND	ORNAMENT		1994	$36.00	$36.00
94-061-0	Ring Master	CR - BLOWN GLASS - POLAND	ORNAMENT	yes	1994	$22.00	$22.00
94-061-1	Ring Master	CR - BLOWN GLASS - POLAND	ORNAMENT	1995	1994	$24.00	$24.00
94-062-0	Li'l Bo Peep	CR - BLOWN GLASS - POLAND	ORNAMENT		1994	$22.00	$22.00
94-062-1	Li'l Bo Peep	CR - BLOWN GLASS - POLAND	ORNAMENT	1995	1994	$22.00	$22.00
94-063-0	Ice Man Cometh	CR - BLOWN GLASS - POLAND	ORNAMENT	1995	1994	$22.00	$35.00
94-089-0	Rosy Lovebirds	CR - BLOWN GLASS - GERMANY	CLIP-ON ORNAMENT		1994	$48.00	$48.00
94-064-0	Perky Pete	CR - BLOWN GLASS - POLAND	CLIP-ON ORNAMENT		1994	$30.00	$30.00
94-064-1	Polly Wanna	CR - BLOWN GLASS - POLAND	CLIP-ON ORNAMENT	1996	1994	$34.00	$34.00
94-065-0	St. Nick	CR - BLOWN GLASS - POLAND	ORNAMENT		1994	$18.00	$18.00
94-065-1	St. Nick	CR - BLOWN GLASS - POLAND	ORNAMENT	1995	1994	$22.00	$22.00
94-066-0	Uncle Max	CR - BLOWN GLASS - POLAND	ORNAMENT	1995	1994	$26.00	$26.00
94-067-0	Squash Man	CR - BLOWN GLASS - POLAND	ORNAMENT		1994	$28.00	$38.00
94-067-1	Squash Man	CR - BLOWN GLASS - POLAND	ORNAMENT		1994	$28.00	$28.00
94-068-0	Jack Clown	CR - BLOWN GLASS - POLAND	ORNAMENT	1995	1994	$22.00	$22.00
94-068-1	Jack Clown	CR - BLOWN GLASS - POLAND	ORNAMENT		1994	$24.00	$24.00
94-069-0	Wings Of Peace	CR - BLOWN GLASS - POLAND	ORNAMENT		1994	$22.00	$22.00
94-069-1	Wings Of Peace	CR - BLOWN GLASS - POLAND	ORNAMENT	1995	1994	$22.00	$22.00
94-070-0	Gifted Santa	CR - BLOWN GLASS - POLAND	PEDIATRIC CANCER FUNDRAISER	1994	1994	$25.00	$65.00
94-070-1	Gifted Santa	CR - BLOWN GLASS - POLAND	ORNAMENT	1996	1994	$28.00	$28.00
94-075-0	Radiant Birth	CR - BLOWN GLASS - GERMANY	STARLIGHT/RISING STAR EXCL.		1994	$76.00	$76.00
94-091-1	Snow Dancing	CR - BLOWN GLASS - GERMANY	ORNAMENT		1994	$38.00	$38.00
94-078-0	Time To Spare	CR - BLOWN GLASS - GERMANY	ORNAMENT		1994	$29.00	$29.00
94-083-0	Mother And Child	CR - BLOWN GLASS - GERMANY	ORNAMENT	1994	1994	$29.00	$29.00
94-086-0	Mountain Church	CR - BLOWN GLASS - GERMANY	STARLIGHT/RISING STAR EXCL.		1994	$42.00	$42.00
94-086-1	Mountain Church	CR - BLOWN GLASS - GERMANY	STARLIGHT/RISING STAR EXCL.		1994	$58.00	$58.00
94-091-0	Snow Dancing	CR - BLOWN GLASS - GERMANY	ORNAMENT		1994	$29.00	$29.00
94-112-0	Pretty Bird	CR - BLOWN GLASS - GERMANY	ORNAMENT		1994	$26.00	$26.00
94-092-0	Circus Band	CR - BLOWN GLASS - GERMANY	ORNAMENT		1994	$34.00	$34.00
94-092-1	Circus Band	CR - BLOWN GLASS - GERMANY	ORNAMENT	1995	1994	$44.00	$44.00
94-094-0	Wedded Bliss	CR - BLOWN GLASS - GERMANY	ORNAMENT		1994	$88.00	$160.00
94-094-1	Wedded Bliss	CR - BLOWN GLASS - GERMANY	ORNAMENT		1994	$100.00	$100.00
94-096-0	Frat Brothers	CR - BLOWN GLASS - GERMANY	ORNAMENT	1994	1994	$22.00	$22.00
94-097-0	Misty	CR - BLOWN GLASS - POLAND	ORNAMENT		1994	$19.00	$19.00
94-097-1	Misty	CR - BLOWN GLASS - POLAND	ORNAMENT	1995	1994	$22.00	$22.00
94-098-0	Ice House	CR - BLOWN GLASS - POLAND	ORNAMENT		1994	$14.00	$14.00
94-098-1	Ice House	CR - BLOWN GLASS - POLAND	ORNAMENT		1994	$16.00	$16.00
94-100-0	Tiny Nautilus	CR - BLOWN GLASS - POLAND	ORNAMENT		1994	$12.00	$12.00
94-100-1	Tiny Nautilus	CR - BLOWN GLASS - POLAND	ORNAMENT		1994	$14.00	$30.00
94-101-0	Oh My Stars	CR - BLOWN GLASS - POLAND	ORNAMENT		1994	$12.00	$12.00
94-101-1	Oh My Stars	CR - BLOWN GLASS - POLAND	ORNAMENT	1995	1994	$14.00	$14.00
94-102-0	Peking Santa	CR - BLOWN GLASS - POLAND	ORNAMENT	1994	1994	$18.00	$25.00
94-108-0	Stocking Sam	CR - BLOWN GLASS - GERMANY	ORNAMENT		1994	$23.00	$55.00
94-108-1	Stocking Sam	CR - BLOWN GLASS - POLAND	ORNAMENT	1995	1994	$22.00	$22.00

Order No.	Title	Type	Theme	Retired	Intro. Year	Retail Price	Secondary Price
94-109-0	Guitar Santa	CR - BLOWN GLASS - GERMANY	ORNAMENT		1994	$28.00	$28.00
94-109-1	Guitar Santa	CR - BLOWN GLASS - GERMANY	ORNAMENT		1994	$32.00	$32.00
94-110-0	Puppy Love	CR - BLOWN GLASS - POLAND	ORNAMENT		1994	$22.00	$22.00
94-110-1	Puppy Love	CR - BLOWN GLASS - GERMANY	ORNAMENT	1995	1994	$22.00	$22.00
94-112-1	Pretty Bird	CR - BLOWN GLASS - GERMANY	CLIP-ON ORNAMENT		1994	$38.00	$38.00
94-113-0	Christmas In Camelot	CR - BLOWN GLASS - GERMANY	ORNAMENT	1995	1994	$27.00	$50.00
94-114-0	Ringing Red Boots	CR - BLOWN GLASS - GERMANY	ORNAMENT		1994	$46.00	$46.00
94-114-1	Ringing Red Boots	CR - BLOWN GLASS - GERMANY	ORNAMENT	1995	1994	$48.00	$48.00
94-123-0	Bunny Hop	CR - BLOWN GLASS - GERMANY	ORNAMENT		1994	$24.00	$24.00
94-200-0	Blue Satin	CR - BLOWN GLASS - POLAND	ORNAMENT	1994	1994	$29.00	$32.00
94-200-1	Blue Satin	CR - BLOWN GLASS - POLAND	ORNAMENT	1995	1994	$32.00	$32.00
94-123-1	Bunny Hop	CR - BLOWN GLASS - GERMANY	ORNAMENT		1994	$24.00	$24.00
94-126-0	Carousel Willy	CR - BLOWN GLASS - GERMANY	ORNAMENT	1994	1994	$74.00	$74.00
94-134-0	Kaiser Pipe	CR - BLOWN GLASS - GERMANY	ORNAMENT		1994	$32.00	$32.00
94-134-1	Kaiser Pipe	CR - BLOWN GLASS - GERMANY	ORNAMENT		1994	$34.00	$34.00
94-135-0	Angelique	CR - BLOWN GLASS - GERMANY	ORNAMENT		1994	$34.00	$34.00
94-135-1	Angelique	CR - BLOWN GLASS - GERMANY	ORNAMENT	1996	1994	$52.00	$52.00
94-136-0	Bright Heavens Above	CR - BLOWN GLASS - GERMANY	ORNAMENT	1994	1994	$56.00	$66.00
94-203-0	Autumn Tapestry	CR - BLOWN GLASS - POLAND	ORNAMENT		1994	$29.00	$32.00
94-138-0	Jack O'Lantern	CR - BLOWN GLASS - GERMANY	ORNAMENT		1994	$39.00	$39.00
94-141-0	Angel Song	CR - BLOWN GLASS - GERMANY	ORNAMENT	1994	1994	$46.00	$46.00
94-142-0	Soldier Boy	CR - BLOWN GLASS - GERMANY	CLIP-ON ORNAMENT		1994	$19.00	$100.00
94-143-0	Sky Dive	CR - BLOWN GLASS - GERMANY	ORNAMENT		1994	$22.00	$22.00
94-143-1	Sky Dive	CR - BLOWN GLASS - GERMANY	ORNAMENT	1995	1994	$22.00	$22.00
94-144-0	Peep's Sheep	CR - BLOWN GLASS - GERMANY	ORNAMENT		1994	$16.00	$16.00
94-144-1	Peep's Sheep	CR - BLOWN GLASS - GERMANY	CLIP-ON ORNAMENT		1994	$18.00	$18.00
94-145-0	Liberty Bell	CR - BLOWN GLASS - GERMANY	ORNAMENT		1994	$22.00	$22.00
94-146-0	Forget Your Troubles	CR - BLOWN GLASS - GERMANY	ORNAMENT	1994	1994	$17.00	$35.00
94-148-0A	Yuletide Bells	CR - BLOWN GLASS - CZECH REP.	ORNAMENT	1994	1994	$12.00	$12.00
94-148-0	Yuletide Bells	CR - BLOWN GLASS - CZECH REP.	ORNAMENT	1994	1994	$12.00	$12.00
94-151-0	Ring Twice	CR - BLOWN GLASS - GERMANY	ORNAMENT		1994	$21.00	$21.00
94-151-1	Ring Twice	CR - BLOWN GLASS - GERMANY	ORNAMENT	1995	1994	$24.00	$24.00
94-155-0	The Los Angeles	CR - BLOWN GLASS - GERMANY	ORNAMENT	1994	1994	$26.00	$35.00
94-156-0	Honey Belle	CR - BLOWN GLASS - GERMANY	STARLIGHT/RISING STAR EXCL.	1994	1994	$74.00	$125.00
94-159-0	Stocking Full	CR - BLOWN GLASS - POLAND	ORNAMENT		1994	$24.00	$32.00
94-161-0	All Wrapped Up	CR - BLOWN GLASS - POLAND	ORNAMENT	1996	1994	$26.00	$28.00
94-163-0	Private Eye	CR - BLOWN GLASS - POLAND	ORNAMENT	1994	1994	$18.00	$30.00
94-165-0	Kayo	CR - BLOWN GLASS - POLAND	ORNAMENT	1994	1994	$14.00	$20.00
94-166-0	Egg Head	CR - BLOWN GLASS - POLAND	ORNAMENT		1994	$19.00	$22.00
94-166-1	Egg Head	CR - BLOWN GLASS - POLAND	ORNAMENT	1996	1994	$22.00	$22.00
94-167-0	Tee Time	CR - BLOWN GLASS - POLAND	ORNAMENT		1994	$16.00	$18.00
94-167-1	Tee Time	CR - BLOWN GLASS - POLAND	ORNAMENT	1995	1994	$18.00	$18.00
94-170-0	Elephant Prince	CR - BLOWN GLASS - POLAND	ORNAMENT	1994	1994	$15.00	$20.00
94-172-0	Liberty Ball	CR - BLOWN GLASS - GERMANY	ORNAMENT		1994	$26.00	$50.00
94-174-0	Metamorphosis	CR - BLOWN GLASS - GERMANY	ORNAMENT	1994	1994	$16.00	$25.00
94-175-0	Mama's Little Angel	CR - BLOWN GLASS - POLAND	ORNAMENT		1994	$23.00	$24.00
94-175-1	Mama's Little Angel	CR - BLOWN GLASS - POLAND	ORNAMENT		1994	$24.00	$24.00
94-183-0	Aunt Kitty	CR - BLOWN GLASS - POLAND	ORNAMENT		1994	$26.00	$26.00
94-183-1	Aunt Kitty	CR - BLOWN GLASS - POLAND	ORNAMENT	1995	1994	$26.00	$26.00
94-188-0	Windswept	CR - BLOWN GLASS - POLAND	ORNAMENT		1994	$29.00	$32.00
94-188-1	Windswept	CR - BLOWN GLASS - POLAND	ORNAMENT	1996	1994	$32.00	$32.00
94-194-0	Hieroglyph	CR - BLOWN GLASS - POLAND	ORNAMENT	1994	1994	$29.00	$62.00
94-196-0	Serenity	CR - BLOWN GLASS - ITALY	ORNAMENT	1994	1994	$44.00	$44.00
94-197-0	White Nights	CR - BLOWN GLASS - CZECH REP.	ORNAMENT	1994	1994	$26.00	$71.00
94-203-1	Autumn Tapestry	CR - BLOWN GLASS - POLAND	ORNAMENT	1996	1994	$32.00	$32.00
94-205-0	Stafford Floral	CR - BLOWN GLASS - POLAND	ORNAMENT	1994	1994	$29.00	$112.00
94-206-0	Top Cat	CR - BLOWN GLASS - POLAND	ORNAMENT	1994	1994	$29.00	$29.00
94-208-0	Angel Bounty	CR - BLOWN GLASS - ITALY	ORNAMENT	1994	1994	$44.00	$60.00
94-210-0	Jolly Stripes	CR - BLOWN GLASS - POLAND	ORNAMENT	1995	1994	$28.00	$28.00
94-211-0	Epiphany Ball	CR - BLOWN GLASS - POLAND	ORNAMENT		1994	$29.00	$34.00
94-211-1	Epiphany Ball	CR - BLOWN GLASS - POLAND	ORNAMENT	1996	1994	$32.00	$34.00
94-212-0	Camille	CR - BLOWN GLASS - POLAND	ORNAMENT		1994	$29.00	$32.00
94-213-0	Valcourt	CR - BLOWN GLASS - POLAND	ORNAMENT		1994	$29.00	$29.00
94-216-0	Christmas Harlequin	CR - BLOWN GLASS - POLAND	ORNAMENT		1994	$29.00	$32.00
94-219-0	Cool Cat	CR - BLOWN GLASS - GERMANY	ORNAMENT	1994	1994	$26.00	$33.00
94-220-0	Chic Of Araby	CR - BLOWN GLASS - POLAND	ORNAMENT		1994	$17.00	$39.00
94-220-1	Chic Of Araby	CR - BLOWN GLASS - POLAND	ORNAMENT	1995	1994	$18.00	$18.00
94-221-0	Messiah	CR - BLOWN GLASS - GERMANY	ORNAMENT		1994	$22.00	$24.00
94-221-1	Messiah	CR - BLOWN GLASS - GERMANY	ORNAMENT	1995	1994	$24.00	$24.00
94-222-0	Crown Of Thorns	CR - BLOWN GLASS - GERMANY	ORNAMENT		1994	$26.00	$30.00
94-222-1	Crown Of Thorns	CR - BLOWN GLASS - GERMANY	ORNAMENT	1995	1994	$30.00	$30.00
94-225-0	Deer-Ring	CR - BLOWN GLASS - GERMANY	ORNAMENT	1994	1994	$16.00	$16.00
94-227-0	Peas On Earth	CR - BLOWN GLASS - POLAND	ORNAMENT		1994	$16.00	$22.00
94-230-0	Moon Mullins	CR - BLOWN GLASS - POLAND	ORNAMENT	1994	1994	$18.00	$32.00
94-232-0	Teddy Roosevelt	CR - BLOWN GLASS - POLAND	ORNAMENT	1995	1994	$22.00	$22.00
94-236-0	Baby Booties/Pink	CR - BLOWN GLASS - POLAND	ORNAMENT	1994	1994	$17.00	$30.00
94-237-0	Snow Bell	CR - BLOWN GLASS - CZECH REP.	ORNAMENT	1994	1994	$12.00	$12.00
94-238-0	Sex Appeal	CR - BLOWN GLASS - POLAND	ORNAMENT		1994	$22.00	$24.00
94-238-1	Sex Appeal	CR - BLOWN GLASS - POLAND	ORNAMENT	1995	1994	$24.00	$24.00
94-239-0	New Year's Babe	CR - BLOWN GLASS - POLAND	ORNAMENT		1994	$21.00	$22.00
94-239-1	New Year's Babe	CR - BLOWN GLASS - POLAND	ORNAMENT	1995	1994	$22.00	$22.00
94-240-0	House Sitting Santa	CR - BLOWN GLASS - POLAND	ORNAMENT		1994	$26.00	$28.00
94-240-1	House Sitting Santa	CR - BLOWN GLASS - POLAND	ORNAMENT		1994	$26.00	$26.00
94-245-0	Tuxedo Carousel	CR - BLOWN GLASS - ITALY	ITALIAN FIGURAL	1996	1994	$52.00	$72.00
94-247-0	On The Run	CR - BLOWN GLASS - ITALY	ITALIAN FIGURAL		1994	$45.00	$100.00
94-247-1	On The Run	CR - BLOWN GLASS - ITALY	ITALIAN FIGURAL		1994	$64.00	$64.00
94-248-0A	My What Big Teeth	CR - BLOWN GLASS - ITALY	ITALIAN FIGURAL		1994	$29.00	$40.00
94-248-0	My What Big Teeth	CR - BLOWN GLASS - ITALY	ITALIAN FIGURAL		1994	$29.00	$40.00
94-248-1	My What Big Teeth	CR - BLOWN GLASS - ITALY	ITALIAN FIGURAL		1994	$40.00	$40.00
94-248-1A	My What Big Teeth	CR - BLOWN GLASS - ITALY	ITALIAN FIGURAL		1994	$40.00	$40.00
94-250-0A	Pinocchio Gets Hitched	CR - BLOWN GLASS - ITALY	ITALIAN FIGURAL		1994	$30.00	$44.00
94-250-0	Pinocchio Gets Hitched	CR - BLOWN GLASS - ITALY	ITALIAN FIGURAL		1994	$30.00	$44.00
94-250-1A	Pinocchio Gets Hitched	CR - BLOWN GLASS - ITALY	ITALIAN FIGURAL		1994	$44.00	$44.00

Order No.	Title	Type	Theme	Retired	Intro. Year	Retial Price	Secondary Price
94-250-1	Pinocchio Gets Hitched	CR - BLOWN GLASS - ITALY	ITALIAN FIGURAL		1994	$44.00	$44.00
94-253-0	King's Guard	CR - BLOWN GLASS - ITALY	ITALIAN FIGURAL		1994	$44.00	$60.00
94-254-0	Bird Brain	CR - BLOWN GLASS - ITALY	ITALIAN FIGURAL	1994	1994	$33.00	$68.00
94-255-0	Chubbs & Slim	CR - BLOWN GLASS - ITALY	ITALIAN FIGURAL	1994	1994	$29.00	$45.00
94-255-0A	Chubbs & Slim	CR - BLOWN GLASS - ITALY	ITALIAN FIGURAL	1994	1994	$29.00	$29.00
94-256-0	Old Sour Puss	CR - BLOWN GLASS - ITALY	ITALIAN FIGURAL	YES	1994	$34.00	$34.00
94-258-0	Bubbly	CR - BLOWN GLASS - ITALY	ITALIAN FIGURAL		1994	$43.00	$48.00
94-260-0	Captain	CR - BLOWN GLASS - ITALY	ITALIAN FIGURAL		1994	$48.00	$145.00
94-260-1	Captain	CR - BLOWN GLASS - ITALY	ITALIAN FIGURAL		1994	$74.00	$74.00
94-261-0	Over The Waves	CR - BLOWN GLASS - ITALY	ITALIAN FIGURAL	1994	1994	$38.00	$38.00
94-262-0	Shivers	CR - BLOWN GLASS - ITALY	ITALIAN FIGURAL	1994	1994	$25.00	$150.00
94-263-0	Ship's Ahoy	CR - BLOWN GLASS - ITALY	ITALIAN FIGURAL	1995	1994	$38.00	$48.00
94-267-0	Bubbles	CR - BLOWN GLASS - ITALY	ITALIAN FIGURAL		1994	$42.00	$54.00
94-267-1	Bubbles	CR - BLOWN GLASS - ITALY	ITALIAN FIGURAL		1994	$54.00	$54.00
94-268-0	Chianti	CR - BLOWN GLASS - ITALY	ITALIAN FIGURAL		1994	$26.00	$26.00
94-269-0	Ollie	CR - BLOWN GLASS - ITALY	ITALIAN FIGURAL		1994	$50.00	$74.00
94-269-1	Ollie	CR - BLOWN GLASS - ITALY	ITALIAN FIGURAL	1996	1994	$74.00	$74.00
94-271-0	Conchita	CR - BLOWN GLASS - ITALY	ITALIAN FIGURAL	1994	1994	$37.00	$55.00
94-272-0	Bird Bath	CR - BLOWN GLASS - ITALY	STARLIGHT/RISING STAR EXCL.	1994	1994	$76.00	$76.00
94-273-0	Wilbur	CR - BLOWN GLASS - ITALY	ITALIAN FIGURAL		1994	$33.00	$48.00
94-273-1	Pork Recipes	CR - BLOWN GLASS - ITALY	ITALIAN FIGURAL	1996	1994	$48.00	$48.00
94-274-0	Party Hopper	CR - BLOWN GLASS - ITALY	ITALIAN FIGURAL	1994	1994	$33.00	$150.00
94-275-0	Glow Worm	CR - BLOWN GLASS - ITALY	ITALIAN FIGURAL		1994	$32.00	$34.00
94-277-0	What A Donkey	CR - BLOWN GLASS - ITALY	ITALIAN FIGURAL	1994	1994	$34.00	$36.00
94-278-0	Swan Fountain	CR - BLOWN GLASS - ITALY	ITALIAN FIGURAL		1994	$44.00	$85.00
94-278-1	Swan Fountain	CR - BLOWN GLASS - ITALY	ITALIAN FIGURAL		1994	$48.00	$48.00
94-279-0	Tomba	CR - BLOWN GLASS - ITALY	ITALIAN FIGURAL		1994	$34.00	$55.00
94-279-1	Downhill Together	CR - BLOWN GLASS - ITALY	ITALIAN FIGURAL		1994	$46.00	$46.00
94-280-0	Mr. Moto	CR - BLOWN GLASS - ITALY	ITALIAN FIGURAL	1994	1994	$36.00	$160.00
94-281-0	Fleet's In	CR - BLOWN GLASS - ITALY	ITALIAN FIGURAL		1994	$38.00	$52.00
94-282-0	Rain Dance	CR - BLOWN GLASS - ITALY	ITALIAN FIGURAL		1994	$34.00	$34.00
94-283-0	Dolly	CR - BLOWN GLASS - ITALY	ITALIAN FIGURAL		1994	$42.00	$60.00
94-283-1	Dolly	CR - BLOWN GLASS - ITALY	ITALIAN FIGURAL		1995	$60.00	$60.00
94-284-0	Cow Poke	CR - BLOWN GLASS - ITALY	ITALIAN FIGURAL		1994	$42.00	$56.00
94-284-1	Cow Poke	CR - BLOWN GLASS - ITALY	ITALIAN FIGURAL		1994	$56.00	$56.00
94-285-0	Cabernet	CR - BLOWN GLASS - ITALY	ITALIAN FIGURAL		1994	$24.00	$24.00
94-285-1	Cabernet	CR - BLOWN GLASS - ITALY	ITALIAN FIGURAL		1994	$24.00	$24.00
94-286-0	Princess	CR - BLOWN GLASS - CZECH REP.	ORNAMENT	1994	1994	$18.00	$18.00
94-287-0	Winter Frolic	CR - BLOWN GLASS - POLAND	ORNAMENT	1995	1994	$18.00	$35.00
94-288-0	Mr. Longneck	CR - BLOWN GLASS - ITALY	ITALIAN FIGURAL	1994	1994	$26.00	$26.00
94-290-0	Lola Ginabridgida	CR - BLOWN GLASS - ITALY	ITALIAN FIGURAL		1994	$44.00	$44.00
94-290-1	Lola Ginabridgida	CR - BLOWN GLASS - ITALY	ITALIAN FIGURAL	1995	1994	$48.00	$48.00
94-291-0	Deercicle	CR - BLOWN GLASS - ITALY	ITALIAN FIGURAL		1994	$29.00	$48.00
94-291-1	Deercicle	CR - BLOWN GLASS - ITALY	ITALIAN FIGURAL		1994	$46.00	$48.00
94-294-0	Piglet	CR - BLOWN GLASS - CZECH REP.	ORNAMENT		1994	$13.00	$13.00
94-294-1	Piglet	CR - BLOWN GLASS - CZECH REP.	ORNAMENT	1995	1994	$17.00	$17.00
94-297-0	Crock O'Dile	CR - BLOWN GLASS - ITALY	ITALIAN FIGURAL		1994	$33.00	$33.00
94-297-1	Crock O'Dile	CR - BLOWN GLASS - ITALY	ITALIAN FIGURAL	1995	1994	$34.00	$33.00
94-298-0	Moon Martian	CR - BLOWN GLASS - ITALY	ITALIAN FIGURAL	1994	1994	$26.00	$80.00
94-299-0	Nighty Night	CR - BLOWN GLASS - ITALY	ITALIAN FIGURAL	1994	1994	$36.00	$120.00
94-300-0	Starry Night	CR - BLOWN GLASS - ITALY	ITALIAN FIGURAL	1994	1994	$31.00	$31.00
94-301-0	Wings And A Snail	CR - BLOWN GLASS - ITALY	ITALIAN FIGURAL		1994	$32.00	$44.00
94-314-0	One Small Step	CR - BLOWN GLASS - ITALY	ITALIAN FIGURAL		1994	$58.00	$72.00
94-301-1	Wings And A Snail	CR - BLOWN GLASS - ITALY	ITALIAN FIGURAL	1995	1994	$44.00	$44.00
94-302-1	Brazilia	CR - BLOWN GLASS - ITALY	ITALIAN FIGURAL	1995	1994	$52.00	$52.00
94-302-0	Brazilia	CR - BLOWN GLASS - ITALY	ITALIAN FIGURAL		1994	$38.00	$48.00
94-303-0	Candelabra	CR - BLOWN GLASS - ITALY	ITALIAN FIGURAL	1994	1994	$33.00	$33.00
94-304-0	Xenon	CR - BLOWN GLASS - ITALY	ITALIAN FIGURAL	1994	1994	$38.00	$175.00
94-306-0	Santa Copter	CR - BLOWN GLASS - ITALY	ITALIAN FIGURAL		1994	$48.00	$48.00
94-306-1	Santa Copter	CR - BLOWN GLASS - ITALY	ITALIAN FIGURAL		1994	$54.00	$54.00
94-307-0	Mexican Hat Dance	CR - BLOWN GLASS - ITALY	ITALIAN FIGURAL	1994	1994	$32.00	$32.00
94-308-0	Bobo	CR - BLOWN GLASS - ITALY	ITALIAN FIGURAL	1994	1994	$31.00	$31.00
94-309-0	Horse Of A Different Color	CR - BLOWN GLASS - ITALY	ITALIAN FIGURAL		1994	$28.00	$28.00
94-310-0	Angel On Board	CR - BLOWN GLASS - ITALY	ITALIAN FIGURAL		1994	$37.00	$37.00
94-310-1	Angel On Board	CR - BLOWN GLASS - ITALY	ITALIAN FIGURAL		1994	$56.00	$56.00
94-311-0	Cheeky Santa	CR - BLOWN GLASS - ITALY	ITALIAN FIGURAL	1994	1994	$22.00	$22.00
94-313-0	Snowy	CR - BLOWN GLASS - ITALY	ITALIAN FIGURAL		1994	$32.00	$44.00
94-314-1	One Small Step	CR - BLOWN GLASS - ITALY	ITALIAN FIGURAL		1994	$72.00	$72.00
94-315-0	Airplane	CR - BLOWN GLASS - ITALY	ITALIAN FIGURAL		1994	$56.00	$76.00
94-315-1	Airplane	CR - BLOWN GLASS - ITALY	ITALIAN FIGURAL		1994	$76.00	$76.00
94-316-0	Nicky	CR - BLOWN GLASS - ITALY	ITALIAN FIGURAL		1994	$24.00	$24.00
94-317-0	Pickled	CR - BLOWN GLASS - ITALY	ITALIAN FIGURAL	1994	1994	$36.00	$45.00
94-318-0	Topo	CR - BLOWN GLASS - ITALY	ITALIAN FIGURAL		1994	$33.00	$42.00
94-318-1	Topo	CR - BLOWN GLASS - ITALY	ITALIAN FIGURAL	1996	1994	$42.00	$42.00
94-321-0	Castanetta	CR - BLOWN GLASS - ITALY	ITALIAN FIGURAL	1994	1994	$37.00	$37.00
94-322-0	From A Distance	CR - BLOWN GLASS - ITALY	ITALIAN FIGURAL		1994	$32.00	$32.00
94-322-1	From A Distance	CR - BLOWN GLASS - ITALY	ITALIAN FIGURAL		1994	$36.00	$36.00
94-323-0	Jean Claude	CR - BLOWN GLASS - ITALY	ITALIAN FIGURAL		1994	$31.00	$31.00
94-323-1	Jean et Marie	CR - BLOWN GLASS - ITALY	ITALIAN FIGURAL	1995	1994	$44.00	$44.00
94-324-0	Just Like Us	CR - BLOWN GLASS - ITALY	ITALIAN FIGURAL	1994	1994	$30.00	$100.00
94-325-0	Surf's Up	CR - BLOWN GLASS - ITALY	ITALIAN FIGURAL		1994	$36.00	$36.00
94-325-1	Surf's Up	CR - BLOWN GLASS - ITALY	ITALIAN FIGURAL	1995	1994	$48.00	$48.00
94-326-0	Martian Holiday	CR - BLOWN GLASS - ITALY	ITALIAN FIGURAL		1994	$42.00	$52.00
94-326-1	Martian Holiday	CR - BLOWN GLASS - ITALY	ITALIAN FIGURAL		1994	$48.00	$48.00
94-327-0	Major Duck	CR - BLOWN GLASS - ITALY	ITALIAN FIGURAL	1994	1994	$58.00	$58.00
94-328-0	Roly Poly Pinocchio	CR - BLOWN GLASS - ITALY	ITALIAN FIGURAL	1996	1994	$54.00	$66.00
94-329-0	Chop Suey	CR - BLOWN GLASS - ITALY	ITALIAN FIGURAL		1994	$34.00	$34.00
94-329-1	The Chop Suey's	CR - BLOWN GLASS - ITALY	ITALIAN FIGURAL	1995	1994	$38.00	$38.00
94-330-0	Quick Draw	CR - BLOWN GLASS - ITALY	ITALIAN FIGURAL	1994	1994	$69.00	$275.00
94-331-0	Kitty Tamer	CR - BLOWN GLASS - ITALY	ITALIAN FIGURAL	1994	1994	$69.00	$250.00
94-332-0	Tangerine	CR - BLOWN GLASS - GERMANY	ORNAMENT		1994	$12.00	$13.00
94-333-0	Strawberry	CR - BLOWN GLASS - GERMANY	ORNAMENT		1994	$12.00	$16.00
94-335-0	Sugar Pear	CR - BLOWN GLASS - CZECH REP.	ORNAMENT		1994	$13.00	$18.00

Order No.	Title	Type	Theme	Retired	Intro. Year	Retail Price	Secondary Price
94-336-0	Corn Husk	CR - BLOWN GLASS - CZECH REP.	ORNAMENT	1994	1994	$13.00	$18.00
94-337-0	Walnut	CR - BLOWN GLASS - GERMANY	ORNAMENT		1994	$11.00	$12.00
94-338-0	Kosher Dill	CR - BLOWN GLASS - GERMANY	ORNAMENT		1994	$12.00	$12.00
94-339-0	Raspberry	CR - BLOWN GLASS - GERMANY	ORNAMENT		1994	$12.00	$12.00
94-339-1	Raspberry	CR - BLOWN GLASS - GERMANY	ORNAMENT		1994	$16.00	$12.00
94-340-0	Blackberry	CR - BLOWN GLASS - GERMANY	ORNAMENT		1994	$14.00	$13.00
94-340-1	Blackberry	CR - BLOWN GLASS - GERMANY	ORNAMENT		1994	$13.00	$13.00
94-341-0	Sugar Berry	CR - BLOWN GLASS - GERMANY	ORNAMENT		1994	$12.00	$12.00
94-342-0	Concord	CR - BLOWN GLASS - GERMANY	ORNAMENT		1994	$16.00	$20.00
94-342-1	Concord	CR - BLOWN GLASS - GERMANY	ORNAMENT		1994	$20.00	$20.00
94-343-0	Sweet Gherkin	CR - BLOWN GLASS - CZECH REP.	ORNAMENT		1994	$12.00	$14.00
94-344-0	Lemon	CR - BLOWN GLASS - GERMANY	ORNAMENT		1994	$15.00	$18.00
94-346-0	Chiquita	CR - BLOWN GLASS - GERMANY	ORNAMENT		1994	$15.00	$16.00
94-346-1	Chiquita	CR - BLOWN GLASS - GERMANY	ORNAMENT		1994	$16.00	$16.00
94-347-0	Purple Plum	CR - BLOWN GLASS - GERMANY	ORNAMENT		1994	$15.00	$15.00
94-347-1	Purple Plum	CR - BLOWN GLASS - GERMANY	ORNAMENT		1994	$18.00	$18.00
94-352-0	Ruby Reflector	CR - BLOWN GLASS - POLAND	ORNAMENT	1994	1994	$26.00	$50.00
94-354-0A	Bloomers	CR - BLOWN GLASS - GERMANY	CLIP-ON ORNAMENT		1994	$19.00	$19.00
94-354-0	Bloomers	CR - BLOWN GLASS - GERMANY	CLIP-ON ORNAMENT		1994	$19.00	$19.00
94-354-1	Bloomers	CR - BLOWN GLASS - GERMANY	CLIP-ON ORNAMENT		1994	$19.00	$19.00
94-354-1A	Bloomers	CR - BLOWN GLASS - GERMANY	CLIP-ON ORNAMENT		1994	$19.00	$19.00
94-359-0	Star Shine	CR - BLOWN GLASS - CZECH REP.	ORNAMENT		1994	$18.00	$18.00
94-359-1	Star Shine	CR - BLOWN GLASS - CZECH REP.	ORNAMENT		1994	$18.00	$18.00
94-360-0	Twinkle Stars	CR - BLOWN GLASS - CZECH REP.	ORNAMENT		1994	$13.00	$13.00
94-360-1	Twinkle Stars	CR - BLOWN GLASS - CZECH REP.	ORNAMENT	1995	1994	$18.00	$18.00
94-364-0	Bow Ties	CR - BLOWN GLASS - CZECH REP.	ORNAMENT		1994	$12.00	$12.00
94-364-1	Bow Ties	CR - BLOWN GLASS - CZECH REP.	ORNAMENT	1995	1994	$15.00	$49.00
94-365-0A	Accordion	CR - BLOWN GLASS - CZECH REP.	ORNAMENT	1994	1994	$22.00	$22.00
94-365-0	Merry Melody	CR - BLOWN GLASS - CZECH REP.	ORNAMENT	1994	1994	$12.00	$12.00
94-366-0	Evergreen	CR - BLOWN GLASS - CZECH REP.	ORNAMENT	1994	1994	$22.00	$22.00
94-367-0	Rock A Bye	CR - BLOWN GLASS - CZECH REP.	ORNAMENT	1994	1994	$18.00	$18.00
94-368-0	Sporting Goods	CR - BLOWN GLASS - CZECH REP.	ORNAMENT	1994	1994	$12.00	$12.00
94-369-0	Shooting Stars	CR - BLOWN GLASS - CZECH REP.	ORNAMENT	1994	1994	$13.00	$13.00
94-372-0	Razzle Dazzle	CR - BLOWN GLASS - POLAND	ORNAMENT		1994	$38.00	$50.00
94-372-1	Razzle Dazzle	CR - BLOWN GLASS - POLAND	ORNAMENT		1994	$50.00	$50.00
94-373-0	Checking It Twice	CR - BLOWN GLASS - POLAND	ORNAMENT		1994	$26.00	$26.00
94-373-1	Checking It Twice	CR - BLOWN GLASS - POLAND	ORNAMENT	1995	1994	$28.00	$28.00
94-374-0	Coffee Break	CR - BLOWN GLASS - CZECH REP.	ORNAMENT	1994	1994	$14.00	$14.00
94-377-0	Crowned Peacock	CR - BLOWN GLASS - CZECH REP.	CLIP-ON ORNAMENT		1994	$15.00	$18.00
94-379-0	Jumbo Harlequin	CR - BLOWN GLASS - POLAND	ORNAMENT		1994	$48.00	$60.00
94-380-0	Pinocchio Finial	CR - BLOWN GLASS - ITALY	FINIAL		1994	$64.00	$64.00
94-381-0	Santa Reflector Finial	CR - BLOWN GLASS - POLAND	FINIAL	1994	1994	$92.00	$92.00
94-382-0	Royale Finial	CR - BLOWN GLASS - CZECH REP.	FINIAL	1994	1994	$64.00	$64.00
94-385-0	My Darling	CR - BLOWN GLASS - GERMANY	ORNAMENT		1994	$88.00	$88.00
94-385-1	My Darling	CR - BLOWN GLASS - GERMANY	ORNAMENT	1995	1994	$24.00	$24.00
94-388-0	French Regency Finial	CR - BLOWN GLASS - POLAND	FINIAL		1994	$78.00	$90.00
94-389-0	Mission Ball Finial	CR - BLOWN GLASS - POLAND	FINIAL		1994	$78.00	$90.00
94-389-1	Mission Ball Finial	CR - BLOWN GLASS - POLAND	FINIAL	1996	1994	$90.00	$90.00
94-391-0	Allegro Finial	CR - BLOWN GLASS - POLAND	ORNAMENT	1994	1994	$74.00	$74.00
94-392-0	Siberian Bear	CR - BLOWN GLASS - POLAND	CLIP-ON ORNAMENT		1994	$24.00	$26.00
94-392-1	Siberian Bear	CR - BLOWN GLASS - POLAND	CLIP-ON ORNAMENT	1996	1994	$26.00	$26.00
94-397-0	Batter Up	CR - BLOWN GLASS - POLAND	ORNAMENT	1994	1994	$13.00	$20.00
94-398-0	Crescent Moon Santa	CR - BLOWN GLASS - POLAND	ORNAMENT		1994	$29.00	$29.00
94-399-0	Holly Jolly	CR - BLOWN GLASS - ITALY	ORNAMENT	1994	1994	$40.00	$40.00
94-401-0	Winter Journey	CR - BLOWN GLASS - POLAND	ORNAMENT		1994	$29.00	$29.00
94-401-1	Winter Journey	CR - BLOWN GLASS - POLAND	ORNAMENT	1995	1994	$32.00	$32.00
94-402-0	Holly Heart	CR - BLOWN GLASS - POLAND	ORNAMENT	1995	1994	$24.00	$24.00
94-413-0	Sugar Cone	CR - BLOWN GLASS - GERMANY	STARLIGHT/RISING STAR EXCL.		1994	$47.00	$86.00
94-413-1	Sugar Cone	CR - BLOWN GLASS - GERMANY	STARLIGHT/RISING STAR EXCL		1994	$86.00	$86.00
94-414-0	Harvest Home	CR - BLOWN GLASS - POLAND	ORNAMENT		1994	$29.00	$29.00
94-414-1	Harvest Home	CR - BLOWN GLASS - POLAND	ORNAMENT	1995	1994	$32.00	$32.00
94-417-0	Faberge Finial	CR - BLOWN GLASS - POLAND	FINIAL		1994	$78.00	$78.00
94-418-0	Star Fire Finial	CR - BLOWN GLASS - POLAND	FINIAL		1994	$84.00	$90.00
94-418-1	Star Fire Finial	CR - BLOWN GLASS - POLAND	FINIAL		1994	$90.00	$90.00
94-419-0	Scotch Pine Finial	CR - BLOWN GLASS - POLAND	FINIAL		1994	$78.00	$90.00
94-420-0	Deep Sea Finial	CR - BLOWN GLASS - POLAND	FINIAL		1994	$78.00	$78.00
94-421-0	Holiday Sparkle Finial	CR - BLOWN GLASS - POLAND	FINIAL		1994	$84.00	$90.00
94-428-0	Angel Star	CR - BLOWN GLASS - POLAND	ORNAMENT	1994	1994	$29.00	$35.00
94-429-0	Damask Rose	CR - BLOWN GLASS - POLAND	ORNAMENT	1994	1994	$29.00	$29.00
94-430-0	Glad Tidings	CR - BLOWN GLASS - ITALY	ORNAMENT	1994	1994	$44.00	$44.00
94-431-0	Picadilly	CR - BLOWN GLASS - POLAND	ORNAMENT	1995	1994	$28.00	$28.00
94-435-0	Partridge Pear	CR - BLOWN GLASS - GERMANY	GARLAND		1994	$68.00	$68.00
94-435-1	Partridge Pear	CR - BLOWN GLASS - GERMANY	GARLAND		1994	$68.00	$68.00
94-440-0	Angel Song	CR - BLOWN GLASS - GERMANY	GARLAND	1994	1994	$64.00	$64.00
94-441-0	Star Of Wonder	CR - BLOWN GLASS - GERMANY	GARLAND		1994	$60.00	$52.00
94-441-1	Star Of Wonder	CR - BLOWN GLASS - GERMANY	GARLAND	1995	1994	$52.00	$52.00
94-442-0	Lantern Lights	CR - BLOWN GLASS - GERMANY	GARLAND	1994	1994	$64.00	$64.00
94-445-0	Forest Holiday	CR - BLOWN GLASS - GERMANY	GARLAND		1994	$64.00	$64.00
94-445-1	Forest Holiday	CR - BLOWN GLASS - GERMANY	GARLAND	1995	1994	$68.00	$68.00
94-446-0	Circus Delight	CR - BLOWN GLASS - GERMANY	GARLAND	1994	1994	$64.00	$64.00
94-453-0	Lady Bug Blossoms	CR - BLOWN GLASS - CZECH REP.	GARLAND		1994	$62.00	$62.00
94-453-1	Lady Bug Blossoms	CR - BLOWN GLASS - CZECH REP.	GARLAND	1995	1994	$64.00	$64.00
94-454-0	Berry Stripes	CR - BLOWN GLASS - CZECH REP.	GARLAND	1995	1994	$48.00	$48.00
94-458-0	Saturn Rings	CR - BLOWN GLASS - GERMANY	GARLAND	1994	1994	$64.00	$64.00
94-460-1	King's Ransom	CR - BLOWN GLASS - GERMANY	GARLAND	1995	1994	$64.00	$64.00
94-SP3	Starbuck Santa	CR - BLOWN GLASS - GERMANY	STARLIGHT MEMBERS ONLY	1994	1994	$75.00	$300.00
94-SP4	Two Turtle Doves	CR - BLOWN GLASS - POLAND	12 DAYS OF CHRISTMAS SERIES	1994	1994	$28.00	$170.00
94-SP5	Frosty Cares	CR - BLOWN GLASS - POLAND	AIDS FUNDRAISER	1994	1994	$25.00	$65.00
95-001-0	Roundup	CR - BLOWN GLASS - POLAND	ORNAMENT	1995	1995	$26.00	$26.00
95-002-0	Annie	CR - BLOWN GLASS - POLAND	ORNAMENT	1995	1995	$26.00	$26.00
95-003-0	Chubby Decker	CR - BLOWN GLASS - POLAND	ORNAMENT		1995	$36.00	$36.00
95-004-0	Aloha	CR - BLOWN GLASS - POLAND	ORNAMENT		1995	$32.00	$32.00
95-005-0	Round About Santa	CR - BLOWN GLASS - POLAND	ORNAMENT		1995	$42.00	$42.00

Order No.	Title	Type	Theme	Retired	Intro. Year	Retial Price	Secondary Price
95-006-0	Little Prince	CR - BLOWN GLASS - GERMANY	ORNAMENT	1995	1995	$38.00	$38.00
95-007-0	Bearly Mooning	CR - BLOWN GLASS - POLAND	ORNAMENT	1996	1995	$26.00	$26.00
95-008-0	High Flying	CR - BLOWN GLASS - POLAND	ORNAMENT	1995	1995	$22.00	$60.00
95-009-0	Rainbow Scallops	CR - BLOWN GLASS - POLAND	ORNAMENT		1995	$16.00	$16.00
95-038-0	Bear Mail	CR - BLOWN GLASS - POLAND	ORNAMENT	1996	1995	$28.00	$28.00
95-010-0	Oktoberfest	CR - BLOWN GLASS - GERMANY	ORNAMENT		1995	$52.00	$52.00
95-011-0	Caribbean Constable	CR - BLOWN GLASS - POLAND	ORNAMENT	1995	1995	$24.00	$48.00
95-012-0	Skater's Waltz	CR - BLOWN GLASS - POLAND	ORNAMENT		1995	$38.00	$38.00
95-013-0	Trick Or Treat	CR - BLOWN GLASS - POLAND	ORNAMENT	1996	1995	$23.00	$23.00
95-014-0	Tennis Anyone?	CR - BLOWN GLASS - POLAND	ORNAMENT	1995	1995	$18.00	$18.00
95-015-0	Bejeweled Balloon	CR - BLOWN GLASS - GERMANY	ORNAMENT	1995	1995	$22.00	$22.00
95-016-0	Pierre	CR - BLOWN GLASS - POLAND	ORNAMENT	1996	1995	$22.00	$22.00
95-017-0	Claudette	CR - BLOWN GLASS - POLAND	ORNAMENT	1995	1995	$28.00	$90.00
95-018-0	Nibbles	CR - BLOWN GLASS - POLAND	ORNAMENT	1996	1995	$24.00	$24.00
95-019-0	Heavy Load	CR - BLOWN GLASS - POLAND	ORNAMENT		1995	$42.00	$42.00
95-020-0	Santa Fantasy	CR - BLOWN GLASS - GERMANY	ORNAMENT	1995	1995	$44.00	$44.00
95-021-0	Buttons	CR - BLOWN GLASS - POLAND	ORNAMENT		1995	$32.00	$32.00
95-022-0	Storytime Santa	CR - BLOWN GLASS - GERMANY	ORNAMENT	1996	1995	$44.00	$44.00
95-023-0	Autumn Oak King	CR - BLOWN GLASS - POLAND	ORNAMENT	1996	1995	$28.00	$28.00
95-024-0	Hooty Hoot	CR - BLOWN GLASS - POLAND	ORNAMENT	1996	1995	$26.00	$26.00
95-025-0	Kaleidoscope Cone	CR - BLOWN GLASS - GERMANY	ORNAMENT		1995	$44.00	$44.00
95-026-0	Frog Lady	CR - BLOWN GLASS - POLAND	ORNAMENT	1995	1995	$24.00	$47.00
95-027-0	Holiday Star Santa	CR - BLOWN GLASS - POLAND	CLIP-ON ORNAMENT		1995	$16.00	$16.00
95-028-0	Helmut's Bells	CR - BLOWN GLASS - GERMANY	ORNAMENT		1995	$18.00	$18.00
95-029-0	Tiny St. Nick	CR - BLOWN GLASS - POLAND	CLIP-ON ORNAMENT		1995	$14.00	$14.00
95-030-0	Lord Is My Shepard	CR - BLOWN GLASS - POLAND	ORNAMENT	1995	1995	$26.00	$26.00
95-031-0	Angel Flight	CR - BLOWN GLASS - GERMANY	ORNAMENT		1995	$44.00	$46.00
95-032-0	Li'l Clem	CR - BLOWN GLASS - POLAND	ORNAMENT		1995	$32.00	$32.00
95-033-0	Christmas Joy	CR - BLOWN GLASS - POLAND	ORNAMENT	1996	1995	$42.00	$42.00
95-034-0	Royal Tiger	CR - BLOWN GLASS - GERMANY	ORNAMENT		1995	$36.00	$36.00
95-035-0	Christmas Cake	CR - BLOWN GLASS - POLAND	ORNAMENT	1996	1995	$24.00	$24.00
95-036-0	Santa's Surprise	CR - BLOWN GLASS - POLAND	ORNAMENT	1996	1995	$34.00	$34.00
95-037-0	Little Drummer Bear	CR - BLOWN GLASS - POLAND	ORNAMENT		1995	$22.00	$22.00
95-039-0	Garden Girls	CR - BLOWN GLASS - POLAND	ORNAMENT	1995	1995	$18.00	$72.00
95-040-0	Snow Song	CR - BLOWN GLASS - POLAND	ORNAMENT		1995	$18.00	$18.00
95-041-0	Pere Noel	CR - BLOWN GLASS - GERMANY	ORNAMENT		1995	$44.00	$44.00
95-042-0	Joy To The World	CR - BLOWN GLASS - GERMANY	ORNAMENT		1995	$68.00	$90.00
95-043-0	Let Freedom Ring	CR - BLOWN GLASS - POLAND	ORNAMENT	1996	1995	$46.00	$46.00
95-044-0	Prince Of Thieves	CR - BLOWN GLASS - POLAND	ORNAMENT	1996	1995	$28.00	$28.00
95-045-0	On The Court	CR - BLOWN GLASS - POLAND	ORNAMENT	1996	1995	$26.00	$26.00
95-046-0	Jingles	CR - BLOWN GLASS - POLAND	ORNAMENT	1996	1995	$26.00	$26.00
95-047-0	Curve Ball	CR - BLOWN GLASS - POLAND	ORNAMENT	1995	1995	$18.00	$18.00
95-048-0	Sky Pilot	CR - BLOWN GLASS - POLAND	ORNAMENT	1995	1995	$18.00	$18.00
95-049-0	Cherub	CR - BLOWN GLASS - GERMANY	ORNAMENT		1995	$32.00	$32.00
95-050-0	Miss Parotte	CR - BLOWN GLASS - POLAND	ORNAMENT	1995	1995	$16.00	$16.00
95-051-0	Downhill Sledding	CR - BLOWN GLASS - GERMANY	ORNAMENT	1995	1995	$36.00	$36.00
95-052-0	Afternoon Tea	CR - BLOWN GLASS - POLAND	ORNAMENT	1995	1995	$22.00	$22.00
95-053-0	Be It Ever So Humble	CR - BLOWN GLASS - POLAND	ORNAMENT	1996	1995	$22.00	$22.00
95-054-0	Delphins	CR - BLOWN GLASS - POLAND	ORNAMENT		1995	$22.00	$22.00
95-055-0	Into The Woods	CR - BLOWN GLASS - POLAND	CLIP-ON ORNAMENT	1995	1995	$32.00	$32.00
95-056-0	David	CR - BLOWN GLASS - POLAND	ORNAMENT	1996	1995	$28.00	$28.00
95-057-0	Willy Clown	CR - BLOWN GLASS - GERMANY	ORNAMENT		1995	$66.00	$66.00
95-058-0	Buster Brown	CR - BLOWN GLASS - GERMANY	ORNAMENT		1995	$32.00	$32.00
95-060-0	Angel Melody	CR - BLOWN GLASS - POLAND	ORNAMENT	1995	1995	$32.00	$32.00
95-061-0	Main Street Al	CR - BLOWN GLASS - GERMANY	ORNAMENT	1996	1995	$42.00	$42.00
95-062-0	Miss Wise	CR - BLOWN GLASS - POLAND	ORNAMENT	1995	1995	$18.00	$18.00
95-063-0	Buford T.	CR - BLOWN GLASS - POLAND	ORNAMENT	1995	1995	$14.00	$14.00
95-064-0	Angels Triumph	CR - BLOWN GLASS - GERMANY	CLIP-ON ORNAMENT		1995	$24.00	$24.00
95-065-0	Night Ride	CR - BLOWN GLASS - POLAND	ORNAMENT	1996	1995	$18.00	$18.00
95-066-0	Drum Major	CR - BLOWN GLASS - POLAND	ORNAMENT	1996	1995	$24.00	$24.00
95-067-0	Autumn Pine	CR - BLOWN GLASS - GERMANY	ORNAMENT		1995	$16.00	$17.00
95-068-0	Jolly Ol'	CR - BLOWN GLASS - POLAND	ORNAMENT	1995	1995	$28.00	$28.00
95-069-0	Parrot Reflector	CR - BLOWN GLASS - POLAND	ORNAMENT		1995	$34.00	$34.00
95-070-0	Bundle Of Toys	CR - BLOWN GLASS - POLAND	ORNAMENT	1996	1995	$34.00	$34.00
95-071-0	Santa Sleighride	CR - BLOWN GLASS - POLAND	ORNAMENT		1995	$34.00	$34.00
95-072-0	According To Elfie	CR - BLOWN GLASS - GERMANY	ORNAMENT	1996	1995	$80.00	$80.00
95-073-0	Al E. Gator	CR - BLOWN GLASS - GERMANY	ORNAMENT	1996	1995	$24.00	$24.00
95-074-0	Can I Keep Him?	CR - BLOWN GLASS - POLAND	ORNAMENT	1996	1995	$22.00	$22.00
95-075-0	Better Watch Out	CR - BLOWN GLASS - POLAND	ORNAMENT	1995	1995	$38.00	$38.00
95-076-0	Polar Express	CR - BLOWN GLASS - POLAND	ORNAMENT		1995	$24.00	$24.00
95-077-0	Holy Mackerel	CR - BLOWN GLASS - GERMANY	ORNAMENT		1995	$42.00	$42.00
95-078-0	Ho Ho Ho	CR - BLOWN GLASS - GERMANY	ORNAMENT		1995	$18.00	$18.00
95-079-0	Kitty Vittles	CR - BLOWN GLASS - POLAND	ORNAMENT	1995	1995	$18.00	$18.00
95-080-0	Winter Cardinal	CR - BLOWN GLASS - POLAND	ORNAMENT	1995	1995	$28.00	$28.00
95-081-0	Santa Heart	CR - BLOWN GLASS - POLAND	ORNAMENT	1995	1995	$24.00	$24.00
95-082-0	Spring Arrival	CR - BLOWN GLASS - GERMANY	ORNAMENT	1995	1995	$44.00	$44.00
95-083-0	Gas Light	CR - BLOWN GLASS - CZECH REP.	ORNAMENT	1995	1995	$48.00	$48.00
95-084-0	Christmas Quarterback	CR - BLOWN GLASS - POLAND	ORNAMENT	1996	1995	$32.00	$32.00
95-085-0	Night Watch	CR - BLOWN GLASS - POLAND	CLIP-ON ORNAMENT	1996	1995	$22.00	$22.00
95-086-0	One On The Way	CR - BLOWN GLASS - POLAND	CLIP-ON ORNAMENT	1995	1995	$24.00	$24.00
95-087-0	Clown Bird	CR - BLOWN GLASS - POLAND	CLIP-ON ORNAMENT	1995	1995	$18.00	$18.00
95-088-0	White Dove	CR - BLOWN GLASS - GERMANY	ORNAMENT	1995	1995	$32.00	$32.00
95-089-0	Wiggle Men	CR - BLOWN GLASS - CZECH REP.	ORNAMENT		1995	$10.00	$10.00
95-090-0	Wild Eagle	CR - BLOWN GLASS - GERMANY	ORNAMENT		1995	$38.00	$38.00
95-091-0	Cock O'Doddle	CR - BLOWN GLASS - GERMANY	ORNAMENT	1995	1995	$19.00	$19.00
95-092-0	Very Berry	CR - BLOWN GLASS - GERMANY	ORNAMENT		1995	$11.00	$11.00
95-093-0	Catch Of The Day	CR - BLOWN GLASS - GERMANY	ORNAMENT		1995	$13.50	$14.00
95-094-0	Beelzebub	CR - BLOWN GLASS - CZECH REP.	ORNAMENT	1995	1995	$14.00	$14.00
95-095-0	Lean And Lanky	CR - BLOWN GLASS - GERMANY	ORNAMENT		1995	$23.00	$23.00
95-096-0	Ski Holiday	CR - BLOWN GLASS - GERMANY	ORNAMENT		1995	$22.00	$22.00
95-097-0	Hi Ho	CR - BLOWN GLASS - GERMANY	ORNAMENT		1995	$56.00	$56.00
95-098-0	Mother Mary	CR - BLOWN GLASS - GERMANY	ORNAMENT	1995	1995	$24.00	$24.00
95-099-0	Sweethearts	CR - BLOWN GLASS - GERMANY	ORNAMENT		1995	$26.00	$26.00

Order No.	Title	Type	Theme	Retired	Intro. Year	Retail Price	Secondary Price
95-100-0	Snow Ball	CR - BLOWN GLASS - GERMANY	ORNAMENT		1995	$28.00	$28.00
95-101-0	Dolly For Susie	CR - BLOWN GLASS - GERMANY	ORNAMENT		1995	$25.00	$25.00
95-102-0	Santa Sam	CR - BLOWN GLASS - POLAND	ORNAMENT	1996	1995	$28.00	$28.00
95-103-0	The Washingtons	CR - BLOWN GLASS - POLAND	ORNAMENT	1996	1995	$28.00	$28.00
95-104-0	Eagle Eye	CR - BLOWN GLASS - POLAND	CLIP-ON ORNAMENT	1996	1995	$26.00	$26.00
95-105-0	American Pride	CR - BLOWN GLASS - POLAND	CLIP-ON ORNAMENT	1996	1995	$24.00	$24.00
95-106-0	Lucy's Goose	CR - BLOWN GLASS - POLAND	ORNAMENT	1996	1995	$28.00	$28.00
95-107-0	Shore Leave	CR - BLOWN GLASS - POLAND	ORNAMENT	1995	1995	$24.00	$24.00
95-108-0	Farmer Boy	CR - BLOWN GLASS - POLAND	ORNAMENT	1995	1995	$28.00	$62.00
95-109-0	Cheery	CR - BLOWN GLASS - GERMANY	ORNAMENT	1995	1995	$52.00	$52.00
95-110-0	Miss Mamie	CR - BLOWN GLASS - GERMANY	ORNAMENT	1995	1995	$34.00	$34.00
95-111-0	Pharaoh	CR - BLOWN GLASS - POLAND	ORNAMENT	1996	1995	$32.00	$32.00
95-112-0	Warm Wishes	CR - BLOWN GLASS - GERMANY	ORNAMENT	1996	1995	$22.00	$22.00
95-113-0	Neptune's Charge	CR - BLOWN GLASS - GERMANY	ORNAMENT		1995	$36.00	$36.00
95-114-0	Slim Pickin's	CR - BLOWN GLASS - POLAND	ORNAMENT		1995	$22.00	$22.00
95-115-0	Glad Tidings To All	CR - BLOWN GLASS - POLAND	ORNAMENT		1995	$44.00	$44.00
95-116-0	Personal Delivery	CR - BLOWN GLASS - GERMANY	ORNAMENT	1995	1995	$36.00	$86.00
95-117-0	His Majesty	CR - BLOWN GLASS - POLAND	CLIP-ON ORNAMENT	1996	1995	$30.00	$30.00
95-118-0	Birds Of A Feather	CR - BLOWN GLASS - GERMANY	CLIP-ON ORNAMENT		1995	$24.00	$24.00
95-119-0	Springtime Sparrow	CR - BLOWN GLASS - GERMANY	CLIP-ON ORNAMENT	1995	1995	$14.00	$14.00
95-120-0	Spring Song	CR - BLOWN GLASS - GERMANY	CLIP-ON ORNAMENT		1995	$22.00	$22.00
95-121-0	Turtle Bird	CR - BLOWN GLASS - POLAND	CLIP-ON ORNAMENT	1995	1995	$22.00	$46.00
95-122-0	Officer Joe	CR - BLOWN GLASS - POLAND	CLIP-ON ORNAMENT	1995	1995	$22.00	$75.00
95-123-0	Holly Santa	CR - BLOWN GLASS - CZECH REP.	ORNAMENT		1995	$18.00	$18.00
95-124-0	Dirigible	CR - BLOWN GLASS - GERMANY	ORNAMENT		1995	$22.00	$22.00
95-125-0	Through The Clouds	CR - BLOWN GLASS - GERMANY	ORNAMENT		1995	$24.00	$24.00
95-126-0	Having A Ball	CR - BLOWN GLASS - GERMANY	ORNAMENT		1995	$26.00	$26.00
95-127-0	The Bishop	CR - BLOWN GLASS - GERMANY	ORNAMENT		1995	$74.00	$90.00
95-128-0	Spellbound	CR - BLOWN GLASS - GERMANY	ORNAMENT		1995	$26.00	$26.00
95-129-0	Veronica's Song	CR - BLOWN GLASS - GERMANY	CLIP-ON ORNAMENT		1995	$18.00	$18.00
95-130-0	Best Friends	CR - BLOWN GLASS - POLAND	ORNAMENT		1995	$22.00	$22.00
95-131-0	Department Store Santa	CR - BLOWN GLASS - POLAND	ORNAMENT		1995	$36.00	$36.00
95-132-0	Flight To Egypt	CR - BLOWN GLASS - POLAND	ORNAMENT		1995	$26.00	$26.00
95-133-0	Carousel Santa	CR - BLOWN GLASS - POLAND	ORNAMENT		1995	$36.00	$36.00
95-134-0	French Lace	CR - BLOWN GLASS - POLAND	ORNAMENT	1995	1995	$24.00	$24.00
95-135-0	Christmas Pie	CR - BLOWN GLASS - GERMANY	ORNAMENT	1996	1995	$54.00	$54.00
95-136-0	Dutch Dolls	CR - BLOWN GLASS - POLAND	ORNAMENT	1995	1995	$22.00	$90.00
95-137-0	J. T. Cricket	CR - BLOWN GLASS - POLAND	ORNAMENT	1996	1995	$22.00	$22.00
95-138-0	Ricky Raccoon	CR - BLOWN GLASS - POLAND	ORNAMENT	1996	1995	$24.00	$24.00
95-139-0	10, 9, 8...	CR - BLOWN GLASS - POLAND	ORNAMENT		1995	$22.00	$22.00
95-140-0	Sister Act	CR - BLOWN GLASS - GERMANY	ORNAMENT	1995	1995	$18.00	$85.00
95-141-0	Christmas Morning	CR - BLOWN GLASS - GERMANY	ORNAMENT	1995	1995	$24.00	$24.00
95-142-0	Rakish Charm	CR - BLOWN GLASS - POLAND	ORNAMENT	1996	1995	$22.00	$22.00
95-143-0	Frosted Santa	CR - BLOWN GLASS - GERMANY	ORNAMENT		1995	$25.00	$30.00
95-144-0	Grandpa Jones	CR - BLOWN GLASS - GERMANY	ORNAMENT	1995	1995	$22.00	$75.00
95-145-0	Winter Sun	CR - BLOWN GLASS - GERMANY	ORNAMENT	1995	1995	$31.00	$31.00
95-146-0	Climbing Higher	CR - BLOWN GLASS - POLAND	ORNAMENT	1996	1995	$26.00	$26.00
95-147-0	Heavenly Peace	CR - BLOWN GLASS - POLAND	ORNAMENT	1996	1995	$32.00	$32.00
95-148-0	My Favorite Chimp	CR - BLOWN GLASS - GERMANY	ORNAMENT		1995	$26.00	$28.00
95-149-0	Drummer Santa	CR - BLOWN GLASS - GERMANY	ORNAMENT		1995	$38.00	$38.00
95-150-0	Sunflower	CR - BLOWN GLASS - GERMANY	CLIP-ON ORNAMENT		1995	$28.00	$28.00
95-151-0	Clown Spin	CR - BLOWN GLASS - GERMANY	ORNAMENT		1995	$38.00	$38.00
95-152-0	Sugar Rose	CR - BLOWN GLASS - GERMANY	CLIP-ON ORNAMENT		1995	$26.00	$26.00
95-153-0	Heartfelt Santa	CR - BLOWN GLASS - GERMANY	ORNAMENT		1995	$38.00	$38.00
95-154-0	Bearly Fits	CR - BLOWN GLASS - POLAND	ORNAMENT	1996	1995	$26.00	$26.00
95-155-0	Boo Boo Kitty	CR - BLOWN GLASS - POLAND	ORNAMENT		1995	$24.00	$24.00
95-156-0	Teddy's Tree	CR - BLOWN GLASS - POLAND	ORNAMENT	1996	1995	$22.00	$22.00
95-157-0	Lavender Light	CR - BLOWN GLASS - GERMANY	ORNAMENT		1995	$28.00	$28.00
95-158-0	Matthew's Game	CR - BLOWN GLASS - CZECH REP.	ORNAMENT		1995	$12.00	$12.00
95-159-0	Little Dreamer	CR - BLOWN GLASS - GERMANY	ORNAMENT		1995	$16.00	$16.00
95-160-0	Another Fine Mess	CR - BLOWN GLASS - POLAND	ORNAMENT		1995	$16.00	$16.00
95-161-0	Al Pine	CR - BLOWN GLASS - POLAND	ORNAMENT	1996	1995	$24.00	$24.00
95-162-0	Together Again	CR - BLOWN GLASS - POLAND	ORNAMENT	1995	1995	$22.00	$22.00
95-163-0	Winter Pooch	CR - BLOWN GLASS - POLAND	ORNAMENT		1995	$22.00	$22.00
95-164-0	House Call	CR - BLOWN GLASS - POLAND	ORNAMENT		1995	$30.00	$30.00
95-165-0	Angel Puck	CR - BLOWN GLASS - POLAND	ORNAMENT		1995	$28.00	$28.00
95-166-0	Twilight Santa Finial	CR - BLOWN GLASS - GERMANY	FINIAL		1995	$80.00	$80.00
95-167-0	Little Toy Maker	CR - BLOWN GLASS - GERMANY	ORNAMENT	1995	1995	$26.00	$62.00
95-168-0	Rummy Tum Tum	CR - BLOWN GLASS - GERMANY	ORNAMENT		1995	$44.00	$44.00
95-169-0	And Snowy Makes Eight	CR - BLOWN GLASS - POLAND	ORNAMENT		1995	$125.00	$125.00
95-170-0	My Bonnie Lass	CR - BLOWN GLASS - POLAND	ORNAMENT	1996	1995	$24.00	$24.00
95-171-0	Wee Piper	CR - BLOWN GLASS - POLAND	ORNAMENT	1996	1995	$24.00	$24.00
95-172-0	Punch	CR - BLOWN GLASS - POLAND	ORNAMENT	1995	1995	$22.00	$22.00
95-173-0	Away We Go	CR - BLOWN GLASS - POLAND	ORNAMENT		1995	$24.00	$24.00
95-174-0	Spring Blossom	CR - BLOWN GLASS - GERMANY	ORNAMENT		1995	$16.00	$16.00
95-175-0	Cockle Bell	CR - BLOWN GLASS - GERMANY	ORNAMENT		1995	$38.00	$38.00
95-176-0	Double Delight	CR - BLOWN GLASS - GERMANY	ORNAMENT		1995	$46.00	$46.00
95-177-0	Fluttering Tulip	CR - BLOWN GLASS - GERMANY	ORNAMENT		1995	$18.00	$18.00
95-178-0	Autumn Berries	CR - BLOWN GLASS - GERMANY	ORNAMENT	1995	1995	$14.00	$14.00
95-179-0	Forest Cabin	CR - BLOWN GLASS - CZECH REP.	ORNAMENT	1996	1995	$15.00	$15.00
95-180-0	Li'l Shroom	CR - BLOWN GLASS - POLAND	ORNAMENT	1995	1995	$16.00	$16.00
95-181-0	Fruit Basket	CR - BLOWN GLASS - GERMANY	ORNAMENT	1995	1995	$14.00	$14.00
95-182-0	Purple Heart	CR - BLOWN GLASS - CZECH REP.	ORNAMENT		1995	$14.00	$14.00
95-183-0	Mugsy	CR - BLOWN GLASS - POLAND	ORNAMENT	1995	1995	$22.00	$60.00
95-184-0	On Parade	CR - BLOWN GLASS - POLAND	ORNAMENT	1995	1995	$24.00	$24.00
95-185-0	Swinging On A Star	CR - BLOWN GLASS - GERMANY	ORNAMENT	1996	1995	$44.00	$44.00
95-186-0	Carousel Star Bell	CR - BLOWN GLASS - GERMANY	ORNAMENT	1995	1995	$60.00	$60.00
95-187-0	Quilted Santa	CR - BLOWN GLASS - GERMANY	ORNAMENT		1995	$68.00	$68.00
95-188-0	Cherub Bell	CR - BLOWN GLASS - GERMANY	ORNAMENT	1995	1995	$58.00	$58.00
95-189-0	Westminster Santa	CR - BLOWN GLASS - POLAND	ORNAMENT		1995	$24.00	$24.00
95-190-0	Butcher Sam	CR - BLOWN GLASS - GERMANY	ORNAMENT	1995	1995	$22.00	$22.00
95-191-0	Every Time A Bell Rings	CR - BLOWN GLASS - GERMANY	ORNAMENT		1995	$50.00	$50.00
95-192-0	Sweet Madame	CR - BLOWN GLASS - GERMANY	ORNAMENT	1995	1995	$48.00	$109.00

Order No.	Title	Type	Theme	Retired	Intro. Year	Retial Price	Secondary Price
95-193-0	Evening Owl	CR - BLOWN GLASS - GERMANY	ORNAMENT	1995	1995	$36.00	$36.00
95-194-0	Aloisius Beer	CR - BLOWN GLASS - GERMANY	ORNAMENT	1995	1995	$75.00	$75.00
95-199-0	String Section	CR - BLOWN GLASS - GERMANY	ORNAMENT		1995	$14.00	$14.00
95-195-0	Along Came A Spider	CR - BLOWN GLASS - POLAND	ORNAMENT	1995	1995	$28.00	$28.00
95-196-0	Jazz Santa	CR - BLOWN GLASS - POLAND	ORNAMENT	1996	1995	$28.00	$28.00
95-197-0	Penelope	CR - BLOWN GLASS - POLAND	ORNAMENT	1995	1995	$26.00	$60.00
95-198-0	Nesting Stork	CR - BLOWN GLASS - CZECH REP.	ORNAMENT	1995	1995	$24.00	$24.00
95-200-0	Jagermeister	CR - BLOWN GLASS - GERMANY	ORNAMENT	1995	1995	$54.00	$54.00
95-201-0	Three Wishes	CR - BLOWN GLASS - GERMANY	ORNAMENT		1995	$42.00	$42.00
95-202-0	Fritz	CR - BLOWN GLASS - POLAND	ORNAMENT	1995	1995	$24.00	$24.00
95-203-0	Gobbles	CR - BLOWN GLASS - GERMANY	ORNAMENT	1995	1995	$52.00	$52.00
95-204-0	Bringing Home The Bacon	CR - BLOWN GLASS - POLAND	ORNAMENT	1995	1995	$26.00	$60.00
95-205-0	Touchdown	CR - BLOWN GLASS - POLAND	ORNAMENT	1996	1995	$19.00	$19.00
95-206-0	Hubbard's The Name	CR - BLOWN GLASS - POLAND	ORNAMENT	1995	1995	$26.00	$108.00
95-207-0	Garden Elves	CR - BLOWN GLASS - GERMANY	ORNAMENT	1996	1995	$56.00	$56.00
95-208-0	The Andrew Jacksons	CR - BLOWN GLASS - POLAND	ORNAMENT	1995	1995	$34.00	$210.00
95-209-0	Santa Cheer	CR - BLOWN GLASS - GERMANY	ORNAMENT	1995	1995	$26.00	$26.00
95-210-0	Foxy Grandpa	CR - BLOWN GLASS - POLAND	ORNAMENT	1996	1995	$30.00	$30.00
95-211-0	Ling-Ling	CR - BLOWN GLASS - POLAND	ORNAMENT		1995	$32.00	$32.00
95-212-0	Peek-A-Boo	CR - BLOWN GLASS - GERMANY	ORNAMENT		1995	$18.00	$18.00
95-213-0	Fruit Nuts	CR - BLOWN GLASS - GERMANY	ORNAMENT	1995	1995	$14.00	$14.00
95-214-0	Little Red	CR - BLOWN GLASS - GERMANY	ORNAMENT	1995	1995	$22.00	$70.00
95-215-0	Spring Nest	CR - BLOWN GLASS - GERMANY	ORNAMENT		1995	$24.00	$24.00
95-216-0	Aslan	CR - BLOWN GLASS - POLAND	ORNAMENT	1996	1995	$30.00	$30.00
95-217-0	Henrietta	CR - BLOWN GLASS - GERMANY	ORNAMENT	1996	1995	$24.00	$24.00
95-218-0	Him Through The Years	CR - BLOWN GLASS - POLAND	ORNAMENT	1996	1995	$30.00	$30.00
95-219-0	Curlycue Santa	CR - BLOWN GLASS - POLAND	ORNAMENT		1995	$30.00	$30.00
95-220-0	Her Through The Years	CR - BLOWN GLASS - POLAND	ORNAMENT	1996	1995	$30.00	$30.00
95-221-0	Hot Head	CR - BLOWN GLASS - GERMANY	ORNAMENT	1996	1995	$18.00	$18.00
95-222-0	Here Boy	CR - BLOWN GLASS - POLAND	ORNAMENT	1995	1995	$12.00	$35.00
95-223-0	Off To Market	CR - BLOWN GLASS - GERMANY	ORNAMENT	1995	1995	$24.00	$60.00
95-224-0	Wise Knight	CR - BLOWN GLASS - GERMANY	ORNAMENT		1995	$22.00	$22.00
95-225-0	Kitty Claus	CR - BLOWN GLASS - POLAND	ORNAMENT	1996	1995	$22.00	$22.00
95-226-0	Ted Of My Heart	CR - BLOWN GLASS - GERMANY	ORNAMENT	1996	1995	$60.00	$60.00
95-227-0	Cockatoo	CR - BLOWN GLASS - GERMANY	ORNAMENT		1995	$18.00	$18.00
95-228-0	Just A Kiss Away	CR - BLOWN GLASS - GERMANY	ORNAMENT		1995	$44.00	$44.00
95-229-0	Santa Bell	CR - BLOWN GLASS - POLAND	ORNAMENT		1995	$16.00	$16.00
95-230-0	Clown Rattle	CR - BLOWN GLASS - POLAND	ORNAMENT	1995	1995	$16.00	$36.00
95-231-0	Pork Chop	CR - BLOWN GLASS - GERMANY	ORNAMENT	1996	1995	$22.00	$22.00
95-232-0	Pencil Santa	CR - BLOWN GLASS - GERMANY	ORNAMENT		1995	$18.00	$18.00
95-233-0	Gunther	CR - BLOWN GLASS - GERMANY	ORNAMENT	1995	1995	$32.00	$125.00
95-234-0	At The Workshop	CR - BLOWN GLASS - POLAND	ORNAMENT		1995	$44.00	$44.00
95-235-0	Grandma Goose	CR - BLOWN GLASS - POLAND	ORNAMENT	1995	1995	$22.00	$22.00
95-236-0	Laugh 'Til You Cry	CR - BLOWN GLASS - POLAND	ORNAMENT	1995	1995	$24.00	$24.00
95-237-0	The Heart Of Christmas	CR - BLOWN GLASS - GERMANY	ORNAMENT		1995	$26.00	$26.00
95-238-0	Blue Dolphin	CR - BLOWN GLASS - GERMANY	ORNAMENT		1995	$22.00	$22.00
95-239-0	Snow Stork	CR - BLOWN GLASS - GERMANY	ORNAMENT	1995	1995	$22.00	$22.00
95-240-0	Imperial Helmut	CR - BLOWN GLASS - POLAND	ORNAMENT	1995	1995	$22.00	$55.00
95-241-0	Stork Lantern	CR - BLOWN GLASS - GERMANY	ORNAMENT	1995	1995	$18.00	$18.00
95-242-0	Autumn Angel	CR - BLOWN GLASS - GERMANY	ORNAMENT	1995	1995	$46.00	$46.00
95-243-0	Santa Rings Twice	CR - BLOWN GLASS - POLAND	ORNAMENT		1995	$22.00	$22.00
95-244-0	Dill Pickle	CR - BLOWN GLASS - GERMANY	ORNAMENT		1995	$16.00	$16.00
95-245-0	Pucker Up	CR - BLOWN GLASS - GERMANY	ORNAMENT		1995	$12.00	$12.00
95-246-0	Banana Split	CR - BLOWN GLASS - POLAND	ORNAMENT		1995	$24.00	$24.00
95-247-0	Bartlett Pear	CR - BLOWN GLASS - POLAND	ORNAMENT		1995	$24.00	$24.00
95-248-0	Sweet Carrot	CR - BLOWN GLASS - GERMANY	ORNAMENT		1995	$22.00	$22.00
95-249-0	Jumbo Walnut	CR - BLOWN GLASS - GERMANY	ORNAMENT	1995	1995	$18.00	$42.00
95-250-0	Pirate Ship	CR - BLOWN GLASS - ITALY	ORNAMENT	1996	1995	$44.00	$44.00
95-251-0	Time For A Bite	CR - BLOWN GLASS - ITALY	ORNAMENT		1995	$62.00	$62.00
95-252-0	In The Sky	CR - BLOWN GLASS - ITALY	ORNAMENT	1996	1995	$36.00	$36.00
95-253-0	Fairy Dust	CR - BLOWN GLASS - ITALY	ORNAMENT		1995	$72.00	$72.00
95-254-0	I Can Fly	CR - BLOWN GLASS - ITALY	ORNAMENT		1995	$60.00	$60.00
95-255-0	Percussion	CR - BLOWN GLASS - ITALY	ORNAMENT		1995	$50.00	$50.00
95-256-0	Hilda	CR - BLOWN GLASS - ITALY	ORNAMENT		1995	$52.00	$52.00
95-257-0	Winter Nest	CR - BLOWN GLASS - ITALY	ORNAMENT		1995	$44.00	$44.00
95-258-0	Sweet Dreams	CR - BLOWN GLASS - ITALY	ORNAMENT		1995	$28.00	$28.00
95-259-0	Youthful Madonna	CR - BLOWN GLASS - ITALY	ORNAMENT		1995	$28.00	$28.00
95-260-0	O Holy Night	CR - BLOWN GLASS - ITALY	ORNAMENT		1995	$52.00	$52.00
95-261-0	Quackers	CR - BLOWN GLASS - ITALY	ORNAMENT		1995	$24.00	$36.00
95-262-0	Celeste	CR - BLOWN GLASS - ITALY	ORNAMENT		1995	$52.00	$52.00
95-263-0	Glorianna	CR - BLOWN GLASS - ITALY	ORNAMENT		1995	$56.00	$56.00
95-264-0	Siamese Slippers	CR - BLOWN GLASS - ITALY	ORNAMENT	1995	1995	$16.00	$16.00
95-265-0	Buon Natale Finial	CR - BLOWN GLASS - ITALY	ORNAMENT		1995	$70.00	$70.00
95-266-0	Buon Natale	CR - BLOWN GLASS - ITALY	ORNAMENT		1995	$36.00	$36.00
95-267-0	Fruit Man Chu	CR - BLOWN GLASS - ITALY	ORNAMENT	1995	1995	$24.00	$24.00
95-268-0	Josephine	CR - BLOWN GLASS - ITALY	ORNAMENT	1996	1995	$38.00	$38.00
95-269-0	Nativity Snowfall	CR - BLOWN GLASS - ITALY	ORNAMENT		1995	$84.00	$84.00
95-270-0	Napoleon	CR - BLOWN GLASS - ITALY	ORNAMENT	1996	1995	$48.00	$48.00
95-271-0	Ivanovich Brothers	CR - BLOWN GLASS - ITALY	ORNAMENT	1996	1995	$48.00	$48.00
95-272-0	Gay Blades	CR - BLOWN GLASS - ITALY	ORNAMENT	1996	1995	$46.00	$46.00
95-273-0	Italian Ice Finial	CR - BLOWN GLASS - ITALY	ORNAMENT		1995	$64.00	$64.00
95-274-0	Cheeky St. Nick	CR - BLOWN GLASS - ITALY	ORNAMENT	1995	1995	$32.00	$32.00
95-275-0	Creole Dancer	CR - BLOWN GLASS - ITALY	ORNAMENT	1996	1995	$52.00	$52.00
95-276-0	Angel In Orbit	CR - BLOWN GLASS - ITALY	ORNAMENT		1995	$56.00	$56.00
95-277-0	Into Mischief	CR - BLOWN GLASS - ITALY	ORNAMENT		1995	$48.00	$48.00
95-278-0	Follow The Leader	CR - BLOWN GLASS - ITALY	ORNAMENT	1996	1995	$44.00	$44.00
95-279-0	Can We Quack	CR - BLOWN GLASS - ITALY	ORNAMENT	1996	1995	$52.00	$52.00
95-280-0	Bobbles	CR - BLOWN GLASS - ITALY	ORNAMENT	1996	1995	$54.00	$54.00
95-281-0	Reflecto	CR - BLOWN GLASS - ITALY	ORNAMENT	1996	1995	$46.00	$46.00
95-282-0	Shy Elephant	CR - BLOWN GLASS - ITALY	ORNAMENT	1995	1995	$32.00	$32.00
95-283-0	Bailey	CR - BLOWN GLASS - ITALY	ORNAMENT	1995	1995	$46.00	$46.00
95-284-0	Rocketeer	CR - BLOWN GLASS - ITALY	ORNAMENT		1995	$44.00	$44.00
95-285-0	One Small Step Finial	CR - BLOWN GLASS - ITALY	FINIAL	1996	1995	$96.00	$96.00

Order No.	Title	Type	Theme	Retired	Intro. Year	Retail Price	Secondary Price
95-286-0	Santa Maria	CR - BLOWN GLASS - ITALY	ORNAMENT	1996	1995	$64.00	$64.00
95-287-0	Chick-a-Dee	CR - BLOWN GLASS - ITALY	ORNAMENT		1995	$38.00	$38.00
95-288-0	Pecky Woodpecker	CR - BLOWN GLASS - ITALY	ORNAMENT	1996	1995	$36.00	$36.00
95-289-0	Nanette En Pointe	CR - BLOWN GLASS - ITALY	ORNAMENT	1996	1995	$38.00	$38.00
95-290-0	With Mary Sure To Go	CR - BLOWN GLASS - ITALY	ORNAMENT	1996	1995	$22.00	$22.00
95-291-0	I'm Late, I'm Late	CR - BLOWN GLASS - ITALY	ORNAMENT		1995	$48.00	$48.00
95-292-0	Papa Bear Reflector	CR - BLOWN GLASS - ITALY	ORNAMENT	1995	1995	$52.00	$52.00
95-293-0	Aqualina	CR - BLOWN GLASS - ITALY	ORNAMENT	1996	1995	$46.00	$46.00
95-294-0	Winter Spray	CR - BLOWN GLASS - POLAND	ORNAMENT	1995	1995	$32.00	$32.00
95-295-0	Ring Of Hearts	CR - BLOWN GLASS - POLAND	ORNAMENT	1995	1995	$32.00	$32.00
95-296-0	Red Lobster	CR - BLOWN GLASS - CZECH REP.	ORNAMENT	1996	1995	$14.00	$14.00
95-297-0	Light Drum	CR - BLOWN GLASS - CZECH REP.	ORNAMENT	1995	1995	$18.00	$18.00
95-298-0	St. Peter's Keys	CR - BLOWN GLASS - CZECH REP.	ORNAMENT	1995	1995	$8.00	$8.00
95-299-0	Hummer	CR - BLOWN GLASS - CZECH REP.	ORNAMENT	1995	1995	$12.00	$12.00
95-300-0	Poinsettia Blossoms	CR - BLOWN GLASS - POLAND	ORNAMENT	1995	1995	$32.00	$32.00
95-301-0	Jeweled Delight	CR - BLOWN GLASS - CZECH REP.	GARLAND	1995	1995	$50.00	$50.00
95-302-0	Rolling Pins	CR - BLOWN GLASS - CZECH REP.	GARLAND	1995	1995	$70.00	$70.00
95-303-0	Soda Pop	CR - BLOWN GLASS - CZECH REP.	GARLAND	1995	1995	$60.00	$60.00
95-304-0	Teddy Hearts	CR - BLOWN GLASS - CZECH REP.	GARLAND		1995	$70.00	$70.00
95-305-0	Sterling Trim	CR - BLOWN GLASS - CZECH REP.	GARLAND		1995	$42.00	$42.00
95-306-0	Autumn Woods	CR - BLOWN GLASS - CZECH REP.	ORNAMENT		1995	$72.00	$72.00
95-307-0	Lavender Berry	CR - BLOWN GLASS - CZECH REP.	GARLAND		1995	$42.00	$42.00
95-308-0	Della Robbia	CR - BLOWN GLASS - GERMANY	GARLAND		1995	$68.00	$68.00
95-309-0	Blue Lucy Finial	CR - BLOWN GLASS - POLAND	FINIAL		1995	$90.00	$90.00
95-310-0	Southern Colonial Finial	CR - BLOWN GLASS - POLAND	FINIAL		1995	$90.00	$90.00
95-311-0	Camille Finial	CR - BLOWN GLASS - POLAND	FINIAL		1995	$90.00	$90.00
95-312-0	Celestial Angel Finial	CR - BLOWN GLASS - GERMANY	FINIAL		1995	$130.00	$130.00
95-901-0	Bordeaux	CR - BLOWN GLASS - GERMANY	ORNAMENT		1995	$18.00	$18.00
95-902-0	Party Time	CR - BLOWN GLASS - POLAND	ORNAMENT	1995	1995	$24.00	$24.00
95-908-0	Gypsy Bear	CR - BLOWN GLASS - POLAND	ORNAMENT		1995	$26.00	$26.00
95-909-0	Prince Philip	CR - BLOWN GLASS - POLAND	ORNAMENT	1995	1995	$22.00	$22.00
95-910-0	My What Big Eyes	CR - BLOWN GLASS - POLAND	ORNAMENT	1995	1995	$22.00	$22.00
95-911-0	Swan Lake	CR - BLOWN GLASS - POLAND	ORNAMENT		1995	$32.00	$32.00
95-912-0	Pine Tree Santa	CR - BLOWN GLASS - POLAND	ORNAMENT		1995	$24.00	$24.00
95-913-0	Midnight Mass	CR - BLOWN GLASS - POLAND	ORNAMENT		1995	$32.00	$32.00
95-914-0	Crescent Moon Santa Finial	CR - BLOWN GLASS - POLAND	FINIAL	1995	1995	$90.00	$90.00
94-915-1	Leader Of The Band	CR - BLOWN GLASS - POLAND	ORNAMENT	1995	1994	$22.00	$22.00
95-NC1	Nutcracker Suite I	CR - BLOWN GLASS - GERMANY	NUTCRACKER SERIES		1995	$90.00	$110.00
95-SP10	On Wings Of Hope	CR - BLOWN GLASS - POLAND	AIDS FUNDRAISER		1995	$30.00	$35.00
95-SP11	Christmas Puppy Love	CR - BLOWN GLASS - POLAND	PEDIATRIC CANCER FUNDRAISER		1995	$30.00	$40.00
95-SP6	On Top Of The World	CR - BLOWN GLASS - GERMANY	10TH ANNIVERSARY PIECE		1995	$32.00	$50.00
95-SP7	Dash Away All	CR - BLOWN GLASS - POLAND	STARLIGHT MEMBERS ONLY	1995	1995	$34.00	$75.00
95-SP8	Purrfect Present	CR - BLOWN GLASS - POLAND	STARLIGHT MEMBERS ONLY	1995	1995		$45.00
95-SP9	Three French Hens	CR - BLOWN GLASS - POLAND	12 DAYS OF CHRISTMAS SERIES		1995	$34.00	$115.00
95-WM	Three Wise Men	CR - BLOWN GLASS - POLAND	NATIVITY SERIES	1995	1995	$90.00	$110.00
86-111-0	Pine Boughs	CR - BLOWN GLASS - POLAND	ORNAMENT	YES	1986	$15.00	$15.00
96-HF	Holy Family	CR - BLOWN GLASS - POLAND	NATIVITY SERIES		1996	$70.00	$70.00
96-HG1	Hansel, Gretel & Witch	CR - BLOWN GLASS - POLAND	SUNDAY BRUNCH SERIES		1996	$50.00	$50.00
96-NC2	The Nutcracker Suite II	CR - BLOWN GLASS - POLAND	NUTCRACKER SERIES		1996	$90.00	$90.00
96-RUS	Russian Rhapsody	CR - BLOWN GLASS - POLAND	RUSSIAN		1996	$150.00	$150.00
96-SP12	Four Calling Birds	CR - BLOWN GLASS - POLAND	12 DAYS OF CHRISTMAS SERIES	1996	1996	$44.00	$120.00
96-SP13	Christmas Magic	CR - BLOWN GLASS - POLAND	STARLIGHT MEMBERS ONLY	1996	1996	$50.00	$50.00
96-SP14	Frosty Weather	CR - BLOWN GLASS - POLAND	STARLIGHT MEMBERS ONLY	1996	1996		$25.00
96-SP15	A Winter Bear's Heart	CR - BLOWN GLASS - POLAND	AIDS FUNDRAISER	1996	1996	$34.00	$34.00
96-SP16	Bearly Awake	CR - BLOWN GLASS - POLAND	PEDIATRIC CANCER FUNDRAISER		1996	$34.00	$34.00
96-SP17	Esquire Santa	CR - BLOWN GLASS - POLAND	STARLIGHT/RISING STAR EXCL.	1996	1996	$150.00	$700.00
96-278-E	Poinsettia Elegance	CR - BLOWN GLASS - POLAND	EVENT PIECE		1996	$32.00	$32.00
86-040-3	Alpine Blush	CR - BLOWN GLASS - POLAND	ORNAMENT		1986	$32.00	$32.00
87-010-4	Rainbow Scarlett	CR - BLOWN GLASS - POLAND	ORNAMENT		1987	$32.00	$32.00
88-101-5	Medium Nautilus	CR - BLOWN GLASS - POLAND	ORNAMENT		1988	$18.00	$18.00
91-112-4A	Plum Russian	CR - BLOWN GLASS - POLAND	RUSSIAN SANTA		1991	$34.00	$34.00
91-112-7	Aqua Russian	CR - BLOWN GLASS - POLAND	RUSSIAN SANTA		1991	$34.00	$34.00
91-112-6	Amber Russian	CR - BLOWN GLASS - POLAND	RUSSIAN SANTA	1996	1991	$34.00	$34.00
91-112-5	Black Russian	CR - BLOWN GLASS - POLAND	RUSSIAN SANTA		1991	$34.00	$34.00
92-101-2	Winter Tree	CR - BLOWN GLASS - POLAND	ORNAMENT		1992	$29.00	$29.00
92-142-2	Southern Colonial	CR - BLOWN GLASS - POLAND	ORNAMENT		1992	$32.00	$32.00
92-198-2	Crimson Scarlett Finial	CR - BLOWN GLASS - POLAND	FINIAL		1992	$90.00	$90.00
93-059-2	Pisces	CR - BLOWN GLASS - CZECH REP.	GARLAND		1993	$76.00	$76.00
93-064-3	Nuts & Berries	CR - BLOWN GLASS - CZECH REP.	GARLAND		1993	$80.00	$80.00
93-099-3	Ski Baby	CR - BLOWN GLASS - GERMANY	ORNAMENT	1996	1993	$24.00	$24.00
93-102-3	Injun Joe	CR - BLOWN GLASS - GERMANY	ORNAMENT		1993	$24.00	$24.00
93-127-3	Santa In Space	CR - BLOWN GLASS - GERMANY	ORNAMENT		1993	$48.00	$48.00
93-144-1	Holiday Sparkle	CR - BLOWN GLASS - POLAND	ORNAMENT		1993	$32.00	$32.00
93-161-1	French Regency Balloon	CR - BLOWN GLASS - POLAND	ORNAMENT		1993	$44.00	$44.00
93-223-2	Wally	CR - BLOWN GLASS - ITALY	ITALIAN FIGURAL		1993	$34.00	$34.00
93-226-2	Teenage Mermaid	CR - BLOWN GLASS - ITALY	ITALIAN FIGURAL		1993	$48.00	$48.00
93-227-3	Siegfred	CR - BLOWN GLASS - ITALY	ITALIAN FIGURAL	1996	1993	$34.00	$34.00
93-232-3	Carnival In Red	CR - BLOWN GLASS - ITALY	ITALIAN FIGURAL	1996	1993	$38.00	$38.00
93-240-2	Maxine	CR - BLOWN GLASS - ITALY	ITALIAN FIGURAL		1993	$32.00	$32.00
93-246-3	Auld Lang Syne	CR - BLOWN GLASS - ITALY	ORNAMENT		1993	$24.00	$24.00
93-278-1	Citrus Twist	CR - BLOWN GLASS - GERMANY	ORNAMENT		1993	$13.00	$13.00
93-292-2	Georgian Santa	CR - BLOWN GLASS - GERMANY	ORNAMENT		1993	$34.00	$34.00
93-335-2	Bavarian Santa	CR - BLOWN GLASS - GERMANY	ORNAMENT		1993	$32.00	$32.00
93-365-3	First Snow	CR - BLOWN GLASS - CZECH REP.	ORNAMENT		1993	$17.00	$17.00
93-394-3	Christmas Express	CR - BLOWN GLASS - CZECH REP.	GARLAND		1993	$80.00	$80.00
93-395-3	Santa By Starlight	CR - BLOWN GLASS - POLAND	GARLAND		1993	$68.00	$68.00
94-025-2	Rajah	CR - BLOWN GLASS - GERMANY	CLIP-ON ORNAMENT	1996	1994	$22.00	$22.00
94-033-2	Shooting The Moon	CR - BLOWN GLASS - GERMANY	ORNAMENT		1994	$28.00	$28.00
94-038-2	Dutch Maiden	CR - BLOWN GLASS - GERMANY	ORNAMENT	1996	1994	$44.00	$44.00
94-056-2	Bag Of Goodies	CR - BLOWN GLASS - POLAND	ORNAMENT	1996	1994	$30.00	$30.00
94-089-1	Rosy Lovebirds	CR - BLOWN GLASS - GERMANY	CLIP-ON ORNAMENT		1994	$56.00	$56.00
94-091-2	Snow Dancing	CR - BLOWN GLASS - POLAND	ORNAMENT	1996	1994	$38.00	$38.00
94-112-2	Pretty Bird	CR - BLOWN GLASS - GERMANY	CLIP-ON ORNAMENT		1994	$38.00	$38.00

Order No.	Title	Type	Theme	Retired	Intro. Year	Retial Price	Secondary Price
94-142-1	Soldier Boy	CR - BLOWN GLASS - GERMANY	CLIP-ON ORNAMENT	1996	1994	$22.00	$22.00
94-145-1	Liberty Bell	CR - BLOWN GLASS - POLAND	ORNAMENT	1996	1994	$26.00	$26.00
94-159-1	Stocking Full	CR - BLOWN GLASS - POLAND	ORNAMENT		1994	$32.00	$32.00
94-159-2	Stocking Full	CR - BLOWN GLASS - POLAND	ORNAMENT	1996	1994	$32.00	$32.00
94-172-1	Liberty Ball	CR - BLOWN GLASS - GERMANY	ORNAMENT	1996	1994	$30.00	$30.00
94-175-2	Mama's Little Angel	CR - BLOWN GLASS - POLAND	ORNAMENT	1996	1994	$24.00	$24.00
94-240-2	House Sitting Santa	CR - BLOWN GLASS - POLAND	ORNAMENT	1996	1994	$26.00	$26.00
94-247-2	On The Run	CR - BLOWN GLASS - ITALY	ITALIAN FIGURAL		1994	$64.00	$64.00
94-258-1	Bubbly	CR - BLOWN GLASS - ITALY	ITALIAN FIGURAL		1994	$48.00	$48.00
94-260-2	Captain	CR - BLOWN GLASS - ITALY	ITALIAN FIGURAL		1994	$74.00	$74.00
94-285-2	Cabernet	CR - BLOWN GLASS - ITALY	ITALIAN FIGURAL		1994	$24.00	$24.00
94-315-2	Airplane	CR - BLOWN GLASS - ITALY	ITALIAN FIGURAL		1994	$76.00	$76.00
94-344-1	Frosty lemon	CR - BLOWN GLASS - GERMANY	ORNAMENT		1994	$18.00	$18.00
94-346-2	Chiquita Ice	CR - BLOWN GLASS - GERMANY	ORNAMENT		1994	$16.00	$16.00
94-354-2A	Bloomers	CR - BLOWN GLASS - GERMANY	CLIP-ON ORNAMENT		1994	$19.00	$19.00
94-354-2	Bloomers	CR - BLOWN GLASS - GERMANY	CLIP-ON ORNAMENT		1994	$19.00	$19.00
94-377-1	Crowned Peacock	CR - BLOWN GLASS - CZECH REP.	CLIP-ON ORNAMENT		1994	$18.00	$18.00
94-388-1	French Regency Finial	CR - BLOWN GLASS - POLAND	FINIAL		1994	$90.00	$90.00
95-903-0	Elfin	CR - BLOWN GLASS - POLAND	ORNAMENT		1995	$24.00	$24.00
95-913-1	Midnight Mass	CR - BLOWN GLASS - POLAND	ORNAMENT		1995	$32.00	$32.00
95-003-1	Chubby Decker	CR - BLOWN GLASS - POLAND	ORNAMENT		1995	$36.00	$36.00
95-005-1	Round About Santa	CR - BLOWN GLASS - POLAND	ORNAMENT	1996	1995	$42.00	$42.00
95-012-1	Skater's Waltz	CR - BLOWN GLASS - POLAND	ORNAMENT	1996	1996	$38.00	$38.00
95-025-1	Kaleidoscope Cone	CR - BLOWN GLASS - GERMANY	ORNAMENT		1995	$44.00	$44.00
95-027-1	White Holiday Star	CR - BLOWN GLASS - POLAND	CLIP-ON ORNAMENT		1995	$16.00	$16.00
95-031-1	Angel Flight	CR - BLOWN GLASS - GERMANY	ORNAMENT		1995	$46.00	$46.00
95-032-1	Li'l Clem	CR - BLOWN GLASS - POLAND	ORNAMENT		1995	$32.00	$32.00
95-037-1	Little Drummer Bear	CR - BLOWN GLASS - POLAND	ORNAMENT	1996	1995	$22.00	$22.00
95-041-1	Pere Noel	CR - BLOWN GLASS - GERMANY	ORNAMENT		1995	$44.00	$44.00
95-042-1	Joy To The World	CR - BLOWN GLASS - GERMANY	ORNAMENT		1995	$72.00	$72.00
95-049-1	Cherub	CR - BLOWN GLASS - GERMANY	ORNAMENT		1995	$32.00	$32.00
95-067-1	Autumn Pine	CR - BLOWN GLASS - GERMANY	ORNAMENT		1995	$17.00	$17.00
95-070-1	Bundle Of Toys	CR - BLOWN GLASS - POLAND	ORNAMENT		1995	$34.00	$34.00
95-071-1	Santa Sleighride	CR - BLOWN GLASS - POLAND	ORNAMENT		1995	$34.00	$34.00
95-077-1	Holy Mackerel	CR - BLOWN GLASS - POLAND	ORNAMENT		1995	$42.00	$42.00
95-078-1	Ho Ho Ho	CR - BLOWN GLASS - POLAND	ORNAMENT	1996	1995	$18.00	$18.00
95-090-1	Wild Eagle	CR - BLOWN GLASS - GERMANY	ORNAMENT	1996	1995	$38.00	$38.00
95-093-1	Catch Of The Day	CR - BLOWN GLASS - GERMANY	ORNAMENT	1996	1995	$14.00	$14.00
95-095-1	Lean and Lanky	CR - BLOWN GLASS - GERMANY	ORNAMENT	1996	1995	$23.00	$23.00
95-096-1	Ski Holiday	CR - BLOWN GLASS - GERMANY	ORNAMENT		1995	$22.00	$22.00
95-097-1	Hi Ho	CR - BLOWN GLASS - GERMANY	ORNAMENT	1996	1995	$56.00	$56.00
95-099-1	Sweethearts	CR - BLOWN GLASS - GERMANY	ORNAMENT		1995	$26.00	$26.00
95-100-1	Snow Ball	CR - BLOWN GLASS - GERMANY	ORNAMENT		1995	$28.00	$28.00
95-101-1	Dolly For Susie	CR - BLOWN GLASS - GERMANY	ORNAMENT	1996	1995	$25.00	$25.00
95-113-1	Neptune's Charge	CR - BLOWN GLASS - GERMANY	ORNAMENT	1996	1995	$36.00	$36.00
95-114-1	Creamy Slim Pickin's	CR - BLOWN GLASS - POLAND	ORNAMENT	1996	1995	$22.00	$22.00
95-114-2	Blue Slim Pickin's	CR - BLOWN GLASS - POLAND	ORNAMENT	1996	1995	$22.00	$22.00
95-114-3	Cranberry Slim Pickin's	CR - BLOWN GLASS - POLAND	ORNAMENT		1995	$22.00	$22.00
95-021-1	Buttons	CR - BLOWN GLASS - POLAND	ORNAMENT		1995	$32.00	$32.00
95-115-1	Glad Tidings To All	CR - BLOWN GLASS - POLAND	ORNAMENT	1996	1995	$44.00	$44.00
95-118-1	Birds Of A Feather	CR - BLOWN GLASS - GERMANY	CLIP-ON ORNAMENT		1995	$24.00	$24.00
95-120-1	Regal Spring	CR - BLOWN GLASS - GERMANY	CLIP-ON ORNAMENT		1995	$22.00	$22.00
95-123-1	Holly Santa	CR - BLOWN GLASS - CZECH REP.	ORNAMENT		1995	$18.00	$18.00
95-125-1	Through The Clouds	CR - BLOWN GLASS - GERMANY	ORNAMENT	1996	1995	$24.00	$24.00
95-126-1	Having A Ball	CR - BLOWN GLASS - GERMANY	ORNAMENT	1996	1995	$26.00	$26.00
95-128-1	Spellbound	CR - BLOWN GLASS - GERMANY	ORNAMENT	1996	1995	$26.00	$26.00
95-129-1	Veronica's Song	CR - BLOWN GLASS - GERMANY	CLIP-ON ORNAMENT		1995	$18.00	$18.00
95-131-1	Department Store Santa	CR - BLOWN GLASS - POLAND	ORNAMENT		1995	$36.00	$36.00
95-132-1	Flight To Egypt	CR - BLOWN GLASS - POLAND	ORNAMENT	1996	1995	$26.00	$26.00
95-139-1	10, 9, 8...	CR - BLOWN GLASS - POLAND	ORNAMENT	1996	1995	$22.00	$22.00
95-143-1	Frosted Santa	CR - BLOWN GLASS - GERMANY	ORNAMENT		1995	$26.00	$26.00
95-148-1	My Favorite Chimp	CR - BLOWN GLASS - GERMANY	ORNAMENT		1995	$28.00	$28.00
95-149-1	Drummer Santa	CR - BLOWN GLASS - GERMANY	ORNAMENT		1995	$36.00	$36.00
95-151-1	Clown Spin	CR - BLOWN GLASS - GERMANY	ORNAMENT	1996	1995	$34.00	$34.00
95-153-1	Heartfelt Santa	CR - BLOWN GLASS - GERMANY	ORNAMENT		1995	$38.00	$38.00
86-050-0	Circus Sphere	CR - BLOWN GLASS - POLAND	ORNAMENT	YES	1986	$15.00	$15.00
93-167-1	Scotch Pine	CR - BLOWN GLASS - POLAND	ORNAMENT	1995	1993	$27.00	$48.00
93-247-1	Rain Dance	CR - BLOWN GLASS - ITALY	ITALIAN FIGURAL	1995	1993	$34.00	$34.00
93-268-2	Bells Are Ringing	CR - BLOWN GLASS - GERMANY	ORNAMENT	1995	1993	$24.00	$24.00
93-268-2A	Bells Are Ringing	CR - BLOWN GLASS - GERMANY	ORNAMENT	1995	1993	$24.00	$24.00
93-268-2B	Bells Are Ringing	CR - BLOWN GLASS - GERMANY	ORNAMENT	1995	1993	$24.00	$24.00
93-334-1	Tiffany Bells	CR - BLOWN GLASS - CZECH REP.	ORNAMENT	1995	1993	$14.00	$14.00
93-360-2	Black Forest Clock	CR - BLOWN GLASS - GERMANY	ORNAMENT	1995	1993	$32.00	$32.00
94-275-1	Glow Worm	CR - BLOWN GLASS - ITALY	ITALIAN FIGURAL	1995	1994	$36.00	$36.00
94-398-1	Ruby Crescent Moon Santa	CR - BLOWN GLASS - POLAND	ORNAMENT	1995	1994	$32.00	$32.00
87-078-0	Twin Peacock Sphere	CR - BLOWN GLASS - POLAND	ORNAMENT	YES	1987	$20.00	$20.00
92-212-2	Christmas Spider	CR - BLOWN GLASS - CZECH REP.	ORNAMENT		1992	$33.00	$33.00
94-054-0	Rainy Day Smile	CR - BLOWN GLASS - POLAND	ORNAMENT		1994	$22.00	$36.00
95-076-SB	Polar Express - South Bend	CR - BLOWN GLASS - POLAND	EVENT PIECE		1995	$27.00	$70.00
94-915-E	Leader Of The Band	CR - BLOWN GLASS - POLAND	EVENT PIECE		1994	$22.00	$350.00
95-DIS-01	Mickey's Tree	CR - BLOWN GLASS - POLAND	ORNAMENT		1995	$45.00	$325.00
95-DIS-02	Pooh's Favorite Gift	CR - BLOWN GLASS - POLAND	ORNAMENT		1995	$45.00	$350.00
95-WB-01	Santa Bugs	CR - BLOWN GLASS - POLAND	ORNAMENT		1995	$45.00	$110.00
95-WB-02	Taz Angel	CR - BLOWN GLASS - POLAND	ORNAMENT		1995	$45.00	$96.00
92-175-0	Floral Cascade Tier Drop	CR - BLOWN GLASS - POLAND	ORNAMENT		1992	$32.00	$75.00
92-092-0	Seahorses	CR - BLOWN GLASS - POLAND	ORNAMENT		1992	$20.00	$86.00
92-093-0	Sitting Bull	CR - BLOWN GLASS - POLAND	ORNAMENT		1992	$26.00	$65.00
94-034-0	Special Delivery	CR - BLOWN GLASS - POLAND	ORNAMENT		1994	$18.00	$32.00
94-266-0	Dancing Harlequin	CR - BLOWN GLASS - ITALY	ITALIAN FIGURAL		1994	$44.00	$65.00
89-073-0	Lucky Fish	CR - BLOWN GLASS - POLAND	ORNAMENT	89	1989	$8.00	$30.00
88-102-EX	Large Nautillis Store Exclusives	CR - BLOWN GLASS - POLAND	ORNAMENT		1988	$8.00	$8.00
91-112-JH	Russian Santa Jolly Holidays Gifts	CR - BLOWN GLASS - POLAND	RUSSIAN SANTA		1991	$34.00	$50.00
91-009-EX	Festive Smitty	CR - BLOWN GLASS - POLAND	ORNAMENT		1991	$15.00	$150.00

Order No.	Title	Type	Theme	Retired	Intro. Year	Retail Price	Secondary Price
92-133-0	Water Lilies	CR - BLOWN GLASS - POLAND	ORNAMENT		1992	$26.00	$175.00
92-225-0	Baby's First Christmas	CR - BLOWN GLASS - CZECH REP.	GARLAND		1992	$48.00	$48.00
93-450-0	1950's Charm Garland	CR - BLOWN GLASS - GERMANY	GARLAND	YES	1993	$38.00	$38.00
93-452-0	Twinkle Little Star garland	CR - BLOWN GLASS - GERMANY	GARLAND	1993	1993	$48.00	$48.00
95-WB-03	Tweety Sprite	CR - BLOWN GLASS - POLAND	ORNAMENT		1995	$40.00	$120.00
96-SP18	A Job Well Done	CR - BLOWN GLASS - POLAND	EVENT PIECE	96	96	$30.00	$30.00
96-SP287-E	Poinsettia Elegance	CR - BLOWN GLASS - POLAND	EVENT PIECE	96	96	$32.00	$32.00
96-001-0	Speed Racer	CR - BLOWN GLASS - CZECH REP.	ORNAMENT		1996	$66.00	
96-002-0	Night Magic	CR - BLOWN GLASS - GERMANY	ORNAMENT		1996	$26.00	
96-003-0	Baby Angel	CR - BLOWN GLASS - GERMANY	ORNAMENT		1996	$22.00	
96-004-0	Charlie Horse	CR - BLOWN GLASS - GERMANY	ORNAMENT		1996	$20.00	
96-005-0	Pumpkin Patch	CR - BLOWN GLASS - GERMANY	ORNAMENT		1996	$26.00	
96-006-0	Fancy Fringe	CR - BLOWN GLASS - GERMANY	ORNAMENT		1996	$18.00	
96-007-0	Starlight	CR - BLOWN GLASS - GERMANY	ORNAMENT		1996	$16.00	
96-008-1	Guilded Wings	CR - BLOWN GLASS - GERMANY	ORNAMENT		1996	$16.00	
96-008-0	Guilded Wings	CR - BLOWN GLASS - GERMANY	ORNAMENT		1996	$16.00	
96-009-0	Seventh Heaven	CR - BLOWN GLASS - GERMANY	ORNAMENT		1996	$26.00	
96-010-1	Rosy Cheek Santa	CR - BLOWN GLASS - GERMANY	ORNAMENT		1996	$20.00	
96-011-0	Home Spun	CR - BLOWN GLASS - GERMANY	ORNAMENT		1996	$14.00	
96-012-0	Dreamy	CR - BLOWN GLASS - GERMANY	ORNAMENT		1996	$17.00	
96-013-1	Lancer	CR - BLOWN GLASS - GERMANY	ORNAMENT		1996	$29.00	
96-014-0	Elfcicle	CR - BLOWN GLASS - GERMANY	ORNAMENT		1996	$28.00	
96-015-0	By The Shore	CR - BLOWN GLASS - GERMANY	ORNAMENT		1996	$16.00	
96-016-1	Tropical Reef	CR - BLOWN GLASS - GERMANY	ORNAMENT		1996	$18.00	
96-017-0	Pumpkin Man	CR - BLOWN GLASS - GERMANY	ORNAMENT		1996	$80.00	
96-018-0	Kringle Cheer	CR - BLOWN GLASS - ITALY	ORNAMENT		1996	$39.00	
96-019-0	Sky Santa Finial	CR - BLOWN GLASS - ITALY	FINIAL		1996	$66.00	
96-020-0	Peppermint Twist	CR - BLOWN GLASS - ITALY	ORNAMENT		1996	$88.00	
96-021-0	Russian Knight	CR - BLOWN GLASS - ITALY	ORNAMENT		1996	$100.00	
96-022-0	Santa Canes	CR - BLOWN GLASS - ITALY	ORNAMENT		1996	$48.00	
96-023-0	Midnight Visit	CR - BLOWN GLASS - ITALY	ORNAMENT		1996	$100.00	
96-024-0	Winter Morning	CR - BLOWN GLASS - ITALY	ORNAMENT		1996	$78.00	
96-025-0	Masquerade	CR - BLOWN GLASS - ITALY	ORNAMENT		1996	$39.00	
96-027-0	Monte Carlo	CR - BLOWN GLASS - ITALY	ORNAMENT		1996	$52.00	
96-028-0	Veronique Magnifique	CR - BLOWN GLASS - ITALY	ORNAMENT		1996	$60.00	
96-029-0	Hipp Hopp	CR - BLOWN GLASS - ITALY	ORNAMENT		1996	$34.00	
96-030-0	Baryschnicow	CR - BLOWN GLASS - ITALY	ORNAMENT		1996	$34.00	
96-031-0	Grizelle	CR - BLOWN GLASS - ITALY	ORNAMENT		1996	$34.00	
96-032-0	Swine Lake	CR - BLOWN GLASS - ITALY	ORNAMENT		1996	$33.00	
96-033-0	Roxanne	CR - BLOWN GLASS - ITALY	ORNAMENT		1996	$40.00	
96-034-0	Goosette	CR - BLOWN GLASS - ITALY	ORNAMENT		1996	$32.00	
96-035-0	Astroman	CR - BLOWN GLASS - ITALY	ORNAMENT		1996	$44.00	
96-035-0	Astropup	CR - BLOWN GLASS - ITALY	ORNAMENT		1996	$32.00	
96-037-0	Super Sonic Santa	CR - BLOWN GLASS - ITALY	ORNAMENT		1996	$48.00	
96-038-0	Rocket Santa	CR - BLOWN GLASS - ITALY	ORNAMENT		1996	$48.00	
96-039-0	To The Stars	CR - BLOWN GLASS - ITALY	ORNAMENT		1996	$86.00	
96-040-0	Crescent Kringle	CR - BLOWN GLASS - ITALY	ORNAMENT		1996	$36.00	
96-041-0	Curly Cue	CR - BLOWN GLASS - ITALY	ORNAMENT		1996	$42.00	
96-042-0	Miss Peanut	CR - BLOWN GLASS - ITALY	STARLIGHT/RISING STAR EXCL		1996	$60.00	
96-043-0	Shuffles	CR - BLOWN GLASS - ITALY	ORNAMENT		1996	$54.00	
96-044-0	Maine Event	CR - BLOWN GLASS - ITALY	ORNAMENT		1996	$60.00	
96-045-0	Polar Love	CR - BLOWN GLASS - GERMANY	ORNAMENT		1996	$22.00	
96-046-0	Fruit Punch	CR - BLOWN GLASS - ITALY	ORNAMENT		1996	$42.00	
96-047-0	Clown Around	CR - BLOWN GLASS - ITALY	ORNAMENT		1996	$58.00	
96-048-0	Santa Joy	CR - BLOWN GLASS - ITALY	ORNAMENT		1996	$42.00	
96-049-0	Old World Santa	CR - BLOWN GLASS - ITALY	ORNAMENT		1996	$76.00	
96-050-0	Lilac Winter	CR - BLOWN GLASS - ITALY	ORNAMENT		1996	$44.00	
96-051-0	Lilac Angel	CR - BLOWN GLASS - ITALY	ORNAMENT		1996	$44.00	
96-052-0	Ragamuffins	CR - BLOWN GLASS - ITALY	ORNAMENT		1996	$39.00	
96-053-0	Yo Ho Ho	CR - BLOWN GLASS - ITALY	ORNAMENT		1996	$48.00	
96-054-0	Ranger and Yosemite Bear	CR - BLOWN GLASS - ITALY	ORNAMENT		1996	$36.00	
96-055-0	Davey	CR - BLOWN GLASS - ITALY	ORNAMENT		1996	$48.00	
96-056-0	Hi Ho Trio	CR - BLOWN GLASS - ITALY	ORNAMENT		1996	$47.00	
96-057-0	Alpine Climber	CR - BLOWN GLASS - ITALY	ORNAMENT		1996	$49.00	
96-058-0	What A Card	CR - BLOWN GLASS - ITALY	ORNAMENT		1996	$44.00	
96-059-0	Carry A Torch	CR - BLOWN GLASS - ITALY	ORNAMENT		1996	$48.00	
96-060-0	Alice	CR - BLOWN GLASS - ITALY	ORNAMENT		1996	$44.00	
96-061-0	Grape Bouquet	CR - BLOWN GLASS - ITALY	ORNAMENT		1996	$33.00	
96-062-0	Winter Holiday	CR - BLOWN GLASS - ITALY	ORNAMENT		1996	$44.00	
96-063-0	Checkered Past	CR - BLOWN GLASS - ITALY	ORNAMENT		1996	$50.00	
96-064-0	Field Blossom	CR - BLOWN GLASS - ITALY	ORNAMENT		1996	$46.00	
96-065-0	Lil Creeper	CR - BLOWN GLASS - ITALY	ORNAMENT		1996	$32.00	
96-066-0	Strong to the Finish	CR - BLOWN GLASS - ITALY	ORNAMENT		1996	$48.00	
96-067-0	His Goil	CR - BLOWN GLASS - ITALY	ORNAMENT		1996	$40.00	
96-068-0	Jolly Pops	CR - BLOWN GLASS - ITALY	ORNAMENT		1996	$24.00	
96-069-0	Puff	CR - BLOWN GLASS - ITALY	ORNAMENT		1996	$48.00	
96-070-0	Off to Bed	CR - BLOWN GLASS - ITALY	ORNAMENT		1996	$24.00	
96-071-0	Lady Wintermeer	CR - BLOWN GLASS - ITALY	ORNAMENT		1996	$44.00	
96-072-0	Love and Valor	CR - BLOWN GLASS - GERMANY	ORNAMENT		1996	$14.50	
96-073-0	Snow Hare	CR - BLOWN GLASS - POLAND	ORNAMENT		1996	$14.00	
96-074-0	Guiding Star	CR - BLOWN GLASS - ITALY	ORNAMENT		1996	$42.00	
96-075-0	Sugar Cane	CR - BLOWN GLASS - ITALY	ORNAMENT		1996	$18.00	
96-076-0	Miss Muffett	CR - BLOWN GLASS - ITALY	ORNAMENT		1996	$48.00	
96-077-0	Sisters Ivanovich	CR - BLOWN GLASS - ITALY	ORNAMENT		1996	$48.00	
96-078-0	Golden Isis	CR - BLOWN GLASS - CZECH REP.	ORNAMENT		1996	$20.00	
96-079-0	Blonde Angel	CR - BLOWN GLASS - ITALY	ORNAMENT		1996	$48.00	
96-080-0	Heavenly Blue	CR - BLOWN GLASS - ITALY	ORNAMENT		1996	$46.00	
96-081-0	Star Angel	CR - BLOWN GLASS - ITALY	ORNAMENT		1996	$46.00	
96-082-0	Celestine	CR - BLOWN GLASS - ITALY	ORNAMENT		1996	$48.00	
96-083-0	Angelina Finial	CR - BLOWN GLASS - ITALY	FINIAL		1996	$64.00	
96-084-0	Catavarius	CR - BLOWN GLASS - ITALY	ORNAMENT		1996	$38.00	
96-085-0	Mandolin Angels	CR - BLOWN GLASS - ITALY	ORNAMENT		1996	$52.00	
96-086-0	For Clara	CR - BLOWN GLASS - GERMANY	ORNAMENT		1996	$32.00	

Order No.	Title	Type	Theme	Retired	Intro. Year	Retial Price	Secondary Price
96-087-0	Miami Ice	CR - BLOWN GLASS - GERMANY	ORNAMENT		1996	$22.00	
96-088-0	Rose Windows	CR - BLOWN GLASS - CZECH REP.	ORNAMENT		1996	$18.00	
96-089-0	Three Little Jigs	CR - BLOWN GLASS - ITALY	ORNAMENT		1996	$48.00	
96-090-0	Gabriel's Horn	CR - BLOWN GLASS - ITALY	ORNAMENT		1996	$76.00	
96-091-0	Royal Crest	CR - BLOWN GLASS - CZECH REP.	ORNAMENT		1996	$14.00	
96-092-0	Royal Guard	CR - BLOWN GLASS - ITALY	ORNAMENT		1996	$48.00	
96-093-0	Fairy Holiday	CR - BLOWN GLASS - ITALY	ORNAMENT		1996	$56.00	
96-094-0	Miss Flurry	CR - BLOWN GLASS - ITALY	ORNAMENT		1996	$38.00	
96-095-0	Winter Bride	CR - BLOWN GLASS - ITALY	ORNAMENT		1996	$58.00	
96-096-0	Nutcracker Finial	CR - BLOWN GLASS - ITALY	FINIAL		1996	$66.00	
96-097-0	Billy Bunny	CR - BLOWN GLASS - POLAND	ORNAMENT		1996	$26.00	
96-098-0	Little Ivanna	CR - BLOWN GLASS - POLAND	ORNAMENT		1996	$24.00	
96-099-0	Village Santa	CR - BLOWN GLASS - POLAND	ORNAMENT		1996	$30.00	
96-100-0	All Heart	CR - BLOWN GLASS - GERMANY	ORNAMENT		1996	$30.00	
96-101-0	Tropical Blue	CR - BLOWN GLASS - GERMANY	ORNAMENT		1996	$17.00	
96-102-0	Crown Jewels	CR - BLOWN GLASS - CZECH REP.	ORNAMENT		1996	$30.00	
96-103-0	Kitty Hawk	CR - BLOWN GLASS - CZECH REP.	ORNAMENT		1996	$32.00	
96-104-0	Czech Express	CR - BLOWN GLASS - CZECH REP.	ORNAMENT		1996	$36.00	
96-105-0	Incantation	CR - BLOWN GLASS - POLAND	ORNAMENT		1996	$24.00	
96-106-0	Autumn Jewels	CR - BLOWN GLASS - GERMANY	ORNAMENT		1996	$14.00	
96-107-0	Casey	CR - BLOWN GLASS - GERMANY	ORNAMENT		1996	$18.00	
96-108-0	Green Tomato	CR - BLOWN GLASS - CZECH REP.	ORNAMENT		1996	$12.00	
96-109-0	Golden Grape	CR - BLOWN GLASS - CZECH REP.	ORNAMENT		1996	$8.00	
96-110-0	Frosted Pear	CR - BLOWN GLASS - CZECH REP.	ORNAMENT		1996	$14.00	
96-111-0	Royal Grape	CR - BLOWN GLASS - CZECH REP.	ORNAMENT		1996	$7.00	
96-112-0	Pineapple Frost	CR - BLOWN GLASS - GERMANY	ORNAMENT		1996	$14.00	
96-113-0	Starship	CR - BLOWN GLASS - GERMANY	ORNAMENT		1996	$28.00	
96-114-0	Cycle Santa	CR - BLOWN GLASS - POLAND	ORNAMENT		1996	$26.00	
96-115-0	Slim Wizard	CR - BLOWN GLASS - GERMANY	ORNAMENT		1996	$18.00	
96-116-0	Velvet Pear	CR - BLOWN GLASS - GERMANY	ORNAMENT		1996	$16.00	
96-117-0	Frosty Peach	CR - BLOWN GLASS - GERMANY	ORNAMENT		1996	$18.00	
96-118-0	Night Lights	CR - BLOWN GLASS - GERMANY	ORNAMENT		1996	$9.00	
96-120-0	Sugar House	CR - BLOWN GLASS - GERMANY	ORNAMENT		1996	$22.00	
96-121-0	Winter Wind	CR - BLOWN GLASS - POLAND	ORNAMENT		1996	$24.00	
96-122-0	Garden Delight	CR - BLOWN GLASS - GERMANY	ORNAMENT		1996	$17.00	
96-123-0	Rainbow Drops	CR - BLOWN GLASS - GERMANY	ORNAMENT		1996	$14.00	
96-124-0	Toy Time	CR - BLOWN GLASS - GERMANY	ORNAMENT		1996	$23.00	
96-125-0	Snow Kitties	CR - BLOWN GLASS - POLAND	ORNAMENT		1996	$26.00	
96-126-0	Polish Winter Wreath	CR - BLOWN GLASS - POLAND	ORNAMENT		1996	$22.00	
96-127-0	Colossal Cone	CR - BLOWN GLASS - GERMANY	ORNAMENT		1996	$40.00	
96-128-0	It's Bo-Bo Bear	CR - BLOWN GLASS - GERMANY	ORNAMENT		1996	$18.00	
96-129-0	Cookin' Up Christmas	CR - BLOWN GLASS - GERMANY	ORNAMENT		1996	$18.00	
96-131-0	Crescent Moon	CR - BLOWN GLASS - GERMANY	ORNAMENT		1996	$13.00	
96-132-0	Way Cool	CR - BLOWN GLASS - GERMANY	ORNAMENT		1996	$22.00	
96-133-0	Waffle Balls	CR - BLOWN GLASS - GERMANY	ORNAMENT		1996	$27.00	
96-134-0	Full of Joy	CR - BLOWN GLASS - GERMANY	ORNAMENT		1996	$12.00	
96-135-0	Angel Prayer	CR - BLOWN GLASS - GERMANY	ORNAMENT		1996	$22.00	
96-136-0	Jumbo Tiffany Bells	CR - BLOWN GLASS - CZECH REP.	ORNAMENT		1996	$18.00	
96-138-0	Red Balloon	CR - BLOWN GLASS - GERMANY	ORNAMENT		1996	$24.00	
96-139-0	Snow Castle	CR - BLOWN GLASS - GERMANY	ORNAMENT		1996	$12.00	
96-140-0	Shoe Shack	CR - BLOWN GLASS - ITALY	ORNAMENT		1996	$44.00	
96-141-0	Circus Seal	CR - BLOWN GLASS - POLAND	ORNAMENT		1996	$22.00	
96-142-0	Prayer of Prayer	CR - BLOWN GLASS - CZECH REP.	ORNAMENT		1996	$16.00	
96-143-0	Starscape Santa	CR - BLOWN GLASS - POLAND	ORNAMENT		1996	$44.00	
96-144-0	Professor Hare	CR - BLOWN GLASS - POLAND	ORNAMENT		1996	$26.00	
96-145-0	Count Dimitri	CR - BLOWN GLASS - POLAND	ORNAMENT		1996	$24.00	
96-146-0	Snow Balling	CR - BLOWN GLASS - POLAND	ORNAMENT		1996	$26.00	
96-147-0	Christmas King	CR - BLOWN GLASS - POLAND	ORNAMENT		1996	$46.00	
96-148-0	Bottoms Up	CR - BLOWN GLASS - POLAND	ORNAMENT		1996	$26.00	
96-149-0	Eggbert	CR - BLOWN GLASS - POLAND	ORNAMENT		1996	$28.00	
96-150-0	Sleighful	CR - BLOWN GLASS - POLAND	ORNAMENT		1996	$34.00	
96-151-0	Return Engagement	CR - BLOWN GLASS - POLAND	ORNAMENT		1996	$38.00	
96-152-0	Caroline	CR - BLOWN GLASS - POLAND	ORNAMENT		1996	$24.00	
96-153-0	Toys for All	CR - BLOWN GLASS - POLAND	ORNAMENT		1996	$44.00	
96-154-0	Jet Elegance	CR - BLOWN GLASS - CZECH REP.	GARLAND		1996	$32.00	
96-155-0	Snowtem Pole	CR - BLOWN GLASS - POLAND	ORNAMENT		1996	$32.00	
96-156-0	Oh Christmas Tree!	CR - BLOWN GLASS - POLAND	ORNAMENT		1996	$42.00	
96-157-0	Eskimo Cheer	CR - BLOWN GLASS - POLAND	ORNAMENT		1996	$22.00	
96-158-0	Sapphire Santa	CR - BLOWN GLASS - POLAND	ORNAMENT		1996	$34.00	
96-159-0	The Clauses	CR - BLOWN GLASS - POLAND	ORNAMENT		1996	$26.00	
96-160-0	Bella D. Snowball	CR - BLOWN GLASS - POLAND	ORNAMENT		1996	$26.00	
96-161-0	Shy Fox	CR - BLOWN GLASS - POLAND	ORNAMENT		1996	$18.00	
96-162-0	Pinecone Bells	CR - BLOWN GLASS - GERMANY	ORNAMENT		1996	$16.00	
96-163-0	Rose Bells	CR - BLOWN GLASS - GERMANY	ORNAMENT		1996	$15.00	
96-164-0	Lady Grey	CR - BLOWN GLASS - ITALY	ORNAMENT		1996	$42.00	
96-165-0	Romanov	CR - BLOWN GLASS - ITALY	ORNAMENT		1996	$100.00	
96-166-0	From Orient Are	CR - BLOWN GLASS - ITALY	ORNAMENT		1996	$54.00	
96-167-0	Minuet	CR - BLOWN GLASS - ITALY	ORNAMENT		1996	$54.00	
96-168-0	Bundle of Joy	CR - BLOWN GLASS - ITALY	ORNAMENT		1996	$36.00	
96-169-0	Midnight Ride	CR - BLOWN GLASS - ITALY	ORNAMENT		1996	$26.00	
96-170-0	Java Jive	CR - BLOWN GLASS - ITALY	ORNAMENT		1996	$34.00	
96-171-0	Snow In Love	CR - BLOWN GLASS - ITALY	ORNAMENT		1996	$42.00	
96-172-0	Smiling Santa	CR - BLOWN GLASS - ITALY	ORNAMENT		1996	$44.00	
96-173-0	Off the Wall	CR - BLOWN GLASS - ITALY	ORNAMENT		1996	$46.00	
96-174-0	High Noon	CR - BLOWN GLASS - POLAND	ORNAMENT		1996	$22.00	
96-175-0	This Bear's for You	CR - BLOWN GLASS - POLAND	ORNAMENT		1996	$44.00	
96-176-0	Sing We Now	CR - BLOWN GLASS - POLAND	ORNAMENT		1996	$22.00	
96-177-0	Blue Princess	CR - BLOWN GLASS - GERMANY	ORNAMENT		1996	$24.00	
96-178-0	Blue Winter	CR - BLOWN GLASS - ITALY	ORNAMENT		1996	$48.00	
96-179-0	Ice Berg	CR - BLOWN GLASS - POLAND	ORNAMENT		1996	$18.00	
96-180-0	Clown Song	CR - BLOWN GLASS - POLAND	ORNAMENT		1996	$24.00	
96-181-0	Celestial Memories	CR - BLOWN GLASS - POLAND	ORNAMENT		1996	$18.00	
96-182-0	Golden Bear	CR - BLOWN GLASS - POLAND	ORNAMENT		1996	$24.00	

Order No.	Title	Type	Theme	Retired	Intro. Year	Retail Price	Secondary Price
96-183-0	Love is in the Air	CR - BLOWN GLASS - POLAND	ORNAMENT		1996	$22.00	
96-184-0	Chicken Little	CR - BLOWN GLASS - GERMANY	ORNAMENT		1996	$9.00	
96-185-0	Heavenly Triumph	CR - BLOWN GLASS - POLAND	ORNAMENT		1996	$22.00	
96-186-0	Here I Go	CR - BLOWN GLASS - POLAND	ORNAMENT		1996	$18.00	
96-187-0	Pookie	CR - BLOWN GLASS - POLAND	ORNAMENT		1996	$16.00	
96-188-0	Singing Armor	CR - BLOWN GLASS - POLAND	ORNAMENT		1996	$22.00	
96-189-0	Merry Matador	CR - BLOWN GLASS - POLAND	ORNAMENT		1996	$22.00	
96-190-0	Early American	CR - BLOWN GLASS - POLAND	ORNAMENT		1996	$22.00	
96-191-0	Steeple Chase	CR - BLOWN GLASS - POLAND	ORNAMENT		1996	$20.00	
96-192-0	Snowy Day	CR - BLOWN GLASS - POLAND	ORNAMENT		1996	$19.00	
96-193-0	Londonberry	CR - BLOWN GLASS - POLAND	ORNAMENT		1996	$44.00	
96-194-0	Dr. Flosswell	CR - BLOWN GLASS - POLAND	ORNAMENT		1996	$18.00	
96-195-0	Shimmering Songbirds	CR - BLOWN GLASS - CZECH REP.	ORNAMENT		1996	$12.00	
96-196-0	Tommy Snowball	CR - BLOWN GLASS - POLAND	ORNAMENT		1996	$24.00	
96-197-0	Iris Dreams	CR - BLOWN GLASS - POLAND	ORNAMENT		1996	$32.00	
96-198-0	Reflections in Blue	CR - BLOWN GLASS - POLAND	ORNAMENT		1996	$32.00	
96-199-0	English Garden	CR - BLOWN GLASS - POLAND	ORNAMENT		1996	$32.00	
96-200-0	Copernicus	CR - BLOWN GLASS - POLAND	ORNAMENT		1996	$34.00	
96-201-0	Jeremiah	CR - BLOWN GLASS - POLAND	ORNAMENT		1996	$26.00	
96-202-0	Jungle Fever	CR - BLOWN GLASS - CZECH REP.	ORNAMENT		1996	$18.00	
96-203-0	Pumpkin Eater	CR - BLOWN GLASS - POLAND	ORNAMENT		1996	$34.00	
96-204-0	Lucinda	CR - BLOWN GLASS - POLAND	ORNAMENT		1996	$38.00	
96-205-0	Bea Witched	CR - BLOWN GLASS - POLAND	ORNAMENT		1996	$38.00	
96-206-0	Trixie Treater	CR - BLOWN GLASS - POLAND	ORNAMENT		1996	$22.00	
96-207-0	Great Gobbles	CR - BLOWN GLASS - POLAND	ORNAMENT		1996	$38.00	
96-208-0	Polar Night	CR - BLOWN GLASS - POLAND	ORNAMENT		1996	$32.00	
96-209-0	Reach for a Star	CR - BLOWN GLASS - POLAND	ORNAMENT		1996	$32.00	
96-210-0	Playful Panda	CR - BLOWN GLASS - POLAND	ORNAMENT		1996	$32.00	
96-211-0	Vincent's Prize	CR - BLOWN GLASS - POLAND	ORNAMENT		1996	$32.00	
96-212-0	Festiva	CR - BLOWN GLASS - POLAND	ORNAMENT		1996	$36.00	
96-213-0	Snowbirds	CR - BLOWN GLASS - POLAND	ORNAMENT		1996	$32.00	
96-214-0	Oriental Porcelain	CR - BLOWN GLASS - POLAND	ORNAMENT		1996	$32.00	
96-215-0	Frosty Cardinal	CR - BLOWN GLASS - POLAND	ORNAMENT		1996	$32.00	
96-216-0	Poinsettia Snow	CR - BLOWN GLASS - POLAND	ORNAMENT		1996	$32.00	
96-217-0	Be My Valetine	CR - BLOWN GLASS - POLAND	ORNAMENT		1996	$18.00	
96-218-0	Astronomy	CR - BLOWN GLASS - CZECH REP.	ORNAMENT		1996	$24.00	
96-219-0	Big Star	CR - BLOWN GLASS - GERMANY	ORNAMENT		1996	$28.00	
96-220-0	Forest Cheer	CR - BLOWN GLASS - CZECH REP.	GARLAND		1996	$32.00	
96-221-0	Little Drummer Bear	CR - BLOWN GLASS - CZECH REP.	GARLAND		1996	$52.00	
96-222-0	Vintage Classics	CR - BLOWN GLASS - CZECH REP.	ORNAMENT		1996	$24.00	
96-223-0	Christmas Past	CR - BLOWN GLASS - CZECH REP.	ORNAMENT		1996	$18.00	
96-224-0	Sweet Tomato	CR - BLOWN GLASS - GERMANY	ORNAMENT		1996	$14.00	
96-225-0	Hot N-Frosty	CR - BLOWN GLASS - GERMANY	ORNAMENT		1996	$10.00	
96-226-0	This Spud's for Yule	CR - BLOWN GLASS - GERMANY	ORNAMENT		1996	$18.00	
96-227-0	Small Gnome Dome	CR - BLOWN GLASS - GERMANY	ORNAMENT		1996	$16.00	
96-228-0	Gnome Dome	CR - BLOWN GLASS - GERMANY	ORNAMENT		1996	$19.00	
96-229-0	Rosegay	CR - BLOWN GLASS - GERMANY	ORNAMENT		1996	$18.00	
96-230-0	What a Hoot	CR - BLOWN GLASS - GERMANY	ORNAMENT		1996	$34.00	
96-231-0	Nantucket Rose	CR - BLOWN GLASS - GERMANY	ORNAMENT		1996	$14.00	
96-232-0	Hedges	CR - BLOWN GLASS - POLAND	ORNAMENT		1996	$22.00	
96-233-0	Lemon Guard	CR - BLOWN GLASS - POLAND	ORNAMENT		1996	$22.00	
96-234-0	Frosty Pepper	CR - BLOWN GLASS - CZECH REP.	ORNAMENT		1996	$12.00	
96-235-0	Baby Buggy	CR - BLOWN GLASS - GERMANY	ORNAMENT		1996	$15.00	
96-236-0	Babushka	CR - BLOWN GLASS - POLAND	ORNAMENT		1996	$25.00	
96-237-0	Persia	CR - BLOWN GLASS - POLAND	ORNAMENT		1996	$18.00	
96-238-0	Elfin Pine	CR - BLOWN GLASS - POLAND	ORNAMENT		1996	$30.00	
96-239-0	Ginger Hearts	CR - BLOWN GLASS - POLAND	ORNAMENT		1996	$28.00	
96-240-0	Magic Munchkin	CR - BLOWN GLASS - POLAND	ORNAMENT		1996	$32.00	
96-241-0	Croc Cutie	CR - BLOWN GLASS - POLAND	ORNAMENT		1996	$22.00	
96-242-0	Romeow	CR - BLOWN GLASS - POLAND	ORNAMENT		1996	$34.00	
96-243-0	Muse	CR - BLOWN GLASS - POLAND	ORNAMENT		1996	$26.00	
96-244-0	Master Jack	CR - BLOWN GLASS - POLAND	ORNAMENT		1996	$26.00	
96-245-0	Ocean Call	CR - BLOWN GLASS - POLAND	ORNAMENT		1996	$18.00	
96-246-0	Every Bead of My Heart	CR - BLOWN GLASS - CZECH REP.	ORNAMENT		1996	$22.00	
96-247-0	Little Birdie	CR - BLOWN GLASS - CZECH REP.	ORNAMENT		1996	$12.00	
96-248-0	Marshmallow	CR - BLOWN GLASS - GERMANY	ORNAMENT		1996	$12.00	
96-249-0	Star Shot	CR - BLOWN GLASS - POLAND	ORNAMENT		1996	$32.00	
96-250-0	Winter Dream	CR - BLOWN GLASS - POLAND	ORNAMENT		1996	$42.00	
96-251-0	Yankee Doodle	CR - BLOWN GLASS - POLAND	ORNAMENT		1996	$34.00	
96-252-0	Santa Hoot	CR - BLOWN GLASS - POLAND	ORNAMENT		1996	$18.00	
96-253-0	Shimmy Down	CR - BLOWN GLASS - POLAND	ORNAMENT		1996	$42.00	
96-254-0	Bear Bundle	CR - BLOWN GLASS - POLAND	ORNAMENT		1996	$22.00	
96-255-0	His Wizardry	CR - BLOWN GLASS - POLAND	ORNAMENT		1996	$22.00	
96-257-0	Flying High	CR - BLOWN GLASS - POLAND	ORNAMENT		1996	$42.00	
96-258-0	Eternal Flame	CR - BLOWN GLASS - POLAND	ORNAMENT		1996	$28.00	
96-256-0	Union Jack	CR - BLOWN GLASS - POLAND	ORNAMENT		1996	$44.00	
96-259-0	Swirl Balloon	CR - BLOWN GLASS - POLAND	ORNAMENT		1996	$24.00	
96-260-0	Rhapsody	CR - BLOWN GLASS - POLAND	ORNAMENT		1996	$60.00	
96-261-0	Harlequin Teardrop	CR - BLOWN GLASS - POLAND	ORNAMENT		1996	$32.00	
96-262-0	Starburst	CR - BLOWN GLASS - CZECH REP.	GARLAND		1996	$52.00	
96-263-0	Santa's Heartstrings	CR - BLOWN GLASS - CZECH REP.	GARLAND		1996	$44.00	
96-264-0	Christmas Colors	CR - BLOWN GLASS - CZECH REP.	GARLAND		1996	$32.00	
96-265-0	Peppermint Joy	CR - BLOWN GLASS - CZECH REP.	GARLAND		1996	$52.00	
96-266-0	Sea Spray	CR - BLOWN GLASS - CZECH REP.	GARLAND		1996	$32.00	
96-267-0	Santa Heart	CR - BLOWN GLASS - CZECH REP.	GARLAND		1996	$54.00	
96-268-0	Baubles and Beads	CR - BLOWN GLASS - CZECH REP.	GARLAND		1996	$48.00	
96-269-0	Drummer Santa	CR - BLOWN GLASS - CZECH REP.	GARLAND		1996	$44.00	
96-270-0	Plum Santa Garland	CR - BLOWN GLASS - CZECH REP.	GARLAND		1996	$44.00	
96-271-0	Clear Polar Night	CR - BLOWN GLASS - POLAND	ORNAMENT		1996	$46.00	
96-272-0	Scherazade	CR - BLOWN GLASS - POLAND	ORNAMENT		1996	$32.00	
96-273-0	Winter Forest	CR - BLOWN GLASS - POLAND	ORNAMENT		1996	$46.00	
96-274-0	'round Midnight	CR - BLOWN GLASS - POLAND	ORNAMENT		1996	$30.00	
96-275-0	Apple Blossom	CR - BLOWN GLASS - POLAND	ORNAMENT		1996	$46.00	

Order No.	Title	Type	Theme	Retired	Intro. Year	Retial Price	Secondary Price
96-276-0	Crimson Stripes	CR - BLOWN GLASS - POLAND	ORNAMENT		1996	$32.00	
96-277-0	Baby Elephants	CR - BLOWN GLASS - POLAND	ORNAMENT		1996	$18.00	
96-278-0	Alpine Blush Finial	CR - BLOWN GLASS - POLAND	FINIAL		1996	$90.00	
96-279-0	Santa Swirl	CR - BLOWN GLASS - POLAND	GARLAND		1996	$44.00	
96-280-0	Large Harlequin	CR - BLOWN GLASS - POLAND	ORNAMENT		1996	$36.00	
96-281-0	Heart's Desire	CR - BLOWN GLASS - POLAND	ORNAMENT		1996	$34.00	
96-282-0	Carnival Star	CR - BLOWN GLASS - POLAND	ORNAMENT		1996	$32.00	
96-283-0	Winter Twilight	CR - BLOWN GLASS - POLAND	ORNAMENT		1996	$46.00	
96-284-0	Winter Blossom	CR - BLOWN GLASS - POLAND	ORNAMENT		1996	$46.00	
96-285-0	Midnight Orchid	CR - BLOWN GLASS - POLAND	ORNAMENT		1996	$32.00	
96-286-0	Up And Away	CR - BLOWN GLASS - POLAND	ORNAMENT		1996	$46.00	
96-288-0	Topolina	CR - BLOWN GLASS - ITALY	ORNAMENT		1996	$42.00	
96-289-0	Twilight Santa Reflector	CR - BLOWN GLASS - POLAND	ORNAMENT		1996	$48.00	
96-290-0	Bossom Bunnies	CR - BLOWN GLASS - ITALY	ORNAMENT		1996	$46.00	
96-291-0	Nativity Snowfall Finial	CR - BLOWN GLASS - ITALY	FINIAL		1996	$170.00	
96-292-0	Santa Deluxe	CR - BLOWN GLASS - POLAND	GARLAND		1996	$44.00	
96-293-0	Grandma Cares	CR - BLOWN GLASS - POLAND	ORNAMENT		1996	$22.00	
96-294-0	Blossom Dairy	CR - BLOWN GLASS - GERMANY	ORNAMENT		1996	$19.00	
96-295-0	Magic World	CR - BLOWN GLASS - GERMANY	ORNAMENT		1996	$23.00	
96-296-0	Ocean Dreams	CR - BLOWN GLASS - GERMANY	ORNAMENT		1996	$14.00	
96-297-0	Winter Games	CR - BLOWN GLASS - POLAND	ORNAMENT		1996	$24.00	
96-298-0	Shell Finial	CR - BLOWN GLASS - GERMANY	FINIAL		1996	$38.00	
96-299-0	Candy Swirl	CR - BLOWN GLASS - GERMANY	ORNAMENT		1996	$24.00	
96-300-0	Snowgift	CR - BLOWN GLASS - CZECH REP.	GARLAND		1996	$54.00	
96-301-0	Church Window	CR - BLOWN GLASS - CZECH REP.	ORNAMENT		1996	$16.00	
96-302-0	Tiffany Rainbow	CR - BLOWN GLASS - CZECH REP.	ORNAMENT		1996	$26.00	
96-305-0	Rainbow Flair	CR - BLOWN GLASS - CZECH REP.	ORNAMENT		1996	$28.00	
96-306-0	Beaded Buggy	CR - BLOWN GLASS - CZECH REP.	ORNAMENT		1996	$24.00	
96-307 -0	Panda Heart	CR - BLOWN GLASS - CZECH REP.	GARLAND		1996	$70.00	
96-308 -0	Ice Sky Garland	CR - BLOWN GLASS - CZECH REP.	GARLAND		1996	$32.00	
96-309-0	Egypt Rings	CR - BLOWN GLASS - GERMANY	ORNAMENT		1996	$13.00	
96-310-0	Delft Rose	CR - BLOWN GLASS - GERMANY	ORNAMENT		1996	$24.00	
96-311-0	Frosty Jewels	CR - BLOWN GLASS - GERMANY	ORNAMENT		1996	$12.00	
96-312-0	By The Sea	CR - BLOWN GLASS - CZECH REP.	ORNAMENT		1996	$52.00	
96-313-0	Under The Sea	CR - BLOWN GLASS - GERMANY	ORNAMENT		1996	$17.00	
96-314-0	Time Flies	CR - BLOWN GLASS - POLAND	ORNAMENT		1996	$28.00	
96-315-0	One For All	CR - BLOWN GLASS - ITALY	ORNAMENT		1996	$76.00	
96-316-0	Seafoam Garland	CR - BLOWN GLASS - CZECH REP.	ORNAMENT		1996	$52.00	
96-303-0	Sail Away	CR - BLOWN GLASS - CZECH REP.	ORNAMENT		1996	$44.00	
96-304-0	Patriot Garland	CR - BLOWN GLASS - CZECH REP.	GARLAND		1996	$32.00	
97-001-0	Angel Light		ORNAMENT		1997	$26.00	
97-002-0	Witch Way		ORNAMENT		1997	$24.00	
97-003-0	Nutcracker Stripes		ORNAMENT		1997	$26.00	
97-004-0	Sweet Melody		ORNAMENT		1997	$27.00	
97-005-0	Hannukah Star		ORNAMENT		1997	$19.00	
97-006-0	Jumbo Plum		ORNAMENT		1997	$17.00	
97-007-0	Vidalia Onion		ORNAMENT		1997	$17.00	
97-008-0	Litle Star Angels		ORNAMENT		1997	$24.00	
97-009-0	Kitty fun		ORNAMENT		1997	$19.50	
97-010-0	Classic Frog		ORNAMENT		1997	$24.00	
97-011-0	Angel On High		ORNAMENT		1997	$33.00	
97-012-0	Little Pen		ORNAMENT		1997	$18.00	
97-013-0	David's Star/Large		ORNAMENT		1997	$17.00	
97-014-0	David's Star/Small		ORNAMENT		1997	$15.00	
97-015-0	Roly Striped Santa		ORNAMENT		1997	$34.00	
97-016-0	Drum Cracker		ORNAMENT		1997	$49.00	
97-017-0	Plum Santa		ORNAMENT		1997	$17.00	
97-018-0	Harvey		ORNAMENT		1997	$53.00	
97-019-0	Ice Cracker		ORNAMENT		1997	$42.00	
97-020-1	Monster Mash		ORNAMENT		1997	$35.00	
97-023-0	Pastel Carousel		ORNAMENT		1997	$35.00	
97-026-0	Woodland Frost		ORNAMENT		1997	$60.00	
97-027-0	Egg La Plante		ORNAMENT		1997	$15.00	
97-028-0	Pomegranate		ORNAMENT		1997	$19.00	
97-029-0	Little Wreath Angels		ORNAMENT		1997	$24.00	
97-030-0	Apple Slice		ORNAMENT		1997	$14.00	
97-031-0	Medium Corn		ORNAMENT		1997	$15.00	
97-032-0	Small ear		ORNAMENT		1997	$11.00	
97-033-0	Frosty Garlic		ORNAMENT		1997	$25.00	
97-034-0	Little Vidalia		ORNAMENT		1997	$13.00	
97-035-0	Garden Spoons		ORNAMENT		1997	$11.00	
97-036-0	Tree Wheelin'		ORNAMENT		1997	$30.00	
97-037-0	Squealbarrow		ORNAMENT		1997	$30.00	
97-038-0	Big Pen		ORNAMENT		1997	$20.00	
97-039-0	Kandy Kringles		ORNAMENT		1997	$25.00	
97-040-0	Darling Angel		ORNAMENT		1997	$20.00	
97-041-0	Little Chapel		ORNAMENT		1997	$17.00	
97-042-0	Frosty Scallops		ORNAMENT		1997	$13.00	
97-043-0	I Didn't Do It		ORNAMENT		1997	$24.00	
97-044-0	Choir Angels		ORNAMENT		1997	$35.00	
97-045-0	Eden Serpent		ORNAMENT		1997	$13.00	
97-046-0	Sea Swirl		ORNAMENT		1997	$13.00	
97-047-0	Little Hopper		ORNAMENT		1997	$11.00	
97-048-0	Frosty Bears		ORNAMENT		1997	$14.00	
97-049-0	Hootie		ORNAMENT		1997	$23.00	
97-050-0	Jewel Hearts		ORNAMENT		1997	$26.00	
97-051-0	Dalia's Star/Large		ORNAMENT		1997	$19.00	
97-052-0	Dalia's Star/Small		ORNAMENT		1997	$17.00	
97-053-0	Gold Trim David's Star		ORNAMENT		1997	$16.00	
97-054-0	Love & Protect		ORNAMENT		1997	$15.00	
97-055-0	A Courtin' Froggy		ORNAMENT		1997	$19.00	
97-056-0	Cozy Kittens		ORNAMENT		1997	$13.00	
97-057-0	Sweetheart Angels		ORNAMENT		1997	$24.00	

Order No.	Title	Type	Theme	Retired	Intro. Year	Retail Price	Secondary Price
97-058-0	Ducky		ORNAMENT		1997	$25.00	
97-059-0	Galaxy Frost		ORNAMENT		1997	$70.00	
97-060-0	Birdhouse		ORNAMENT		1997	$17.00	
97-061-0	Snow Kids		ORNAMENT		1997	$13.00	
97-062-0	Winter Chapel		ORNAMENT		1997	$19.00	
97-063-0	Pining Santa		ORNAMENT		1997	$15.00	
97-064-0	Holly Berry Santa		ORNAMENT		1997	$24.00	
97-065-0	Spring elves		ORNAMENT		1997	$26.00	
97-066-0	Toyland Santa		ORNAMENT		1997	$47.00	
97-067-0	Conic Emeralds		ORNAMENT		1997	$36.00	
97-069-0	Concertina		ORNAMENT		1997	$23.00	
97-070-0	Pinewoods Santa		ORNAMENT		1997	$45.00	
97-071-0	Rainbow Iris		ORNAMENT		1997	$40.00	
97-072-0	Munchkin Blossom		ORNAMENT		1997	$36.00	
97-073-0	Rose Bouquet		ORNAMENT		1997	$26.00	
97-074-0	Love Struck		ORNAMENT		1997	$17.00	
97-075-0	Comet		ORNAMENT		1997	$15.00	
97-076-0	Fancy Flight		ORNAMENT		1997	$24.00	
97-077-0	Ruby Star Finial		FINIAL		1997	$82.00	
97-078-0	Blood Orange		ORNAMENT		1997	$14.00	
97-079-0	Ruby Orange		ORNAMENT		1997	$17.00	
97-080-0	Heaven Tree		ORNAMENT		1997	$67.00	
97-081-0	Star Gazing Finial		FINIAL		1997	$105.00	
97-082-0	Ruby Star Drop		ORNAMENT		1997	$80.00	
97-083-0	Ruby Star		ORNAMENT		1997	$26.00	
97-084-0	Star Horizons		ORNAMENT		1997	$17.00	
97-085-0	Golden Star/Large		ORNAMENT		1997	$15.00	
97-086-0	Royal Claus		ORNAMENT		1997	$47.00	
97-087-0	Hanukkah Ball		ORNAMENT		1997	$34.00	
97-088-0	Golden Teardrop		ORNAMENT		1997	$24.00	
97-087-0	Hanukkah Ball		ORNAMENT		1997	$34.00	
97-089-0	Chilly Charlie		ORNAMENT		1997	$28.00	
97-090-0	Christmas Cloudhoppers		ORNAMENT		1997	$70.00	
97-091-0	Santa Medallion		ORNAMENT		1997	$17.00	
97-092-0	April Bunny		ORNAMENT		1997	$36.00	
97-093-0	Lucky Ted		ORNAMENT		1997	$32.00	
97-094-0	Sky Kringle		ORNAMENT		1997	$29.00	
97-095-0	General Cracker		ORNAMENT		1997	$36.00	
97-096-0	Santa Tree Finial		FINIAL		1997	$76.00	
97-097-0	Deluxe Nutcracker Finial		FINIAL		1997	$70.00	
97-098-0	Coburg Cracker		ORNAMENT		1997	$36.00	
97-099-0	Valentine Finial		FINIAL		1997	$50.00	
97-CIR-1	Moscow Circus		ORNAMENT		1997	$90.00	
97-EGY-1	Ramses		ORNAMENT		1997	$50.00	
97-HG-2	Nibble Nibble		ORNAMENT		1997	$60.00	
97-HOU-1	Sugar Hill		ORNAMENT		1997	$145.00	
97-NAT-3	Shepherds prayer, Gloria		ORNAMENT		1997	$90.00	
97-NC-3	Nutcracker III		ORNAMENT		1997	$90.00	
97-PAT-1	General Lafayaette		ORNAMENT		1997	$35.00	
97-SP-19	Five Gold Rings		ORNAMENT		1997	$62.00	
97-SP-20	Enchanted Evening		ORNAMENT		1997	$55.00	
97-SP-21	Li'l Miss Angel		ORNAMENT		1997		
97-SP-22	A Caring Clown		ORNAMENT		1997	$36.00	
97-SP-23	Kitty Cares		ORNAMENT		1997	$30.00	
97-SP-24	Regency Santa		ORNAMENT		1997	$185.00	
97-SP-25	Yippy Yi Yo		ORNAMENT		1997	$70.00	
97-SP-26	Watch Over Me		ORNAMENT		1997	$28.00	
97-100-0	Strawberry Santa		ORNAMENT		1997	$47.00	
97-101-0	Rose Red		ORNAMENT		1997	$17.00	
97-102-0	Boutonniere Bloom		ORNAMENT		1997	$17.00	
97-103-0	Joyful Ted Finial		FINIAL		1997	$65.00	
97-104-0	Porcelain Pony		ORNAMENT		1997	$24.00	
97-105-0	Orange Frost		ORNAMENT		1997	$17.00	
97-106-0	Apple Snap		ORNAMENT		1997	$17.00	
97-107-0	Pepper's Frost		ORNAMENT		1997	$16.00	
97-108-0	Winter Stocking		ORNAMENT		1997	$15.00	
97-109-0	Sleigh Bears		ORNAMENT		1997	$19.00	
97-110-0	Vineyard Frost		ORNAMENT		1997	$23.00	
97-111-0	Juicey Frost		ORNAMENT		1997	$17.00	
97-112-0	Green Grapes		ORNAMENT		1997	$11.00	
97-113-0	Timber Claus		ORNAMENT		1997	$34.00	
97-114-0	Old World Angel		ORNAMENT		1997	$26.00	
97-115-0	Baby Berries		ORNAMENT		1997	$11.00	
97-116-0	Candy Claus		ORNAMENT		1997	$30.00	
97-117-0	Kiddie Clown		ORNAMENT		1997	$34.00	
97-119-0	Shroom Shack		ORNAMENT		1997	$19.00	
97-120-0	Kitty Flight		ORNAMENT		1997	$41.00	
97-121-0	Gardening Angels		ORNAMENT		1997	$36.00	
97-122-0	Autumn Birds		ORNAMENT		1997	$24.00	
97-123-0	Winter Birds		ORNAMENT		1997	$24.00	
97-124-0	Love Reflections		ORNAMENT		1997	$45.00	
97-125-0	Sunrise Sunset		ORNAMENT		1997	$19.00	
97-126-0	Jumbo Lemon		ORNAMENT		1997	$17.00	
97-127-0	Jumbo Lime		ORNAMENT		1997	$17.00	
97-128-0	Tiny Chiquita		ORNAMENT		1997	$13.00	
97-129-0	Jumbo Corn		ORNAMENT		1997	$26.00	
97-130-0	Frosty Cardinal Finial		FINIAL		1997	$96.00	
97-131-0	Candy Starship		ORNAMENT		1997	$45.00	
97-132-0	Willy Wobble		ORNAMENT		1997	$53.00	
97-133-0	Fauntleroy		ORNAMENT		1997	$32.00	
97-134-0	Laddie		ORNAMENT		1997	$35.00	
97-135-0	Holly Frost		ORNAMENT		1997	$24.00	
97-136-0	Cranberry Frost		ORNAMENT		1997	$24.00	

Order No.	Title	Type	Theme	Retired	Intro. Year	Retial Price	Secondary Price
97-137-0	Dutch Date		ORNAMENT		1997	$59.00	
97-138-0	Basketball		ORNAMENT		1997	$23.00	
97-139-0	Pageantry		ORNAMENT		1997	$36.00	
97-140-0	De Milo		ORNAMENT		1997	$42.00	
97-141-0	Safari Santa		ORNAMENT		1997	$40.00	
97-142-0	Poney Express		ORNAMENT		1997	$43.00	
97-143-0	Hopper B. Topper		ORNAMENT		1997	$47.00	
97-144-0	The Duke		ORNAMENT		1997	$41.00	
97-145-0	Quintessa		ORNAMENT		1997	$57.00	
97-146-0	Jeb And Hannah Zuill		ORNAMENT		1997	$70.00	
97-147-0	Sun Kissed		ORNAMENT		1997	$18.00	
97-148-0	Jolly Elf		ORNAMENT		1997	$40.00	
97-149-0	Homerun Holiday		ORNAMENT		1997	$45.00	
97-150-0	Peachtree Polka		ORNAMENT		1997	$53.00	
97-151-0	Jolly Jalopy		ORNAMENT		1997	$51.00	
97-152-0	Spruced-Up Spruce		ORNAMENT		1997	$45.00	
97-153-0	Enchanter		ORNAMENT		1997	$39.00	
97-155-0	Persian Delight		ORNAMENT		1997	$38.00	
97-156-0	Letter To My Love		ORNAMENT		1997	$34.00	
97-159-0	Chow Cows		ORNAMENT		1997	$37.00	
97-160-0	Bird Go 'Round Garland		GARLAND		1997	$50.00	
97-161-0	Huggy Bear		ORNAMENT		1997	$54.00	
97-162-0	Miss Marina		ORNAMENT		1997	$36.00	
97-163-0	Monkey Shines		ORNAMENT		1997	$60.00	
97-164-0	Billy Joe N' Bessie Jean		ORNAMENT		1997	$70.00	
97-165-0	Mr. Lincoln		ORNAMENT		1997	$40.00	
97-166-0	General George		ORNAMENT		1997	$49.00	
97-167-0	Northern Knights		ORNAMENT		1997	$40.00	
97-168-0	Frosty Wise		ORNAMENT		1997	$30.00	
97-169-0	Snuggle Buddies		ORNAMENT		1997	$26.00	
97-170-0	Shore Light		ORNAMENT		1997	$34.00	
97-171-0	Good Night Prayer		ORNAMENT		1997	$45.00	
97-172-0	Mountain Pine		ORNAMENT		1997	$42.00	
97-173-0	Candy Corn		ORNAMENT		1997	$29.00	
97-175-0	Winning Smile		ORNAMENT		1997	$40.00	
97-176-0	Bright Eyes & Bushy Tail		ORNAMENT		1997	$38.00	
97-177-0	Nutty		ORNAMENT		1997	$30.00	
97-178-0	Kitty Clown		ORNAMENT		1997	$24.00	
97-179-0	Manchester		ORNAMENT		1997	$26.00	
97-180-0	Golden Collie		ORNAMENT		1997	$25.00	
97-181-0	Kitty Basket		ORNAMENT		1997	$23.00	
97-182-0	Dainty Jane		ORNAMENT		1997	$34.00	
97-183-0	Pearly		ORNAMENT		1997	$40.00	
97-184-0	Rock Lobster		ORNAMENT		1997	$26.00	
97-185-0	Rocket Man		ORNAMENT		1997	$28.00	
97-188-0	To The Moon		ORNAMENT		1997	$30.00	
97-189-0	Daisy Darling		ORNAMENT		1997	$30.00	
97-190-0	Harvest Day		ORNAMENT		1997	$50.00	
97-191-0	Shroom With A View		ORNAMENT		1997	$48.00	
97-192-0	Spring Debut		ORNAMENT		1997	$19.00	
97-193-0	Cock A Doddle Doo		ORNAMENT		1997	$30.00	
97-194-0	Hoo-Dunnit		ORNAMENT		1997	$34.00	
97-196-0	Wabbit Wobbles		ORNAMENT		1997	$54.00	
97-197-0	Elfkin		ORNAMENT		1997	$30.00	
97-198-0	Bunmobile		ORNAMENT		1997	$36.00	
97-199-0	Sabrina		ORNAMENT		1997	$24.00	
97-200-0	Pumpkin Pete		ORNAMENT		1997	$34.00	
97-201-0	Harp Song		ORNAMENT		1997	$26.00	
97-203-0	Traditions		ORNAMENT		1997	$48.00	
97-204-0	Emerald Isle		ORNAMENT		1997	$36.00	
97-205-0	Whispers Of Joy		ORNAMENT		1997	$64.00	
97-206-0	Stars & Stripes Aloft		ORNAMENT		1997	$47.00	
97-207-0	A Loving Heart		ORNAMENT		1997	$44.00	
97-208-0	Noel's Bells		ORNAMENT		1997	$35.00	
97-209-0	Enough For All		ORNAMENT		1997	$80.00	
97-210-0	Gather 'Round		ORNAMENT		1997	$38.00	
97-211-0	Rockaway Sweethearts		ORNAMENT		1997	$30.00	
97-212-0	Goldie		ORNAMENT		1997	$24.00	
97-215-0	Chapel Hill		ORNAMENT		1997	$32.00	
97-216-0	One More Stop		ORNAMENT		1997	$42.50	
97-217-0	Big Nick		ORNAMENT		1997	$85.00	
97-218-0	Chimney Cheer		ORNAMENT		1997	$39.00	
97-219-0	Goldie And Son		ORNAMENT		1997	$26.00	
97-220-0	Felina		ORNAMENT		1997	$24.00	
97-221-0	Christmas Filly		ORNAMENT		1997	$47.00	
97-222-0	Making A List		ORNAMENT		1997	$42.00	
97-223-0	Hey Diddle Diddle		ORNAMENT		1997	$55.00	
97-224-0	Snowy Owl		ORNAMENT		1997	$28.00	
97-225-0	Evening Owl		ORNAMENT		1997	$28.00	
97-226-0	Sleepy Hollowhead		ORNAMENT		1997	$48.00	
97-227-0	Rosey O'hare		ORNAMENT		1997	$45.00	
97-228-0	Lillie-Mae		ORNAMENT		1997	$30.00	
97-229-0	My Little Monkey		ORNAMENT		1997	$36.00	
97-230-0	Aunt Peggy		ORNAMENT		1997	$30.00	
97-231-0	Santa's Workshop		ORNAMENT		1997	$49.00	
97-232-0	A Cool Surprise		ORNAMENT		1997	$34.00	
97-233-0	Rooftops Of London		ORNAMENT		1997	$80.00	
97-234-0	Piled Mile High		ORNAMENT		1997	$49.00	
97-236-0	Santa Serenade		ORNAMENT		1997	$48.00	
97-237-0	Merry Tune		ORNAMENT		1997	$48.00	
97-238-0	All Ready To Go		ORNAMENT		1997	$45.00	
97-239-0	Heart Ride		ORNAMENT		1997	$28.00	
97-240-0	Roy Rabbit		ORNAMENT		1997	$47.00	

Order No.	Title	Type	Theme	Retired	Intro. Year	Retail Price	Secondary Price
97-241-0	Punkin' Pal		ORNAMENT		1997	$45.00	
97-242-0	Snow Gent		ORNAMENT		1997	$35.00	
97-244-0	Teacher's Pet		ORNAMENT		1997	$40.00	
97-245-0	Teddy For President		ORNAMENT		1997	$34.00	
97-246-0	Sledin' To My House		ORNAMENT		1997	$51.00	
97-247-0	Santa Delivers		ORNAMENT		1997	$59.00	
97-248-0	Bobsquad		ORNAMENT		1997	$46.00	
97-249-0	Sky Ride		ORNAMENT		1997	$45.00	
97-250-0	Heartlight Express		ORNAMENT		1997	$49.00	
97-251-0	Squeezebox Santa		ORNAMENT		1997	$40.00	
97-252-0	Holly Jolly		ORNAMENT		1997	$49.00	
97-253-0	Sack O'Plenty		ORNAMENT		1997	$40.00	
97-255-0	Elfin Magic		ORNAMENT		1997	$35.00	
97-256-0	Oxford Santa		ORNAMENT		1997	$50.00	
97-257-0	Gold Balmoral Santa		ORNAMENT		1997	$85.00	
97-257-1	Blue Balmoral Santa		ORNAMENT		1997	$84.00	
97-258-0	Dublin Way Santa		ORNAMENT		1997	$69.00	
97-259-0	Winter Wisdom		ORNAMENT		1997	$68.00	
97-260-0	Glasgow Santa		ORNAMENT		1997	$49.00	
97-261-E	Little Golden Hood		ORNAMENT		1997	$39.00	
97-262-0	Last Stop		ORNAMENT		1997	$55.00	
97-263-0	Scooting Star		ORNAMENT		1997	$50.00	
97-264-0	Harvest Santa		ORNAMENT		1997	$38.00	
97-265-0	Snowflake		ORNAMENT		1997	$15.00	
97-266-0	Splash		ORNAMENT		1997	$26.00	
97-267-0	Who?		ORNAMENT		1997	$30.00	
97-268-0	Little Ralph		ORNAMENT		1997	$19.00	
97-270-0	Wee Berry House		ORNAMENT		1997	$25.00	
97-271-0	Henry Chesterfield		ORNAMENT		1997	$26.00	
97-272-0	Hawaii Gold		ORNAMENT		1997	$25.00	
97-273-0	Razzle Berry		ORNAMENT		1997	$11.00	
97-274-0	Sparkle Cone		ORNAMENT		1997	$9.00	
97-275-0	Merry Monks		ORNAMENT		1997	$55.00	
97-276-0	Santa Swift		ORNAMENT		1997	$63.00	
97-277-0	Forest Nut		ORNAMENT		1997	$11.00	
97-278-0	Napolean II		ORNAMENT		1997	$34.00	
97-279-0	Miss Holiday		ORNAMENT		1997	$21.00	
97-280-0	Toychest		ORNAMENT		1997	$47.00	
97-281-0	Masha		ORNAMENT		1997	$29.50	
97-282-0	Angel's Song		ORNAMENT		1997	$26.00	
97-283-0	Rufus T. Dawg		ORNAMENT		1997	$30.00	
97-284-0	Sea Shells		ORNAMENT		1997	$15.00	
97-285-0	Day Or Night		ORNAMENT		1997	$23.00	
97-286-0	The Bunny Tones		ORNAMENT		1997	$92.00	
97-288-0	Gold Winter Blossom Finial		FINIAL		1997	$105.00	
97-288-1	White Winter Blossom Finial		FINIAL		1997	$105.00	
97-288-2	Pink Winter Blossom Finial		EVENT PIECE		1997	$105.00	
97-288-3	Blue Winter Blossom Finial		FINIAL		1997	$105.00	
97-289-0	Nick Of Time		ORNAMENT		1997	$74.00	
97-292-0	Snowfall		ORNAMENT		1997	$49.00	
97-293-0	Let It Snow		ORNAMENT		1997	$53.00	
97-295-0	Circus Chief		ORNAMENT		1997	$45.00	
97-297-0	Merry Measure		ORNAMENT		1997	$25.00	
97-299-0	Sweet Cakes		ORNAMENT		1997	$40.00	
97-300-0	Candy Garland		GARLAND		1997	$65.00	
97-301-0	Crimson Stripes Deluxe		ORNAMENT		1997	$105.00	
97-302-0	Frosty Mist		ORNAMENT		1997	$52.00	
97-303-0	Royal Crown		ORNAMENT		1997	$26.00	
97-304-0	Santa's Sleigh '97		ORNAMENT		1997	$46.00	
97-305-0	Persian Magic		ORNAMENT		1997	$48.00	
97-306-0	Madras Magic		ORNAMENT		1997	$48.00	
97-307-0	Jumbo Field Blossom		ORNAMENT		1997	$48.00	
97-308-0	Our Nations Father		ORNAMENT		1997	$36.00	
97-309-0	Sunnyside		ORNAMENT		1997	$48.00	
97-310-0	Spiral Fantasies		ORNAMENT		1997	$44.00	
97-311-0	Gem Spirals		ORNAMENT		1997	$35.00	
97-312-0	Emporium		ORNAMENT		1997	$59.00	
97-313-0	Milano Finial		ORNAMENT		1997	$135.00	
97-314-0	From The Orchard		ORNAMENT		1997	$38.00	
97-315-0	Simon's Dreidel		ORNAMENT		1997	$36.00	
97-316-0	Me Big Chief		ORNAMENT		1997	$50.00	
97-317-0	Kit 'N Boots		ORNAMENT		1997	$36.00	
97-318-0	Been A Good Girl		ORNAMENT		1997	$63.00	
97-319-0	Santa's Herald		ORNAMENT		1997	$63.00	
97-320-0	Santa Ho!		ORNAMENT		1997	$62.00	
97-321-0	Miss Valentine		ORNAMENT		1997	$76.00	
97-322-0	Jasmine Dancer		ORNAMENT		1997	$125.00	
97-323-0	Centaur		ORNAMENT		1997	$95.00	
97-324-0	Balancing Betty		ORNAMENT		1997	$80.00	
97-325-0	Rudy, Cubby & Max		ORNAMENT		1997	$29.00	
97-326-0	Holly Berry Ball		ORNAMENT		1997	$48.00	
97-327-0	Midnight Tidings		ORNAMENT		1997	$36.00	
97-328-0	Humperdink		ORNAMENT		1997	$53.00	
97-329-0	Wintersaurus		ORNAMENT		1997	$47.00	
97-330-0	Rex Dance		ORNAMENT		1997	$48.00	
97-331-0	Neptune		ORNAMENT		1997	$65.00	
97-333-0	Sea Stars		ORNAMENT		1997	$25.00	
97-334-0	Sonya Honey		ORNAMENT		1997	$67.00	
97-335-0	Grape Expectations		ORNAMENT		1997	$46.00	
97-336-0	Kings Herald		ORNAMENT		1997	$49.00	
97-337-0	Pampered Pussycats		ORNAMENT		1997	$34.00	
97-338-0	Christmas Lace		ORNAMENT		1997	$46.00	
97-339-0	Rockwell		ORNAMENT		1997	$46.00	

Order No.	Title	Type	Theme	Retired	Intro. Year	Retial Price	Secondary Price
97-341-0	Winter Skate		ORNAMENT		1997	$67.00	
97-342-0	Flora Diva		ORNAMENT		1997	$57.00	
97-343-0	Angel Smiles		ORNAMENT		1997	$29.00	
97-344-0	Cupid Flight Garland		ORNAMENT		1997	$50.00	
97-344-0	Cupid Flight Garland		GARLAND		1997	$50.00	
97-345-0	Grape Expectations		ORNAMENT		1997	$46.00	
97-346-0	Kings Herald		ORNAMENT		1997	$49.00	
97-347-0	Pampered Pussycats		ORNAMENT		1997	$34.00	
97-348-0	Christmas Lace		ORNAMENT		1997	$46.00	
97-349-0	Carnival Harlequin		ORNAMENT		1997	$50.00	
97-350-0	Balancing Act		ORNAMENT		1997	$35.00	
97-351-0	Spring Ripple		ORNAMENT		1997	$24.00	
97-352-0	Autumn Ripple		ORNAMENT		1997	$24.00	
97-353-0	Classic Ripple		ORNAMENT		1997	$24.00	
97-354-0	Rainbow Ripple I		ORNAMENT		1997	$26.00	
97-355-0	Rainbow Ripple II		ORNAMENT		1997	$26.00	
97-356-0	Off The Wall Jumbo		ORNAMENT		1997	$64.00	
97-357-0	Miss Bluebell		ORNAMENT		1997	$68.00	
97-358-0	Little Jewel Tassels		ORNAMENT		1997	$13.00	
97-359-0	Jazz Ball		ORNAMENT		1997	$35.00	
97-360-0	Winter Whiz		ORNAMENT		1997	$38.00	
97-361-0	Rockin' Ted		ORNAMENT		1997	$40.00	
97-362-0	Sweet Serenity		ORNAMENT		1997	$50.00	
97-363-0	Country Winter		ORNAMENT		1997	$55.00	
97-364-0	Swiss Snow House		ORNAMENT		1997	$48.00	
97-365-0	Snowbear		ORNAMENT		1997	$29.00	
97-366-0	Missy Mouse		ORNAMENT		1997	$50.00	
97-367-0	Holiday Dreamers		ORNAMENT		1997	$25.00	
97-368-0	Comin' To Town		ORNAMENT		1997	$63.00	
97-369-0	Winter Acorns		ORNAMENT		1997	$6.00	
97-370-0	Wagon		ORNAMENT		1997	$38.00	
97-371-0	Harvest Home		ORNAMENT		1997	$11.00	
97-372-0	Winter Windmill		ORNAMENT		1997	$19.00	
97-373-0	Chilly Tangerine		ORNAMENT		1997	$13.00	
97-374-0	Toy Zeppelin		ORNAMENT		1997	$13.00	
97-376-0	Jewelled Carriage		ORNAMENT		1997	$50.00	
97-377-0	Constellations		ORNAMENT		1997	$37.00	
97-378-0	Christmas Constellations		ORNAMENT		1997	$37.00	
97-379-0	Big Wiggles		ORNAMENT		1997	$34.00	
97-380-0	Walnuts		ORNAMENT		1997	$7.00	
97-381-0	Snow Boot		ORNAMENT		1997	$11.00	
97-382-0	Stage Coach		ORNAMENT		1997	$43.00	
97-383-0	Pacific Pastels		ORNAMENT		1997	$13.00	
97-384-0	Om For The Holidays		ORNAMENT		1997	$13.00	
97-385-0	Home Harvest		ORNAMENT		1997	$11.00	
97-386-0	Wonderful World		ORNAMENT		1997	$17.00	
97-387-0	Star Blossoms		ORNAMENT		1997	$13.00	
97-388-0	Arthur's Chapel		ORNAMENT		1997	$32.00	
97-389-0	Star Flare		ORNAMENT		1997	$22.00	
97-390-0	Floral Frost		ORNAMENT		1997	$32.00	
97-391-0	Jeweled Tassel		ORNAMENT		1997	$16.00	
97-392-0	Angelic Accord		ORNAMENT		1997	$47.00	
97-393-0	Almost Angels		ORNAMENT		1997	$38.00	
97-394-0	Chapel Ball		ORNAMENT		1997	$43.00	
97-395-0	Mice Capades		ORNAMENT		1997	$46.00	
97-396-0	Ever Homeward		ORNAMENT		1997	$47.00	
97-398-0	Rain Dance		ORNAMENT		1997	$47.00	
97-399-0	Corinthian		ORNAMENT		1997	$90.00	
97-400-0	Winter Clear I		ORNAMENT		1997	$40.00	
97-402-0	Blessed Family		ORNAMENT		1997	$43.00	
97-403-0	Watchful Shepherds		ORNAMENT		1997	$32.00	
97-404-0	Glory		ORNAMENT		1997	$50.00	
97-405-0	Royal Journey		ORNAMENT		1997	$64.00	
97-406-0	Blessed Journey		ORNAMENT		1997	$67.00	
97-407-0	Jewel Tones		ORNAMENT		1997	$36.00	
97-408-0	Fly By Night		ORNAMENT		1997	$44.00	
97-409-0	Black Cat		ORNAMENT		1997	$29.00	
97-410-0	Festival Harlequin		ORNAMENT		1997	$47.00	
97-410-1	Pastel Festival Harlequin		ORNAMENT		1997	$47.00	
97-411-0	Winter Wreath Garland		GARLAND		1997	$65.00	
97-412-0	Tug Boat Parade Garland		GARLAND		1997	$65.00	
97-413-0	Star Lights		ORNAMENT		1997	$34.00	
97-414-0	Rosedown		ORNAMENT		1997	$43.00	
97-415-0	Rosedown Finial		FINIAL		1997	$105.00	
97-416-0	Christmas Bells		ORNAMENT		1997	$40.00	
97-417-0	Christmas Blossom		ORNAMENT		1997	$30.00	
97-418-0	Nativity Portrait		ORNAMENT		1997	$63.00	
97-419-0	Golden Star/Small		ORNAMENT		1997	$17.00	
97-420-0	Heavenly Music Finial		FINIAL		1997	$110.00	
97-421-0	Maidens Fair & Bright		ORNAMENT		1997	$85.00	
97-423-0	Spot		ORNAMENT		1997	$35.00	
97-427-0	Winter Clear		ORNAMENT		1997	$36.00	
97-428-0	Crystal Frost		ORNAMENT		1997	$73.00	
97-429-0	Silver Squirrel		ORNAMENT		1997	$73.00	
97-430-0	Fireworks		ORNAMENT		1997	$73.00	
97-431-0	Frosty Friends		ORNAMENT		1997	$47.00	
97-432-0	Firebird		ORNAMENT		1997	$47.00	
97-433-0	Royal Game		ORNAMENT		1997	$80.00	
97-434-0	Sky Beauty		ORNAMENT		1997	$38.00	
97-435-0	Mad About Yule		ORNAMENT		1997	$46.00	
97-436-0	Peanut Gallery		ORNAMENT		1997	$59.00	
97-437-0	The French L. Ephants		ORNAMENT		1997	$63.00	
97-438-0	Mint Cane		ORNAMENT		1997	$30.00	

Order No.	Title	Type	Theme	Retired	Intro. Year	Retail Price	Secondary Price
97-439-0	Dandy Canes		ORNAMENT		1997	$50.00	
97-440-0	Jumpin' Jersey		ORNAMENT		1997	$50.00	
97-441-0	Run Always		ORNAMENT		1997	$47.00	
97-444-0	Miss Merriweather		ORNAMENT		1997	$68.00	
97-445-0	Princely Pride		ORNAMENT		1997	$70.00	
97-449-0	Slip N' Slide		ORNAMENT		1997	$15.00	
97-451-0	Babykins		ORNAMENT		1997	$19.00	
97-452-0	Bear Go 'Round Garland		GARLAND		1997	$68.00	
97-453-0	Carnivale Garland		GARLAND		1997	$70.00	
97-454-0	Penny Candy Garland		GARLAND		1997	$60.00	
97-455-0	Santa Trees Garland		GARLAND		1997	$70.00	
97-456-0	Holiday Pear		ORNAMENT		1997	$17.00	
97-457-0	Apple A Day		ORNAMENT		1997	$15.00	
93-059-2	Pisces	CR - BLOWN GLASS - CZECH REP.	ORNAMENT		1993		
96-DIS-3	Noel Pluto		ORNAMENT		96		
96-DIS-4	Ready For Sea		ORNAMENT		96		
96-DIS-5	A Goofy Surprise		ORNAMENT		96		
96-DIS-8	Holiday Skaters		ORNAMENT		96		
96-193-1	Lilac Londonberry	CR - BLOWN GLASS - POLAND	ORNAMENT		1996		
96-204-1	Matilda	CR - BLOWN GLASS - POLAND	ORNAMENT		1996	$38.00	
96-250-1	Autumn Dream	CR - BLOWN GLASS - POLAND	ORNAMENT		1996	$42.00	
96-286-1	Far and Away	CR - BLOWN GLASS - POLAND	ORNAMENT		1996	$50.00	

HALLMARK KEEPSAKE ORNAMENTS

Order No.	Title	Type	Theme	Retired	Intro. Year	Retail Price	Secondary Price
1973-XHD83-2	Boy Caroler	CC - ORNAMENT	ORNAMENT		1973	$1.25	$24.00
1973-XHD84-5	Green Girl	CC - ORNAMENT	ORNAMENT		1973	$1.25	$27.50
1973-XHD85-2	Blue Girl	CC - ORNAMENT	ORNAMENT		1973	$1.25	$24.00
1974-QX111-1	Norman Rockwell (Santa)	CC - ORNAMENT	ORNAMENT		1974	$2.50	$80.00
1974-QX106-1	Norman Rockwell (Tree)	CC - ORNAMENT	ORNAMENT		1974	$2.50	$78.00
1974-QX108-1	Betsey Clark - 2nd	CC - ORNAMENT	ORNAMENT		1974	$2.50	$65.00
1974-QX109-1	Charmers	CC - ORNAMENT	ORNAMENT		1974	$2.50	$36.00
1974-QX107-1	Snowgoose	CC - ORNAMENT	ORNAMENT		1974	$2.50	$78.00
1974-QX110-1	Angel (Ball)	CC - ORNAMENT	ORNAMENT		1974	$2.50	$75.00
1974-QX114-1	Raggedy Ann And Raggedy Andy	CC - ORNAMENT	ORNAMENT		1974	$4.50	$75.00
1974-QX115-1	Little Miracles	CC - ORNAMENT	ORNAMENT		1974	$4.50	$55.00
1974-QX113-1	Buttons & Bo	CC - ORNAMENT	ORNAMENT		1974	$3.50	$53.00
1974-QX112-1	Currier & Ives	CC - ORNAMENT	ORNAMENT		1974	$3.50	$52.00
1974-QX100-1	Mrs. Santa	CC - ORNAMENT	ORNAMENT		1974	$1.50	$24.50
1974-QX101-1	Elf	CC - ORNAMENT	ORNAMENT		1974	$1.50	$27.00
1974-XHD102-1	Soldier	CC - ORNAMENT	ORNAMENT		1974	$1.50	$24.00
1974-QX103-1	Angel (Yarn)	CC - ORNAMENT	ORNAMENT		1974	$1.50	$30.00
1974-XHD104-1	Snowman	CC - ORNAMENT	ORNAMENT		1974	$1.50	$23.00
1974-QX105-1	Santa	CC - ORNAMENT	ORNAMENT		1974	$1.50	$25.00
1975-QX168-1	Betsey Clark	CC - ORNAMENT	ORNAMENT		1975	$4.50	$42.00
1975-QX167-1	Betsey Clark	CC - ORNAMENT	ORNAMENT		1975	$3.50	$40.00
1975-QX163-1	Betsey Clark	CC - ORNAMENT	ORNAMENT		1975	$2.50	$32.00
1975-QX133-1	Betsey Clark - 3rd	CC - ORNAMENT	ORNAMENT		1975	$3.00	$61.00
1975-QX164-1	Currier & Ives	CC - ORNAMENT	ORNAMENT		1975	$2.50	$35.00
1975-QX137-1	Currier & Ives	CC - ORNAMENT	ORNAMENT		1975	$4.00	$37.00
1975-QX138-1	Raggedy Ann And Raggedy Andy	CC - ORNAMENT	ORNAMENT		1975	$4.00	$55.00
1975-QX165-1	Raggedy Ann (Ball)	CC - ORNAMENT	ORNAMENT		1975	$2.50	$45.00
1975-QX166-1	Norman Rockwell	CC - ORNAMENT	ORNAMENT		1975	$2.50	$42.00
1975-QX134-1	Norman Rockwell	CC - ORNAMENT	ORNAMENT		1975	$3.00	$40.00
1975-QX135-1	Charmers	CC - ORNAMENT	ORNAMENT		1975	$3.00	$38.50
1993-QK114-5	Mistletoe Kiss	CC - ORNAMENT	ORNAMENT		1993	$13.75	$29.00
1993-QK115-2	Christmas Feast	CC - ORNAMENT	ORNAMENT		1993	$13.75	$29.00
1993-QK114-2	Joy of Sharing	CC - ORNAMENT	ORNAMENT		1993	$13.75	$29.00
1993-QK116-2	N. Rockwell Jolly Postman	CC - ORNAMENT	ORNAMENT		1993	$13.75	$29.00
1993-QK115-5	N. Rockwell Fllng the Stocking	CC - ORNAMENT	ORNAMENT		1993	$13.75	$29.00
1993-QK104-5	Riding the Wind (Goose)	CC - ORNAMENT	ORNAMENT		1993	$15.75	$55.00
1993-QK107-2	Santa Claus	CC - ORNAMENT	ORNAMENT		1993	$16.75	$190.00
1993-QK106-5	Riding the Woods (Fox)	CC - ORNAMENT	ORNAMENT		1993	$15.75	$65.00
1993-QK105-5	Polar Bear Adventure	CC - ORNAMENT	ORNAMENT		1993	$15.00	$57.00
1993-QK105-2	Angel in Flight	CC - ORNAMENT	ORNAMENT		1993	$15.75	$45.00
1993-QK108-5	Silver Stars & Holly	CC - ORNAMENT	ORNAMENT		1993	$24.75	$28.00
1993-QK107-5	Silver Dove of Peace	CC - ORNAMENT	ORNAMENT		1993	$24.75	$26.00
1993-QK108-2	Silver Sleigh	CC - ORNAMENT	ORNAMENT		1993	$24.75	$28.00
1993-QK109-2	Silver Santa	CC - ORNAMENT	ORNAMENT		1993	$24.75	$46.00
1993-QK100-5	Visions of Sugarplums	CC - ORNAMENT	ORNAMENT		1993	$13.75	$28.00
1993-QK102-5	The Magi	CC - ORNAMENT	ORNAMENT		1993	$13.75	$31.00
1993-QK101-2	Journey to the Forest	CC - ORNAMENT	ORNAMENT		1993	$13.75	$27.50
1993-QK104-2	Bringing Home the Tree	CC - ORNAMENT	ORNAMENT		1993	$13.75	$32.00
1993-QK103-2	Angelic Messengers	CC - ORNAMENT	ORNAMENT		1993	$13.75	$33.50
1994-QK104-3	Peaceful Dove	CC - ORNAMENT	ORNAMENT		1994	$11.75	$18.00
1994-QK103-6	Joyful Lamb	CC - ORNAMENT	ORNAMENT		1994	$11.75	$18.00
1994-QK105-3	Dapper Snowman	CC - ORNAMENT	ORNAMENT		1994	$13.75	$17.50
1994-QK103-3	Graceful Fawn	CC - ORNAMENT	ORNAMENT		1994	$11.75	$15.50
1994-QK104-6	Jolly Santa	CC - ORNAMENT	ORNAMENT		1994	$13.75	$23.00
1994-QK119-3	Rarin' To Go	CC - ORNAMENT	ORNAMENT		1994	$15.75	$28.00
1994-QK116-6	Going to Town	CC - ORNAMENT	ORNAMENT		1994	$15.75	$28.00
1994-QK117-6	Roundup Time	CC - ORNAMENT	ORNAMENT		1994	$16.75	$34.00
1994-QK118-3	Catching 40 Winks	CC - ORNAMENT	ORNAMENT		1994	$16.75	$28.00
1994-QK117-3	Racing through the Snow	CC - ORNAMENT	ORNAMENT		1994	$15.75	$36.00
1994-QK100-6	Silver Poinsettia	CC - ORNAMENT	ORNAMENT		1994	$24.75	$36.00
1994-QK102-3	Silver Bows	CC - ORNAMENT	ORNAMENT		1994	$24.75	$29.00
1994-QK101-6	Silver Snowflakes	CC - ORNAMENT	ORNAMENT		1994	$24.75	$29.00
1994-QK102-6	Silver Bells	CC - ORNAMENT	ORNAMENT		1994	$24.75	$29.00
1994-QK110-6	Peaceful Village	CC - ORNAMENT	ORNAMENT		1994	$15.75	$32.00
1994-QK111-6	Moonbeams	CC - ORNAMENT	ORNAMENT		1994	$15.75	$25.00
1994-QK112-6	Mother and Child	CC - ORNAMENT	ORNAMENT		1994	$15.75	$17.50
1994-QK112-3	Home for the Holidays	CC - ORNAMENT	ORNAMENT		1994	$15.75	$23.00
1994-EXP094-1	Golden Santa (EXPO Ornament)	CC - ORNAMENT	ORNAMENT		1994	$10.00	$34.00

Order No.	Title	Type	Theme	Retired	Intro. Year	Retial Price	Secondary Price
1994-EXPO94-2	Golden Stars and Holly (EXPO)	CC - ORNAMENT	ORNAMENT		1994	$10.00	$22.50
1994-EXPO94-3	Golden Sleigh (EXPO Ornament)	CC - ORNAMENT	ORNAMENT		1994	$10.00	$42.00
1994-EXPO94-4	Golden Bows (EXPO Ornament)	CC - ORNAMENT	ORNAMENT		1994	$10.00	$35.00
1994-EXPO94-5	Golden Poinsettia (EXPO)	CC - ORNAMENT	ORNAMENT		1994	$10.00	$36.00
1994-EXPO94-6	Golden Dove of Peace (EXPO	CC - ORNAMENT	ORNAMENT		1994	$10.00	$20.00
1995-QK102-7	Turn-of-the-Century - 1st	CC - ORNAMENT	ORNAMENT		1995	$16.95	$34.00
1995-QK109-7	Away in a Manger	CC - ORNAMENT	ORNAMENT		1995	$13.95	$22.00
1995-QK109-9	Following the Star	CC - ORNAMENT	ORNAMENT		1995	$13.95	$20.00
1995-QK106-7	Raising a Family	CC - ORNAMENT	ORNAMENT		1995	$18.95	$30.00
1995-QK107-9	Violets and Butterflies	CC - ORNAMENT	ORNAMENT		1995	$16.95	$28.00
1995-QK106-9	Backyard Orchard	CC - ORNAMENT	ORNAMENT		1995	$18.95	$30.00
1995-QK107-7	Christmas Cardinal	CC - ORNAMENT	ORNAMENT		1995	$18.95	$46.00
1995-QK113-7	Joy	CC - ORNAMENT	ORNAMENT		1995	$12.95	$27.00
1995-QK113-9	Noelle	CC - ORNAMENT	ORNAMENT		1995	$12.95	$28.00
1995-QK114-7	Carole	CC - ORNAMENT	ORNAMENT		1995	$12.95	$19.00
1995-QK103-7	Guiding Santa	CC - ORNAMENT	ORNAMENT		1995	$18.95	$37.50
1995-QK103-9	Fishing Party	CC - ORNAMENT	ORNAMENT		1995	$15.95	$31.00
1995-QK104-7	Learning to Skate	CC - ORNAMENT	ORNAMENT		1995	$14.95	$31.00
1995-QK105-7	Fetching the Firewood	CC - ORNAMENT	ORNAMENT		1995	$15.95	$31.00
1995-QK108-7	Jolly Santa	CC - ORNAMENT	ORNAMENT		1995	$15.95	$22.00
1995-QK108-9	Sweet Song	CC - ORNAMENT	ORNAMENT		1995	$15.95	$22.00
1995-QK111-9	Victorian Home Teapot	CC - ORNAMENT	ORNAMENT		1995	$15.95	$22.00
1995-QK112-7	Cozy Cottage Teapot	CC - ORNAMENT	ORNAMENT		1995	$15.95	$25.00
1995-QK112-9	European Castle Teapot	CC - ORNAMENT	ORNAMENT		1995	$15.95	$22.00
1995-QK115-9	Angel of Light	CC - ORNAMENT	ORNAMENT		1995	$11.95	$20.00
1995-QK115-7	Gentle Lullaby	CC - ORNAMENT	ORNAMENT		1995	$11.95	$22.00
1995-QXC105-9	Home from the Woods	CC - ORNAMENT	ORNAMENT		1995	$15.95	$32.00
1973-XHD100-2	Betsey Clark	CC - ORNAMENT	ORNAMENT		1973	$2.50	$79.00
1973-XHD110-2	Betsey Clark - 1st	CC - ORNAMENT	ORNAMENT		1973	$2.50	$113.00
1973-XHD102-2	Manger Scene	CC - ORNAMENT	ORNAMENT		1973	$2.50	$87.00
1973-XHD106-2	Christmas Is Love	CC - ORNAMENT	ORNAMENT		1973	$2.50	$70.00
1973-XHD101-5	Santa With Elves	CC - ORNAMENT	ORNAMENT		1973	$2.50	$82.00
1973-XHD103-5	Elves	CC - ORNAMENT	ORNAMENT		1973	$2.50	$72.00
1973-XHD74-5	Mr. Santa	CC - ORNAMENT	ORNAMENT		1973	$1.25	$24.00
1973-XHD75-2	Mrs. Santa	CC - ORNAMENT	ORNAMENT		1973	$1.25	$24.00
1973-XHD76-5	Mr. Snowman	CC - ORNAMENT	ORNAMENT		1973	$1.25	$24.00
1973-XHD77-2	Mrs. Snowman	CC - ORNAMENT	ORNAMENT		1973	$1.25	$24.00
1973-XHD78-5	Angel	CC - ORNAMENT	ORNAMENT		1973	$1.25	$29.00
1973-XHD79-2	Elf	CC - ORNAMENT	ORNAMENT		1973	$1.25	$27.00
1973-XHD80-5	Choir Boy	CC - ORNAMENT	ORNAMENT		1973	$1.25	$24.00
1973-XHD81-2	Soldier	CC - ORNAMENT	ORNAMENT		1973	$1.00	$22.00
1973-XHD82-5	Little Girl	CC - ORNAMENT	ORNAMENT		1973	$1.25	$24.00
1975-QX136-1	Marty Links	CC - ORNAMENT	ORNAMENT		1975	$3.00	$42.50
1975-QX139-1	Buttons & Bo	CC - ORNAMENT	ORNAMENT		1975	$5.00	$42.00
1975-QX140-1	Little Miracles	CC - ORNAMENT	ORNAMENT		1975	$5.00	$38.00
1975-QX121-1	Raggedy Ann (Yarn)	CC - ORNAMENT	ORNAMENT		1975	$1.75	$34.00
1975-QX122-1	Raggedy Andy (Yarn)	CC - ORNAMENT	ORNAMENT		1975	$1.75	$34.00
1975-QX123-1	Drummer Boy (Yarn)	CC - ORNAMENT	ORNAMENT		1975	$1.75	$25.00
1975-QX124-1	Santa (Yarn)	CC - ORNAMENT	ORNAMENT		1975	$1.75	$25.00
1975-QX125-1	Mrs. Santa (Yarn)	CC - ORNAMENT	ORNAMENT		1975	$1.75	$24.00
1975-QX126-1	Little Girl	CC - ORNAMENT	ORNAMENT		1975	$1.75	$23.00
1975-QX127-1	Locomotive	CC - ORNAMENT	ORNAMENT		1975	$3.50	$156.00
1975-QX128-1	Rocking Horse (Nostalgia)	CC - ORNAMENT	ORNAMENT		1975	$3.50	$143.00
1975-QX129-1	Santa And Sleigh (Nostalgia)	CC - ORNAMENT	ORNAMENT		1975	$3.50	$230.00
1975-QX130-1	Drummer Boy (Nostalgia)	CC - ORNAMENT	ORNAMENT		1975	$3.50	$156.00
1975-QX131-1	Peace On Earth	CC - ORNAMENT	ORNAMENT		1975	$3.50	$144.00
1975-QX132-1	Joy (Nostalgia)	CC - ORNAMENT	ORNAMENT		1975	$3.50	$225.00
1975-QX155-1	Santa (Adorable)	CC - ORNAMENT	ORNAMENT		1975	$2.50	$192.00
1975-QX156-1	Mrs. Santa (Adorable)	CC - ORNAMENT	ORNAMENT		1975	$2.50	$192.00
1975-QX157-1	Betsey Clark (Adorable)	CC - ORNAMENT	ORNAMENT		1975	$2.50	$227.00
1975-QX159-1	Raggedy Ann (Adorable)	CC - ORNAMENT	ORNAMENT		1975	$2.50	$325.00
1975-QX160-1	Raggedy Andy (Adorable)	CC - ORNAMENT	ORNAMENT		1975	$2.50	$350.00
1975-QX161-1	Drummer Boy (Adorable)	CC - ORNAMENT	ORNAMENT		1975	$2.50	$202.00
1976-QX211-1	Baby's First Christmas	CC - ORNAMENT	ORNAMENT		1976	$1.50	$119.00
1976-QX203-1	Bicentennial '76 Commemorative	CC - ORNAMENT	ORNAMENT		1976	$2.50	$50.00
1976-QX198-1	Bicentennial Charmers	CC - ORNAMENT	ORNAMENT		1976	$3.00	$34.00
1976-QX208-1	Colonial Children	CC - ORNAMENT	ORNAMENT		1976	$4.00	$42.00
1976-QX195-1	Betsey Clark - 4th	CC - ORNAMENT	ORNAMENT		1976	$3.00	$88.00
1976-QX210-1	Betsey Clark	CC - ORNAMENT	ORNAMENT		1976	$2.50	$42.00
1976-QX218-1	Betsey Clark	CC - ORNAMENT	ORNAMENT		1976	$4.50	$45.00
1976-QX209-1	Currier & Ives (Col. House)	CC - ORNAMENT	ORNAMENT		1976	$2.50	$41.00
1976-QX197-1	Currier & Ives (Amer. Winter)	CC - ORNAMENT	ORNAMENT		1976	$3.00	$40.00
1976-QX196-1	Norman Rockwell	CC - ORNAMENT	ORNAMENT		1976	$3.00	$65.00
1976-QX213-1	Rudolph And Santa	CC - ORNAMENT	ORNAMENT		1976	$2.50	$80.00
1976-QX212-1	Raggedy Ann (Ball)	CC - ORNAMENT	ORNAMENT		1976	$2.50	$60.00
1976-QX207-1	Marty Links	CC - ORNAMENT	ORNAMENT		1976	$4.00	$35.00
1976-QX216-1	Happy The Snowman	CC - ORNAMENT	ORNAMENT		1976	$3.50	$46.00
1976-QX215-1	Charmers	CC - ORNAMENT	ORNAMENT		1976	$3.50	$47.00
1976-QX204-1	Chickadees	CC - ORNAMENT	ORNAMENT		1976	$2.25	$45.00
1976-QX205-1	Cardinals	CC - ORNAMENT	ORNAMENT		1976	$2.25	$40.00
1976-QX181-1	Train (Yesteryears)	CC - ORNAMENT	ORNAMENT		1976	$5.00	$120.50
1976-QX182-1	Santa (Yesteryears)	CC - ORNAMENT	ORNAMENT		1976	$5.00	$155.00
1976-QX183-1	Partridge (Yesteryears)	CC - ORNAMENT	ORNAMENT		1976	$5.00	$118.00
1976-QX184-1	Drummer Boy (Yesteryears)	CC - ORNAMENT	ORNAMENT		1976	$5.00	$135.00
1976-QX171-1	Angel (Twirl-About)	CC - ORNAMENT	ORNAMENT		1976	$4.50	$140.00
1976-QX172-1	Santa (Twirl-About)	CC - ORNAMENT	ORNAMENT		1976	$4.50	$110.00
1976-QX173-1	Soldier (Twirl-About)	CC - ORNAMENT	ORNAMENT		1976	$4.50	$92.00
1976-QX174-1	Partridge (Twirl-About)	CC - ORNAMENT	ORNAMENT		1976	$4.50	$160.00
1976-QX175-1	Shepherd (Tree Treats)	CC - ORNAMENT	ORNAMENT		1976	$3.00	$112.00
1976-QX176-1	Angel (Tree Treats)	CC - ORNAMENT	ORNAMENT		1976	$3.00	$145.00
1976-QX177-1	Santa (Tree Treats)	CC - ORNAMENT	ORNAMENT		1976	$3.00	$195.00
1976-QX178-1	Reindeer (Tree Treats)	CC - ORNAMENT	ORNAMENT		1976	$3.00	$95.00
1975-QX128-1	Rocking Horse (Nostalgia)	CC - ORNAMENT	ORNAMENT		1976	$4.00	$125.00

Order No.	Title	Type	Theme	Retired	Intro. Year	Retail Price	Secondary Price
1975-QX130-1	Drummer Boy (Nostalgia)	CC - ORNAMENT	ORNAMENT		1976	$4.00	$120.00
1976-QX222-1	Locomotive (Nostalgia)	CC - ORNAMENT	ORNAMENT		1976	$4.00	$135.00
1976-QX223-1	Peace On Earth (Nostalgia)	CC - ORNAMENT	ORNAMENT		1976	$4.00	$170.00
1976-QX121-1	Raggedy Ann (Yarn)	CC - ORNAMENT	ORNAMENT		1976	$1.75	$38.00
1976-QX122-1	Raggedy Andy (Yarn)	CC - ORNAMENT	ORNAMENT		1976	$1.75	$37.00
1976-QX123-1	Drummer Boy (Yarn)	CC - ORNAMENT	ORNAMENT		1976	$1.75	$25.00
1976-QX124-1	Santa (Yarn)	CC - ORNAMENT	ORNAMENT		1976	$1.75	$24.00
1976-QX125-1	Mrs. Santa	CC - ORNAMENT	ORNAMENT		1976	$1.75	$22.00
1976-QX126-1	Caroler	CC - ORNAMENT	ORNAMENT		1976	$1.75	$21.00
1977-QX131-5	Baby's First Christmas	CC - ORNAMENT	ORNAMENT		1977	$3.50	$68.00
1977-QX208-2	Granddaughter	CC - ORNAMENT	ORNAMENT		1977	$3.50	$24.00
1977-QX209-5	Grandson	CC - ORNAMENT	ORNAMENT		1977	$3.50	$24.00
1977-QX261-5	Mother	CC - ORNAMENT	ORNAMENT		1977	$3.50	$21.00
1977-QX260-2	Grandmother	CC - ORNAMENT	ORNAMENT		1977	$3.50	$41.00
1977-QX132-2	First Christmas Together	CC - ORNAMENT	ORNAMENT		1977	$3.50	$55.00
1977-QX262-2	Love	CC - ORNAMENT	ORNAMENT		1977	$3.50	$24.00
1977-QX263-5	For Your New Home	CC - ORNAMENT	ORNAMENT		1977	$3.50	$34.00
1977-QX153-5	Charmers	CC - ORNAMENT	ORNAMENT		1977	$3.50	$49.00
1977-QX130-2	Currier & Ives	CC - ORNAMENT	ORNAMENT		1977	$3.50	$45.00
1977-QX151-5	Norman Rockwell	CC - ORNAMENT	ORNAMENT		1977	$3.50	$6.00
1977-QX133-5	Disney (Mickey in Wreath)	CC - ORNAMENT	ORNAMENT		1977	$3.50	$47.00
1977-QX137-5	Disney	CC - ORNAMENT	ORNAMENT		1977	$4.00	$44.00
1977-QX264-2	Betsey Clark - 5th	CC - ORNAMENT	ORNAMENT		1977	$3.50	$420.00
1977-QX162-2	Peanuts	CC - ORNAMENT	ORNAMENT		1977	$2.50	$54.00
1977-QX135-5	Peanuts	CC - ORNAMENT	ORNAMENT		1977	$3.50	$68.00
1977-QX163-5	Peanuts	CC - ORNAMENT	ORNAMENT		1977	$4.00	$79.00
1977-QX150-2	Grandma Moses	CC - ORNAMENT	ORNAMENT		1977	$3.50	$80.00
1977-QX154-2	Bell (Ball)	CC - ORNAMENT	ORNAMENT		1977	$3.50	$35.00
1977-QX155-5	Ornaments	CC - ORNAMENT	ORNAMENT		1977	$3.50	$35.00
1977-QX157-5	Mandolin	CC - ORNAMENT	ORNAMENT		1977	$3.50	
1977-QX156-2	Wreath (Ball)	CC - ORNAMENT	ORNAMENT		1977	$3.50	
1977-QX158-2	Mountains	CC - ORNAMENT	ORNAMENT		1977	$2.50	
1977-QX159-5	Desert	CC - ORNAMENT	ORNAMENT		1977	$2.50	$13.00
1977-QX160-2	Seashore	CC - ORNAMENT	ORNAMENT		1977	$2.50	$24.00
1977-QX161-5	Wharf	CC - ORNAMENT	ORNAMENT		1977	$2.50	$24.00
1977-QX139-5	Rabbit	CC - ORNAMENT	ORNAMENT		1977	$2.50	$95.00
1977-QX138-2	Squirrel	CC - ORNAMENT	ORNAMENT		1977	$2.50	$95.00
1977-QX134-2	Christmas Mouse	CC - ORNAMENT	ORNAMENT		1977	$3.50	
1977-QX152-2	Stained Glass	CC - ORNAMENT	ORNAMENT		1977	$3.50	
1977-QX200-2	Bell (Colors of Christmas)	CC - ORNAMENT	ORNAMENT		1977	$3.50	
1977-QX201-5	Joy (Colors of Christmas)	CC - ORNAMENT	ORNAMENT		1977	$3.50	$53.00
1977-QX202-2	Wreath (Colors of Christmas)	CC - ORNAMENT	ORNAMENT		1977	$3.50	$55.00
1977-QX203-5	Candle	CC - ORNAMENT	ORNAMENT		1977	$3.50	$58.00
1977-QX310-2	Joy (Acrylic)	CC - ORNAMENT	ORNAMENT		1977	$3.50	$64.00
1977-QX311-5	Peace On Earth	CC - ORNAMENT	ORNAMENT		1977	$3.50	
1977-QX312-2	Drummer Boy	CC - ORNAMENT	ORNAMENT		1977	$3.50	$62.00
1977-QX313-5	Star	CC - ORNAMENT	ORNAMENT		1977	$3.50	$49.00
1977-QX210-2	Snowflake Collection	CC - ORNAMENT	ORNAMENT		1977	$5.00	$94.00
1977-QX190-2	Snowman (Twirl-About)	CC - ORNAMENT	ORNAMENT		1977	$4.50	$75.00
1977-QX191-5	Weather House (Twirl-About)	CC - ORNAMENT	ORNAMENT		1977	$6.00	$95.00
1977-QX192-2	Bellringer	CC - ORNAMENT	ORNAMENT		1977	$6.00	$52.00
1977-QX193-5	Della Robia Wreath	CC - ORNAMENT	ORNAMENT		1977	$4.50	$115.00
1977-QX182-2	Angel (Nostalgia)	CC - ORNAMENT	ORNAMENT		1977	$5.00	$99.00
1977-QX183-5	Toys (Nostalgia)	CC - ORNAMENT	ORNAMENT		1977	$5.00	$147.00
1977-QX180-2	Antique Car (Nostalgia)	CC - ORNAMENT	ORNAMENT		1977	$5.00	$58.00
1977-QX181-5	Nativity (Nostalgia)	CC - ORNAMENT	ORNAMENT		1977	$5.00	$145.00
1977-QX182-2	Angel (Yesteryears)	CC - ORNAMENT	ORNAMENT		1977	$6.00	$114.00
1977-QX173-5	Reindeer (Yesteryears)	CC - ORNAMENT	ORNAMENT		1977	$6.00	$113.00
1977-QX171-5	Jack-in-the-Box (Yesteryears)	CC - ORNAMENT	ORNAMENT		1977	$6.00	$98.00
1977-QX170-2	House (Yesteryears)	CC - ORNAMENT	ORNAMENT		1977	$6.00	$105.00
1977-QX220-2	Angel (Cloth)	CC - ORNAMENT	ORNAMENT		1977	$1.75	$95.00
1977-QX221-5	Santa	CC - ORNAMENT	ORNAMENT		1977	$1.75	$65.00
1978-QX200-3	Baby's First Christmas	CC - ORNAMENT	ORNAMENT		1978	$3.50	$68.00
1978-QX216-3	Granddaughter	CC - ORNAMENT	ORNAMENT		1978	$3.50	$32.00
1978-QX215-6	Grandson	CC - ORNAMENT	ORNAMENT		1978	$3.50	$45.00
1978-QX218-3	First Christmas Together	CC - ORNAMENT	ORNAMENT		1978	$3.50	$44.00
1978-QX269-6	25th Christmas Together	CC - ORNAMENT	ORNAMENT		1978	$3.50	$23.00
1978-QX268-3	Love	CC - ORNAMENT	ORNAMENT		1978	$3.50	$52.00
1978-QX267-6	Grandmother	CC - ORNAMENT	ORNAMENT		1978	$3.50	$45.00
1978-QX266-3	Mother	CC - ORNAMENT	ORNAMENT		1978	$3.50	$38.00
1978-QX217-6	For Your New Home	CC - ORNAMENT	ORNAMENT		1978	$3.50	$25.00
1978-QX204-3	Peanuts	CC - ORNAMENT	ORNAMENT		1978	$2.50	$65.00
1978-QX205-6	Peanuts	CC - ORNAMENT	ORNAMENT		1978	$3.50	$63.00
1978-QX206-3	Peanuts	CC - ORNAMENT	ORNAMENT		1978	$3.50	$54.00
1978-QX203-6	Peanuts	CC - ORNAMENT	ORNAMENT		1978	$2.50	$55.00
1978-QX201-6	Betsey Clark - 6th	CC - ORNAMENT	ORNAMENT		1978	$3.50	$55.00
1978-QX221-6	Joan Walsh Anglund	CC - ORNAMENT	ORNAMENT		1978	$3.50	$64.00
1978-QX219-6	Spencer Sparrow	CC - ORNAMENT	ORNAMENT		1978	$3.50	$50.00
1978-QX207-6	Disney	CC - ORNAMENT	ORNAMENT		1978	$3.50	$75.00
1978-QX202-3	Merry Christmas (Santa)	CC - ORNAMENT	ORNAMENT		1978	$3.50	$47.00
1978-QX220-3	Hallmark's Antique Card Coll.	CC - ORNAMENT	ORNAMENT		1978	$3.50	$39.00
1978-QX250-3	Yesterday's Toys	CC - ORNAMENT	ORNAMENT		1978	$3.50	$24.00
1978-QX253-6	Nativity	CC - ORNAMENT	ORNAMENT		1978	$3.50	$85.00
1978-QX251-6	The Quail	CC - ORNAMENT	ORNAMENT		1978	$3.50	$45.00
1978-QX252-3	Drummer Boy (Ball)	CC - ORNAMENT	ORNAMENT		1978	$3.50	$27.00
1978-QX254-3	Joy (Ball)	CC - ORNAMENT	ORNAMENT		1978	$3.50	$35.00
1978-QX307-6	Santa (Holiday Highlights)	CC - ORNAMENT	ORNAMENT		1978	$3.50	$68.00
1978-QX308-3	Snowflake	CC - ORNAMENT	ORNAMENT		1978	$3.50	$55.00
1978-QX309-6	Nativity (Holiday Highlights)	CC - ORNAMENT	ORNAMENT		1978	$3.50	$79.00
1978-QX310-3	Dove (Holiday Highlights)	CC - ORNAMENT	ORNAMENT		1978	$3.50	$122.50
1978-QX320-3	Reindeer Chimes	CC - ORNAMENT	ORNAMENT		1978	$4.50	$41.00
1978-QX133-6	Thimble - 1st	CC - ORNAMENT	ORNAMENT		1978	$2.50	$278.00
1978-QX135-6	Santa (Little Trimmer)	CC - ORNAMENT	ORNAMENT		1978	$2.50	$52.00

Order No.	Title	Type	Theme	Retired	Intro. Year	Retial Price	Secondary Price
1978-QX134-3	Praying Angel	CC - ORNAMENT	ORNAMENT		1978	$2.50	$87.00
1978-QX136-3	Drummer Boy (Little Trimmer)	CC - ORNAMENT	ORNAMENT		1978	$2.50	$68.00
1978-QX132-3	Little Trimmer Collection	CC - ORNAMENT	ORNAMENT		1978	$9.00	$310.00
1978-QX355-6	Merry Christmas (C of C)	CC - ORNAMENT	ORNAMENT		1978	$3.50	$50.00
1978-QX356-3	Locomotive	CC - ORNAMENT	ORNAMENT		1978	$3.50	$50.00
1978-QX354-3	Angel (Colors of Christmas)	CC - ORNAMENT	ORNAMENT		1978	$3.50	$42.00
1978-QX357-6	Candle	CC - ORNAMENT	ORNAMENT		1978	$3.50	$85.00
1978-QX190-3	Dove (Twirl-About)	CC - ORNAMENT	ORNAMENT		1978	$4.50	
1978-QX147-6	Holly And Poinsettia Ball	CC - ORNAMENT	ORNAMENT		1978	$6.00	$82.50
1978-QX152-3	Schneeberg Bell	CC - ORNAMENT	ORNAMENT		1978	$8.00	$250.00
1978-QX150-3	Angels	CC - ORNAMENT	ORNAMENT		1978	$8.00	$290.00
1978-QX146-3	Carrousel - 1st	CC - ORNAMENT	ORNAMENT		1978	$6.00	$380.00
1978-QX138-3	Joy	CC - ORNAMENT	ORNAMENT		1978	$4.50	$78.00
1978-QX139-6	Angel (Dough-Look)	CC - ORNAMENT	ORNAMENT		1978	$4.50	$84.50
1978-QX137-6	Calico Mouse	CC - ORNAMENT	ORNAMENT		1978	$4.50	$167.00
1978-QX144-3	Red Cardinal	CC - ORNAMENT	ORNAMENT		1978	$4.50	$158.00
1978-QX145-6	Panorama Ball	CC - ORNAMENT	ORNAMENT		1978	$6.00	$132.00
1978-QX142-3	Skating Raccoon	CC - ORNAMENT	ORNAMENT		1978	$6.00	$78.00
1978-QX148-3	Rocking Horse	CC - ORNAMENT	ORNAMENT		1978	$6.00	$90.00
1978-QX149-6	Animal House	CC - ORNAMENT	ORNAMENT		1978	$6.00	$150.00
1978-QX123-1	Green Boy	CC - ORNAMENT	ORNAMENT		1978	$2.00	$15.00
1978-QX125-1	Mrs. Claus	CC - ORNAMENT	ORNAMENT		1978	$2.00	$15.00
1978-QX126-1	Green Girl	CC - ORNAMENT	ORNAMENT		1978	$2.00	$15.00
1978-QX340-3	Mr. Claus	CC - ORNAMENT	ORNAMENT		1978	$2.00	$15.00
1979-QX208-7	Baby's First Christmas	CC - ORNAMENT	ORNAMENT		1979	$3.50	$25.00
1979-QX154-7	Baby's First Christmas	CC - ORNAMENT	ORNAMENT		1979	$8.00	$124.00
1979-QX210-7	Grandson	CC - ORNAMENT	ORNAMENT		1979	$3.50	$28.00
1979-QX211-9	Granddaughter	CC - ORNAMENT	ORNAMENT		1979	$3.50	$29.00
1979-QX251-9	Mother	CC - ORNAMENT	ORNAMENT		1979	$3.50	$29.00
1979-QX252-7	Grandmother	CC - ORNAMENT	ORNAMENT		1979	$3.50	$27.00
1979-QX209-9	Our First Christmas Together	CC - ORNAMENT	ORNAMENT		1979	$3.50	$52.00
1979-QX250-7	Our Twenty-Fifth Anniversary	CC - ORNAMENT	ORNAMENT		1979	$3.50	$16.00
1979-QX258-7	Love	CC - ORNAMENT	ORNAMENT		1979	$3.50	$33.00
1979-QX203-9	Friendship	CC - ORNAMENT	ORNAMENT		1979	$3.50	$31.00
1979-QX213-9	Teacher	CC - ORNAMENT	ORNAMENT		1979	$3.50	$18.00
1979-QX212-7	New Home	CC - ORNAMENT	ORNAMENT		1979	$3.50	$38.00
1979-QX201-9	Betsey Clark - 7th	CC - ORNAMENT	ORNAMENT		1979	$3.50	$32.00
1979-QX202-7	Peanuts (Time to Trim)	CC - ORNAMENT	ORNAMENT		1979	$3.50	$39.00
1979-QX200-7	Spencer Sparrow	CC - ORNAMENT	ORNAMENT		1979	$3.50	$31.00
1979-QX205-9	Joan Walsh Anglund	CC - ORNAMENT	ORNAMENT		1979	$3.50	$35.00
1979-QX206-7	Winnie-the-Pooh	CC - ORNAMENT	ORNAMENT		1979	$3.50	$43.00
1979-QX254-7	Mary Hamilton	CC - ORNAMENT	ORNAMENT		1979	$3.50	$28.00
1979-QX214-7	Night Before Christmas	CC - ORNAMENT	ORNAMENT		1979	$3.50	$41.00
1979-QX204-7	Christmas Chickadees	CC - ORNAMENT	ORNAMENT		1979	$3.50	$34.00
1979-QX255-9	Behold The Star	CC - ORNAMENT	ORNAMENT		1979	$3.50	$34.00
1979-QX253-9	Christmas Traditions	CC - ORNAMENT	ORNAMENT		1979	$3.50	$34.00
1979-QX257-9	Christmas Collage	CC - ORNAMENT	ORNAMENT		1979	$3.50	$26.00
1979-QX207-9	Black Angel	CC - ORNAMENT	ORNAMENT		1979	$3.50	$20.00
1979-QX256-7	The Light Of Christmas	CC - ORNAMENT	ORNAMENT		1979	$3.50	$27.00
1979-QX300-7	Christmas Angel	CC - ORNAMENT	ORNAMENT		1979	$3.50	$88.00
1979-QX301-9	Snowflake	CC - ORNAMENT	ORNAMENT		1979	$3.50	$38.00
1979-QX302-7	Christmas Tree	CC - ORNAMENT	ORNAMENT		1979	$3.50	$59.00
1979-QX303-9	Christmas Cheer	CC - ORNAMENT	ORNAMENT		1979	$3.50	$65.00
1979-QX304-7	Love (Holiday Highlights)	CC - ORNAMENT	ORNAMENT		1979	$3.50	$89.00
1979-QX350-7	Words Of Christmas	CC - ORNAMENT	ORNAMENT		1979	$3.50	$72.00
1979-QX353-9	Holiday Wreath	CC - ORNAMENT	ORNAMENT		1979	$3.50	$37.00
1979-QX351-9	Partridge In A Pear Tree	CC - ORNAMENT	ORNAMENT		1979	$3.50	$37.00
1979-QX352-7	Star Over Bethlehem	CC - ORNAMENT	ORNAMENT		1979	$3.50	$65.00
1979-QX133-6	Little Trimmers/Thimble - 1st	CC - ORNAMENT	ORNAMENT		1979	$3.00	$290.00
1979-QX135-6	Santa	CC - ORNAMENT	ORNAMENT		1979	$3.00	$50.00
1979-QX132-7	A Matchless Christmas	CC - ORNAMENT	ORNAMENT		1979	$4.00	$64.00
1979-QX130-7	Angel Delight	CC - ORNAMENT	ORNAMENT		1979	$3.00	$85.00
1979-QX152-7	Holiday Scrimshaw	CC - ORNAMENT	ORNAMENT		1979	$4.00	$200.00
1979-QX140-7	Christmas Heart	CC - ORNAMENT	ORNAMENT		1979	$6.50	$90.00
1979-QX157-9	Christmas Eve Surprise	CC - ORNAMENT	ORNAMENT		1979	$6.50	$55.00
1979-QX138-7	Santa's Here (Twirl-About)	CC - ORNAMENT	ORNAMENT		1979	$5.00	$65.00
1979-QX142-3	Skating Raccoon	CC - ORNAMENT	ORNAMENT		1979	$6.50	$89.00
1979-QX145-9	The Downhill Run	CC - ORNAMENT	ORNAMENT		1979	$6.50	$145.00
1979-QX143-9	The Drummer Boy	CC - ORNAMENT	ORNAMENT		1979	$8.00	$122.00
1979-QX150-7	Outdoor Fun	CC - ORNAMENT	ORNAMENT		1979	$8.00	$110.00
1979-QX134-7	A Christmas Treat	CC - ORNAMENT	ORNAMENT		1979	$5.00	$62.00
1979-QX139-9	The Skating Snowman	CC - ORNAMENT	ORNAMENT		1979	$5.00	$75.00
1979-QX135-9	Christmas Is for Children	CC - ORNAMENT	ORNAMENT		1979	$5.00	$78.00
1979-QX133-9	Ready For Christmas	CC - ORNAMENT	ORNAMENT		1979	$6.50	$120.00
1979-QX146-7	Carrousel - 2nd	CC - ORNAMENT	ORNAMENT		1979	$6.50	$168.00
1979-QX131-9	A Christmas Salute/Thimble - 2nd	CC - ORNAMENT	ORNAMENT		1979	$3.00	$149.00
1979-QX141-9	Snoopy And Friends - 1st	CC - ORNAMENT	ORNAMENT		1979	$8.00	$115.00
1979-QX155-9	Here Comes Santa - 1st	CC - ORNAMENT	ORNAMENT		1979	$9.00	$615.00
1979-QX147-9	The Bellringer - 1st	CC - ORNAMENT	ORNAMENT		1979	$10.00	$305.00
1979-QX320-3	Reindeer Chimes	CC - ORNAMENT	ORNAMENT		1979	$4.50	$39.00
1979-QX137-9	Star Chimes	CC - ORNAMENT	ORNAMENT		1979	$4.50	$55.00
1979-QX340-7	The Rocking Horse	CC - ORNAMENT	ORNAMENT		1979	$2.00	$20.00
1979-QX342-7	Merry Santa	CC - ORNAMENT	ORNAMENT		1979	$2.00	$19.00
1979-QX341-9	Stuffed Full Stocking	CC - ORNAMENT	ORNAMENT		1979	$2.00	$18.00
1979-QX343-9	Angel Music	CC - ORNAMENT	ORNAMENT		1979	$2.00	$18.00
1979-QX123-1	Green Boy	CC - ORNAMENT	ORNAMENT		1979	$2.00	$19.00
1979-QX125-1	Mrs. Claus	CC - ORNAMENT	ORNAMENT		1979	$2.00	$21.00
1979-QX126-1	Green Girl	CC - ORNAMENT	ORNAMENT		1979	$2.00	$19.00
1979-QX340-3	Mr. Claus	CC - ORNAMENT	ORNAMENT		1979	$2.00	$21.00
1980-QX200-1	Baby's First Christmas	CC - ORNAMENT	ORNAMENT		1980	$4.00	$18.00
1980-QX229-4	Black Baby's First Christmas	CC - ORNAMENT	ORNAMENT		1980	$4.00	$24.00
1980-QX156-1	Baby's First Christmas	CC - ORNAMENT	ORNAMENT		1980	$12.00	$42.00
1980-QX201-4	Grandson	CC - ORNAMENT	ORNAMENT		1980	$4.00	$28.00

Order No.	Title	Type	Theme	Retired	Intro. Year	Retail Price	Secondary Price
1980-QX202-1	Granddaughter	CC - ORNAMENT	ORNAMENT		1980	$4.00	$27.00
1980-QX211-4	Son	CC - ORNAMENT	ORNAMENT		1980	$4.00	$27.00
1980-QX212-1	Daughter	CC - ORNAMENT	ORNAMENT		1980	$4.00	$28.00
1980-QX214-1	Dad	CC - ORNAMENT	ORNAMENT		1980	$4.00	$15.00
1980-QX203-4	Mother	CC - ORNAMENT	ORNAMENT		1980	$4.00	$22.00
1980-QX230-1	Mother And Dad	CC - ORNAMENT	ORNAMENT		1980	$4.00	$28.50
1980-QX204-1	Grandmother	CC - ORNAMENT	ORNAMENT		1980	$4.00	$18.00
1980-QX231-4	Grandfather	CC - ORNAMENT	ORNAMENT		1980	$4.00	$19.00
1980-QX213-4	Grandparents	CC - ORNAMENT	ORNAMENT		1980	$4.00	$18.00
1980-QX206-1	25th Christmas Together	CC - ORNAMENT	ORNAMENT		1980	$4.00	$44.00
1980-QX205-4	First Christmas Together	CC - ORNAMENT	ORNAMENT		1980	$4.00	$19.00
1980-QX207-4	Christmas Love	CC - ORNAMENT	ORNAMENT		1980	$4.00	$38.00
1980-QX208-1	Friendship	CC - ORNAMENT	ORNAMENT		1980	$4.00	$18.00
1980-QX210-1	Christmas At Home	CC - ORNAMENT	ORNAMENT		1980	$4.00	$23.50
1980-QX209-4	Teacher	CC - ORNAMENT	ORNAMENT		1980	$4.00	$16.00
1980-QX302-1	Love	CC - ORNAMENT	ORNAMENT		1980	$4.00	$53.00
1980-QX303-4	Beauty Of Friendship	CC - ORNAMENT	ORNAMENT		1980	$4.00	$42.00
1980-QX305-4	First Christmas Together	CC - ORNAMENT	ORNAMENT		1980	$4.00	$34.00
1980-QX304-1	Mother	CC - ORNAMENT	ORNAMENT		1980	$4.00	$24.00
1980-QX215-4	Betsey Clark - 8th	CC - ORNAMENT	ORNAMENT		1980	$4.00	$28.00
1980-QX307-4	Betsey Clark	CC - ORNAMENT	ORNAMENT		1980	$6.50	$52.00
1980-QX149-4	Betsey Clark's Christmas	CC - ORNAMENT	ORNAMENT		1980	$7.50	$28.00
1980-QX216-1	Peanuts	CC - ORNAMENT	ORNAMENT		1980	$4.00	$34.50
1980-QX217-4	Joan Walsh Anglund	CC - ORNAMENT	ORNAMENT		1980	$4.00	$23.00
1980-QX218-1	Disney	CC - ORNAMENT	ORNAMENT		1980	$4.00	$28.00
1980-QX219-4	Mary Hamilton	CC - ORNAMENT	ORNAMENT		1980	$4.00	$19.00
1980-QX220-1	Muppets	CC - ORNAMENT	ORNAMENT		1980	$4.00	$25.00
1980-QX221-4	Marty Links	CC - ORNAMENT	ORNAMENT		1980	$4.00	$18.00
1980-QX228-1	Christmas Choir	CC - ORNAMENT	ORNAMENT		1980	$4.00	$74.00
1980-QX225-4	Nativity	CC - ORNAMENT	ORNAMENT		1980	$4.00	$38.00
1980-QX226-1	Christmas Time	CC - ORNAMENT	ORNAMENT		1980	$4.00	$28.00
1980-QX223-4	Santa's Workshop	CC - ORNAMENT	ORNAMENT		1980	$4.00	$24.00
1980-QX222-1	Happy Christmas	CC - ORNAMENT	ORNAMENT		1980	$4.00	$28.00
1980-QX227-4	Jolly Santa	CC - ORNAMENT	ORNAMENT		1980	$4.00	$25.00
1980-QX224-1	Christmas Cardinals	CC - ORNAMENT	ORNAMENT		1980	$4.00	$28.00
1980-QX300-1	Three Wise Men	CC - ORNAMENT	ORNAMENT		1980	$4.00	$25.00
1980-QX301-4	Wreath	CC - ORNAMENT	ORNAMENT		1980	$4.00	$75.00
1980-QX350-1	Joy (Colors of Christmas)	CC - ORNAMENT	ORNAMENT		1980	$4.00	$21.00
1980-QX309-4	Drummer Boy (Frosted Images)	CC - ORNAMENT	ORNAMENT		1980	$4.00	$23.00
1980-QX310-1	Santa (Frosted Images)	CC - ORNAMENT	ORNAMENT		1980	$4.00	$19.00
1980-QX308-1	Dove (Frosted Images)	CC - ORNAMENT	ORNAMENT		1980	$4.00	$36.00
1980-QX134-1	Clothespin Soldier	CC - ORNAMENT	ORNAMENT		1980	$3.50	$36.00
1980-QX135-4	Christmas Teddy	CC - ORNAMENT	ORNAMENT		1980	$2.50	$105.00
1980-QX160-1	Merry Redbird	CC - ORNAMENT	ORNAMENT		1980	$3.50	$55.00
1980-QX130-1	Swingin' On A Star	CC - ORNAMENT	ORNAMENT		1980	$4.00	$72.00
1980-QX131-4	Christmas Owl	CC - ORNAMENT	ORNAMENT		1980	$4.00	$42.00
1980-QX131-9	Thimble - 2nd	CC - ORNAMENT	ORNAMENT		1980	$4.00	$149.00
1980-QX133-4	The Snowflake Swing	CC - ORNAMENT	ORNAMENT		1980	$4.00	$44.00
1980-QX146-1	Santa 1980	CC - ORNAMENT	ORNAMENT		1980	$5.50	$82.00
1980-QX147-4	Drummer Boy (Dough-Look)	CC - ORNAMENT	ORNAMENT		1980	$5.50	$88.00
1980-QX135-9	Christmas Is for Children	CC - ORNAMENT	ORNAMENT		1980	$5.50	$79.00
1980-QX134-7	A Christmas Treat	CC - ORNAMENT	ORNAMENT		1980	$5.50	$64.00
1980-QX139-9	Skating Snowman	CC - ORNAMENT	ORNAMENT		1980	$5.50	$78.00
1980-QX139-4	A Heavenly Nap	CC - ORNAMENT	ORNAMENT		1980	$6.50	$45.00
1980-QX152-1	Heavenly Sounds	CC - ORNAMENT	ORNAMENT		1980	$7.50	$88.00
1980-QX140-1	Caroling Bear	CC - ORNAMENT	ORNAMENT		1980	$7.50	$132.00
1980-QX138-1	Santa's Flight	CC - ORNAMENT	ORNAMENT		1980	$5.50	$105.00
1980-QX150-1	The Animal's Christmas	CC - ORNAMENT	ORNAMENT		1980	$8.00	$54.00
1980-QX153-4	A Spot Of Christmas Cheer	CC - ORNAMENT	ORNAMENT		1980	$8.00	$133.00
1980-QX142-1	Elfin Antics	CC - ORNAMENT	ORNAMENT		1980	$9.00	$202.00
1980-QX144-1	A Christmas Vigil	CC - ORNAMENT	ORNAMENT		1980	$9.00	$115.00
1980-QX156-7	Heavenly Minstrel - SE	CC - ORNAMENT	ORNAMENT		1980	$15.00	$285.00
1980-QX158-4	Checking It Twice - SE	CC - ORNAMENT	ORNAMENT		1980	$20.00	$195.00
1980-QX165-4	Snowflake Chimes	CC - ORNAMENT	ORNAMENT		1980	$5.50	$27.00
1980-QX320-3	Reindeer Chimes	CC - ORNAMENT	ORNAMENT		1980	$5.50	$44.00
1980-QX136-1	Santa Mobile	CC - ORNAMENT	ORNAMENT		1980	$5.50	$37.00
1980-QX306-1	Norman Rockwell - 1st	CC - ORNAMENT	ORNAMENT		1980	$6.50	$210.00
1980-QX137-4	Frosty Friends - 1st	CC - ORNAMENT	ORNAMENT		1980	$6.50	$625.00
1980-QX154-1	Snoopy And Friends - 2nd	CC - ORNAMENT	ORNAMENT		1980	$9.00	$105.00
1980-QX141-4	Carrousel - 3rd	CC - ORNAMENT	ORNAMENT		1980	$7.50	$145.00
1980-QX132-1	Thimble - 3rd	CC - ORNAMENT	ORNAMENT		1980	$4.00	$147.00
1980-QX143-4	Here Comes Santa - 2nd	CC - ORNAMENT	ORNAMENT		1980	$12.00	$182.00
1980-QX157-4	The Bellringer - 2nd	CC - ORNAMENT	ORNAMENT		1980	$15.00	$77.00
1980-QX161-4	Santa (Yarn)	CC - ORNAMENT	ORNAMENT		1980	$3.00	$8.00
1980-QX162-1	Angel	CC - ORNAMENT	ORNAMENT		1980	$3.00	$9.00
1980-QX163-4	Snowman	CC - ORNAMENT	ORNAMENT		1980	$3.00	$8.00
1980-QX164-1	Soldier	CC - ORNAMENT	ORNAMENT		1980	$3.00	$8.00
1980-QX340-7	The Rocking Horse	CC - ORNAMENT	ORNAMENT		1980	$2.00	$22.00
1980-QX342-7	Merry Santa	CC - ORNAMENT	ORNAMENT		1980	$2.00	$21.00
1980-QX341-9	Stuffed Full Stocking	CC - ORNAMENT	ORNAMENT		1980	$2.00	$23.00
1980-QX343-9	Angel Music	CC - ORNAMENT	ORNAMENT		1980	$2.00	$15.00
1981-QX600-2	Baby's First Christmas - Girl	CC - ORNAMENT	ORNAMENT		1981	$4.50	$18.00
1981-QX601-5	Baby's First Christmas - Boy	CC - ORNAMENT	ORNAMENT		1981	$4.50	$23.00
1981-QX602-2	Baby's First Christmas - Black	CC - ORNAMENT	ORNAMENT		1981	$4.50	$22.00
1981-QX516-2	Baby's First Christmas	CC - ORNAMENT	ORNAMENT		1981	$5.50	$28.00
1981-QX513-5	Baby's First Christmas	CC - ORNAMENT	ORNAMENT		1981	$8.50	$15.00
1981-QX440-2	Baby's First Christmas	CC - ORNAMENT	ORNAMENT		1981	$13.00	$47.00
1981-QX603-5	Godchild	CC - ORNAMENT	ORNAMENT		1981	$4.50	$18.00
1981-QX604-2	Grandson	CC - ORNAMENT	ORNAMENT		1981	$4.50	$19.00
1981-QX605-5	Granddaughter	CC - ORNAMENT	ORNAMENT		1981	$4.50	$19.00
1981-QX607-5	Daughter	CC - ORNAMENT	ORNAMENT		1981	$4.50	$28.00
1981-QX606-2	Son	CC - ORNAMENT	ORNAMENT		1981	$4.50	$28.00
1981-QX608-2	Mother	CC - ORNAMENT	ORNAMENT		1981	$4.50	$12.00

Order No.	Title	Type	Theme	Retired	Intro. Year	Retial Price	Secondary Price
1981-QX609-5	Father	CC - ORNAMENT	ORNAMENT		1981	$4.50	$18.00
1981-QX700-2	Mother And Dad	CC - ORNAMENT	ORNAMENT		1981	$4.50	$14.00
1981-QX704-2	Friendship	CC - ORNAMENT	ORNAMENT		1981	$4.50	$22.00
1981-QX705-5	The Gift Of Love	CC - ORNAMENT	ORNAMENT		1981	$4.50	$23.00
1981-QX709-5	Home	CC - ORNAMENT	ORNAMENT		1981	$4.50	$18.00
1981-QX800-2	Teacher	CC - ORNAMENT	ORNAMENT		1981	$4.50	$12.50
1981-QX701-5	Grandfather	CC - ORNAMENT	ORNAMENT		1981	$4.50	$18.00
1981-QX702-2	Grandmother	CC - ORNAMENT	ORNAMENT		1981	$4.50	$12.00
1981-QX703-5	Grandparents	CC - ORNAMENT	ORNAMENT		1981	$4.50	$18.00
1981-QX706-2	First Christmas Together	CC - ORNAMENT	ORNAMENT		1981	$4.50	$28.00
1981-QX707-5	25th Christmas Together	CC - ORNAMENT	ORNAMENT		1981	$4.50	$18.00
1981-QX708-2	50th Christmas	CC - ORNAMENT	ORNAMENT		1981	$4.50	$18.00
1981-QX502-2	Love	CC - ORNAMENT	ORNAMENT		1981	$5.50	$42.00
1981-QX503-5	Friendship	CC - ORNAMENT	ORNAMENT		1981	$5.00	$28.00
1981-QX505-5	First Christmas Together	CC - ORNAMENT	ORNAMENT		1981	$5.50	$22.00
1981-QX504-2	25th Christmas Together	CC - ORNAMENT	ORNAMENT		1981	$5.50	$18.00
1981-QX512-2	Betsey Clark	CC - ORNAMENT	ORNAMENT		1981	$8.50	$23.00
1981-QX423-5	Betsey Clark	CC - ORNAMENT	ORNAMENT		1981	$9.00	$72.00
1981-QX802-2	Betsey Clark - 9th	CC - ORNAMENT	ORNAMENT		1981	$4.50	$25.00
1981-QX807-5	Muppets	CC - ORNAMENT	ORNAMENT		1981	$4.50	$28.00
1981-QX424-2	Kermit The Frog	CC - ORNAMENT	ORNAMENT		1981	$9.00	$87.00
1981-QX425-5	The Divine Miss Piggy	CC - ORNAMENT	ORNAMENT		1981	$12.00	$82.00
1981-QX806-2	Mary Hamilton	CC - ORNAMENT	ORNAMENT		1981	$4.50	$17.00
1981-QX808-2	Marty Links	CC - ORNAMENT	ORNAMENT		1981	$4.50	$18.00
1981-QX803-5	Peanuts	CC - ORNAMENT	ORNAMENT		1981	$4.50	$29.00
1981-QX804-2	Joan Walsh Anglund	CC - ORNAMENT	ORNAMENT		1981	$4.50	$28.00
1981-QX805-5	Disney	CC - ORNAMENT	ORNAMENT		1981	$4.50	$25.00
1981-QX809-5	Christmas 1981- Schneeberg	CC - ORNAMENT	ORNAMENT		1981	$4.50	$18.50
1981-QX810-2	Christmas Magic	CC - ORNAMENT	ORNAMENT		1981	$4.50	$15.50
1981-QX801-5	Traditional (Black Santa)	CC - ORNAMENT	ORNAMENT		1981	$4.50	$85.00
1981-QX811-5	Let Us Adore Him	CC - ORNAMENT	ORNAMENT		1981	$4.50	$45.00
1981-QX812-2	Santa's Coming	CC - ORNAMENT	ORNAMENT		1981	$4.50	$25.00
1981-QX813-5	Christmas In The Forest	CC - ORNAMENT	ORNAMENT		1981	$4.50	$95.00
1981-QX814-2	Merry Christmas	CC - ORNAMENT	ORNAMENT		1981	$4.50	$19.00
1981-QX815-5	Santa's Surprise	CC - ORNAMENT	ORNAMENT		1981	$4.50	$23.00
1981-QX507-5	Angel (Acrylic)	CC - ORNAMENT	ORNAMENT		1981	$4.50	$24.00
1981-QX515-5	Tree Photoholder	CC - ORNAMENT	ORNAMENT		1981	$5.50	$21.00
1981-QX516-5	Unicorn	CC - ORNAMENT	ORNAMENT		1981	$8.50	$16.00
1981-QX508-2	Mouse	CC - ORNAMENT	ORNAMENT		1981	$4.00	$15.00
1981-QX509-5	Angel (Frosted Images)	CC - ORNAMENT	ORNAMENT		1981	$4.00	$52.00
1981-QX510-2	Snowman (Frosted Images)	CC - ORNAMENT	ORNAMENT		1981	$4.00	$24.00
1981-QX500-2	Shepherd Scene	CC - ORNAMENT	ORNAMENT		1981	$5.50	$23.00
1981-QX501-5	Christmas Star	CC - ORNAMENT	ORNAMENT		1981	$5.50	$18.00
1981-QX406-2	Puppy Love	CC - ORNAMENT	ORNAMENT		1981	$3.50	$31.00
1981-QX407-5	Jolly Snowman	CC - ORNAMENT	ORNAMENT		1981	$3.50	$48.00
1981-QX409-5	Perky Penguin	CC - ORNAMENT	ORNAMENT		1981	$3.50	$45.00
1981-QX408-2	Clothespin Drummer Boy	CC - ORNAMENT	ORNAMENT		1981	$4.50	$39.00
1981-QX412-2	The Stocking Mouse	CC - ORNAMENT	ORNAMENT		1981	$4.50	$90.00
1981-QX430-2	Space Santa	CC - ORNAMENT	ORNAMENT		1981	$6.50	$93.00
1981-QX418-2	Candyville Express	CC - ORNAMENT	ORNAMENT		1981	$7.50	$99.00
1981-QX431-5	Ice Fairy	CC - ORNAMENT	ORNAMENT		1981	$6.50	$82.00
1981-QX421-5	Star Swing	CC - ORNAMENT	ORNAMENT		1981	$5.50	$34.00
1981-QX139-4	A Heavenly Nap	CC - ORNAMENT	ORNAMENT		1981	$6.50	$52.00
1981-QX139-6	Dough Angel	CC - ORNAMENT	ORNAMENT		1981	$5.50	$82.00
1981-QX429-5	Topsy-Turvy Tunes	CC - ORNAMENT	ORNAMENT		1981	$7.50	$74.00
1981-QX154-7	A Well-Stocked Stocking	CC - ORNAMENT	ORNAMENT		1981	$9.00	$75.00
1981-QX434-2	The Friendly Fiddler	CC - ORNAMENT	ORNAMENT		1981	$8.00	$68.00
1981-QX432-2	The Ice Sculptor	CC - ORNAMENT	ORNAMENT		1981	$8.00	$82.00
1981-QX437-5	Christmas Dreams	CC - ORNAMENT	ORNAMENT		1981	$12.00	$202.00
1981-QX155-4	Christmas Fantasy	CC - ORNAMENT	ORNAMENT		1981	$13.00	$73.00
1981-QX439-5	Sailing Santa	CC - ORNAMENT	ORNAMENT		1981	$13.00	$254.00
1981-QX425-2	Love And Joy (Porc. Chimes)	CC - ORNAMENT	ORNAMENT		1981	$9.00	$84.00
1981-QX148-1	Drummer Boy	CC - ORNAMENT	ORNAMENT		1981	$2.50	$42.00
1981-QX446-2	St. Nicholas	CC - ORNAMENT	ORNAMENT		1981	$5.50	$49.50
1981-QX448-5	Mr. & Mrs. Claus	CC - ORNAMENT	ORNAMENT		1981	$12.00	$108.00
1981-QX158-4	Checking It Twice - SE	CC - ORNAMENT	ORNAMENT		1981	$22.50	$195.00
1981-QX445-5	Snowman Chimes	CC - ORNAMENT	ORNAMENT		1981	$5.50	$28.00
1981-QX136-1	Santa Mobile	CC - ORNAMENT	ORNAMENT		1981	$5.50	$40.00
1981-QX165-4	Snowflake Chimes	CC - ORNAMENT	ORNAMENT		1981	$5.50	$30.00
1981-QX422-2	Rocking Horse - 1st	CC - ORNAMENT	ORNAMENT		1981	$9.00	$560.00
1981-QX441-5	The Bellringer - 3rd	CC - ORNAMENT	ORNAMENT		1981	$15.00	$82.50
1981-QX511-5	Norman Rockwell - 2nd	CC - ORNAMENT	ORNAMENT		1981	$8.50	$38.00
1981-QX438-2	Here Comes Santa - 3rd	CC - ORNAMENT	ORNAMENT		1981	$13.00	$260.00
1981-QX427-5	Carrousel - 4th	CC - ORNAMENT	ORNAMENT		1981	$9.00	$80.00
1981-QX436-2	Snoopy And Friends - 3rd	CC - ORNAMENT	ORNAMENT		1981	$12.00	$80.00
1981-QX413-5	Angel/Thimble - 4th	CC - ORNAMENT	ORNAMENT		1981	$4.50	$133.00
1981-QX433-5	Frosty Friends - 2nd	CC - ORNAMENT	ORNAMENT		1981	$8.00	$345.00
1981-QX400-2	Cardinal Cutie	CC - ORNAMENT	ORNAMENT		1981	$3.00	$28.00
1981-QX401-5	Peppermint Mouse	CC - ORNAMENT	ORNAMENT		1981	$3.00	$28.00
1981-QX402-2	Gingham Dog	CC - ORNAMENT	ORNAMENT		1981	$3.00	$15.00
1981-QX403-5	Calico Kitty	CC - ORNAMENT	ORNAMENT		1981	$3.00	$19.00
1981-QX161-4	Santa	CC - ORNAMENT	ORNAMENT		1981	$3.00	$8.00
1981-QX162-1	Angel (Yarn)	CC - ORNAMENT	ORNAMENT		1981	$3.00	$8.00
1981-QX163-4	Snowman (Yarn)	CC - ORNAMENT	ORNAMENT		1981	$3.00	$8.00
1981-QX164-1	Soldier	CC - ORNAMENT	ORNAMENT		1981	$3.00	$8.00
1981-QX404-2	Christmas Teddy	CC - ORNAMENT	ORNAMENT		1981	$5.50	$19.00
1981-QX405-5	Raccoon Tunes	CC - ORNAMENT	ORNAMENT		1981	$5.50	$17.00
1982-QX312-6	Baby's First Christmas - Photo	CC - ORNAMENT	ORNAMENT		1982	$6.50	$23.00
1982-QX455-3	Baby's First Christmas	CC - ORNAMENT	ORNAMENT		1982	$13.00	$45.00
1982-QX216-3	Baby's First Christmas (Boy)	CC - ORNAMENT	ORNAMENT		1982	$4.50	$22.00
1982-QX207-3	Baby's First Christmas (Girl)	CC - ORNAMENT	ORNAMENT		1982	$4.50	$25.00
1982-QX222-6	Godchild	CC - ORNAMENT	ORNAMENT		1982	$4.50	$18.00
1982-QX224-6	Grandson	CC - ORNAMENT	ORNAMENT		1982	$4.50	$27.00

Order No.	Title	Type	Theme	Retired	Intro. Year	Retail Price	Secondary Price
1982-QX224-3	Granddaughter	CC - ORNAMENT	ORNAMENT		1982	$4.50	$21.00
1982-QX204-3	Son	CC - ORNAMENT	ORNAMENT		1982	$4.50	$14.00
1982-QX204-6	Daughter	CC - ORNAMENT	ORNAMENT		1982	$4.50	$21.00
1982-QX205-6	Father	CC - ORNAMENT	ORNAMENT		1982	$4.50	$28.00
1982-QX205-3	Mother	CC - ORNAMENT	ORNAMENT		1982	$4.50	$15.00
1982-QX222-3	Mother And Dad	CC - ORNAMENT	ORNAMENT		1982	$4.50	$15.00
1982-QX208-3	Sister	CC - ORNAMENT	ORNAMENT		1982	$4.50	$19.00
1982-QX200-3	Grandmother	CC - ORNAMENT	ORNAMENT		1982	$4.50	$22.00
1982-QX207-6	Grandfather	CC - ORNAMENT	ORNAMENT		1982	$4.50	$18.50
1982-QX214-6	Grandparents	CC - ORNAMENT	ORNAMENT		1982	$4.50	$17.50
1982-QX306-6	First Christmas Together	CC - ORNAMENT	ORNAMENT		1982	$8.50	$32.00
1982-QX211-3	First Christmas Together	CC - ORNAMENT	ORNAMENT		1982	$4.50	$27.00
1982-QX456-3	First Christmas Together - Lkt	CC - ORNAMENT	ORNAMENT		1982	$15.00	$25.00
1982-QX311-6	Christmas Memories	CC - ORNAMENT	ORNAMENT		1982	$6.50	$16.00
1982-QX214-3	Teacher	CC - ORNAMENT	ORNAMENT		1982	$4.50	$13.50
1982-QX212-6	New Home	CC - ORNAMENT	ORNAMENT		1982	$4.50	$15.00
1982-QX312-3	Teacher	CC - ORNAMENT	ORNAMENT		1982	$6.50	$12.50
1982-QX211-6	25th Christmas Together	CC - ORNAMENT	ORNAMENT		1982	$4.50	$12.50
1982-QX212-3	50th Christmas Together	CC - ORNAMENT	ORNAMENT		1982	$4.50	$14.50
1982-QX209-3	Moments Of Love	CC - ORNAMENT	ORNAMENT		1982	$4.50	$13.50
1982-QX209-6	Love	CC - ORNAMENT	ORNAMENT		1982	$4.50	$15.00
1982-QX208-6	Friendship	CC - ORNAMENT	ORNAMENT		1982	$4.50	$15.50
1982-QX301-6	Teacher - Apple	CC - ORNAMENT	ORNAMENT		1982	$5.50	$12.50
1982-QX302-3	Baby's First Christmas	CC - ORNAMENT	ORNAMENT		1982	$5.50	$28.00
1982-QX302-6	First Christmas Together	CC - ORNAMENT	ORNAMENT		1982	$5.50	$16.00
1982-QX304-3	Love	CC - ORNAMENT	ORNAMENT		1982	$5.50	$26.00
1982-QX304-6	Friendship	CC - ORNAMENT	ORNAMENT		1982	$5.50	$18.00
1982-QX218-3	Miss Piggy And Kermit	CC - ORNAMENT	ORNAMENT		1982	$4.50	$38.00
1982-QX218-6	Muppets Party	CC - ORNAMENT	ORNAMENT		1982	$4.50	$37.00
1982-QX495-6	Kermit The Frog	CC - ORNAMENT	ORNAMENT		1982	$11.00	$85.00
1982-QX425-5	The Divine Miss Piggy	CC - ORNAMENT	ORNAMENT		1982	$12.00	$92.50
1982-QX305-6	Betsey Clark	CC - ORNAMENT	ORNAMENT		1982	$8.50	$25.00
1982-QX305-3	Norman Rockwell - 3rd	CC - ORNAMENT	ORNAMENT		1982	$8.50	$23.50
1982-QX215-6	Betsey Clark - 10th	CC - ORNAMENT	ORNAMENT		1982	$4.50	$33.00
1982-QX202-3	Norman Rockwell	CC - ORNAMENT	ORNAMENT		1982	$4.50	$25.00
1982-QX200-6	Peanuts	CC - ORNAMENT	ORNAMENT		1982	$4.50	$34.50
1982-QX217-3	Disney	CC - ORNAMENT	ORNAMENT		1982	$4.50	$33.00
1982-QX217-6	Mary Hamilton	CC - ORNAMENT	ORNAMENT		1982	$4.50	$20.00
1982-QX219-3	Joan Walsh Anglund	CC - ORNAMENT	ORNAMENT		1982	$4.50	$18.00
1982-QX226-3	Old World Angels	CC - ORNAMENT	ORNAMENT		1982	$4.50	$29.00
1982-QX226-6	Patterns Of Christmas	CC - ORNAMENT	ORNAMENT		1982	$4.50	$19.00
1982-QX227-6	Old Fashioned Christmas	CC - ORNAMENT	ORNAMENT		1982	$4.50	$38.00
1982-QX228-3	Stained Glass	CC - ORNAMENT	ORNAMENT		1982	$4.50	$20.00
1982-QX225-6	Merry Christmas	CC - ORNAMENT	ORNAMENT		1982	$4.50	$17.00
1982-QX203-6	Twelve Days of Christmas	CC - ORNAMENT	ORNAMENT		1982	$4.50	$23.00
1982-QX220-6	Christmas Angel	CC - ORNAMENT	ORNAMENT		1982	$4.50	$18.50
1982-QX221-6	Santa	CC - ORNAMENT	ORNAMENT		1982	$4.50	$13.50
1982-QX201-3	Currier & Ives	CC - ORNAMENT	ORNAMENT		1982	$4.50	$17.50
1982-QX221-3	Season For Caring	CC - ORNAMENT	ORNAMENT		1982	$4.50	$19.50
1982-QX308-3	Nativity	CC - ORNAMENT	ORNAMENT		1982	$4.50	$30.00
1982-QX308-6	Santa's Flight	CC - ORNAMENT	ORNAMENT		1982	$4.50	$28.00
1982-QX300-6	Snowy Seal	CC - ORNAMENT	ORNAMENT		1982	$4.00	$17.50
1982-QX300-3	Arctic Penguin	CC - ORNAMENT	ORNAMENT		1982	$4.00	$18.00
1982-QX309-3	Christmas Sleigh	CC - ORNAMENT	ORNAMENT		1982	$5.50	$62.00
1982-QX309-6	Angel	CC - ORNAMENT	ORNAMENT		1982	$5.50	$28.00
1982-QX311-3	Christmas Magic	CC - ORNAMENT	ORNAMENT		1982	$5.50	$29.00
1982-QX307-3	Three Kings	CC - ORNAMENT	ORNAMENT		1982	$8.50	$21.00
1982-QX456-6	Baroque Angel	CC - ORNAMENT	ORNAMENT		1982	$15.00	$145.00
1982-QX145-4	Cloisonne Angel	CC - ORNAMENT	ORNAMENT		1982	$12.00	$87.00
1982-QX467-6	Santa And Reindeer	CC - ORNAMENT	ORNAMENT		1982	$9.00	$42.00
1982-QX460-6	Brass Bell	CC - ORNAMENT	ORNAMENT		1982	$12.00	$23.00
1982-QX478-6	Santa's Sleigh	CC - ORNAMENT	ORNAMENT		1982	$9.00	$25.00
1982-QX452-6	The Spirit Of Christmas	CC - ORNAMENT	ORNAMENT		1982	$10.00	$117.00
1982-QX457-6	Jogging Santa	CC - ORNAMENT	ORNAMENT		1982	$8.00	$42.00
1982-QX148-7	Santa Bell	CC - ORNAMENT	ORNAMENT		1982	$15.00	$51.00
1982-QX450-3	Santa's Workshop	CC - ORNAMENT	ORNAMENT		1982	$10.00	$74.00
1982-QX435-5	Cycling Santa	CC - ORNAMENT	ORNAMENT		1982	$20.00	$132.00
1982-QX155-4	Christmas Fantasy	CC - ORNAMENT	ORNAMENT		1982	$13.00	$75.00
1982-QX480-6	Cowboy Snowman	CC - ORNAMENT	ORNAMENT		1982	$8.00	$51.00
1982-QX461-3	Pinecone Home	CC - ORNAMENT	ORNAMENT		1982	$8.00	$155.00
1982-QX479-3	Raccoon Surprises	CC - ORNAMENT	ORNAMENT		1982	$9.00	$155.00
1982-QX457-3	Elfin Artist	CC - ORNAMENT	ORNAMENT		1982	$9.00	$42.00
1982-QX432-2	Ice Sculptor	CC - ORNAMENT	ORNAMENT		1982	$8.00	$78.00
1982-QX483-6	Tin Soldier	CC - ORNAMENT	ORNAMENT		1982	$6.50	$45.50
1982-QX419-5	Peeking Elf	CC - ORNAMENT	ORNAMENT		1982	$6.50	$27.00
1982-QX465-3	Jolly Christmas Elf	CC - ORNAMENT	ORNAMENT		1982	$6.50	$81.00
1982-QX494-6	Embroidered Tree	CC - ORNAMENT	ORNAMENT		1982	$6.50	$24.00
1982-QX454-6	Cookie Mouse	CC - ORNAMENT	ORNAMENT		1982	$4.50	$52.00
1982-QX459-6	Musical Angel	CC - ORNAMENT	ORNAMENT		1982	$5.50	$145.00
1982-QX415-5	Merry Moose	CC - ORNAMENT	ORNAMENT		1982	$5.50	$47.00
1982-QX131-4	Christmas Owl	CC - ORNAMENT	ORNAMENT		1982	$4.50	$52.50
1982-QX462-3	Dove Love	CC - ORNAMENT	ORNAMENT		1982	$4.50	$45.00
1982-QX409-5	Perky Penguin	CC - ORNAMENT	ORNAMENT		1982	$4.00	$50.00
1982-QX454-3	Christmas Kitten	CC - ORNAMENT	ORNAMENT		1982	$4.00	$30.50
1982-QX477-6	Jingling Teddy	CC - ORNAMENT	ORNAMENT		1982	$4.00	$35.00
1982-QX313-3	Holiday Wildlife - 1st	CC - ORNAMENT	ORNAMENT		1982	$7.00	$382.00
1982-QX460-3	Tin Locomotive - 1st	CC - ORNAMENT	ORNAMENT		1982	$13.00	$530.00
1982-QX458-3	Clothespin Soldier - 1st	CC - ORNAMENT	ORNAMENT		1982	$5.00	$188.00
1982-QX455-6	The Bellringer - 4th	CC - ORNAMENT	ORNAMENT		1982	$15.00	$78.00
1982-QX478-3	Carrousel - 5th	CC - ORNAMENT	ORNAMENT		1982	$10.00	$83.00
1982-QX480-3	Snoopy And Friends - 4th	CC - ORNAMENT	ORNAMENT		1982	$13.00	$93.00
1982-QX464-3	Here Comes Santa - 4th	CC - ORNAMENT	ORNAMENT		1982	$15.00	$128.00
1982-QX502-3	Rocking Horse - 2nd	CC - ORNAMENT	ORNAMENT		1982	$10.00	$350.00

Order No.	Title	Type	Theme	Retired	Intro. Year	Retial Price	Secondary Price
1982-QX451-3	Thimble - 5th	CC - ORNAMENT	ORNAMENT		1982	$5.00	$59.50
1982-QX452-3	Frosty Friends - 3rd	CC - ORNAMENT	ORNAMENT		1982	$8.00	$170.00
1982-QX484-6	Tree Chimes	CC - ORNAMENT	ORNAMENT		1982	$5.50	$43.00
1982-QX494-3	Bell Chimes	CC - ORNAMENT	ORNAMENT		1982	$5.50	$25.00
1982-QX502-6	Angel Chimes	CC - ORNAMENT	ORNAMENT		1982	$5.50	$24.50
1983-QX301-9	Baby's First Christmas	CC - ORNAMENT	ORNAMENT		1983	$7.50	$11.50
1983-QX402-7	Baby's First Christmas	CC - ORNAMENT	ORNAMENT		1983	$14.00	$32.50
1983-QX200-7	Baby's First Christmas - Girl	CC - ORNAMENT	ORNAMENT		1983	$4.50	$19.00
1983-QX200-9	Baby's First Christmas - Boy	CC - ORNAMENT	ORNAMENT		1983	$4.50	$18.00
1983-QX302-9	Baby's First Christmas (Photo)	CC - ORNAMENT	ORNAMENT		1983	$7.00	$22.00
1983-QX430-9	Grandchild's First Christmas	CC - ORNAMENT	ORNAMENT		1983	$14.00	$32.00
1983-QX226-9	Child's Third Christmas	CC - ORNAMENT	ORNAMENT		1983	$4.50	$22.00
1983-QX312-9	Grandchild's First Christmas	CC - ORNAMENT	ORNAMENT		1983	$6.00	$18.50
1983-QX226-7	Baby's Second Christmas	CC - ORNAMENT	ORNAMENT		1983	$4.50	$25.00
1983-QX202-7	Granddaughter	CC - ORNAMENT	ORNAMENT		1983	$4.50	$24.00
1983-QX201-9	Grandson	CC - ORNAMENT	ORNAMENT		1983	$4.50	$26.00
1983-QX202-9	Son	CC - ORNAMENT	ORNAMENT		1983	$4.50	$32.00
1983-QX203-7	Daughter	CC - ORNAMENT	ORNAMENT		1983	$4.50	$34.00
1983-QX201-7	Godchild	CC - ORNAMENT	ORNAMENT		1983	$4.50	$17.50
1983-QX205-7	Grandmother	CC - ORNAMENT	ORNAMENT		1983	$4.50	$18.00
1983-QX429-7	Mom And Dad	CC - ORNAMENT	ORNAMENT		1983	$6.50	$23.00
1983-QX206-9	Sister	CC - ORNAMENT	ORNAMENT		1983	$4.50	$21.00
1983-QX429-9	Grandparents	CC - ORNAMENT	ORNAMENT		1983	$6.50	$15.50
1983-QX208-9	First Christmas Together	CC - ORNAMENT	ORNAMENT		1983	$4.50	$22.00
1983-QX310-7	First Christmas Together	CC - ORNAMENT	ORNAMENT		1983	$6.00	$20.00
1983-QX301-7	First Christmas Together	CC - ORNAMENT	ORNAMENT		1983	$7.50	$17.50
1983-QX432-9	First Christmas Together - Lkt	CC - ORNAMENT	ORNAMENT		1983	$15.00	$32.50
1983-QX223-9	Love Is A Song	CC - ORNAMENT	ORNAMENT		1983	$4.50	$24.00
1983-QX422-7	Love	CC - ORNAMENT	ORNAMENT		1983	$13.00	$24.00
1983-QX310-9	Love	CC - ORNAMENT	ORNAMENT		1983	$6.00	$33.00
1983-QX207-9	Love	CC - ORNAMENT	ORNAMENT		1983	$4.50	$24.00
1983-QX304-9	Teacher	CC - ORNAMENT	ORNAMENT		1983	$6.00	$11.00
1983-QX306-9	First Christmas Together	CC - ORNAMENT	ORNAMENT		1983	$6.00	$19.50
1983-QX305-9	Friendship	CC - ORNAMENT	ORNAMENT		1983	$6.00	$16.50
1983-QX305-7	Love	CC - ORNAMENT	ORNAMENT		1983	$6.00	$15.50
1983-QX306-7	Mother	CC - ORNAMENT	ORNAMENT		1983	$6.00	$18.00
1983-QX224-7	25th Christmas Together	CC - ORNAMENT	ORNAMENT		1983	$4.50	$17.00
1983-QX224-9	Teacher	CC - ORNAMENT	ORNAMENT		1983	$4.50	$15.00
1983-QX207-7	Friendship	CC - ORNAMENT	ORNAMENT		1983	$4.50	$18.00
1983-QX210-7	New Home	CC - ORNAMENT	ORNAMENT		1983	$4.50	$28.00
1983-QX430-7	Tenth Christmas Together	CC - ORNAMENT	ORNAMENT		1983	$6.50	$28.50
1983-QX404-7	Betsey Clark	CC - ORNAMENT	ORNAMENT		1983	$6.50	$21.50
1983-QX440-1	Betsey Clark	CC - ORNAMENT	ORNAMENT		1983	$9.00	$29.00
1983-QX211-9	Betsey Clark - 11th	CC - ORNAMENT	ORNAMENT		1983	$4.50	$29.00
1983-QX212-7	Peanuts	CC - ORNAMENT	ORNAMENT		1983	$4.50	$32.00
1983-QX212-9	Disney	CC - ORNAMENT	ORNAMENT		1983	$4.50	$35.00
1983-QX214-9	Shirt Tales	CC - ORNAMENT	ORNAMENT		1983	$4.50	$23.00
1983-QX213-7	Mary Hamilton	CC - ORNAMENT	ORNAMENT		1983	$4.50	$29.50
1983-QX405-7	Miss Piggy	CC - ORNAMENT	ORNAMENT		1983	$13.00	$186.00
1983-QX214-7	The Muppets	CC - ORNAMENT	ORNAMENT		1983	$4.50	$45.00
1983-QX495-6	Kermit The Frog	CC - ORNAMENT	ORNAMENT		1983	$11.00	$90.00
1983-QX300-7	Norman Rockwell - 4th	CC - ORNAMENT	ORNAMENT		1983	$7.50	$29.00
1983-QX215-7	Norman Rockwell	CC - ORNAMENT	ORNAMENT		1983	$4.50	$40.00
1983-QX215-9	Currier & Ives	CC - ORNAMENT	ORNAMENT		1983	$4.50	$14.50
1983-QX216-9	Christmas Joy	CC - ORNAMENT	ORNAMENT		1983	$4.50	$25.00
1983-QX217-7	Here Comes Santa	CC - ORNAMENT	ORNAMENT		1983	$4.50	$28.00
1983-QX218-7	Oriental Butterflies	CC - ORNAMENT	ORNAMENT		1983	$4.50	$24.50
1983-QX219-7	Angels	CC - ORNAMENT	ORNAMENT		1983	$5.00	$22.00
1983-QX219-9	Season's Greetings	CC - ORNAMENT	ORNAMENT		1983	$4.50	$18.50
1983-QX220-9	1983	CC - ORNAMENT	ORNAMENT		1983	$4.50	$22.50
1983-QX220-7	The Wise Men	CC - ORNAMENT	ORNAMENT		1983	$4.50	$43.50
1983-QX221-9	Christmas Wonderland	CC - ORNAMENT	ORNAMENT		1983	$4.50	$82.00
1983-QX217-9	An Old Fashioned Christmas	CC - ORNAMENT	ORNAMENT		1983	$4.50	$23.00
1983-QX216-7	The Annunciation	CC - ORNAMENT	ORNAMENT		1983	$4.50	$23.50
1983-QX303-9	Christmas Stocking	CC - ORNAMENT	ORNAMENT		1983	$6.00	$35.00
1983-QX304-7	Star Of Peace	CC - ORNAMENT	ORNAMENT		1983	$6.00	$16.00
1983-QX307-7	Time For Sharing	CC - ORNAMENT	ORNAMENT		1983	$6.00	$38.00
1983-QX311-9	Enameled Christmas Wreath	CC - ORNAMENT	ORNAMENT		1983	$9.00	$13.50
1983-QX303-7	Memories To Treasure	CC - ORNAMENT	ORNAMENT		1983	$7.00	$17.50
1983-QX302-7	Mother And Child	CC - ORNAMENT	ORNAMENT		1983	$7.50	$36.00
1983-QX308-7	Santa	CC - ORNAMENT	ORNAMENT		1983	$4.00	$21.50
1983-QX307-9	Heart	CC - ORNAMENT	ORNAMENT		1983	$4.00	$33.50
1983-QX479-6	Embroidered Stocking	CC - ORNAMENT	ORNAMENT		1983	$6.50	$16.50
1983-QX421-7	Embroidered Heart	CC - ORNAMENT	ORNAMENT		1983	$6.50	$22.00
1983-QX424-9	Scrimshaw Reindeer	CC - ORNAMENT	ORNAMENT		1983	$8.00	$27.00
1983-QX407-9	Jack Frost	CC - ORNAMENT	ORNAMENT		1983	$9.00	$47.50
1983-QX426-7	Unicorn	CC - ORNAMENT	ORNAMENT		1983	$10.00	$50.00
1983-QX423-7	Porcelain Doll, Diana	CC - ORNAMENT	ORNAMENT		1983	$9.00	$21.00
1983-QX423-9	Brass Santa	CC - ORNAMENT	ORNAMENT		1983	$9.00	$18.50
1983-QX426-9	Santa's On His Way	CC - ORNAMENT	ORNAMENT		1983	$10.00	$32.00
1983-QX409-9	Old-Fashioned Santa	CC - ORNAMENT	ORNAMENT		1983	$11.00	$55.00
1983-QX435-5	Cycling Santa	CC - ORNAMENT	ORNAMENT		1983	$20.00	$120.00
1983-QX450-3	Santa's Workshop	CC - ORNAMENT	ORNAMENT		1983	$10.00	$75.00
1983-QX418-7	Ski Lift Santa	CC - ORNAMENT	ORNAMENT		1983	$8.00	$63.00
1983-QX424-7	Hitchhiking Santa	CC - ORNAMENT	ORNAMENT		1983	$8.00	$28.50
1983-QX407-7	Mountain Climbing Santa	CC - ORNAMENT	ORNAMENT		1983	$6.50	$32.50
1983-QX425-9	Jolly Santa	CC - ORNAMENT	ORNAMENT		1983	$3.50	$28.50
1983-QX311-7	Santa's Many Faces	CC - ORNAMENT	ORNAMENT		1983	$6.00	$27.50
1983-QX422-9	Baroque Angels	CC - ORNAMENT	ORNAMENT		1983	$13.00	$72.00
1983-QX428-7	Madonna And Child	CC - ORNAMENT	ORNAMENT		1983	$12.00	$26.00
1983-QX413-7	Mouse On Cheese	CC - ORNAMENT	ORNAMENT		1983	$6.50	$43.00
1983-QX408-9	Peppermint Penguin	CC - ORNAMENT	ORNAMENT		1983	$6.50	$35.00
1983-QX409-7	Skating Rabbit	CC - ORNAMENT	ORNAMENT		1983	$8.00	$43.00

Order No.	Title	Type	Theme	Retired	Intro. Year	Retail Price	Secondary Price
1983-QX420-7	Skiing Fox	CC - ORNAMENT	ORNAMENT		1983	$8.00	$37.00
1983-QX419-7	Mouse In Bell	CC - ORNAMENT	ORNAMENT		1983	$10.00	$57.00
1983-QX415-7	Mailbox Kitten	CC - ORNAMENT	ORNAMENT		1983	$6.50	$48.00
1983-QX414-9	Tin Rocking Horse	CC - ORNAMENT	ORNAMENT		1983	$6.50	$48.00
1983-QX420-9	Bell Wreath	CC - ORNAMENT	ORNAMENT		1983	$6.50	$26.00
1983-QX408-7	Angel Messenger	CC - ORNAMENT	ORNAMENT		1983	$6.50	$93.00
1983-QX412-7	Holiday Puppy	CC - ORNAMENT	ORNAMENT		1983	$3.50	$24.00
1983-QX416-7	Rainbow Angel	CC - ORNAMENT	ORNAMENT		1983	$5.50	$107.00
1983-QX400-9	Sneaker Mouse	CC - ORNAMENT	ORNAMENT		1983	$4.50	$29.50
1983-QX419-9	Christmas Koala	CC - ORNAMENT	ORNAMENT		1983	$4.00	$29.00
1983-QX411-7	Caroling Owl	CC - ORNAMENT	ORNAMENT		1983	$4.50	$35.50
1983-QX454-3	Christmas Kitten	CC - ORNAMENT	ORNAMENT		1983	$4.00	$29.00
1983-QX403-9	The Bellringer - 5th	CC - ORNAMENT	ORNAMENT		1983	$15.00	$125.00
1983-QX309-9	Holiday Wildlife - 2nd	CC - ORNAMENT	ORNAMENT		1983	$7.00	$68.00
1983-QX403-7	Here Comes Santa - 5th	CC - ORNAMENT	ORNAMENT		1983	$13.00	$270.00
1983-QX416-9	Snoopy And Friends - 5th/Final	CC - ORNAMENT	ORNAMENT		1983	$13.00	$81.50
1983-QX401-9	Carrousel - 6th and Final	CC - ORNAMENT	ORNAMENT		1983	$11.00	$48.00
1983-QX428-9	Porcelain Bear - 1st	CC - ORNAMENT	ORNAMENT		1983	$7.00	$69.00
1983-QX402-9	Clothespin Soldier - 2nd	CC - ORNAMENT	ORNAMENT		1983	$5.00	$47.00
1983-QX417-7	Rocking Horse - 3rd	CC - ORNAMENT	ORNAMENT		1983	$10.00	$273.00
1983-QX400-7	Frosty Friends - 4th	CC - ORNAMENT	ORNAMENT		1983	$8.00	$265.00
1983-QX401-7	Elf/Thimble - 6th	CC - ORNAMENT	ORNAMENT		1983	$5.00	$34.00
1983-QX404-9	Tin Locomotive - 2nd	CC - ORNAMENT	ORNAMENT		1983	$13.00	$257.50
1984-QX904-1	Baby's First Christmas	CC - ORNAMENT	ORNAMENT		1984	$16.00	$40.00
1984-QX438-1	Baby's First Christmas	CC - ORNAMENT	ORNAMENT		1984	$14.00	$38.00
1984-QX300-1	Baby's First Christmas (Photo)	CC - ORNAMENT	ORNAMENT		1984	$7.00	$13.50
1984-QX340-1	Baby's First Christmas	CC - ORNAMENT	ORNAMENT		1984	$6.00	$33.00
1984-QX240-4	Baby's First Christmas - Boy	CC - ORNAMENT	ORNAMENT		1984	$4.50	$21.00
1984-QX240-1	Baby's First Christmas - Girl	CC - ORNAMENT	ORNAMENT		1984	$4.50	$20.00
1984-QX241-1	Baby's Second Christmas	CC - ORNAMENT	ORNAMENT		1984	$4.50	$22.00
1984-QX261-1	Child's Third Christmas	CC - ORNAMENT	ORNAMENT		1984	$4.50	$22.00
1984-QX460-1	Grandchild's First Christmas	CC - ORNAMENT	ORNAMENT		1984	$11.00	$19.00
1984-QX257-4	Grandchild's First Christmas	CC - ORNAMENT	ORNAMENT		1984	$4.50	$15.50
1984-QX242-1	Godchild	CC - ORNAMENT	ORNAMENT		1984	$4.50	$17.00
1984-QX242-4	Grandson	CC - ORNAMENT	ORNAMENT		1984	$4.50	$25.00
1984-QX243-1	Granddaughter	CC - ORNAMENT	ORNAMENT		1984	$4.50	$25.00
1984-QX256-1	Grandparents	CC - ORNAMENT	ORNAMENT		1984	$4.50	$11.00
1984-QX244-1	Grandmother	CC - ORNAMENT	ORNAMENT		1984	$4.50	$17.50
1984-QX257-1	Father	CC - ORNAMENT	ORNAMENT		1984	$6.00	$11.00
1984-QX343-4	Mother	CC - ORNAMENT	ORNAMENT		1984	$6.00	$13.50
1984-QX258-1	Mother And Dad	CC - ORNAMENT	ORNAMENT		1984	$6.50	$15.00
1984-QX259-4	Sister	CC - ORNAMENT	ORNAMENT		1984	$6.50	$23.00
1984-QX244-4	Daughter	CC - ORNAMENT	ORNAMENT		1984	$4.50	$29.00
1984-QX243-4	Son	CC - ORNAMENT	ORNAMENT		1984	$4.00	$25.00
1984-QX342-4	The Miracle of Love	CC - ORNAMENT	ORNAMENT		1984	$6.00	$28.00
1984-QX342-1	First Christmas Together	CC - ORNAMENT	ORNAMENT		1984	$6.00	$29.00
1984-QX904-4	First Christmas Together	CC - ORNAMENT	ORNAMENT		1984	$16.00	$35.50
1984-QX436-4	First Christmas Together	CC - ORNAMENT	ORNAMENT		1984	$15.00	$26.00
1984-QX340-4	First Christmas Together	CC - ORNAMENT	ORNAMENT		1984	$7.50	$16.00
1984-QX245-1	First Christmas Together	CC - ORNAMENT	ORNAMENT		1984	$4.50	$22.00
1984-QX443-4	Heartful of Love	CC - ORNAMENT	ORNAMENT		1984	$10.00	$43.00
1984-QX247-4	Love...the Spirit of Christmas	CC - ORNAMENT	ORNAMENT		1984	$4.50	$39.00
1984-QX255-4	Love	CC - ORNAMENT	ORNAMENT		1984	$4.50	$20.00
1984-QX258-4	Ten Years Together	CC - ORNAMENT	ORNAMENT		1984	$6.50	$28.00
1984-QX259-1	Twenty-Five Years Together	CC - ORNAMENT	ORNAMENT		1984	$6.50	$29.00
1984-QX344-4	Gratitude	CC - ORNAMENT	ORNAMENT		1984	$6.00	$11.50
1984-QX343-1	The Fun of Friendship	CC - ORNAMENT	ORNAMENT		1984	$6.00	$29.50
1984-QX248-1	Friendship	CC - ORNAMENT	ORNAMENT		1984	$4.50	$15.50
1984-QX260-4	A Gift of Friendship	CC - ORNAMENT	ORNAMENT		1984	$4.50	$17.50
1984-QX245-4	New Home	CC - ORNAMENT	ORNAMENT		1984	$4.50	$54.00
1984-QX248-4	From Our Home to Yours	CC - ORNAMENT	ORNAMENT		1984	$4.50	$29.50
1984-QX249-1	Teacher	CC - ORNAMENT	ORNAMENT		1984	$4.50	$10.00
1984-QX253-1	Baby-sitter	CC - ORNAMENT	ORNAMENT		1984	$4.50	$12.50
1984-QX462-4	Betsey Clark Angel	CC - ORNAMENT	ORNAMENT		1984	$9.00	$28.00
1984-QX463-1	Katybeth	CC - ORNAMENT	ORNAMENT		1984	$9.00	$26.00
1984-QX252-1	Peanuts	CC - ORNAMENT	ORNAMENT		1984	$4.50	$39.00
1984-QX250-4	Disney	CC - ORNAMENT	ORNAMENT		1984	$4.50	$33.00
1984-QX251-4	The Muppets	CC - ORNAMENT	ORNAMENT		1984	$4.50	$29.00
1984-QX251-1	Norman Rockwell	CC - ORNAMENT	ORNAMENT		1984	$4.50	$28.00
1984-QX250-1	Currier & Ives	CC - ORNAMENT	ORNAMENT		1984	$4.50	$18.00
1984-QX252-4	Shirt Tales	CC - ORNAMENT	ORNAMENT		1984	$4.50	$15.00
1984-QX439-1	Snoopy and Woodstock	CC - ORNAMENT	ORNAMENT		1984	$7.50	$93.00
1984-QX442-1	Muffin	CC - ORNAMENT	ORNAMENT		1984	$5.50	$24.00
1984-QX453-4	Kit	CC - ORNAMENT	ORNAMENT		1984	$5.50	$23.00
1984-QX905-1	White Christmas	CC - ORNAMENT	ORNAMENT		1984	$16.00	$80.00
1984-QX415-9	Twelve Days of Christmas	CC - ORNAMENT	ORNAMENT		1984	$15.00	$70.00
1984-QX451-1	Gift of Music	CC - ORNAMENT	ORNAMENT		1984	$15.00	$80.00
1984-QX432-1	Amanda	CC - ORNAMENT	ORNAMENT		1984	$9.00	$23.00
1984-QX437-4	Holiday Jester	CC - ORNAMENT	ORNAMENT		1984	$11.00	$29.00
1984-QX449-1	Uncle Sam	CC - ORNAMENT	ORNAMENT		1984	$6.00	$42.00
1984-QX451-4	Chickadee	CC - ORNAMENT	ORNAMENT		1984	$6.00	$42.00
1984-QX455-1	Cuckoo Clock	CC - ORNAMENT	ORNAMENT		1984	$10.00	$38.00
1984-QX452-1	Alpine Elf	CC - ORNAMENT	ORNAMENT		1984	$6.00	$25.00
1984-QX442-4	Nostalgic Sled	CC - ORNAMENT	ORNAMENT		1984	$6.00	$20.00
1984-QX436-1	Santa Sulky Driver	CC - ORNAMENT	ORNAMENT		1984	$9.00	$21.00
1984-QX346-4	Old Fashioned Rocking Horse	CC - ORNAMENT	ORNAMENT		1984	$7.50	$13.00
1984-QX344-1	Madonna and Child	CC - ORNAMENT	ORNAMENT		1984	$6.00	$33.00
1984-QX445-1	Holiday Friendship	CC - ORNAMENT	ORNAMENT		1984	$13.00	$26.00
1984-QX341-4	Peace on Earth	CC - ORNAMENT	ORNAMENT		1984	$7.50	$28.00
1984-QX254-1	A Savior is Born	CC - ORNAMENT	ORNAMENT		1984	$4.50	$24.50
1984-QX253-4	Holiday Starburst	CC - ORNAMENT	ORNAMENT		1984	$5.00	$17.00
1984-QX458-4	Santa	CC - ORNAMENT	ORNAMENT		1984	$7.50	$12.50
1984-QX459-4	Needlepoint Wreath	CC - ORNAMENT	ORNAMENT		1984	$6.50	$13.50

Order No.	Title	Type	Theme	Retired	Intro. Year	Retial Price	Secondary Price
1984-QX300-4	Christmas Memories Photoholder	CC - ORNAMENT	ORNAMENT		1984	$6.50	$16.50
1984-QX421-7	Embroidered Heart	CC - ORNAMENT	ORNAMENT		1984	$6.50	$24.50
1984-QX479-6	Embroidered Stocking	CC - ORNAMENT	ORNAMENT		1984	$6.50	$19.50
1984-QX443-1	Bell Ringer Squirrel	CC - ORNAMENT	ORNAMENT		1984	$10.00	$29.50
1984-QX447-4	Raccoon's Christmas	CC - ORNAMENT	ORNAMENT		1984	$9.00	$46.00
1984-QX431-1	Three Kittens in a Mitten	CC - ORNAMENT	ORNAMENT		1984	$8.00	$42.00
1984-QX456-4	Marathon Santa	CC - ORNAMENT	ORNAMENT		1984	$8.00	$35.00
1984-QX450-4	Santa Star	CC - ORNAMENT	ORNAMENT		1984	$5.50	$37.50
1984-QX431-4	Snowmobile Santa	CC - ORNAMENT	ORNAMENT		1984	$6.50	$32.00
1984-QX453-1	Snowshoe Penguin	CC - ORNAMENT	ORNAMENT		1984	$6.50	$42.50
1984-QX444-1	Christmas Owl	CC - ORNAMENT	ORNAMENT		1984	$6.00	$27.00
1984-QX434-4	Musical Angel	CC - ORNAMENT	ORNAMENT		1984	$5.50	$62.00
1984-QX435-1	Napping Mouse	CC - ORNAMENT	ORNAMENT		1984	$5.50	$47.50
1984-QX457-1	Roller Skating Rabbit	CC - ORNAMENT	ORNAMENT		1984	$5.00	$26.50
1984-QX444-4	Frisbee Puppy	CC - ORNAMENT	ORNAMENT		1984	$5.00	$46.00
1984-QX254-4	Reindeer Racetrack	CC - ORNAMENT	ORNAMENT		1984	$4.50	$18.50
1984-QX246-1	A Christmas Prayer	CC - ORNAMENT	ORNAMENT		1984	$4.50	$19.00
1984-QX256-4	Flights of Fantasy	CC - ORNAMENT	ORNAMENT		1984	$4.50	$18.00
1984-QX430-1	Polar Bear Drummer	CC - ORNAMENT	ORNAMENT		1984	$4.50	$35.00
1984-QX433-4	Santa Mouse	CC - ORNAMENT	ORNAMENT		1984	$4.50	$44.00
1984-QX450-1	Snowy Seal	CC - ORNAMENT	ORNAMENT		1984	$4.00	$19.00
1984-QX452-4	Fortune Cookie Elf	CC - ORNAMENT	ORNAMENT		1984	$4.50	$37.00
1984-QX456-1	Peppermint 1984	CC - ORNAMENT	ORNAMENT		1984	$4.50	$47.50
1984-QX407-7	Mountain Climbing Santa	CC - ORNAMENT	ORNAMENT		1984	$6.50	$33.00
1984-QX459-1	Classical Angel - LE	CC - ORNAMENT	ORNAMENT		1984	$27.50	$85.00
1984-QX448-1	Nost. Houses And Shops - 1st	CC - ORNAMENT	ORNAMENT		1984	$13.00	$182.00
1984-QX439-4	Wood Childhood Ornaments - 1st	CC - ORNAMENT	ORNAMENT		1984	$6.50	$35.00
1984-QX348-4	Twelve Days of Chrstmas - 1st	CC - ORNAMENT	ORNAMENT		1984	$6.00	$165.00
1984-QX349-4	Art Masterpiece - 1st	CC - ORNAMENT	ORNAMENT		1984	$6.50	$17.00
1984-QX454-1	Porcelain Bear - 2nd	CC - ORNAMENT	ORNAMENT		1984	$7.00	$32.00
1984-QX440-4	Tin Locomotive - 3rd	CC - ORNAMENT	ORNAMENT		1984	$14.00	$74.00
1984-QX447-1	Clothespin Soldier - 3rd	CC - ORNAMENT	ORNAMENT		1984	$5.00	$22.00
1984-QX347-4	Holiday Wildlife - 3rd	CC - ORNAMENT	ORNAMENT		1984	$7.25	$25.00
1984-QX435-4	Rocking Horse - 4th	CC - ORNAMENT	ORNAMENT		1984	$10.00	$63.50
1984-QX437-1	Frosty Friends - 5th	CC - ORNAMENT	ORNAMENT		1984	$8.00	$72.00
1984-QX341-1	Norman Rockwell - 5th	CC - ORNAMENT	ORNAMENT		1984	$7.50	$32.00
1984-QX432-4	Here Comes Santa - 6th	CC - ORNAMENT	ORNAMENT		1984	$13.00	$82.00
1984-QX438-4	The Bellringer - 6th and Final	CC - ORNAMENT	ORNAMENT		1984	$15.00	$36.00
1984-QX430-4	Thimble - 7th	CC - ORNAMENT	ORNAMENT		1984	$5.00	$49.00
1984-QX249-4	Betsey Clark - 12th	CC - ORNAMENT	ORNAMENT		1984	$5.00	$28.00
1985-QX499-5	Baby's First Christmas	CC - ORNAMENT	ORNAMENT		1985	$16.00	$32.00
1985-QX499-2	Baby's First Christmas	CC - ORNAMENT	ORNAMENT		1985	$15.00	$45.00
1985-QX401-2	Baby Locket	CC - ORNAMENT	ORNAMENT		1985	$16.00	$18.00
1985-QX370-2	Baby's First Christmas	CC - ORNAMENT	ORNAMENT		1985	$5.75	$14.00
1985-QX478-2	Baby's First Christmas	CC - ORNAMENT	ORNAMENT		1985	$7.00	$15.00
1985-QX260-2	Baby's First Christmas	CC - ORNAMENT	ORNAMENT		1985	$5.00	$18.00
1985-QX478-5	Baby's Second Christmas	CC - ORNAMENT	ORNAMENT		1985	$6.00	$28.00
1985-QX475-5	Child's Third Christmas	CC - ORNAMENT	ORNAMENT		1985	$6.00	$28.00
1985-QX260-5	Grandchild's First Christmas	CC - ORNAMENT	ORNAMENT		1985	$5.00	$17.00
1985-QX495-5	Grandchild's First Christmas	CC - ORNAMENT	ORNAMENT		1985	$11.00	$18.00
1985-QX380-5	Grandparents	CC - ORNAMENT	ORNAMENT		1985	$7.00	$7.00
1985-QX520-5	Niece	CC - ORNAMENT	ORNAMENT		1985	$5.75	$7.00
1985-QX372-2	Mother	CC - ORNAMENT	ORNAMENT		1985	$6.75	$9.00
1985-QX509-2	Mother And Dad	CC - ORNAMENT	ORNAMENT		1985	$7.75	$18.00
1985-QX376-2	Father	CC - ORNAMENT	ORNAMENT		1985	$6.50	$8.00
1985-QX506-5	Sister	CC - ORNAMENT	ORNAMENT		1985	$7.25	$18.00
1985-QX503-2	Daughter	CC - ORNAMENT	ORNAMENT		1985	$5.50	$12.00
1985-QX380-2	Godchild	CC - ORNAMENT	ORNAMENT		1985	$6.75	$9.50
1985-QX502-5	Son	CC - ORNAMENT	ORNAMENT		1985	$5.50	$27.00
1985-QX262-5	Grandmother	CC - ORNAMENT	ORNAMENT		1985	$4.75	$17.00
1985-QX262-2	Grandson	CC - ORNAMENT	ORNAMENT		1985	$4.75	$22.00
1985-QX263-5	Granddaughter	CC - ORNAMENT	ORNAMENT		1985	$4.75	$25.00
1985-QX400-5	First Christmas Together	CC - ORNAMENT	ORNAMENT		1985	$16.75	$22.00
1985-QX371-5	Love At Christmas	CC - ORNAMENT	ORNAMENT		1985	$5.75	$26.00
1985-QX370-5	First Christmas Together	CC - ORNAMENT	ORNAMENT		1985	$6.75	$22.00
1985-QX493-5	First Christmas Together	CC - ORNAMENT	ORNAMENT		1985	$13.00	$23.00
1985-QX498-2	Holiday Heart	CC - ORNAMENT	ORNAMENT		1985	$8.00	$18.00
1985-QX507-2	First Christmas Together	CC - ORNAMENT	ORNAMENT		1985	$8.00	$10.00
1985-QX378-2	Heart Full of Love	CC - ORNAMENT	ORNAMENT		1985	$6.75	$12.00
1985-QX261-2	First Christmas Together	CC - ORNAMENT	ORNAMENT		1985	$4.75	$22.00
1985-QX500-5	Twenty-Five Years Together	CC - ORNAMENT	ORNAMENT		1985	$8.00	$16.00
1985-QX506-2	Friendship	CC - ORNAMENT	ORNAMENT		1985	$7.75	$11.00
1985-QX378-5	Friendship	CC - ORNAMENT	ORNAMENT		1985	$6.75	$13.50
1985-QX520-2	From Our House to Yours	CC - ORNAMENT	ORNAMENT		1985	$7.75	$10.00
1985-QX505-2	Teacher	CC - ORNAMENT	ORNAMENT		1985	$6.00	$14.00
1985-QX375-2	With Appreciation	CC - ORNAMENT	ORNAMENT		1985	$6.75	$9.50
1985-QX372-5	Special Friends	CC - ORNAMENT	ORNAMENT		1985	$5.75	$9.50
1985-QX269-5	New Home	CC - ORNAMENT	ORNAMENT		1985	$4.75	$24.00
1985-QX264-2	Baby-sitter	CC - ORNAMENT	ORNAMENT		1985	$4.75	$11.00
1985-QX265-2	Good Friends	CC - ORNAMENT	ORNAMENT		1985	$4.75	$22.00
1985-QX491-5	Snoopy and Woodstock (Hockey)	CC - ORNAMENT	ORNAMENT		1985	$7.50	$60.00
1985-QX483-5	Muffin the Angel	CC - ORNAMENT	ORNAMENT		1985	$5.75	$23.00
1985-QX484-5	Kit the Shepherd	CC - ORNAMENT	ORNAMENT		1985	$5.75	$22.50
1985-QX508-5	Betsey Clark	CC - ORNAMENT	ORNAMENT		1985	$8.50	$26.00
1985-QX271-5	Hugga Bunch	CC - ORNAMENT	ORNAMENT		1985	$5.00	$27.00
1985-QX265-5	Fraggle Rock Holiday	CC - ORNAMENT	ORNAMENT		1985	$4.75	$28.00
1985-QX266-5	Peanuts	CC - ORNAMENT	ORNAMENT		1985	$4.75	$29.00
1985-QX266-2	Norman Rockwell	CC - ORNAMENT	ORNAMENT		1985	$4.75	$22.00
1985-QX268-2	Rainbow Brite and Friends	CC - ORNAMENT	ORNAMENT		1985	$4.75	$23.00
1985-QX271-2	A Disney Christmas	CC - ORNAMENT	ORNAMENT		1985	$4.75	$28.00
1985-QX267-2	Merry Shirt Tales	CC - ORNAMENT	ORNAMENT		1985	$4.75	$19.50
1985-QX479-5	Porcelain Bird	CC - ORNAMENT	ORNAMENT		1985	$6.50	$31.00
1985-QX379-5	Sewn Photoholder	CC - ORNAMENT	ORNAMENT		1985	$7.00	$25.00

Order No.	Title	Type	Theme	Retired	Intro. Year	Retail Price	Secondary Price
1985-QX374-2	Candle Cameo	CC - ORNAMENT	ORNAMENT		1985	$6.75	$12.50
1985-QX494-2	Santa Pipe	CC - ORNAMENT	ORNAMENT		1985	$9.50	$18.00
1985-QX373-5	Old-Fashioned Wreath	CC - ORNAMENT	ORNAMENT		1985	$7.50	$18.00
1985-QX373-2	Peaceful Kingdom	CC - ORNAMENT	ORNAMENT		1985	$5.75	$18.00
1985-QX507-5	Christmas Treats	CC - ORNAMENT	ORNAMENT		1985	$5.50	$15.00
1985-QX498-5	The Spirit of Santa Claus - SE	CC - ORNAMENT	ORNAMENT		1985	$22.50	$80.00
1985-QX442-4	Nostalgic Sled	CC - ORNAMENT	ORNAMENT		1985	$6.00	$33.00
1985-QX449-4	Night Before Christmas	CC - ORNAMENT	ORNAMENT		1985	$13.00	$32.00
1985-QX264-5	Nativity Scene	CC - ORNAMENT	ORNAMENT		1985	$4.75	$25.00
1985-QX496-2	Santa's Ski Trip	CC - ORNAMENT	ORNAMENT		1985	$12.00	$55.00
1985-QX476-2	Mouse Wagon	CC - ORNAMENT	ORNAMENT		1985	$5.75	$56.00
1985-QX490-5	Children in the Shoe	CC - ORNAMENT	ORNAMENT		1985	$9.50	$39.00
1985-QX481-2	Do Not Disturb Bear	CC - ORNAMENT	ORNAMENT		1985	$7.75	$23.50
1985-QX492-2	Sun and Fun Santa	CC - ORNAMENT	ORNAMENT		1985	$7.75	$33.00
1985-QX481-5	Bottlecap Fun Bunnies	CC - ORNAMENT	ORNAMENT		1985	$7.75	$29.00
1985-QX480-2	Lamb in Legwarmers	CC - ORNAMENT	ORNAMENT		1985	$7.00	$19.00
1985-QX470-5	Candy Apple Mouse	CC - ORNAMENT	ORNAMENT		1985	$6.50	$58.00
1985-QX473-2	Skateboard Raccoon	CC - ORNAMENT	ORNAMENT		1985	$6.50	$28.00
1985-QX475-2	Stardust Angel	CC - ORNAMENT	ORNAMENT		1985	$5.75	$290.00
1985-QX477-5	Soccer Beaver	CC - ORNAMENT	ORNAMENT		1985	$6.50	$21.00
1985-QX480-5	Beary Smooth Ride	CC - ORNAMENT	ORNAMENT		1985	$6.50	$28.00
1985-QX492-5	Swinging Angel Bell	CC - ORNAMENT	ORNAMENT		1985	$11.00	$32.00
1985-QX474-2	Doggy in a Stocking	CC - ORNAMENT	ORNAMENT		1985	$5.50	$26.00
1985-QX473-5	Engineering Mouse	CC - ORNAMENT	ORNAMENT		1985	$5.50	$19.50
1985-QX474-5	Kitty Mischief	CC - ORNAMENT	ORNAMENT		1985	$5.00	$25.00
1985-QX491-2	Baker Elf	CC - ORNAMENT	ORNAMENT		1985	$5.75	$28.00
1985-QX476-5	Ice-Skating Owl	CC - ORNAMENT	ORNAMENT		1985	$5.00	$18.50
1985-QX477-2	Dapper Penguin	CC - ORNAMENT	ORNAMENT		1985	$5.00	$26.00
1985-QX471-2	Trumpet Panda	CC - ORNAMENT	ORNAMENT		1985	$4.50	$17.00
1985-QX403-2	Merry Mouse	CC - ORNAMENT	ORNAMENT		1985	$4.50	$22.00
1985-QX470-2	Snow-Pitching Snowman	CC - ORNAMENT	ORNAMENT		1985	$4.50	$21.00
1985-QX431-1	Three Kittens in a Mitten	CC - ORNAMENT	ORNAMENT		1985	$8.00	$42.50
1985-QX457-1	Roller Skating Rabbit	CC - ORNAMENT	ORNAMENT		1985	$5.00	$29.50
1985-QX450-1	Snowy Seal	CC - ORNAMENT	ORNAMENT		1985	$4.00	$22.00
1985-QX519-5	Old-Fashioned Doll	CC - ORNAMENT	ORNAMENT		1985	$14.50	$32.50
1985-QX518-5	Country Goose	CC - ORNAMENT	ORNAMENT		1985	$7.75	$11.00
1985-QX518-2	Rocking Horse Memories	CC - ORNAMENT	ORNAMENT		1985	$10.00	$11.00
1985-QX519-2	Whirligig Santa	CC - ORNAMENT	ORNAMENT		1985	$12.50	$21.00
1985-QX517-5	Sheep at Christmas	CC - ORNAMENT	ORNAMENT		1985	$8.25	$20.00
1985-QX514-5	Keepsake Basket	CC - ORNAMENT	ORNAMENT		1985	$15.00	$18.00
1985-QX513-2	Victorian Lady	CC - ORNAMENT	ORNAMENT		1985	$9.50	$19.00
1985-QX512-5	Charming Angel	CC - ORNAMENT	ORNAMENT		1985	$9.75	$22.00
1985-QX511-2	Lacy Heart	CC - ORNAMENT	ORNAMENT		1985	$8.75	$22.00
1985-QX510-5	Snowflake	CC - ORNAMENT	ORNAMENT		1985	$6.50	$18.00
1985-QX405-2	Heavenly Trumpeter - LE	CC - ORNAMENT	ORNAMENT		1985	$27.50	$73.00
1985-QX490-2	Windows of the World - 1st	CC - ORNAMENT	ORNAMENT		1985	$9.75	$79.00
1985-QX482-5	Miniature Creche - 1st	CC - ORNAMENT	ORNAMENT		1985	$8.75	$25.50
1985-QX497-5	Nost. Houses And Shops - 2nd	CC - ORNAMENT	ORNAMENT		1985	$13.75	$99.00
1985-QX377-2	Art Masterpiece - 2nd	CC - ORNAMENT	ORNAMENT		1985	$6.75	$15.00
1985-QX472-2	Wood Childhood Ornaments - 2nd	CC - ORNAMENT	ORNAMENT		1985	$7.00	$42.00
1985-QX371-2	Twelve Days of Chrstmas - 2nd	CC - ORNAMENT	ORNAMENT		1985	$6.50	$62.00
1985-QX479-2	Porcelain Bear - 3rd	CC - ORNAMENT	ORNAMENT		1985	$7.50	$68.00
1985-QX497-2	Tin Locomotive - 4th	CC - ORNAMENT	ORNAMENT		1985	$14.75	$76.00
1985-QX376-5	Holiday Wildlife - 4th	CC - ORNAMENT	ORNAMENT		1985	$7.50	$22.50
1985-QX471-5	Clothespin Soldier - 4th	CC - ORNAMENT	ORNAMENT		1985	$5.50	$50.00
1985-QX493-2	Rocking Horse - 5th	CC - ORNAMENT	ORNAMENT		1985	$10.75	$44.00
1985-QX374-5	Norman Rockwell - 6th	CC - ORNAMENT	ORNAMENT		1985	$7.50	$40.00
1985-QX496-5	Here Comes Santa - 7th	CC - ORNAMENT	ORNAMENT		1985	$14.00	$57.00
1985-QX482-2	Frosty Friends - 6th	CC - ORNAMENT	ORNAMENT		1985	$8.50	$45.00
1985-QX263-2	Betsey Clark - 13th and Final	CC - ORNAMENT	ORNAMENT		1985	$5.00	$20.00
1985-QX472-5	Thimble - 8th	CC - ORNAMENT	ORNAMENT		1985	$5.50	$32.00
1986-QX412-6	Baby's First Christmas	CC - ORNAMENT	ORNAMENT		1986	$9.00	$33.00
1986-QX379-2	Baby's First Christmas - Photo	CC - ORNAMENT	ORNAMENT		1986	$8.00	$17.00
1986-QX380-3	Baby's First Christmas	CC - ORNAMENT	ORNAMENT		1986	$6.00	$22.00
1986-QX271-3	Baby's First Christmas	CC - ORNAMENT	ORNAMENT		1986	$5.50	$16.50
1986-QX411-6	Grandchild's First Christmas	CC - ORNAMENT	ORNAMENT		1986	$10.00	$20.00
1986-QX413-3	Baby's Second Christmas	CC - ORNAMENT	ORNAMENT		1986	$6.50	$25.00
1986-QX413-6	Child's Third Christmas	CC - ORNAMENT	ORNAMENT		1986	$6.50	$19.00
1986-QX412-3	Baby Locket	CC - ORNAMENT	ORNAMENT		1986	$16.00	$16.00
1986-QX383-6	Husband	CC - ORNAMENT	ORNAMENT		1986	$8.00	$12.00
1986-QX380-6	Sister	CC - ORNAMENT	ORNAMENT		1986	$6.75	$14.00
1986-QX431-6	Mother And Dad	CC - ORNAMENT	ORNAMENT		1986	$7.50	$15.00
1986-QX382-6	Mother	CC - ORNAMENT	ORNAMENT		1986	$7.00	$17.00
1986-QX431-3	Father	CC - ORNAMENT	ORNAMENT		1986	$6.50	$13.00
1986-QX430-6	Daughter	CC - ORNAMENT	ORNAMENT		1986	$5.75	$35.00
1986-QX430-3	Son	CC - ORNAMENT	ORNAMENT		1986	$5.75	$32.00
1986-QX426-6	Niece	CC - ORNAMENT	ORNAMENT		1986	$6.00	$9.00
1986-QX381-3	Nephew	CC - ORNAMENT	ORNAMENT		1986	$6.25	$10.00
1986-QX274-3	Grandmother	CC - ORNAMENT	ORNAMENT		1986	$4.75	$12.00
1986-QX432-3	Grandparents	CC - ORNAMENT	ORNAMENT		1986	$7.50	$15.00
1986-QX273-6	Granddaughter	CC - ORNAMENT	ORNAMENT		1986	$4.75	$17.50
1986-QX273-3	Grandson	CC - ORNAMENT	ORNAMENT		1986	$4.75	$21.50
1986-QX271-6	Godchild	CC - ORNAMENT	ORNAMENT		1986	$4.75	$12.00
1986-QX400-3	First Christmas Together	CC - ORNAMENT	ORNAMENT		1986	$16.00	$16.00
1986-QX409-6	First Christmas Together	CC - ORNAMENT	ORNAMENT		1986	$12.00	$27.00
1986-QX379-3	First Christmas Together	CC - ORNAMENT	ORNAMENT		1986	$7.00	$19.00
1986-QX270-3	First Christmas Together	CC - ORNAMENT	ORNAMENT		1986	$4.75	$16.00
1986-QX401-3	Ten Years Together	CC - ORNAMENT	ORNAMENT		1986	$7.50	$16.00
1986-QX410-3	Twenty-Five Years Together	CC - ORNAMENT	ORNAMENT		1986	$8.00	$18.00
1986-QX400-6	Fifty Years Together	CC - ORNAMENT	ORNAMENT		1986	$10.00	$15.00
1986-QX409-3	Loving Memories	CC - ORNAMENT	ORNAMENT		1986	$9.00	$24.50
1986-QX379-6	Timeless Love	CC - ORNAMENT	ORNAMENT		1986	$6.00	$15.00
1986-QX408-6	Sweetheart	CC - ORNAMENT	ORNAMENT		1986	$11.00	$43.00

Order No.	Title	Type	Theme	Retired	Intro. Year	Retial Price	Secondary Price
1986-QX270-6	Season of the Heart	CC - ORNAMENT	ORNAMENT		1986	$4.75	$15.00
1986-QX427-3	Friendship Greeting	CC - ORNAMENT	ORNAMENT		1986	$8.00	$13.00
1986-QX382-3	Joy of Friends	CC - ORNAMENT	ORNAMENT		1986	$6.75	$12.00
1986-QX381-6	Friendship's Gift	CC - ORNAMENT	ORNAMENT		1986	$6.00	$11.00
1986-QX383-3	From Our Home to Yours	CC - ORNAMENT	ORNAMENT		1986	$6.00	$13.00
1986-QX432-6	Gratitude	CC - ORNAMENT	ORNAMENT		1986	$6.00	$6.50
1986-QX272-3	Friends Are Fun	CC - ORNAMENT	ORNAMENT		1986	$4.75	$31.00
1986-QX274-6	New Home	CC - ORNAMENT	ORNAMENT		1986	$4.75	$25.00
1986-QX275-3	Teacher	CC - ORNAMENT	ORNAMENT		1986	$4.75	$8.50
1986-QX275-6	Baby-Sitter	CC - ORNAMENT	ORNAMENT		1986	$4.75	$10.00
1986-QX384-3	The Statue of Liberty	CC - ORNAMENT	ORNAMENT		1986	$6.00	$22.00
1986-QX434-6	Snoopy and Woodstock (Sled)	CC - ORNAMENT	ORNAMENT		1986	$8.00	$38.00
1986-QX436-3	Heathcliff	CC - ORNAMENT	ORNAMENT		1986	$7.50	$22.00
1986-QX435-3	Katybeth	CC - ORNAMENT	ORNAMENT		1986	$7.00	$17.00
1986-QX435-6	Paddington Bear	CC - ORNAMENT	ORNAMENT		1986	$6.00	$35.00
1986-QX276-3	Norman Rockwell	CC - ORNAMENT	ORNAMENT		1986	$4.75	$26.00
1986-QX276-6	Peanuts	CC - ORNAMENT	ORNAMENT		1986	$4.75	$28.00
1986-QX277-3	Shirt Tales Parade	CC - ORNAMENT	ORNAMENT		1986	$4.75	$16.00
1986-QX426-3	Santa's Hot Tub	CC - ORNAMENT	ORNAMENT		1986	$12.00	$49.00
1986-QX425-3	Playful Possum	CC - ORNAMENT	ORNAMENT		1986	$11.00	$24.00
1986-QX425-6	Treetop Trio	CC - ORNAMENT	ORNAMENT		1986	$11.00	$27.50
1986-QX424-6	Wynken, Blynken and Nod	CC - ORNAMENT	ORNAMENT		1986	$9.75	$37.00
1986-QX424-3	Acorn Inn	CC - ORNAMENT	ORNAMENT		1986	$8.50	$28.00
1986-QX423-3	Touchdown Santa	CC - ORNAMENT	ORNAMENT		1986	$8.00	$31.50
1986-QX423-6	Snowbuddies	CC - ORNAMENT	ORNAMENT		1986	$8.00	$31.00
1986-QX422-6	Open Me First	CC - ORNAMENT	ORNAMENT		1986	$7.25	$28.00
1986-QX421-6	Rah Rah Rabbit	CC - ORNAMENT	ORNAMENT		1986	$7.00	$27.50
1986-QX418-6	Tipping the Scales	CC - ORNAMENT	ORNAMENT		1986	$6.75	$19.00
1986-QX419-3	Li'l Jingler	CC - ORNAMENT	ORNAMENT		1986	$6.75	$32.00
1986-QX420-6	Ski Tripper	CC - ORNAMENT	ORNAMENT		1986	$6.75	$17.00
1986-QX421-3	Popcorn Mouse	CC - ORNAMENT	ORNAMENT		1986	$6.75	$35.00
1986-QX420-3	Puppy's Best Friend	CC - ORNAMENT	ORNAMENT		1986	$6.50	$21.00
1986-QX418-3	Happy Christmas to Owl	CC - ORNAMENT	ORNAMENT		1986	$6.00	$15.50
1986-QX419-6	Walnut Shell Rider	CC - ORNAMENT	ORNAMENT		1986	$6.00	$17.50
1986-QX417-3	Heavenly Dreamer	CC - ORNAMENT	ORNAMENT		1986	$5.75	$29.00
1986-QX416-6	Mouse In The Moon	CC - ORNAMENT	ORNAMENT		1986	$5.50	$20.00
1986-QX415-3	Merry Koala	CC - ORNAMENT	ORNAMENT		1986	$5.00	$19.00
1986-QX417-6	Chatty Penguin	CC - ORNAMENT	ORNAMENT		1986	$5.75	$18.50
1986-QX415-6	Special Delivery	CC - ORNAMENT	ORNAMENT		1986	$5.00	$19.50
1986-QX483-2	Jolly Hiker	CC - ORNAMENT	ORNAMENT		1986	$5.00	$18.00
1986-QX414-6	Cookies for Santa	CC - ORNAMENT	ORNAMENT		1986	$4.50	$24.00
1986-QX403-2	Merry Mouse	CC - ORNAMENT	ORNAMENT		1986	$4.50	$24.00
1986-QX473-2	Skateboard Raccoon	CC - ORNAMENT	ORNAMENT		1986	$6.50	$25.00
1986-QX480-5	Beary Smooth Ride	CC - ORNAMENT	ORNAMENT		1986	$6.50	$22.00
1986-QX470-2	Snow-Pitching Snowman	CC - ORNAMENT	ORNAMENT		1986	$4.50	$21.00
1986-QX474-5	Kitty Mischief	CC - ORNAMENT	ORNAMENT		1986	$5.00	$24.50
1986-QX477-5	Soccer Beaver	CC - ORNAMENT	ORNAMENT		1986	$6.50	$22.00
1986-QX481-2	Do Not Disturb Bear	CC - ORNAMENT	ORNAMENT		1986	$7.75	$23.00
1986-QX429-6	Jolly St. Nick - S.E.	CC - ORNAMENT	ORNAMENT		1986	$22.50	$59.00
1986-QX429-3	Magical Unicorn - L.E.	CC - ORNAMENT	ORNAMENT		1986	$27.50	$90.00
1986-QX513-6	Joyful Carolers	CC - ORNAMENT	ORNAMENT		1986	$9.75	$28.00
1986-QX513-3	Festive Treble Clef	CC - ORNAMENT	ORNAMENT		1986	$8.75	$18.00
1986-QX514-3	Favorite Tin Drum	CC - ORNAMENT	ORNAMENT		1986	$8.50	$24.00
1986-QX512-6	Christmas Guitar	CC - ORNAMENT	ORNAMENT		1986	$7.00	$19.00
1986-QX514-6	Holiday Horn	CC - ORNAMENT	ORNAMENT		1986	$8.00	$28.00
1986-QX511-3	Country Sleigh	CC - ORNAMENT	ORNAMENT		1986	$10.00	$21.00
1986-QX510-6	Remembering Christmas	CC - ORNAMENT	ORNAMENT		1986	$8.75	$26.00
1986-QX511-6	Little Drummers	CC - ORNAMENT	ORNAMENT		1986	$12.50	$24.00
1986-QX512-3	Nutcracker Santa	CC - ORNAMENT	ORNAMENT		1986	$10.00	$48.00
1986-QX510-3	Welcome, Christmas	CC - ORNAMENT	ORNAMENT		1986	$8.25	$24.00
1986-QX404-6	Holiday Jingle Bell	CC - ORNAMENT	ORNAMENT		1986	$16.00	$42.00
1986-QX427-6	Memories to Cherish	CC - ORNAMENT	ORNAMENT		1986	$7.50	$26.00
1986-QX428-3	Bluebird	CC - ORNAMENT	ORNAMENT		1986	$7.25	$43.00
1986-QX428-6	Glowing Christmas Tree	CC - ORNAMENT	ORNAMENT		1986	$7.00	$12.50
1986-QX515-3	Heirloom Snowflake	CC - ORNAMENT	ORNAMENT		1986	$6.75	$13.50
1986-QX322-3	Christmas Beauty	CC - ORNAMENT	ORNAMENT		1986	$6.00	$8.00
1986-QX322-6	Star Brighteners	CC - ORNAMENT	ORNAMENT		1986	$6.00	$12.00
1986-QX272-6	The Magi	CC - ORNAMENT	ORNAMENT		1986	$4.75	$16.00
1986-QX275-2	Mary Emmerling: Amer. Country	CC - ORNAMENT	ORNAMENT		1986	$7.95	$19.00
1986-QX402-6	Mr. And Mrs. Claus - 1st	CC - ORNAMENT	ORNAMENT		1986	$13.00	$101.00
1986-QX422-3	Reindeer Champs - 1st	CC - ORNAMENT	ORNAMENT		1986	$7.50	$122.50
1986-QX277-6	Betsey Clark - 1st	CC - ORNAMENT	ORNAMENT		1986	$5.00	$28.00
1986-QX408-3	Windows of the World - 2nd	CC - ORNAMENT	ORNAMENT		1986	$10.00	$45.00
1986-QX407-6	Miniature Creche - 2nd	CC - ORNAMENT	ORNAMENT		1986	$9.00	$55.00
1986-QX403-3	Nost. Houses And Shops - 3rd	CC - ORNAMENT	ORNAMENT		1986	$13.75	$258.00
1986-QX407-3	Wood Childhood Ornaments - 3rd	CC - ORNAMENT	ORNAMENT		1986	$7.50	$23.00
1986-QX378-6	Twelve Days of Chrstmas - 3rd	CC - ORNAMENT	ORNAMENT		1986	$6.50	$38.00
1986-QX350-6	Art Masterpiece - 3rd/Final	CC - ORNAMENT	ORNAMENT		1986	$6.75	$20.00
1986-QX405-6	Porcelain Bear - 4th	CC - ORNAMENT	ORNAMENT		1986	$7.75	$31.00
1986-QX403-6	Tin Locomotive - 5th	CC - ORNAMENT	ORNAMENT		1986	$14.75	$63.50
1986-QX321-6	Holiday Wildlife - 5th	CC - ORNAMENT	ORNAMENT		1986	$7.50	$23.00
1986-QX406-3	Clothespin Soldier - 5th	CC - ORNAMENT	ORNAMENT		1986	$5.50	$22.00
1986-QX401-6	Rocking Horse - 6th	CC - ORNAMENT	ORNAMENT		1986	$10.75	$56.00
1986-QX321-3	Norman Rockwell - 7th	CC - ORNAMENT	ORNAMENT		1986	$7.75	$17.00
1986-QX405-3	Frosty Friends - 7th	CC - ORNAMENT	ORNAMENT		1986	$8.50	$55.00
1986-QX404-3	Here Comes Santa - 8th	CC - ORNAMENT	ORNAMENT		1986	$14.00	$50.00
1986-QX406-6	Thimble - 9th	CC - ORNAMENT	ORNAMENT		1986	$5.75	$20.00
1987-QX411-3	Baby's First Christmas	CC - ORNAMENT	ORNAMENT		1987	$9.75	$22.00
1987-QX461-9	Baby's First Christmas Photo	CC - ORNAMENT	ORNAMENT		1987	$7.50	$27.00
1987-QX372-9	Baby's First Christmas	CC - ORNAMENT	ORNAMENT		1987	$6.00	$14.00
1987-QX274-7	Baby's First Christmas - Girl	CC - ORNAMENT	ORNAMENT		1987	$4.75	$13.00
1987-QX274-9	Baby's First Christmas - Boy	CC - ORNAMENT	ORNAMENT		1987	$4.75	$32.00
1987-QX460-9	Grandchild's First Christmas	CC - ORNAMENT	ORNAMENT		1987	$9.00	$17.00

Order No.	Title	Type	Theme	Retired	Intro. Year	Retail Price	Secondary Price
1987-QX460-7	Baby's Second Christmas	CC - ORNAMENT	ORNAMENT		1987	$5.75	$28.00
1987-QX459-9	Child's Third Christmas	CC - ORNAMENT	ORNAMENT		1987	$5.75	$20.50
1987-QX461-7	Baby Locket	CC - ORNAMENT	ORNAMENT		1987	$15.00	$23.00
1987-QX462-7	Mother And Dad	CC - ORNAMENT	ORNAMENT		1987	$7.00	$18.00
1987-QX373-7	Mother	CC - ORNAMENT	ORNAMENT		1987	$6.50	$7.00
1987-QX462-9	Dad	CC - ORNAMENT	ORNAMENT		1987	$6.00	$34.50
1987-QX373-9	Husband	CC - ORNAMENT	ORNAMENT		1987	$7.00	$9.00
1987-QX474-7	Sister	CC - ORNAMENT	ORNAMENT		1987	$6.00	$11.00
1987-QX463-7	Daughter	CC - ORNAMENT	ORNAMENT		1987	$5.75	$19.00
1987-QX463-9	Son	CC - ORNAMENT	ORNAMENT		1987	$5.75	$31.00
1987-QX275-9	Niece	CC - ORNAMENT	ORNAMENT		1987	$4.75	$9.00
1987-QX277-9	Grandmother	CC - ORNAMENT	ORNAMENT		1987	$4.75	$10.00
1987-QX277-7	Grandparents	CC - ORNAMENT	ORNAMENT		1987	$4.75	$17.00
1987-QX276-9	Grandson	CC - ORNAMENT	ORNAMENT		1987	$4.75	$20.00
1987-QX374-7	Granddaughter	CC - ORNAMENT	ORNAMENT		1987	$6.00	$15.50
1987-QX276-7	Godchild	CC - ORNAMENT	ORNAMENT		1987	$4.75	$12.00
1987-QX446-9	First Christmas Together	CC - ORNAMENT	ORNAMENT		1987	$15.00	$25.00
1987-QX446-7	First Christmas Together	CC - ORNAMENT	ORNAMENT		1987	$9.50	$21.50
1987-QX445-9	First Christmas Together	CC - ORNAMENT	ORNAMENT		1987	$8.00	$27.00
1987-QX371-9	First Christmas Together	CC - ORNAMENT	ORNAMENT		1987	$6.50	$15.00
1987-QX272-9	First Christmas Together	CC - ORNAMENT	ORNAMENT		1987	$4.75	$10.00
1987-QX444-7	Ten Years Together	CC - ORNAMENT	ORNAMENT		1987	$7.00	$23.00
1987-QX443-9	Twenty-Five Years Together	CC - ORNAMENT	ORNAMENT		1987	$7.50	$23.00
1987-QX443-7	Fifty Years Together	CC - ORNAMENT	ORNAMENT		1987	$8.00	$19.00
1987-QX447-7	Word of Love	CC - ORNAMENT	ORNAMENT		1987	$8.00	$16.50
1987-QX372-7	Heart in Blossom	CC - ORNAMENT	ORNAMENT		1987	$6.00	$18.50
1987-QX447-9	Sweetheart	CC - ORNAMENT	ORNAMENT		1987	$11.00	$24.00
1987-QX278-7	Love Is Everywhere	CC - ORNAMENT	ORNAMENT		1987	$4.75	$20.00
1987-QX375-7	Holiday Greetings	CC - ORNAMENT	ORNAMENT		1987	$6.00	$12.50
1987-QX375-9	Warmth of Friendship	CC - ORNAMENT	ORNAMENT		1987	$6.00	$10.50
1987-QX280-7	Time for Friends	CC - ORNAMENT	ORNAMENT		1987	$4.75	$17.00
1987-QX279-9	From Our Home to Yours	CC - ORNAMENT	ORNAMENT		1987	$4.75	$34.50
1987-QX376-7	New Home	CC - ORNAMENT	ORNAMENT		1987	$6.00	$24.00
1987-QX279-7	Babysitter	CC - ORNAMENT	ORNAMENT		1987	$4.75	$13.50
1987-QX466-7	Teacher	CC - ORNAMENT	ORNAMENT		1987	$5.75	$17.00
1987-QX472-9	Snoopy and Woodstock (Tree)	CC - ORNAMENT	ORNAMENT		1987	$7.25	$40.00
1987-QX473-7	Bright Christmas Dreams	CC - ORNAMENT	ORNAMENT		1987	$7.25	$85.00
1987-QX440-7	Joy Ride	CC - ORNAMENT	ORNAMENT		1987	$11.50	$67.00
1987-QX448-9	Pretty Kitty	CC - ORNAMENT	ORNAMENT		1987	$11.00	$20.00
1987-QX457-9	Santa at Bat	CC - ORNAMENT	ORNAMENT		1987	$7.75	$20.00
1987-QX457-7	Jogging Through The Snow	CC - ORNAMENT	ORNAMENT		1987	$7.25	$22.00
1987-QX449-9	Jack Frosting	CC - ORNAMENT	ORNAMENT		1987	$7.00	$48.00
1987-QX458-7	Raccoon Biker	CC - ORNAMENT	ORNAMENT		1987	$7.00	$19.50
1987-QX459-7	Treetop Dreams	CC - ORNAMENT	ORNAMENT		1987	$6.75	$22.50
1987-QX451-7	Night Before Christmas	CC - ORNAMENT	ORNAMENT		1987	$6.50	$25.00
1987-QX455-9	Owliday Wish	CC - ORNAMENT	ORNAMENT		1987	$6.50	$17.00
1987-QX458-9	Let It Snow	CC - ORNAMENT	ORNAMENT		1987	$6.50	$17.00
1987-QX471-9	Hot Dogger	CC - ORNAMENT	ORNAMENT		1987	$6.50	$16.00
1987-QX452-9	Spots 'n Stripes	CC - ORNAMENT	ORNAMENT		1987	$5.50	$18.00
1987-QX454-9	Seasoned Greetings	CC - ORNAMENT	ORNAMENT		1987	$6.25	$22.00
1987-QX456-7	Chocolate Chipmunk	CC - ORNAMENT	ORNAMENT		1987	$6.00	$43.00
1987-QX449-7	Fudge Forever	CC - ORNAMENT	ORNAMENT		1987	$5.00	$32.00
1987-QX450-7	Sleepy Santa	CC - ORNAMENT	ORNAMENT		1987	$6.25	$23.00
1987-QX452-7	Reindoggy	CC - ORNAMENT	ORNAMENT		1987	$5.75	$28.00
1987-QX453-7	Christmas Cuddle	CC - ORNAMENT	ORNAMENT		1987	$5.75	$44.00
1987-QX472-7	Paddington Bear	CC - ORNAMENT	ORNAMENT		1987	$5.50	$24.00
1987-QX273-9	Nature's Decorations	CC - ORNAMENT	ORNAMENT		1987	$4.75	$24.00
1987-QX278-3	Dr. Seuss: The Grinch's Xmas	CC - ORNAMENT	ORNAMENT		1987	$4.75	$42.00
1987-QX283-9	Jammie Pies	CC - ORNAMENT	ORNAMENT		1987	$4.75	$13.50
1987-QX281-9	Peanuts	CC - ORNAMENT	ORNAMENT		1987	$4.75	$26.50
1987-QX456-9	Happy Santa	CC - ORNAMENT	ORNAMENT		1987	$4.75	$25.50
1987-QX450-9	Icy Treat	CC - ORNAMENT	ORNAMENT		1987	$4.50	$20.00
1987-QX416-6	Mouse in the Moon	CC - ORNAMENT	ORNAMENT		1987	$5.50	$20.00
1987-QX419-3	Li'l Jingler	CC - ORNAMENT	ORNAMENT		1987	$6.75	$48.00
1987-QX419-6	Walnut Shell Rider	CC - ORNAMENT	ORNAMENT		1987	$6.00	$19.00
1987-QX425-6	Treetop Trio	CC - ORNAMENT	ORNAMENT		1987	$11.00	$27.00
1987-QX483-2	Jolly Hiker	CC - ORNAMENT	ORNAMENT		1987	$5.00	$20.00
1987-QX415-3	Merry Kaola	CC - ORNAMENT	ORNAMENT		1987	$5.00	$21.00
1987-QX377-7	The Constitution	CC - ORNAMENT	ORNAMENT		1987	$6.50	$15.50
1987-QX468-9	Nostalgic Rocker	CC - ORNAMENT	ORNAMENT		1987	$6.50	$22.00
1987-QX469-9	Little Whittler	CC - ORNAMENT	ORNAMENT		1987	$6.00	$26.00
1987-QX470-9	Country Wreath	CC - ORNAMENT	ORNAMENT		1987	$5.75	$18.00
1987-QX469-7	In a Nutshell	CC - ORNAMENT	ORNAMENT		1987	$5.50	$18.00
1987-QX474-9	Folk Art Santa	CC - ORNAMENT	ORNAMENT		1987	$5.25	$27.00
1987-QX467-7	Doc Holiday	CC - ORNAMENT	ORNAMENT		1987	$8.00	$28.00
1987-QX467-9	Christmas Fun Puzzle	CC - ORNAMENT	ORNAMENT		1987	$8.00	$17.00
1987-QX466-9	Jolly Follies	CC - ORNAMENT	ORNAMENT		1987	$8.50	$28.00
1987-QX453-9	St. Louie Nick	CC - ORNAMENT	ORNAMENT		1987	$7.75	$25.00
1987-QX470-7	Holiday Hourglass	CC - ORNAMENT	ORNAMENT		1987	$8.00	$20.00
1987-QX468-7	Mistletoad	CC - ORNAMENT	ORNAMENT		1987	$7.00	$21.00
1987-QX471-7	Happy Holidata	CC - ORNAMENT	ORNAMENT		1987	$6.50	$22.00
1987-QX464-9	Goldfinch	CC - ORNAMENT	ORNAMENT		1987	$7.00	$62.00
1987-QX465-9	Heavenly Harmony	CC - ORNAMENT	ORNAMENT		1987	$15.00	$28.00
1987-QX464-7	Special Memories Photoholder	CC - ORNAMENT	ORNAMENT		1987	$6.75	$19.00
1987-QX465-7	Joyous Angels	CC - ORNAMENT	ORNAMENT		1987	$7.75	$21.00
1987-QX374-9	Promise of Peace	CC - ORNAMENT	ORNAMENT		1987	$6.50	$19.00
1987-QX473-9	Christmas Keys	CC - ORNAMENT	ORNAMENT		1987	$5.75	$26.00
1987-QX278-9	I Remember Santa	CC - ORNAMENT	ORNAMENT		1987	$4.75	$25.00
1987-QX282-7	Norman Rockwell: Xmas Scenes	CC - ORNAMENT	ORNAMENT		1987	$4.75	$21.00
1987-QX282-9	Currier & Ives: Amer. Farm	CC - ORNAMENT	ORNAMENT		1987	$4.75	$20.00
1987-QX442-9	Christmas Time Mime - L.E.	CC - ORNAMENT	ORNAMENT		1987	$27.50	$46.00
1987-QX444-9	Christmas Is Gentle - L.E.	CC - ORNAMENT	ORNAMENT		1987	$17.50	$66.00
1987-QX445-7	Favorite Santa - S.E.	CC - ORNAMENT	ORNAMENT		1987	$22.50	$32.00

Order No.	Title	Type	Theme	Retired	Intro. Year	Retial Price	Secondary Price
1987-QX454-7	Three Men in a Tub	CC - ORNAMENT	ORNAMENT		1987	$8.00	$24.00
1987-QX451-9	Wee Chimney Sweep	CC - ORNAMENT	ORNAMENT		1987	$6.25	$23.00
1987-QX448-7	December Showers	CC - ORNAMENT	ORNAMENT		1987	$5.50	$23.00
1987-QX455-7	Beary Special	CC - ORNAMENT	ORNAMENT		1987	$4.75	$32.00
1987-QX485-7	Holiday Heirloom - 1st - L.E.	CC - ORNAMENT	ORNAMENT		1987	$25.00	$31.00
1987-QX481-7	Collector's Plate - 1st	CC - ORNAMENT	ORNAMENT		1987	$8.00	$62.00
1987-QX483-7	Mr. And Mrs. Claus - 2nd	CC - ORNAMENT	ORNAMENT		1987	$13.25	$45.00
1987-QX480-9	Reindeer Champs - 2nd	CC - ORNAMENT	ORNAMENT		1987	$7.50	$45.00
1987-QX272-7	Betsey Clark - 2nd	CC - ORNAMENT	ORNAMENT		1987	$5.00	$26.00
1987-QX482-7	Windows of the World - 3rd	CC - ORNAMENT	ORNAMENT		1987	$10.00	$18.50
1987-QX481-9	Miniature Creche - 3rd	CC - ORNAMENT	ORNAMENT		1987	$9.00	$22.00
1987-QX483-9	Nost. Houses And Shops - 4th	CC - ORNAMENT	ORNAMENT		1987	$14.00	$69.00
1987-QX370-9	Twelve Days of Chrstmas - 4th	CC - ORNAMENT	ORNAMENT		1987	$6.50	$26.50
1987-QX441-7	Wood Childhood Ornaments - 4th	CC - ORNAMENT	ORNAMENT		1987	$7.50	$19.00
1987-QX442-7	Porcelain Bear - 5th	CC - ORNAMENT	ORNAMENT		1987	$7.75	$20.00
1987-QX484-9	Tin Locomotive - 6th	CC - ORNAMENT	ORNAMENT		1987	$14.75	$58.00
1987-QX371-7	Holiday Wildlife - 6th	CC - ORNAMENT	ORNAMENT		1987	$7.50	$15.50
1987-QX480-7	Clothespin Soldier - 6th/Final	CC - ORNAMENT	ORNAMENT		1987	$5.50	$21.00
1987-QX440-9	Frosty Friends - 8th	CC - ORNAMENT	ORNAMENT		1987	$8.50	$49.00
1987-QX482-9	Rocking Horse - 7th	CC - ORNAMENT	ORNAMENT		1987	$10.75	$58.00
1987-QX370-7	Norman Rockwell - 8th	CC - ORNAMENT	ORNAMENT		1987	$7.75	$19.00
1987-QX484-7	Here Comes Santa - 9th	CC - ORNAMENT	ORNAMENT		1987	$14.00	$66.00
1987-QX441-9	Thimble - 10th	CC - ORNAMENT	ORNAMENT		1987	$5.75	$19.00
1988-QX470-1	Baby's First Christmas	CC - ORNAMENT	ORNAMENT		1988	$9.75	$25.00
1988-QX470-4	Baby's First Christmas Photo	CC - ORNAMENT	ORNAMENT		1988	$7.50	$22.00
1988-QX372-1	Baby's First Christmas	CC - ORNAMENT	ORNAMENT		1988	$6.00	$13.50
1988-QX272-1	Baby's First Christmas - Boy	CC - ORNAMENT	ORNAMENT		1988	$4.75	$12.00
1988-QX272-4	Baby's First Christmas - Girl	CC - ORNAMENT	ORNAMENT		1988	$4.75	$10.00
1988-QX471-1	Baby's Second Christmas	CC - ORNAMENT	ORNAMENT		1988	$6.00	$26.00
1988-QX471-4	Child's Third Christmas	CC - ORNAMENT	ORNAMENT		1988	$6.00	$13.50
1988-QX415-1	Daughter	CC - ORNAMENT	ORNAMENT		1988	$5.75	$45.00
1988-QX415-4	Son	CC - ORNAMENT	ORNAMENT		1988	$5.75	$29.50
1988-QX375-1	Mother	CC - ORNAMENT	ORNAMENT		1988	$6.50	$9.00
1988-QX414-1	Dad	CC - ORNAMENT	ORNAMENT		1988	$7.00	$19.00
1988-QX414-4	Mother And Dad	CC - ORNAMENT	ORNAMENT		1988	$8.00	$12.00
1988-QX499-4	Sister	CC - ORNAMENT	ORNAMENT		1988	$8.00	$16.00
1988-QX276-4	Grandmother	CC - ORNAMENT	ORNAMENT		1988	$4.75	$7.00
1988-QX277-1	Grandparents	CC - ORNAMENT	ORNAMENT		1988	$4.75	$7.00
1988-QX277-4	Granddaughter	CC - ORNAMENT	ORNAMENT		1988	$4.75	$12.00
1988-QX278-1	Grandson	CC - ORNAMENT	ORNAMENT		1988	$4.75	$15.00
1988-QX278-4	Godchild	CC - ORNAMENT	ORNAMENT		1988	$4.75	$10.00
1988-QX490-1	Sweetheart	CC - ORNAMENT	ORNAMENT		1988	$9.75	$12.50
1988-QX489-4	First Christmas Together	CC - ORNAMENT	ORNAMENT		1988	$9.00	$19.00
1988-QX373-1	First Christmas Together	CC - ORNAMENT	ORNAMENT		1988	$6.75	$13.00
1988-QX274-1	First Christmas Together	CC - ORNAMENT	ORNAMENT		1988	$4.75	$13.00
1988-QX274-4	Five Years Together	CC - ORNAMENT	ORNAMENT		1988	$4.75	$12.00
1988-QX275-1	Ten Years Together	CC - ORNAMENT	ORNAMENT		1988	$4.75	$14.00
1988-QX373-4	Twenty-Five Years Together	CC - ORNAMENT	ORNAMENT		1988	$6.75	$7.00
1988-QX374-1	Fifty Years Together	CC - ORNAMENT	ORNAMENT		1988	$6.75	$10.00
1988-QX374-4	Love Fills the Heart	CC - ORNAMENT	ORNAMENT		1988	$6.00	$15.00
1988-QX275-4	Love Grows	CC - ORNAMENT	ORNAMENT		1988	$4.75	$16.50
1988-QX276-1	Spirit of Christmas	CC - ORNAMENT	ORNAMENT		1988	$4.75	$20.00
1988-QX416-4	Year to Remember	CC - ORNAMENT	ORNAMENT		1988	$7.00	$14.00
1988-QX375-4	Gratitude	CC - ORNAMENT	ORNAMENT		1988	$6.00	$10.00
1988-QX376-1	New Home	CC - ORNAMENT	ORNAMENT		1988	$6.00	$14.00
1988-QX279-4	From Our Home To Yours	CC - ORNAMENT	ORNAMENT		1988	$4.75	$9.00
1988-QX279-1	Babysitter	CC - ORNAMENT	ORNAMENT		1988	$4.75	$6.00
1988-QX280-1	Peanuts	CC - ORNAMENT	ORNAMENT		1988	$4.75	$17.00
1988-QX417-1	Teacher	CC - ORNAMENT	ORNAMENT		1988	$6.25	$16.00
1988-QX477-4	Jingle Bell Clown	CC - ORNAMENT	ORNAMENT		1988	$15.00	$24.00
1988-QX477-1	Travels with Santa	CC - ORNAMENT	ORNAMENT		1988	$10.00	$28.00
1988-QX476-1	Party Line	CC - ORNAMENT	ORNAMENT		1988	$8.75	$19.00
1988-QX476-4	Goin' Cross Country	CC - ORNAMENT	ORNAMENT		1988	$8.50	$15.50
1988-QX478-1	Winter Fun	CC - ORNAMENT	ORNAMENT		1988	$8.50	$17.50
1988-QX417-4	Go For The Gold	CC - ORNAMENT	ORNAMENT		1988	$8.00	$16.00
1988-QX475-1	Soft Landing	CC - ORNAMENT	ORNAMENT		1988	$7.00	$15.00
1988-QX416-1	Feliz Navidad (Donkey)	CC - ORNAMENT	ORNAMENT		1988	$6.75	$22.00
1988-QX475-4	Squeaky Clean	CC - ORNAMENT	ORNAMENT		1988	$6.75	$14.00
1988-QX372-4	Christmas Memories Photoholder	CC - ORNAMENT	ORNAMENT		1988	$6.50	$21.00
1988-QX474-4	Purrfect Snuggle	CC - ORNAMENT	ORNAMENT		1988	$6.25	$18.00
1988-QX474-1	Snoopy and Woodstck (Stocking)	CC - ORNAMENT	ORNAMENT		1988	$6.00	$30.50
1988-QX473-4	The Town Crier	CC - ORNAMENT	ORNAMENT		1988	$5.50	$16.00
1988-QX273-1	Norman Rockwell: Xmas Scenes	CC - ORNAMENT	ORNAMENT		1988	$4.75	$15.50
1988-QX473-1	Jolly Walrus	CC - ORNAMENT	ORNAMENT		1988	$4.50	$18.00
1988-QX472-4	Slipper Spaniel	CC - ORNAMENT	ORNAMENT		1988	$4.25	$11.00
1988-QX472-1	Arctic Tenor	CC - ORNAMENT	ORNAMENT		1988	$4.00	$13.00
1988-QX453-9	St. Louie Nick	CC - ORNAMENT	ORNAMENT		1988	$7.75	
1988-QX468-7	Mistletoad	CC - ORNAMENT	ORNAMENT		1988	$7.00	$24.00
1988-QX459-7	Treetop Dreams	CC - ORNAMENT	ORNAMENT		1988	$6.75	$24.00
1988-QX451-7	Night Before Christmas	CC - ORNAMENT	ORNAMENT		1988	$6.50	
1988-QX455-9	Owliday Wish	CC - ORNAMENT	ORNAMENT		1988	$6.50	$19.00
1988-QX471-7	Happy Holidata	CC - ORNAMENT	ORNAMENT		1988	$6.50	
1988-QX452-7	Reindoggy	CC - ORNAMENT	ORNAMENT		1988	$5.75	
1988-QX469-7	In a Nutshell	CC - ORNAMENT	ORNAMENT		1988	$5.50	
1988-QX411-4	The Wonderful Santacycle - SE	CC - ORNAMENT	ORNAMENT		1988	$22.50	$34.00
1988-QX480-1	Christmas Cuckoo	CC - ORNAMENT	ORNAMENT		1988	$8.00	$18.00
1988-QX487-1	Peek-a-Boo Kitties	CC - ORNAMENT	ORNAMENT		1988	$7.50	$18.00
1988-QX487-4	Cool Juggler	CC - ORNAMENT	ORNAMENT		1988	$6.50	$16.00
1988-QX483-4	Santa Flamingo	CC - ORNAMENT	ORNAMENT		1988	$4.75	$19.50
1988-QX479-1	Par for Santa	CC - ORNAMENT	ORNAMENT		1988	$5.00	$14.00
1988-QX422-1	Hoe-Hoe-Hoe!	CC - ORNAMENT	ORNAMENT		1988	$5.00	$20.00
1988-QX422-4	Nick the Kick	CC - ORNAMENT	ORNAMENT		1988	$5.00	$12.50
1988-QX423-1	Holiday Hero	CC - ORNAMENT	ORNAMENT		1988	$5.00	$15.00

Order No.	Title	Type	Theme	Retired	Intro. Year	Retail Price	Secondary Price
1988-QX478-4	Polar Bowler	CC - ORNAMENT	ORNAMENT		1988	$5.00	$12.50
1988-QX479-4	Gone Fishing	CC - ORNAMENT	ORNAMENT		1988	$5.00	$14.00
1988-QX486-4	Love Santa	CC - ORNAMENT	ORNAMENT		1988	$5.00	$11.00
1988-QX486-1	Kiss the Klaus	CC - ORNAMENT	ORNAMENT		1988	$5.00	$16.00
1988-QX418-4	Sweet Star	CC - ORNAMENT	ORNAMENT		1988	$5.00	$21.00
1988-QX419-1	Filled with Fudge	CC - ORNAMENT	ORNAMENT		1988	$4.75	$25.00
1988-QX418-1	Teeny Taster	CC - ORNAMENT	ORNAMENT		1988	$4.75	$18.00
1988-QX482-1	A Kiss From Santa	CC - ORNAMENT	ORNAMENT		1988	$4.50	$24.00
1988-QX481-4	Oreo Chocolate Sndwich Cookies	CC - ORNAMENT	ORNAMENT		1988	$4.00	$12.50
1988-QX488-4	Uncle Sam Nutcracker	CC - ORNAMENT	ORNAMENT		1988	$7.00	$26.00
1988-QX497-1	Old-Fashioned Schoolhouse	CC - ORNAMENT	ORNAMENT		1988	$4.00	$17.00
1988-QX498-1	Old-Fashioned Church	CC - ORNAMENT	ORNAMENT		1988	$4.00	$15.50
1988-QX490-4	Noah's Ark	CC - ORNAMENT	ORNAMENT		1988	$8.50	$28.50
1988-QX491-1	Sailing! Sailing!	CC - ORNAMENT	ORNAMENT		1988	$8.50	$23.00
1988-QX488-1	Americana Drum	CC - ORNAMENT	ORNAMENT		1988	$7.75	$25.50
1988-QX496-1	Kringle Portrait	CC - ORNAMENT	ORNAMENT		1988	$7.50	$26.00
1988-QX495-4	Kringle Tree	CC - ORNAMENT	ORNAMENT		1988	$6.50	$38.00
1988-QX495-1	Kringle Moon	CC - ORNAMENT	ORNAMENT		1988	$5.50	$26.00
1988-QX492-1	Glowing Wreath	CC - ORNAMENT	ORNAMENT		1988	$6.00	$12.00
1988-QX493-1	Sparkling Tree	CC - ORNAMENT	ORNAMENT		1988	$6.00	$16.00
1988-QX492-4	Shiny Sleigh	CC - ORNAMENT	ORNAMENT		1988	$5.75	$16.00
1988-QX493-4	Loving Bear	CC - ORNAMENT	ORNAMENT		1988	$4.75	$13.00
1988-QX494-4	Starry Angel	CC - ORNAMENT	ORNAMENT		1988	$4.75	$17.00
1988-QX494-1	Christmas Cardinal	CC - ORNAMENT	ORNAMENT		1988	$4.75	$13.00
1988-QX423-4	Merry-Mint Unicorn	CC - ORNAMENT	ORNAMENT		1988	$8.50	$14.00
1988-QX408-1	Little Jack Horner	CC - ORNAMENT	ORNAMENT		1988	$8.00	$19.00
1988-QX410-4	Midnight Snack	CC - ORNAMENT	ORNAMENT		1988	$6.00	$16.00
1988-QX411-1	Cymbals of Christmas	CC - ORNAMENT	ORNAMENT		1988	$5.50	$19.00
1988-QX409-1	Very Strawbeary	CC - ORNAMENT	ORNAMENT		1988	$4.75	$12.50
1988-QX410-1	Baby Redbird	CC - ORNAMENT	ORNAMENT		1988	$5.00	$11.00
1988-QX407-4	Mary's Angels - 1st	CC - ORNAMENT	ORNAMENT		1988	$5.00	$34.00
1988-QX406-1	Collector's Plate - 2nd	CC - ORNAMENT	ORNAMENT		1988	$8.00	$26.00
1988-QX401-1	Mr. And Mrs. Claus - 3rd	CC - ORNAMENT	ORNAMENT		1988	$13.00	$46.00
1988-QX405-1	Reindeer Champs - 3rd	CC - ORNAMENT	ORNAMENT		1988	$7.50	$32.00
1988-QX271-4	Betsey Clark - 3rd	CC - ORNAMENT	ORNAMENT		1988	$5.00	$13.00
1988-QX402-1	Windows of the World - 4th	CC - ORNAMENT	ORNAMENT		1988	$10.00	$15.00
1988-QX403-4	Miniature Creche - 4th	CC - ORNAMENT	ORNAMENT		1988	$8.50	$18.50
1988-QX401-4	Nost. Houses And Shops - 5th	CC - ORNAMENT	ORNAMENT		1988	$14.50	$42.00
1988-QX404-1	Wood Childhood Ornaments - 5th	CC - ORNAMENT	ORNAMENT		1988	$7.50	$18.00
1988-QX371-4	Twelve Days of Chrstmas - 5th	CC - ORNAMENT	ORNAMENT		1988	$6.50	$20.00
1988-QX404-4	Porcelain Bear - 6th	CC - ORNAMENT	ORNAMENT		1988	$8.00	$26.00
1988-QX400-4	Tin Locomotive - 7th	CC - ORNAMENT	ORNAMENT		1988	$14.75	$44.00
1988-QX371-1	Holiday Wildlife - 7th/Final	CC - ORNAMENT	ORNAMENT		1988	$7.75	$14.00
1988-QX402-4	Rocking Horse - 8th	CC - ORNAMENT	ORNAMENT		1988	$10.75	$13.50
1988-QX403-1	Frosty Friends - 9th	CC - ORNAMENT	ORNAMENT		1988	$8.75	$45.00
1988-QX370-4	Norman Rockwell - 9th/Final	CC - ORNAMENT	ORNAMENT		1988	$7.75	$15.00
1988-QX400-1	Here Comes Santa - 10th	CC - ORNAMENT	ORNAMENT		1988	$14.00	$36.00
1988-QX405-4	Thimble - 11th	CC - ORNAMENT	ORNAMENT		1988	$5.75	$18.00
1989-QX468-2	Baby's First Christmas Photo	CC - ORNAMENT	ORNAMENT		1989	$6.25	$33.50
1989-QX272-2	Baby's First Christmas - Girl	CC - ORNAMENT	ORNAMENT		1989	$4.75	$16.50
1989-QX272-5	Baby's First Christmas - Boy	CC - ORNAMENT	ORNAMENT		1989	$4.75	$17.00
1989-QX381-5	Baby's First Christmas	CC - ORNAMENT	ORNAMENT		1989	$6.75	$13.50
1989-QX382-2	Granddaughter's First Chrstmas	CC - ORNAMENT	ORNAMENT		1989	$6.75	$18.00
1989-QX382-5	Grandson's First Christmas	CC - ORNAMENT	ORNAMENT		1989	$6.75	$12.00
1989-QX449-2	Baby's First Christmas	CC - ORNAMENT	ORNAMENT		1989	$7.25	$63.00
1989-QX449-5	Baby's Second Christmas	CC - ORNAMENT	ORNAMENT		1989	$6.75	$29.00
1989-QX469-5	Child's Third Christmas	CC - ORNAMENT	ORNAMENT		1989	$6.75	$17.00
1989-QX543-2	Child's Fourth Christmas	CC - ORNAMENT	ORNAMENT		1989	$6.75	$16.50
1989-QX543-5	Child's Fifth Christmas	CC - ORNAMENT	ORNAMENT		1989	$6.75	$16.50
1989-QX440-5	Mother	CC - ORNAMENT	ORNAMENT		1989	$9.75	$22.00
1989-QX442-5	Mom and Dad	CC - ORNAMENT	ORNAMENT		1989	$9.75	$18.00
1989-QX441-2	Dad	CC - ORNAMENT	ORNAMENT		1989	$7.25	$9.00
1989-QX443-2	Daughter	CC - ORNAMENT	ORNAMENT		1989	$6.25	$8.00
1989-QX444-5	Son	CC - ORNAMENT	ORNAMENT		1989	$6.25	$15.00
1989-QX445-2	Brother	CC - ORNAMENT	ORNAMENT		1989	$7.25	$12.50
1989-QX279-2	Sister	CC - ORNAMENT	ORNAMENT		1989	$4.75	$10.00
1989-QX277-2	Grandparents	CC - ORNAMENT	ORNAMENT		1989	$4.75	$15.00
1989-QX277-5	Grandmother	CC - ORNAMENT	ORNAMENT		1989	$4.75	$12.00
1989-QX278-2	Granddaughter	CC - ORNAMENT	ORNAMENT		1989	$4.75	$17.00
1989-QX278-5	Grandson	CC - ORNAMENT	ORNAMENT		1989	$4.75	$20.00
1989-QX311-2	Godchild	CC - ORNAMENT	ORNAMENT		1989	$6.25	$10.00
1989-QX486-5	Sweetheart	CC - ORNAMENT	ORNAMENT		1989	$9.75	$24.00
1989-QX485-2	First Christmas Together	CC - ORNAMENT	ORNAMENT		1989	$9.75	$22.00
1989-QX383-2	First Christmas Together	CC - ORNAMENT	ORNAMENT		1989	$6.75	$22.00
1989-QX273-2	First Christmas Together	CC - ORNAMENT	ORNAMENT		1989	$4.75	$16.00
1989-QX273-5	Five Years Together	CC - ORNAMENT	ORNAMENT		1989	$4.75	$15.00
1989-QX274-2	Ten Years Together	CC - ORNAMENT	ORNAMENT		1989	$4.75	$15.00
1989-QX485-5	Twenty-Five Yrs Together Photo	CC - ORNAMENT	ORNAMENT		1989	$8.75	$14.00
1989-QX545-2	Forty Years Together Photo	CC - ORNAMENT	ORNAMENT		1989	$8.75	$16.00
1989-QX486-2	Fifty Years Together Photo	CC - ORNAMENT	ORNAMENT		1989	$8.75	$16.50
1989-QX383-5	Language of Love	CC - ORNAMENT	ORNAMENT		1989	$6.25	$18.00
1989-QX274-5	World of Love	CC - ORNAMENT	ORNAMENT		1989	$4.75	$28.00
1989-QX413-2	Friendship Time	CC - ORNAMENT	ORNAMENT		1989	$9.75	$28.00
1989-QX412-5	Teacher	CC - ORNAMENT	ORNAMENT		1989	$5.75	$24.00
1989-QX275-5	New Home	CC - ORNAMENT	ORNAMENT		1989	$4.75	$9.00
1989-QX384-2	Festive Year	CC - ORNAMENT	ORNAMENT		1989	$7.75	$15.00
1989-QX385-2	Gratitude	CC - ORNAMENT	ORNAMENT		1989	$6.75	$17.00
1989-QX384-5	From Our Home to Yours	CC - ORNAMENT	ORNAMENT		1989	$6.25	$15.00
1989-QX437-2	Joyful Trio	CC - ORNAMENT	ORNAMENT		1989	$9.75	$11.50
1989-QX434-5	Old-World Gnome	CC - ORNAMENT	ORNAMENT		1989	$7.75	$15.00
1989-QX469-2	Hoppy Holidays	CC - ORNAMENT	ORNAMENT		1989	$7.75	$18.00
1989-QX547-5	The First Christmas	CC - ORNAMENT	ORNAMENT		1989	$7.75	$13.50
1989-QX548-5	Gentle Fawn	CC - ORNAMENT	ORNAMENT		1989	$7.75	$16.00

Order No.	Title	Type	Theme	Retired	Intro. Year	Retial Price	Secondary Price
1989-QX431-2	Spencer Sparrow, Esq.	CC - ORNAMENT	ORNAMENT		1989	$6.75	$17.00
1989-QX433-2	Snoopy and Woodstock (Top Hat)	CC - ORNAMENT	ORNAMENT		1989	$6.75	$26.00
1989-QX438-5	Sweet Memories Photoholder	CC - ORNAMENT	ORNAMENT		1989	$6.75	$19.00
1989-QX456-5	Stocking Kitten	CC - ORNAMENT	ORNAMENT		1989	$6.75	$13.50
1989-QX386-2	George Washington Bicentennial	CC - ORNAMENT	ORNAMENT		1989	$6.25	$13.00
1989-QX439-2	Feliz Navidad (Pinata)	CC - ORNAMENT	ORNAMENT		1989	$6.75	$22.00
1989-QX426-2	Cranberry Bunny	CC - ORNAMENT	ORNAMENT		1989	$5.75	$10.00
1989-QX426-5	Deer Disguise	CC - ORNAMENT	ORNAMENT		1989	$5.75	$20.00
1989-QX429-2	Paddington Bear	CC - ORNAMENT	ORNAMENT		1989	$5.75	$18.00
1989-QX420-5	Snowplow Santa	CC - ORNAMENT	ORNAMENT		1989	$5.75	$12.00
1989-QX424-5	Kristy Claus	CC - ORNAMENT	ORNAMENT		1989	$5.75	$10.00
1989-QX545-5	Here's the Pitch	CC - ORNAMENT	ORNAMENT		1989	$5.75	$13.00
1989-QX546-2	North Pole Jogger	CC - ORNAMENT	ORNAMENT		1989	$5.75	$9.00
1989-QX546-5	Camera Claus	CC - ORNAMENT	ORNAMENT		1989	$5.75	$8.50
1989-QX415-2	Sea Santa	CC - ORNAMENT	ORNAMENT		1989	$5.75	$20.00
1989-QX418-5	Gym Dandy	CC - ORNAMENT	ORNAMENT		1989	$5.75	$9.00
1989-QX419-2	On the Links	CC - ORNAMENT	ORNAMENT		1989	$5.75	$12.50
1989-QX432-5	Special Delivery	CC - ORNAMENT	ORNAMENT		1989	$5.75	$16.00
1989-QX430-5	Hang in There	CC - ORNAMENT	ORNAMENT		1989	$5.25	$25.00
1989-QX436-5	Owliday Greetings	CC - ORNAMENT	ORNAMENT		1989	$4.00	$11.00
1989-QX276-2	Norman Rockwell	CC - ORNAMENT	ORNAMENT		1989	$4.75	$17.00
1989-QX276-5	Peanuts - A Charlie Brown Xmas	CC - ORNAMENT	ORNAMENT		1989	$4.75	$35.00
1989-QX476-1	Party Line	CC - ORNAMENT	ORNAMENT		1989	$8.75	$25.00
1989-QX487-1	Peek-a-Boo Kitties	CC - ORNAMENT	ORNAMENT		1989	$7.50	$19.00
1989-QX478-4	Polar Bowler	CC - ORNAMENT	ORNAMENT		1989	$5.75	$15.00
1989-QX479-4	Gone Fishing	CC - ORNAMENT	ORNAMENT		1989	$5.75	
1989-QX418-1	Teeny Taster	CC - ORNAMENT	ORNAMENT		1989	$4.75	$22.00
1989-QX482-1	A Kiss From Santa	CC - ORNAMENT	ORNAMENT		1989	$4.50	
1989-QX481-4	Oreo Chocolate Sndwich Cookies	CC - ORNAMENT	ORNAMENT		1989	$4.00	
1989-QX547-2	Sparkling Snowflake	CC - ORNAMENT	ORNAMENT		1989	$7.75	$19.00
1989-QX463-5	Festive Angel	CC - ORNAMENT	ORNAMENT		1989	$6.75	$17.00
1989-QX464-2	Graceful Swan	CC - ORNAMENT	ORNAMENT		1989	$6.75	$16.00
1989-QX466-5	Nostalgic Lamb	CC - ORNAMENT	ORNAMENT		1989	$6.75	$8.00
1989-QX463-2	Horse Weathervane	CC - ORNAMENT	ORNAMENT		1989	$5.75	$15.00
1989-QX467-5	Rooster Weathervane	CC - ORNAMENT	ORNAMENT		1989	$5.75	$12.00
1989-QX467-2	Country Cat	CC - ORNAMENT	ORNAMENT		1989	$6.25	$14.00
1989-QX465-2	Nutshell Holiday	CC - ORNAMENT	ORNAMENT		1989	$5.75	$22.00
1989-QX465-5	Nutshell Dreams	CC - ORNAMENT	ORNAMENT		1989	$5.75	$16.00
1989-QX487-2	Nutshell Workshop	CC - ORNAMENT	ORNAMENT		1989	$5.75	$22.00
1989-QX488-5	Claus Construction	CC - ORNAMENT	ORNAMENT		1989	$7.75	$15.00
1989-QX411-2	Cactus Cowboy	CC - ORNAMENT	ORNAMENT		1989	$6.75	$30.00
1989-QX407-2	Rodney Reindeer	CC - ORNAMENT	ORNAMENT		1989	$6.75	$12.00
1989-QX488-2	Let's Play	CC - ORNAMENT	ORNAMENT		1989	$7.25	$27.50
1989-QX409-2	TV Break	CC - ORNAMENT	ORNAMENT		1989	$6.25	$16.00
1989-QX489-5	Balancing Elf	CC - ORNAMENT	ORNAMENT		1989	$6.75	$15.00
1989-QX489-2	Wiggly Snowman	CC - ORNAMENT	ORNAMENT		1989	$6.75	$18.00
1989-QX487-5	Cool Swing	CC - ORNAMENT	ORNAMENT		1989	$6.25	$21.00
1989-QX410-5	Goin' South	CC - ORNAMENT	ORNAMENT		1989	$4.25	$21.00
1989-QX450-5	Peppermint Clown	CC - ORNAMENT	ORNAMENT		1989	$24.75	$21.00
1989-QX447-2	Merry-Go-Round Unicorn	CC - ORNAMENT	ORNAMENT		1989	$10.75	$17.50
1989-QX451-5	Carousel Zebra	CC - ORNAMENT	ORNAMENT		1989	$9.25	$12.00
1989-QX452-2	Mail Call	CC - ORNAMENT	ORNAMENT		1989	$8.75	$15.00
1989-QX452-5	Baby Partridge	CC - ORNAMENT	ORNAMENT		1989	$6.75	$19.00
1989-QX453-5	Playful Angel	CC - ORNAMENT	ORNAMENT		1989	$6.75	$19.00
1989-QX453-2	Cherry Jubilee	CC - ORNAMENT	ORNAMENT		1989	$5.00	$15.00
1989-QX454-2	Bear-i-Tone	CC - ORNAMENT	ORNAMENT		1989	$4.75	$10.00
1989-QX580-5	The Ornament Express - S.E.	CC - ORNAMENT	ORNAMENT		1989	$22.00	$36.00
1989-QX544-5	Christmas Kitty - 1st	CC - ORNAMENT	ORNAMENT		1989	$14.75	$23.00
1989-QX427-2	Winter Surprise - 1st	CC - ORNAMENT	ORNAMENT		1989	$10.75	$17.00
1989-QX455-5	Hark! It's Herald - 1st	CC - ORNAMENT	ORNAMENT		1989	$6.75	$15.00
1989-QX435-2	Crayola Crayon - 1st	CC - ORNAMENT	ORNAMENT		1989	$8.75	$45.00
1989-QX279-5	The Gift Bringers - 1st	CC - ORNAMENT	ORNAMENT		1989	$5.00	$14.00
1989-QX454-5	Mary's Angels - 2nd	CC - ORNAMENT	ORNAMENT		1989	$5.75	$53.00
1989-QX461-2	Collector's Plate - 3rd	CC - ORNAMENT	ORNAMENT		1989	$8.25	$18.00
1989-QX457-5	Mr. And Mrs. Claus - 4th	CC - ORNAMENT	ORNAMENT		1989	$13.25	$45.00
1989-QX456-2	Reindeer Champs - 4th	CC - ORNAMENT	ORNAMENT		1989	$7.75	$16.00
1989-QX230-2	Betsey Clark - 4th	CC - ORNAMENT	ORNAMENT		1989	$5.00	$18.00
1989-QX462-5	Windows of the World - 5th	CC - ORNAMENT	ORNAMENT		1989	$10.75	$18.00
1989-QX459-2	Miniature Creche - 5th/Final	CC - ORNAMENT	ORNAMENT		1989	$9.25	$22.00
1989-QX458-2	Nost. Houses And Shops - 6th	CC - ORNAMENT	ORNAMENT		1989	$14.25	$50.00
1989-QX459-5	Wood Childhood Ornaments - 6th	CC - ORNAMENT	ORNAMENT		1989	$7.75	$17.00
1989-QX381-2	Twelve Days of Chrstmas - 6th	CC - ORNAMENT	ORNAMENT		1989	$6.75	$14.00
1989-QX461-5	Porcelain Bear - 7th	CC - ORNAMENT	ORNAMENT		1989	$8.75	$18.00
1989-QX460-2	Tin Locomotive - 8th and Final	CC - ORNAMENT	ORNAMENT		1989	$14.75	$45.00
1989-QX462-2	Rocking Horse - 9th	CC - ORNAMENT	ORNAMENT		1989	$10.75	$25.50
1989-QX457-2	Frosty Friends - 10th	CC - ORNAMENT	ORNAMENT		1989	$9.25	$28.00
1989-QX458-5	Here Comes Santa - 11th	CC - ORNAMENT	ORNAMENT		1989	$14.75	$42.00
1989-QX455-2	Thimble - 12th and Final	CC - ORNAMENT	ORNAMENT		1989	$5.75	$17.50
1990-QX485-3	Baby's First Christmas	CC - ORNAMENT	ORNAMENT		1990	$9.75	$16.00
1990-QX484-3	Baby's First Christmas Photo	CC - ORNAMENT	ORNAMENT		1990	$7.75	$17.00
1990-QX206-3	Baby's First Christmas - Boy	CC - ORNAMENT	ORNAMENT		1990	$4.75	$12.00
1990-QX206-6	Baby's First Christmas - Girl	CC - ORNAMENT	ORNAMENT		1990	$4.75	$12.00
1990-QX303-6	Baby's First Christmas	CC - ORNAMENT	ORNAMENT		1990	$6.75	$15.00
1990-QX306-3	Grandson's First Christmas	CC - ORNAMENT	ORNAMENT		1990	$6.75	$13.00
1990-QX310-6	Granddaughter's First Chrstmas	CC - ORNAMENT	ORNAMENT		1990	$6.75	$16.00
1990-QX485-6	Baby's First Christmas	CC - ORNAMENT	ORNAMENT		1990	$7.75	$24.00
1990-QX486-3	Baby's Second Christmas	CC - ORNAMENT	ORNAMENT		1990	$6.75	$21.00
1990-QX486-6	Child's Third Christmas	CC - ORNAMENT	ORNAMENT		1990	$6.75	$150.00
1990-QX487-3	Child's Fourth Christmas	CC - ORNAMENT	ORNAMENT		1990	$6.75	$18.00
1990-QX487-6	Child's Fifth Christmas	CC - ORNAMENT	ORNAMENT		1990	$6.75	$15.00
1990-QX491-6	Mom-to-Be	CC - ORNAMENT	ORNAMENT		1990	$5.75	$17.00
1990-QX491-3	Dad-to-Be	CC - ORNAMENT	ORNAMENT		1990	$5.75	$16.00
1990-QX453-6	Mother	CC - ORNAMENT	ORNAMENT		1990	$8.75	$9.00

Order No.	Title	Type	Theme	Retired	Intro. Year	Retail Price	Secondary Price
1990-QX453-3	Dad	CC - ORNAMENT	ORNAMENT		1990	$6.75	$12.00
1990-QX459-3	Mom and Dad	CC - ORNAMENT	ORNAMENT		1990	$8.75	$14.00
1990-QX451-6	Son	CC - ORNAMENT	ORNAMENT		1990	$5.75	$9.00
1990-QX449-6	Daughter	CC - ORNAMENT	ORNAMENT		1990	$5.75	$15.00
1990-QX227-3	Sister	CC - ORNAMENT	ORNAMENT		1990	$4.75	$8.50
1990-QX449-3	Brother	CC - ORNAMENT	ORNAMENT		1990	$5.75	$10.50
1990-QX223-6	Grandmother	CC - ORNAMENT	ORNAMENT		1990	$4.75	$12.50
1990-QX225-3	Grandparents	CC - ORNAMENT	ORNAMENT		1990	$4.75	$12.00
1990-QX229-3	Grandson	CC - ORNAMENT	ORNAMENT		1990	$4.75	$11.00
1990-QX228-6	Granddaughter	CC - ORNAMENT	ORNAMENT		1990	$4.75	$12.00
1990-QX317-6	Godchild	CC - ORNAMENT	ORNAMENT		1990	$6.75	$9.00
1990-QX489-3	Sweetheart	CC - ORNAMENT	ORNAMENT		1990	$11.75	$16.00
1990-QX488-3	First Christmas Together	CC - ORNAMENT	ORNAMENT		1990	$9.75	$12.00
1990-QX488-6	First Christmas Together Photo	CC - ORNAMENT	ORNAMENT		1990	$7.75	$15.00
1990-QX314-6	First Christmas Together	CC - ORNAMENT	ORNAMENT		1990	$6.75	$17.00
1990-QX213-6	First Christmas Together	CC - ORNAMENT	ORNAMENT		1990	$4.75	$19.00
1990-QX210-3	Five Years Together	CC - ORNAMENT	ORNAMENT		1990	$4.75	$12.00
1990-QX215-3	Ten Years Together	CC - ORNAMENT	ORNAMENT		1990	$4.75	$6.00
1990-QX489-6	Twenty-Five Years Together	CC - ORNAMENT	ORNAMENT		1990	$9.75	$10.00
1990-QX490-3	Forty Years Together	CC - ORNAMENT	ORNAMENT		1990	$9.75	$9.00
1990-QX490-6	Fifty Years Together	CC - ORNAMENT	ORNAMENT		1990	$9.75	$16.00
1990-QX213-3	Time for Love	CC - ORNAMENT	ORNAMENT		1990	$4.75	$10.00
1990-QX210-6	Peaceful Kingdom	CC - ORNAMENT	ORNAMENT		1990	$4.75	$14.00
1990-QX315-6	Jesus Loves Me	CC - ORNAMENT	ORNAMENT		1990	$6.75	$11.50
1990-QX448-6	Copy of Cheer	CC - ORNAMENT	ORNAMENT		1990	$7.75	$10.00
1990-QX414-3	Friendship Kitten	CC - ORNAMENT	ORNAMENT		1990	$6.75	$17.50
1990-QX317-3	Across the Miles	CC - ORNAMENT	ORNAMENT		1990	$6.75	$8.50
1990-QX434-3	New Home	CC - ORNAMENT	ORNAMENT		1990	$6.75	$12.50
1990-QX216-6	From Our Home to Yours	CC - ORNAMENT	ORNAMENT		1990	$4.75	$13.00
1990-QX448-3	Teacher	CC - ORNAMENT	ORNAMENT		1990	$7.75	$6.00
1990-QX316-6	Child Care Giver	CC - ORNAMENT	ORNAMENT		1990	$6.75	$5.50
1990-QX549-3	Stocking Pals	CC - ORNAMENT	ORNAMENT		1990	$10.75	$18.00
1990-QX548-3	Bearback Rider	CC - ORNAMENT	ORNAMENT		1990	$9.75	$19.00
1990-QX548-6	Baby Unicorn	CC - ORNAMENT	ORNAMENT		1990	$9.75	$16.00
1990-QX549-6	Spoon Rider	CC - ORNAMENT	ORNAMENT		1990	$9.75	$12.00
1990-QX547-6	Lovable Dears	CC - ORNAMENT	ORNAMENT		1990	$8.75	$16.00
1990-QX444-6	Meow Mart	CC - ORNAMENT	ORNAMENT		1990	$7.75	$19.00
1990-QX469-3	Perfect Catch	CC - ORNAMENT	ORNAMENT		1990	$7.75	$12.00
1990-QX518-6	Stitches of Joy	CC - ORNAMENT	ORNAMENT		1990	$7.75	$15.00
1990-QX523-3	Little Drummer Boy	CC - ORNAMENT	ORNAMENT		1990	$7.75	$17.00
1990-QX523-6	Goose Cart	CC - ORNAMENT	ORNAMENT		1990	$7.75	$9.00
1990-QX550-3	Joy Is in the Air	CC - ORNAMENT	ORNAMENT		1990	$7.75	$22.00
1990-QX468-3	Jolly Dolphin	CC - ORNAMENT	ORNAMENT		1990	$6.75	$25.00
1990-QX473-3	Beary Good Deal	CC - ORNAMENT	ORNAMENT		1990	$6.75	$12.00
1990-QX471-3	Hang in There	CC - ORNAMENT	ORNAMENT		1990	$6.75	$17.00
1990-QX471-6	Kitty's Best Pal	CC - ORNAMENT	ORNAMENT		1990	$6.75	$18.00
1990-QX470-3	Long Winter's Nap	CC - ORNAMENT	ORNAMENT		1990	$6.75	$16.00
1990-QX517-3	Feliz Navidad (Chili Pepper)	CC - ORNAMENT	ORNAMENT		1990	$6.75	$17.00
1990-QX518-3	Home for the Owlidays	CC - ORNAMENT	ORNAMENT		1990	$6.75	$10.50
1990-QX519-3	Nutshell Chat	CC - ORNAMENT	ORNAMENT		1990	$6.75	$10.00
1990-QX503-3	Gingerbread Elf	CC - ORNAMENT	ORNAMENT		1990	$5.75	$14.00
1990-QX472-3	Snoopy and Woodstock (Hug)	CC - ORNAMENT	ORNAMENT		1990	$6.75	$25.00
1990-QX223-3	Peanuts	CC - ORNAMENT	ORNAMENT		1990	$4.75	$22.00
1990-QX229-6	Norman Rockwell Art	CC - ORNAMENT	ORNAMENT		1990	$4.75	$18.00
1990-QX524-3	Holiday Cardinals	CC - ORNAMENT	ORNAMENT		1990	$7.75	$17.50
1990-QX464-5	Happy Voices	CC - ORNAMENT	ORNAMENT		1990	$6.75	$10.50
1990-QX524-6	Christmas Partridge	CC - ORNAMENT	ORNAMENT		1990	$7.75	$10.00
1990-QX488-5	Claus Construction	CC - ORNAMENT	ORNAMENT		1990	$7.75	
1990-QX456-5	Stocking Kitten	CC - ORNAMENT	ORNAMENT		1990	$6.75	$14.50
1990-QX431-2	Spencer Sparrow, Esq.	CC - ORNAMENT	ORNAMENT		1990	$6.75	$17.00
1990-QX465-2	Nutshell Holiday	CC - ORNAMENT	ORNAMENT		1990	$5.75	
1990-QX468-6	S. Claus Taxi	CC - ORNAMENT	ORNAMENT		1990	$11.75	$24.50
1990-QX499-3	Coyote Carols	CC - ORNAMENT	ORNAMENT		1990	$8.75	$16.50
1990-QX410-6	King Klaus	CC - ORNAMENT	ORNAMENT		1990	$7.75	$13.50
1990-QX496-3	Golf's My Bag	CC - ORNAMENT	ORNAMENT		1990	$7.75	$15.00
1990-QX497-6	Hot Dogger	CC - ORNAMENT	ORNAMENT		1990	$7.75	$11.00
1990-QX498-6	Poolside Walrus	CC - ORNAMENT	ORNAMENT		1990	$7.75	$16.00
1990-QX499-6	Three Little Piggies	CC - ORNAMENT	ORNAMENT		1990	$7.75	$16.50
1990-QX519-6	Billboard Bunny	CC - ORNAMENT	ORNAMENT		1990	$7.75	$11.00
1990-QX497-3	Pepperoni Mouse	CC - ORNAMENT	ORNAMENT		1990	$6.75	$14.00
1990-QX493-3	Mooy Christmas	CC - ORNAMENT	ORNAMENT		1990	$6.75	$19.00
1990-QX436-6	Chiming In	CC - ORNAMENT	ORNAMENT		1990	$9.75	$13.50
1990-QX504-3	Born to Dance	CC - ORNAMENT	ORNAMENT		1990	$7.75	$10.00
1990-QX230-3	Garfield	CC - ORNAMENT	ORNAMENT		1990	$4.75	$12.00
1990-QX496-6	Cozy Goose	CC - ORNAMENT	ORNAMENT		1990	$5.75	$12.00
1990-QX492-6	Two Peas in a Pod	CC - ORNAMENT	ORNAMENT		1990	$4.75	$30.00
1990-QX515-6	Polar Sport	CC - ORNAMENT	ORNAMENT		1990	$7.75	$15.00
1990-QX516-6	Polar TV	CC - ORNAMENT	ORNAMENT		1990	$7.75	$11.00
1990-QX462-6	Polar Pair	CC - ORNAMENT	ORNAMENT		1990	$5.75	$13.00
1990-QX463-3	Polar Video	CC - ORNAMENT	ORNAMENT		1990	$5.75	$11.50
1990-QX466-3	Polar V.I.P.	CC - ORNAMENT	ORNAMENT		1990	$5.75	$11.50
1990-QX466-6	Polar Jogger	CC - ORNAMENT	ORNAMENT		1990	$5.75	$9.50
1990-QX437-3	Christmas Croc	CC - ORNAMENT	ORNAMENT		1990	$7.75	$11.00
1990-QX498-3	Santa Schnoz	CC - ORNAMENT	ORNAMENT		1990	$6.75	$18.00
1990-QX482-3	Donder's Diner	CC - ORNAMENT	ORNAMENT		1990	$13.75	$11.50
1990-QX477-3	Welcome, Santa	CC - ORNAMENT	ORNAMENT		1990	$11.75	$16.00
1990-QX476-3	Happy Woodcutter	CC - ORNAMENT	ORNAMENT		1990	$9.75	$13.50
1990-QX474-6	Angel Kitty	CC - ORNAMENT	ORNAMENT		1990	$8.75	$14.00
1990-QX475-3	Mouseboat	CC - ORNAMENT	ORNAMENT		1990	$7.75	$12.00
1990-QX475-6	Gentle Dreamers	CC - ORNAMENT	ORNAMENT		1990	$8.75	$10.00
1990-QX505-6	Dickens Caroler Bell - 1st	CC - ORNAMENT	ORNAMENT		1990	$21.75	$33.00
1990-QX473-6	Merry Olde Santa - 1st	CC - ORNAMENT	ORNAMENT		1990	$14.75	$62.50
1990-QX472-6	Heart of Christmas - 1st	CC - ORNAMENT	ORNAMENT		1990	$13.75	$65.00

Order No.	Title	Type	Theme	Retired	Intro. Year	Retial Price	Secondary Price
1990-QX446-6	Fabulous Decade - 1st	CC - ORNAMENT	ORNAMENT		1990	$7.75	$35.00
1990-QX465-6	Greatest Story - 1st	CC - ORNAMENT	ORNAMENT		1990	$12.75	$22.00
1990-QX450-6	Christmas Kitty - 2nd	CC - ORNAMENT	ORNAMENT		1990	$14.75	$20.00
1990-QX444-3	Winter Surprise - 2nd	CC - ORNAMENT	ORNAMENT		1990	$10.75	$18.00
1990-QX458-6	Crayola Crayon - 2nd	CC - ORNAMENT	ORNAMENT		1990	$8.75	$35.00
1990-QX446-3	Hark! It's Herald - 2nd	CC - ORNAMENT	ORNAMENT		1990	$6.75	$16.00
1990-QX280-3	The Gift Bringers - 2nd	CC - ORNAMENT	ORNAMENT		1990	$5.00	$9.00
1990-QX442-3	Mary's Angels - 3rd	CC - ORNAMENT	ORNAMENT		1990	$5.75	$23.00
1990-QX443-6	Collector's Plate - 4th	CC - ORNAMENT	ORNAMENT		1990	$8.75	$18.00
1990-QX439-3	Mr. And Mrs. Claus - 5th	CC - ORNAMENT	ORNAMENT		1990	$13.75	$50.00
1990-QX443-3	Reindeer Champs - 5th	CC - ORNAMENT	ORNAMENT		1990	$7.75	$20.00
1990-QX203-3	Betsey Clark - 5th	CC - ORNAMENT	ORNAMENT		1990	$5.00	$14.00
1990-QX463-6	Windows of the World - 6th/F	CC - ORNAMENT	ORNAMENT		1990	$10.75	$15.00
1990-QX469-6	Nost. Houses And Shops - 7th	CC - ORNAMENT	ORNAMENT		1990	$14.75	$45.50
1990-QX303-3	Twelve Days of Chrstmas - 7th	CC - ORNAMENT	ORNAMENT		1990	$6.75	$17.00
1990-QX442-6	Porcelain Bear - 8th and Final	CC - ORNAMENT	ORNAMENT		1990	$8.75	$18.00
1990-QX464-6	Rocking Horse - 10th	CC - ORNAMENT	ORNAMENT		1990	$10.75	$62.00
1990-QX439-6	Frosty Friends - 11th	CC - ORNAMENT	ORNAMENT		1990	$9.75	$27.00
1991-QX510-7	Baby's First Christmas	CC - ORNAMENT	ORNAMENT		1991	$17.75	$25.00
1991-QX486-9	Baby's First Christmas Photo	CC - ORNAMENT	ORNAMENT		1991	$7.75	$21.50
1991-QX222-7	Baby's First Christmas - Girl	CC - ORNAMENT	ORNAMENT		1991	$4.75	$13.00
1991-QX221-7	Baby's First Christmas - Boy	CC - ORNAMENT	ORNAMENT		1991	$4.75	$13.00
1991-QX511-7	Grandson's First Christmas	CC - ORNAMENT	ORNAMENT		1991	$6.75	$18.00
1991-QX511-9	Granddaughter's First Chrstmas	CC - ORNAMENT	ORNAMENT		1991	$6.75	$19.00
1991-QX488-7	A Child's Christmas	CC - ORNAMENT	ORNAMENT		1991	$9.75	$12.50
1991-QX488-9	Baby's First Christmas	CC - ORNAMENT	ORNAMENT		1991	$7.75	$17.00
1991-QX489-7	Baby's Second Christmas	CC - ORNAMENT	ORNAMENT		1991	$6.75	$13.00
1991-QX489-9	Child's Third Christmas	CC - ORNAMENT	ORNAMENT		1991	$6.75	$21.50
1991-QX490-7	Child's Fourth Christmas	CC - ORNAMENT	ORNAMENT		1991	$6.75	$9.00
1991-QX490-9	Child's Fifth Christmas	CC - ORNAMENT	ORNAMENT		1991	$6.75	$34.00
1991-QX487-7	Mom-to-Be	CC - ORNAMENT	ORNAMENT		1991	$5.75	$16.00
1991-QX487-9	Dad-to-Be	CC - ORNAMENT	ORNAMENT		1991	$5.75	$9.00
1991-QX545-7	Mother	CC - ORNAMENT	ORNAMENT		1991	$9.75	$24.00
1991-QX512-7	Dad	CC - ORNAMENT	ORNAMENT		1991	$7.75	$13.50
1991-QX546-7	Mom and Dad	CC - ORNAMENT	ORNAMENT		1991	$9.75	$18.00
1991-QX547-7	Daughter	CC - ORNAMENT	ORNAMENT		1991	$5.75	$13.50
1991-QX546-9	Son	CC - ORNAMENT	ORNAMENT		1991	$5.75	$13.00
1991-QX548-7	Sister	CC - ORNAMENT	ORNAMENT		1991	$6.75	$12.50
1991-QX547-9	Brother	CC - ORNAMENT	ORNAMENT		1991	$6.75	$14.00
1991-QX230-7	Grandmother	CC - ORNAMENT	ORNAMENT		1991	$4.75	$8.50
1991-QX230-9	Grandparents	CC - ORNAMENT	ORNAMENT		1991	$4.75	$7.00
1991-QX229-9	Granddaughter	CC - ORNAMENT	ORNAMENT		1991	$4.75	$10.50
1991-QX229-7	Grandson	CC - ORNAMENT	ORNAMENT		1991	$4.75	$11.00
1991-QX548-9	Godchild	CC - ORNAMENT	ORNAMENT		1991	$6.75	$13.00
1991-QX495-7	Sweetheart	CC - ORNAMENT	ORNAMENT		1991	$9.75	$21.00
1991-QX491-9	First Christmas Together	CC - ORNAMENT	ORNAMENT		1991	$8.75	$12.50
1991-QX313-9	First Christmas Together	CC - ORNAMENT	ORNAMENT		1991	$6.75	$19.00
1991-QX222-9	First Christmas Together	CC - ORNAMENT	ORNAMENT		1991	$4.75	$8.50
1991-QX491-7	First Christmas Together Photo	CC - ORNAMENT	ORNAMENT		1991	$8.75	$13.00
1991-QX493-7	Twenty-Five Yrs Together Photo	CC - ORNAMENT	ORNAMENT		1991	$8.75	$12.00
1991-QX494-7	Fifty Years Together Photo	CC - ORNAMENT	ORNAMENT		1991	$8.75	$12.50
1991-QX492-7	Five Years Together	CC - ORNAMENT	ORNAMENT		1991	$7.75	$10.00
1991-QX492-9	Ten Years Together	CC - ORNAMENT	ORNAMENT		1991	$7.75	$10.50
1991-QX493-9	Forty Years Together	CC - ORNAMENT	ORNAMENT		1991	$7.75	$13.00
1991-QX494-9	Under the Mistletoe	CC - ORNAMENT	ORNAMENT		1991	$8.75	$16.00
1991-QX314-7	Jesus Loves Me	CC - ORNAMENT	ORNAMENT		1991	$7.75	$10.50
1991-QX528-9	Friends Are Fun	CC - ORNAMENT	ORNAMENT		1991	$9.75	$17.50
1991-QX227-9	Extra-Special Friends	CC - ORNAMENT	ORNAMENT		1991	$4.75	$22.00
1991-QX315-7	Across the Miles	CC - ORNAMENT	ORNAMENT		1991	$6.75	$9.00
1991-QX228-7	From Our Home to Yours	CC - ORNAMENT	ORNAMENT		1991	$4.75	$12.00
1991-QX544-9	New Home	CC - ORNAMENT	ORNAMENT		1991	$6.75	$19.00
1991-QX530-9	Terrific Teacher	CC - ORNAMENT	ORNAMENT		1991	$6.75	$12.00
1991-QX228-9	Teacher	CC - ORNAMENT	ORNAMENT		1991	$4.75	$7.00
1991-QX532-7	The Big Cheese	CC - ORNAMENT	ORNAMENT		1991	$6.75	$13.50
1991-QX531-9	Gift of Joy	CC - ORNAMENT	ORNAMENT		1991	$8.75	$13.00
1991-QX535-9	Folk Art Reindeer	CC - ORNAMENT	ORNAMENT		1991	$8.75	$13.00
1991-QX536-9	Joyous Memories Photoholder	CC - ORNAMENT	ORNAMENT		1991	$6.75	$24.00
1991-QX526-9	Snowy Owl	CC - ORNAMENT	ORNAMENT		1991	$7.75	$18.00
1991-QX519-9	Cuddly Lamb	CC - ORNAMENT	ORNAMENT		1991	$6.75	$15.00
1991-QX517-6	Nutshell Nativity	CC - ORNAMENT	ORNAMENT		1991	$6.75	$16.00
1991-QX527-9	Feliz Navidad (Sombrero)	CC - ORNAMENT	ORNAMENT		1991	$6.75	$18.00
1991-QX517-7	Garfield	CC - ORNAMENT	ORNAMENT		1991	$7.75	$17.50
1991-QX519-7	Snoopy and Woodstock (Pizza)	CC - ORNAMENT	ORNAMENT		1991	$6.75	$17.50
1991-QX225-7	Peanuts	CC - ORNAMENT	ORNAMENT		1991	$5.00	$15.00
1991-QX225-9	Norman Rockwell Art	CC - ORNAMENT	ORNAMENT		1991	$5.00	$16.00
1991-QX431-7	Old-Fashioned Sled	CC - ORNAMENT	ORNAMENT		1991	$8.75	$12.50
1991-QX537-7	Basket Bell Players	CC - ORNAMENT	ORNAMENT		1991	$7.75	$15.00
1991-QX527-7	Dinoclaus	CC - ORNAMENT	ORNAMENT		1991	$7.75	$14.00
1991-QX533-9	Chilly Chap	CC - ORNAMENT	ORNAMENT		1991	$6.75	$15.00
1991-QX528-7	Polar Classic	CC - ORNAMENT	ORNAMENT		1991	$6.75	$14.50
1991-QX532-9	All-Star	CC - ORNAMENT	ORNAMENT		1991	$6.75	$15.00
1991-QX544-7	Ski Lift Bunny	CC - ORNAMENT	ORNAMENT		1991	$6.75	$17.00
1991-QX535-7	Notes of Cheer	CC - ORNAMENT	ORNAMENT		1991	$5.75	$12.00
1991-QX483-3	Nutty Squirrel	CC - ORNAMENT	ORNAMENT		1991	$5.75	$12.00
1991-QX479-9	Merry Carolers	CC - ORNAMENT	ORNAMENT		1991	$29.75	$55.00
1991-QX498-9	Ebenezer Scrooge	CC - ORNAMENT	ORNAMENT		1991	$13.75	$15.50
1991-QX499-7	Bob Cratchit	CC - ORNAMENT	ORNAMENT		1991	$13.75	$16.00
1991-QX499-9	Mrs. Cratchitt	CC - ORNAMENT	ORNAMENT		1991	$13.75	$14.50
1991-QX503-7	Tiny Tim	CC - ORNAMENT	ORNAMENT		1991	$10.75	$15.00
1991-QX557-9	Christopher Robin	CC - ORNAMENT	ORNAMENT		1991	$9.75	$29.00
1991-QX556-9	Winnie-the-Pooh	CC - ORNAMENT	ORNAMENT		1991	$9.75	$42.00
1991-QX557-7	Piglet and Eeyore	CC - ORNAMENT	ORNAMENT		1991	$9.75	$47.00
1991-QX560-7	Rabbit	CC - ORNAMENT	ORNAMENT		1991	$9.75	$30.00

Order No.	Title	Type	Theme	Retired	Intro. Year	Retail Price	Secondary Price
1991-QX560-9	Tigger	CC - ORNAMENT	ORNAMENT		1991	$9.75	$106.00
1991-QX561-7	Kanga and Roo	CC - ORNAMENT	ORNAMENT		1991	$9.75	$42.00
1991-QX497-9	Snow Twins	CC - ORNAMENT	ORNAMENT		1991	$8.75	$15.00
1991-QX496-7	Yule Logger	CC - ORNAMENT	ORNAMENT		1991	$8.75	$19.00
1991-QX496-9	Glee Club Bears	CC - ORNAMENT	ORNAMENT		1991	$8.75	$17.00
1991-QX497-7	Plum Delightful	CC - ORNAMENT	ORNAMENT		1991	$8.75	$18.50
1991-QX495-9	Look Out Below	CC - ORNAMENT	ORNAMENT		1991	$8.75	$18.50
1991-QX498-7	Loving Stitches	CC - ORNAMENT	ORNAMENT		1991	$8.75	$23.00
1991-QX533-7	Fanfare Bear	CC - ORNAMENT	ORNAMENT		1991	$8.75	$14.00
1991-QX538-9	Evergreen Inn	CC - ORNAMENT	ORNAMENT		1991	$8.75	$8.50
1991-QX539-7	Santa's Studio	CC - ORNAMENT	ORNAMENT		1991	$8.75	$10.00
1991-QX539-9	Holiday Cafe	CC - ORNAMENT	ORNAMENT		1991	$8.75	$9.00
1991-QX529-9	Christmas Welcome	CC - ORNAMENT	ORNAMENT		1991	$9.75	$18.00
1991-QX530-7	Night Before Christmas	CC - ORNAMENT	ORNAMENT		1991	$9.75	$15.00
1991-QX529-7	Partridge in a Pear Tree	CC - ORNAMENT	ORNAMENT		1991	$9.75	$18.00
1991-QX541-9	Jolly Wolly Santa	CC - ORNAMENT	ORNAMENT		1991	$7.75	$23.00
1991-QX542-7	Jolly Wolly Snowman	CC - ORNAMENT	ORNAMENT		1991	$7.75	$19.50
1991-QX542-9	Jolly Wolly Soldier	CC - ORNAMENT	ORNAMENT		1991	$7.75	$18.00
1991-QX486-7	Noah's Ark	CC - ORNAMENT	ORNAMENT		1991	$13.75	$37.00
1991-QX439-9	Polar Circus Wagon	CC - ORNAMENT	ORNAMENT		1991	$13.75	$23.00
1991-QX438-9	Santa Sailor	CC - ORNAMENT	ORNAMENT		1991	$9.75	$15.00
1991-QX439-7	Tramp and Laddie	CC - ORNAMENT	ORNAMENT		1991	$7.75	$21.00
1991-QX438-7	Fiddlin' Around	CC - ORNAMENT	ORNAMENT		1991	$7.75	$12.50
1991-QX410-9	Hooked on Santa	CC - ORNAMENT	ORNAMENT		1991	$7.75	$16.00
1991-QX503-9	Dickens Caroler Bell - 2nd	CC - ORNAMENT	ORNAMENT		1991	$21.75	$39.00
1991-QX431-9	Classic American Cars - 1st	CC - ORNAMENT	ORNAMENT		1991	$12.75	$186.00
1991-QX512-9	Peace On Earth - 1st	CC - ORNAMENT	ORNAMENT		1991	$11.75	$18.50
1991-QX436-7	Heavenly Angels - 1st	CC - ORNAMENT	ORNAMENT		1991	$7.75	$19.00
1991-QX537-9	Puppy Love - 1st	CC - ORNAMENT	ORNAMENT		1991	$7.75	$41.00
1991-QX435-9	Merry Olde Santa - 2nd	CC - ORNAMENT	ORNAMENT		1991	$14.75	$73.00
1991-QX435-7	Heart of Christmas - 2nd	CC - ORNAMENT	ORNAMENT		1991	$13.75	$23.50
1991-QX412-9	Greatest Story - 2nd	CC - ORNAMENT	ORNAMENT		1991	$12.75	$19.00
1991-QX411-9	Fabulous Decade - 2nd	CC - ORNAMENT	ORNAMENT		1991	$7.75	$26.50
1991-QX437-7	Christmas Kitty - 3rd/Final	CC - ORNAMENT	ORNAMENT		1991	$14.75	$28.00
1991-QX427-7	Winter Surprise - 3rd	CC - ORNAMENT	ORNAMENT		1991	$10.75	$21.00
1991-QX421-9	Crayola Crayon - 3rd	CC - ORNAMENT	ORNAMENT		1991	$9.75	$24.00
1991-QX437-9	Hark! It's Herald - 3rd	CC - ORNAMENT	ORNAMENT		1991	$6.75	$18.00
1991-QX211-7	The Gift Bringers - 3rd	CC - ORNAMENT	ORNAMENT		1991	$5.00	$11.00
1991-QX427-9	Mary's Angels - 4th	CC - ORNAMENT	ORNAMENT		1991	$6.75	$23.00
1991-QX436-9	Collector's Plate - 5th	CC - ORNAMENT	ORNAMENT		1991	$8.75	$23.00
1991-QX433-9	Mr. And Mrs. Claus - 6th	CC - ORNAMENT	ORNAMENT		1991	$13.75	$26.00
1991-QX434-7	Reindeer Champs - 6th	CC - ORNAMENT	ORNAMENT		1991	$7.75	$20.50
1991-QX210-9	Betsey Clark - 6th/Final	CC - ORNAMENT	ORNAMENT		1991	$5.00	$17.00
1991-QX413-9	Nost. Houses And Shops - 8th	CC - ORNAMENT	ORNAMENT		1991	$14.75	$38.00
1991-QX308-9	Twelve Days of Christmas - 8th	CC - ORNAMENT	ORNAMENT		1991	$6.75	$16.50
1991-QX414-7	Rocking Horse - 11th	CC - ORNAMENT	ORNAMENT		1991	$10.75	$29.00
1991-QX434-9	Here Comes Santa - 13th	CC - ORNAMENT	ORNAMENT		1991	$14.75	$38.00
1991-QX432-7	Frosty Friends - 12th	CC - ORNAMENT	ORNAMENT		1991	$9.75	$27.50
1990-QX492-3	Here Comes Santa - 12th	CC - ORNAMENT	ORNAMENT		1990	$14.75	$30.00
1991-QLX719-9	Starship Enterprise	CC - ORNAMENT	ORNAMENT		1991	$20.00	$275.00
1983-QX110-9	Silver Bell	CC - ORNAMENT	ORNAMENT		1983	$12.00	$35.00
1987-XPR933-3	North Pole Power & Light	CC - ORNAMENT	ORNAMENT		1987	$2.95	$19.00
1990-QX504-6	Country Angel	CC - ORNAMENT	ORNAMENT		1990	$6.75	$71.00
1976-QX225-1	Happy Holidays Kissing Ball	CC - ORNAMENT	ORNAMENT		1976		
1977-QSD230-2	Angel Tree Topper	CC - ORNAMENT	ORNAMENT		1977	$9.00	$400.00
1977-QHD320-2	Holly & Poinsettia Table Dec.	CC - ORNAMENT	ORNAMENT		1977	$8.00	$130.00
1977-QX225-2	Mr. & Mrs. Snwman Kissing Ball	CC - ORNAMENT	ORNAMENT		1977	$5.00	$99.00
1977-QX225-5	Old Fash. Customs Kissing Ball	CC - ORNAMENT	ORNAMENT		1977	$5.00	
1978-QX702-3	Christmas Star Tree Topper	CC - ORNAMENT	ORNAMENT		1978	$7.50	$32.00
1978-QHD921-9	Heavenly Minstrel Tabletop	CC - ORNAMENT	ORNAMENT		1978	$35.00	$300.00
1978-QHD900-3	Holiday Memories Kissing Ball	CC - ORNAMENT	ORNAMENT		1978	$5.00	$80.00
1979-QHD950-7	Creche Tabletop Decoration	CC - ORNAMENT	ORNAMENT		1979	$25.00	$145.00
1979-QX159-9	Little Trimmer Set	CC - ORNAMENT	ORNAMENT		1979	$9.00	$280.00
1979-QX703-7	Tiffany Angel Tree Topper	CC - ORNAMENT	ORNAMENT		1979	$10.00	$26.00
1980-QX705-4	Brass Star Tree Topper	CC - ORNAMENT	ORNAMENT		1980	$25.00	$65.00
1980-QX353-4	Christmas Kitten Test Ornament	CC - ORNAMENT	ORNAMENT		1980	$4.00	
1980-QX352-1	Dove Test Ornament	CC - ORNAMENT	ORNAMENT		1980	$4.00	$195.00
1980-QHD925-4	Santa's Workshop Tabletop Dec.	CC - ORNAMENT	ORNAMENT		1980	$40.00	$152.00
1982-QMB900-7	Baby's First Christmas	CC - ORNAMENT	ORNAMENT		1982	$16.00	$77.00
1982-ITEM1	Brass Promotional Ornament	CC - ORNAMENT	ORNAMENT		1982	$3.50	$22.00
1982-QMB901-9	First Christmas Together	CC - ORNAMENT	ORNAMENT		1982	$16.00	$80.00
1982-QMB900-9	Love	CC - ORNAMENT	ORNAMENT		1982	$16.00	$70.00
1983-QMB903-9	Baby's First Christmas	CC - ORNAMENT	ORNAMENT		1983	$16.00	$71.00
1983-QMB904-7	Friendship	CC - ORNAMENT	ORNAMENT		1983	$16.00	$105.00
1983-QMB904-9	Nativity	CC - ORNAMENT	ORNAMENT		1983	$16.00	$77.00
1983-QHD406-9	St. Nicholas	CC - ORNAMENT	ORNAMENT		1983	$27.50	$90.00
1983-QMB415-9	Twelve Days Of Christmas Muscl	CC - ORNAMENT	ORNAMENT		1983	$15.00	$84.50
1984-QLX704-4	All Are Precious	CC - ORNAMENT	ORNAMENT		1984	$8.00	$21.00
1984-QTT710-1	Angel Tree Topper	CC - ORNAMENT	ORNAMENT		1984	$24.50	$35.00
1984-QLX702-1	Village Church	CC - ORNAMENT	ORNAMENT		1984	$15.00	$45.00
1984-QLX701-1	Sugarplum Cottage	CC - ORNAMENT	ORNAMENT		1984	$11.00	$45.00
1984-QLX701-4	City Lights	CC - ORNAMENT	ORNAMENT		1984	$10.00	$40.00
1984-QLX700-4	Santa's Workshop	CC - ORNAMENT	ORNAMENT		1984	$13.00	$45.00
1984-QLX702-4	Santa's Arrival	CC - ORNAMENT	ORNAMENT		1984	$13.00	$55.00
1984-QLX700-1	Nativity	CC - ORNAMENT	ORNAMENT		1984	$12.00	$21.00
1984-QLX703-1	Stained Glass	CC - ORNAMENT	ORNAMENT		1984	$8.00	$22.00
1984-QLX703-4	Christmas In The Forest	CC - ORNAMENT	ORNAMENT		1984	$8.00	$21.00
1984-QLX707-1	Brass Carousel	CC - ORNAMENT	ORNAMENT		1984	$9.00	$67.00
1985-QLX700-5	Baby's First Christmas	CC - ORNAMENT	ORNAMENT		1985	$16.50	$30.00
1985-QLX710-2	Katybeth	CC - ORNAMENT	ORNAMENT		1985	$10.75	$35.50
1985-QLX703-2	Chris Mouse - 1st	CC - ORNAMENT	ORNAMENT		1985	$12.50	$82.00
1985-QLX706-5	Swiss Cheese Lane	CC - ORNAMENT	ORNAMENT		1985	$13.00	$40.00
1985-QLX705-2	Mr. And Mrs. Santa	CC - ORNAMENT	ORNAMENT		1985	$14.50	$60.00

Order No.	Title	Type	Theme	Retired	Intro. Year	Retial Price	Secondary Price
1985-QLX711-2	Little Red Schoolhouse	CC - ORNAMENT	ORNAMENT		1985	$15.75	$85.00
1985-QLX702-5	Love Wreath	CC - ORNAMENT	ORNAMENT		1985	$8.50	$20.00
1985-QLX701-1	Sugarplum Cottage	CC - ORNAMENT	ORNAMENT		1985	$11.00	$44.00
1985-QLX702-1	Village Church	CC - ORNAMENT	ORNAMENT		1985	$15.00	$55.00
1985-QLX700-4	Santa's Workshop	CC - ORNAMENT	ORNAMENT		1985	$13.00	$55.00
1985-QLX700-1	Nativity	CC - ORNAMENT	ORNAMENT		1985	$12.00	
1985-QLX704-4	All Are Precious	CC - ORNAMENT	ORNAMENT		1985	$8.00	
1985-QLX710-5	Christmas Eve Visit	CC - ORNAMENT	ORNAMENT		1985	$12.00	$22.00
1985-QLX712-2	Season of Beauty	CC - ORNAMENT	ORNAMENT		1985	$8.00	$20.00
1985-QX300-5	Santa Claus	CC - ORNAMENT	ORNAMENT		1985	$6.75	$6.00
1985-QX300-2	Santa's Village	CC - ORNAMENT	ORNAMENT		1985	$6.75	$7.00
1986-QLX710-3	Baby's First Christmas	CC - ORNAMENT	ORNAMENT		1986	$19.50	$40.00
1986-QLX707-3	First Christmas Together	CC - ORNAMENT	ORNAMENT		1986	$14.00	$30.00
1986-QLX703-3	Santa And Sparky - 1st	CC - ORNAMENT	ORNAMENT		1986	$22.00	$70.00
1986-QLX704-3	Christmas Classics - 1st	CC - ORNAMENT	ORNAMENT		1986	$17.50	$68.00
1986-QLX705-6	Chris Mouse - 2nd	CC - ORNAMENT	ORNAMENT		1986	$13.00	$69.00
1986-QLX707-2	Village Express	CC - ORNAMENT	ORNAMENT		1986	$24.50	$72.50
1986-QLX701-2	Christmas Sleigh Ride	CC - ORNAMENT	ORNAMENT		1986	$24.50	$110.00
1986-QLX711-5	Santa's On His Way	CC - ORNAMENT	ORNAMENT		1986	$15.00	$50.00
1986-QLX705-3	General Store	CC - ORNAMENT	ORNAMENT		1986	$15.75	$49.00
1986-QLX708-3	Gentle Blessings	CC - ORNAMENT	ORNAMENT		1986	$15.00	$139.00
1986-QLX707-6	Keep On Glowin'!	CC - ORNAMENT	ORNAMENT		1986	$10.00	$35.00
1986-QLX706-6	Santa's Snack	CC - ORNAMENT	ORNAMENT		1986	$10.00	$47.00
1986-QLX709-3	Merry Christmas Bell	CC - ORNAMENT	ORNAMENT		1986	$8.50	$18.50
1986-QLX706-3	Sharing Friendship	CC - ORNAMENT	ORNAMENT		1986	$8.50	$17.00
1986-QLX705-2	Mr. And Mrs. Santa	CC - ORNAMENT	ORNAMENT		1986	$14.50	$99.00
1986-QLX701-1	Sugarplum Cottage	CC - ORNAMENT	ORNAMENT		1986	$11.00	$44.50
1986-QX0440-6	Santa And His Reindeer	CC - ORNAMENT	ORNAMENT		1986	$9.75	$29.00
1986-QX0279-6	Coca-Cola Santa	CC - ORNAMENT	ORNAMENT		1986	$4.75	$16.50
1986-QX0440-3	Old-Fashioned Santa	CC - ORNAMENT	ORNAMENT		1986	$12.75	$45.00
1986-QX0441-3	Santa's Panda Pal	CC - ORNAMENT	ORNAMENT		1986	$5.00	$17.50
1986-QX402-3	Marionette Angel	CC - ORNAMENT	ORNAMENT		1986	$8.50	$400.00
1986-QSP420-1	On The Right Track	CC - ORNAMENT	ORNAMENT		1986	$15.00	$31.00
1986-QT700-6	Santa Tree Topper	CC - ORNAMENT	ORNAMENT		1986	$18.00	$37.50
1986-QTT709-6	Shining Star Tree Topper	CC - ORNAMENT	ORNAMENT		1986	$17.50	$35.00
1987-QLX704-9	Baby's First Christmas	CC - ORNAMENT	ORNAMENT		1987	$13.50	$33.00
1987-QLX708-7	First Christmas Together	CC - ORNAMENT	ORNAMENT		1987	$11.50	$39.00
1987-QLX701-9	Santa And Sparky - 2nd	CC - ORNAMENT	ORNAMENT		1987	$19.50	$55.00
1987-QLX702-9	Christmas Classics - 2nd	CC - ORNAMENT	ORNAMENT		1987	$16.00	$48.00
1987-QLX705-7	Chris Mouse - 3rd	CC - ORNAMENT	ORNAMENT		1987	$11.00	$53.00
1987-QLX701-3	Christmas Morning	CC - ORNAMENT	ORNAMENT		1987	$24.50	$34.00
1987-QLX701-6	Loving Holiday	CC - ORNAMENT	ORNAMENT		1987	$22.00	$48.00
1987-QLX711-3	Angelic Messengers	CC - ORNAMENT	ORNAMENT		1987	$18.75	$61.00
1987-QLX704-6	Good Cheer Blimp	CC - ORNAMENT	ORNAMENT		1987	$16.00	$50.00
1987-QLX703-9	Train Station	CC - ORNAMENT	ORNAMENT		1987	$12.75	$41.00
1987-QLX704-7	Keeping Cozy	CC - ORNAMENT	ORNAMENT		1987	$11.75	$25.00
1987-QLX709-7	Lacy Brass Snowflake	CC - ORNAMENT	ORNAMENT		1987	$11.50	$19.00
1987-QLX708-9	Meowy Christmas!	CC - ORNAMENT	ORNAMENT		1987	$10.00	$55.00
1987-QLX706-7	Memories Are Forever Photo	CC - ORNAMENT	ORNAMENT		1987	$8.50	$22.00
1987-QLX706-9	Season For Friendship	CC - ORNAMENT	ORNAMENT		1987	$8.50	$18.00
1987-QLX705-9	Bright Noel	CC - ORNAMENT	ORNAMENT		1987	$7.00	$28.00
1987-QLX707-2	Village Express	CC - ORNAMENT	ORNAMENT		1987	$24.50	$110.00
1987-QLX707-6	Keep On Glowin'!	CC - ORNAMENT	ORNAMENT		1987	$10.00	$44.00
1987-QXC580-9	Wreath of Memories	CC - ORNAMENT	ORNAMENT		1987		$47.00
1987-QXC581-7	Carousel Reindeer	CC - ORNAMENT	ORNAMENT		1987	$8.00	$52.00
1987-QSP930-9	Emil Painter Elf	CC - ORNAMENT	ORNAMENT		1987	$10.00	$33.00
1987-QSP930-7	Hans Carpenter Elf	CC - ORNAMENT	ORNAMENT		1987	$10.00	$22.00
1987-QSP931-7	Kurt Blue Print Elf	CC - ORNAMENT	ORNAMENT		1987	$10.00	$20.00
1987-QSP927-9	Filling The Stocking	CC - ORNAMENT	ORNAMENT		1987	$50.00	$125.00
1988-QLX718-4	Baby's First Christmas	CC - ORNAMENT	ORNAMENT		1988	$24.00	$34.00
1988-QLX702-7	First Christmas Together	CC - ORNAMENT	ORNAMENT		1988	$12.00	$22.00
1988-QLX719-1	Santa And Sparky - 3rd/Final	CC - ORNAMENT	ORNAMENT		1988	$19.50	$29.00
1988-QLX716-1	Christmas Classics - 3rd	CC - ORNAMENT	ORNAMENT		1988	$15.00	$29.00
1988-QLX715-4	Chris Mouse - 4th	CC - ORNAMENT	ORNAMENT		1988	$8.75	$55.00
1988-QLX719-4	Parade of Toys	CC - ORNAMENT	ORNAMENT		1988	$24.50	$34.50
1988-QLX720-1	Skater's Waltz	CC - ORNAMENT	ORNAMENT		1988	$24.50	$39.00
1988-QLX718-1	Last-Minute Hug	CC - ORNAMENT	ORNAMENT		1988	$22.00	$37.00
1988-QLX716-4	Kitty Capers	CC - ORNAMENT	ORNAMENT		1988	$13.00	$35.50
1988-QLX717-1	Christmas Is Magic	CC - ORNAMENT	ORNAMENT		1988	$12.00	$37.00
1988-QLX711-4	Heavenly Glow	CC - ORNAMENT	ORNAMENT		1988	$11.75	$18.00
1988-QLX712-1	Radiant Tree	CC - ORNAMENT	ORNAMENT		1988	$11.75	$19.00
1988-QLX720-4	Festive Feeder	CC - ORNAMENT	ORNAMENT		1988	$11.50	$35.00
1988-QLX712-4	Circling The Globe	CC - ORNAMENT	ORNAMENT		1988	$10.50	$28.00
1988-QLX715-1	Bearly Reaching	CC - ORNAMENT	ORNAMENT		1988	$9.50	$28.00
1988-QLX713-4	Moonlit Nap	CC - ORNAMENT	ORNAMENT		1988	$8.75	$21.00
1988-QLX710-4	Tree Of Friendship	CC - ORNAMENT	ORNAMENT		1988	$8.50	$15.00
1988-QLX711-1	Song Of Christmas	CC - ORNAMENT	ORNAMENT		1988	$8.50	$16.50
1988-QLX701-3	Christmas Morning	CC - ORNAMENT	ORNAMENT		1988	$24.50	
1988-QLX721-1	Country Express	CC - ORNAMENT	ORNAMENT		1988	$24.50	$44.00
1988-QXC580-4	Our Clubhouse	CC - ORNAMENT	ORNAMENT		1988		$32.00
1988-QXC580-1	Sleighful Of Dreams	CC - ORNAMENT	ORNAMENT		1988	$8.00	$42.00
1988-QX406-4	Holiday Heirloom - 2nd - L.E.	CC - ORNAMENT	ORNAMENT		1988	$25.00	$25.00
1988-QX408-4	Angelic Minstrel - L.E.	CC - ORNAMENT	ORNAMENT		1988	$29.50	$35.00
1988-QX407-1	Christmas Is Sharing - L.E.	CC - ORNAMENT	ORNAMENT		1988	$17.50	$32.00
1988-QLX701-7	Kringle's Toy Shop	CC - ORNAMENT	ORNAMENT		1988	$24.50	$37.00
1989-QLX727-2	Baby's First Christmas	CC - ORNAMENT	ORNAMENT		1989	$30.00	$40.00
1989-QLX734-2	First Christmas Together	CC - ORNAMENT	ORNAMENT		1989	$17.50	$29.50
1989-QLX728-2	Forest Frolics - 1st	CC - ORNAMENT	ORNAMENT		1989	$24.50	$58.00
1989-QLX724-2	Christmas Classics - 4th	CC - ORNAMENT	ORNAMENT		1989	$13.50	$30.00
1989-QLX722-5	Chris Mouse - 5th	CC - ORNAMENT	ORNAMENT		1989	$9.50	$45.50
1989-QLX729-5	Joyous Carolers	CC - ORNAMENT	ORNAMENT		1989	$30.00	$52.00
1989-QLX717-4	Tiny Tinker	CC - ORNAMENT	ORNAMENT		1989	$19.50	$33.00
1989-QLX725-2	Rudolph The Red-Nosed Reindeer	CC - ORNAMENT	ORNAMENT		1989	$19.50	$48.00

Order No.	Title	Type	Theme	Retired	Intro. Year	Retail Price	Secondary Price
1989-QLX726-2	Loving Spoonful	CC - ORNAMENT	ORNAMENT		1989	$19.50	$28.00
1989-QLX722-2	Holiday Bell	CC - ORNAMENT	ORNAMENT		1989	$17.50	$25.00
1989-QLX724-5	Busy Beaver	CC - ORNAMENT	ORNAMENT		1989	$17.50	$40.00
1989-QLX721-5	Backstage Bear	CC - ORNAMENT	ORNAMENT		1989	$13.50	$23.00
1989-QLX723-2	The Animals Speak	CC - ORNAMENT	ORNAMENT		1989	$13.50	$75.00
1989-QLX720-2	Angel Melody	CC - ORNAMENT	ORNAMENT		1989	$9.50	$16.50
1989-QLX723-5	Unicorn Fantasy	CC - ORNAMENT	ORNAMENT		1989	$9.50	$16.50
1989-QLX713-4	Moonlit Nap	CC - ORNAMENT	ORNAMENT		1989	$8.75	$25.00
1989-QLX701-7	Kringle's Toy Shop	CC - ORNAMENT	ORNAMENT		1989	$24.50	$55.00
1989-QLX727-5	Metro Express	CC - ORNAMENT	ORNAMENT		1989	$28.00	$52.00
1989-QLX728-5	Spirit Of St. Nick	CC - ORNAMENT	ORNAMENT		1989	$24.50	$52.00
1989-QXC580-2	Visit From Santa	CC - ORNAMENT	ORNAMENT		1989		$31.00
1989-QXC428-5	Collect A Dream	CC - ORNAMENT	ORNAMENT		1989	$9.00	$41.00
1989-QXC451-2	Christmas Is Peaceful - L.E.	CC - ORNAMENT	ORNAMENT		1989	$18.50	$30.00
1989-QXC448-3	Noelle - L.E.	CC - ORNAMENT	ORNAMENT		1989	$19.75	$41.00
1989-QXC460-5	Holiday Heirloom - 3rd/F - LE	CC - ORNAMENT	ORNAMENT		1989	$25.00	$25.00
1989-XPR971-9	Snow, Carousel Horse	CC - ORNAMENT	ORNAMENT		1989	$3.95	$23.00
1989-XPR972-2	Holly, Carousel Horse	CC - ORNAMENT	ORNAMENT		1989	$3.95	$16.00
1989-XPR972-0	Star, Carousel Horse	CC - ORNAMENT	ORNAMENT		1989	$3.95	$16.50
1989-XPR972-1	Ginger, Carousel Horse	CC - ORNAMENT	ORNAMENT		1989	$3.95	$18.00
1989-XPR972-3	Carousel Display Stand	CC - ORNAMENT	ORNAMENT		1989	$1.00	$9.00
1990-QLX724-6	Baby's First Christmas	CC - ORNAMENT	ORNAMENT		1990	$28.00	$38.00
1990-QLX725-5	First Christmas Together	CC - ORNAMENT	ORNAMENT		1990	$18.00	$30.00
1990-QLX723-6	Forest Frolics - 2nd	CC - ORNAMENT	ORNAMENT		1990	$25.00	$42.00
1990-QLX730-3	Christmas Classics - 5th/Final	CC - ORNAMENT	ORNAMENT		1990	$14.00	$26.00
1990-QLX729-6	Chris Mouse - 6th	CC - ORNAMENT	ORNAMENT		1990	$10.00	$28.00
1990-QLX727-6	Christmas Memories	CC - ORNAMENT	ORNAMENT		1990	$25.00	$38.00
1990-QLX725-6	Santa's Ho-Ho-Hoedown	CC - ORNAMENT	ORNAMENT		1990	$25.00	$63.00
1990-QLX726-3	Mrs. Santa's Kitchen	CC - ORNAMENT	ORNAMENT		1990	$25.00	$43.00
1990-QLX725-3	Song And Dance	CC - ORNAMENT	ORNAMENT		1990	$20.00	$69.50
1990-QLX726-5	Elfin Whittler	CC - ORNAMENT	ORNAMENT		1990	$20.00	$34.00
1990-QLX733-6	Starship Christmas	CC - ORNAMENT	ORNAMENT		1990	$18.00	$38.00
1990-QLX721-3	Deer Crossing	CC - ORNAMENT	ORNAMENT		1990	$18.00	$34.00
1990-QLX733-3	Holiday Flash	CC - ORNAMENT	ORNAMENT		1990	$18.00	$28.00
1990-QLX722-6	Letter To Santa	CC - ORNAMENT	ORNAMENT		1990	$14.00	$19.00
1990-QLX730-6	Starlight Angel	CC - ORNAMENT	ORNAMENT		1990	$14.00	$21.00
1990-QLX736-3	Blessings of Love	CC - ORNAMENT	ORNAMENT		1990	$14.00	$35.00
1990-QLX721-2	Partridges In A Pear	CC - ORNAMENT	ORNAMENT		1990	$14.00	$19.00
1990-QLX732-6	Beary Short Nap	CC - ORNAMENT	ORNAMENT		1990	$10.00	$19.50
1990-QLX735-6	Elf Of The Year	CC - ORNAMENT	ORNAMENT		1990	$10.00	$16.00
1990-QLX724-3	Children's Express	CC - ORNAMENT	ORNAMENT		1990	$28.00	$46.00
1990-QLX735-3	Hop 'N Pop Popper	CC - ORNAMENT	ORNAMENT		1990	$20.00	$70.00
1990-QXC445-6	Club Hollow	CC - ORNAMENT	ORNAMENT		1990		$23.00
1990-QXC445-3	Armful Of Joy	CC - ORNAMENT	ORNAMENT		1990	$9.75	$30.00
1990-QXC447-6	Dove Of Peace - L.E.	CC - ORNAMENT	ORNAMENT		1990	$24.75	$46.50
1990-QXC447-3	Sugar Plum Fairy - L.E.	CC - ORNAMENT	ORNAMENT		1990	$27.75	$39.50
1990-QXC476-6	Christmas Limited - L.E.	CC - ORNAMENT	ORNAMENT		1990	$19.75	$84.00
1991-QX223-7	Mary Englebreit	CC - ORNAMENT	ORNAMENT		1991	$4.75	$13.50
1991-QX534-7	On a Roll	CC - ORNAMENT	ORNAMENT		1991	$6.75	$13.50
1991-QX504-7	Up 'N' Down Journey	CC - ORNAMENT	ORNAMENT		1991	$9.75	$16.00
1991-QX536-7	Sweet Talk	CC - ORNAMENT	ORNAMENT		1991	$8.75	$16.00
1991-QLX724-7	Baby's First Christmas	CC - ORNAMENT	ORNAMENT		1991	$30.00	$50.50
1991-QLX713-7	First Christmas Together	CC - ORNAMENT	ORNAMENT		1991	$25.00	$28.00
1991-QLX716-9	Friendship Tree	CC - ORNAMENT	ORNAMENT		1991	$10.00	$17.50
1991-QLX722-9	Peanuts - 1st	CC - ORNAMENT	ORNAMENT		1991	$18.00	$51.00
1991-QLX721-9	Forest Frolics - 3rd	CC - ORNAMENT	ORNAMENT		1991	$25.00	$49.00
1991-QLX720-7	Chris Mouse - 7th	CC - ORNAMENT	ORNAMENT		1991	$10.00	$32.00
1991-QLX732-3	Jingle Bears	CC - ORNAMENT	ORNAMENT		1991	$25.00	$24.50
1991-QLX724-9	Bringing Home The Tree	CC - ORNAMENT	ORNAMENT		1991	$28.00	$42.00
1991-QLX726-6	Ski Trip	CC - ORNAMENT	ORNAMENT		1991	$28.00	$41.50
1991-QLX711-9	Kringle's Bumper Cars	CC - ORNAMENT	ORNAMENT		1991	$25.00	$41.50
1991-QLX712-9	Toyland Tower	CC - ORNAMENT	ORNAMENT		1991	$20.00	$33.00
1991-QLX723-7	It's A Wonderful Life	CC - ORNAMENT	ORNAMENT		1991	$20.00	$50.50
1991-QLX714-9	Mole Family Home	CC - ORNAMENT	ORNAMENT		1991	$20.00	$33.00
1991-QLX715-9	Santa's Hot Line	CC - ORNAMENT	ORNAMENT		1991	$18.00	$30.00
1991-QLX715-7	Sparkling Angel	CC - ORNAMENT	ORNAMENT		1991	$18.00	$25.50
1991-QLX714-7	Father Christmas	CC - ORNAMENT	ORNAMENT		1991	$14.00	$32.00
1991-QLX717-7	Holiday Glow	CC - ORNAMENT	ORNAMENT		1991	$14.00	$25.00
1991-QLX717-9	Festive Brass Church	CC - ORNAMENT	ORNAMENT		1991	$14.00	$20.00
1991-QLX720-9	Elfin Engineer	CC - ORNAMENT	ORNAMENT		1991	$10.00	$14.50
1991-QLX727-3	Salvation Army Band	CC - ORNAMENT	ORNAMENT		1991	$30.00	$47.00
1991-QLX711-7	Arctic Dome	CC - ORNAMENT	ORNAMENT		1991	$25.00	$36.00
1991-QLX716-7	Santa Special - S.E.	CC - ORNAMENT	ORNAMENT		1991	$40.00	$58.00
1991-QXC476-9	Hidden Treasure	CC - ORNAMENT	ORNAMENT		1991	$15.00	$28.50
1991-QXC725-9	Beary Artistic	CC - ORNAMENT	ORNAMENT		1991	$10.00	$35.00
1991-QXC479-7	Secrets For Santa - L.E.	CC - ORNAMENT	ORNAMENT		1991	$23.75	$50.00
1991-QXC477-9	Galloping Into Christmas - LE	CC - ORNAMENT	ORNAMENT		1991	$19.75	$65.00
1991-QXC315-9	Five Years Together	CC - ORNAMENT	ORNAMENT		1991		$34.00
1991-QX523-7	Santa's Premiere	CC - ORNAMENT	ORNAMENT		1991	$10.75	$30.00
1991-XPR973-3	Caboose, Claus & Co. R.R.	CC - ORNAMENT	ORNAMENT		1991	$3.95	$12.50
1991-XPR973-1	Gift Car, Claus & Co. R.R.	CC - ORNAMENT	ORNAMENT		1991	$3.95	$12.50
1991-XPR973-0	Locomotive, Claus & Co. R.R.	CC - ORNAMENT	ORNAMENT		1991	$3.95	$28.00
1991-XPR973-2	Passenger Car, Claus & Co. RR	CC - ORNAMENT	ORNAMENT		1991	$3.95	$12.00
1991-XPR973-4	Trestle, Claus & Co. R.R.	CC - ORNAMENT	ORNAMENT		1991	$2.95	$8.50
1991-QX524-9	Flag Of Liberty	CC - ORNAMENT	ORNAMENT		1991	$6.75	$9.50
1991-ITEM2	Kansas City Santa - S.E.	CC - ORNAMENT	ORNAMENT		1991		$825.00
1992-QX489-1	Tobin Fraley Carousel - 1st	CC - ORNAMENT	ORNAMENT		1992	$28.00	$33.00
1992-QX454-4	Owliver - 1st	CC - ORNAMENT	ORNAMENT		1992	$7.75	$15.00
1992-QX210-4	Betsey's Country Christmas-1st	CC - ORNAMENT	ORNAMENT		1992	$5.00	$22.00
1992-QX428-4	Classic American Cars - 2nd	CC - ORNAMENT	ORNAMENT		1992	$12.75	$40.00
1992-QX517-4	Peace On Earth - 2nd	CC - ORNAMENT	ORNAMENT		1992	$11.75	$36.00
1992-QX445-4	Heavenly Angels - 2nd	CC - ORNAMENT	ORNAMENT		1992	$7.75	$17.00
1992-QX448-4	Puppy Love - 2nd	CC - ORNAMENT	ORNAMENT		1992	$7.75	$38.00

Order No.	Title	Type	Theme	Retired	Intro. Year	Retial Price	Secondary Price
1992-QX441-4	Merry Olde Santa - 3rd	CC - ORNAMENT	ORNAMENT		1992	$14.75	$23.00
1992-QX441-1	Heart of Christmas - 3rd	CC - ORNAMENT	ORNAMENT		1992	$13.75	$23.00
1992-QX424-4	Fabulous Decade - 3rd	CC - ORNAMENT	ORNAMENT		1992	$7.75	$34.00
1992-QX426-4	Crayola Crayon - 4th	CC - ORNAMENT	ORNAMENT		1992	$9.75	$32.00
1992-QX212-4	The Gift Bringers - 4th	CC - ORNAMENT	ORNAMENT		1992	$5.00	$15.50
1992-QX427-4	Mary's Angels - 5th	CC - ORNAMENT	ORNAMENT		1992	$6.75	$45.00
1992-QX429-4	Mr. And Mrs. Claus - 7th	CC - ORNAMENT	ORNAMENT		1992	$14.75	$32.00
1992-QX528-4	Reindeer Champs - 7th	CC - ORNAMENT	ORNAMENT		1992	$8.75	$26.00
1992-QX425-4	Nost. Houses And Shops - 9th	CC - ORNAMENT	ORNAMENT		1992	$14.75	$34.00
1992-QX303-1	Twelve Days of Chrstmas - 9th	CC - ORNAMENT	ORNAMENT		1992	$6.75	$16.00
1992-QX426-1	Rocking Horse - 12th	CC - ORNAMENT	ORNAMENT		1992	$10.75	$28.00
1992-QX429-1	Frosty Friends - 13th	CC - ORNAMENT	ORNAMENT		1992	$9.75	$23.00
1992-QX434-1	Here Comes Santa - 14th	CC - ORNAMENT	ORNAMENT		1992	$14.75	$25.00
1992-QX425-1	Greatest Story - 3rd and Final	CC - ORNAMENT	ORNAMENT		1992	$12.75	$18.00
1992-QX427-1	Winter Surprise - 4th/Final	CC - ORNAMENT	ORNAMENT		1992	$11.75	$23.00
1992-QX446-4	Hark! It's Herald - 4th/Final	CC - ORNAMENT	ORNAMENT		1992	$7.75	$14.00
1992-QX446-1	Collector's Plate - 6th/Final	CC - ORNAMENT	ORNAMENT		1992	$8.75	$16.00
1992-QX498-4	Mother Goose	CC - ORNAMENT	ORNAMENT		1992	$13.75	$23.50
1992-QX593-1	Elfin Marionette	CC - ORNAMENT	ORNAMENT		1992	$11.75	$20.00
1992-QX491-4	Polar Post	CC - ORNAMENT	ORNAMENT		1992	$8.75	$18.00
1992-QX499-1	Turtle Dreams	CC - ORNAMENT	ORNAMENT		1992	$8.75	$18.00
1992-QX500-1	Uncle Art's Ice Cream	CC - ORNAMENT	ORNAMENT		1992	$8.75	$19.00
1992-QX593-4	Stocked With Joy	CC - ORNAMENT	ORNAMENT		1992	$7.75	$17.00
1992-QX455-4	Dickens Caroler Bell - 3rd	CC - ORNAMENT	ORNAMENT		1992	$21.75	$28.00
1992-QX458-1	Baby's First Christmas	CC - ORNAMENT	ORNAMENT		1992	$18.75	$28.00
1992-QX464-1	Baby's First Christmas Photo	CC - ORNAMENT	ORNAMENT		1992	$7.75	$22.00
1992-QX220-4	Baby's First Christmas - Girl	CC - ORNAMENT	ORNAMENT		1992	$4.75	$12.00
1992-QX219-1	Baby's First Christmas - Boy	CC - ORNAMENT	ORNAMENT		1992	$4.75	$12.00
1992-QX518-4	For My Grandma Photoholder	CC - ORNAMENT	ORNAMENT		1992	$7.75	$11.50
1992-QX457-4	A Child's Christmas	CC - ORNAMENT	ORNAMENT		1992	$9.75	$18.00
1992-QX462-1	Grandson's First Christmas	CC - ORNAMENT	ORNAMENT		1992	$6.75	$12.50
1992-QX463-4	Granddaughter's First Chrstmas	CC - ORNAMENT	ORNAMENT		1992	$6.75	$15.00
1992-QX461-4	Mom-To-Be	CC - ORNAMENT	ORNAMENT		1992	$6.75	$15.00
1992-QX461-1	Dad-To-Be	CC - ORNAMENT	ORNAMENT		1992	$6.75	$10.00
1992-QX464-4	Baby's First Christmas	CC - ORNAMENT	ORNAMENT		1992	$7.75	$19.00
1992-QX465-1	Baby's Second Christmas	CC - ORNAMENT	ORNAMENT		1992	$6.75	$18.00
1992-QX465-4	Child's Third Christmas	CC - ORNAMENT	ORNAMENT		1992	$6.75	$16.50
1992-QX466-1	Child's Fourth Christmas	CC - ORNAMENT	ORNAMENT		1992	$6.75	$19.00
1992-QX466-4	Child's Fifth Christmas	CC - ORNAMENT	ORNAMENT		1992	$6.75	$15.00
1992-QX484-4	For The One I Love	CC - ORNAMENT	ORNAMENT		1992	$9.75	$18.00
1992-QX506-1	Our First Christmas Together	CC - ORNAMENT	ORNAMENT		1992	$9.75	$14.00
1992-QX469-4	Our First Christmas Tog. Photo	CC - ORNAMENT	ORNAMENT		1992	$8.75	$14.50
1992-QX301-1	Our First Christmas Together	CC - ORNAMENT	ORNAMENT		1992	$6.75	$8.50
1992-QX484-1	Love To Skate	CC - ORNAMENT	ORNAMENT		1992	$8.75	$14.00
1992-QX485-1	Anniversary Year Photoholder	CC - ORNAMENT	ORNAMENT		1992	$9.75	$13.00
1992-QX467-4	Dad	CC - ORNAMENT	ORNAMENT		1992	$7.75	$12.00
1992-QX516-4	Mom	CC - ORNAMENT	ORNAMENT		1992	$7.75	$14.50
1992-QX468-4	Brother	CC - ORNAMENT	ORNAMENT		1992	$6.75	$10.00
1992-QX468-1	Sister	CC - ORNAMENT	ORNAMENT		1992	$6.75	$14.50
1992-QX502-4	Son	CC - ORNAMENT	ORNAMENT		1992	$6.75	$17.50
1992-QX503-1	Daughter	CC - ORNAMENT	ORNAMENT		1992	$6.75	$14.00
1992-QX467-1	Mom And Dad	CC - ORNAMENT	ORNAMENT		1992	$9.75	$35.00
1992-QX200-4	Grandparents	CC - ORNAMENT	ORNAMENT		1992	$4.75	$12.00
1992-QX201-1	Grandmother	CC - ORNAMENT	ORNAMENT		1992	$4.75	$12.00
1992-QX594-1	Godchild	CC - ORNAMENT	ORNAMENT		1992	$6.75	$9.50
1992-QX560-4	Granddaughter	CC - ORNAMENT	ORNAMENT		1992	$6.75	$15.00
1992-QX561-1	Grandson	CC - ORNAMENT	ORNAMENT		1992	$6.75	$16.00
1992-QX503-4	Friendship Line	CC - ORNAMENT	ORNAMENT		1992	$9.75	$26.00
1992-QX504-1	Friendly Greetings	CC - ORNAMENT	ORNAMENT		1992	$7.75	$11.00
1992-QX519-1	New Home	CC - ORNAMENT	ORNAMENT		1992	$8.75	$15.50
1992-QX304-4	Across The Miles	CC - ORNAMENT	ORNAMENT		1992	$6.75	$12.00
1992-QX213-1	From Our Home To Yours	CC - ORNAMENT	ORNAMENT		1992	$4.75	$9.50
1992-QX542-4	Secret Pal	CC - ORNAMENT	ORNAMENT		1992	$7.75	$12.50
1992-QX226-4	Teacher	CC - ORNAMENT	ORNAMENT		1992	$4.75	$12.00
1992-QX505-4	World-Class Teacher	CC - ORNAMENT	ORNAMENT		1992	$7.75	$15.50
1992-QX505-1	V.P. Of Important Stuff	CC - ORNAMENT	ORNAMENT		1992	$6.75	$13.00
1992-QX504-4	Holiday Memo	CC - ORNAMENT	ORNAMENT		1992	$7.75	$12.00
1992-QX542-1	Special Dog Photoholder	CC - ORNAMENT	ORNAMENT		1992	$7.75	$22.00
1992-QX541-4	Special Cat Photoholder	CC - ORNAMENT	ORNAMENT		1992	$7.75	$13.00
1992-QX524-4	Eric The Baker	CC - ORNAMENT	ORNAMENT		1992	$8.75	$17.00
1992-QX525-4	Otto The Carpenter	CC - ORNAMENT	ORNAMENT		1992	$8.75	$18.00
1992-QX525-1	Max The Tailor	CC - ORNAMENT	ORNAMENT		1992	$8.75	$18.00
1992-QX526-1	Franz The Artist	CC - ORNAMENT	ORNAMENT		1992	$8.75	$19.00
1992-QX526-4	Frieda The Animals' Friend	CC - ORNAMENT	ORNAMENT		1992	$8.75	$18.00
1992-QX528-1	Ludwig The Musician	CC - ORNAMENT	ORNAMENT		1992	$8.75	$17.00
1992-QX532-4	Silver Star	CC - ORNAMENT	ORNAMENT		1992	$28.00	$51.00
1992-QX531-1	Locomotive, Christmas Sky Line	CC - ORNAMENT	ORNAMENT		1992	$9.75	$33.00
1992-QX540-1	Coal Car, Christmas Sky Line	CC - ORNAMENT	ORNAMENT		1992	$9.75	$17.00
1992-QX531-4	Stock Car, Christmas Sky Line	CC - ORNAMENT	ORNAMENT		1992	$9.75	$17.50
1992-QX532-1	Caboose, Christmas Sky Line	CC - ORNAMENT	ORNAMENT		1992	$9.75	$19.00
1992-QX510-4	North Pole Fire Fighter	CC - ORNAMENT	ORNAMENT		1992	$9.75	$18.50
1992-QX509-4	Rapid Delivery	CC - ORNAMENT	ORNAMENT		1992	$8.75	$15.00
1992-QX517-1	Gone Wishin'	CC - ORNAMENT	ORNAMENT		1992	$8.75	$16.50
1992-QX521-4	Skiing 'Round	CC - ORNAMENT	ORNAMENT		1992	$8.75	$17.00
1992-QX510-1	Green Thumb Santa	CC - ORNAMENT	ORNAMENT		1992	$7.75	$13.00
1992-QX598-4	Golf's A Ball	CC - ORNAMENT	ORNAMENT		1992	$6.75	$18.00
1992-QX599-1	A Santa-Full!	CC - ORNAMENT	ORNAMENT		1992	$9.75	$24.00
1992-QX599-4	Tasty Christmas	CC - ORNAMENT	ORNAMENT		1992	$9.75	$17.50
1992-QX508-4	Santa's Roundup	CC - ORNAMENT	ORNAMENT		1992	$8.75	$18.00
1992-QX520-4	Deck The Hogs	CC - ORNAMENT	ORNAMENT		1992	$8.75	$19.00
1992-QX523-4	Partridge IN A Pear Tree	CC - ORNAMENT	ORNAMENT		1992	$8.75	$14.50
1992-QX523-1	Spirit Of Christmas Stress	CC - ORNAMENT	ORNAMENT		1992	$8.75	$14.50
1992-QX529-1	Please Pause Here	CC - ORNAMENT	ORNAMENT		1992	$14.75	$25.00

Order No.	Title	Type	Theme	Retired	Intro. Year	Retail Price	Secondary Price
1992-QX595-4	Snoopy And Woodstock (Skating)	CC - ORNAMENT	ORNAMENT		1992	$8.75	$26.00
1992-QX537-4	Garfield	CC - ORNAMENT	ORNAMENT		1992	$7.75	$17.00
1992-QX222-4	Norman Rockwell Art	CC - ORNAMENT	ORNAMENT		1992	$5.00	$17.00
1992-QX224-4	Peanuts	CC - ORNAMENT	ORNAMENT		1992	$5.00	$15.00
1992-QX561-4	Owl	CC - ORNAMENT	ORNAMENT		1992	$9.75	$17.50
1992-QX507-4	Santa Maria	CC - ORNAMENT	ORNAMENT		1992	$12.75	$16.00
1992-QX513-4	Fun On A Big Scale	CC - ORNAMENT	ORNAMENT		1992	$10.75	$17.00
1992-QX537-1	Genius At Work	CC - ORNAMENT	ORNAMENT		1992	$10.75	$18.00
1992-QX514-1	Hello-Ho-Ho	CC - ORNAMENT	ORNAMENT		1992	$9.75	$16.50
1992-QX515-4	Cheerful Santa	CC - ORNAMENT	ORNAMENT		1992	$9.75	$21.00
1992-QX516-1	Memories To Cherish Photohlder	CC - ORNAMENT	ORNAMENT		1992	$10.75	$15.00
1992-QX509-1	Tread Bear	CC - ORNAMENT	ORNAMENT		1992	$8.75	$18.00
1992-QX511-4	Merry Swiss Mouse	CC - ORNAMENT	ORNAMENT		1992	$7.75	$13.50
1992-QX506-4	Honest George	CC - ORNAMENT	ORNAMENT		1992	$7.75	$17.00
1992-QX507-1	Bear Bell Champ	CC - ORNAMENT	ORNAMENT		1992	$7.75	$12.50
1992-QX512-1	Egg Nog Nest	CC - ORNAMENT	ORNAMENT		1992	$7.75	$14.50
1992-QX302-4	Jesus Loves Me	CC - ORNAMENT	ORNAMENT		1992	$7.75	$11.50
1992-QX515-1	Loving Shepherd	CC - ORNAMENT	ORNAMENT		1992	$7.75	$14.00
1992-QX545-9	Toboggan Tail	CC - ORNAMENT	ORNAMENT		1992	$7.75	$16.50
1992-QX514-4	Down-Under Holiday	CC - ORNAMENT	ORNAMENT		1992	$7.75	$13.00
1992-QX513-1	Holiday Wishes	CC - ORNAMENT	ORNAMENT		1992	$7.75	$14.00
1992-QX518-1	Feliz Navidad (Guitar)	CC - ORNAMENT	ORNAMENT		1992	$6.75	$17.50
1992-QX543-1	Holiday Teatime	CC - ORNAMENT	ORNAMENT		1992	$14.75	$22.00
1992-QX543-4	Santa's Hook Shot	CC - ORNAMENT	ORNAMENT		1992	$12.75	$21.00
1992-QX547-4	Cool Fliers	CC - ORNAMENT	ORNAMENT		1992	$10.75	$16.50
1992-QLX721-4	Peanuts - 2nd	CC - ORNAMENT	ORNAMENT		1992	$18.00	$30.00
1992-QLX725-4	Forest Frolics - 4th	CC - ORNAMENT	ORNAMENT		1992	$28.00	$55.00
1992-QLX707-4	Chris Mouse - 8th	CC - ORNAMENT	ORNAMENT		1992	$12.00	$28.00
1992-QLX716-7	Santa Special - S.E.	CC - ORNAMENT	ORNAMENT		1992	$40.00	$79.00
1992-QLX726-4	Continental Express	CC - ORNAMENT	ORNAMENT		1992	$32.00	$61.00
1992-QLX709-4	Look! It's Santa	CC - ORNAMENT	ORNAMENT		1992	$14.00	$26.00
1992-QLX726-1	The Dancing Nutcracker	CC - ORNAMENT	ORNAMENT		1992	$30.00	$45.00
1992-QLX727-4	Enchanted Clock	CC - ORNAMENT	ORNAMENT		1992	$30.00	$50.00
1992-QLX727-1	Christmas Parade	CC - ORNAMENT	ORNAMENT		1992	$30.00	$51.00
1992-QLX724-4	Good Sledding Ahead	CC - ORNAMENT	ORNAMENT		1992	$28.00	$45.00
1992-QLX731-4	Yuletide Rider	CC - ORNAMENT	ORNAMENT		1992	$28.00	$45.00
1992-QLX724-1	Santa's Answering Machine	CC - ORNAMENT	ORNAMENT		1992	$22.00	$23.50
1992-QLX728-1	Baby's First Christmas	CC - ORNAMENT	ORNAMENT		1992	$22.00	$75.00
1992-QLX722-1	Our First Christmas Together	CC - ORNAMENT	ORNAMENT		1992	$20.00	$38.00
1992-QLX732-1	Santa Sub	CC - ORNAMENT	ORNAMENT		1992	$18.00	$38.00
1992-QLX723-1	Lighting The Way	CC - ORNAMENT	ORNAMENT		1992	$18.00	$35.00
1992-QLX732-4	Under Construction	CC - ORNAMENT	ORNAMENT		1992	$18.00	$32.00
1992-QLX709-1	Feathered Friends	CC - ORNAMENT	ORNAMENT		1992	$14.00	$27.00
1992-QLX708-4	Watch Owls	CC - ORNAMENT	ORNAMENT		1992	$12.00	$20.00
1992-QLX708-1	Nut Sweet Nut	CC - ORNAMENT	ORNAMENT		1992	$10.00	$18.00
1991-QLT723-9	Angel Of Light	CC - ORNAMENT	ORNAMENT		1991	$30.00	$43.00
1992-QXC508-1	Rodney Takes Flight	CC - ORNAMENT	ORNAMENT		1992		$19.00
1992-QXC729-1	Santa's Club List	CC - ORNAMENT	ORNAMENT		1992	$15.00	$27.00
1992-QXC406-7	Victorian Skater - L.E.	CC - ORNAMENT	ORNAMENT		1992	$25.00	$52.00
1992-QXC546-4	Christmas Treasures - L.E.	CC - ORNAMENT	ORNAMENT		1992	$22.00	$155.00
1992-QLX733-1	Shuttlecraft Galileo	CC - ORNAMENT	ORNAMENT		1992	$24.00	$45.00
1992-QX562-4	Elvis	CC - ORNAMENT	ORNAMENT		1992	$14.75	$21.50
1986-QSP420-4	Toymaker - 1st - L.E.	CC - ORNAMENT	ORNAMENT		1986		$74.00
1987-QSP433-7	Toymaker - 2nd - L.E.	CC - ORNAMENT	ORNAMENT		1987	$27.50	$50.00
1988-QSP413-1	Toymaker - 3rd - L.E.	CC - ORNAMENT	ORNAMENT		1988	$27.50	$45.00
1989-QSP9302	Toymaker - 4th - L.E.	CC - ORNAMENT	ORNAMENT		1989		$42.50
1987-QSP927-7	Special Delivery - L.E.	CC - ORNAMENT	ORNAMENT		1987		$80.00
1987-QSP925-7	The Journey Begins - L.E.	CC - ORNAMENT	ORNAMENT		1987		$73.50
1985-QTT625	Angel - Country	CC - ORNAMENT	ORNAMENT		1985		$26.00
1989-QEC9261	First Noel Porcelain Creche	CC - ORNAMENT	ORNAMENT		1989		$49.00
1986-QTT711-6	Angel	CC - ORNAMENT	ORNAMENT		1986		$59.50
1986-QTT712	Country Holiday Goose	CC - ORNAMENT	ORNAMENT		1986		$45.00
1986-QLT709	Tree Topper	CC - ORNAMENT	ORNAMENT		1986		
1993-QX561-2	Tannenbaum's Dept Store	CC - ORNAMENT	ORNAMENT		1993	$26.00	$37.00
1993-QX567-5	Shopping With Santa	CC - ORNAMENT	ORNAMENT		1993	$24.00	$24.50
1993-QX568-2	Frosty Friends	CC - ORNAMENT	ORNAMENT		1993	$20.00	$31.00
1993-QX528-2	Mother Goose - 1st	CC - ORNAMENT	ORNAMENT		1993	$13.75	$26.00
1993-QX529-2	U.S. Christmas Stamps - 1st	CC - ORNAMENT	ORNAMENT		1993	$10.75	$23.00
1993-QX531-5	The Peanuts Gang - 1st	CC - ORNAMENT	ORNAMENT		1993	$9.75	$35.50
1993-QX550-2	Tobin Fraley Carousel - 2nd	CC - ORNAMENT	ORNAMENT		1993	$28.00	$31.50
1993-QX542-5	Owliver - 2nd	CC - ORNAMENT	ORNAMENT		1993	$7.75	$16.50
1993-QX206-2	Betsey's Country Christmas-2nd	CC - ORNAMENT	ORNAMENT		1993	$5.00	$14.00
1993-QX527-5	Classic American Cars - 3rd	CC - ORNAMENT	ORNAMENT		1993	$12.75	$30.00
1993-QX504-5	Puppy Love - 3rd	CC - ORNAMENT	ORNAMENT		1993	$7.75	$16.00
1993-QX448-2	Heart of Christmas - 4th	CC - ORNAMENT	ORNAMENT		1993	$14.75	$25.00
1993-QX484-2	Merry Olde Santa - 4th	CC - ORNAMENT	ORNAMENT		1993	$14.75	$22.00
1993-QX447-5	Fabulous Decade - 4th	CC - ORNAMENT	ORNAMENT		1993	$7.75	$13.50
1993-QX442-2	Crayola Crayon - 5th	CC - ORNAMENT	ORNAMENT		1993	$10.75	$16.50
1993-QX428-2	Mary's Angels - 6th	CC - ORNAMENT	ORNAMENT		1993	$6.75	$16.00
1993-QX420-2	Mr. And Mrs. Claus - 8th	CC - ORNAMENT	ORNAMENT		1993	$14.75	$22.00
1993-QX417-5	Nost. Houses And Shops - 10th	CC - ORNAMENT	ORNAMENT		1993	$14.75	$26.00
1993-QX301-2	Twelve Days of Chrstmas - 10th	CC - ORNAMENT	ORNAMENT		1993	$6.75	$12.00
1993-QX416-2	Rocking Horse - 13th	CC - ORNAMENT	ORNAMENT		1993	$10.75	$30.00
1993-QX414-2	Frosty Friends - 14th	CC - ORNAMENT	ORNAMENT		1993	$9.75	$19.50
1993-QX410-2	Here Comes Santa - 15th	CC - ORNAMENT	ORNAMENT		1993	$14.75	$27.00
1993-QX524-2	Peace On Earth - 3rd and Final	CC - ORNAMENT	ORNAMENT		1993	$11.75	$18.00
1993-QX494-5	Heavenly Angels - 3rd/Final	CC - ORNAMENT	ORNAMENT		1993	$7.75	$14.00
1993-QX206-5	The Gift Bringers - 5th/Final	CC - ORNAMENT	ORNAMENT		1993	$5.00	$17.00
1993-QX433-1	Reindeer Champs - 8th/Final	CC - ORNAMENT	ORNAMENT		1993	$8.75	$17.50
1993-QX526-5	On Her Toes	CC - ORNAMENT	ORNAMENT		1993	$8.75	$16.00
1993-QX526-2	Wake-Up Call	CC - ORNAMENT	ORNAMENT		1993	$8.75	$14.00
1993-QX525-5	Howling Good Time	CC - ORNAMENT	ORNAMENT		1993	$9.75	$14.50
1993-QX525-2	Bird-Watcher	CC - ORNAMENT	ORNAMENT		1993	$9.75	$12.00

Order No.	Title	Type	Theme	Retired	Intro. Year	Retial Price	Secondary Price
1993-QX524-5	Peek-A-Boo Tree	CC - ORNAMENT	ORNAMENT		1993	$10.75	$22.00
1993-QX529-5	Julianne and Teddy	CC - ORNAMENT	ORNAMENT		1993	$21.75	$28.00
1993-QX550-5	Dickens Caroler Bell - 4th/F	CC - ORNAMENT	ORNAMENT		1993	$21.75	$30.00
1993-QX551-2	Baby's First Christmas	CC - ORNAMENT	ORNAMENT		1993	$18.75	$25.00
1993-QX551-5	Baby's First Christmas	CC - ORNAMENT	ORNAMENT		1993	$10.75	$17.00
1993-QX209-2	Baby's First Christmas - Girl	CC - ORNAMENT	ORNAMENT		1993	$4.75	$13.00
1993-QX210-5	Baby's First Christmas - Boy	CC - ORNAMENT	ORNAMENT		1993	$4.75	$15.00
1993-QX552-2	Baby's First Christmas - Photo	CC - ORNAMENT	ORNAMENT		1993	$7.75	$15.00
1993-QX588-2	A Child's Christmas	CC - ORNAMENT	ORNAMENT		1993	$9.75	$16.00
1993-QX555-2	Grandchild's First Christmas	CC - ORNAMENT	ORNAMENT		1993	$6.75	$8.00
1993-QX555-5	To My Grandma	CC - ORNAMENT	ORNAMENT		1993	$7.75	$10.00
1993-QX553-5	Mom-to-Be	CC - ORNAMENT	ORNAMENT		1993	$6.75	$9.00
1993-QX553-2	Dad-to-Be	CC - ORNAMENT	ORNAMENT		1993	$6.75	$9.00
1993-QX552-5	Baby's First Christmas	CC - ORNAMENT	ORNAMENT		1993	$7.75	$21.00
1993-QX599-2	Baby's Second Christmas	CC - ORNAMENT	ORNAMENT		1993	$6.75	$15.00
1993-QX599-5	Child's Third Christmas	CC - ORNAMENT	ORNAMENT		1993	$6.75	$15.00
1993-QX521-5	Child's Fourth Christmas	CC - ORNAMENT	ORNAMENT		1993	$6.75	$13.50
1993-QX522-2	Child's Fifth Christmas	CC - ORNAMENT	ORNAMENT		1993	$6.75	$13.50
1993-QX595-5	Our First Christmas Together	CC - ORNAMENT	ORNAMENT		1993	$18.75	$32.00
1993-QX564-2	Our First Christmas Together	CC - ORNAMENT	ORNAMENT		1993	$9.75	$12.00
1993-QX595-2	Our First Chrstms Tog. - Photo	CC - ORNAMENT	ORNAMENT		1993	$8.75	$17.50
1993-QX301-5	Our First Christmas Together	CC - ORNAMENT	ORNAMENT		1993	$6.75	$14.00
1993-QX594-2	Our Christmas Together	CC - ORNAMENT	ORNAMENT		1993	$10.75	$15.00
1993-QX596-5	Strange and Wonderful Love	CC - ORNAMENT	ORNAMENT		1993	$8.75	$12.00
1993-QX597-2	Anniversary Year - Photoholder	CC - ORNAMENT	ORNAMENT		1993	$9.75	$12.50
1993-QX584-5	Mom and Dad	CC - ORNAMENT	ORNAMENT		1993	$9.75	$12.50
1993-QX585-5	Dad	CC - ORNAMENT	ORNAMENT		1993	$7.75	$10.00
1993-QX585-2	Mom	CC - ORNAMENT	ORNAMENT		1993	$7.75	$15.50
1993-QX586-5	Son	CC - ORNAMENT	ORNAMENT		1993	$6.75	$9.00
1993-QX587-2	Daughter	CC - ORNAMENT	ORNAMENT		1993	$6.75	$10.00
1993-QX554-2	Brother	CC - ORNAMENT	ORNAMENT		1993	$6.75	$10.00
1993-QX554-5	Sister	CC - ORNAMENT	ORNAMENT		1993	$6.75	$15.50
1993-QX588-5	Sister to Sister	CC - ORNAMENT	ORNAMENT		1993	$9.75	$37.50
1993-QX589-2	Our Family - Photoholder	CC - ORNAMENT	ORNAMENT		1993	$7.75	$12.00
1993-QX573-2	Niece	CC - ORNAMENT	ORNAMENT		1993	$6.75	$9.00
1993-QX573-5	Nephew	CC - ORNAMENT	ORNAMENT		1993	$6.75	$8.00
1993-QX208-5	Grandparents	CC - ORNAMENT	ORNAMENT		1993	$4.75	$10.00
1993-QX566-5	Grandmother	CC - ORNAMENT	ORNAMENT		1993	$6.75	$9.50
1993-QX563-5	Granddaughter	CC - ORNAMENT	ORNAMENT		1993	$6.75	$11.00
1993-QX563-2	Grandson	CC - ORNAMENT	ORNAMENT		1993	$6.75	$11.00
1993-QX587-5	Godchild	CC - ORNAMENT	ORNAMENT		1993	$8.75	$13.50
1993-QX523-5	Special Cat - Photoholder	CC - ORNAMENT	ORNAMENT		1993	$7.75	$9.50
1993-QX596-2	Special Dog - Photoholder	CC - ORNAMENT	ORNAMENT		1993	$7.75	$14.00
1993-QX589-5	Warm and Special Friends	CC - ORNAMENT	ORNAMENT		1993	$10.75	$17.00
1993-QX591-2	Across the Miles	CC - ORNAMENT	ORNAMENT		1993	$8.75	$10.50
1993-QX590-5	New Home	CC - ORNAMENT	ORNAMENT		1993	$7.75	$33.00
1993-QX590-2	Apple for Teacher	CC - ORNAMENT	ORNAMENT		1993	$7.75	$8.00
1993-QX564-5	Star Teacher - Photoholder	CC - ORNAMENT	ORNAMENT		1993	$5.75	$7.50
1993-QX593-5	Coach	CC - ORNAMENT	ORNAMENT		1993	$6.75	$7.50
1993-QX593-2	People Friendly	CC - ORNAMENT	ORNAMENT		1993	$8.75	$12.00
1993-QX592-5	Top Banana	CC - ORNAMENT	ORNAMENT		1993	$7.75	$10.00
1993-QX540-5	Sylvester and Tweety	CC - ORNAMENT	ORNAMENT		1993	$9.75	$21.00
1993-QX541-2	Bugs Bunny	CC - ORNAMENT	ORNAMENT		1993	$8.75	$19.00
1993-QX549-5	Elmer Fudd	CC - ORNAMENT	ORNAMENT		1993	$8.75	$13.00
1993-QX565-2	Porky Pig	CC - ORNAMENT	ORNAMENT		1993	$8.75	$16.50
1993-QX571-5	Winnie the Pooh	CC - ORNAMENT	ORNAMENT		1993	$9.75	$24.00
1993-QX567-2	Kanga and Roo	CC - ORNAMENT	ORNAMENT		1993	$9.75	$18.50
1993-QX569-5	Owl	CC - ORNAMENT	ORNAMENT		1993	$9.75	$15.00
1993-QX570-2	Rabbit	CC - ORNAMENT	ORNAMENT		1993	$9.75	$15.00
1993-QX570-5	Tigger and Piglet	CC - ORNAMENT	ORNAMENT		1993	$9.75	$42.00
1993-QX571-2	Eeyore	CC - ORNAMENT	ORNAMENT		1993	$9.75	$16.00
1993-QX561-5	Tin Hot Air Balloon	CC - ORNAMENT	ORNAMENT		1993	$7.75	$15.00
1993-QX562-2	Tin Airplane	CC - ORNAMENT	ORNAMENT		1993	$7.75	$20.00
1993-QX562-5	Tin Blimp	CC - ORNAMENT	ORNAMENT		1993	$7.75	$15.00
1993-QX577-5	Making Waves	CC - ORNAMENT	ORNAMENT		1993	$9.75	$18.00
1993-QX579-5	Putt-Putt Penguin	CC - ORNAMENT	ORNAMENT		1993	$9.75	$15.00
1993-QX583-5	Icicle Bicycle	CC - ORNAMENT	ORNAMENT		1993	$9.75	$15.50
1993-QX584-2	Big On Gardening	CC - ORNAMENT	ORNAMENT		1993	$9.75	$12.00
1993-QX557-2	Fills the Bill	CC - ORNAMENT	ORNAMENT		1993	$8.75	$12.00
1993-QX577-2	Perfect Match	CC - ORNAMENT	ORNAMENT		1993	$8.75	$12.00
1993-QX556-2	Home for Christmas	CC - ORNAMENT	ORNAMENT		1993	$7.75	$15.00
1993-QX556-5	Bowling for ZZZs	CC - ORNAMENT	ORNAMENT		1993	$7.75	$12.00
1993-QX557-5	Dunkin' Roo	CC - ORNAMENT	ORNAMENT		1993	$7.75	$12.00
1993-QX576-2	Beary Gifted	CC - ORNAMENT	ORNAMENT		1993	$7.75	$12.50
1993-QX576-5	Snowbird	CC - ORNAMENT	ORNAMENT		1993	$7.75	$15.00
1993-QX582-5	Christmas Break	CC - ORNAMENT	ORNAMENT		1993	$7.75	$13.00
1993-QX579-2	Quick as a Fox	CC - ORNAMENT	ORNAMENT		1993	$8.75	$13.50
1993-QX578-2	Faithful Fire Fighter	CC - ORNAMENT	ORNAMENT		1993	$7.75	$12.00
1993-QX578-5	Caring Nurse	CC - ORNAMENT	ORNAMENT		1993	$6.75	$10.50
1993-QX598-2	Star Of Wonder	CC - ORNAMENT	ORNAMENT		1993	$6.75	$30.00
1993-QX536-2	He is Born	CC - ORNAMENT	ORNAMENT		1993	$9.75	$29.00
1993-QX537-5	Water Bed Snooze	CC - ORNAMENT	ORNAMENT		1993	$9.75	$14.00
1993-QX538-2	Room for One More	CC - ORNAMENT	ORNAMENT		1993	$8.75	$30.00
1993-QX538-5	Maxine	CC - ORNAMENT	ORNAMENT		1993	$8.75	$18.50
1993-QX575-2	Superman	CC - ORNAMENT	ORNAMENT		1993	$12.75	$31.00
1993-QX575-5	The Pink Panther	CC - ORNAMENT	ORNAMENT		1993	$12.75	$18.00
1993-QX207-2	Peanuts	CC - ORNAMENT	ORNAMENT		1993	$5.00	$13.00
1993-QX534-2	One-Elf Marching Band	CC - ORNAMENT	ORNAMENT		1993	$12.75	$18.00
1993-QX528-5	Curly 'n' Kingly	CC - ORNAMENT	ORNAMENT		1993	$10.75	$15.00
1993-QX534-5	That's Entertainment	CC - ORNAMENT	ORNAMENT		1993	$8.75	$16.00
1993-QX535-2	Big Roller	CC - ORNAMENT	ORNAMENT		1993	$8.75	$13.50
1993-QX535-5	Snow Bear Angel	CC - ORNAMENT	ORNAMENT		1993	$7.75	$13.00
1993-QX574-2A	Playful Pals	CC - ORNAMENT	ORNAMENT		1993	$14.75	$21.50

Order No.	Title	Type	Theme	Retired	Intro. Year	Retail Price	Secondary Price
1993-QX574-2B	Lou Rankin Polar Bear	CC - ORNAMENT	ORNAMENT		1993	$9.75	$24.50
1993-QX207-5	Mary Engelbreit	CC - ORNAMENT	ORNAMENT		1993	$5.00	$13.50
1993-QX532-2	Peep Inside	CC - ORNAMENT	ORNAMENT		1993	$13.75	$21.00
1993-QX568-5	Look for the Wonder	CC - ORNAMENT	ORNAMENT		1993	$12.75	$18.00
1993-QX530-5	Silvery Noel	CC - ORNAMENT	ORNAMENT		1993	$12.75	$18.00
1993-QX531-2	Snowy Hideaway	CC - ORNAMENT	ORNAMENT		1993	$9.75	$10.50
1993-QX532-5	Makin' Music	CC - ORNAMENT	ORNAMENT		1993	$9.75	$14.00
1993-QX533-5	Smile! It's Christmas - Photo	CC - ORNAMENT	ORNAMENT		1993	$9.75	$14.50
1993-QX533-2	High Top-purr	CC - ORNAMENT	ORNAMENT		1993	$8.75	$19.50
1993-QX536-5	Feliz Navidad (Mission)	CC - ORNAMENT	ORNAMENT		1993	$8.75	$13.00
1993-QX512-4	Ready for Fun	CC - ORNAMENT	ORNAMENT		1993	$7.75	$14.50
1993-QX566-2	Clever Cookie	CC - ORNAMENT	ORNAMENT		1993	$7.75	$14.50
1993-QX537-2	Little Drummer Boy	CC - ORNAMENT	ORNAMENT		1993	$8.75	$12.50
1993-QX539-2	Popping Good Times	CC - ORNAMENT	ORNAMENT		1993	$14.75	$20.00
1993-QX539-5	The Swat Team	CC - ORNAMENT	ORNAMENT		1993	$12.75	$22.00
1993-QX540-2	Great Connections	CC - ORNAMENT	ORNAMENT		1993	$10.75	$19.50
1993-QLX715-5	Peanuts - 3rd	CC - ORNAMENT	ORNAMENT		1993	$18.00	$34.00
1993-QLX716-5	Forest Frolics - 5th	CC - ORNAMENT	ORNAMENT		1993	$25.00	$32.00
1993-QLX715-2	Chris Mouse - 9th	CC - ORNAMENT	ORNAMENT		1993	$12.00	$21.00
1993-QLX741-5	Road Runner & Wile. E. Coyote	CC - ORNAMENT	ORNAMENT		1993	$30.00	$66.00
1993-QLX742-2	Winnie the Pooh	CC - ORNAMENT	ORNAMENT		1993	$24.00	$38.00
1993-QLX739-5	Home on the Range	CC - ORNAMENT	ORNAMENT		1993	$32.00	$42.00
1993-QLX737-5	Santa's Workshop	CC - ORNAMENT	ORNAMENT		1993	$28.00	$38.00
1993-QLX738-5	Last-Minute Shopping	CC - ORNAMENT	ORNAMENT		1993	$28.00	$35.00
1993-QLX740-2	Bells are Ringing	CC - ORNAMENT	ORNAMENT		1993	$28.00	$55.00
1993-QLX736-5	Baby's First Christmas	CC - ORNAMENT	ORNAMENT		1993	$22.00	$27.00
1993-QLX735-5	Our First Christmas Together	CC - ORNAMENT	ORNAMENT		1993	$20.00	$35.00
1993-QLX739-2	North Pole Merrython	CC - ORNAMENT	ORNAMENT		1993	$25.00	$45.00
1993-QLX740-5	Song of the Chimes	CC - ORNAMENT	ORNAMENT		1993	$25.00	$35.00
1993-QLX736-2	Radio News Flash	CC - ORNAMENT	ORNAMENT		1993	$22.00	$33.00
1993-QLX737-2	Dollhouse Dreams	CC - ORNAMENT	ORNAMENT		1993	$22.00	$38.00
1993-QLX719-2	The Lamplighter	CC - ORNAMENT	ORNAMENT		1993	$18.00	$28.00
1993-QLX717-2	Dog's Best Friend	CC - ORNAMENT	ORNAMENT		1993	$12.00	$22.00
1993-QLX735-2	Santa's Snow Getter	CC - ORNAMENT	ORNAMENT		1993	$18.00	$28.00
1993-QLX718-5	Raiding the Fridge	CC - ORNAMENT	ORNAMENT		1993	$16.00	$26.00
1993-QLX741-2	U.S.S. Enterprise - Next Gen.	CC - ORNAMENT	ORNAMENT		1993	$24.00	$42.50
1993-QX572-5	Holiday Barbie - 1st	CC - ORNAMENT	ORNAMENT		1993	$14.75	$105.00
1993-QLX747-6	Messages of Christmas	CC - ORNAMENT	ORNAMENT		1993	$35.00	$33.00
1993-QXC527-2	It's In the Mail	CC - ORNAMENT	ORNAMENT		1993		$19.00
1993-QXC433-2	Trimmed with Memories	CC - ORNAMENT	ORNAMENT		1993		$31.50
1993-ITEM3	Sharing Christmas - L.E.	CC - ORNAMENT	ORNAMENT		1993	$20.00	$34.00
1993-QXC544-2	Gentle Tidings	CC - ORNAMENT	ORNAMENT		1993		$41.50
1992-XPR973-5	Dasher/Dancer-Santa & His Rndr	CC - ORNAMENT	ORNAMENT		1992	$4.95	$23.00
1992-XPR973-7	Comet/Cupid-Santa & His Rndr	CC - ORNAMENT	ORNAMENT		1992	$4.95	$15.00
1992-XPR973-8	Donder/Blitzen-Snta & His Rndr	CC - ORNAMENT	ORNAMENT		1992	$4.95	$23.00
1992-XPR973-6	Prancer/Vixen-Santa & His Rndr	CC - ORNAMENT	ORNAMENT		1992	$4.95	$15.50
1992-XPR973-9	Santa Claus-Santa & His Rndr	CC - ORNAMENT	ORNAMENT		1992	$4.95	$19.00
1993-ITEM4	Santa's Favorite Stop	CC - ORNAMENT	ORNAMENT		1993	$55.00	$415.00
1993-ITEM5	Circle of Friendship	CC - ORNAMENT	ORNAMENT		1993		$202.00
1993-XPR974-6	Papa Bearinger	CC - ORNAMENT	ORNAMENT		1993	$4.95	$8.00
1993-XPR974-5	Mama Bearinger	CC - ORNAMENT	ORNAMENT		1993	$4.95	$10.00
1993-XPR974-7	Abearnathy	CC - ORNAMENT	ORNAMENT		1993	$4.95	$10.00
1993-XPR974-8	Bearnadette	CC - ORNAMENT	ORNAMENT		1993	$4.95	$10.00
1993-XPR974-9	Flckering Fireplce, Bearingers	CC - ORNAMENT	ORNAMENT		1993	$4.95	$10.00
1993-QX569-2	You're Always Welcome	CC - ORNAMENT	ORNAMENT		1993		$55.00
1992-QX541-1	O Christmas Tree Premier Bell	CC - ORNAMENT	ORNAMENT		1992	$10.75	$28.00
1993-ITEM6	K.C. Angel	CC - ORNAMENT	ORNAMENT		1993		$545.00
1994-QXC482-3	Holiday Pursuit	CC - ORNAMENT	ORNAMENT		1994		$15.50
1994-QXC485-3	On Cloud Nine	CC - ORNAMENT	ORNAMENT		1994	$12.00	$25.00
1994-ITEM7	Majestic Deer - L.E.	CC - ORNAMENT	ORNAMENT		1994	$25.00	$35.00
1994-ITEM8	Jolly Holly Santa - L.E.	CC - ORNAMENT	ORNAMENT		1994	$22.00	$40.00
1994-QX531-6	Yuletide Central - 1st	CC - ORNAMENT	ORNAMENT		1994	$18.95	$31.00
1994-QX542-6	Kiddie Car Classics - 1st	CC - ORNAMENT	ORNAMENT		1994	$13.95	$45.00
1994-QX532-3	Baseball Heroes - 1st	CC - ORNAMENT	ORNAMENT		1994	$12.95	$40.00
1994-QHX909-4	1956 Garton Kidillac Pedal Car	CC - ORNAMENT	ORNAMENT		1994	$50.00	$65.00
1994-QX531-3	Cat Naps - 1st	CC - ORNAMENT	ORNAMENT		1994	$7.95	$20.00
1994-QX521-3	Mother Goose - 2nd	CC - ORNAMENT	ORNAMENT		1994	$13.95	$25.00
1994-QX520-6	U.S. Christmas Stamps - 2nd	CC - ORNAMENT	ORNAMENT		1994	$10.95	$20.50
1994-QX520-3	The Peanuts Gang - 2nd	CC - ORNAMENT	ORNAMENT		1994	$9.95	$15.00
1994-QX522-3	Tobin Fraley Carousel - 3rd	CC - ORNAMENT	ORNAMENT		1994	$28.00	$44.00
1994-QX542-2	Classic American Cars - 4th	CC - ORNAMENT	ORNAMENT		1994	$12.95	$36.00
1994-QX525-3	Puppy Love - 4th	CC - ORNAMENT	ORNAMENT		1994	$7.95	$16.00
1994-QX525-6	Merry Olde Santa - 5th	CC - ORNAMENT	ORNAMENT		1994	$14.95	$20.00
1994-QX526-3	Fabulous Decade - 5th	CC - ORNAMENT	ORNAMENT		1994	$7.95	$18.00
1994-QX527-3	Crayola Crayon - 6th	CC - ORNAMENT	ORNAMENT		1994	$10.95	$17.00
1994-QX527-6	Mary's Angels - 7th	CC - ORNAMENT	ORNAMENT		1994	$6.95	$14.50
1994-QX528-3	Mr. And Mrs. Claus - 9th	CC - ORNAMENT	ORNAMENT		1994	$14.95	$22.00
1994-QX528-6	Nost. Houses And Shops - 11th	CC - ORNAMENT	ORNAMENT		1994	$14.95	$24.00
1994-QX318-3	Twelve Days of Chrstmas - 11th	CC - ORNAMENT	ORNAMENT		1994	$6.95	$12.00
1994-QX501-6	Rocking Horse - 14th	CC - ORNAMENT	ORNAMENT		1994	$10.95	$20.00
1994-QX529-3	Frosty Friends - 15th	CC - ORNAMENT	ORNAMENT		1994	$9.95	$18.00
1994-QX529-6	Here Comes Santa - 16th	CC - ORNAMENT	ORNAMENT		1994	$14.95	$45.50
1994-QX522-6	Owliver - 3rd and Final	CC - ORNAMENT	ORNAMENT		1994	$7.95	$14.00
1994-QX240-3	Betsey's Country Christmas-3rd	CC - ORNAMENT	ORNAMENT		1994	$5.00	$13.50
1994-QX526-6	Heart of Christmas - 5th/F	CC - ORNAMENT	ORNAMENT		1994	$14.95	$25.00
1994-QX542-3	Happy Birthday, Jesus	CC - ORNAMENT	ORNAMENT		1994	$12.95	$21.00
1994-QX541-6	Kitty's Catamaran	CC - ORNAMENT	ORNAMENT		1994	$10.95	$15.00
1994-QX539-6	Cock-a-Doodle Christmas	CC - ORNAMENT	ORNAMENT		1994	$8.95	$18.00
1994-QX540-3	Making It Bright	CC - ORNAMENT	ORNAMENT		1994	$8.95	$13.00
1994-QX541-3	Keep on Mowin'	CC - ORNAMENT	ORNAMENT		1994	$8.95	$14.00
1994-QX481-3	Lucinda and Teddy	CC - ORNAMENT	ORNAMENT		1994	$21.75	$32.00
1994-QX563-3	Baby's First Christmas	CC - ORNAMENT	ORNAMENT		1994	$18.95	$28.00
1994-QX574-3	Baby's First Christmas	CC - ORNAMENT	ORNAMENT		1994	$12.95	$14.00

Order No.	Title	Type	Theme	Retired	Intro. Year	Retial Price	Secondary Price
1994-QX243-3	Baby's First Christmas - Girl	CC - ORNAMENT	ORNAMENT		1994	$5.00	$12.00
1994-QX243-6	Baby's First Christmas - Boy	CC - ORNAMENT	ORNAMENT		1994	$5.00	$11.00
1994-QX563-6	Baby's First Xmas Photoholder	CC - ORNAMENT	ORNAMENT		1994	$7.95	$16.00
1994-QX567-6	Grandchild's First Christmas	CC - ORNAMENT	ORNAMENT		1994	$7.95	$14.00
1994-QX550-6	Mom-to-Be	CC - ORNAMENT	ORNAMENT		1994	$7.95	$17.00
1994-QX547-3	Dad-to-Be	CC - ORNAMENT	ORNAMENT		1994	$7.95	$11.00
1994-QX561-3	For My Grandma	CC - ORNAMENT	ORNAMENT		1994	$6.95	$11.00
1994-QX561-6	Grandpa	CC - ORNAMENT	ORNAMENT		1994	$7.95	$11.00
1994-QX571-3	Baby's First Christmas	CC - ORNAMENT	ORNAMENT		1994	$7.95	$15.50
1994-QX571-6	Baby's Second Christmas	CC - ORNAMENT	ORNAMENT		1994	$7.95	$15.00
1994-QX572-3	Child's Third Christmas	CC - ORNAMENT	ORNAMENT		1994	$6.95	$11.00
1994-QX572-6	Child's Fourth Christmas	CC - ORNAMENT	ORNAMENT		1994	$6.95	$13.00
1994-QX573-3	Child's Fifth Christmas	CC - ORNAMENT	ORNAMENT		1994	$6.95	$10.00
1994-QX570-6	Our First Christmas Together	CC - ORNAMENT	ORNAMENT		1994	$18.95	$24.00
1994-QX564-3	Our First Christmas Together	CC - ORNAMENT	ORNAMENT		1994	$9.95	$14.00
1994-QX565-3	Our First Christmas Together	CC - ORNAMENT	ORNAMENT		1994	$8.95	$15.00
1994-QX318-6	Our First Christmas Together	CC - ORNAMENT	ORNAMENT		1994	$6.95	$10.00
1994-QX481-6	Our Christmas Together	CC - ORNAMENT	ORNAMENT		1994	$9.95	$14.00
1994-QX564-6	Tou Can Love	CC - ORNAMENT	ORNAMENT		1994	$8.95	$15.50
1994-QX568-3	Anniversary Year Photoholder	CC - ORNAMENT	ORNAMENT		1994	$10.95	$15.00
1994-QX566-6	Mom and Dad	CC - ORNAMENT	ORNAMENT		1994	$9.95	$14.50
1994-QX546-6	Mom	CC - ORNAMENT	ORNAMENT		1994	$7.95	$12.00
1994-QX546-3	Dad	CC - ORNAMENT	ORNAMENT		1994	$7.95	$12.00
1994-QX562-3	Daughter	CC - ORNAMENT	ORNAMENT		1994	$6.95	$11.00
1994-QX562-6	Son	CC - ORNAMENT	ORNAMENT		1994	$6.95	$13.50
1994-QX551-3	Sister	CC - ORNAMENT	ORNAMENT		1994	$6.95	$11.50
1994-QX551-6	Brother	CC - ORNAMENT	ORNAMENT		1994	$6.95	$11.50
1994-QX553-3	Sister to Sister	CC - ORNAMENT	ORNAMENT		1994	$9.95	$16.00
1994-QX557-6	Our Family Photoholder	CC - ORNAMENT	ORNAMENT		1994	$7.95	$10.50
1994-QX554-3	Niece	CC - ORNAMENT	ORNAMENT		1994	$7.95	$15.50
1994-QX554-6	Nephew	CC - ORNAMENT	ORNAMENT		1994	$7.95	$10.00
1994-QX242-6	Grandparents	CC - ORNAMENT	ORNAMENT		1994	$5.00	$10.00
1994-QX567-3	Grandmother	CC - ORNAMENT	ORNAMENT		1994	$7.95	$13.00
1994-QX552-3	Granddaughter	CC - ORNAMENT	ORNAMENT		1994	$6.95	$12.50
1994-QX552-6	Grandson	CC - ORNAMENT	ORNAMENT		1994	$6.95	$11.50
1994-QX242-3	Godparent	CC - ORNAMENT	ORNAMENT		1994	$5.00	$9.00
1994-QX445-3	Godchild	CC - ORNAMENT	ORNAMENT		1994	$8.95	$16.00
1994-QX560-3	Special Dog	CC - ORNAMENT	ORNAMENT		1994	$7.95	$13.00
1994-QX560-6	Special Cat	CC - ORNAMENT	ORNAMENT		1994	$7.95	$13.00
1994-QX569-3	Thick 'n' Thin	CC - ORNAMENT	ORNAMENT		1994	$10.95	$18.00
1994-QX568-6	Friendly Push	CC - ORNAMENT	ORNAMENT		1994	$8.95	$13.00
1994-QX573-6	Secret Santa	CC - ORNAMENT	ORNAMENT		1994	$7.95	$12.00
1994-QX565-6	Across the Miles	CC - ORNAMENT	ORNAMENT		1994	$8.95	$16.50
1994-QX566-3	New Home	CC - ORNAMENT	ORNAMENT		1994	$8.95	$18.00
1994-QX576-6	Out of this World Teacher	CC - ORNAMENT	ORNAMENT		1994	$7.95	$12.00
1994-QX583-6	Champion Teacher	CC - ORNAMENT	ORNAMENT		1994	$6.95	$11.00
1994-QX593-3	Coach	CC - ORNAMENT	ORNAMENT		1994	$7.95	$9.00
1994-QX590-6	Child Care Giver	CC - ORNAMENT	ORNAMENT		1994	$7.95	$13.00
1994-QX570-3	Stamp of Approval	CC - ORNAMENT	ORNAMENT		1994	$7.95	$14.00
1994-QX569-6	Open-and-Shut Holiday	CC - ORNAMENT	ORNAMENT		1994	$9.95	$15.00
1994-QX582-3	Caring Doctor	CC - ORNAMENT	ORNAMENT		1994	$8.95	$13.50
1994-QX597-3	Gentle Nurse	CC - ORNAMENT	ORNAMENT		1994	$6.95	$10.00
1994-QX582-6	Holiday Patrol	CC - ORNAMENT	ORNAMENT		1994	$8.95	$14.00
1994-QX583-3	Extra-Special Delivery	CC - ORNAMENT	ORNAMENT		1994	$7.95	$11.00
1994-QX584-3	Red Hot Holiday	CC - ORNAMENT	ORNAMENT		1994	$7.95	$12.00
1994-QX560-2	Road Runner and Wile E. Coyote	CC - ORNAMENT	ORNAMENT		1994	$12.95	$20.00
1994-QX560-5	Tasmanian Devil	CC - ORNAMENT	ORNAMENT		1994	$8.95	$42.00
1994-QX541-5	Daffy Duck	CC - ORNAMENT	ORNAMENT		1994	$8.95	$15.00
1994-QX534-3	Speedy Gonzales	CC - ORNAMENT	ORNAMENT		1994	$8.95	$16.00
1994-QX534-6	Yosemite Sam	CC - ORNAMENT	ORNAMENT		1994	$8.95	$17.00
1994-QX543-3	Dorothy and Toto	CC - ORNAMENT	ORNAMENT		1994	$10.95	$36.00
1994-QX543-6	The Scarecrow	CC - ORNAMENT	ORNAMENT		1994	$9.95	$24.00
1994-QX544-3	The Tin Man	CC - ORNAMENT	ORNAMENT		1994	$9.95	$26.00
1994-QX544-6	The Cowardly Lion	CC - ORNAMENT	ORNAMENT		1994	$9.95	$22.00
1994-QX537-3	The Beatles	CC - ORNAMENT	ORNAMENT		1994	$48.00	$73.00
1994-QX535-6	Relaxing Moment	CC - ORNAMENT	ORNAMENT		1994	$14.95	$22.00
1994-QX476-6	Friendship Sundae	CC - ORNAMENT	ORNAMENT		1994	$10.95	$19.00
1994-QX241-3	Norman Rockwell Art	CC - ORNAMENT	ORNAMENT		1994	$5.00	$13.50
1994-QX241-6	Mary Engelbreit	CC - ORNAMENT	ORNAMENT		1994	$5.00	$15.50
1994-QX244-3	The Tale of Peter Rabbit	CC - ORNAMENT	ORNAMENT		1994	$5.00	$12.00
1994-QX574-6	Winnie the Pooh and Tigger	CC - ORNAMENT	ORNAMENT		1994	$12.95	$33.00
1994-QX500-3	Fred and Barney	CC - ORNAMENT	ORNAMENT		1994	$14.95	$20.00
1994-QX575-3	Garfield	CC - ORNAMENT	ORNAMENT		1994	$12.95	$18.00
1994-QX545-3	Santa's Lego Sleigh	CC - ORNAMENT	ORNAMENT		1994	$10.95	$19.00
1994-QX545-6	Lou Rankin Seal	CC - ORNAMENT	ORNAMENT		1994	$9.95	$12.00
1994-QX585-3	Batman	CC - ORNAMENT	ORNAMENT		1994	$12.95	$22.50
1994-QX587-3	Big Shot	CC - ORNAMENT	ORNAMENT		1994	$7.95	$12.00
1994-QX592-3	All Pumped Up	CC - ORNAMENT	ORNAMENT		1994	$8.95	$12.00
1994-QX587-6	Busy Batter	CC - ORNAMENT	ORNAMENT		1994	$7.95	$11.50
1994-QX592-6	Reindeer Pro	CC - ORNAMENT	ORNAMENT		1994	$7.95	$14.50
1994-QX591-6	Kickin' Roo	CC - ORNAMENT	ORNAMENT		1994	$7.95	$12.00
1994-QX591-3	Merry Fishmas	CC - ORNAMENT	ORNAMENT		1994	$8.95	$12.00
1994-QX586-6	Thrill a Minute	CC - ORNAMENT	ORNAMENT		1994	$8.95	$15.00
1994-QX586-3	Practice Makes Perfect	CC - ORNAMENT	ORNAMENT		1994	$8.95	$12.50
1994-QX585-6	It's a Strike	CC - ORNAMENT	ORNAMENT		1994	$8.95	$12.50
1994-QX588-6	Kringle's Kayak	CC - ORNAMENT	ORNAMENT		1994	$7.95	$14.00
1994-QX589-3	Colors of Joy	CC - ORNAMENT	ORNAMENT		1994	$7.95	$17.50
1994-QX577-3	A Sharp Flat	CC - ORNAMENT	ORNAMENT		1994	$10.95	$18.00
1994-QX584-6	Follow the Sun	CC - ORNAMENT	ORNAMENT		1994	$8.95	$14.00
1994-QX594-6	Ice Show	CC - ORNAMENT	ORNAMENT		1994	$7.95	$13.00
1994-QX581-6	A Feline of a Christmas	CC - ORNAMENT	ORNAMENT		1994	$8.95	$21.00
1994-QX589-6	Angel Hare	CC - ORNAMENT	ORNAMENT		1994	$8.95	$16.50
1994-QX595-3	Feelin' Groovy	CC - ORNAMENT	ORNAMENT		1994	$7.95	$15.00

Order No.	Title	Type	Theme	Retired	Intro. Year	Retail Price	Secondary Price
1994-QX578-6	Cheery Cyclists	CC - ORNAMENT	ORNAMENT		1994	$12.95	$19.50
1994-QX576-3	In the Pink	CC - ORNAMENT	ORNAMENT		1994	$9.95	$17.50
1994-QX575-6	Jump-Along Jackalope	CC - ORNAMENT	ORNAMENT		1994	$8.95	$13.00
1994-QX579-3	Feliz Navidad (Dog in Pot)	CC - ORNAMENT	ORNAMENT		1994	$8.95	$13.00
1994-QX579-6	Cheers to You!	CC - ORNAMENT	ORNAMENT		1994	$10.95	$20.00
1994-QX440-6	Hearts in Harmony	CC - ORNAMENT	ORNAMENT		1994	$10.95	$18.00
1994-QX447-3	Joyous Song	CC - ORNAMENT	ORNAMENT		1994	$8.95	$12.00
1994-QX553-6	Helpful Shepherd	CC - ORNAMENT	ORNAMENT		1994	$8.95	$13.00
1994-QX581-3	Time of Peace	CC - ORNAMENT	ORNAMENT		1994	$7.95	$13.50
1994-QX598-3	Tulip Time	CC - ORNAMENT	ORNAMENT		1994	$9.95	$14.00
1994-QX598-6	Daisy Days	CC - ORNAMENT	ORNAMENT		1994	$9.95	$13.00
1994-QX599-3	Harvest Joy	CC - ORNAMENT	ORNAMENT		1994	$9.95	$14.50
1994-QX597-6	Yuletide Cheer	CC - ORNAMENT	ORNAMENT		1994	$9.95	$14.50
1994-QX578-3	Jingle Bell Band	CC - ORNAMENT	ORNAMENT		1994	$10.95	$26.00
1994-QX577-6	Candy Caper	CC - ORNAMENT	ORNAMENT		1994	$8.95	$15.00
1994-QX588-3	Magic Carpet Ride	CC - ORNAMENT	ORNAMENT		1994	$7.95	$21.00
1994-QX580-6	Dear Santa Mouse	CC - ORNAMENT	ORNAMENT		1994	$14.95	$20.00
1994-QX599-6	Mistletoe Surprise	CC - ORNAMENT	ORNAMENT		1994	$12.95	$21.50
1994-QX580-3	Sweet Greeting	CC - ORNAMENT	ORNAMENT		1994	$10.95	$21.00
1994-QLX749-6	Tobin Fraley Hldy Carousel-1st	CC - ORNAMENT	ORNAMENT		1994	$32.00	$50.00
1994-QLX740-6	Peanuts - 4th	CC - ORNAMENT	ORNAMENT		1994	$20.00	$38.00
1994-QLX743-6	Forest Frolics - 6th	CC - ORNAMENT	ORNAMENT		1994	$28.00	$35.00
1994-QLX739-3	Chris Mouse - 10th	CC - ORNAMENT	ORNAMENT		1994	$12.00	$20.00
1994-QLX738-2	Gingerbread Fantasy	CC - ORNAMENT	ORNAMENT		1994	$44.00	$68.00
1994-QLX748-6	The Eagle Has Landed	CC - ORNAMENT	ORNAMENT		1994	$24.00	$34.00
1994-QLX749-3	Winnie the Pooh Parade	CC - ORNAMENT	ORNAMENT		1994	$32.00	$55.00
1994-QLX746-3	White Christmas	CC - ORNAMENT	ORNAMENT		1994	$28.00	$48.00
1994-QLX747-3	Santa's Sing-Along	CC - ORNAMENT	ORNAMENT		1994	$24.00	$47.00
1994-QLX750-3	Maxine	CC - ORNAMENT	ORNAMENT		1994	$20.00	$28.00
1994-QLX746-6	Baby's First Christmas	CC - ORNAMENT	ORNAMENT		1994	$20.00	$30.00
1994-QLX743-3	Feliz Navidad	CC - ORNAMENT	ORNAMENT		1994	$28.00	$38.00
1994-QLX742-6	Conversations with Santa	CC - ORNAMENT	ORNAMENT		1994	$28.00	$36.00
1994-QLX744-3	Very Merry Minutes	CC - ORNAMENT	ORNAMENT		1994	$24.00	$38.00
1994-QLX741-6	Country Showtime	CC - ORNAMENT	ORNAMENT		1994	$22.00	$28.00
1994-QLX742-3	Peekaboo Pup	CC - ORNAMENT	ORNAMENT		1994	$20.00	$29.00
1994-QLX741-3	Kringle Trolley	CC - ORNAMENT	ORNAMENT		1994	$20.00	$42.00
1994-QLX740-3	Rock Candy Miner	CC - ORNAMENT	ORNAMENT		1994	$20.00	$38.00
1994-QLX737-6	Candy Cane Lookout	CC - ORNAMENT	ORNAMENT		1994	$18.00	$45.00
1994-QLX738-3	Away in a Manger	CC - ORNAMENT	ORNAMENT		1994	$16.00	$35.00
1994-QX533-6	Eager for Christmas	CC - ORNAMENT	ORNAMENT		1994	$15.00	$30.00
1994-QXC484-1	Mrs. Claus' Cupboard	CC - ORNAMENT	ORNAMENT		1994	$55.00	$175.00
1994-QLX738-6	Klingon Bird of Prey	CC - ORNAMENT	ORNAMENT		1994	$24.00	$37.00
1994-QX500-6	Barbie - 1st	CC - ORNAMENT	ORNAMENT		1994	$14.95	$27.00
1994-QX521-6	Holiday Barbie - 2nd	CC - ORNAMENT	ORNAMENT		1994	$14.95	$40.00
1994-QLX750-6	Barney	CC - ORNAMENT	ORNAMENT		1994	$24.00	$29.00
1994-QLX751-3A	Simba, Sarabi, & Mufasa-L&M	CC - ORNAMENT	ORNAMENT		1994	$32.00	$73.00
1994-QX540-6	Mufasa and Simba	CC - ORNAMENT	ORNAMENT		1994	$14.95	$23.00
1994-QX530-3	Simba and Nala	CC - ORNAMENT	ORNAMENT		1994	$12.95	$21.00
1994-QX536-6	Timon and Pumbaa	CC - ORNAMENT	ORNAMENT		1994	$8.95	$18.00
1994-QX596-6	Barney	CC - ORNAMENT	ORNAMENT		1994	$9.95	$37.00
1994-XPR945-0	Country Church-Sarah, Plain...	CC - ORNAMENT	ORNAMENT		1994	$7.95	$21.00
1994-XPR945-1	Mrs. Parkley's Gen Store-Sarah	CC - ORNAMENT	ORNAMENT		1994	$7.95	$16.00
1994-XPR945-2	The Hays Train Station-Sarah..	CC - ORNAMENT	ORNAMENT		1994	$7.95	$15.50
1994-XPR945-3	Sarah's Prairie Home-Sarah...	CC - ORNAMENT	ORNAMENT		1994	$7.95	$17.50
1994-XPR945-4	Sarah's Maine Home-Sarah...	CC - ORNAMENT	ORNAMENT		1994	$7.95	$18.00
1991-ITEM9	Claus & Co. R.R. (5-pc set)	CC - ORNAMENT	ORNAMENT		1991	$18.75	$50.00
1989-ITEM10	Carousel Horses (5-piece set)	CC - ORNAMENT	ORNAMENT		1989	$16.80	$62.00
1992-ITEM11	Santa And His Reindeer (5 pc)	CC - ORNAMENT	ORNAMENT		1992	$24.75	$64.00
1993-ITEM12	The Bearingers (5-piece set)	CC - ORNAMENT	ORNAMENT		1993	$24.75	$41.50
1995-QXC411-7	Collecting Memories	CC - ORNAMENT	ORNAMENT		1995		$19.50
1995-QXC520-7	Fishing for Fun	CC - ORNAMENT	ORNAMENT		1995		$17.50
1995-QXC416-7	1958 Ford Edsel Citation Conv.	CC - ORNAMENT	ORNAMENT		1995	$12.95	$57.00
1995-QXC539-7	Barbie, Brunette Debut - 1959	CC - ORNAMENT	ORNAMENT		1995	$14.95	$51.00
1995-QX585-9	Wish List	CC - ORNAMENT	ORNAMENT		1995	$15.00	$21.00
1995-QXC404-9	Christmas Eve Bake-Off	CC - ORNAMENT	ORNAMENT		1995	$60.00	$125.00
1995-QXI617-9	Percy, Flit and Meeko	CC - ORNAMENT	ORNAMENT		1995	$9.95	$15.00
1995-QXI619-7	Pocahontas and Capt John Smith	CC - ORNAMENT	ORNAMENT		1995	$14.95	$20.00
1995-QXI616-9	Captain John Smith and Meeko	CC - ORNAMENT	ORNAMENT		1995	$12.95	$15.00
1995-QXI617-7	Pocahontas	CC - ORNAMENT	ORNAMENT		1995	$12.95	$15.00
1995-QXI504-9	Barbie - 2nd (Solo/Spotlight)	CC - ORNAMENT	ORNAMENT		1995	$14.95	$27.00
1995-QXI505-7	Holiday Barbie - 3rd	CC - ORNAMENT	ORNAMENT		1995	$14.95	$33.50
1995-QXI573-7	Captain Jean-Luc Picard	CC - ORNAMENT	ORNAMENT		1995	$13.95	$18.50
1995-QXI553-9	Captain James T. Kirk	CC - ORNAMENT	ORNAMENT		1995	$13.95	$19.50
1995-QXI726-7	Romulan Warbird	CC - ORNAMENT	ORNAMENT		1995	$24.00	$30.00
1995-QXI575-9	Football Legends - 1st	CC - ORNAMENT	ORNAMENT		1995	$14.95	$38.00
1995-QXI551-7	Hoop Stars - 1st	CC - ORNAMENT	ORNAMENT		1995	$14.95	$29.50
1995-QX508-7	Christmas Visitors - 1st	CC - ORNAMENT	ORNAMENT		1995	$14.95	$20.00
1995-QX552-7	All-American Trucks - 1st	CC - ORNAMENT	ORNAMENT		1995	$13.95	$28.00
1995-QX507-7	Celebration of Angels - 1st	CC - ORNAMENT	ORNAMENT		1995	$12.95	$21.00
1995-QX507-9	Yuletide Central - 2nd	CC - ORNAMENT	ORNAMENT		1995	$18.95	$24.00
1995-QX502-7	Kiddie Car Classics - 2nd	CC - ORNAMENT	ORNAMENT		1995	$13.95	$26.50
1995-QX502-9	Baseball Heroes - 2nd	CC - ORNAMENT	ORNAMENT		1995	$12.95	$18.00
1995-QX509-7	Cat Naps - 2nd	CC - ORNAMENT	ORNAMENT		1995	$7.95	$14.00
1995-QX509-9	Mother Goose - 3rd	CC - ORNAMENT	ORNAMENT		1995	$13.95	$19.00
1995-QX505-9	The Peanuts Gang - 3rd	CC - ORNAMENT	ORNAMENT		1995	$9.95	$16.00
1995-QX523-9	Classic American Cars - 5th	CC - ORNAMENT	ORNAMENT		1995	$12.95	$18.00
1995-QX513-7	Puppy Love - 5th	CC - ORNAMENT	ORNAMENT		1995	$7.95	$13.50
1995-QX513-9	Merry Olde Santa - 6th	CC - ORNAMENT	ORNAMENT		1995	$14.95	$21.00
1995-QX514-7	Fabulous Decade - 6th	CC - ORNAMENT	ORNAMENT		1995	$7.95	$13.00
1995-QX524-7	Crayola Crayon - 7th	CC - ORNAMENT	ORNAMENT		1995	$10.95	$17.00
1995-QX514-9	Mary's Angels - 8th	CC - ORNAMENT	ORNAMENT		1995	$6.95	$13.50
1995-QX515-9	Nost. Houses And Shops - 12th	CC - ORNAMENT	ORNAMENT		1995	$14.95	$21.00
1995-QX508-9	Accessories for Nost. H & S	CC - ORNAMENT	ORNAMENT		1995	$8.95	$15.00

Order No.	Title	Type	Theme	Retired	Intro. Year	Retial Price	Secondary Price
1995-QX517-9	Here Comes Santa - 17th	CC - ORNAMENT	ORNAMENT		1995	$14.95	$24.00
1995-QX516-9	Frosty Friends - 16th	CC - ORNAMENT	ORNAMENT		1995	$10.95	$15.00
1995-QX516-7	Rocking Horse - 15th	CC - ORNAMENT	ORNAMENT		1995	$10.95	$19.00
1995-QX506-9	Tobin Fraley Carousel - 4th/F	CC - ORNAMENT	ORNAMENT		1995	$28.00	$37.50
1995-QX506-7	U.S. Christmas Stamps - 3rd/F	CC - ORNAMENT	ORNAMENT		1995	$10.95	$18.00
1995-QX300-9	Twelve Days of Christmas-12th/F	CC - ORNAMENT	ORNAMENT		1995	$6.95	$11.50
1995-QX515-7	Mr. And Mrs. Claus - 10th/F	CC - ORNAMENT	ORNAMENT		1995	$14.95	$21.00
1995-QX520-9	Our Little Blessings	CC - ORNAMENT	ORNAMENT		1995	$12.95	$16.50
1995-QX518-9	Barrel-Back Rider	CC - ORNAMENT	ORNAMENT		1995	$9.95	$11.00
1995-QX616-7	Pewter Rocking Horse	CC - ORNAMENT	ORNAMENT		1995	$20.00	$35.00
1995-QX525-9	Beverly And Teddy	CC - ORNAMENT	ORNAMENT		1995	$21.75	$28.00
1995-QX501-7	Sylvester And Tweety	CC - ORNAMENT	ORNAMENT		1995	$13.95	$20.00
1995-QX501-9	Bugs Bunny	CC - ORNAMENT	ORNAMENT		1995	$8.95	$14.50
1995-QX525-7	Popeye	CC - ORNAMENT	ORNAMENT		1995	$10.95	$19.00
1995-QX240-7	Norman Rockwell Art	CC - ORNAMENT	ORNAMENT		1995	$5.00	$9.00
1995-QX240-9	Mary Engelbreit	CC - ORNAMENT	ORNAMENT		1995	$5.00	$10.00
1995-QX500-9	Winnie the Pooh and Tigger	CC - ORNAMENT	ORNAMENT		1995	$12.95	$21.00
1995-QX541-7	Betty And Wilma	CC - ORNAMENT	ORNAMENT		1995	$14.95	$19.00
1995-QX500-7	Garfield	CC - ORNAMENT	ORNAMENT		1995	$10.95	$16.00
1995-QX476-9	Lego Fireplace with Santa	CC - ORNAMENT	ORNAMENT		1995	$10.95	$16.00
1995-QX406-9	Lou Rankin Bear	CC - ORNAMENT	ORNAMENT		1995	$9.95	$14.00
1995-QX525-8	Forever Friends Bear	CC - ORNAMENT	ORNAMENT		1995	$8.95	$13.00
1995-QX553-7	Vera the Mouse	CC - ORNAMENT	ORNAMENT		1995	$8.95	$10.50
1995-QX406-7	Refreshing Gift	CC - ORNAMENT	ORNAMENT		1995	$14.95	$26.50
1995-QX526-7	Pez Santa	CC - ORNAMENT	ORNAMENT		1995	$7.95	$13.00
1995-QX620-9	Dudley the Dragon	CC - ORNAMENT	ORNAMENT		1995	$10.95	$14.00
1995-QX551-9	Colorful World	CC - ORNAMENT	ORNAMENT		1995	$10.95	$16.50
1995-QX574-9	Glinda, Witch of the North	CC - ORNAMENT	ORNAMENT		1995	$13.95	$21.00
1995-QX584-9	The Magic School Bus	CC - ORNAMENT	ORNAMENT		1995	$10.95	$15.50
1995-QX585-7	Thomas the Tank Engine-No. 1	CC - ORNAMENT	ORNAMENT		1995	$9.95	$16.00
1995-QX573-9	Batmobile	CC - ORNAMENT	ORNAMENT		1995	$14.95	$22.00
1995-QX615-9	Simba, Pumbaa and Timon	CC - ORNAMENT	ORNAMENT		1995	$12.95	$19.50
1995-QX618-7	Wheel of Fortune	CC - ORNAMENT	ORNAMENT		1995	$12.95	$21.00
1995-QX316-9	The Olympic Spirit	CC - ORNAMENT	ORNAMENT		1995	$7.95	$12.00
1995-QX587-9	Bobbin' Along	CC - ORNAMENT	ORNAMENT		1995	$8.95	$18.00
1995-QX588-7	Gopher Fun	CC - ORNAMENT	ORNAMENT		1995	$9.95	$16.00
1995-QX588-9	The Winning Play	CC - ORNAMENT	ORNAMENT		1995	$7.95	$12.00
1995-QX590-9	Ski Hound	CC - ORNAMENT	ORNAMENT		1995	$8.95	$11.00
1995-QX590-7	Tennis, Anyone?	CC - ORNAMENT	ORNAMENT		1995	$7.95	$14.50
1995-QX589-9	Catch the Spirit	CC - ORNAMENT	ORNAMENT		1995	$7.95	$13.00
1995-QX589-7	Faithful Fan	CC - ORNAMENT	ORNAMENT		1995	$8.95	$11.00
1995-QX591-7	Hockey Pup	CC - ORNAMENT	ORNAMENT		1995	$9.95	$14.00
1995-QX591-9	Bingo Bear	CC - ORNAMENT	ORNAMENT		1995	$7.95	$11.50
1995-QX592-7	Perfect Balance	CC - ORNAMENT	ORNAMENT		1995	$7.95	$11.00
1995-QX592-9	Acorn 500	CC - ORNAMENT	ORNAMENT		1995	$10.95	$15.00
1995-QX593-7	Roller Whiz	CC - ORNAMENT	ORNAMENT		1995	$7.95	$10.00
1995-QX602-7	Merry RV	CC - ORNAMENT	ORNAMENT		1995	$12.95	$18.00
1995-QX602-9	Takin' a Hike	CC - ORNAMENT	ORNAMENT		1995	$7.95	$14.00
1995-QX604-7	On the Ice	CC - ORNAMENT	ORNAMENT		1995	$7.95	$14.00
1995-QX603-9	Water Sports	CC - ORNAMENT	ORNAMENT		1995	$14.95	$21.00
1995-QX604-9	In Time with Christmas	CC - ORNAMENT	ORNAMENT		1995	$12.95	$14.00
1995-QX599-9	Cows of Bali	CC - ORNAMENT	ORNAMENT		1995	$8.95	$12.00
1995-QX600-9	Muletide Greetings	CC - ORNAMENT	ORNAMENT		1995	$7.95	$15.00
1995-QX600-7	Dream On	CC - ORNAMENT	ORNAMENT		1995	$10.95	$12.00
1995-QX601-7	Santa's Serenade	CC - ORNAMENT	ORNAMENT		1995	$8.95	$12.50
1995-QX601-9	Surfin' Santa	CC - ORNAMENT	ORNAMENT		1995	$9.95	$12.00
1995-QX586-9	Feliz Navidad	CC - ORNAMENT	ORNAMENT		1995	$7.95	$16.00
1995-QX587-7	Santa in Paris	CC - ORNAMENT	ORNAMENT		1995	$8.95	$15.00
1995-QX586-7	Joy to the World	CC - ORNAMENT	ORNAMENT		1995	$8.95	$12.00
1995-QX597-9	Three Wishes	CC - ORNAMENT	ORNAMENT		1995	$7.95	$12.50
1995-QX605-7	Heaven's Gift	CC - ORNAMENT	ORNAMENT		1995	$20.00	$20.00
1995-QX598-7	Rejoice!	CC - ORNAMENT	ORNAMENT		1995	$10.95	$20.00
1995-QX610-6	Waiting up for Santa	CC - ORNAMENT	ORNAMENT		1995	$8.95	$14.00
1995-QX611-7	Polar Coaster	CC - ORNAMENT	ORNAMENT		1995	$8.95	$14.50
1995-QX599-7	Christmas Morning	CC - ORNAMENT	ORNAMENT		1995	$10.95	$14.50
1995-QX603-7	Happy Wrappers	CC - ORNAMENT	ORNAMENT		1995	$10.95	$12.00
1995-QX554-7	Baby's First Christmas	CC - ORNAMENT	ORNAMENT		1995	$18.95	$25.00
1995-QX555-7	Baby's First Christmas	CC - ORNAMENT	ORNAMENT		1995	$9.95	$14.00
1995-QX231-7	Baby's First Christmas - Girl	CC - ORNAMENT	ORNAMENT		1995	$5.00	$9.00
1995-QX231-9	Baby's First Christmas - Boy	CC - ORNAMENT	ORNAMENT		1995	$5.00	$9.00
1995-QX563-9	Packed with Memories	CC - ORNAMENT	ORNAMENT		1995	$7.95	$10.00
1995-QX554-9	Baby's First Christmas	CC - ORNAMENT	ORNAMENT		1995	$7.95	$12.00
1995-QX555-9	Baby's First Christmas	CC - ORNAMENT	ORNAMENT		1995	$7.95	$12.50
1995-QX556-7	Baby's Second Christmas	CC - ORNAMENT	ORNAMENT		1995	$7.95	$12.50
1995-QX562-7	Child's Third Christmas	CC - ORNAMENT	ORNAMENT		1995	$7.95	$15.50
1995-QX562-9	Child's Fourth Christmas	CC - ORNAMENT	ORNAMENT		1995	$6.95	$11.00
1995-QX563-7	Child's Fifth Christmas	CC - ORNAMENT	ORNAMENT		1995	$6.95	$8.00
1995-QX579-7	Our First Christmas Together	CC - ORNAMENT	ORNAMENT		1995	$16.95	$22.00
1995-QX579-9	Our First Christmas Together	CC - ORNAMENT	ORNAMENT		1995	$8.95	$12.00
1995-QX580-7	Our First Christmas Together	CC - ORNAMENT	ORNAMENT		1995	$8.95	$11.50
1995-QX317-7	Our First Christmas Together	CC - ORNAMENT	ORNAMENT		1995	$6.95	$14.00
1995-QX580-9	Our Christmas Together	CC - ORNAMENT	ORNAMENT		1995	$9.95	$14.00
1995-QX581-7	In A Heartbeat	CC - ORNAMENT	ORNAMENT		1995	$8.95	$15.00
1995-QX581-9	Anniversary Year	CC - ORNAMENT	ORNAMENT		1995	$8.95	$11.50
1995-QX565-7	Mom and Dad	CC - ORNAMENT	ORNAMENT		1995	$9.95	$17.50
1995-QX564-7	Mom	CC - ORNAMENT	ORNAMENT		1995	$7.95	$11.50
1995-QX564-9	Dad	CC - ORNAMENT	ORNAMENT		1995	$7.95	$12.00
1995-QX565-9	Mom-to-Be	CC - ORNAMENT	ORNAMENT		1995	$7.95	$10.00
1995-QX566-7	Dad-to-Be	CC - ORNAMENT	ORNAMENT		1995	$7.95	$10.00
1995-QX567-7	Daughter	CC - ORNAMENT	ORNAMENT		1995	$6.95	$10.00
1995-QX566-9	Son	CC - ORNAMENT	ORNAMENT		1995	$6.95	$11.00
1995-QX568-7	Sister	CC - ORNAMENT	ORNAMENT		1995	$6.95	$10.50
1995-QX567-9	Brother	CC - ORNAMENT	ORNAMENT		1995	$6.95	$10.50

Order No.	Title	Type	Theme	Retired	Intro. Year	Retail Price	Secondary Price
1995-QX568-9	Sister to Sister	CC - ORNAMENT	ORNAMENT		1995	$8.95	$11.50
1995-QX570-9	Our Family	CC - ORNAMENT	ORNAMENT		1995	$7.95	$11.00
1995-QX241-7	Godparent	CC - ORNAMENT	ORNAMENT		1995	$5.00	$6.00
1995-QX570-7	Godchild	CC - ORNAMENT	ORNAMENT		1995	$7.95	$12.50
1995-QX571-9	Special Dog	CC - ORNAMENT	ORNAMENT		1995	$7.95	$10.00
1995-QX571-7	Special Cat	CC - ORNAMENT	ORNAMENT		1995	$7.95	$11.00
1995-QX241-9	Grandparents	CC - ORNAMENT	ORNAMENT		1995	$5.00	$6.00
1995-QX576-7	Grandmother	CC - ORNAMENT	ORNAMENT		1995	$7.95	$12.00
1995-QX572-9	For My Grandma	CC - ORNAMENT	ORNAMENT		1995	$6.95	$12.00
1995-QX576-9	Grandpa	CC - ORNAMENT	ORNAMENT		1995	$8.95	$10.00
1995-QX577-9	Granddaughter	CC - ORNAMENT	ORNAMENT		1995	$6.95	$12.50
1995-QX578-7	Grandson	CC - ORNAMENT	ORNAMENT		1995	$6.95	$10.00
1995-QX577-7	Grandchild's First Christmas	CC - ORNAMENT	ORNAMENT		1995	$7.95	$12.00
1995-QX582-9	Two for Tea	CC - ORNAMENT	ORNAMENT		1995	$9.95	$16.50
1995-QX582-7	Friendly Boost	CC - ORNAMENT	ORNAMENT		1995	$8.95	$18.00
1995-QX410-7	Delivering Kisses	CC - ORNAMENT	ORNAMENT		1995	$10.95	$20.00
1995-QX583-9	New Home	CC - ORNAMENT	ORNAMENT		1995	$8.95	$12.00
1995-QX584-7	Across the Miles	CC - ORNAMENT	ORNAMENT		1995	$8.95	$11.50
1995-QX594-7	Important Memo	CC - ORNAMENT	ORNAMENT		1995	$8.95	$13.50
1995-QX594-9	Number One Teacher	CC - ORNAMENT	ORNAMENT		1995	$7.95	$10.00
1995-QX595-7	North Pole 911	CC - ORNAMENT	ORNAMENT		1995	$10.95	$11.00
1995-QX595-9	Christmas Patrol	CC - ORNAMENT	ORNAMENT		1995	$7.95	$15.50
1995-QX596-7	Christmas Fever	CC - ORNAMENT	ORNAMENT		1995	$7.95	$9.00
1995-QX597-7	Air Express	CC - ORNAMENT	ORNAMENT		1995	$7.95	$11.00
1995-QLX726-9	Tobin Fraley Hldy Carousel-2nd	CC - ORNAMENT	ORNAMENT		1995	$32.00	$45.00
1995-QLX730-7	Chris Mouse - 11th	CC - ORNAMENT	ORNAMENT		1995	$12.50	$23.50
1995-QLX729-9	Forest Frolics - 7th and Final	CC - ORNAMENT	ORNAMENT		1995	$28.00	$37.00
1995-QLX727-7	Peanuts - 5th and Final	CC - ORNAMENT	ORNAMENT		1995	$24.50	$38.00
1995-QLX735-7	Victorian Toy Box	CC - ORNAMENT	ORNAMENT		1995	$42.00	$50.00
1995-QLX736-9	Coming to See Santa	CC - ORNAMENT	ORNAMENT		1995	$32.00	$48.00
1995-QLX728-9	Fred and Dino	CC - ORNAMENT	ORNAMENT		1995	$28.00	$47.00
1995-QLX727-9	My First Hot Wheels	CC - ORNAMENT	ORNAMENT		1995	$28.00	$34.00
1995-QLX730-9	Superman	CC - ORNAMENT	ORNAMENT		1995	$28.00	$34.00
1995-QLX739-6	Space Shuttle	CC - ORNAMENT	ORNAMENT		1995	$24.50	$34.00
1995-QLX729-7	Winnie the Pooh-Too Much Hunny	CC - ORNAMENT	ORNAMENT		1995	$24.50	$40.00
1995-QLX734-7	Jumping for Joy	CC - ORNAMENT	ORNAMENT		1995	$28.00	$42.00
1995-QLX733-7	Santa's Diner	CC - ORNAMENT	ORNAMENT		1995	$24.50	$27.00
1995-QLX732-9	Wee Little Christmas	CC - ORNAMENT	ORNAMENT		1995	$22.00	$30.00
1995-QLX732-7	Headin' Home	CC - ORNAMENT	ORNAMENT		1995	$22.00	$37.00
1995-QLX731-7	Baby's First Christmas	CC - ORNAMENT	ORNAMENT		1995	$22.00	$29.00
1995-QLX731-9	Holiday Swim	CC - ORNAMENT	ORNAMENT		1995	$18.50	$20.00
1995-QLX736-7	Goody Gumballs!	CC - ORNAMENT	ORNAMENT		1995	$12.50	$29.00
1995-QLX734-9	Friends Share Fun	CC - ORNAMENT	ORNAMENT		1995	$16.50	$24.50
1995-ITEM13	Joe Montana, Kansas Cty Chiefs	CC - ORNAMENT	ORNAMENT		1995		$95.00
1995-QRP4207	Charlie Brown, Chrlie Brn Xmas	CC - ORNAMENT	ORNAMENT		1995	$4.95	$16.00
1995-QRP4209	Lucy, A Charlie Brown Xmas	CC - ORNAMENT	ORNAMENT		1995	$4.95	$12.50
1995-QRP4217	Linus, A Charlie Brown Xmas	CC - ORNAMENT	ORNAMENT		1995	$4.95	$12.50
1995-QRP4219	Snoopy, A Charlie Brown Xmas	CC - ORNAMENT	ORNAMENT		1995	$4.95	$15.00
1995-QRP4227	Snow Scene, A Chrlie Brn Xmas	CC - ORNAMENT	ORNAMENT		1995	$4.95	$18.00
1995-XPF340-7	Holiday Memories Barbie - 2nd	CC - ORNAMENT	ORNAMENT		1995	$45.00	$65.00
1995-QX630-7	Happy Holidays Photo Album	CC - ORNAMENT	ORNAMENT		1995	$2.95	$10.00
1995-ITEM14	Goin' Fishin'-1995 Premiere	CC - ORNAMENT	ORNAMENT		1995		$16.00
1995-ITEM15	A Charlie Brown Xmas (5-piece)	CC - ORNAMENT	ORNAMENT		1995		$57.00
1994-ITEM16	Sarah, Plain & Tall (5-piece)	CC - ORNAMENT	ORNAMENT		1994		$75.50
1994-ITEM17	Collector's Survival Kit, 1994	CC - ORNAMENT	ORNAMENT		1994		$28.00
1994-ITEM18	Here's Your Fortune - '94 EXPO	CC - ORNAMENT	ORNAMENT		1994		$19.00
1994-XPF354-6	Victorian Elegance Barbie Doll	CC - ORNAMENT	ORNAMENT		1994	$40.00	$105.00
1994-QLX751-3B	Simba, Sarabi, & Mufasa-Light	CC - ORNAMENT	ORNAMENT		1994	$20.00	$33.50
1992-ITEM19	Christmas Skyline, 4-piece set	CC - ORNAMENT	ORNAMENT		1992		$66.00
1994-ITEM20	Holiday Hello	CC - ORNAMENT	ORNAMENT		1994		$22.50
1995-ITEM21	EXPO Christmas Tree Cookie	CC - ORNAMENT	ORNAMENT		1995	$12.95	$19.00
1995-ITEM22	EXPO Keepsake Artists	CC - ORNAMENT	ORNAMENT		1995	$7.95	$19.50
1995-ITEM23	NFL Football Helmets (Set-10)	CC - ORNAMENT	ORNAMENT		1995		
1995-QSR624-7	Washington Redskins Ftbl Helmt	CC - ORNAMENT	ORNAMENT		1995		$25.00
1995-ITEM24	Chicago Bears Football Helmet	CC - ORNAMENT	ORNAMENT		1995		$25.00
1995-QSR625-9	Philadelphia Eagles Ftbl Hlmt	CC - ORNAMENT	ORNAMENT		1995		$25.50
1995-QSR623-9	San Francisco 49ers Ftbl Hlmt	CC - ORNAMENT	ORNAMENT		1995		$23.50
1995-ITEM25	Kansas City Chiefs Ftbll Hlmt	CC - ORNAMENT	ORNAMENT		1995		$41.00
1995-QSR622-7	Carolina Panthers Ftbl Hlmt	CC - ORNAMENT	ORNAMENT		1995		$26.00
1995-QSR622-9	New England Patriots Ftbl Hlmt	CC - ORNAMENT	ORNAMENT		1995		$30.00
1995-ITEM26	Detroit Redskins Football Hlmt	CC - ORNAMENT	ORNAMENT		1995		$26.50
1995-QSR626-7	Minnesota Vikings Ftbll Hlmt	CC - ORNAMENT	ORNAMENT		1995		$26.00
1995-QSR621-7	Dallas Cowboys Football Helmet	CC - ORNAMENT	ORNAMENT		1995		$47.00
1995-QSR624-9	Los Angeles Raiders Ftbl Hlmt	CC - ORNAMENT	ORNAMENT		1995		$26.50
1996-QK1171	Language of the Flowers - 1st	CC - ORNAMENT	ORNAMENT		1996	$15.95	$15.95
1996-QK1084	Turn-of-the-Century - 2nd	CC - ORNAMENT	ORNAMENT		1996	$16.95	$16.95
1996-QK1094	The Holly Basket	CC - ORNAMENT	ORNAMENT		1996	$18.95	$24.00
1996-QK1104	Christmas Bunny	CC - ORNAMENT	ORNAMENT		1996	$18.95	$24.00
1996-QK1114	The Birds' Christmas Tree	CC - ORNAMENT	ORNAMENT		1996	$18.95	$24.00
1996-QK1124	Santa's Gifts	CC - ORNAMENT	ORNAMENT		1996	$18.95	$24.00
1996-QK1204	Mrs. Claus	CC - ORNAMENT	ORNAMENT		1996	$18.95	$24.00
1996-QK1134	Caroling Angel	CC - ORNAMENT	ORNAMENT		1996	$16.95	$23.00
1996-QK1174	Balthasar (Frankincense)	CC - ORNAMENT	ORNAMENT		1996	$13.95	$17.00
1996-QK1181	Melchior (Gold)	CC - ORNAMENT	ORNAMENT		1996	$13.95	$13.95
1996-QK1184	Caspar (Myrrh)	CC - ORNAMENT	ORNAMENT		1996	$13.95	$13.95
1996-QK1144	Madonna and Child	CC - ORNAMENT	ORNAMENT		1996	$15.95	$15.95
1996-QK1154	Praying Madonna	CC - ORNAMENT	ORNAMENT		1996	$15.95	$15.95
1996-QK1161	Clyde	CC - ORNAMENT	ORNAMENT		1996	$15.95	$15.95
1996-QK1164	Carmen	CC - ORNAMENT	ORNAMENT		1996	$15.95	$15.95
1996-QXC4164	Santa	CC - ORNAMENT	ORNAMENT		1996		
1996-QXC7341	Rudolph the Red-Nosed Reindeer	CC - ORNAMENT	ORNAMENT		1996		
1996-QXC1	1988 Happy Holidays Barbie	CC - ORNAMENT	ORNAMENT		1996	$14.95	$14.95
1996-QXC2	1937 Steelcraft Auburn	CC - ORNAMENT	ORNAMENT		1996	$15.95	$15.95

Order No.	Title	Type	Theme	Retired	Intro. Year	Retial Price	Secondary Price
1996-QXC3	The Wizard of Oz	CC - ORNAMENT	ORNAMENT		1996	$12.95	$12.95
1996-QXC4	Airmail for Santa	CC - ORNAMENT	ORNAMENT		1996		$18.00
1996-QX6331	Welcome Sign	CC - ORNAMENT	ORNAMENT		1996	$15.00	$15.00
1996-HOOKED	Get Hooked on Collecting	CC - ORNAMENT	ORNAMENT		1996	$7.99	$7.99
1996-QXC4201	Toy Shop Santa	CC - ORNAMENT	ORNAMENT		1996	$60.00	$60.00
1996-QXE7444	Lighting the Flame	CC - ORNAMENT	ORNAMENT		1996	$28.00	$30.00
1996-QXE5511	Invitation to the Games	CC - ORNAMENT	ORNAMENT		1996	$14.95	$14.95
1996-QXE5731	Olympic Triumph	CC - ORNAMENT	ORNAMENT		1996	$10.95	$16.00
1996-QXE5724	Izzy - The Mascot	CC - ORNAMENT	ORNAMENT		1996	$9.95	$12.00
1996-QXE5741	Parade of Nations	CC - ORNAMENT	ORNAMENT		1996	$10.95	$16.00
1996-QXI6541	Barbie - 3rd	CC - ORNAMENT	ORNAMENT		1996	$14.95	$14.95
1996-QXI5371	Holiday Barbie - 4th	CC - ORNAMENT	ORNAMENT		1996	$14.95	$20.00
1996-QXI6341	Quasimodo	CC - ORNAMENT	ORNAMENT		1996	$9.95	$9.95
1996-QXI6354	Laverne, Victor and Hugo	CC - ORNAMENT	ORNAMENT		1996	$12.95	$12.95
1996-QXI6351	Esmeralda and Djali	CC - ORNAMENT	ORNAMENT		1996	$14.95	$14.95
1996-QXI7534	Star Trek	CC - ORNAMENT	ORNAMENT		1996	$45.00	$45.00
1996-QXI7544	U.S.S. Voyager	CC - ORNAMENT	ORNAMENT		1996	$24.00	$24.00
1996-QXI5544	Mr. Spock	CC - ORNAMENT	ORNAMENT		1996	$14.95	$14.95
1996-QXI5551	Commander William T. Riker	CC - ORNAMENT	ORNAMENT		1996	$14.95	$14.95
1996-QXI5711	At the Ballpark - 1st	CC - ORNAMENT	ORNAMENT		1996	$14.95	$14.95
1996-QXI5014	Hoop Stars - 2nd	CC - ORNAMENT	ORNAMENT		1996	$14.95	$14.95
1996-QXI5021	Football Legends - 2nd	CC - ORNAMENT	ORNAMENT		1996	$14.95	$14.95
1996-QXI6531	It's a Wonderful Life	CC - ORNAMENT	ORNAMENT		1996	$14.95	$14.95
1996-QX5531	Lionel Train - 1st	CC - ORNAMENT	ORNAMENT		1996	$18.95	$18.95
1996-QX5561	Dolls of the World - 1st	CC - ORNAMENT	ORNAMENT		1996	$14.95	$14.95
1996-QX6311	Madame Alexander - 1st	CC - ORNAMENT	ORNAMENT		1996	$14.95	$22.00
1996-QX5564	All God's Children - 1st	CC - ORNAMENT	ORNAMENT		1996	$12.95	$18.00
1996-QX5631	Christmas Visitors - 2nd	CC - ORNAMENT	ORNAMENT		1996	$14.95	$14.95
1996-QX5241	All-American Trucks - 2nd	CC - ORNAMENT	ORNAMENT		1996	$13.95	$13.95
1996-QX5634	A Celebration of Angels - 2nd	CC - ORNAMENT	ORNAMENT		1996	$12.95	$14.50
1996-QX5011	Yuletide Central - 3rd	CC - ORNAMENT	ORNAMENT		1996	$18.95	$18.95
1996-QX5364	Kiddie Car Classics - 3rd	CC - ORNAMENT	ORNAMENT		1996	$13.95	$18.00
1996-QX5304	Baseball Heroes - 3rd	CC - ORNAMENT	ORNAMENT		1996	$12.95	$12.95
1996-QX5641	Cat Naps - 3rd	CC - ORNAMENT	ORNAMENT		1996	$7.95	$8.50
1996-QX5644	Mother Goose - 4th	CC - ORNAMENT	ORNAMENT		1996	$13.95	$13.95
1996-QX5651	Puppy Love - 6th	CC - ORNAMENT	ORNAMENT		1996	$7.95	$7.95
1996-QX5384	Classic American Cars - 6th	CC - ORNAMENT	ORNAMENT		1996	$12.95	$16.00
1996-QX5654	Merry Olde Santa - 7th	CC - ORNAMENT	ORNAMENT		1996	$14.95	$14.95
1996-QX5661	Fabulous Decade - 7th	CC - ORNAMENT	ORNAMENT		1996	$7.95	$7.95
1996-QX5391	Crayola Crayon - 8th	CC - ORNAMENT	ORNAMENT		1996	$10.95	$16.00
1996-QX5664	Mary's Angels - 9th	CC - ORNAMENT	ORNAMENT		1996	$6.95	$6.95
1996-QX5681	Frosty Friends - 17th	CC - ORNAMENT	ORNAMENT		1996	$10.95	$14.00
1996-QX5671	Nostalgic Houses & Shops-13th	CC - ORNAMENT	ORNAMENT		1996	$14.95	$14.95
1996-QX5684	Here Comes Santa - 18th	CC - ORNAMENT	ORNAMENT		1996	$14.95	$14.95
1996-QX5381	The Peanuts Gang - 4th & Final	CC - ORNAMENT	ORNAMENT		1996	$9.95	$9.95
1996-QX5674	Rocking Horse - 16th and Final	CC - ORNAMENT	ORNAMENT		1996	$10.95	$10.95
1996-QX5714	Evergreen Santa	CC - ORNAMENT	ORNAMENT		1996	$22.00	$26.00
1996-QX5757	Spider-Man	CC - ORNAMENT	ORNAMENT		1996	$12.95	$12.95
1996-QX5941	Wonder Woman	CC - ORNAMENT	ORNAMENT		1996	$12.95	$12.95
1996-QX5444	Foghorn Leghorn & Henery Hawk	CC - ORNAMENT	ORNAMENT		1996	$13.95	$13.95
1996-QX5451	Marvin the Martian	CC - ORNAMENT	ORNAMENT		1996	$10.95	$10.95
1996-QX5481	Olive Oyl and Swee' Pea	CC - ORNAMENT	ORNAMENT		1996	$10.95	$10.95
1996-QX6524	Ziggy	CC - ORNAMENT	ORNAMENT		1996	$9.95	$9.95
1996-QX5521	Yogi Bear and Boo Boo	CC - ORNAMENT	ORNAMENT		1996	$12.95	$12.95
1996-QX5454	Winnie the Pooh and Piglet	CC - ORNAMENT	ORNAMENT		1996	$12.95	$12.95
1996-QX5507	A Tree for Snoopy	CC - ORNAMENT	ORNAMENT		1996	$8.95	$8.95
1996-QX5554	Witch of the West	CC - ORNAMENT	ORNAMENT		1996	$13.95	$13.95
1996-QX6314	Percy the Small Engine-No. 6	CC - ORNAMENT	ORNAMENT		1996	$9.95	$9.95
1996-QX6321	Tonka Mighty Dump Truck	CC - ORNAMENT	ORNAMENT		1996	$13.95	$13.95
1996-QX5394	Welcome Guest	CC - ORNAMENT	ORNAMENT		1996	$14.95	$14.95
1996-QX6534	Pez Snowman	CC - ORNAMENT	ORNAMENT		1996	$7.95	$7.95
1996-QX5504	Little Spooners	CC - ORNAMENT	ORNAMENT		1996	$12.95	$13.00
1996-QX5464	Time for a Treat	CC - ORNAMENT	ORNAMENT		1996	$11.95	$11.95
1996-QX6214	Christmas Snowman	CC - ORNAMENT	ORNAMENT		1996	$9.95	$9.95
1996-QX5891	I Dig Golf	CC - ORNAMENT	ORNAMENT		1996	$10.95	$10.95
1996-QX6031	Bounce Pass	CC - ORNAMENT	ORNAMENT		1996	$7.95	$7.95
1996-QX5904	Happy Holi-doze	CC - ORNAMENT	ORNAMENT		1996	$9.95	$9.95
1996-QX5914	This Big!	CC - ORNAMENT	ORNAMENT		1996	$9.95	$9.95
1996-QX5924	Fan-tastic Season	CC - ORNAMENT	ORNAMENT		1996	$9.95	$11.00
1996-QX6001	Goal Line Glory	CC - ORNAMENT	ORNAMENT		1996	$12.95	$16.00
1996-QX6014	Bowl 'em Over	CC - ORNAMENT	ORNAMENT		1996	$7.95	$7.95
1996-QX6034	Polar Cycle	CC - ORNAMENT	ORNAMENT		1996	$12.95	$12.95
1996-QX6011	Pup-Tenting	CC - ORNAMENT	ORNAMENT		1996	$7.95	$7.95
1996-QX5541	Growth of a Leader	CC - ORNAMENT	ORNAMENT		1996	$9.95	$9.95
1996-QX5884	Merry Carpoolers	CC - ORNAMENT	ORNAMENT		1996	$14.95	$14.95
1996-QX5901	Antlers Aweigh!	CC - ORNAMENT	ORNAMENT		1996	$9.95	$13.00
1996-QX5921	Sew Sweet	CC - ORNAMENT	ORNAMENT		1996	$8.95	$8.95
1996-QX5911	Jackpot Jingle	CC - ORNAMENT	ORNAMENT		1996	$9.95	$9.95
1996-QX6004	Star of the Show	CC - ORNAMENT	ORNAMENT		1996	$8.95	$8.95
1996-QX6054	Yuletide Cheer	CC - ORNAMENT	ORNAMENT		1996	$7.95	$7.95
1996-QX6061	Matchless Memories	CC - ORNAMENT	ORNAMENT		1996	$9.95	$9.95
1996-QX6121	Apple for Teacher	CC - ORNAMENT	ORNAMENT		1996	$7.95	$7.95
1996-QX6114	Tender Lovin' Care	CC - ORNAMENT	ORNAMENT		1996	$7.95	$10.00
1996-QX6074	Hurrying Downstairs	CC - ORNAMENT	ORNAMENT		1996	$8.95	$8.95
1996-QX6071	Child Care Giver	CC - ORNAMENT	ORNAMENT		1996	$8.95	$12.00
1996-QX6271	Making His Rounds	CC - ORNAMENT	ORNAMENT		1996	$14.95	$14.95
1996-QX6274	Kindly Shepherd	CC - ORNAMENT	ORNAMENT		1996	$12.95	$14.00
1996-QX6301	Tamika	CC - ORNAMENT	ORNAMENT		1996	$7.95	$7.95
1996-QX6304	Feliz Navidad	CC - ORNAMENT	ORNAMENT		1996	$9.95	$9.95
1996-QX6324	Madonna and Child	CC - ORNAMENT	ORNAMENT		1996	$12.95	$13.00
1996-QX6124	Lighting the Way	CC - ORNAMENT	ORNAMENT		1996	$12.95	$12.95
1996-QX6244	Come All Ye Faithful	CC - ORNAMENT	ORNAMENT		1996	$12.95	$12.95
1996-QX6241	Christmas Joy	CC - ORNAMENT	ORNAMENT		1996	$14.95	$14.95

Order No.	Title	Type	Theme	Retired	Intro. Year	Retail Price	Secondary Price
1996-QX6251	Precious Child	CC - ORNAMENT	ORNAMENT		1996	$8.95	$8.95
1996-QX6231	Glad Tidings	CC - ORNAMENT	ORNAMENT		1996	$14.95	$14.95
1996-QX6261	Prayer for Peace	CC - ORNAMENT	ORNAMENT		1996	$7.95	$15.00
1996-QX6264	Welcome Him	CC - ORNAMENT	ORNAMENT		1996	$8.95	$8.95
1996-QX6131	Woodland Santa	CC - ORNAMENT	ORNAMENT		1996	$12.95	$12.95
1996-QX6221	Jolly Wolly Ark	CC - ORNAMENT	ORNAMENT		1996	$12.95	$12.95
1996-QX6201	Holiday Haul	CC - ORNAMENT	ORNAMENT		1996	$14.95	$14.95
1996-QX6134	Hillside Express	CC - ORNAMENT	ORNAMENT		1996	$12.95	$12.95
1996-QX6224	Maxine	CC - ORNAMENT	ORNAMENT		1996	$9.95	$9.95
1996-QX6064	High Style	CC - ORNAMENT	ORNAMENT		1996	$8.95	$8.95
1996-QX6234	Peppermint Surprise	CC - ORNAMENT	ORNAMENT		1996	$7.95	$7.95
1996-QX6211	A Little Song and Dance	CC - ORNAMENT	ORNAMENT		1996	$9.95	$9.95
1996-QX6204	Regal Cardinal	CC - ORNAMENT	ORNAMENT		1996	$9.95	$12.00
1996-QX5744	Baby's First Christmas	CC - ORNAMENT	ORNAMENT		1996	$18.95	$18.95
1996-QX5751	Baby's First Christmas	CC - ORNAMENT	ORNAMENT		1996	$10.95	$10.95
1996-QX5754	Baby's First Christmas	CC - ORNAMENT	ORNAMENT		1996	$9.95	$9.95
1996-QX5761	Baby's First Christmas	CC - ORNAMENT	ORNAMENT		1996	$7.95	$7.95
1996-QX5764	Baby's First Christmas	CC - ORNAMENT	ORNAMENT		1996	$7.95	$7.95
1996-QX5771	Baby's Second Christmas	CC - ORNAMENT	ORNAMENT		1996	$7.95	$7.95
1996-QX5774	Child's Third Christmas	CC - ORNAMENT	ORNAMENT		1996	$7.95	$7.95
1996-QX5781	Child's Fourth Christmas	CC - ORNAMENT	ORNAMENT		1996	$7.95	$7.95
1996-QX5784	Child's Fifth Christmas	CC - ORNAMENT	ORNAMENT		1996	$6.95	$6.95
1996-QX5794	Our Christmas Together	CC - ORNAMENT	ORNAMENT		1996	$18.95	$18.95
1996-QX5804	Our Christmas Together-Photo	CC - ORNAMENT	ORNAMENT		1996	$8.95	$8.95
1996-QX5801	Our First Christmas Together	CC - ORNAMENT	ORNAMENT		1996	$10.95	$10.95
1996-QX5811	Our First Christmas Together	CC - ORNAMENT	ORNAMENT		1996	$9.95	$9.95
1996-QX3051	Our First Christmas Together	CC - ORNAMENT	ORNAMENT		1996	$6.95	$6.95
1996-QX5814	Hearts Full of Love	CC - ORNAMENT	ORNAMENT		1996	$9.95	$9.95
1996-QX5824	Mom	CC - ORNAMENT	ORNAMENT		1996	$7.95	$7.95
1996-QX5831	Dad	CC - ORNAMENT	ORNAMENT		1996	$7.95	$7.95
1996-QX5821	Mom and Dad	CC - ORNAMENT	ORNAMENT		1996	$9.95	$9.95
1996-QX6077	Daughter	CC - ORNAMENT	ORNAMENT		1996	$8.95	$8.95
1996-QX5791	Mom-to-Be	CC - ORNAMENT	ORNAMENT		1996	$7.95	$7.95
1996-QX6079	Son	CC - ORNAMENT	ORNAMENT		1996	$8.95	$8.95
1996-QX5834	Sister to Sister	CC - ORNAMENT	ORNAMENT		1996	$9.95	$9.95
1996-QX5697	Granddaughter	CC - ORNAMENT	ORNAMENT		1996	$7.95	$7.95
1996-QX5699	Grandson	CC - ORNAMENT	ORNAMENT		1996	$7.95	$7.95
1996-QX5844	Grandma	CC - ORNAMENT	ORNAMENT		1996	$8.95	$8.95
1996-QX5851	Grandpa	CC - ORNAMENT	ORNAMENT		1996	$8.95	$8.95
1996-QX5854	Thank You, Santa Photo Holder	CC - ORNAMENT	ORNAMENT		1996	$7.95	$7.95
1996-QX5861	On My Way Photo Holder	CC - ORNAMENT	ORNAMENT		1996	$7.95	$7.95
1996-QX5864	Special Dog Photo Holder	CC - ORNAMENT	ORNAMENT		1996	$7.95	$7.95
1996-QX5841	Godchild	CC - ORNAMENT	ORNAMENT		1996	$8.95	$11.00
1996-QX5874	Close-Knit Friends	CC - ORNAMENT	ORNAMENT		1996	$9.95	$9.95
1996-QX5881	New Home	CC - ORNAMENT	ORNAMENT		1996	$8.95	$8.95
1996-QLX7524	Journeys into Space - 1st	CC - ORNAMENT	ORNAMENT		1996	$24.00	$24.00
1996-QLX7371	Chris Mouse - 12th	CC - ORNAMENT	ORNAMENT		1996	$14.50	$14.50
1996-QLX7461	Tobin Fraley Hldy Carousel-3rd	CC - ORNAMENT	ORNAMENT		1996	$32.00	$34.00
1996-QLX7471	North Pole Volunteers	CC - ORNAMENT	ORNAMENT		1996	$42.00	$42.00
1996-QLX7421	The Statue of Liberty	CC - ORNAMENT	ORNAMENT		1996	$24.50	$29.00
1996-QLX7474	Millenium Falcon	CC - ORNAMENT	ORNAMENT		1996	$24.00	$24.00
1996-QLX7454	Emerald City	CC - ORNAMENT	ORNAMENT		1996	$32.00	$32.00
1996-QLX7411	The Jetsons	CC - ORNAMENT	ORNAMENT		1996	$28.00	$34.00
1996-QLX7394	Peanuts	CC - ORNAMENT	ORNAMENT		1996	$18.50	$18.50
1996-QLX7414	Slippery Day (Winnie the Pooh)	CC - ORNAMENT	ORNAMENT		1996	$24.50	$24.50
1996-QLX7404	Baby's First Christmas	CC - ORNAMENT	ORNAMENT		1996	$22.00	$22.00
1996-QLX7451	Pinball Wonder	CC - ORNAMENT	ORNAMENT		1996	$28.00	$28.00
1996-QLX7431	Video Party	CC - ORNAMENT	ORNAMENT		1996	$28.00	$28.00
1996-QLX7339	Jukebox Party	CC - ORNAMENT	ORNAMENT		1996	$24.50	$31.00
1996-QLX7424	Sharing a Soda	CC - ORNAMENT	ORNAMENT		1996	$24.50	$24.50
1996-QLX7491	Chicken Coop Chorus	CC - ORNAMENT	ORNAMENT		1996	$24.50	$24.50
1996-QLX7391	Father Time	CC - ORNAMENT	ORNAMENT		1996	$24.50	$24.50
1996-QLX7384	Treasured Memories	CC - ORNAMENT	ORNAMENT		1996	$18.50	$18.50
1996-QLX7381	Let Us Adore Him	CC - ORNAMENT	ORNAMENT		1996	$16.50	$15.50
1996-QLX7374	Over the Rooftops	CC - ORNAMENT	ORNAMENT		1996	$14.50	$14.50
1996-YR	Yuletide Romance Barbie Doll	CC - ORNAMENT	ORNAMENT		1996		
1996-TSS	Toy Shop Santa	CC - ORNAMENT	ORNAMENT		1996	$14.95	$14.95
1996-101	Dalmation, 101 Dalmations	CC - ORNAMENT	ORNAMENT		1996	$12.95	$12.95
1997-QX1401-2	Meg and Pegasus	CC - ORNAMENT	ORNAMENT		1997	$16.95	
1997-QX1407-2	Ariel, The Little Mermaid	CC - ORNAMENT	ORNAMENT		1997	$12.95	
1997-QX1548-4	Luke Skywalker #1	CC - ORNAMENT	ORNAMENT		1997	$13.95	
1997-QX1753-1	Darth Vader	CC - ORNAMENT	ORNAMENT		1997	$24.00	
1997-QX1426-5	C-3PO and R2-D2-STARWARS	CC - ORNAMENT	ORNAMENT		1997	$12.95	
1997-QX1635-5	Yoda	CC - ORNAMENT	ORNAMENT		1997	$9.95	
1997-QX1618-2	Wedding Day-BARBIE #4	CC - ORNAMENT	ORNAMENT		1997	$15.95	
1997-QX1618-5	Barbie and Ken-Wedding	CC - ORNAMENT	ORNAMENT		1997	$35.00	
1997-QX1621-2	Holiday BARBIE #5	CC - ORNAMENT	ORNAMENT		1997	$15.95	
1997-QX1613-5	Victorian Christmas #1	CC - ORNAMENT	ORNAMENT		1997	$10.95	
1997-QX1754-5	The Warmth of Home	CC - ORNAMENT	ORNAMENT		1997	$18.95	
1997-QX1634-5	Commander Data	CC - ORNAMENT	ORNAMENT		1997	$14.95	
1997-QX1635-2	Dr. Leonard H. McCoy	CC - ORNAMENT	ORNAMENT		1997	$14.95	
1997-QX1748-1	U.S.S. Defiant	CC - ORNAMENT	ORNAMENT		1997	$24.00	
1997-QX1645-5	1997 Corvette	CC - ORNAMENT	ORNAMENT		1997	$13.95	
1997-QX1432-2	Miniature 1994 Corvette	CC - ORNAMENT	ORNAMENT		1997	$6.95	
1997-QX1616-5	Jeff Gordon #1	CC - ORNAMENT	ORNAMENT		1997	$14.95	
1997-QX1627-5	Wayne Gretzky #1	CC - ORNAMENT	ORNAMENT		1997	$14.95	
1997-QX1615-2	Hank Aaron #2	CC - ORNAMENT	ORNAMENT		1997	$14.95	
1997-QX1618-2	Joe Namath #3	CC - ORNAMENT	ORNAMENT		1997	$14.95	
1997-QX1683-2	Magic Johnson #3	CC - ORNAMENT	ORNAMENT		1997	$14.95	
1997-QX557-4	The Flight at Kitty Hawk #1	CC - ORNAMENT	ORNAMENT		1997	$14.95	
1997-QX557-4	The Flight at Kitty Hawk #1	CC - ORNAMENT	ORNAMENT		1997	$14.95	
1997-QX570-4	Marilyn Monroe #1	CC - ORNAMENT	ORNAMENT		1997	$14.95	
1997-QX612-5	Scarlett O'Hara #1	CC - ORNAMENT	ORNAMENT		1997	$14.95	

Order No.	Title	Type	Theme	Retired	Intro. Year	Retial Price	Secondary Price
1997-QX611-2	The Clauses on Vacation #1	CC - ORNAMENT	ORNAMENT		1997	$14.95	
1997-QX614-2	Nikki-All God's Children #2	CC - ORNAMENT	ORNAMENT		1997	$12.95	
1997-QX569-4	Snowshoe Rabbits in Winter	CC - ORNAMENT	ORNAMENT		1997	$12.95	
1997-QX569-4	Snowshoe Rabbits in Winter	CC - ORNAMENT	ORNAMENT		1997	$12.95	
1997-QX615-5	Little Red Riding Hood-1991 #2	CC - ORNAMENT	ORNAMENT		1997	$14.95	
1997-QX616-2	Chinese BARBIE #2	CC - ORNAMENT	ORNAMENT		1997	$14.95	
1997-QX109-5	Snowdrop Angel #2	CC - ORNAMENT	ORNAMENT		1997	$15.95	
1997-QX614-5	1959 Sante Fe F3 Diesel Locomotive #2	CC - ORNAMENT	ORNAMENT		1997	$18.95	
1997-LX753-2	Friendship 7 #2	CC - ORNAMENT	ORNAMENT		1997	$24.00	
1997-QX610-5	1953 GMC #3	CC - ORNAMENT	ORNAMENT		1997	$13.95	
1997-QX617-5	A Celebration of Angels #3	CC - ORNAMENT	ORNAMENT		1997	$13.95	
1997-QX620-5	Cat Naps #4	CC - ORNAMENT	ORNAMENT		1997	$8.95	
1997-QX619-5	Murray Dumpt Truck #4	CC - ORNAMENT	ORNAMENT		1997	$13.95	
1997-QX581-2	Yuletide Central #4	CC - ORNAMENT	ORNAMENT		1997	$18.95	
1997-QX622-2	Puppy Love #7	CC - ORNAMENT	ORNAMENT		1997	$7.95	
1997-QX610-2	1969 Hurst Oldsmobile 442 #7	CC - ORNAMENT	ORNAMENT		1997	$13.95	
1997-QX623-2	Fabulous Decade #8	CC - ORNAMENT	ORNAMENT		1997	$12.95	
1997-QX622-5	Merry Olde Santa #8	CC - ORNAMENT	ORNAMENT		1997	$14.95	
1997-QX623-5	Bright Rocking Colors #8	CC - ORNAMENT	ORNAMENT		1997	$12.95	
1997-QX624-2	Daisy-Mary's Angels #10	CC - ORNAMENT	ORNAMENT		1997	$7.95	
1997-QX624-5	Cafe #14	CC - ORNAMENT	ORNAMENT		1997	$16.95	
1997-QX6255	Frosty Friends #18	CC - ORNAMENT	ORNAMENT		1997	$10.95	
1997-QX626-2	The Claus-Mobile #19	CC - ORNAMENT	ORNAMENT		1997	$14.95	
1997-QX617-2	Kolydad #3	CC - ORNAMENT	ORNAMENT		1997	$16.95	
1997-QX121-5	Santa Claus #3	CC - ORNAMENT	ORNAMENT		1997	$16.95	
1997-QX620-2	Jackie Robinson #4	CC - ORNAMENT	ORNAMENT		1997	$12.95	
1997-QX621-5	Little Boy Blue #5	CC - ORNAMENT	ORNAMENT		1997	$13.95	
1997-LX752-5	Chris Mouse Luminaria #13	CC - ORNAMENT	ORNAMENT		1997	$14.95	
1997-QX572-1	The Night Before Christmas	CC - ORNAMENT	ORNAMENT		1997	$24.00	
1997-QX667-2	Santa's Magical Sleigh	CC - ORNAMENT	ORNAMENT		1997	$24.00	
1997-QXD402-2	Bandleader Mickey #1	CC - ORNAMENT	ORNAMENT		1997	$13.95	
1997-QXD402-5	Donald's Surprising Gift #1	CC - ORNAMENT	ORNAMENT		1997	$12.95	
1997-QXD403-2	New Pair of Skates	CC - ORNAMENT	ORNAMENT		1997	$13.95	
1997-QXD404-2	Goofey's Ski Adventure	CC - ORNAMENT	ORNAMENT		1997	$12.95	
1997-QXD403-5	Mickey's Snow Angel	CC - ORNAMENT	ORNAMENT		1997	$9.95	
1997-QXD641-2	Mickey's Long Shot	CC - ORNAMENT	ORNAMENT		1997	$9.95	
1997-QXD404-5	Cinderella #1	CC - ORNAMENT	ORNAMENT		1997	$14.95	
1997-QXD405-2	Gus & Jaq, Cinderella	CC - ORNAMENT	ORNAMENT		1997	$12.95	
1997-QXD405-5	Snow White, Anniversary Edition	CC - ORNAMENT	ORNAMENT		1997	$16.95	
1997-QXD636-5	Waitin' on Santa, Winnie the Pooh	CC - ORNAMENT	ORNAMENT		1997	$12.95	
1997-QXD425-5	Honey of a Gift-Winnie the Pooh	CC - ORNAMENT	ORNAMENT		1997	$6.96	
1997-QXD406-2	Jasmine & Aladdin, King of Thieves	CC - ORNAMENT	ORNAMENT		1997	$14.95	
1997-QXD406-5	Timon & Tumbaa, The Lion King	CC - ORNAMENT	ORNAMENT		1997	$12.95	
1997-QXD634-4	Phoebus & Esmeralda, Hunchback	CC - ORNAMENT	ORNAMENT		1997	$14.95	
1997-QXD401-5	Two-tone, 101 Dalmations	CC - ORNAMENT	ORNAMENT		1997	$9.95	
1997-QXD636-2	Tonka Might Front Loader	CC - ORNAMENT	ORNAMENT		1997	$13.95	
1997-LX752-2	The Lincoln Memorial	CC - ORNAMENT	ORNAMENT		1997	$24.00	
1997-QX637-2	Miss Gulch	CC - ORNAMENT	ORNAMENT		1997	$13.95	
1997-QX627-2	Howdy Doody	CC - ORNAMENT	ORNAMENT		1997	$12.95	
1997-QX626-5	The Lone Ranger	CC - ORNAMENT	ORNAMENT		1997	$12.95	
1997-QX633-5	Mr. Potato Head	CC - ORNAMENT	ORNAMENT		1997	$10.95	
1997-LX747-5	SNOOPY Plays Santa	CC - ORNAMENT	ORNAMENT		1997	$22.00	
1997-QX547-1	The Incredible Hulk	CC - ORNAMENT	ORNAMENT		1997	$12.95	
1997-LX750-2	Decorator Taz	CC - ORNAMENT	ORNAMENT		1997	$30.00	
1997-QX633-2	Michigan J. Frog	CC - ORNAMENT	ORNAMENT		1997	$9.95	
1997-QX632-5	Sweet Discovery	CC - ORNAMENT	ORNAMENT		1997	$11.95	
1997-QX630-5	Taking A Break	CC - ORNAMENT	ORNAMENT		1997	$14.95	
1997-QX634-2	Marbles Champion	CC - ORNAMENT	ORNAMENT		1997	$10.95	
1997-QSR550-5	ARIZONA CARDINALS	CC - ORNAMENT	ORNAMENT		1997	$9.95	
1997-QSR530-5	ATLANTA FALCONS	CC - ORNAMENT	ORNAMENT		1997	$9.95	
1997-QSR535-2	BALTIMORE RAVENS	CC - ORNAMENT	ORNAMENT		1997	$9.95	
1997-QSR531-2	BUFFALO BILLS	CC - ORNAMENT	ORNAMENT		1997	$9.95	
1997-QSR531-5	CAROLINA PANTHERS	CC - ORNAMENT	ORNAMENT		1997	$9.95	
1997-QSR532-2	CHICAGO BEARS	CC - ORNAMENT	ORNAMENT		1997	$9.95	
1997-QSR532-5	CINCINNATI BENGALS	CC - ORNAMENT	ORNAMENT		1997	$9.95	
1997-QSR535-5	DALLAS COWBOYS	CC - ORNAMENT	ORNAMENT		1997	$9.95	
1997-QSR536-2	DENVER BRONCOS	CC - ORNAMENT	ORNAMENT		1997	$9.95	
1997-QSR536-5	DETROIT LIONS	CC - ORNAMENT	ORNAMENT		1997	$9.95	
1997-QSR537-2	GREEN BAY PACKERS	CC - ORNAMENT	ORNAMENT		1997	$9.95	
1997-QSR537-5	HOUSTON OILERS	CC - ORNAMENT	ORNAMENT		1997	$9.95	
1997-QSR541-1	INDIANAPOLIS COLTS	CC - ORNAMENT	ORNAMENT		1997	$9.95	
1997-QSR541-5	JACKSONVILLE JAGUARS	CC - ORNAMENT	ORNAMENT		1997	$9.95	
1997-QSR530-2	KANSAS CITY CHIEFS	CC - ORNAMENT	ORNAMENT		1997	$9.95	
1997-QSR547-2	MIAMI DOLPHINS	CC - ORNAMENT	ORNAMENT		1997	$9.95	
1997-QSR547-7	MINNESOTA VIKINGS	CC - ORNAMENT	ORNAMENT		1997	$9.95	
1997-QSR548-2	NEW ENGLAND PATRIOTS	CC - ORNAMENT	ORNAMENT		1997	$9.95	
1997-QSR548-5	NEW ORLEANS SAINTS	CC - ORNAMENT	ORNAMENT		1997	$9.95	
1997-QSR549-2	NEW YORK GIANTS	CC - ORNAMENT	ORNAMENT		1997	$9.95	
1997-QSR549-5	NEW YORK JETS	CC - ORNAMENT	ORNAMENT		1997	$9.95	
1997-QSR542-2	OAKLAND RAIDERS	CC - ORNAMENT	ORNAMENT		1997	$9.95	
1997-QSR550-2	PHILADELPHIA EAGLES	CC - ORNAMENT	ORNAMENT		1997	$9.95	
1997-QSR551-2	PITTSBURGH STEELERS	CC - ORNAMENT	ORNAMENT		1997	$9.95	
1997-QSR542-5	ST. LOUIS RAMS	CC - ORNAMENT	ORNAMENT		1997	$9.95	
1997-QSR551-5	SAN DIEGO CHARGERS	CC - ORNAMENT	ORNAMENT		1997	$9.95	
1997-QSR552-2	SAN FRANCISCO 49ERS	CC - ORNAMENT	ORNAMENT		1997	$9.95	
1997-QSR552-5	SEATTLE SEAHAWKS	CC - ORNAMENT	ORNAMENT		1997	$9.95	
1997-QSR553-2	TAMPA BAY BUCCANEERS	CC - ORNAMENT	ORNAMENT		1997	$9.95	
1997-QSR553-5	WASHINGTON REDSKINS	CC - ORNAMENT	ORNAMENT		1997	$9.95	
1997-QSR122-2	CHARLOTTE HORNETS	CC - ORNAMENT	ORNAMENT		1997	$9.95	
1997-QSR123-2	CHICAGO BULLS	CC - ORNAMENT	ORNAMENT		1997	$9.95	
1997-QSR124-2	DETROIT PISTONS	CC - ORNAMENT	ORNAMENT		1997	$9.95	
1997-QSR124-5	HOUSTON ROCKETS	CC - ORNAMENT	ORNAMENT		1997	$9.95	
1997-QSR125-2	INDIANA PACERS	CC - ORNAMENT	ORNAMENT		1997	$9.95	

Order No.	Title	Type	Theme	Retired	Intro. Year	Retail Price	Secondary Price
1997-QSR126-2	LOS ANGELES LAKERS	CC - ORNAMENT	ORNAMENT		1997	$9.95	
1997-QSR127-2	NEW YORK KNICKERBOCKERS	CC - ORNAMENT	ORNAMENT		1997	$9.95	
1997-QSR128-2	ORLANDO MAGIC	CC - ORNAMENT	ORNAMENT		1997	$9.95	
1997-QSR129-2	PHOENIX SUNS	CC - ORNAMENT	ORNAMENT		1997	$9.95	
1997-QSR129-2	PHOENIX SUNS	CC - ORNAMENT	ORNAMENT		1997	$9.95	
1997-QSR129-5	SEATTLE SUPERSONICS	CC - ORNAMENT	ORNAMENT		1997	$9.95	
1997-QX653-5	Baby's First Christmas	CC - ORNAMENT	ORNAMENT		1997	$14.95	
1997-QX648-5	Baby's First Christmas	CC - ORNAMENT	ORNAMENT		1997	$9.95	
1997-QX649-2	Baby's First Christmas	CC - ORNAMENT	ORNAMENT		1997	$9.95	
1997-QX648-2	Baby's First Christmas	CC - ORNAMENT	ORNAMENT		1997	$7.95	
1997-QX649-5	Baby's First Christmas	CC - ORNAMENT	ORNAMENT		1997	$7.95	
1997-QX650-2	Baby's Second Christmas	CC - ORNAMENT	ORNAMENT		1997	$7.95	
1997-QX650-5	Baby's Third Christmas	CC - ORNAMENT	ORNAMENT		1997	$7.95	
1997-QX651-2	Baby's Fourth Christmas	CC - ORNAMENT	ORNAMENT		1997	$7.95	
1997-QX651-5	Baby's Fifth Christmas	CC - ORNAMENT	ORNAMENT		1997	$7.95	
1997-QX650-5	Child's Third Christmas	CC - ORNAMENT	ORNAMENT		1997	$7.95	
1997-QX651-2	Child's Fourth Christmas	CC - ORNAMENT	ORNAMENT		1997	$7.95	
1997-QX651-5	Child's Fifth Christmas	CC - ORNAMENT	ORNAMENT		1997	$7.95	
1997-QX647-5	Our First Christmas Together	CC - ORNAMENT	ORNAMENT		1997	$16.95	
1997-QX646-5	Our First Christmas Together	CC - ORNAMENT	ORNAMENT		1997	$8.95	
1997-QX647-2	Our First Christmas Together	CC - ORNAMENT	ORNAMENT		1997	$8.95	
1997-QX318-2	Our First Christmas Together	CC - ORNAMENT	ORNAMENT		1997	$7.95	
1997-QX652-5	Mom	CC - ORNAMENT	ORNAMENT		1997	$8.95	
1997-QX653-2	Dad	CC - ORNAMENT	ORNAMENT		1997	$8.95	
1997-QX652-2	Mom and Dad	CC - ORNAMENT	ORNAMENT		1997	$9.95	
1997-QX660-5	Son	CC - ORNAMENT	ORNAMENT		1997	$7.95	
1997-QX661-2	Daughter	CC - ORNAMENT	ORNAMENT		1997	$7.95	
1997-QX663-5	Sister to Sister	CC - ORNAMENT	ORNAMENT		1997	$9.95	
1997-QX662-5	Grandma	CC - ORNAMENT	ORNAMENT		1997	$8.95	
1997-QX661-5	Grandson	CC - ORNAMENT	ORNAMENT		1997	$7.95	
1997-QX662-2	Granddaughter	CC - ORNAMENT	ORNAMENT		1997	$7.95	
1997-QX664-5	Book of the Year	CC - ORNAMENT	ORNAMENT		1997	$7.95	
1997-QX663-2	Special Dog	CC - ORNAMENT	ORNAMENT		1997	$7.95	
1997-QX666-2	Godchild	CC - ORNAMENT	ORNAMENT		1997	$7.95	
1997-QX665-2	New Home	CC - ORNAMENT	ORNAMENT		1997	$8.95	
1997-QX665-5	Friendship Blend	CC - ORNAMENT	ORNAMENT		1997	$9.95	
1997-QX642-5	Cycling Santa	CC - ORNAMENT	ORNAMENT		1997	$14.95	
1997-QX642-2	Santa's Ski Adventure	CC - ORNAMENT	ORNAMENT		1997	$12.95	
1997-QX643-2	Elegance on Ice	CC - ORNAMENT	ORNAMENT		1997	$9.95	
1997-QX671-2	Catch of the Day	CC - ORNAMENT	ORNAMENT		1997	$9.95	
1997-QX644-5	Clever Camper	CC - ORNAMENT	ORNAMENT		1997	$7.95	
1997-QX639-2	All-Round Sports Fan	CC - ORNAMENT	ORNAMENT		1997	$8.95	
1997-QX641-5	All-Weather Walker	CC - ORNAMENT	ORNAMENT		1997	$8.95	
1997-QX644-2	What a Deal!	CC - ORNAMENT	ORNAMENT		1997	$8.95	
1997-QX639-5	Snow Bowling	CC - ORNAMENT	ORNAMENT		1997	$6.95	
1997-QX643-5	Love to Sew	CC - ORNAMENT	ORNAMENT		1997	$7.95	
1997-QX645-2	Tomorrow's Leader	CC - ORNAMENT	ORNAMENT		1997	$9.95	
1997-QX638-2	Bucket Brigade	CC - ORNAMENT	ORNAMENT		1997	$8.95	
1997-QX638-5	Christmas Checkup	CC - ORNAMENT	ORNAMENT		1997	$7.95	
1997-QX637-5	Expressly for Teacher	CC - ORNAMENT	ORNAMENT		1997	$7.95	
1997-QX655-2	King Noor-First King	CC - ORNAMENT	ORNAMENT		1997	$12.95	
1997-QX655-5	Stealing a Kiss	CC - ORNAMENT	ORNAMENT		1997	$14.95	
1997-QX656-2	Snowgirl	CC - ORNAMENT	ORNAMENT		1997	$7.95	
1997-QX666-5	Feliz Navidad	CC - ORNAMENT	ORNAMENT		1997	$8.95	
1997-QX654-5	Madonna del Rosario	CC - ORNAMENT	ORNAMENT		1997	$12.95	
1997-QX654-2	Praise Him	CC - ORNAMENT	ORNAMENT		1997	$8.95	
1997-LX742-5	Madonna and Child	CC - ORNAMENT	ORNAMENT		1997	$19.95	
1997-LX743-5	Glowing Angel	CC - ORNAMENT	ORNAMENT		1997	$18.95	
1997-QX679-2	God's Gift of Love	CC - ORNAMENT	ORNAMENT		1997	$16.95	
1997-QX680-5	Classic Cross	CC - ORNAMENT	ORNAMENT		1997	$13.95	
1997-QX679-5	Heavenly Song	CC - ORNAMENT	ORNAMENT		1997	$12.95	
1997-QX658-5	The Spirit of Christmas	CC - ORNAMENT	ORNAMENT		1997	$9.95	
1997-QX657-5	Nativity Tree	CC - ORNAMENT	ORNAMENT		1997	$14.95	
1997-QX660-2	Lion and Lamb	CC - ORNAMENT	ORNAMENT		1997	$7.95	
1997-QX659-2	Playful Shepherd	CC - ORNAMENT	ORNAMENT		1997	$9.95	
1997-QX659-5	Juggling Stars	CC - ORNAMENT	ORNAMENT		1997	$9.95	
1997-QLX746-5	Santa's Showboat	CC - ORNAMENT	ORNAMENT		1997	$42.00	
1997-QLX749-5	Motorcycle Chums	CC - ORNAMENT	ORNAMENT		1997	$24.00	
1997-QLX748-2	Teapot Party	CC - ORNAMENT	ORNAMENT		1997	$18.95	
1997-QLX751-2	Joy to the World	CC - ORNAMENT	ORNAMENT		1997	$14.95	
1997-QLX667-5	Prize Topiary	CC - ORNAMENT	ORNAMENT		1997	$14.95	
1997-QLX668-2	Biking Buddies	CC - ORNAMENT	ORNAMENT		1997	$12.95	
1997-QLX677-5	Swinging in the Snow	CC - ORNAMENT	ORNAMENT		1997	$12.95	
1997-QLX670-2	Santa Mail	CC - ORNAMENT	ORNAMENT		1997	$10.95	
1997-QLX669-5	Jingle Bell Jester	CC - ORNAMENT	ORNAMENT		1997	$9.95	
1997-QLX670-5	Downhill Run	CC - ORNAMENT	ORNAMENT		1997	$9.95	
1997-QLX672-2	Breezin' Along	CC - ORNAMENT	ORNAMENT		1997	$8.95	
1997-QLX673-2	Sweet Dreamer	CC - ORNAMENT	ORNAMENT		1997	$6.95	
1997-QLX745-5	Santa's Secret Gift	CC - ORNAMENT	ORNAMENT		1997	$24.00	
1997-QLX678-2	Leading the Way	CC - ORNAMENT	ORNAMENT		1997	$16.95	
1997-QLX678-5	Santa's Merry Path	CC - ORNAMENT	ORNAMENT		1997	$16.95	
1997-QLX668-5	Santa's Friend	CC - ORNAMENT	ORNAMENT		1997	$12.95	
1997-QLX748-5	Holiday Serenade	CC - ORNAMENT	ORNAMENT		1997	$24.00	
1997-QLX674-5	Honored Guests	CC - ORNAMENT	ORNAMENT		1997	$14.95	
1997-QLX675-2	Garden Bouquet	CC - ORNAMENT	ORNAMENT		1997	$14.95	
1997-QLX675-5	Santa's Polar Friend	CC - ORNAMENT	ORNAMENT		1997	$16.95	
1997-QLX676-2	Angel Friend	CC - ORNAMENT	ORNAMENT		1997	$14.95	
1997-QLX676-5	Sailor Bear	CC - ORNAMENT	ORNAMENT		1997	$14.95	
1997-QLX677-2	Porcelain Hinged Box	CC - ORNAMENT	ORNAMENT		1997	$14.95	
1997-QLX671-5	Meadow Snowman	CC - ORNAMENT	ORNAMENT		1997	$12.95	
1997-QXM418-5	Antique Tractors #1	CC - ORNAMENT	ORNAMENT		1997	$6.95	
1997-QXM420-5	Welcome Friends #1	CC - ORNAMENT	ORNAMENT		1997	$6.95	
1997-QXM419-2	Snowflake Ballet #1	CC - ORNAMENT	ORNAMENT		1997	$5.95	

Order No.	Title	Type	Theme	Retired	Intro. Year	Retial Price	Secondary Price
1997-QXM421-5	Teddy-Bear Style #1	CC - ORNAMENT	ORNAMENT		1997	$5.95	
1997-QXM413-5	Herr Drosselmeyer #2	CC - ORNAMENT	ORNAMENT		1997	$5.95	
1997-QXM413-2	Murry Inc. Pursuit Airplant #3	CC - ORNAMENT	ORNAMENT		1997	$6.95	
1997-QXM414-2	White Rabbit #3	CC - ORNAMENT	ORNAMENT		1997	$6.95	
1997-QXM415-5	Miniature Clothespin Soldier #3	CC - ORNAMENT	ORNAMENT		1997	$4.95	
1997-QXM416-2	Christmas Bells #3	CC - ORNAMENT	ORNAMENT		1997	$4.95	
1997-QXM416-5	Nutcracker Guild #4	CC - ORNAMENT	ORNAMENT		1997	$6.95	
1997-QXM429-5	Centuries of Santa #4	CC - ORNAMENT	ORNAMENT		1997	$6.95	
1997-QXM417-2	On the Road #5	CC - ORNAMENT	ORNAMENT		1997	$5.95	
1997-QXM417-5	Candy Car #9	CC - ORNAMENT	ORNAMENT		1997	$6.95	
1997-QXM415-2	Santa's Little Big Top #3	CC - ORNAMENT	ORNAMENT		1997	$6.95	
1997-QXM418-2	Village Depot #10	CC - ORNAMENT	ORNAMENT		1997	$6.95	
1997-QXM430-2	Rocking Horse #10	CC - ORNAMENT	ORNAMENT		1997	$4.95	
1997-QXM427-5	Our Lady of Guadalupe	CC - ORNAMENT	ORNAMENT		1997	$8.95	
1997-QXM427-2	Casablanca	CC - ORNAMENT	ORNAMENT		1997	$19.95	
1997-QXM426-2	King of the Forest	CC - ORNAMENT	ORNAMENT		1997	$24.00	
1997-QXM425-2	Ice Cold Coca-Cola	CC - ORNAMENT	ORNAMENT		1997	$6.95	
1997-QXM423-4	He Is Born	CC - ORNAMENT	ORNAMENT		1997	$7.95	
1997-QXM424-2	Seeds of Joy	CC - ORNAMENT	ORNAMENT		1997	$6.95	
1997-QXM419-5	Sew Talented	CC - ORNAMENT	ORNAMENT		1997	$5.95	
1997-QXM421-2	Shutterbug	CC - ORNAMENT	ORNAMENT		1997	$5.95	
1997-QXM428-2	Tiny Home Improvers	CC - ORNAMENT	ORNAMENT		1997	$29.00	
1997-QXM422-1	Gentle Giraffes	CC - ORNAMENT	ORNAMENT		1997	$5.95	
1997-QXM423-2	Home Sweet Home	CC - ORNAMENT	ORNAMENT		1997	$5.95	
1997-QXM423-2	Future Star	CC - ORNAMENT	ORNAMENT		1997	$5.95	
1997-QXM429-2	Heavenly Music	CC - ORNAMENT	ORNAMENT		1997	$5.95	
1997-QXM430-5	Victorian Skater	CC - ORNAMENT	ORNAMENT		1997	$5.95	
1997-QXM431-2	Peppermint Painter	CC - ORNAMENT	ORNAMENT		1997	$4.95	
1997-QXM431-5	Snowboard Bunny	CC - ORNAMENT	ORNAMENT		1997	$4.95	
1997-QXM443-2	Polar Buddies	CC - ORNAMENT	ORNAMENT		1997	$4.95	
1997-QXM433-2	Polar Buddies	CC - ORNAMENT	ORNAMENT		1997	$4.95	
1997-QXM414-1	Shining Star Tree Topper	CC - ORNAMENT	ORNAMENT		1997	$9.95	
JUNE MCKENNA							
123	UP ON THE ROOFTOP	SANTA FIGURINES	JM - SPECIAL LIMITED EDITION	91	90	$280.00	
124	SANTA'S REINDEER	SANTA FIGURINES	JM - SPECIAL LIMITED EDITION	93	90	$400.00	
125	CHRISTMAS DREAMS/HASSOCK	SANTA FIGURINES	JM - SPECIAL LIMITED EDITION	93	90	$280.00	
126	CHRISTMAS DREAMS/CHAIR	SANTA FIGURINES	JM - SPECIAL LIMITED EDITION	92	90	$280.00	
127	BEDTIME STORIES	SANTA FIGURINES	JM - SPECIAL LIMITED EDITION		91	$500.00	
128	SANTA'S ARRIVAL	SANTA FIGURINES	JM - SPECIAL LIMITED EDITION		92	$300.00	
129	BAKING COOKIES	SANTA FIGURINES	JM - SPECIAL LIMITED EDITION		93	$450.00	$450.00
130	FATHER CHRISTMAS	SANTA FIGURINES	JM - LIMITED EDITIONS SANTA/4,000	85	83	$120.00	$3,250.00
131	OLD SAINT NICK	SANTA FIGURINES	JM - LIMITED EDITIONS SANTA/4,000	86	84	$100.00	$1,500.00
132	WOODLAND	SANTA FIGURINES	JM - LIMITED EDITIONS SANTA/4,000	87	85	$140.00	$1,900.00
133	VICTORIAN	SANTA FIGURINES	JM - LIMITED EDITIONS SANTA/4,000	88	86	$150.00	$600.00
134	CHRISTMAS EVE	SANTA FIGURINES	JM - LIMITED EDITIONS SANTA/4,000	89	87	$170.00	$575.00
135	BRINGING HOME CHRISTMAS	SANTA FIGURINES	JM - LIMITED EDITIONS SANTA/4,000	90	88		
136	SEASON'S GREETINGS	SANTA FIGURINES	JM - LIMITED EDITIONS SANTA/4,000	92	89	$200.00	$325.00
137	WILDERNESS	SANTA FIGURINES	JM - LIMITED EDITIONS SANTA/4,000		90	$200.00	$200.00
138	COMING TO TOWN	SANTA FIGURINES	JM - LIMITED EDITIONS SANTA/4,000		89	$220.00	$220.00
139	CHRISTMAS GATHERING	SANTA FIGURINES	JM - LIMITED EDITIONS SANTA/4,000	96	92	$220.00	$220.00
140	THE PATRIOT	SANTA FIGURINES	JM - LIMITED EDITIONS SANTA/4,000		93	$250.00	$250.00
142	WHITE CHRISTMAS	SANTA FIGURINES	JM - REGISTERED EDITION SANTA	87	87	$170.00	$1,500.00
143	JOLLY OLE' ST. NICK	SANTA FIGURINES	JM - REGISTERED EDITION SANTA	90	98	$170.00	$250.00
144	TRADITIONAL	SANTA FIGURINES	JM - REGISTERED EDITION SANTA	91	89	$180.00	$220.00
145	THE TOY MAKER	SANTA FIGURINES	JM - REGISTERED EDITION SANTA	93	90	$200.00	$200.00
146	CHECKING HIS LIST	SANTA FIGURINES	JM - REGISTERED EDITION SANTA	93	91	$240.00	$230.00
147	FORTY WINKS	SANTA FIGURINES	JM - REGISTERED EDITION SANTA	93	92	$250.00	$250.00
148	LITTLE GUARDIAN ANGEL	SANTA FIGURINES	JM - REGISTERED EDITION SANTA	92	92	$160.00	
149	TOMORROW'S CHRISTMAS	SANTA FIGURINES	JM - REGISTERED EDITION SANTA		93	$245.00	$250.00
150	CHRISTMAS MEMORIES	SANTA FIGURINES	JM - LARGE LIMITED ED./7,500 SERIES	91	88		
151	JOYFUL CHRISTMAS	SANTA FIGURINES	JM - LARGE LIMITED ED./7,500 SERIES	91	88		
152	SANTA'S BAG OF SURPRISES	SANTA FIGURINES	JM - LARGE LIMITED ED./7,500 SERIES	91	88	$100.00	
153	OLD FASHIONED SANTA	SANTA FIGURINES	JM - LARGE LIMITED ED./7,500 SERIES	91	89		
154	CHRISTMAS DELIGHT	SANTA FIGURINES	JM - LARGE LIMITED ED./7,500 SERIES	92	90		
155	ETHNIC	SANTA FIGURINES	JM - LARGE LIMITED ED./7,500 SERIES	92	90		
156	CHRISTMAS BISHOP	SANTA FIGURINES	JM - LARGE LIMITED ED./7,500 SERIES	93	91		
157	CHRISTMAS WIZARD	SANTA FIGURINES	JM - LARGE LIMITED ED./7,500 SERIES		92		
158	CHRISTMAS CHEER	SANTA FIGURINES	JM - LARGE LIMITED ED./7,500 SERIES		93	$120.00	$180.00
159	MYSTICAL SANTA	FLATBACK	JM - LIMITED EDITION SANTA/10,000	91	88	$30.00	
160	TOYS OF JOY	FLATBACK	JM - LIMITED EDITION SANTA/10,000	91	88	$30.00	$100.00
161	BLUE CHRISTMAS	FLATBACK	JM - LIMITED EDITION SANTA/10,000	91	89	$32.00	
162	VICTORIAN	FLATBACK	JM - LIMITED EDITION SANTA/10,000	91	89	$32.00	
163	MEDIEVAL SANTA	FLATBACK	JM - LIMITED EDITION SANTA/10,000	92	90	$32.00	
164	OLD TIME SANTA	FLATBACK	JM - LIMITED EDITION SANTA/10,000	92	90	$32.00	
165	FAREWELL SANTA	FLATBACK	JM - LIMITED EDITION SANTA/10,000	92	91	$40.00	
166	SANTA'S BAG OF SURPRISES	FLATBACK	JM - LIMITED EDITION SANTA/10,000	93	91	$40.00	
167	DECK THE HALLS	FLATBACK	JM - LIMITED EDITION SANTA/10,000		92	$40.00	
168	GOOD TIDINGS	FLATBACK	JM - LIMITED EDITION SANTA/10,000		92	$40.00	
169	BELLS OF CHRISTMAS	SANTA FIGURINES	JM - LIMITED EDITION SANTA/10,000		93	$40.00	$40.00
171	FATHER CHRISTMAS	SANTA FIGURINES	JM - PERSONAL APPEARANCE SANTA	93	89	$22.50	
164	OLD TIME SANTA	FLATBACK	JM - LIMITED EDITION SANTA/10,000		90	$32.00	
173	WOODLAND	SANTA FIGURINES	JM - PERSONAL APPEARANCE SANTA		91	$30.00	
174	VICTORIAN	SANTA FIGURINES	JM - PERSONAL APPEARANCE SANTA		92	$30.00	
175	CHRISTMAS EVE	SANTA FIGURINES	JM - PERSONAL APPEARANCE SANTA		93	$35.00	$40.00
168	FATHER TIME	THREE DIMENSIONAL	JM - ASSORTED	91	85	$40.00	$165.00
177	L'IL ST. NICK	THREE DIMENSIONAL	JM - ASSORTED	90	85	$40.00	
170	SANTA'S LOVE	FLATBACK	JM - LIMITED EDITION SANTA/10,000	89	93	$40.00	$40.00
179	BOY CAROLER	THREE DIMENSIONAL	JM - CAROLERS	89	85	$36.00	$80.00
180	MAN CAROLER	THREE DIMENSIONAL	JM - CAROLERS	89	85	$36.00	$80.00
181	WOMAN CAROLER	THREE DIMENSIONAL	JM - CAROLERS	89	85	$36.00	
182	PATRIOTIC SANTA	THREE DIMENSIONAL	JM - SANTA	96	86	$44.00	

Order No.	Title	Type	Theme	Retired	Intro. Year	Retail Price	Secondary Price
183	MALE ANGEL	THREE DIMENSIONAL	JM - ANGEL	86	86	$44.00	$1,500.00
184	MR. SANTA	THREE DIMENSIONAL	JM - SANTA	91	87	$44.00	$100.00
185	MRS. SANTA	THREE DIMENSIONAL	JM - SANTA	89	87	$40.00	
186	JOLLY OLE SANTA	THREE DIMENSIONAL	JM - SANTA	91	91	$44.00	
187	16TH CENTURY SANTA/BLUE	THREE DIMENSIONAL	JM - SANTA	91	89	$60.00	
188	16TH CENTURY SANTA/GREEN	THREE DIMENSIONAL	JM - SANTA	89	89	$60.00	
189	16TH CENTURY SANTA/LIGHT GREEN	THREE DIMENSIONAL	JM - SANTA	89	89	$60.00	
190	17TH CENTURY SANTA	THREE DIMENSIONAL	JM - SANTA	91	89	$70.00	
191	NOEL	THREE DIMENSIONAL	JM - ASSORTED	92	90	$50.00	
192	CHRISTMAS SANTA	THREE DIMENSIONAL	JM - SANTA	93	92	$70.00	
193	TAKING A BREAK	THREE DIMENSIONAL	JM - SANTA		92	$60.00	$70.00
194	SANTA AND FRIENDS	THREE DIMENSIONAL	JM - SANTA	96	93	$70.00	$70.00
195	A GOOD NIGHT'S SLEEP	THREE DIMENSIONAL	JM - SANTA		93	$70.00	$70.00
056	SANTA WITH BANNER	ORNAMENTS	JM - SANTA	92	91	$20.00	
057	ELF JOEY	ORNAMENTS	JM - ELF	93	91	$20.00	$20.00
001	FATHER BEAR IN SUIT/GRAY	ORNAMENTS	JM - BEARS	88	83	$12.00	
002	FATHER BEAR IN SUIT/MUSHROOM	ORNAMENTS	JM - BEARS	88	83	$12.00	
004	BABY BEAR IN VEST/RED	ORNAMENTS	JM - BEARS	88	83	$11.00	$50.00
003	FATHER BEAR IN SUIT/GREEN	ORNAMENTS	JM - BEARS	88	83	$12.00	
005	BABY BEAR IN VEST/GREEN	ORNAMENTS	JM - BEARS	88	83	$11.00	$50.00
006	BABY BEAR IN VEST/LIGHT BLUE	ORNAMENTS	JM - BEARS	88	83	$11.00	$50.00
007	BABY BEAR IN VEST/NAVY BLUE	ORNAMENTS	JM - BEARS	88	83	$11.00	$50.00
008	BABY BEAR IN VEST/MUSHROOM	ORNAMENTS	JM - BEARS	88	83	$11.00	$50.00
009	GIRL RAG DOLL/BLUE DRESS	ORNAMENTS	JM - RAG DOLL	83	83	$11.00	$425.00
010	GIRL RAG DOLL/RED SHIRT	ORNAMENTS	JM - RAG DOLL	83	83	$11.00	$425.00
011	BOY RAG DOLL/BLUE SHIRT	ORNAMENTS	JM - RAG DOLL	83	83	$11.00	
013	ST. NICK WITH LANTERN	ORNAMENTS	JM - ST. NICK	88	83	$13.00	$75.00
014	GLORIA ANGEL	ORNAMENTS	JM - ANGEL	84	84	$13.00	$475.00
015	BABY/PINK	ORNAMENTS	JM - BABY	88	84	$11.00	
012	BOY RAG DOLL/RED SHIRT	ORNAMENTS	JM - RAG DOLL	83	83	$11.00	
016	BABY/BLUE	ORNAMENTS	JM - BABY	88	84	$11.00	
017	ANGEL WITH HORN	ORNAMENTS	JM - ANGEL	88	84	$13.00	$75.00
018	MR. CLAUS	ORNAMENTS	JM - SANTA	88	84	$13.00	$65.00
019	MRS. CLAUS	ORNAMENTS	JM - SANTA	88	84	$13.00	$60.00
022	COUNTRY GIRL/PINK DRESS	ORNAMENTS	JM - COUNTRY KIDS	88	84	$13.00	
023	COUNTRY GIRL/BLUE DRESS	ORNAMENTS	JM - COUNTRY KIDS	88	84	$13.00	
020	COUNTRY BOY/MUSTARD PANTS	ORNAMENTS	JM - COUNTRY KIDS	88	84	$13.00	
021	COUNTRY BOY/GRAY PANTS	ORNAMENTS	JM - COUNTRY KIDS	88	84	$13.00	
024	OLD WORLD SANTA/RED	ORNAMENTS	JM - SANTA	89	84	$13.00	$60.00
025	OLD WORLD SANTA/BLUE	ORNAMENTS	JM - SANTA	89	84	$13.00	$60.00
026	OLD WORLD SANTA/GOLD	ORNAMENTS	JM - SANTA	89	84	$13.00	$60.00
027	BABY PIG	ORNAMENTS	JM - ANIMALS	88	85	$11.00	$50.00
028	FATHER PIG	ORNAMENTS	JM - ANIMALS	88	85	$12.00	$75.00
029	MOTHER PIG	ORNAMENTS	JM - ANIMALS	88	85	$12.00	$125.00
032	PRIMITVE SANTA	ORNAMENTS	JM - SANTA	89	85	$13.00	
037	SANTA WITH BELLS/BLUE	ORNAMENTS	JM - SANTA	89	86	$14.00	
038	SANTA WITH BELLS/GREEN	ORNAMENTS	JM - SANTA	87	86	$14.00	$425.00
039	SANTA WITH BEAR	ORNAMENTS	JM - SANTA	91	87	$14.00	
040	SANTA WITH BAG	ORNAMENTS	JM - SANTA	89	87	$16.00	
041	GUARDIAN ANGEL	ORNAMENTS	JM - ANGEL	91	88	$16.00	
042	1776 SANTA	ORNAMENTS	JM - SANTA	91	88	$17.00	$40.00
043	SANTA WITH BOOK/BLUE	ORNAMENTS	JM - SANTA	88	88	$17.00	$250.00
044	SANTA WITH BOOK/RED	ORNAMENTS	JM - SANTA	88	88	$17.00	$250.00
046	SANTA WITH WREATH	ORNAMENTS	JM - SANTA	91	88	$17.00	
045	SANTA WITH TOYS	ORNAMENTS	JM - SANTA	91	88	$17.00	$115.00
047	GLORIA ANGEL	ORNAMENTS	JM - ANGEL	92	89	$17.00	$475.00
048	SANTA WITH STAFF	ORNAMENTS	JM - SANTA	91	89	$17.00	
049	SANTA WITH TREE	ORNAMENTS	JM - SANTA	91	89	$17.00	$40.00
050	WINKING SANTA	ORNAMENTS	JM - SANTA	91	90	$17.00	
051	Ho Ho Ho	ORNAMENTS	JM - SANTA	92	90	$17.00	$40.00
052	ELF JEFFREY	ORNAMENTS	JM - ELF	92	90	$17.00	$40.00
053	HARVEST SANTA	ORNAMENTS	JM - SANTA	92	90	$17.00	$40.00
054	SANTA WITH LIGHTS/BLACK	ORNAMENTS	JM - SANTA	92	91	$20.00	$20.00
055	SANTA WITH LIGHTS/WHITE	ORNAMENTS	JM - SANTA	92	91	$20.00	
058	BOY ANGEL/VANILLA	ORNAMENTS	JM - ANGEL	92	91	$20.00	
059	BOY ANGEL/WHITE	ORNAMENTS	JM - ANGEL	91	91	$20.00	$120.00
05	GIRL ANGEL/VANILLA	ORNAMENTS	JM - ANGEL	93	91	$20.00	$20.00
061	GIRL ANGEL/WHITE	ORNAMENTS	JM - ANGEL	91	91	$20.00	$130.00
062	SANTA WITH BASKET	ORNAMENTS	JM - SANTA	93	92	$25.00	$25.00
063	SANTA WITH SACK	ORNAMENTS	JM - SANTA	93	92	$25.00	$25.00
064	NORTH POLE NEWS	ORNAMENTS	JM - ASSORTED	93	92	$25.00	
065	ELF SCOTTY	ORNAMENTS	JM - ELF		92	$25.00	$25.00
066	PRAYING ANGEL	ORNAMENTS	JM - ANGEL	93	92	$25.00	$25.00
067	OLD LAMPLIGHTER	ORNAMENTS	JM - ASSORTED	93	93	$30.00	$30.00
068	CHRISTMAS TREAT	ORNAMENTS	JM - ASSORTED	93	93	$30.00	
069	FINAL NOTES	ORNAMENTS	JM - ASSORTED	93	93	$30.00	$30.00
070	ELF BERNIE	ORNAMENTS	JM - ELF		93	$30.00	$30.00
071	ANGEL OF PEACE/VANILLA	ORNAMENTS	JM - ANGEL		93	$30.00	
073	TREE TOPPER ANGEL	ORNAMENTS	JM - ANGEL	87	84	$70.00	$225.00
074	SANTA WITH TOYS	ORNAMENTS	JM - SANTA	88	82	$13.00	$80.00
075	MAMA BEAR/BLUE CAP	ORNAMENTS	JM - BEARS	84	82	$11.00	$90.00
076	MAMA BEAR/RED CAP	ORNAMENTS	JM - BEARS	84	82	$11.00	$90.00
077	BABY BEAR/WHITE SHIRT	ORNAMENTS	JM - BEARS	84	82	$11.00	$150.00
078	CANDY CANE	ORNAMENTS	JM - ASSORTED	84	82	$10.00	$375.00
091	ANGEL WITH TOYS	ORNAMENTS	JM - ANGEL	88	82	$14.00	$125.00
095	GRANDPA/CINNAMON	ORNAMENTS	JM - ASSORTED	88	83	$12.00	$80.00
97	GRANDPA/MUSHROOM	ORNAMENTS	JM - ASSORTED	88	83	$12.00	
98	GRANDPA/BLUE	ORNAMENTS	JM - ASSORTED	88	83	$12.00	
101	NAME PLAQUE	FLATBACK	JM - ASSORTED	92	87	$50.00	$125.00
102	NATIVITY SET	FLATBACK	JM - NATIVITY AND OTHER FLATBACKS		88	$130.00	
103	THREE WISE MAN SET	FLATBACK	JM - NATIVITY AND OTHER FLATBACKS		89	$70.00	
104	SHEEP AND SHEPHERDS SET	FLATBACK	JM - NATIVITY AND OTHER FLATBACKS		91	$60.00	
105	WOMAN AND BOY CAROLERS	FLATBACK	JM - CAROLERS		91	$50.00	$65.00

Order No.	Title	Type	Theme	Retired	Intro. Year	Retial Price	Secondary Price
106	MAN AND GIRL CAROLERS	FLATBACK	JM - CAROLERS		91	$50.00	$65.00
107	GRANPARENT CAROLERS	FLATBACK	JM - CAROLERS		92	$70.00	$85.00
108	LET IT SNOW	FLATBACK	JM - ASSORTED	96	92	$60.00	
109	CHOIR OF ANGELS	FLATBACK	JM - ANGEL	93	92	$60.00	
110	THE SNOW FAMILY	FLATBACK	JM - SNOW MEN	90	93	$40.00	$40.00
111	MR. SNOW MAN	FLATBACK	JM - SNOW MEN		93	$40.00	$40.00
112	ANGEL NAME PLAQUE	FLATBACK	JM - ANGEL		93	$70.00	$70.00
113	SANTA NAME PLAQUE	FLATBACK	JM - SANTA		93	$70.00	$70.00
114	CHILDREN ICE SKATERS	FLATBACK	JM - ICE SKATERS		93	$70.00	$70.00
115	COW	FLATBACK	JM - NATIVITY AND OTHER FLATBACKS		93	$30.00	$30.00
116	KRIS KRINGLE	SANTA FIGURINES	JM - LARGE LIMITED EDITION SANTA	90	87	$350.00	$800.00
117	REMEMBRANCE OF CHRISTMAS PAST	SANTA FIGURINES	JM - LARGE LIMITED EDITION SANTA	92	88	$420.00	$500.00
118	SANTA'S WARDROBE	SANTA FIGURINES	JM - LARGE LIMITED EDITION SANTA	92	89	$750.00	$750.00
119	NIGHT BEFORE CHRISTMAS	SANTA FIGURINES	JM - LARGE LIMITED EDITION SANTA	93	90	$750.00	$750.00
121	SANTA AND HIS MAGIC SLEIGH	SANTA FIGURINES	JM - SPECIAL LIMITED EDITION	92	89	$280.00	
122	LAST GENTLE NUDGE	SANTA FIGURINES	JM - SPECIAL LIMITED EDITION	91	89	$280.00	
072	ANGEL OF PEACE/PINK	ORNAMENTS	JM - ANGEL		93	$30.00	$30.00
060	GIRL ANGEL/VANILLA	ORNAMENTS	JM - ANGEL	93	91	$20.00	
092	GRANDMA/CINNAMON	ORNAMENTS	JM - ASSORTED	88	83	$12.00	$70.00
093	GRANDMA/MUSHROOM	ORNAMENTS	JM - ASSORTED	88	83	$12.00	$70.00
094	GRANDMA/RED	ORNAMENTS	JM - ASSORTED	88	83	$12.00	$70.00
096	GRANDPA/MUSHROOM	ORNAMENTS	JM - ASSORTED	88	83	$12.00	$80.00
097	GRANDPA/BLUE	ORNAMENTS	JM - ASSORTED	88	83	$12.00	$80.00
158A	DANCING TO THE TUNE	SANTA FIGURINES	JM - LARGE LIMITED EDITION/7,500 SERIES	96	94	$120.00	$120.00
158B	SANTA'S ONE MAN BAND	SANTA FIGURINES	JM - LARGE LIMITED EDITION/7,500 SERIES	96	94	$120.00	$120.00
158C	CHRISTMAS LULLABY/RED	SANTA FIGURINES	JM - LARGE LIMITED EDITION/7,500 SERIES	96	95	$120.00	
158D	CHRISTMAS LULLABY/BLUE	SANTA FIGURINES	JM - LARGE LIMITED EDITION/7,500 SERIES		95	$120.00	
158E	POLAR BEAR EXPRESS	SANTA FIGURINES	JM - LIMITED EDITIONS SANTA/4,000		96	$120.00	
140A	ST. NICHOLAS	SANTA FIGURINES	JM - LIMITED EDITIONS SANTA/4,000	96	94	$250.00	$250.00
140B	PEACEFUL JOURNEY	SANTA FIGURINES	JM - LIMITED EDITIONS SANTA/4,000		95	$250.00	
140C	MAGIC OF CHRISTMAS	FLATBACK	JM - LIMITED EDITION SANTA/4,000		96	$250.00	
178	GIRL CAROLER	THREE DIMENSIONAL	JM - ASSORTED	89	85	$36.00	$80.00
176	FATHER TIME	THREE DIMENSIONAL	JM - ASSORTED	91	85	$40.00	
172	OLD SAINT NICK	SANTA FIGURINES	JM - PERSONAL APPEARANCE SANTA		89	$25.00	
170A	NOT ONCE, BUT TWICE	FLATBACK	JM - LIMITED EDITION SANTA/10,000	96	94	$40.00	$40.00
170B	POST MARKED NORTH POLE	FLATBACK	JM - LIMITED EDITION SANTA/10,000	96	94	$40.00	$40.00
170C	CHRISTMAS DELIVERY	FLATBACK	JM - LIMITED EDITION SANTA/10,000		95	$40.00	$40.00
170D	LIGHT OF CHRISTMAS	FLATBACK	JM - LIMITED EDITION SANTA/10,000		95	$40.00	$40.00
170E	HAPPY HOLIDAYS	FLATBACK	JM - LIMITED EDITION SANTA/3,000		96	$40.00	$40.00
170F	YULETIDE JOY	FLATBACK	JM - LIMITED EDITION SANTA/3,000		96	$40.00	$40.00
129A	WELCOME TO THE WORLD	SANTA FIGURINES	JM - SPECIAL LIMITED EDITION	95	94	$400.00	$4,000.00
129B	INTERNATIONAL SANTA	SANTA FIGURINES	JM - SPECIAL LIMITED EDITION	96	96	$100.00	
129C	SHOW MY THE WAY	SANTA FIGURINES	JM - SPECIAL LIMITED EDITION		96	$500.00	
149A	SAY CHEESE, PLEASE	SANTA FIGURINES	JM - REGISTERED EDITION SANTA	96	94	$250.00	$250.00
149B	CHRISTMAS DOWN ON THE FARM	SANTA FIGURINES	JM - REGISTERED EDITION SANTA		95	$260.00	$260.00
149C	A CHRISTMAS TREAT FOR ALL	SANTA FIGURINES	JM - REGISTERED EDITION SANTA		95	$260.00	$260.00
149D	CHRISTMAS OVERLOAD	SANTA FIGURINES	JM - REGISTERED EDITION SANTA		96	$260.00	$260.00
120	SANTA'S HOT AIR BALLOON	SANTA FIGURINES	JM - LARGE LIMITED EDITION SANTA	93	92	$800.00	$800.00
175A	BRINGING HOME CHRISTMAS	SANTA FIGURINES	JM - PERSONAL APPEARANCE SANTA		94	$35.00	$30.00
175B	SEASON'S GREETINGS	SANTA FIGURINES	JM - PERSONAL APPEARANCE SANTA		95	$35.00	
175C	WILDERNESS SANTA	SANTA FIGURINES	JM - PERSONAL APPEARANCE SANTA		96	$35.00	
196	BUST OF FATHER CHRISTMAS	SANTA FIGURINES	JM - LIMITED EDITIONS SANTA/4,000		94	$30.00	
197	BLUE BUST OF FATHER CHRISTMAS	SANTA FIGURINES	JM - ANNUAL FESTIVAL SERIES		95	$35.00	
115A	RAM & EWE	FLATBACK	JM - NATIVITY AND OTHER FLATBACKS		93	$30.00	$30.00
115B	DONKEY	FLATBACK	JM - NATIVITY AND OTHER FLATBACKS		93	$30.00	$30.00
115C	NATIVITY (STOCK #N-96)	FLATBACK	JM - NATIVITY AND OTHER FLATBACKS		96	$150.00	$150.00
199	ENGINE AND COAL CAR SET/2	FLATBACK	JM - NORTH POLE EXPRESS SERIES		94	$500.00	
200	TOY CAR	FLATBACK	JM - NORTH POLE EXPRESS SERIES	95	95	$250.00	
201	LOGGING CAR	FLATBACK	JM - NORTH POLE EXPRESS SERIES	96	95	$250.00	
195A	CONDUCTOR/ALL ABOARD, SANTA	THREE DIMENSIONAL	JM - SANTA		94	$70.00	$70.00
195B	DECORATING FOR CHRISTMAS	THREE DIMENSIONAL	JM - SANTA	96	94	$70.00	$70.00
195C	FINISHING TOUCH	THREE DIMENSIONAL	JM - SANTA		95	$70.00	
195D	A SURPRISE FOR JOEY	THREE DIMENSIONAL	JM - SANTA	96	95	$70.00	
195E	HELPFUL FRIENDS-SNOWMAN	THREE DIMENSIONAL	JM - SANTA		96	$90.00	
195F	MR. SANTA WITH RAD DOLL	THREE DIMENSIONAL	JM - SANTA		96	$70.00	
195G	MRS. SANTA WITH RAG DOLL	THREE DIMENSIONAL	JM - SANTA		96	$70.00	
195H	SET OF THREE TREES	THREE DIMENSIONAL	JM - SANTA		96	$60.00	
115D	CHILDREN CAROLERS	FLATBACK	JM - NATIVITY AND OTHER FLATBACKS	96	94	$90.00	$90.00
115E	SNOWMAN AND CHILD	FLATBACK	JM - NATIVITY AND OTHER FLATBACKS	96	94	$70.00	$70.00
115F	STAR OF BETHLEHEM--ANGEL	FLATBACK	JM - NATIVITY AND OTHER FLATBACKS	96	94	$40.00	$40.00
115G	SANTA--CAROLING	FLATBACK	JM - NATIVITY AND OTHER FLATBACKS	96	95	$60.00	$65.00
115H	SANTA--TREE TOPPER	FLATBACK	JM - NATIVITY AND OTHER FLATBACKS	96	95	$70.00	
115I	TRAVEL PLANS	FLATBACK	JM - NATIVITY AND OTHER FLATBACKS	96	95	$70.00	$70.00
202	ANGEL--LONG RED HAIR	ORNAMENTS	JM - ICICLES		96	$17.00	
203	ANGEL--SHORT BLONDE HAIR	ORNAMENTS	JM - ICICLES		96	$17.00	
204	ANGEL--SHORT BROWN HAIR	ORNAMENTS	JM - ICICLES		96	$17.00	
205	BLACK ANGEL	ORNAMENTS	JM - ICICLES		96	$17.00	
206	SANTA WITH HAT	ORNAMENTS	JM - ICICLES		96	$17.00	
207	SANTA WITH PIPE	ORNAMENTS	JM - ICICLES		96	$17.00	$17.00
208	SNOWMAN	ORNAMENTS	JM - ICICLES		96	$17.00	
209	PRIMITIVE	ORNAMENTS	JM - SANTA HEAD ORNAMENTS		94	$17.00	
210	QUICK AS A WINK	ORNAMENTS	JM - SANTA HEAD ORNAMENTS		94	$17.00	
211	WHISPERING	ORNAMENTS	JM - SANTA HEAD ORNAMENTS		94	$17.00	
212	CHRISTMAS KISS	ORNAMENTS	JM - SANTA HEAD ORNAMENTS	96	95	$17.00	
213	HELPING HAND	ORNAMENTS	JM - SANTA HEAD ORNAMENTS		95	$17.00	
214	I LOVE YOU	ORNAMENTS	JM - SANTA HEAD ORNAMENTS	96	95	$17.00	
215	MOON SHAPE SANTA	ORNAMENTS	JM - SANTA HEAD ORNAMENTS		95	$17.00	
216	SANTA WITH HOLLY	ORNAMENTS	JM - SANTA HEAD ORNAMENTS		95	$17.00	
217	SANTA WITH PIPE	ORNAMENTS	JM - SANTA HEAD ORNAMENTS		95	$17.00	
218	PATRIOTIC SANTA	ORNAMENTS	JM - SANTA HEAD ORNAMENTS		96	$17.00	
219	SANTA WITH TASSEL	ORNAMENTS	JM - SANTA HEAD ORNAMENTS		96	$17.00	
220	SNOWMAN	ORNAMENTS	JM - SANTA HEAD ORNAMENTS		96	$17.00	
100A	ANGEL'S GUIDING LIGHT/PINK	ORNAMENTS	JM - ANGEL	95	94	$30.00	

Order No.	Title	Type	Theme	Retired	Intro. Year	Retail Price	Secondary Price
100B	ANGEL'S GUIDING LIGHT/GREEN	ORNAMENTS	JM - ANGEL	95	94	$30.00	$30.00
100C	ANGEL'S GUIDING LIGHT/WHITE	ORNAMENTS	JM - ANGEL	95	94	$30.00	$30.00
100D	ELF RICKY	ORNAMENTS	JM - ELF	95	94	$30.00	$30.00
100E	ELF TAMMY	ORNAMENTS	JM - ELF	95	94	$30.00	$30.00
100F	MRS. KLAUS	ORNAMENTS	JM - SANTA	96	94	$30.00	
100G	NUTCRACKER	ORNAMENTS	JM - ASSORTED	95	94	$30.00	$30.00
100H	RINGING IN CHRISTMAS	ORNAMENTS	JM - ASSORTED	95	94	$30.00	$50.00
100I	SANTA WITH PIPE	ORNAMENTS	JM - SANTA	96	94	$30.00	$30.00
100J	SANTA WITH SKIS	ORNAMENTS	JM - SANTA	96	94	$30.00	$30.00
100K	SNOW SHOWERS	ORNAMENTS	JM - ASSORTED	96	94	$30.00	$30.00
100L	ANGEL W/TEDDY	ORNAMENTS	JM - ASSORTED	96	95	$30.00	$30.00
100M	ANGEL W/WREATH	ORNAMENTS	JM - ANGEL		95	$30.00	$30.00
100N	COUNTRY SANTA	ORNAMENTS	JM - SANTA		95	$30.00	$30.00
100-O	ELF DANNY	ORNAMENTS	JM - ELF	96	95	$30.00	$30.00
100-P	SANTA AND HELPER/BROWN	ORNAMENTS	JM - SANTA	95	95	$30.00	$65.00
100Q	SANTA NUTCRACKER	ORNAMENTS	JM - SANTA	96	95	$30.00	$30.00
100R	SANTA TEACHER	ORNAMENTS	JM - SANTA		95	$30.00	$30.00
100S	WHO'S THIS FROSTY	ORNAMENTS	JM - ASSORTED	96	95	$30.00	$30.00
100T	ANGEL WITH HORN--MARY	ORNAMENTS	JM - ANGEL		96	$30.00	$30.00
100U	ANGEL WITH HARP--ELIZABETH	ORNAMENTS	JM - ANGEL		96	$30.00	$30.00
100V	ANGEL WITH LYRE--KATHLEEN	ORNAMENTS	JM - ANGEL		96	$30.00	$30.00
100W	ANOTHER TEDDY--SANTA	ORNAMENTS	JM - SANTA		96	$30.00	
100X	CHRISTMAS TREAT/RED	ORNAMENTS	JM - ASSORTED	96	96	$30.00	
100Y	ELF-CADDY	ORNAMENTS	JM - ASSORTED		96	$30.00	$30.00
100Z	FIREMAN	ORNAMENTS	JM - ASSORTED		96	$30.00	$30.00
100AA	FISHING	ORNAMENTS	JM - ASSORTED		96	$30.00	$30.00
100AB	GOLFING	ORNAMENTS	JM - ASSORTED		96	$30.00	$30.00
100AC	NUTCRACKER	ORNAMENTS	JM - ASSORTED	96	96	$30.00	$30.00
100AD	MRS. SANTA--A GOODBYE KISS	ORNAMENTS	JM - SANTA		96	$30.00	$30.00
100AE	SANTA--A GOODBYE KISS	ORNAMENTS	JM - SANTA		96	$30.00	$30.00
100AF	SANTA AND HELPER/WHITE	ORNAMENTS	JM - SANTA	96	96	$30.00	$30.00
100AG	SNOWMAN	ORNAMENTS	JM - SNOW MEN		96	$30.00	$30.00
221	ALL I WANT FOR CHRISTMAS	THREE DIMENSIONAL	JM - BLACK FOLK ART COLLECTION		96	$70.00	
222	I'VE GOT THE TREE	THREE DIMENSIONAL	JM - BLACK FOLK ART COLLECTION		96	$70.00	
223	UNCLE TOM'S CHRISTMAS	THREE DIMENSIONAL	JM - BLACK FOLK ART COLLECTION		96	$80.00	
224	A GIFT FROM SANTA	THREE DIMENSIONAL	JM - COLLECTORS SOCIETY PIECES	95	94	$70.00	
225	DASHING THROUGH THE SNOW	THREE DIMENSIONAL	JM - COLLECTORS SOCIETY PIECES	96	95	$60.00	
226	WHITE CHRISTMAS	THREE DIMENSIONAL	JM - COLLECTORS SOCIETY PIECES	96	95		
227	AHH...SOOTHING BUBBLES	THREE DIMENSIONAL	JM - COLLECTORS SOCIETY PIECES		96	$70.00	
228	JOLLY OLD ST. NICK	THREE DIMENSIONAL	JM - COLLECTORS SOCIETY PIECES		96		
230	SHEPHERDS WITH SHEEP	FLATBACK	JM - NATIVITY AND OTHER FLATBACKS		91	$60.00	
231	SAMICHLAUS	SANTA FIGURINES	JM - INTERNATIONAL SANTAS		97	$100.00	
232	NORTH POLE EXPRESS	THREE DIMENSIONAL	JM - NORTH POLE EXPRESS SERIES		97	$300.00	
233	LIGHTING THE WAY	THREE DIMENSIONAL	JM - LIMITED EDITIONS SANTA/4,000		97	$260.00	
234	ALL I WANT FOR CHRISTMAS	THREE DIMENSIONAL	JM - LIMITED EDITION SANTA/2,500		97	$120.00	
235	CHRISTMAS JOY	FLATBACK	JM - LIMITED EDITION SANTA/3,000		97	$40.00	
236	MERRY CHRISTMAS	FLATBACK	JM - LIMITED EDITION SANTA/3,000		97	$40.00	
237	FOREST FRIENDS	THREE DIMENSIONAL	JM - REGISTERED EDITION SANTA		97	$260.00	
238	A GIFT FOR CLARA	THREE DIMENSIONAL	JM - ASSORTED		97	$70.00	
239	SNOWMAN AND ANGEL	THREE DIMENSIONAL	JM - ASSORTED		97	$70.00	
240	CHRISTMAS WINDOW	FLATBACK	JM - ASSORTED		97	$70.00	
241	NEW CHILDREN CAROLERS	FLATBACK	JM - CAROLERS		97	$70.00	
242	NEW MAN & WOMAN CAROLERS	FLATBACK	JM - CAROLERS		97	$70.00	
243	JANUARY/PARTY	SANTA FIGURINES	JM - ANNIVERSARY SERIES		97	$30.00	
244	FEBRUARY/VALENTINE'S DAY	SANTA FIGURINES	JM - ANNIVERSARY SERIES		97	$30.00	
245	MARCH/ST. PATRICK DAY	SANTA FIGURINES	JM - ANNIVERSARY SERIES		97	$30.00	
246	APRIL/EASTER	SANTA FIGURINES	JM - ANNIVERSARY SERIES		97	$30.00	
247	MAY/FLOWERS	SANTA FIGURINES	JM - ANNIVERSARY SERIES		97	$30.00	
248	JUNE/GRADUATION	SANTA FIGURINES	JM - ANNIVERSARY SERIES		97	$30.00	
250	AUGUST/BEACH	SANTA FIGURINES	JM - ANNIVERSARY SERIES		97	$30.00	
251	SEPTEMBER/BACK TO SCHOOL	SANTA FIGURINES	JM - ANNIVERSARY SERIES		97	$30.00	
252	OCTOBER/HALLOWEEN	SANTA FIGURINES	JM - ANNIVERSARY SERIES		97	$30.00	
253	NOVEMBER/THANKSGIVING	SANTA FIGURINES	JM - ANNIVERSARY SERIES		97	$30.00	
254	DECEMBER/CHRISTMAS	SANTA FIGURINES	JM - ANNIVERSARY SERIES		97	$30.00	
255	SABRINA'S ANGEL	FLATBACK ORNAMENTS	JM - ANGEL		97	$30.00	
256	DOCTOR/SANTA	FLATBACK ORNAMENTS	JM - SANTA		97	$30.00	
257	OLD WORLD SANTA	FLATBACK ORNAMENTS	JM - SANTA		97	$30.00	
258	TENNIS SANTA	FLATBACK ORNAMENTS	JM - SANTA		97	$30.00	
259	NUTCRACKER WITH HORN	FLATBACK ORNAMENTS	JM - ASSORTED		97	$30.00	
260	ALL I WANT FOR CHRISTMAS	THREE DIMENSIONAL	JM - BLACK FOLK ART COLLECTION		97	$70.00	
261	ALL I WANT FOR CHRISTMAS	THREE DIMENSIONAL	JM - BLACK FOLK ART COLLECTION		97	$70.00	
262	I'VE GOT THE TREE	THREE DIMENSIONAL	JM - BLACK FOLK ART COLLECTION		97	$70.00	
	16TH CENTURY SANTA/GOLD	THREE DIMENSIONAL	JM - SANTA		89	$60.00	$290.00

LYNN HANEY

Order No.	Title	Type	Theme	Retired	Intro. Year	Retail Price	Secondary Price
6198	18 IN. MR. GINGERBREAD	SANTAS	LH - OTHER		96	$240.00	
6199	18 IN. MRS. GINGERBREAD	SANTAS	LH - OTHER		96	$240.00	
179	18 IN. WINTER'S EVE SANTA	SANTAS	LH - OTHER		95	$240.00	
6202	21 IN. SANTA OF SNOWY RIVER	SANTAS	LH - OTHER		96	$350.00	
102	18 IN. COUNTRY FATHER CHRISTMAS/BURGUNDY	SANTAS	LH - OTHER	90	87	$150.00	
155	18 IN. CHRISTMAS ELEGANCE/GREEN	SANTAS	LH - OTHER		94	$220.00	
215	24 IN. BIRD PEDDLER	OTHER	LH - OTHER	92	90	$500.00	
217	24 IN. FORESTER	OTHER	LH - OTHER	91	90	$500.00	
219	24 IN. OLD WORLD FATHER CHRISTMAS/BURGUNDY	SANTAS	LH - OTHER	93	90	$600.00	
219	24 IN. OLD WORLD FATHER CHRISTMAS/GREEN	SANTAS	LH - OTHER	93	90	$600.00	
219	24 IN. OLD WORLD FATHER CHRISTMAS/RED	SANTAS	LH - OTHER	93	90	$600.00	
305	24 IN. LACE PEDDLER/BLUE	OTHER	LH - LIMITED EDITION	91	90	$750.00	
144	18 IN. SYLVAN SATA WITH DEER	OTHER	LH - OTHER	93	91	$300.00	
152	18 IN. HAT PEDDLER/BLUE	OTHER	LH - OTHER	92	91	$210.00	
152	18 IN. HAT PEDDLER/ROSE	OTHER	LH - OTHER	92	91	$300.00	
156	18 IN. SITTING JOLLY SANTA WITH CHAIR/BURGUNDY	OTHER	LH - LIMITED EDITION	94	91	$210.00	
158	18 IN. EDWARDIAN FATHER CHRISTMAS/BURGUNDY	SANTAS	LH - OTHER	93	91	$210.00	

Order No.	Title	Type	Theme	Retired	Intro. Year	Retial Price	Secondary Price
158	18 IN. EDWARDIAN FATHER CHRISTMAS/GREEN	SANTAS	LH - OTHER	93	91	$210.00	
158	18 IN. EDWARDIAN FATHER CHRISTMAS/IVORY	SANTAS	LH - OTHER	93	91	$210.00	
158	18 IN. EDWARDIAN FATHER CHRISTMAS/ROSE	SANTAS	LH - OTHER	93	91	$210.00	
160	18 IN. OLD WORLD FATHR CHRISTMAS IN SLEIGH/BURGUNDY	SANTAS	LH - LIMITED EDITION	94	91	$300.00	
160	18 IN. OLD WORLD FATHR CHRISTMAS IN SLEIGH/RED	SANTAS	LH - LIMITED EDITION	94	91	$300.00	
162	18 IN. MRS. CLAUS/BURGUNDY	SANTAS	LH - OTHER	94	91	$210.00	
162	18 IN. MRS. CLAUS/RED	SANTAS	LH - OTHER	94	91	$210.00	
164	18 IN. BLACK JOLLY SANTA (AFRICAN AMERICAN)	SANTAS	LH - OTHER	93	91	$210.00	
166	18 IN. GENTLE ST. NICK/BURGUNDY	SANTAS	LH - OTHER	94	91	$210.00	
166	18 IN. GENTLE ST. NICK/GREEN	SANTAS	LH - OTHER	94	91	$210.00	
166	18 IN. GENTLE ST. NICK/RED	SANTAS	LH - OTHER	94	91	$210.00	
166	18 IN. GENTLE ST. NICK/IVORY	SANTAS	LH - OTHER	94	91	$210.00	
155	18 IN. CHRISTMAS ELEGANCE/RED	SANTAS	LH - OTHER		94	$220.00	
155	18 IN. CHRISTMAS ELEGANCE	SANTAS	LH - OTHER		94	$220.00	
6203	21 IN. PATCHWORK FATHER CHRISTMAS	SANTAS	LH - OTHER	97	96	$350.00	
149	18 IN. SANTA OF CHRISTMAS VILLAGE/BLACK	SANTAS	LH - HUNGARIAN FOLK ART		94	$230.00	
149	18 IN. SANTA OF CHRISTMAS VILLAGE/IVORY	SANTAS	LH - HUNGARIAN FOLK ART		94	$230.00	
149	18 IN. SANTA OF CHRISTMAS VILLAGE/RED	SANTAS	LH - HUNGARIAN FOLK ART		94	$230.00	
149	18 IN. SANTA OF CHRISTMAS VILLAGE/BLACK	SANTAS	LH - HUNGARIAN FOLK ART			$230.00	
163	18 IN. HOLLY VILLAGE SANTA/RED	SANTAS	LH - HUNGARIAN FOLK ART		95	$240.00	
181	18 IN. GIFTS OF HOLLY	SANTAS	LH - HUNGARIAN FOLK ART		96	$240.00	
163	18 IN. HOLLY VILLAGE SANTA/IVORY	SANTAS	LH - HUNGARIAN FOLK ART		95	$240.00	
185	18 IN. SNOWFLAKE SANTA/IVORY/RED	SANTAS	LH - HUNGARIAN FOLK ART		96	$240.00	
311	21 IN. BOUGHS OF HOLLY SANTA	SANTAS	LH - HUNGARIAN FOLK ART		95	$350.00	
157	18 IN. SANTA OF THE OLD COUNTRY/IVORY/RED	SANTAS	LH - HUNGARIAN FOLK ART		94	$230.00	
183	18 IN. HEART AND HOLLY	SANTAS	LH - HUNGARIAN FOLK ART		96	$240.00	
157	18 IN. SANTA OF THE OLD COUNTRY/IVORY/GREEN	SANTAS	LH - HUNGARIAN FOLK ART		94	$230.00	
237	24 IN. TIMBERLAND SANTA ON SLED(SEATED)	SANTAS	LH - OTHER		93	$550.00	
175	18 IN. SANTA OF THE EVERGREENS	SANTAS	LH - OTHER		95	$240.00	
171	18 IN. OLD FRIENDS/RED	SANTAS	LH - OTHER		95	$240.00	
245	24 IN. MOUNTAIN MAN	SANTAS	LH - OTHER	97	94	$500.00	
171	18 IN. OLD FRIENDS/BURGUNDY	SANTAS	LH - OTHER			$240.00	
303	21 IN. AMERICAN SANTA	SANTAS	LH - OTHER			$350.00	
125	18 IN. WILDERNESS SANTA (IN 30 IN. CANOE)	SANTAS	LH - OTHER		93	$340.00	
153	18 IN. SANTA OF THE TUNDRA	SANTAS	LH - OTHER		94	$220.00	
6201	21 IN. SANTA OF DEER MOUNTAIN	SANTAS	LH - OTHER		96	$350.00	
161	18 IN. GARDENING SANTA	SANTAS	LH - OTHER	96	94	$220.00	
121	18 IN. COUNTRY CLUB SANTA (IN RED/GOLD CREST)	SANTAS	LH - OTHER			$250.00	
121	18 IN. GOLFING SANTA (IN RED/GREEN ARGYLE)	SANTAS	LH - OTHER		93	$230.00	
145	18 IN. FLYING BUDDIES	SANTAS	LH - OTHER		94	$220.00	
119	18 IN. GOURMET SANTA/RED	SANTAS	LH - OTHER		93	$220.00	
147	18 IN. COWBOY SANTA	SANTAS	LH - OTHER		94	$220.00	
186	18 IN. MOUNTAIN LODGE SANTA	SANTAS	LH - OTHER			$240.00	
127	18 IN. FISHING SANTA	SANTAS	LH - OTHER		94	$220.00	
6101	18 IN. TIDINGS OF JOY (AFRICAN-AMERICAN) RED	SANTAS	LH - OTHER		96	$240.00	
6101	18 IN. TIDINGS OF JOY (AFRICAN-AMERICAN) BURGUNDY	SANTAS	LH - OTHER		96	$240.00	
6101	18 IN. TIDINGS OF JOY (AFRICAN-AMERICAN) GREEN	SANTAS	LH - OTHER		96	$240.00	
177	18 IN. HERITAGE SANTA (AFRICAN AMERICAN)RED	SANTAS	LH - OTHER		95	$240.00	
177	18 IN. HERITAGE SANTA/BURGUNDY	SANTAS	LH - OTHER			$240.00	
6301	24 IN. CHRISTMAS TRIMMINGS	SANTAS	LH - OTHER		96	$500.00	
191	18 IN. SPIRIT OF CHRISTMAS	SANTAS	LH - OTHER		96	$240.00	
195	18 IN. HOLIDAY TREASURES/RED	SANTAS	LH - OTHER		96	$240.00	
6302	24 IN. SANTA OF REINDEER VILLAGE	SANTAS	LH - OTHER		96	$500.00	
189	18 IN. CHRISTMAS BEARS FOR EVERYONE/RED	SANTAS	LH - OTHER		96	$240.00	
307	21 IN.TANNENBAUM FATHER CHRISTMAS/GREEN	SANTAS	LH - OTHER	97	95	$350.00	
247	24 IN. CHRISTMAS TREASURES/RED	SANTAS	LH - OTHER		95	$530.00	
309	21 IN. SANTA OF GOOD TIDINGS/RED	SANTAS	LH - OTHER		95	$530.00	
189	18 IN. CHRISTMAS BEARS FOR EVERYONE/GREEN	SANTAS	LH - OTHER			$240.00	
401	18 IN. WISE MAN #1 - MELCHIOR/BLUE	NATIVITY	LH - LIMITED EDITION	97		$240.00	
402	18 IN. WISEMAN #2 - KASPAR/GREEN	NATIVITY	LH - LIMITED EDITION		96	$240.00	
4037	18 IN. WISEMAN #3 - BALTHASAR/PURPLE	NATIVITY	LH - LIMITED EDITION		97	$240.00	
153	18 IN. SANTA OF THE TUNDRA	SANTAS	LH - OTHER		94	$220.00	
157	18 IN. SANTA OF THE OLD COUNTRY/BLACK/RED	SANTAS	LH - HUNGARIAN FOLK ART	96	94	$230.00	
157	18 IN. SANTA OF THE OLD COUNTRY/RED/BLACK	SANTAS	LH - HUNGARIAN FOLK ART	96	94	$230.00	
185	18 IN. SNOWFLAKE SANTA/RED/GREEN	SANTAS	LH - HUNGARIAN FOLK ART		96	$240.00	
307	21 IN.TANNENBAUM W/MUSIC BOX	SANTAS	LH - OTHER	96	95	$350.00	
104	18 IN. LACE FATHER CHRISTMAS/RED	SANTAS	LH - OTHER	89	87	$150.00	
104	18 IN. LACE FATHER CHRISTMAS/BLUE	SANTAS	LH - OTHER	89	87	$150.00	
104	18 IN. LACE FATHER CHRISTMAS/GREEN	SANTAS	LH - OTHER	89	87	$150.00	
104	18 IN. LACE FATHER CHRISTMAS/WHITE	SANTAS	LH - OTHER	89	87	$150.00	
102	18 IN. COUNTRY FATHER CHRISTMAS/BLUE	SANTAS	LH - OTHER	90	87	$150.00	
102	18 IN. COUNTRY FATHER CHRISTMAS/GREEN	SANTAS	LH - OTHER	90	87	$150.00	
106	18 IN. VICTORIAN FATHER CHRISTMAS/BURGUNDY	SANTAS	LH - OTHER	91	88	$200.00	
110	18 IN. MERLIN WIZARD/BLACK	OTHER	LH - OTHER	91	88	$160.00	
110	18 IN. MERLIN WIZARD/BLUE	OTHER	LH - OTHER	91	88	$160.00	
110	18 IN. MERLIN WIZARD/PURPLE	OTHER	LH - OTHER	91	88	$160.00	
112	18 IN. MADAM	OTHER	LH - OTHER	89	88	$160.00	
114	18 IN. WOODLAND SANTA/GREEN	SANTAS	LH - OTHER	91	89	$190.00	
114	18 IN. WOODLAND SANTA/RED	SANTAS	LH - OTHER	91	89	$190.00	
116	18 IN. FATHER CHRISTMAS IN SLEIGH/BURGUNDY	SANTAS	LH - LIMITED EDITION	91	89	$300.00	
116	18 IN. FATHER CHRISTMAS IN SLEIGH/RED	SANTAS	LH - LIMITED EDITION	91	89	$300.00	
118	18 IN. WIZARD OF THE FOREST	OTHER	LH - OTHER	93	89	$170.00	
120	18 IN. EZRA THE TRAVELER	OTHER	LH - OTHER	90	89	$170.00	
203	24 IN. JACK FROST	OTHER	LH - OTHER	91	89	$500.00	
205	24 IN. SNOW QUEEN	OTHER	LH - OTHER	91	89	$500.00	
207	24 IN. HARVESTER	OTHER	LH - OTHER	90	89	$500.00	
209	24 IN. TAPESTRY WIZARD	OTHER	LH - OTHER	92	89	$500.00	
301	36 IN.YOUNG WILLIAM	OTHER	LH - LIMITED EDITION	91	89	$750.00	
303	36 IN. BIRD PEDDLER	OTHER	LH - LIMITED EDITION	91	89	$750.00	
122	18 IN. HARVESTER	OTHER	LH - OTHER	92	90	$200.00	
124	18 IN. JOLLY OLD SANTA/BURGUNDY	SANTAS	LH - OTHER	96	90	$210.00	
130	18 IN. SHELL COLLECTOR	OTHER	LH - OTHER	94	90	$200.00	
132	18 IN. SAINT FRANCIS	OTHER	LH - OTHER	91	90	$210.00	

Order No.	Title	Type	Theme	Retired	Intro. Year	Retail Price	Secondary Price
124	18 IN. JOLLY OLD SANTA/IVORY	SANTAS	LH - OTHER	96	90	$210.00	
124	18 IN. JOLLY OLD SANTA/RED	SANTAS	LH - OTHER	96	90	$210.00	
134	18 IN. WIZARD OF LIGHT	OTHER	LH - OTHER	93	90	$180.00	
136	18 IN. STARKEEPER	OTHER	LH - OTHER	93	90	$180.00	
138	18 IN. KRIS KRINGLE/BURGUNDY	SANTAS	LH - OTHER	93	90	$210.00	
138	18 IN. KRIS KRINGLE/RED	SANTAS	LH - OTHER	93	90	$210.00	
138	18 IN. KRIS KRINGLE/GREEN	SANTAS	LH - OTHER	93	90	$210.00	
140	18 IN. PERE NOEL/BLUE	SANTAS	LH - OTHER	92	90	$210.00	
140	18 IN. PERE NOEL/IVORY	SANTAS	LH - OTHER	92	90	$210.00	
140	18 IN. PERE NOEL/IVORY	SANTAS	LH - OTHER		90	$210.00	
140	18 IN. PERE NOEL/RED	SANTAS	LH - OTHER		90	$210.00	
142	18 IN. WINTER FANTASY-WHITE SLEIGH	SANTAS	LH - LIMITED EDITION	92	90	$300.00	
144	18 IN. HERB PEDDLER	OTHER	LH - OTHER	91	90	$200.00	
221	24 IN. FLOWER PEDDLER/BLACK	OTHER	LH - OTHER	93	91	$500.00	
221	24 IN. FLOWER PEDDLER/BLUE	OTHER	LH - OTHER	93	91	$500.00	
221	24 IN. FLOWER PEDDLER/IVORY	OTHER	LH - OTHER	93	91	$500.00	
223	24 IN. VICTORIAN FATHER CHRISTMAS/BURGUNDY	SANTAS	LH - OTHER	94	91	$500.00	
223	24 IN. VICTORIAN FATHER CHRISTMAS/GREEN	SANTAS	LH - OTHER	94	91	$500.00	
223	24 IN. VICTORIAN FATHER CHRISTMAS/RED	SANTAS	LH - OTHER	94	91	$500.00	
225	24 IN. TWILIGHT FATHER CHRISTMAS	SANTAS	LH - OTHER	94	91	$500.00	
402	18 IN. YANKEE DOODLE SANTA	SANTAS	LH - OTHER	93	91	$300.00	
404	18 IN. COWBOY SANTA	SANTAS	LH - OTHER	93	91	$200.00	
406	18 IN. ROCKY MOUNTAIN SANTA	SANTAS	LH - OTHER	93	91	$300.00	
408	18 IN. SANTA OF THE NORTH WOODS	SANTAS	LH - OTHER	93	91	$300.00	
168	18 IN. LADY FLOWER PEDDLER	OTHER	LH - OTHER	94	92	$210.00	
170	18 IN. LADY BIRD PEDDLER	OTHER	LH - OTHER	93	92	$220.00	
194	18 IN. ALMOST TIME FOR CHRISTMAS	SANTAS	LH - LIMITED EDITION	95	92	$300.00	
501	18 IN. OLD WORLD FATHER CHRISTMAS/RUST	SANTAS	LH - LIMITED EDITION	93	92	$300.00	
503	18 IN. OLD WORLD FATHER CHRISTMAS/GREEN	SANTAS	LH - LIMITED EDITION	93	92	$300.00	
505	18 IN. OLD WORLD FATHER CHRISTMAS/BURGUNDY	SANTAS	LH - LIMITED EDITION	94	92	$300.00	
101	18 IN. VICTORIAN FATHER CHRISTMAS/BURGUNDY	SANTAS	LH - OTHER	94	93	$200.00	
103	18 IN. RENAISSANCE FATHER CHRISTMAS/BURGUNDY	SANTAS	LH - OTHER	94	93	$220.00	
101	18 IN. VICTORIAN FATHER CHRISTMAS/IVORY	SANTAS	LH - OTHER	94	93	$220.00	
101	18 IN. VICTORIAN FATHER CHRISTMAS/RED	SANTAS	LH - OTHER	94	93	$200.00	
103	18 IN. RENAISSANCE FATHER CHRISTMAS/IVORY	SANTAS	LH - OTHER	94	93	$220.00	
103	18 IN. RENAISSANCE FATHER CHRISTMAS/GREEN	SANTAS	LH - OTHER	94	93	$220.00	
107	18 IN. TWIG CHAIR SANTA	SANTAS	LH - OTHER	94	93	$330.00	
109	18 IN. SANTA OF CHRISTMAS MOUNTAIN	SANTAS	LH - OTHER	94	93	$220.00	
111	18 IN. CHRISTMAS TRAVELER/BURGUNDY	SANTAS	LH - OTHER	96	93	$220.00	
111	18 IN. CHRISTMAS TRAVELER/RED	SANTAS	LH - OTHER	96	93	$220.00	
123	18 IN. SANTA OF THE PINEY WOODS	SANTAS	LH - OTHER	96	93	$220.00	
196	18 IN. UST MAKING BEARS	OTHER	LH - LIMITED EDITION	96	93	$300.00	
229	24 IN. RADIANCE SANTA	SANTAS	LH - OTHER	96	93	$530.00	
231	24 IN. NORTHERN TERRITORY	SANTAS	LH - OTHER	96	93	$500.00	
233	24 IN. CROSS COUNTRY SANTA IN SWEATER	SANTAS	LH - OTHER	94	93	$500.00	
235	24 IN. MERLIN THE GOOD WIZARD	OTHER	LH - OTHER	94	93	$500.00	
507	36 IN. NORTHERN TERRITORY SANTA	OTHER	LH - LIMITED EDITION	95	93	$1,600.00	
509	36 IN. REGAL FATHER CHRISTMAS	OTHER	LH - LIMITED EDITION	95	93	$1,600.00	
131	18 IN. CELESTIAL SANTA/BLUE	SANTAS	LH - OTHER	96	94	$240.00	
133	18 IN. CELESTIAL SANTA/BLUE	SANTAS	LH - OTHER	96	94	$240.00	
133	18 IN. CELESTIAL SANTA/BURGUNDY	SANTAS	LH - OTHER	96	94	$240.00	
135	18 IN. CHRISTMAS JOURNEY/BURGUNDY	SANTAS	LH - OTHER	96	94	$240.00	
135	18 IN. CHRISTMAS JOURNEY/RED	SANTAS	LH - OTHER	96	94	$240.00	
151	18 IN. CHRISTMAS MAJESTY	SANTAS	LH - OTHER	96	94	$220.00	
155	18 IN. CHRISTMAS ELEGANCE WITH NO FUR/BURGUNDY	SANTAS	LH - OTHER	95	94	$245.00	
155	18 IN. CHRISTMAS ELEGANCE/BURGUNDY	SANTAS	LH - OTHER		94	$220.00	
155	18 IN. CHRISTMAS ELEGANCE/GREEN	SANTAS	LH - OTHER		94	$220.00	
155	18 IN. CHRISTMAS ELEGANCE/RED	SANTAS	LH - OTHER		94	$220.00	
157	18 IN. SANTA OF THE OLD COUNTRY/IVORY/GREEN	SANTAS	LH - HUNGARIAN FOLK ART		94	$230.00	
157	18 IN. SANTA OF THE OLD COUNTRY/IVORY/RED	SANTAS	LH - HUNGARIAN FOLK ART		94	$230.00	
157	18 IN. SANTA OF THE OLD COUNTRY/BLACK/RED	SANTAS	LH - HUNGARIAN FOLK ART	96	94	$230.00	
157	18 IN. SANTA OF THE OLD COUNTRY/RED/BLACK	SANTAS	LH - HUNGARIAN FOLK ART	96	94	$230.00	
159	18 IN. WIZARD OF DREMS	SANTAS	LH - OTHER	96	94	$220.00	
169	18 IN. FATHER CHRISTMAS W/MUSIC BOX	SANTAS	LH - OTHER	95	94	$230.00	
239	24 IN. WOODLAND TRAIL	SANTAS	LH - OTHER	96	94	$500.00	
241	24 IN. STORYBOOK SANTA	SANTAS	LH - LIMITED EDITION	96	94	$530.00	
243	24 IN. SANTA OF THE WINTER WOODS	SANTAS	LH - OTHER	96	94	$500.00	
301	21 IN. SANTA OF PEACE	SANTAS	LH - OTHER	96	94	$300.00	
301	21 IN. SANTA OF PEACE	SANTAS	LH - OTHER	NO	94	$300.00	
305	21 IN. YULETIDE FATHER CHRISTMAS/BURGUNDY	SANTAS	LH - OTHER	96	94	$350.00	
511	36 IN. SANTA OF THE PEACEABLE KINGDOM	SANTAS	LH - LIMITED EDITION	95	94	$1,600.00	
305	21 IN. YULETIDE FATHER CHRISTMAS/RED	SANTAS	LH - OTHER	96	94	$350.00	
513	36 IN. MEMORIES OF CHRISTMAS	SANTAS	LH - LIMITED EDITION	95	94	$1,600.00	
121	18 IN. COUNTRY CLUB SANTA/RED	SANTAS	LH - OTHER	NO	95	$250.00	
121	18 IN. COUNTRY CLUB SANTA/GOLD	SANTAS	LH - OTHER	NO	95	$250.00	
155	18 IN. VICTORIAN COLLECTOR	SANTAS	LH - OTHER	96	95	$240.00	
187	18 IN. CANTIQUE DE NOEL WITH MUSIC BOX	SANTAS	LH - OTHER	96	95	$240.00	
195	18 IN. BLOOMINGDALE SANTA	SANTAS	LH - OTHER	96	95	$230.00	
313	21 IN. ENCHANTED TREASURES/BURGUNDY	OTHER	LH - OTHER	96	95	$350.00	
313	21 IN. ENCHANTED TREASURES/GREEN	OTHER	LH - OTHER	96	95	$350.00	
515	36 IN. VICTORIAN TREASURES	OTHER	LH - OTHER	97	95	$1,600.00	
6201	21 IN. SANTA OF DEER MOUNTAIN	SANTAS	LH - OTHER	NO	95	$350.00	
197	18 IN. SAINT NICHOLAS	SANTAS	LH - OTHER	NO	96	$240.00	
3057	24 IN. CHRISTMAS DREAMS	SANTAS	LH - OTHER	NO	96	$500.00	
3067	24 IN. HANGING THE GARLAND SANTA	SANTAS	LH - OTHER	NO	96	$500.00	
6102	18 IN. MR. GUMDROP	SANTAS	LH - OTHER	NO	96	$240.00	
6104	18 IN. CHRISTMAS BOX SANTA	SANTAS	LH - OTHER	97	96	$240.00	
6106	18 IN. CHRISTMAS CELEBRATION/PATCHWORK	SANTAS	LH - OTHER	97	96	$240.00	
6107	18 IN. VICTORIAN MEMORY	SANTAS	LH - OTHER	97	96	$240.00	
6114	18 IN. HUSKER SANTA	SANTAS	LH - OTHER	NO	96	$240.00	
6116	18 IN. CHRISTMAS GOODIES	SANTAS	LH - OTHER	NO	96	$240.00	
6117	18 IN. ROCKY MOUNTAIN SANTA/IVORY	SANTAS	LH - OTHER	NO	96	$240.00	
6117	18 IN. ROCKY MOUNTAIN SANTA/RED	SANTAS	LH - OTHER	NO	96	$240.00	

Order No.	Title	Type	Theme	Retired	Intro. Year	Retial Price	Secondary Price
6204	21 IN. VICTORIAN MEMORIES	SANTAS	LH - OTHER	NO	96	$350.00	
6206	21 IN. SANTA OF THE NORTHWEST JOURNEY	SANTAS	LH - OTHER	NO	96	$350.00	
6304	24 IN. SLEIGH RIDE/GREEN SLEIGH	SANTAS	LH - OTHER	97	96	$1,500.00	
6517	36 IN. NOEL SANTA	SANTAS	LH - LIMITED EDITION	NO	96	$1,600.00	
1017	18 IN. STARRY NIGHT SANTA	SANTAS	LH - HUNGARIAN FOLK ART	NO	97	$240.00	
1027	18 IN. SANTA OF DEER VALLEY/RED/BLACK	SANTAS	LH - HUNGARIAN FOLK ART	NO	97	$240.00	
1027	18 IN. SANTA OF DEER VALLEY/RED/IVORY	SANTAS	LH - HUNGARIAN FOLK ART	NO	97	$240.00	
1047	18 IN. MRS. GUMDROP	OTHER	LH - HUNGARIAN FOLK ART	NO	97	$240.00	
1057	18 IN. LET IT SNOW	OTHER	LH - OTHER	NO	97	$240.00	
1067	18 IN. SANTA OF TOY HAMLET	OTHER	LH - HUNGARIAN FOLK ART	NO	97	$240.00	
1077	18 IN. SAMPLER SANTA/BLACK	OTHER	LH - HUNGARIAN FOLK ART	NO	97	$240.00	
1077	18 IN. SAMPLER SANTA/RED	OTHER	LH - HUNGARIAN FOLK ART	NO	97	$240.00	
1087	18 IN. SANTA OF THE WHITE WOODS	OTHER	LH - HUNGARIAN FOLK ART	NO	97	$240.00	
1097	18 IN. CHRISTMAS COTTAGE/GREEN	OTHER	LH - OTHER	NO	97	$240.00	
1097	18 IN. CHRISTMAS COTTAGE/RED	OTHER	LH - OTHER	NO	97	$240.00	
1117	18 IN. SNOW COUNTRY SANTA	SANTAS	LH - OTHER	NO	97	$240.00	
1107	18 IN. CHRISTMA PICKLE	SANTAS	LH - OTHER	NO	97	$240.00	
1127	18 IN. ONWARD	SANTAS	LH - LIMITED EDITION	NO	97	$270.00	
2017	21 IN. CHRISTMAS BERRIES	SANTAS	LH - OTHER	NO	97	$350.00	
2037	21 IN. SANTA OF CHRISTMAS PAST	SANTAS	LH - OTHER	NO	97	$330.00	
2047	21 IN. STARLIGHT FATHER CHRISTMAS	SANTAS	LH - OTHER	NO	97	$330.00	
2057	21 IN. HOMESTEAD SANTA/SITTING/QUILTED	SANTAS	LH - OTHER	NO	97	$330.00	
3017	24 IN. MAGIC SLEIGH RIDE/BURGUNDY	SANTAS	LH - LIMITED EDITION	NO	97	$1,600.00	
3027	24 IN. RIDE THROUGH THE COUNTRY/BROWN SLEIGH	SANTAS	LH - LIMITED EDITION	NO	97	$530.00	
3037	24 IN. FIRESIDE SANTA	SANTAS	LH - OTHER	NO	97	$530.00	
3047	24 IN. CHRISTMAS FANTASY/SITTING	SANTAS	LH - OTHER	NO	97	$450.00	
4047	18 IN. MELCHIOR--WISEMAN #1/SECOND EDITION	SANTAS	LH - LIMITED EDITION	NO	97	$240.00	
5017	36 IN. SLEIGH BELL SANTA	SANTAS	LH - LIMITED EDITION	NO	97	$1,600.00	
6115	18 IN. VINEYARD SANTA	SANTAS	LH - OTHER	NO	97	$240.00	
			LYNN WEST				
3546	OLD TIME SANTA AND TREE/3RD IN SERIES	LW DESIGNS/AMAR/LSTNGENDRMENTS	LW - OLD TIME SANTAS	95	94	$650.00	$925.00
4221	ASTEROID	LW DESIGNS/AMAR/LSTNGENDRMENTS	LW - FAERIES	95	94	$284.00	$284.00
4222	CADENCE	LW DESIGNS/AMAR/LSTNGENDRMENTS	LW - FAERIES	95	94	$284.00	$284.00
4275	CHRISTMAS PEACE	LW DESIGNS/AMAR/LSTNGENDRMENTS	LW - SANTAS & FATHER CHRISTMAS	95	94	$1,450.00	$2,955.00
3501	HOLLY 1989	LW DESIGNS/AMAR/LSTNGENDRMENTS	LW - ELVES	89	89	$250.00	$250.00
8102	NATE	LW DESIGNS/AMAR/LSTNGENDRMENTS	LW - ELVES	94	94	$220.00	$210.00
4605	PATCHES	LW DESIGNS/AMAR/LSTNGENDRMENTS	LW - ELVES	93	92	$278.00	$500.00
2303	WASSAIL	LW DESIGNS/AMAR/LSTNGENDRMENTS	LW - ELVES	88	88	$230.00	$250.00
3502	WASSAIL	LW DESIGNS/AMAR/LSTNGENDRMENTS	LW - ELVES	89	89	$250.00	$380.00
4532	WOLFIE	LW DESIGNS/AMAR/LSTNGENDRMENTS	LW - ELVES	95	93	$390.00	$390.00
3600	ANGEL	LW DESIGNS/AMAR/LSTNGENDRMENTS	LW - CHRISTMAS SCENES	89	89	$500.00	$500.00
2305	UP ON THE ROOF TOP	LW DESIGNS/AMAR/LSTNGENDRMENTS	LW - CHRISTMAS SCENES	91	89	$1,300.00	$1,300.00
4224	BOREALIS	LW DESIGNS/AMAR/LSTNGENDRMENTS	LW - FAERIES	95	95	$310.00	$315.00
4230	DREAMWEAVER	LW DESIGNS/AMAR/LSTNGENDRMENTS	LW - FAERIES		96	$330.00	$330.00
4112	EGGBURT	LW DESIGNS/AMAR/LSTNGENDRMENTS	LW - FAERIES	93	91	$278.00	$425.00
5219	EVERGREEN	LW DESIGNS/AMAR/LSTNGENDRMENTS	LW - FAERIES	94	93	$284.00	
4225	FIGARO	LW DESIGNS/AMAR/LSTNGENDRMENTS	LW - FAERIES	95	95	$310.00	$315.00
	SEAN-CUSTOM FAERIE/NEIMAN	LW DESIGNS/AMAR/LSTNGENDRMENTS	LW - FAERIES	95	95	$310.00	$312.00
4223	SERENADE	LW DESIGNS/AMAR/LSTNGENDRMENTS	LW - FAERIES	95	95	$310.00	$310.00
	WINSOR-CUSTOM FAERIE/NEIMAN	LW DESIGNS/AMAR/LSTNGENDRMENTS	LW - FAERIES	95	95	$310.00	$315.00
2300	CHRISTMAS MAJESTY	LW DESIGNS/AMAR/LSTNGENDRMENTS	LW - SANTAS & FATHER CHRISTMAS	89	88	$750.00	$750.00
4270	CHRISTMAS MAJESTY/SPECIAL EDITION	LW DESIGNS/AMAR/LSTNGENDRMENTS	LW - SPECIAL EDITION	93	93	$1,590.00	$2,490.00
4340	OLD WORLD SANTA	LW DESIGNS/AMAR/LSTNGENDRMENTS	LW - SANTAS & FATHER CHRISTMAS		96	$750.00	$740.00
4255	VICTORIAN ST. NICHOLAS	LW DESIGNS/AMAR/LSTNGENDRMENTS	LW - OLD WORLD SANTA SERIES	95	94	$1,300.00	$2,300.00
7006	FREDERICK-MUSIC SCHOOL	LW DESIGNS/AMAR/LSTNGENDRMENTS	LW - MAGICAL FOREST FAERIES	95	95	$490.00	$485.00
7005	PROFESSER WIND CHIME	LW DESIGNS/AMAR/LSTNGENDRMENTS	LW - MAGICAL FOREST FAERIES	95	95	$1,190.00	$1,185.00
4110	SULLIVAN	LW DESIGNS/AMAR/LSTNGENDRMENTS	LW - MAGICAL FOREST FAERIES	92	91	$480.00	$475.00
7035	FERN	LW DESIGNS/AMAR/LSTNGENDRMENTS	LW - LYNNIPUTS	95	95	$450.00	$450.00
3555	FRANZ, SANTA'S HELPER/3RD IN SERIES	LW DESIGNS/AMAR/LSTNGENDRMENTS	LW - ELVES	95	95	$330.00	$330.00
3602	HERBIE, HOLIDAY HELPER/3RD IN SERIES	LW DESIGNS/AMAR/LSTNGENDRMENTS	LW - ELVES		96	$350.00	$350.00
1115	KRIS KRINGLE/SPECIAL EDITION	LW DESIGNS/AMAR/LSTNGENDRMENTS	LW - SPECIAL EDITION	88	88	$2,000.00	$2,000.00
6005BRD	LAST MINUTE DETAILS W/BEARD	LW DESIGNS/AMAR/LSTNGENDRMENTS	LW - SANTAS & FATHER CHRISTMAS	92	91	$550.00	$695.00
6005MD	LAST MINUTE DETAILS-M.B.	LW DESIGNS/AMAR/LSTNGENDRMENTS	LW - SANTAS & FATHER CHRISTMAS	92	91	$430.00	$425.00
2301	SPENCER	LW DESIGNS/AMAR/LSTNGENDRMENTS	LW - SANTAS & FATHER CHRISTMAS	91	88	$850.00	$845.00
9002	STANDING SANTA W/TOY PACK	LW DESIGNS/AMAR/LSTNGENDRMENTS	LW - SANTAS & FATHER CHRISTMAS	94	94	$450.00	$445.00
3601	WOODLAND SANTA ON WOODEN BASE	LW DESIGNS/AMAR/LSTNGENDRMENTS	LW - SANTAS & FATHER CHRISTMAS		96	$690.00	$685.00
	CRYSTAL THE ELF	LW DESIGNS/AMAR/LSTNGENDRMENTS	LW - ELVES		88	$2,000.00	
	FHARANTINO	LW DESIGNS/AMAR/LSTNGENDRMENTS	LW -		88	$3,150.00	
	SILVER/GREEN BALLOON	LW DESIGNS/AMAR/LSTNGENDRMENTS	LW -		88	$1,050.00	
	CHRISTMAS FAIRY	LW DESIGNS/AMAR/LSTNGENDRMENTS	LW - FAERIES		89	$600.00	
	ERNST THE ELF	LW DESIGNS/AMAR/LSTNGENDRMENTS	LW - ELVES		89	$1,700.00	
	ICICLE FAIRY	LW DESIGNS/AMAR/LSTNGENDRMENTS	LW - FAERIES		89	$600.00	
	IVAN HEART	LW DESIGNS/AMAR/LSTNGENDRMENTS	LW -		89	$3,150.00	
	CHRISTMAS ROSE FAIRY	LW DESIGNS/AMAR/LSTNGENDRMENTS	LW - FAERIES		90	$650.00	
	DECO BUBBLE FAIRY	LW DESIGNS/AMAR/LSTNGENDRMENTS	LW - FAERIES		90	$650.00	
	FOXGLOVE FAIRY	LW DESIGNS/AMAR/LSTNGENDRMENTS	LW - FAERIES		90	$600.00	
	GOLDEN STAR FAIRY	LW DESIGNS/AMAR/LSTNGENDRMENTS	LW - FAERIES		90	$650.00	
	LARGE YULETIDE FAIRY	LW DESIGNS/AMAR/LSTNGENDRMENTS	LW - FAERIES		90	$1,700.00	
	MASQUERADE DOLL	LW DESIGNS/AMAR/LSTNGENDRMENTS	LW - DOLLS		90	$2,200.00	
	MAUVE MAGNOLIA FAIRY	LW DESIGNS/AMAR/LSTNGENDRMENTS	LW - FAERIES		90	$600.00	
	PISTACHIO DOLL	LW DESIGNS/AMAR/LSTNGENDRMENTS	LW - DOLLS		90	$2,200.00	
	REINDEER HOLLY FAIRY	LW DESIGNS/AMAR/LSTNGENDRMENTS	LW - FAERIES		90	$650.00	
	ANTIQUE HOLLY FAIRY	LW DESIGNS/AMAR/LSTNGENDRMENTS	LW - FAERIES		91	$650.00	
	BURGUNDY GOLD/CHRISTMAS BALLOON	LW DESIGNS/AMAR/LSTNGENDRMENTS	LW -		91	$900.00	
	COUNTRY SPRING FAIRY	LW DESIGNS/AMAR/LSTNGENDRMENTS	LW - FAERIES		91	$700.00	
	JACAMO THE CLOWN	LW DESIGNS/AMAR/LSTNGENDRMENTS	LW -		91	$2,200.00	
	POINSETTA FAIRY	LW DESIGNS/AMAR/LSTNGENDRMENTS	LW - FAERIES		91	$650.00	
	RED/GREEN CHRISTMAS BALLOON	LW DESIGNS/AMAR/LSTNGENDRMENTS	LW -		91	$900.00	
	RUSSIAN FAIRY WITH SWAN	LW DESIGNS/AMAR/LSTNGENDRMENTS	LW - FAERIES		91	$650.00	
	SEBASTIAN	LW DESIGNS/AMAR/LSTNGENDRMENTS	LW - FAERIES		91	$1,390.00	
	SPRING AIR BALLOON	LW DESIGNS/AMAR/LSTNGENDRMENTS	LW -		91	$850.00	

Order No.	Title	Type	Theme	Retired	Intro. Year	Retail Price	Secondary Price
	SPRINGTIME MELODY FAIRY	LW DESIGNS/AMAR/LSTNGENDRMENTS	LW - FAERIES		91	$650.00	
	VICTORIAN ROSE ST. NICK	LW DESIGNS/AMAR/LSTNGENDRMENTS	LW - SANTAS & FATHER CHRISTMAS		91	$1,500.00	
	BUBBLES THE CLOWN	LW DESIGNS/AMAR/LSTNGENDRMENTS	LW -		92	$2,300.00	
	CHRISTMAS TREASURES	LW DESIGNS/AMAR/LSTNGENDRMENTS	LW -		92	$1,750.00	
	ESHBACH THE ELF	LW DESIGNS/AMAR/LSTNGENDRMENTS	LW - ELVES		92	$1,550.00	
	FEMALE FAIRY	LW DESIGNS/AMAR/LSTNGENDRMENTS	LW - FAERIES		92	$750.00	
	JEWEL THE HARLEQUIN	LW DESIGNS/AMAR/LSTNGENDRMENTS	LW -		92	$2,300.00	
	MALE CHRISTMAS GOOSE FAIRY	LW DESIGNS/AMAR/LSTNGENDRMENTS	LW - FAERIES		92	$500.00	
	OLD WORLD SANTA	LW DESIGNS/AMAR/LSTNGENDRMENTS	LW - SANTAS & FATHER CHRISTMAS		92	$1,590.00	
4540	JOLLY HOLIDAY	LW DESIGNS/AMAR/LSTNGENDRMENTS	LW - ELVES		94	$950.00	$950.00
4220	TIMBER	LW DESIGNS/AMAR/LSTNGENDRMENTS	LW - FAERIES	95	94	$284.00	$285.00
4541	KRISTER	LW DESIGNS/AMAR/LSTNGENDRMENTS	LW - ELVES		94	$510.00	$510.00
4330	ANNIVERSARY FATHER CHRISTMAS	LW DESIGNS/AMAR/LSTNGENDRMENTS	LW - SANTAS & FATHER CHRISTMAS	95	94	$750.00	$750.00
7025	CAPTAIN SUREWOOD	LW DESIGNS/AMAR/LSTNGENDRMENTS	LW - MAGICAL FOREST FAERIES	95	94	$950.00	$950.00
7032	CHESTNUT	LW DESIGNS/AMAR/LSTNGENDRMENTS	LW - LYNNIPUTS	95	94	$450.00	$450.00
7033	NOEL	LW DESIGNS/AMAR/LSTNGENDRMENTS	LW - LYNNIPUTS	95	94	$390.00	$450.00
7031	POPS	LW DESIGNS/AMAR/LSTNGENDRMENTS	LW - LYNNIPUTS	95	94	$390.00	$450.00
7030	NESTER	LW DESIGNS/AMAR/LSTNGENDRMENTS	LW - LYNNIPUTS	95	94	$390.00	$450.00
7020	MENDICINO	LW DESIGNS/AMAR/LSTNGENDRMENTS	LW - FAERIES	95	94	$510.00	$515.00
2350	CHECKING IT TWICE	LW DESIGNS/AMAR/LSTNGENDRMENTS	LW - CHRISTMAS SCENES	95	93	$3,590.00	$3,590.00
4250	FATHER CHRISTMAS WITH STAFF	LW DESIGNS/AMAR/LSTNGENDRMENTS	LW - SANTAS & FATHER CHRISTMAS	94	93	$1,300.00	$2,115.00
4400	LARGE TRADITIONAL SANTA	LW DESIGNS/AMAR/LSTNGENDRMENTS	LW - SANTAS & FATHER CHRISTMAS	93	90	$700.00	
4505	D'LIGHT	LW DESIGNS/AMAR/LSTNGENDRMENTS	LW - ELVES	92	91	$500.00	$500.00
4500	RUSSEL THE WRAPPER	LW DESIGNS/AMAR/LSTNGENDRMENTS	LW - ELVES	92	90	$480.00	$475.00
4305	FATHER NIKOLAI	LW DESIGNS/AMAR/LSTNGENDRMENTS	LW - OLD WORLD SANTA SERIES	93	91	$750.00	$750.00
2400	MERRY LITTLE CHRISTMAS	LW DESIGNS/AMAR/LSTNGENDRMENTS	LW - CHRISTMAS SCENES	93	91	$1,990.00	$1,990.00
6000	SAINT NICK	LW DESIGNS/AMAR/LSTNGENDRMENTS	LW - SANTAS & FATHER CHRISTMAS	91	91	$370.00	$375.00
4203	SNOW FLAKE	LW DESIGNS/AMAR/LSTNGENDRMENTS	LW - FAERIES	91	90	$278.00	$280.00
4201	BERRY	LW DESIGNS/AMAR/LSTNGENDRMENTS	LW - FAERIES	91	90	$278.00	$475.00
4202	JINGLES	LW DESIGNS/AMAR/LSTNGENDRMENTS	LW - FAERIES	92	90	$248.00	$280.00
4603	HALF NOTE	LW DESIGNS/AMAR/LSTNGENDRMENTS	LW - ELVES	92	90	$278.00	
4602	ROCKY	LW DESIGNS/AMAR/LSTNGENDRMENTS	LW - ELVES	92	89	$278.00	$278.00
4604	RUMP-PAPA-PUM	LW DESIGNS/AMAR/LSTNGENDRMENTS	LW - ELVES	92	91	$278.00	$275.00
4601	SKEETER	LW DESIGNS/AMAR/LSTNGENDRMENTS	LW - ELVES	92	90	$278.00	$275.00
3520	GRAND FATHER CHRISTMAS	LW DESIGNS/AMAR/LSTNGENDRMENTS	LW - SANTAS & FATHER CHRISTMAS	91	89	$750.00	$740.00
4300	WINTER MAJESTY	LW DESIGNS/AMAR/LSTNGENDRMENTS	LW - SANTAS & FATHER CHRISTMAS	92	90	$750.00	$945.00
3535	SANTA AT THE NORTH POLE	LW DESIGNS/AMAR/LSTNGENDRMENTS	LW - SANTAS & FATHER CHRISTMAS	91	89	$450.00	$455.00
4204	TWEETLE BERRY	LW DESIGNS/AMAR/LSTNGENDRMENTS	LW - FAERIES	92	91	$284.00	$285.00
4205	MISTLETOE	LW DESIGNS/AMAR/LSTNGENDRMENTS	LW - FAERIES	93	91	$284.00	$432.00
5001	MRS. SANTA B. CLAWS	LW DESIGNS/AMAR/LSTNGENDRMENTS	LW - BEARS	91	91	$500.00	
5000	MR. SANTA B. CLAWS	LW DESIGNS/AMAR/LSTNGENDRMENTS	LW - BEARS		91	$500.00	$500.00
4101	BLUEBERRY	LW DESIGNS/AMAR/LSTNGENDRMENTS	LW - FAERIES	90	90	$270.00	$275.00
4102	EMERALD	LW DESIGNS/AMAR/LSTNGENDRMENTS	LW - FAERIES	92	90	$270.00	$275.00
4103	DUSTY	LW DESIGNS/AMAR/LSTNGENDRMENTS	LW - FAERIES	91	90	$270.00	$270.00
4000	WEE WILLIE	LW DESIGNS/AMAR/LSTNGENDRMENTS	LW - MAGICAL FOREST FAERIES	91	90	$480.00	$580.00
4111	RADDISH	LW DESIGNS/AMAR/LSTNGENDRMENTS	LW - FAERIES	92	91	$278.00	$432.00
5006	SARA BEARSLEY	LW DESIGNS/AMAR/LSTNGENDRMENTS	LW - BEARS	91	89	$500.00	$500.00
5005	ASHLEY BEARSLEY	LW DESIGNS/AMAR/LSTNGENDRMENTS	LW - BEARS	91	91	$500.00	$500.00
4320	SPECIAL DELIVERY/8TH IN SERIES	LW DESIGNS/AMAR/LSTNGENDRMENTS	LW - OLD WORLD SANTA SERIES	93	93	$750.00	$750.00
3545	STILL FITS/2ND IN SERIES	LW DESIGNS/AMAR/LSTNGENDRMENTS	LW - OLD TIME SANTAS	93	93	$700.00	$890.00
4520	T'WINKLE	LW DESIGNS/AMAR/LSTNGENDRMENTS	LW - ELVES	94	93	$950.00	$1,300.00
4530	RAFFAEL	LW DESIGNS/AMAR/LSTNGENDRMENTS	LW - ELVES	94	93	$390.00	$390.00
4531	DOMINICK	LW DESIGNS/AMAR/LSTNGENDRMENTS	LW - ELVES	94	93	$420.00	$420.00
7015	WHISKERS AND WINK	LW DESIGNS/AMAR/LSTNGENDRMENTS	LW - MAGICAL FOREST FAERIES	93	93	$690.00	$795.00
7010	HERMES	LW DESIGNS/AMAR/LSTNGENDRMENTS	LW - MAGICAL FOREST FAERIES	93	93	$790.00	$785.00
4218	JACK	LW DESIGNS/AMAR/LSTNGENDRMENTS	LW - FAERIES	94	93	$284.00	$425.00
4265	YULETIDE SAINT NICK/4TH IN SERIES	LW DESIGNS/AMAR/LSTNGENDRMENTS	LW - SANTAS & FATHER CHRISTMAS		96	$1,450.00	$1,450.00
4266	NATHANIEL/CAROLER ANGEL	LW DESIGNS/AMAR/LSTNGENDRMENTS	LW - ANGELS		96	$590.00	$590.00
4267	KATHERINE/CAROLER ANGEL	LW DESIGNS/AMAR/LSTNGENDRMENTS	LW - ANGELS		96	$590.00	$590.00
4231	JUBILEE	LW DESIGNS/AMAR/LSTNGENDRMENTS	LW - FAERIES		96	$330.00	$325.00
4232	GARDINO	LW DESIGNS/AMAR/LSTNGENDRMENTS	LW - FAERIES		96	$330.00	$330.00
4233	GUMDROP	LW DESIGNS/AMAR/LSTNGENDRMENTS	LW - FAERIES		96	$330.00	$330.00
4260	VICTORIAN WINTER FATHER CHRISTMAS/3RD IN SERIES	LW DESIGNS/AMAR/LSTNGENDRMENTS	LW - COLLECTIBLE SANTA SERIES		95	$1,450.00	
4262	ANNA-VICTORIAN WINTER ANGEL BABY	LW DESIGNS/AMAR/LSTNGENDRMENTS	LW - ANGELS		95	$590.00	$590.00
3600	WOODLAND SANTA CLAUS AND HERBIE	LW DESIGNS/AMAR/LSTNGENDRMENTS	LW - SANTAS & FATHER CHRISTMAS		96	$1,650.00	$1,650.00
3550	LYNN WEST'S SANTA CLAUS	LW DESIGNS/AMAR/LSTNGENDRMENTS	LW - SANTAS & FATHER CHRISTMAS		95	$550.00	$555.00
7034	FROSTIE	LW DESIGNS/AMAR/LSTNGENDRMENTS	LW - LYNNIPUTS		95	$450.00	$450.00
4210	FIDDLER	LW DESIGNS/AMAR/LSTNGENDRMENTS	LW - FAERIES	93	92	$284.00	$425.00
4211	BAUBLES	LW DESIGNS/AMAR/LSTNGENDRMENTS	LW - FAERIES	93	92	$284.00	$425.00
4212	WOODIE	LW DESIGNS/AMAR/LSTNGENDRMENTS	LW - FAERIES	93	92	$284.00	$285.00
4213	CARDINAL	LW DESIGNS/AMAR/LSTNGENDRMENTS	LW - FAERIES	93	92	$284.00	$285.00
4510	PEPE MINT	LW DESIGNS/AMAR/LSTNGENDRMENTS	LW - ELVES	92	92	$850.00	$845.00
4310	CHRISTMAS GLORY/7TH IN SERIES	LW DESIGNS/AMAR/LSTNGENDRMENTS	LW - OLD WORLD SANTA SERIES	93	92	$750.00	$750.00
3540	OLD TIME SANTA/1ST IN SERIES	LW DESIGNS/AMAR/LSTNGENDRMENTS	LW - OLD TIME SANTAS	93	92	$530.00	$795.00
2450	CHRISTMAS MEMORIES/SET	LW DESIGNS/AMAR/LSTNGENDRMENTS	LW - CHRISTMAS MEMORIES	94	92	$2,390.00	$2,390.00
2451	CLASSIC SANTA WITH KINGS CHAIR	LW DESIGNS/AMAR/LSTNGENDRMENTS	LW - SANTAS & FATHER CHRISTMAS	93	92	$1,450.00	$1,875.00
2452	OLIVER	LW DESIGNS/AMAR/LSTNGENDRMENTS	LW - ELVES	93	92	$470.00	$470.00
2453	TIMOTHY	LW DESIGNS/AMAR/LSTNGENDRMENTS	LW - ELVES	94	92	$590.00	$585.00
4215	SPRING MIST	LW DESIGNS/AMAR/LSTNGENDRMENTS	LW - FAERIES	93	92	$284.00	$285.00
4216	LUDWIG	LW DESIGNS/AMAR/LSTNGENDRMENTS	LW - FAERIES	93	92	$284.00	$284.00
4217	TEALBERRY	LW DESIGNS/AMAR/LSTNGENDRMENTS	LW - FAERIES	94	92	$284.00	$285.00
4214	GOLDEN FROST	LW DESIGNS/AMAR/LSTNGENDRMENTS	LW - FAERIES	93	92	$284.00	$285.00
7002	LEOPOLE	LW DESIGNS/AMAR/LSTNGENDRMENTS	LW - MAGICAL FOREST FAERIES	93	92	$470.00	$785.00
7000	FATHER EARTH	LW DESIGNS/AMAR/LSTNGENDRMENTS	LW - MAGICAL FOREST FAERIES	93	92	$830.00	$825.00
7001	TELLTALE AND TEABU	LW DESIGNS/AMAR/LSTNGENDRMENTS	LW - MAGICAL FOREST FAERIES	93	90	$670.00	$1,300.00
4261	ANDRE-VICTORIAN	LW DESIGNS/AMAR/LSTNGENDRMENTS	LW - ANGELS		95	$590.00	$590.00
4900	DUCHESS TINCHIN	LW DESIGNS/AMAR/LSTNGENDRMENTS	LW - BEARS	90	90	$750.00	$750.00
3100	PRINCESS SIMSONG AND PI	LW DESIGNS/AMAR/LSTNGENDRMENTS	LW - BEARS	89	89	$750.00	$750.00
9001	SU-LIN AND SON	LW DESIGNS/AMAR/LSTNGENDRMENTS	LW - BEARS	94	94	$300.00	$300.00
2500	WEE WOO WONG	LW DESIGNS/AMAR/LSTNGENDRMENTS	LW - BEARS	88	89	$750.00	$750.00
2304	BAYBERRY	LW DESIGNS/AMAR/LSTNGENDRMENTS	LW - ELVES	88	88	$250.00	$500.00
3503	BAYBERRY	LW DESIGNS/AMAR/LSTNGENDRMENTS	LW - ELVES	89	89	$278.00	$500.00
8103	BRANDY	LW DESIGNS/AMAR/LSTNGENDRMENTS	LW - ELVES	94	94	$230.00	$225.00

Order No.	Title	Type	Theme	Retired	Intro. Year	Retial Price	Secondary Price
8101	FORREST	LW DESIGNS/AMAR/LSTNGENDRMENTS	LW - ELVES	94	94	$210.00	$210.00
4515	GIUSEPPE-CHRISTMAS ELF	LW DESIGNS/AMAR/LSTNGENDRMENTS	LW - ELVES		95	$900.00	$900.00
4525	GOLDWIN	LW DESIGNS/AMAR/LSTNGENDRMENTS	LW - ELVES	95	95	$950.00	$475.00
2302	HOLLY 1988	LW DESIGNS/AMAR/LSTNGENDRMENTS	LW - ELVES	88	88	$230.00	$230.00
	SILVER/GOLD AIR BALLOON	LW DESIGNS/AMAR/LSTNGENDRMENTS	LW -		92	$950.00	
	SPRING MONET AIR BALLOON	LW DESIGNS/AMAR/LSTNGENDRMENTS	LW -		92	$900.00	
	VICTORIAN AIR BALLOON	LW DESIGNS/AMAR/LSTNGENDRMENTS	LW -		92	$950.00	
	ALAKAZAM! THE MAGICIAN/LARGE	LW DESIGNS/AMAR/LSTNGENDRMENTS	LW -		93	$1,590.00	
	ALAKAZAM! THE MAGICIAN/SMALL	LW DESIGNS/AMAR/LSTNGENDRMENTS	LW -		93	$500.00	
	BRIAN O'BRENNON	LW DESIGNS/AMAR/LSTNGENDRMENTS	LW -		93	$1,500.00	
	CELESTIAL JEWEL ANGEL	LW DESIGNS/AMAR/LSTNGENDRMENTS	LW - ANGELS		93	$2,300.00	
	HARP BERRY FAIRY	LW DESIGNS/AMAR/LSTNGENDRMENTS	LW - FAERIES		93	$700.00	
	HOLLY BERRY FAIRY	LW DESIGNS/AMAR/LSTNGENDRMENTS	LW - FAERIES		93	$990.00	
	HOLLY BERRY SANTA	LW DESIGNS/AMAR/LSTNGENDRMENTS	LW - SANTAS & FATHER CHRISTMAS		93	$1,590.00	
	HOLLY BERRY BALLOON	LW DESIGNS/AMAR/LSTNGENDRMENTS	LW -		93	$990.00	
	HOLLY ROCKINGHORSE FAIRY	LW DESIGNS/AMAR/LSTNGENDRMENTS	LW - FAERIES		93	$790.00	
	MOZART FAIRY	LW DESIGNS/AMAR/LSTNGENDRMENTS	LW - FAERIES		93	$1,650.00	
	SPRING FAIRY WITH BIRDCAGE	LW DESIGNS/AMAR/LSTNGENDRMENTS	LW - FAERIES		93	$700.00	
	ST. NICHOLAS WITH PACK	LW DESIGNS/AMAR/LSTNGENDRMENTS	LW - SANTAS & FATHER CHRISTMAS		93	$1,590.00	
	AIR BALLOON SANTA	LW DESIGNS/AMAR/LSTNGENDRMENTS	LW - SANTAS & FATHER CHRISTMAS		94	$990.00	
	ANGEL BABIES-WHITE	LW DESIGNS/AMAR/LSTNGENDRMENTS	LW - ANGELS		94	$2,990.00	
	IRIS HARLEQUIN DOLL	LW DESIGNS/AMAR/LSTNGENDRMENTS	LW - DOLLS		94	$2,300.00	
	LIFE SIZE ELVES/CUSTOM	LW DESIGNS/AMAR/LSTNGENDRMENTS	LW - ELVES		94	$7,000.00	
	LIFE SIZE ST. NICK	LW DESIGNS/AMAR/LSTNGENDRMENTS	LW - SANTAS & FATHER CHRISTMAS		94	$12,000	
	PEONY HARLEQUIN DOLL	LW DESIGNS/AMAR/LSTNGENDRMENTS	LW - DOLLS		94	$2,300.00	
8010	MR. SANTA	LW DESIGNS/AMAR/LSTNGENDRMENTS	LW - ORNAMENTS	95	94	$110.00	$110.00
8020	ST. NICK/BURGUNDY	LW DESIGNS/AMAR/LSTNGENDRMENTS	LW - ORNAMENTS	95	94	$120.00	$120.00
8030	ANGEL	LW DESIGNS/AMAR/LSTNGENDRMENTS	LW - ORNAMENTS	95	94	$120.00	$120.00
8040	JESTER	LW DESIGNS/AMAR/LSTNGENDRMENTS	LW - ORNAMENTS	95	94	$120.00	$345.00
8015	MRS. CLAUS	LW DESIGNS/AMAR/LSTNGENDRMENTS	LW - ORNAMENTS	95	95	$110.00	$110.00
8045	HARLEQUIN	LW DESIGNS/AMAR/LSTNGENDRMENTS	LW - ORNAMENTS	95	95	$110.00	$110.00
8025	ST. NICK/WHITE	LW DESIGNS/AMAR/LSTNGENDRMENTS	LW - ORNAMENTS	95	95	$120.00	$120.00
9003	DAY AFTER CHRISTMAS	LW DESIGNS/AMAR/LSTNGENDRMENTS	LW -		89	$590.00	
9004	DUCHESS TINCHIN	LW DESIGNS/AMAR/LSTNGENDRMENTS	LW -		89	$750.00	
9005	OLD TIME SANTA	LW DESIGNS/AMAR/LSTNGENDRMENTS	LW - SANTAS & FATHER CHRISTMAS	89	89	$530.00	
9006	SPENCER	LW DESIGNS/AMAR/LSTNGENDRMENTS	LW -		89	$850.00	
9007	LARGE SANTA	LW DESIGNS/AMAR/LSTNGENDRMENTS	LW - SANTAS & FATHER CHRISTMAS		90	$700.00	$700.00
9008	SKEETER W/BEARDS	LW DESIGNS/AMAR/LSTNGENDRMENTS	LW - ELVES		90	$270.00	
9009	SARA BEARSLEY		LW - BEARS		91	$500.00	
9019	ANGEL ORNAMENT		LW - ANGELS		94	$120.00	
9011	MR. SANTA ORNAMENT				94	$110.00	
9012	BEAR FOR ALL SEASONS	LW DESIGNS/AMAR/LSTNGENDRMENTS	LW - BEARS		84	$348.00	
9013	CHESTER BEAR WAND	LW DESIGNS/AMAR/LSTNGENDRMENTS	LW - BEARS		84	$108.00	
9014	CHESTER RABBIT WAND	LW DESIGNS/AMAR/LSTNGENDRMENTS	LW -		84	$108.00	
9015	CHRISTMAS BALLOON	LW DESIGNS/AMAR/LSTNGENDRMENTS	LW -		84	$290.00	
9016	CLOWN AIR BALLOON	LW DESIGNS/AMAR/LSTNGENDRMENTS	LW -		84	$290.00	
9017	COW BEAR	LW DESIGNS/AMAR/LSTNGENDRMENTS	LW - BEARS		84	$380.00	
9018	FAIRY	LW DESIGNS/AMAR/LSTNGENDRMENTS	LW - FAERIES		84	$134.00	
9019	NOEL ON SLED	LW DESIGNS/AMAR/LSTNGENDRMENTS	LW -		84	$114.00	
9020	SANTA IN ROCKER	LW DESIGNS/AMAR/LSTNGENDRMENTS	LW - SANTAS & FATHER CHRISTMAS		84	$198.00	
9021	SPRING BASKET	LW DESIGNS/AMAR/LSTNGENDRMENTS	LW -		84	$198.00	
9022	ANGELA	LW DESIGNS/AMAR/LSTNGENDRMENTS	LW -		85	$370.00	
9033	BUDDY BALLOON	LW DESIGNS/AMAR/LSTNGENDRMENTS	LW -		85	$350.00	
9044	CHESTER ORNAMENT	LW DESIGNS/AMAR/LSTNGENDRMENTS	LW -		85	$64.00	
9045	CHRISTMAS AIR BALLOON	LW DESIGNS/AMAR/LSTNGENDRMENTS	LW -		85	$290.00	
9046	GIRL FAIRY	LW DESIGNS/AMAR/LSTNGENDRMENTS	LW - FAERIES		85	$150.00	
9047	HOLLY BERRY FAIRY	LW DESIGNS/AMAR/LSTNGENDRMENTS	LW - FAERIES		85	$150.00	
9048	LARGE FLOWER FAIRY	LW DESIGNS/AMAR/LSTNGENDRMENTS	LW - FAERIES		85		
9049	MRS. SANTA HEAD BURGUNDY ORNAMENT	LW DESIGNS/AMAR/LSTNGENDRMENTS	LW - SANTAS & FATHER CHRISTMAS		85	$35.00	
9050	MRS. SANTA HEAD RED ORNAMETN	LW DESIGNS/AMAR/LSTNGENDRMENTS	LW - SANTAS & FATHER CHRISTMAS		85	$35.00	
9051	NICOLE BALLOON	LW DESIGNS/AMAR/LSTNGENDRMENTS	LW -		85	$350.00	
9052	NOEL ON A SLED	LW DESIGNS/AMAR/LSTNGENDRMENTS	LW - SANTAS & FATHER CHRISTMAS		85		
9053	RENAISSANCE ANGEL	LW DESIGNS/AMAR/LSTNGENDRMENTS	LW - ANGELS		85	$38.00	
9054	SANTA HEAD BURGUNDY ORNAMENT	LW DESIGNS/AMAR/LSTNGENDRMENTS	LW - SANTAS & FATHER CHRISTMAS		85	$35.00	
9055	SANTA HEAD RED ORNAMENT	LW DESIGNS/AMAR/LSTNGENDRMENTS	LW - SANTAS & FATHER CHRISTMAS		85	$35.00	
9056	SANTA ROCKER	LW DESIGNS/AMAR/LSTNGENDRMENTS	LW - SANTAS & FATHER CHRISTMAS		85	$290.00	
9057	SMALL FLOWER FAIRY	LW DESIGNS/AMAR/LSTNGENDRMENTS	LW - FAERIES		85		
9058	ST. NICHOLAS ORNAMENT	LW DESIGNS/AMAR/LSTNGENDRMENTS	LW - SANTAS & FATHER CHRISTMAS		85	$45.00	
9059	STANDING SANTA	LW DESIGNS/AMAR/LSTNGENDRMENTS	LW - SANTAS & FATHER CHRISTMAS		85		
9060	SWAN AND FAIRY	LW DESIGNS/AMAR/LSTNGENDRMENTS	LW - FAERIES		85	$320.00	
9062	TALLULAH	LW DESIGNS/AMAR/LSTNGENDRMENTS	LW -		85	$370.00	
9063	FATHER CHRISTMAS	LW DESIGNS/AMAR/LSTNGENDRMENTS	LW - SANTAS & FATHER CHRISTMAS		86	$590.00	
9064	FATHER CHRISTMAS ORNAMENT BALL	LW DESIGNS/AMAR/LSTNGENDRMENTS	LW - SANTAS & FATHER CHRISTMAS		86	$65.00	
9065	FATHER CHRISTMAS POUCH ORNAMENT	LW DESIGNS/AMAR/LSTNGENDRMENTS	LW - SANTAS & FATHER CHRISTMAS		86	$65.00	
9066	HANS THE TOYMAKER	LW DESIGNS/AMAR/LSTNGENDRMENTS	LW -		86	$700.00	
9067	HOLLY AND GOLF BALL ORNAMENT	LW DESIGNS/AMAR/LSTNGENDRMENTS	LW -		86	$65.00	
9068	HOLLY WREATH ORNAMENT	LW DESIGNS/AMAR/LSTNGENDRMENTS	LW -		86	$65.00	
9069	UNCLE THEO JESTER BEAR	LW DESIGNS/AMAR/LSTNGENDRMENTS	LW -		86	$650.00	
9070	VICTORIAN AIR BALLOON	LW DESIGNS/AMAR/LSTNGENDRMENTS	LW -		86		
9071	WHITE AND GOLD FAIRY	LW DESIGNS/AMAR/LSTNGENDRMENTS	LW - FAERIES		86	$180.00	
9072	ABIGAIL BUNNYCOAT	LW DESIGNS/AMAR/LSTNGENDRMENTS	LW -		87	$560.00	
9073	ALOUISHOUS T. BUNNCOAT	LW DESIGNS/AMAR/LSTNGENDRMENTS	LW -		87	$520.00	
9074	ANGEL MAROTIE	LW DESIGNS/AMAR/LSTNGENDRMENTS	LW - ANGELS		87	$250.00	
9075	AUNT PHOEBE	LW DESIGNS/AMAR/LSTNGENDRMENTS	LW -		87	$750.00	
9076	BLINK (BAKER)	LW DESIGNS/AMAR/LSTNGENDRMENTS	LW -		87	$650.00	
9077	BURGUNDY FAIRY	LW DESIGNS/AMAR/LSTNGENDRMENTS	LW - FAERIES		87	$164.00	
9078	COUNT ALEXI BEARINSKI	LW DESIGNS/AMAR/LSTNGENDRMENTS	LW - BEARS		87	$700.00	
9079	CROCUS FAIRY	LW DESIGNS/AMAR/LSTNGENDRMENTS	LW - FAERIES		87	$164.00	
9080	CRYSTAL ANGEL	LW DESIGNS/AMAR/LSTNGENDRMENTS	LW - ANGELS		87	$1,500.00	
9081	DAY AFTER CHRISTMAS	LW DESIGNS/AMAR/LSTNGENDRMENTS	LW -		87	$590.00	
9082	DINKER (DECORATOR)	LW DESIGNS/AMAR/LSTNGENDRMENTS	LW -		87	$250.00	
9083	DOUGLAS COURTLY FAERIE	LW DESIGNS/AMAR/LSTNGENDRMENTS	LW - FAERIES		87	$250.00	
9084	EARL COURTLY FAERIE	LW DESIGNS/AMAR/LSTNGENDRMENTS	LW - FAERIES		87	$250.00	

Order No.	Title	Type	Theme	Retired	Intro. Year	Retail Price	Secondary Price
9085	FATHER CHRISTMAS (SPECIAL EDITION)	LW DESIGNS/AMAR/LSTNGENDRMENTS	LW - SANTAS & FATHER CHRISTMAS		87	$2,000.00	
9086	FATHER CHRISTMAS MAROTIE (ORNAMENT)	LW DESIGNS/AMAR/LSTNGENDRMENTS	LW - SANTAS & FATHER CHRISTMAS		87	$250.00	
9087	FOREST FAIRY	LW DESIGNS/AMAR/LSTNGENDRMENTS	LW - FAERIES		87	$164.00	
9088	GAYLORD AND BEEWISE	LW DESIGNS/AMAR/LSTNGENDRMENTS	LW -		87	$900.00	
9089	JESTER MAROTIE	LW DESIGNS/AMAR/LSTNGENDRMENTS	LW-		87	$250.00	
9090	JOSHUA GRIZZLYNN	LW DESIGNS/AMAR/LSTNGENDRMENTS	LW BEARS		87	$290.00	
9091	KING RUFUS	LW DESIGNS/AMAR/LSTNGENDRMENTS	LW -		87	$700.00	
9092	KRIS KRINGLE	LW DESIGNS/AMAR/LSTNGENDRMENTS	LW - SANTAS & FATHER CHRISTMAS		87	$590.00	
90093	MARCEL	LW DESIGNS/AMAR/LSTNGENDRMENTS	LW -		87	$1,050.00	
9094	MAUVE FAIRY	LW DESIGNS/AMAR/LSTNGENDRMENTS	LW - FAERIES		87	$164.00	
9095	MIMI	LW DESIGNS/AMAR/LSTNGENDRMENTS	LW -		87	$750.00	
9096	MONIQUE	LW DESIGNS/AMAR/LSTNGENDRMENTS	LW -		87	$1,050.00	
9097	NAVY BLUE FAIRY	LW DESIGNS/AMAR/LSTNGENDRMENTS	LW - FAERIES		87	$164.00	
9098	NELLIE BEARA GRIZZLYN	LW DESIGNS/AMAR/LSTNGENDRMENTS	LW - BEARS		87	$410.00	
9099	PASTEL WOODLAND BASKET	LW DESIGNS/AMAR/LSTNGENDRMENTS	LW -		87	$450.00	
9100	PRINCE NICHOLAI	LW DESIGNS/AMAR/LSTNGENDRMENTS	LW -		87	$700.00	
9101	PROFESSOR GRIZZLYNN	LW DESIGNS/AMAR/LSTNGENDRMENTS	LW - BEARS		87	$410.00	
9102	PUCK AND GANDER	LW DESIGNS/AMAR/LSTNGENDRMENTS	LW -		87	$1,190.00	
9103	PUNCH	LW DESIGNS/AMAR/LSTNGENDRMENTS	LW -		87	$1,050.00	
9104	RED FAERIE	LW DESIGNS/AMAR/LSTNGENDRMENTS	LW - FAERIES		87	$164.00	
9105	RED WOODLAND BASKET	LW DESIGNS/AMAR/LSTNGENDRMENTS	LW -		87	$450.00	
9106	SANTA AND A TREE	LW DESIGNS/AMAR/LSTNGENDRMENTS	LW - SANTAS & FATHER CHRISTMAS		87	$490.00	
9107	SHAYNA GRIZZLYNN	LW DESIGNS/AMAR/LSTNGENDRMENTS	LW - BEARS		87	$290.00	
9108	SILVER AND WHITE FAERIE	LW DESIGNS/AMAR/LSTNGENDRMENTS	LW - FAERIES		87	$180.00	
9109	SLATE GRAY FAERIE	LW DESIGNS/AMAR/LSTNGENDRMENTS	LW - FAERIES		87	$164.00	
9110	SLEEPING SANTA ROCKER	LW DESIGNS/AMAR/LSTNGENDRMENTS	LW - SANTAS & FATHER CHRISTMAS		87	$320.00	
9112	SONYA GRIZZLYNN BEARINSKI	LW DESIGNS/AMAR/LSTNGENDRMENTS	LW - BEARS		87	$700.00	
9113	ST. NICHOLAS AND SLEIGH	LW DESIGNS/AMAR/LSTNGENDRMENTS	LW - SANTAS & FATHER CHRISTMAS		87	$358.00	
9114	STANDING SANTA	LW DESIGNS/AMAR/LSTNGENDRMENTS	LW - SANTAS & FATHER CHRISTMAS		87	$250.00	
9115	STANDING ST. NICK	LW DESIGNS/AMAR/LSTNGENDRMENTS	LW - SANTAS & FATHER CHRISTMAS		87	$250.00	
9116	TINKER (TOYMAKER)	LW DESIGNS/AMAR/LSTNGENDRMENTS	LW -		87	$250.00	
9117	TOYLAND SLEIGH	LW DESIGNS/AMAR/LSTNGENDRMENTS	LW -		87	$140.00	
9118	TYRONNE COURTLY FAERIE	LW DESIGNS/AMAR/LSTNGENDRMENTS	LW - FAERIES		87	$250.00	
9119	UNCLE THEO HARE BEAR	LW DESIGNS/AMAR/LSTNGENDRMENTS	LW - BEARS		87	$430.00	
9120	VICTORIAN ANGEL	LW DESIGNS/AMAR/LSTNGENDRMENTS	LW - ANGELS		87	$1,500.00	
9122	YVONNE POLARI	LW DESIGNS/AMAR/LSTNGENDRMENTS	LW -		87	$650.00	
9123	BARK	LW DESIGNS/AMAR/LSTNGENDRMENTS	LW -		88	$184.00	
9124	CHECKERS	LW DESIGNS/AMAR/LSTNGENDRMENTS	LW -		88	$1,050.00	
9125	ERBIE	LW DESIGNS/AMAR/LSTNGENDRMENTS	LW -		88	$450.00	
9126	JOLLY TROLLY	LW DESIGNS/AMAR/LSTNGENDRMENTS	LW -		88	$350.00	
9127	MOSS	LW DESIGNS/AMAR/LSTNGENDRMENTS	LW -		88	$184.00	
9128	TOYLAND EXPRESS	LW DESIGNS/AMAR/LSTNGENDRMENTS	LW -		88	$370.00	
9129	UP ON THE ROOFTOP	LW DESIGNS/AMAR/LSTNGENDRMENTS	LW -		88		
9130	WILD FLOWER	LW DESIGNS/AMAR/LSTNGENDRMENTS	LW -		88	$184.00	
9121	WILD WOOLY GRIZZLYNN	LW DESIGNS/AMAR/LSTNGENDRMENTS	LW - BEARS		87	$450.00	
			MARGARET FURLONG DESIGNS				
AM-D	2" MINIATURE DAISY	ANGELS	MF - 2" ANGELS		96	$10.00	
	1986 THE HALLEJUAH ANGEL	ANGELS	MF - GIFTS FROM GOD	86	86	$45.00	$850.00
	1987 THE ANGEL OF LIGHT	ANGELS	MF - GIFTS FROM GOD	87	87	$45.00	$500.00
	1988 THE CELESTIAL ANGEL	ANGELS	MF - GIFTS FROM GOD	88	88	$45.00	$500.00
	1989 THE CORONATION ANGEL	ANGELS	MF - GIFTS FROM GOD	89	89	$45.00	$450.00
	1990 THE CELEBRATION ANGEL	ANGELS	MF - JOYEUX NOEL	90	90	$45.00	$200.00
	1991 THANKSGIVING ANGEL	ANGELS	MF - JOYEUX NOEL	91	91	$45.00	$210.00
	1992 JOYEUX NOEL	ANGELS	MF - JOYEUX NOEL	94	92	$45.00	$200.00
	1993 STAR OF BETHLEHEM	ANGELS	MF - JOYEUX NOEL	94	93	$45.00	$225.00
	1994 MESSIAH ANGEL	ANGELS	MF - JOYEUX NOEL	94	94	$45.00	$450.00
	1980 THE CAROLER	ANGELS	MF - MUSICAL SERIES	80	80	$50.00	$500.00
	1981 THE LYRIST	ANGELS	MF - MUSICAL SERIES	81	81	$45.00	$750.00
	1982 THE LUTIST	ANGELS	MF - MUSICAL SERIES	82	82	$45.00	$700.00
	1983 THE CONERTINIST	ANGELS	MF - MUSICAL SERIES	83	83	$45.00	$650.00
	1984 THE HERALD ANGEL	ANGELS	MF - MUSICAL SERIES	84	84	$45.00	$500.00
AM-W	2" MINIATURE WREATH	ANGELS	MF - 2" ANGELS		95	$10.00	
AM-HT	2" MINIATURE HEART	ANGELS	MF - 2" ANGELS		94	$10.00	
AM-C	2" MINIATURE CELESTIAL	ANGELS	MF - 2" ANGELS		93	$10.00	
A1-MG	3" MORNING GLORY	ANGELS	MF - 3" ANGELS		96	$12.00	
A1-FG	3" FLOWER GARLAND	ANGELS	MF - 3" ANGELS		95	$12.00	
A1-SN	3" SUN	ANGELS	MF - 3" ANGELS		94	$12.00	
A1-C	3" CROSS	ANGELS	MF - 3" ANGELS		93	$12.00	
A1-N	3" NOEL	ANGELS	MF - 3" ANGELS	97	92	$12.00	
A1-G	3" GIFT	ANGELS	MF - 3" ANGELS		91	$12.00	
A1-CT	3" CHRISTMAS TREE	ANGELS	MF - 3" ANGELS		90	$12.00	
A1-SF	3" SNOWFLAKE	ANGELS	MF - 3" ANGELS		89	$12.00	
A1-B	3" BOUQUET	ANGELS	MF - 3" ANGELS		87	$12.00	
A1-HT	3" HEART	ANGELS	MF - 3" ANGELS		86	$12.00	
A1-W	3" WREATH	ANGELS	MF - 3" ANGELS		85	$12.00	
A1-H	3" HOLLY	ANGELS	MF - 3" ANGELS		83	$12.00	
A2-SR	4" SUNFLOWER/SPECIAL EDITION	ANGELS	MF - 4" ANGELS		96	$21.00	
A2-FG	4" FLOWER GARLAND	ANGELS	MF - 4" ANGELS		95	$21.00	
A2-SN	4" SUN	ANGELS	MF - 4" ANGELS		94	$21.00	
A2-C	4" CROSS	ANGELS	MF - 4" ANGELS		93	$21.00	
A2-N	4" NOEL	ANGELS	MF - 4" ANGELS	97	92	$21.00	
A2-G	4" GIFT	ANGELS	MF - 4" ANGELS		91	$21.00	
A2-CT	4" CHRISTMAS TREE	ANGELS	MF - LIMITED EDITION		90	$21.00	
A2-SF	4" SNOWFLAKE	ANGELS	MF - 4" ANGELS		89	$21.00	
A2-B	4" BOUQUET	ANGELS	MF - 4" ANGELS		87	$21.00	
A2-HT	4" HEART	ANGELS	MF - 4" ANGELS		86	$21.00	
A2-W	4" WREATH	ANGELS	MF - 4" ANGELS		85	$21.00	
A2-H	4" HOLLY	ANGELS	MF - 4" ANGELS		83	$21.00	
MC-96	6.5" MADONNA OF THE CROSS/FIRST IN 3 YR. SERIES	ANGELS	MF - MADONNA AND CHILD	96	96	$80.00	$80.00
A1-T	3" TRUMPETER ANGEL	ANGELS	MF - 3" ANGELS	94	80	$12.00	$80.00

Order No.	Title	Type	Theme	Retired	Intro. Year	Retial Price	Secondary Price
AC-1	4.5" ACORN	ANGELS	MF - PORCELAIN ORNAMENTS		96	$12.00	
F-1	4" SHELL FISH	ANGELS	MF - PORCELAIN ORNAMENTS		94	$11.00	
FGL-1	4" GOLD FISH	ANGELS	MF - PORCELAIN ORNAMENTS		94	$19.00	
HH-1	2" HANDFUL OF HEARTS (SET OF 6)	ANGELS	MF - PORCELAIN ORNAMENTS		87	$20.00	
H-4	2" OH SWEETEST HEART	ANGELS	MF - PORCELAIN ORNAMENTS		87	$5.00	
HL-1	2.5" WINGS OF LOVE	ANGELS	MF - PORCELAIN ORNAMENTS		95	$6.00	
HL-4	2.5" ALL FOUR LOVE (SET OF 4)	ANGELS	MF - PORCELAIN ORNAMENTS		96	$22.00	
I-1	4.5" ICICLE	ANGELS	MF - PORCELAIN ORNAMENTS	97	95	$12.00	
ICL-1	4.5" ICICLE (COPPER)	ANGELS	MF - PORCELAIN ORNAMENTS	97	95	$18.00	
IGL-1	4.5" ICICLE (GOLD)	ANGELS	MF - PORCELAIN ORNAMENTS	97	95	$18.00	
ISL-1	4.5" ICICLE (SILVER)	ANGELS	MF - PORCELAIN ORNAMENTS	97	95	$18.00	
S-1	3" MORNING STAR	ANGELS	MF - PORCELAIN ORNAMENTS		80	$6.00	
GLS-1	3" MORNING STAR (GOLD)	ANGELS	MF - PORCELAIN ORNAMENTS		92	$12.00	
S-2	6.5" TREE TOP STAR (RETIRING)	ANGELS	MF - PORCELAIN ORNAMENTS	96	84	$30.00	
S-3	2" A POCKETFUL OF STARS (SET OF 6)	ANGELS	MF - PORCELAIN ORNAMENTS		85	$20.00	
S-4	2" CATCH A FALLING STAR	ANGELS	MF - PORCELAIN ORNAMENTS		87	$5.00	
GLS-4	2" CATCH A FALLING STAR (GOLD)	ANGELS	MF - PORCELAIN ORNAMENTS		93	$10.00	
S-7	2.5" A STAR IN THE NIGHT	ANGELS	MF - PORCELAIN ORNAMENTS		91	$10.00	
GLS-7	2.5" A STAR IN THE NIGHT (GOLD)	ANGELS	MF - PORCELAIN ORNAMENTS		92	$10.00	
S-8	5" EVENING STAR	ANGELS	MF - PORCELAIN ORNAMENTS		92	$9.00	
GLS-8	5" EVENING STAR (GOLD)	ANGELS	MF - PORCELAIN ORNAMENTS		92	$16.00	
SF-1	2" WINTER'S JEWELS (SET OF 6)	ANGELS	MF - PORCELAIN ORNAMENTS		89	$20.00	
SF-4	2" A WINTER JEWEL	ANGELS	MF - PORCELAIN ORNAMENTS		89	$5.00	
SS-1	2" SUNSHELL	ANGELS	MF - PORCELAIN ORNAMENTS		93	$5.00	
GSS-1	2"SUNSHELL (GOLD)	ANGELS	MF - PORCELAIN ORNAMENTS		93	$10.00	
T-1	5" SHELL TASSEL	ANGELS	MF - PORCELAIN ORNAMENTS		94	$16.00	
TGL-1	5" SHELL TASSEL (GOLD)	ANGELS	MF - PORCELAIN ORNAMENTS		94	$24.00	
T-2	5" CORAL TASSEL	ANGELS	MF - PORCELAIN ORNAMENTS		95	$16.00	
TCL-2	5" CORAL TASSEL (COPPER)	ANGELS	MF - PORCELAIN ORNAMENTS		95	$24.00	
TGL-2	5" CORAL TASSEL (GOLD)	ANGELS	MF - PORCELAIN ORNAMENTS		95	$24.00	
W-2	3" OAK & ACORN WREATH	ANGELS	MF - PORCELAIN ORNAMENTS		96	$8.00	
GLW-2	3" OAK & ACORN WREATH (GOLD)	ANGELS	MF - WREATH		96	$16.00	
TF-1	7" TREE TOP FINIAL (GOLD)	ANGELS	MF - PORCELAIN ORNAMENTS		95	$24.00	
P1-C	CROSS	ANGELS	MF - PINS			$6.00	
P1-H	HOLLY	ANGELS	MF - PINS			$6.00	
P1-R	ROSES	ANGELS	MF - PINS			$6.00	
P1-SF	SNOWFLAKE	ANGELS	MF - PINS			$6.00	
P1-SH	SMALL HEART	ANGELS	MF - PINS			$6.00	
P1-SM	CELESTIAL	ANGELS	MF - PINS			$6.00	
P1-SN	STARRY NIGHT	ANGELS	MF - PINS			$6.00	
P1-SS	SUN	ANGELS	MF - PINS			$6.00	
P1-V	VICTORIAN HEART	ANGELS	MF - PINS			$6.00	
P1-W	WREATH	ANGELS	MF - PINS			$6.00	
HW-2	4" HEART WREATH	ANGELS	MF - PORCELAIN ORNAMENTS	96	86	$20.00	
A1-BS	3" BUTTERFLY ANGEL	ANGELS	MF - 3" ANGELS	96	88	$12.00	$55.00
A2-BS	4" BUTTERFLY ANGEL	ANGELS	MF - 4" ANGELS	96	88	$21.00	$70.00
A2-VH	4" VICTORIA HEART ANGEL/EXCLUSIVE VICTORIA MAG.	ANGELS	MF - 4" ANGELS		94	$25.00	
A2-VL	4" VICTORIA LILLY ANGEL/EXCLUSIVE VICTORIA MAG.	ANGELS	MF - 4" ANGELS		94	$25.00	
A2-SR	4" SUNFLOWER ANGEL	ANGELS	MF - 4" ANGELS	96	96	$21.00	$21.00
S-5I	STARS BY THE YARD/IVORY	ANGELS	MF - PORCELAIN ORNAMENTS	94	87	$20.00	
S-5R	STARS BY THE YARD/RED	ANGELS	MF - PORCELAIN ORNAMENTS	94	87	$20.00	
S-5G	STARS BY THE YARD/GOLD	ANGELS	MF - PORCELAIN ORNAMENTS	94	87	$20.00	
GC-SN	STARRY NIGHT COLLECTION (ANGEL W/4STARS)	ANGELS	MF - PORCELAIN ORNAMENTS	96	95	$24.00	
A-95	5" FAITH ANGEL	ANGELS	MF - FLORA ANGELICA/LTD EDITION	95	95	$45.00	$90.00
A-96	5" HOPE ANGEL/SOLD OUT	ANGELS	MF - FLORA ANGELICA	96	95	$45.00	$70.00
A2-T	4" TRUMPETER ANGEL	ANGELS	MF - 4" ANGELS	94	80	$21.00	$110.00
A1-S	3" STAR ANGEL	ANGELS	MF - 3" ANGELS	94	82	$12.00	$80.00
A2-S	4" STAR ANGEL	ANGELS	MF - 3" ANGELS	94	82	$21.00	$110.00
A1-D	3" DOVE ANGEL	ANGELS	MF - 3" ANGELS	95	84	$12.00	$75.00
A2-D	4" DOVE ANGEL	ANGELS	MF - FLORA ANGELICA/LTD EDITION	95	84	$21.00	$85.00
AM-V	2" MINIATURE VIOLA	ANGELS	MF - 2" ANGELS		97	$11.50	
A1-DW	3" DOGWOOD	ANGELS	MF - 3" ANGELS		97	$13.50	
A2-97	4" IRIS	ANGELS	MF - 4" ANGELS		97	$23.00	
A-97	5" CHARITY ANGEL	ANGELS	MF - MADONNA AND CHILD		97	$50.00	
HF-1	2.5" FROM THE HEART	ANGELS	MF - PORCELAIN ORNAMENTS		97	$8.00	
	1985 THE CHARIS ANGEL	ANGELS	MF - GIFTS FROM GOD	85	85		$700.00

OLD WORLD CHRISTMAS

Order No.	Title	Type	Theme	Retired	Intro. Year	Retial Price	Secondary Price
141	GUARDING MY CHILDREN/ LIMITED TO 5,000	OLD MOLD GLASS ORNAMENTS	ANIMALS	96	96	$65.00	$65.00
1018	VICTORIAN ANGEL (A)	OLD MOLD GLASS ORNAMENTS	ANGELS & FEMALE FIGURES	96	89	$8.25	$9.00
1022	SMALL GIRL HEAD	OLD MOLD GLASS ORNAMENTS	ANGELS & FEMALE FIGURES	96	90	$7.00	$7.00
1026	ANTIQUE STYLE DOLL HEAD	OLD MOLD GLASS ORNAMENTS	ANGELS & FEMALE FIGURES	96	90	$9.00	$9.00
1030	GIRL IN POLKA DOT DRESS	OLD MOLD GLASS ORNAMENTS	ANGELS & FEMALE FIGURES	96	90	$12.50	$13.00
1040	GARDEN GIRL	OLD MOLD GLASS ORNAMENTS	ANGELS & FEMALE FIGURES	96	92	$8.25	$8.90
1042227	GIRL IN BLUE DRESS	OLD MOLD GLASS ORNAMENTS	ANGELS & FEMALE FIGURES	96	85	$7.00	$7.00
1045	GIRL W/WHITE KITTY	OLD MOLD GLASS ORNAMENTS	ANGELS & FEMALE FIGURES	96	92	$9.25	$10.00
1057	CHUBBY MUSHROOM GIRL	OLD MOLD GLASS ORNAMENTS	ANGELS & FEMALE FIGURES	96	93	$8.00	$8.00
1037	LITTLE TYROLEAN GIRL	OLD MOLD GLASS ORNAMENTS	ANGELS & FEMALE FIGURES	96	91	$7.00	$7.00
1234356	MATTE GOLD BEAR W/HEART	OLD MOLD GLASS ORNAMENTS	ANIMALS	96	85	$7.00	$7.00
1249	GOLD FISH	OLD MOLD GLASS ORNAMENTS	ANIMALS	96	91	$7.00	$7.00
1250	PROUD PUG	OLD MOLD GLASS ORNAMENTS	ANIMALS	96	92	$9.25	$9.90
1626	MESSENGER BIRD	OLD MOLD GLASS ORNAMENTS	BIRDS FOR HANGING	96	92	$6.75	$7.00
1808	GOLDFINCH	OLD MOLD GLASS ORNAMENTS	BIRDS WITH CLIP	96	87	$8.55	$9.00
1852	CARNIVAL CANARY	OLD MOLD GLASS ORNAMENTS	BIRDS WITH CLIP	96	93	$9.45	$10.00
2838	FRUIT BASKET	OLD MOLD GLASS ORNAMENTS	FRUITS & VEGTABLES	96	90	$7.75	$8.00
3819	LARGE BELL WITH HOLLY	OLD MOLD GLASS ORNAMENTS	MUSICAL INSTRUMENTS	96	93	$50.00	$50.00
5014	LARGE SPIRE W/REFELCTOR	OLD MOLD GLASS ORNAMENTS	TREE TOPS	9	905	$70.00	$70.00
5017	VERY LARGE REFLECTOR TREETOP	OLD MOLD GLASS ORNAMENTS	TREE TOPS	96	93	$65.00	$65.00
1311	WOODLAND CHRISTMAS GARLAND	OLD MOLD GLASS ORNAMENTS	BEAD GARLANDS	96	94	$65.00	$66.00
1322	SANTA'S/ CANDY GARLAND	OLD MOLD GLASS ORNAMENTS	BEAD GARLANDS	96	96	$110.00	$110.00
1323	POINSETTIA GARLAND	OLD MOLD GLASS ORNAMENTS	BEAD GARLANDS	96	96	$100.00	$100.00
1324	CHRISTMAS CANDY GARLAND	OLD MOLD GLASS ORNAMENTS	BEAD GARLANDS	96	96	$110.00	$110.00

Order No.	Title	Type	Theme	Retired	Intro. Year	Retail Price	Secondary Price
1325	SHINY GOLD GARLAND	OLD MOLD GLASS ORNAMENTS	BEAD GARLANDS	96	96	$135.00	$135.00
1542	FATHER CHRISTMAS ON BALLOON	OLD MOLD GLASS ORNAMENTS	MUSEUM COLLECTION	96	94		$9.00
3628	CLIP-ON PINK ROSE	OLD MOLD GLASS ORNAMENTS	MISCELLANEOUS FORMS	96	90	$10.50	$10.50
1001	LITTLE RED RIDING HOOD	OLD MOLD GLASS ORNAMENTS	ANGELS & FEMALE FIGURES	93	85	$10.00	$15.95
1002	PINK ANGEL WITH WINGS	OLD MOLD GLASS ORNAMENTS	ANGELS & FEMALE FIGURES	88	85	$9.00	$16.00
1006	MUSHROOM GIRL	OLD MOLD GLASS ORNAMENTS	ANGELS & FEMALE FIGURES	94	87	$9.90	$11.90
1007	GIRL ON SNOWBALL WITH TEDDY	OLD MOLD GLASS ORNAMENTS	ANGELS & FEMALE FIGURES	95	87	$9.00	$14.95
1081	MRS. SANTA CLAUS	OLD MOLD GLASS ORNAMENTS	ANGELS & FEMALE FIGURES			$8.95	$23.95
1209	CINNAMON BEAR	OLD MOLD GLASS ORNAMENTS	ANIMALS		85		$8.00
121042	PINK PIG	OLD MOLD GLASS ORNAMENTS	ANIMALS	96	85	$7.80	$8.00
1234	PASTEL FISH	OLD MOLD GLASS ORNAMENTS	ANIMALS	96	90	$6.75	$7.00
1245	LOBSTER	OLD MOLD GLASS ORNAMENTS	ANIMALS	96	91		$26.00
1259	MINIATURE FROG	OLD MOLD GLASS ORNAMENTS	ANIMALS			$6.00	$10.90
1266	BUSTER	OLD MOLD GLASS ORNAMENTS	ANIMALS	96	93	$8.25	$8.90
1271	BRILLIANT BUTTERFLY ON FORM	OLD MOLD GLASS ORNAMENTS	ANIMALS			$10.75	$10.95
1620	BIRDIE	OLD MOLD GLASS ORNAMENTS	BIRDS FOR HANGING	96	92	$8.80	$9.00
1623	EXOTIC BIRD	OLD MOLD GLASS ORNAMENTS	BIRDS FOR HANGING	96	92	$10.30	$11.00
1624	LARGE GERMAN SONGBIRD	OLD MOLD GLASS ORNAMENTS	BIRDS FOR HANGING	96	92	$11.25	$11.95
1625	BRILLIANT HANGING SNOWBIRD	OLD MOLD GLASS ORNAMENTS	BIRDS FOR HANGING	96	92	$10.00	$10.00
1630	HANGING PASTEL BIRD	OLD MOLD GLASS ORNAMENTS	BIRDS FOR HANGING	96	93	$10.50	$10.75
1631	HANGING PARROT	OLD MOLD GLASS ORNAMENTS	BIRDS FOR HANGING	96	93	$96.00	$10.00
181083	NIGHTINGALE	OLD MOLD GLASS ORNAMENTS	BIRDS WITH CLIP	96	85	$5.55	$6.00
1831	ROOSTER	OLD MOLD GLASS ORNAMENTS	BIRDS WITH CLIP	96	91	$10.50	$11.00
1842	LARGE NIGHTINGALE	OLD MOLD GLASS ORNAMENTS	BIRDS WITH CLIP	96	92	$8.00	$8.00
1845	BLUE BIRD WITH TOPNOTCH	OLD MOLD GLASS ORNAMENTS	BIRDS WITH CLIP	96	92	$9.45	$10.00
1846	LARGE WOODPECKER	OLD MOLD GLASS ORNAMENTS	BIRDS WITH CLIP	96	92	$11.15	$12.00
1854	TROPICAL SONGBIRD	OLD MOLD GLASS ORNAMENTS	BIRDS WITH CLIP	96	93	$7.55	$8.00
1868	HARVEST BIRD	OLD MOLD GLASS ORNAMENTS	BIRDS WITH CLIP	96	95	$7.50	$8.00
1870	CRANBERRY PEACOCK	OLD MOLD GLASS ORNAMENTS	BIRDS WITH CLIP	96	95	$13.95	$14.00
2003	FARM HOUSE	OLD MOLD GLASS ORNAMENTS	CHURCHES AND HOUSES	96	85	$8.45	$9.00
2024	MISSION WITH SEA GULL	OLD MOLD GLASS ORNAMENTS	CHURCHES AND HOUSES	96	91	$9.45	$10.00
2027	WATCH TOWER	OLD MOLD GLASS ORNAMENTS	CHURCHES AND HOUSES	96	92	$9.25	$10.00
2029	CASTLE TOWER	OLD MOLD GLASS ORNAMENTS	CHURCHES AND HOUSES	96	92	$9.45	$10.15
2204	SHINING SUN	OLD MOLD GLASS ORNAMENTS	CELESTIAL FIGURES	96	90	$7.00	$7.00
2209	COMET ON FORM	OLD MOLD GLASS ORNAMENTS	CELESTIAL FIGURES	96	93	$7.65	$7.90
2211	HIGH NOON	OLD MOLD GLASS ORNAMENTS	CELESTIAL FIGURES	96	93	$5.75	$6.00
2401	INDIAN IN CANOE	OLD MOLD GLASS ORNAMENTS	CLOWNS & MALE FIGURES	96	85	$10.00	$11.00
241005	CLOWN PLAYING BASS FIDDLE	OLD MOLD GLASS ORNAMENTS	CLOWNS & MALE FIGURES	96	84	$7.75	$8.00
241008	INDIAN CHIEF W/PEACE PIPE	OLD MOLD GLASS ORNAMENTS	CLOWNS & MALE FIGURES	96	84	$7.50	$8.00
2412	CLOWN HEAD IN DRUM	OLD MOLD GLASS ORNAMENTS	CLOWNS & MALE FIGURES	96	85	$10.50	$10.75
2420	JOLLY SNOWMAN	OLD MOLD GLASS ORNAMENTS	CLOWNS & MALE FIGURES	96	87	$8.00	$8.00
2449	BAKER	OLD MOLD GLASS ORNAMENTS	CLOWNS & MALE FIGURES	96	92	$8.25	$9.00
2451	PIRATE	OLD MOLD GLASS ORNAMENTS	CLOWNS & MALE FIGURES	96	92	$7.50	$8.00
2435	WINKING LEPRECHAUN	OLD MOLD GLASS ORNAMENTS	CLOWNS & MALE FIGURES	96	93	$6.50	$9.95
2454	BOXER	OLD MOLD GLASS ORNAMENTS	CLOWNS & MALE FIGURES	96	93	$5.30	$12.95
2457	SAILOR	OLD MOLD GLASS ORNAMENTS	CLOWNS & MALE FIGURES	96	93	$8.00	$8.00
2462	SMALL SNOWMAN	OLD MOLD GLASS ORNAMENTS	CLOWNS & MALE FIGURES	95	93	$6.00	$5.90
2469	SNOWMAN ON ICICLE	OLD MOLD GLASS ORNAMENTS	CLOWNS & MALE FIGURES	96	93		$10.95
2471	JACK HORNER	OLD MOLD GLASS ORNAMENTS	CLOWNS & MALE FIGURES	96	94	$6.50	$7.00
2474	MY BUDDY	OLD MOLD GLASS ORNAMENTS	CLOWNS & MALE FIGURES	96	94	$7.80	$8.00
2489	PUNCH WITH LEGS	OLD MOLD GLASS ORNAMENTS	CLOWNS & MALE FIGURES			$8.75	$9.00
2493	JESTER ON SPIRAL	OLD MOLD GLASS ORNAMENTS	CLOWNS & MALE FIGURES	96	95		$8.90
2881	LARGE SUGAR PEAR	OLD MOLD GLASS ORNAMENTS	FRUITS & VEGTABLES	96	93	$13.00	$13.00
2882	LARGE CANDIED APPLE	OLD MOLD GLASS ORNAMENTS	FRUITS & VEGTABLES	96	93	$13.00	$13.00
2887	GRAPES WITH BUTTERFLY	OLD MOLD GLASS ORNAMENTS	FRUITS & VEGTABLES	96	94	$9.75	$9.95
3211	FLAPPER PURSE	OLD MOLD GLASS ORNAMENTS	HOUSEHOLD ITEMS	96	92	$9.00	$10.00
3212	CHRISTMAS SHOE	OLD MOLD GLASS ORNAMENTS	HOUSEHOLD ITEMS		92	$8.00	$8.25
3222	CHEERS!	OLD MOLD GLASS ORNAMENTS	HOUSEHOLD ITEMS	96	94	$7.00	$7.00
3612	MR. SUNFLOWER	OLD MOLD GLASS ORNAMENTS	MISCELLANEOUS FORMS	96	89	$7.80	$7.75
3632	CHRISTMAS SHAMROCK	OLD MOLD GLASS ORNAMENTS	MISCELLANEOUS FORMS	96	91	$9.25	$10.00
3633	LARGE RIBBED BALL W/ROSES	OLD MOLD GLASS ORNAMENTS	MISCELLANEOUS FORMS	96	91	$7.00	$6.50
3639	GARDEN FLOWERS	OLD MOLD GLASS ORNAMENTS	MISCELLANEOUS FORMS	96	92	$9.00	$9.00
3654	TUDOR CROWN	OLD MOLD GLASS ORNAMENTS	MISCELLANEOUS FORMS	96	94	$9.00	$9.00
3657	STARS AND STRIPES	OLD MOLD GLASS ORNAMENTS	MISCELLANEOUS FORMS	96	94	$9.00	$8.75
3663	FIRECRACKER	OLD MOLD GLASS ORNAMENTS	MISCELLANEOUS FORMS	96	95	$6.95	$7.00
3808	LARGE CHRISTMAS BELL	OLD MOLD GLASS ORNAMENTS	MUSICAL INSTRUMENTS	95	90	$10.25	$11.00
3810	ZITHER	OLD MOLD GLASS ORNAMENTS	MUSICAL INSTRUMENTS	96	90		$8.50
3820	HARMONICA	OLD MOLD GLASS ORNAMENTS	MUSICAL INSTRUMENTS	96	94	$8.00	$7.75
401064	ST. NICHOLAS ON HORSE	OLD MOLD GLASS ORNAMENTS	SANTAS	96	85	$14.00	$14.00
4027	SMALL VICTORIAN SANTA HEAD	OLD MOLD GLASS ORNAMENTS	SANTAS	96	90	$7.35	$8.00
4037	VERY LARGE BELZNICKLE	OLD MOLD GLASS ORNAMENTS	SANTAS	96	90	$22.50	$23.50
4040	OLD-FASHIONED ST. NICHOLAS	OLD MOLD GLASS ORNAMENTS	SANTAS	96	90	$11.00	$11.00
4042	LARGE WEIHNACHTSMANN	OLD MOLD GLASS ORNAMENTS	SANTAS	96	91	$10.00	$12.95
4044	OLD BAVARIAN SANTA	OLD MOLD GLASS ORNAMENTS	SANTAS	96	91	$12.50	$13.00
4045	VICTORIAN FATHER CHRISTMAS	OLD MOLD GLASS ORNAMENTS	SANTAS	96	91	$10.00	$10.50
4046	FATHER CHRISTMAS ON FORM	OLD MOLD GLASS ORNAMENTS	SANTAS	96	91	$11.00	$11.00
4048	SANTA IN MUSHROOM	OLD MOLD GLASS ORNAMENTS	SANTAS	96	91	$8.70	$8.75
4049	SMALL SANTA ON FORM	OLD MOLD GLASS ORNAMENTS	SANTAS	96	91	$8.00	$8.00
4052	GOLD WEIHNACTSMANN	OLD MOLD GLASS ORNAMENTS	SANTAS	96	92	$9.80	$9.75
4056	SNOWY PURPLE SANTA	OLD MOLD GLASS ORNAMENTS	SANTAS				$10.95
4058	SANTA IN WALNUT	OLD MOLD GLASS ORNAMENTS	SANTAS	96	93	$7.00	$7.00
4090	FESTIVE OLD WORLD SANTA	OLD MOLD GLASS ORNAMENTS	SANTAS			$11.00	$10.75
4205	STRAWBERRY IN REFLECTOR	OLD MOLD GLASS ORNAMENTS	REFLECTORS	96	90	$9.25	$9.90
4208	PEACOCK IN REFLECTOR	OLD MOLD GLASS ORNAMENTS	REFLECTORS	96	91	$9.25	$10.00
4209	PEARS IN REFLECTOR	OLD MOLD GLASS ORNAMENTS	REFLECTORS	96	91	$9.25	$9.75
4218	PATRIOTIC REFLECTOR	OLD MOLD GLASS ORNAMENTS	REFLECTORS	96	95	$8.95	$9.00
4404	SOCCER BALL	OLD MOLD GLASS ORNAMENTS	TOYS	96	85	$7.00	$7.00
4414	GIDDY-UP	OLD MOLD GLASS ORNAMENTS	TOYS	96	94	$12.00	$12.00
467265	ZEPPELIN	OLD MOLD GLASS ORNAMENTS	TRANSPORTATION	96	85		$7.00
4811	PINE CONE MAN	OLD MOLD GLASS ORNAMENTS	TREES & CONES	96	90	$8.25	$8.50
4815	LARGE CHRISTMAS TREE	OLD MOLD GLASS ORNAMENTS	TREES & CONES	96	92	$8.00	$8.50
1020	LITTLE WITCH	OLD MOLD GLASS ORNAMENTS	ANGELS & FEMALE FIGURES		89	$8.25	$9.00
1258	MONKEY WITH APPLE	OLD MOLD GLASS ORNAMENTS	ANIMALS	96	93	$9.00	$9.00

Order No.	Title	Type	Theme	Retired	Intro. Year	Retial Price	Secondary Price
2431	GNOME IN A TREE	OLD MOLD GLASS ORNAMENTS	CLOWNS & MALE FIGURES	96	87	$7.75	$7.75
131	O' TANNENBAUM	OMGO-BIRGITS CHRISTMAS CLLCTN	MISCELLANEOUS FORMS	96	96	$35.00	$35.00
133	OLD CHRISTMAS BARN	OMGO-BIRGITS CHRISTMAS CLLCTN	MISCELLANEOUS FORMS	96	96	$50.00	$50.00
1004	CLIP-ON ANGEL WINGS	OLD MOLD GLASS ORNAMENTS	ANGELS & FEMALE FIGURES	96	85	$10.00	$10.95
1009	BABY	OLD MOLD GLASS ORNAMENTS	ANGELS & FEMALE FIGURES	95	87	$5.25	$6.00
1010	GIRL IN GRAPES	OLD MOLD GLASS ORNAMENTS	ANGELS & FEMALE FIGURES	95	87	$8.45	$19.95
101029	SMALL GIRL WITH TREE	OLD MOLD GLASS ORNAMENTS	ANGELS & FEMALE FIGURES	95	85	$5.80	$5.90
1010306	GOLD GIRL WITH TREE	OLD MOLD GLASS ORNAMENTS	ANGELS & FEMALE FIGURES	95	85	$8.00	$11.90
1010309	RED GIRL WITH TREE	OLD MOLD GLASS ORNAMENTS	ANGELS & FEMALE FIGURES	95	85	$8.25	$13.00
101035	VICTORIAN GIRL	OLD MOLD GLASS ORNAMENTS	ANGELS & FEMALE FIGURES	89	85	$5.25	$15.95
101052	LT. BLUE ANGEL WITH WINGS	OLD MOLD GLASS ORNAMENTS	ANGELS & FEMALE FIGURES	94	85	$9.30	$13.90
101062	CAROLING GIRL	OLD MOLD GLASS ORNAMENTS	ANGELS & FEMALE FIGURES	90	85	$6.65	$18.90
101069	GIRL WITH FLOWERS	OLD MOLD GLASS ORNAMENTS	ANGELS & FEMALE FIGURES	93	85	$7.50	$12.95
1012	LARGE BLUE ANGEL	OLD MOLD GLASS ORNAMENTS	ANGELS & FEMALE FIGURES	94	87	$13.50	$17.00
1013	LARGE DOLL HEAD	OLD MOLD GLASS ORNAMENTS	ANGELS & FEMALE FIGURES	95	87	$11.50	$12.00
1014	GIRL UNDER TREE	OLD MOLD GLASS ORNAMENTS	ANGELS & FEMALE FIGURES	95	87	$7.75	$8.00
1015	BABY IN BUNTING	OLD MOLD GLASS ORNAMENTS	ANGELS & FEMALE FIGURES	90	87	$7.70	$14.00
1025	PRAYING GIRL	OLD MOLD GLASS ORNAMENTS	ANGELS & FEMALE FIGURES	93	90	$7.90	$11.90
1027	MINI. MRS. CLAUS	OLD MOLD GLASS ORNAMENTS	ANGELS & FEMALE FIGURES	95	90	$4.90	$4.90
1031	BAROQUE ANGEL	OLD MOLD GLASS ORNAMENTS	ANGELS & FEMALE FIGURES	95	91	$12.95	$13.00
103209	DOLL HEAD	OLD MOLD GLASS ORNAMENTS	ANGELS & FEMALE FIGURES	89	85	$6.40	$10.90
1033	ANGEL OF PEACE	OLD MOLD GLASS ORNAMENTS	ANGELS & FEMALE FIGURES	95	91	$9.25	$7.00
1036	BABY JESUS	OLD MOLD GLASS ORNAMENTS	ANGELS & FEMALE FIGURES	95	91		$9.95
1042	HONEY CHILD	OLD MOLD GLASS ORNAMENTS	ANGELS & FEMALE FIGURES	95	92	$7.50	$8.00
1043	GUARDIAN ANGEL	OLD MOLD GLASS ORNAMENTS	ANGELS & FEMALE FIGURES	95	92	$8.00	$8.90
1044	ANGEL ON FORM	OLD MOLD GLASS ORNAMENTS	ANGELS & FEMALE FIGURES	95	92	$9.75	$9.80
1059	FRAU SCHNEEMANN	OLD MOLD GLASS ORNAMENTS	ANGELS & FEMALE FIGURES	95	93	$6.75	$16.95
1202	PLAYING CAT	OLD MOLD GLASS ORNAMENTS	ANIMALS	94	85	$8.80	$10.00
1203	BEAR IN CRIB	OLD MOLD GLASS ORNAMENTS	ANIMALS	94	85	$9.00	$11.95
1204	CAT IN BAG	OLD MOLD GLASS ORNAMENTS	ANIMALS	95	85	$9.00	$9.00
1206	SITTING DOG WITH PIPE	OLD MOLD GLASS ORNAMENTS	ANIMALS	95	85	$7.80	$11.25
121004	KITTEN	OLD MOLD GLASS ORNAMENTS	ANIMALS	95	84	$7.00	$7.00
121009	THREE-SIDED:OWL, DOG, CAT	OLD MOLD GLASS ORNAMENTS	ANIMALS	94	84	$8.55	$13.00
121010	PUPPY	OLD MOLD GLASS ORNAMENTS	ANIMALS	94	84	$6.90	$8.90
121021	CIRCUS DOG	OLD MOLD GLASS ORNAMENTS	ANIMALS	94	84	$8.90	$11.90
121041	SNAIL	OLD MOLD GLASS ORNAMENTS	ANIMALS	93	85	$6.70	$18.00
121088	IARGE THREE-SIDED HEAD	OLD MOLD GLASS ORNAMENTS	ANIMALS	94	85	$12.90	$22.95
121089	LARGE TEDDY BEAR	OLD MOLD GLASS ORNAMENTS	ANIMALS	88	85	$13.00	$17.95
121090	SMALL BUNNY	OLD MOLD GLASS ORNAMENTS	ANIMALS	94	85	$5.20	$8.00
1211	MOUSE	OLD MOLD GLASS ORNAMENTS	ANIMALS	95	87	$10.00	$10.00
121103	CAT IN SHOE	OLD MOLD GLASS ORNAMENTS	ANIMALS	94	85	$7.75	$11.00
1213	JUMBO ELEPHANT	OLD MOLD GLASS ORNAMENTS	ANIMALS	95	87	$9.00	$10.00
1214	LARGE FISH	OLD MOLD GLASS ORNAMENTS	ANIMALS	93	87	$10.75	$14.00
1218	TEDDY BEAR WITH BOW	OLD MOLD GLASS ORNAMENTS	ANIMALS	90	89	$6.65	$17.25
1219	RABBIT IN TREE	OLD MOLD GLASS ORNAMENTS	ANIMALS	95	89	$8.25	$9.00
1221	CAT AND THE FIDDLE	OLD MOLD GLASS ORNAMENTS	ANIMALS	94	89	$7.75	$10.90
1222	KING CHARLES SPANIEL	OLD MOLD GLASS ORNAMENTS	ANIMALS	95	89	$10.00	$10.00
1223	FAT FISH	OLD MOLD GLASS ORNAMENTS	ANIMALS	95	89	$5.75	$5.90
1227	PINK POODLE	OLD MOLD GLASS ORNAMENTS	ANIMALS	94	90	$8.75	$10.90
1228	SITTING BLACK CAT	OLD MOLD GLASS ORNAMENTS	ANIMALS	95	90	$7.00	$7.00
1232	WEST HIGHLAND TERRIER	OLD MOLD GLASS ORNAMENTS	ANIMALS	93	90	$7.45	$15.25
123420	GREY ELEPHANT	OLD MOLD GLASS ORNAMENTS	ANIMALS	95	85	$7.00	$6.90
1237447	BUTTERFLY ON FORM	OLD MOLD GLASS ORNAMENTS	ANIMALS	95	85	$7.00	$8.00
1241	LARGE PUPPY WITH BASKET	OLD MOLD GLASS ORNAMENTS	ANIMALS	93	91	$13.25	$22.00
1244	RABBIT ON HEART	OLD MOLD GLASS ORNAMENTS	ANIMALS	96	91	$8.00	$8.00
1246	SITTING PUPPY	OLD MOLD GLASS ORNAMENTS	ANIMALS	94	91	$6.75	$9.00
1265	GRIZZLY BEAR	OLD MOLD GLASS ORNAMENTS	ANIMALS	95	92	$8.25	$9.00
1268	PASTEL BUTTERFLY	OLD MOLD GLASS ORNAMENTS	ANIMALS	95	92	$8.45	$10.00
1276	MY DARLING	OLD MOLD GLASS ORNAMENTS	ANIMALS	96	93	$6.25	$7.00
1279	BEAR ABOVE REFLECTOR	OLD MOLD GLASS ORNAMENTS	ANIMALS	95	93	$32.75	$35.00
1301	CLOWN & DRUM GARLAND	OLD MOLD GLASS ORNAMENTS	BEAD GARLANDS	93	93	$55.00	$66.50
1304	PICKLE GARLAND	OLD MOLD GLASS ORNAMENTS	BEAD GARLANDS	93	93	$55.00	$110.00
1305	FROG & FISH GARLAND	OLD MOLD GLASS ORNAMENTS	BEAD GARLANDS	93	93	$55.00	$96.00
1306	ANGEL GARLAND	OLD MOLD GLASS ORNAMENTS	BEAD GARLANDS	93	93	$55.00	$85.50
1308	SANTA GARLAND	OLD MOLD GLASS ORNAMENTS	BEAD GARLANDS	93	93	$55.00	$110.00
1492	SANTA IN MOON (CLUB)	OLD MOLD GLASS ORNAMENTS	LIMITED EDITION	94	93		$9.90
1493	LG. SANTA IN CHIMNEY (CLUB)	OLD MOLD GLASS ORNAMENTS	LIMITED EDITION	94	93	$42.50	$80.00
1501	NIGHT BEFORE CHRISTMAS BALL	OLD MOLD GLASS ORNAMENTS	LIMITED EDITION	93	90	$73.00	$170.00
1502	SANTA'S VISIT	OLD MOLD GLASS ORNAMENTS	LIMITED EDITION	94	91	$73.00	$99.00
1503	SANTA'S DEPARTURE	OLD MOLD GLASS ORNAMENTS	LIMITED EDITION	94	92	$73.00	$99.00
1510	'92 NUTCRACKER ORNAMENT	OLD MOLD GLASS ORNAMENTS	LIMITED EDITION	93	92	$33.75	$175.00
1511	93 HANSEL & GRETAL/LIMITED TO 2,400	OLD MOLD GLASS ORNAMENTS	LIMITED EDITION	93	93	$45.00	$115.00
1512	'94 SANTA IN MOON ON DISC	OLD MOLD GLASS ORNAMENTS	LIMITED EDITION	94	94	$32.50	$40.00
1513	95 CHRISTMAS TREE WITH STAR	OLD MOLD GLASS ORNAMENTS	LIMITED EDITION	95	95	$53.00	$80.00
1521	SANTA WITH TINSEL WIRE	OLD MOLD GLASS ORNAMENTS	LIMITED EDITION	93	91	$55.00	$90.00
1522	ANGEL WITH TINSEL WIRE	OLD MOLD GLASS ORNAMENTS	LIMITED EDITION	93	91	$55.00	$85.00
1523	SNOWMAN WITH TINSEL WIRE	OLD MOLD GLASS ORNAMENTS	LIMITED EDITION	93	91		$82.50
1547	PARACHUTING SANTA	OLD MOLD GLASS ORNAMENTS	LIMITED EDITION	95	95	$60.00	$60.00
1550	FLYING PEACOCK WITH WINGS	OLD MOLD GLASS ORNAMENTS	LIMITED EDITION	95	92	$22.50	$23.50
1563	HEAVENLY ANGEL	OLD MOLD GLASS ORNAMENTS	LIMITED EDITION	94	93	$20.00	$19.50
1570	SANTA WITH HOT AIR BALLOON	OLD MOLD GLASS ORNAMENTS	LIMITED EDITION	94	93	$39.00	$39.00
1582	WITCH	OLD MOLD GLASS ORNAMENTS	LIMITED EDITION	95	95	$35.00	$800.00
1587	CHRISTMAS CAROUSEL	OLD MOLD GLASS ORNAMENTS	LIMITED EDITION	95	95	$80.00	$95.00
1593	CHRISTMAS HEART	OLD MOLD GLASS ORNAMENTS	LIMITED EDITION	93	93	$10.00	$50.00
1599	DEVIL BELL	OLD MOLD GLASS ORNAMENTS	LIMITED EDITION	95	95	$35.00	
1601	OWL ON FORM	OLD MOLD GLASS ORNAMENTS	BIRDS FOR HANGING	95	85	$11.00	$11.00
1602	SONGBIRDS ON BALL	OLD MOLD GLASS ORNAMENTS	BIRDS FOR HANGING	94	85	$9.25	$10.90
1603	ROOSTER ON FORM	OLD MOLD GLASS ORNAMENTS	BIRDS FOR HANGING	89	85	$6.65	$8.90
1604	LARGE OWL WITH STEIN	OLD MOLD GLASS ORNAMENTS	BIRDS FOR HANGING	89	85	$10.00	$44.00
1605	SWAN ON FORM	OLD MOLD GLASS ORNAMENTS	BIRDS FOR HANGING	95	85	$8.35	$9.50
1610	FAT ROOSTER	OLD MOLD GLASS ORNAMENTS	BIRDS FOR HANGING	95	87	$10.35	$10.95
161012	COCK ROBIN	OLD MOLD GLASS ORNAMENTS	BIRDS FOR HANGING	95	84	$7.00	$7.50
161098	CARDINAL WITH WINGS	OLD MOLD GLASS ORNAMENTS	BIRDS FOR HANGING	94	85	$11.00	$11.00

Order No.	Title	Type	Theme	Retired	Intro. Year	Retail Price	Secondary Price
161058	TURKEY	OLD MOLD GLASS ORNAMENTS	BIRDS FOR HANGING	89	85	$8.00	$12.90
1611	BIRD HOUSE	OLD MOLD GLASS ORNAMENTS	BIRDS FOR HANGING	95	87	$10.50	$11.00
161100	BLUE BIRD WITH WINGS	OLD MOLD GLASS ORNAMENTS	BIRDS FOR HANGING	91	85	$7.65	$9.75
1612	SWANS ON LAKE	OLD MOLD GLASS ORNAMENTS	BIRDS FOR HANGING	95	87	$7.75	$8.00
1613	DUCK	OLD MOLD GLASS ORNAMENTS	BIRDS FOR HANGING	95	89	$6.20	$7.50
1614	SONGBIRD ON FORM	OLD MOLD GLASS ORNAMENTS	BIRDS FOR HANGING	94	90	$8.80	$9.90
1617	LARGE PARROT ON BALL	OLD MOLD GLASS ORNAMENTS	BIRDS FOR HANGING	95	90	$11.00	$11.50
1618	SONGBIRD ON HEART	OLD MOLD GLASS ORNAMENTS	BIRDS FOR HANGING	93	91	$8.25	$10.80
1619	CHICK ON FORM	OLD MOLD GLASS ORNAMENTS	BIRDS FOR HANGING	93	91	$8.00	$11.75
1551	FLYING SONGBIRD WITH WINGS	OLD MOLD GLASS ORNAMENTS	LIMITED EDITION	95	92	$22.00	$22.00
1556	ANGEL WITH WINGS	OLD MOLD GLASS ORNAMENTS	LIMITED EDITION	93	93	$12.75	$85.00
1247	CHRISTMAS BUTTERFLY	OLD MOLD GLASS ORNAMENTS	ANIMALS	94	91	$7.00	$8.90
1801	BIRD IN NEST	OLD MOLD GLASS ORNAMENTS	BIRDS WITH CLIP	95	85	$9.38	$10.00
1802	CLIP-ON ROOSTER	OLD MOLD GLASS ORNAMENTS	BIRDS WITH CLIP	89	86	$8.00	$32.00
1803	GOLD BIRD WITH TINSEL TAIL	OLD MOLD GLASS ORNAMENTS	BIRDS WITH CLIP	94	85	$7.45	$70.00
1805	WHITE COCKATOO	OLD MOLD GLASS ORNAMENTS	BIRDS WITH CLIP	95	85	$7.80	$8.00
1807	SHINY GOLD BIRD	OLD MOLD GLASS ORNAMENTS	BIRDS WITH CLIP	95	87	$5.55	$6.00
1809	SMALL PURPLE BIRD	OLD MOLD GLASS ORNAMENTS	BIRDS WITH CLIP	95	87	$7.00	$7.00
1810	RED SNOWBIRD	OLD MOLD GLASS ORNAMENTS	BIRDS WITH CLIP	93	87	$8.70	$13.00
181025	LARGE COCKATOO	OLD MOLD GLASS ORNAMENTS	BIRDS WITH CLIP	94	84	$13.95	$16.00
181073	FANCY PEACOCK	OLD MOLD GLASS ORNAMENTS	BIRDS WITH CLIP	93	85	$13.50	$16.00
181075	FANTASY BIRD WITH TINSEL TAIL	OLD MOLD GLASS ORNAMENTS	BIRDS WITH CLIP	95	85	$8.00	$8.00
181076	NUTHATCH	OLD MOLD GLASS ORNAMENTS	BIRDS WITH CLIP	95	85	$7.00	$8.00
181077	COCKATOO	OLD MOLD GLASS ORNAMENTS	BIRDS WITH CLIP	95	85	$8.55	$9.00
181078	BLUE BIRD	OLD MOLD GLASS ORNAMENTS	BIRDS WITH CLIP	95	85	$6.65	$8.00
181080	SNOWBIRD	OLD MOLD GLASS ORNAMENTS	BIRDS WITH CLIP	93	85	$8.00	$14.00
181082	PINK BIRD WITH BLUE WINGS	OLD MOLD GLASS ORNAMENTS	BIRDS WITH CLIP	94	85	$5.55	$8.00
181085	LARGE GOLDFINCH	OLD MOLD GLASS ORNAMENTS	BIRDS WITH CLIP	94	85	$9.25	$11.00
181086	MAGNIFICENT SONGBIRD	OLD MOLD GLASS ORNAMENTS	BIRDS WITH CLIP	94	85	$13.95	$10.00
181096	FANCY PINK PEACOCK	OLD MOLD GLASS ORNAMENTS	BIRDS WITH CLIP	95	85	$13.95	$14.00
1811	LILAC BIRD	OLD MOLD GLASS ORNAMENTS	BIRDS WITH CLIP	95	87	$8.70	$10.00
181101	BIRD OF PARADISE	OLD MOLD GLASS ORNAMENTS	BIRDS WITH CLIP	94	85	$7.80	$10.00
1813	FAT BURGUNDY BIRD	OLD MOLD GLASS ORNAMENTS	BIRDS WITH CLIP	95	87	$7.80	$10.00
1814	PARTRIDGE	OLD MOLD GLASS ORNAMENTS	BIRDS WITH CLIP	94	87	$8.00	$11.00
1816	SNOW OWL	OLD MOLD GLASS ORNAMENTS	BIRDS WITH CLIP	94	87	$9.90	$13.95
1819	ROBIN	OLD MOLD GLASS ORNAMENTS	BIRDS WITH CLIP	93	87	$8.80	$13.00
1822	CARDINAL	OLD MOLD GLASS ORNAMENTS	BIRDS WITH CLIP	95	90	$9.90	$10.00
1823	SMALL RED-HEADED SONGBIRD	OLD MOLD GLASS ORNAMENTS	BIRDS WITH CLIP	95	90	$7.00	$7.00
1824	CHRISTMAS BIRD	OLD MOLD GLASS ORNAMENTS	BIRDS WITH CLIP	95	90	$7.00	$7.00
1825	MINIATURE PEACOCK	OLD MOLD GLASS ORNAMENTS	BIRDS WITH CLIP	94	90	$8.35	$12.50
1830	LARGE PEACOCK WITH CROWN	OLD MOLD GLASS ORNAMENTS	BIRDS WITH CLIP	94	91	$13.95	$19.00
1826	TROPICAL PARROT	OLD MOLD GLASS ORNAMENTS	BIRDS WITH CLIP	94	90	$10.35	$13.25
1828	MINIATURE PARROT	OLD MOLD GLASS ORNAMENTS	BIRDS WITH CLIP	95	90	$8.45	$9.00
1832	FESTIVE BIRD	OLD MOLD GLASS ORNAMENTS	BIRDS WITH CLIP	95	91	$6.00	$6.00
1833	SILLY BIRD	OLD MOLD GLASS ORNAMENTS	BIRDS WITH CLIP	94	91	$6.75	$12.00
1834	CANARY	OLD MOLD GLASS ORNAMENTS	BIRDS WITH CLIP	94	91	$7.35	$10.00
1837	ADVENT BIRD	OLD MOLD GLASS ORNAMENTS	BIRDS WITH CLIP	95	91	$8.00	$8.00
1838	COCKATIEL	OLD MOLD GLASS ORNAMENTS	BIRDS WITH CLIP	94	91	$9.25	$10.00
1841	BRILLIANT SONGBIRD	OLD MOLD GLASS ORNAMENTS	BIRDS WITH CLIP	95	91	$7.35	$8.00
1843	CHRISTMAS FINCH	OLD MOLD GLASS ORNAMENTS	BIRDS WITH CLIP	95	92	$7.65	$8.00
187215	MEDIUM PEACOCK WITH TINSEL TAIL	OLD MOLD GLASS ORNAMENTS	BIRDS WITH CLIP	85	85	$9.00	$10.00
1901	BUTTERFLY, WHITE W/RED	OLD MOLD GLASS ORNAMENTS	BUTTERFLIES	91	87	$20.95	$30.00
1902	BUTTERFLY, WHITE W/BLUE	OLD MOLD GLASS ORNAMENTS	BUTTERFLIES	91	87	$20.95	$30.00
1903	BUTTERFLY, RED W/CREAM	OLD MOLD GLASS ORNAMENTS	BUTTERFLIES	91	87	$20.95	$30.00
1904	BUTTERFLY, ORANGE W/ORANGE	OLD MOLD GLASS ORNAMENTS	BUTTERFLIES	91	87	$20.95	$30.00
1905	BUTTERFLY, BLUE W/BLUE	OLD MOLD GLASS ORNAMENTS	BUTTERFLIES	91	87	$20.95	$30.00
1906	BUTTERFLY, GOLD W/GOLD	OLD MOLD GLASS ORNAMENTS	BUTTERFLIES	91	87	$20.95	$30.00
2001	GINGERBREAD HOUSE	OLD MOLD GLASS ORNAMENTS	CHURCHES AND HOUSES	89	86	$6.55	$16.25
2004	HOUSE WITH PEACOCK	OLD MOLD GLASS ORNAMENTS	CHURCHES AND HOUSES	87	85	$7.45	$16.00
2006	WINDMILL ON FORM	OLD MOLD GLASS ORNAMENTS	CHURCHES AND HOUSES	88	85	$7.45	$22.00
2008	CHURCH/TREE ON FORM	OLD MOLD GLASS ORNAMENTS	CHURCHES AND HOUSES	95	89	$8.35	$9.00
201040	SQUARE HOUSE	OLD MOLD GLASS ORNAMENTS	CHURCHES AND HOUSES	95	85	$7.80	$9.00
201051	RATHAUS	OLD MOLD GLASS ORNAMENTS	CHURCHES AND HOUSES	89	85	$7.00	$14.00
201059	BAVARIAN HOUSE	OLD MOLD GLASS ORNAMENTS	CHURCHES AND HOUSES	94	85	$8.00	$13.00
2011	GARDEN HOUSE WITH GNOME	OLD MOLD GLASS ORNAMENTS	CHURCHES AND HOUSES	93	90	$7.80	$14.00
2014	CHRISTMAS CHALET	OLD MOLD GLASS ORNAMENTS	CHURCHES AND HOUSES	95	90	$8.00	$9.00
2019	THATCHED COTTAGE	OLD MOLD GLASS ORNAMENTS	CHURCHES AND HOUSES	95	91	$7.35	$8.00
2020	CHRISTMAS SHOP	OLD MOLD GLASS ORNAMENTS	CHURCHES AND HOUSES	95	91	$9.45	$10.00
2023	LARGE LIGHTHOUSE MILL	OLD MOLD GLASS ORNAMENTS	CHURCHES AND HOUSES	95	91	$11.00	$11.00
206790	MATTE CREAM CHURCH	OLD MOLD GLASS ORNAMENTS	CHURCHES AND HOUSES	93	85	$6.45	$11.00
2201	SHOOTING STAR ON BALL	OLD MOLD GLASS ORNAMENTS	CELESTIAL FIGURES	93	85	$6.65	$11.90
221027	SUN/MOON	OLD MOLD GLASS ORNAMENTS	CELESTIAL FIGURES	93	85	$7.00	$9.75
2237139	LG. GOLD STAR WITH GLITTER	OLD MOLD GLASS ORNAMENTS	CELESTIAL FIGURES	93	85	$7.00	$9.90
2402	AVIATOR	OLD MOLD GLASS ORNAMENTS	CLOWNS & MALE FIGURES	93	85	$7.75	$11.00
2404	SAILOR HEAD	OLD MOLD GLASS ORNAMENTS	CLOWNS & MALE FIGURES	90	85		$28.90
2405	BABY	OLD MOLD GLASS ORNAMENTS	CLOWNS & MALE FIGURES	89	85	$6.75	$19.00
2406	PIXIE WITH ACCORDION	OLD MOLD GLASS ORNAMENTS	CLOWNS & MALE FIGURES	89	85	$5.00	$15.95
2407	CLOWN WITH BANJO	OLD MOLD GLASS ORNAMENTS	CLOWNS & MALE FIGURES	95	85	$7.00	$8.00
2409	CLOWN WITH ACCORDION	OLD MOLD GLASS ORNAMENTS	CLOWNS & MALE FIGURES	95	85	$10.00	$11.00
241003	KEYSTONE COP	OLD MOLD GLASS ORNAMENTS	CLOWNS & MALE FIGURES	94	84	$10.00	$19.00
241011	SHORTY CLOWN	OLD MOLD GLASS ORNAMENTS	CLOWNS & MALE FIGURES	88	84	$5.65	$13.95
241015	ROLY-POLY KEYSTONE COP	OLD MOLD GLASS ORNAMENTS	CLOWNS & MALE FIGURES	88	84	$9.90	$25.50
241017	SCOTSMAN	OLD MOLD GLASS ORNAMENTS	CLOWNS & MALE FIGURES	88	84	$6.25	$19.95
241019	STOP KEYSTONE COP	OLD MOLD GLASS ORNAMENTS	CLOWNS & MALE FIGURES	89	84	$6.50	$30.00
241032	BOY IN YELLOW SWEATER	OLD MOLD GLASS ORNAMENTS	CLOWNS & MALE FIGURES	88	85	$6.75	$14.95
241047	WAITER IN TUXEDO	OLD MOLD GLASS ORNAMENTS	CLOWNS & MALE FIGURES	89	85	$7.00	$23.95
2415	SCHOOL BOY	OLD MOLD GLASS ORNAMENTS	CLOWNS & MALE FIGURES	89	85	$5.00	$12.95
2416	CLIP-ON BOY HEAD	OLD MOLD GLASS ORNAMENTS	CLOWNS & MALE FIGURES	89	85	$6.50	$12.50
2417	GNOME UNDER MUSHROOM	OLD MOLD GLASS ORNAMENTS	CLOWNS & MALE FIGURES	93	85	$6.95	$11.75
2418	CLOWN HEAD WITH BURGUNDY HAT	OLD MOLD GLASS ORNAMENTS	CLOWNS & MALE FIGURES	94	85	$7.00	$9.95
2421	KING	OLD MOLD GLASS ORNAMENTS	CLOWNS & MALE FIGURES	95	87	$10.50	$10.50
2426	MR. BIG NOSE	OLD MOLD GLASS ORNAMENTS	CLOWNS & MALE FIGURES	93	87	$8.00	$18.90
2427	SCROOGE	OLD MOLD GLASS ORNAMENTS	CLOWNS & MALE FIGURES	95	87	$8.50	$10.95

Order No.	Title	Type	Theme	Retired	Intro. Year	Retial Price	Secondary Price
2429	JOLLY CLOWN HEAD	OLD MOLD GLASS ORNAMENTS	CLOWNS & MALE FIGURES	94	87	$13.00	$13.00
2430	MUSHROOM GNOME	OLD MOLD GLASS ORNAMENTS	CLOWNS & MALE FIGURES	89	87	$6.25	$112.95
2432	HARPO	OLD MOLD GLASS ORNAMENTS	CLOWNS & MALE FIGURES	91	87	$6.25	$25.00
243321	DUTCH BOY	OLD MOLD GLASS ORNAMENTS	CLOWNS & MALE FIGURES	93	85	$7.50	$16.00
2436	SMALL CLOWN HEAD	OLD MOLD GLASS ORNAMENTS	CLOWNS & MALE FIGURES	93	89	$6.75	$10.95
2439	BLACK BOY	OLD MOLD GLASS ORNAMENTS	CLOWNS & MALE FIGURES	95	90	$9.00	$11.95
2440	SCOUT	OLD MOLD GLASS ORNAMENTS	CLOWNS & MALE FIGURES	95	90	$9.25	$10.00
2442	ENGLISH BOBBY	OLD MOLD GLASS ORNAMENTS	CLOWNS & MALE FIGURES	94	90	$8.75	$12.00
2442265	FAT BOY WITH SWEATER & CAP	OLD MOLD GLASS ORNAMENTS	CLOWNS & MALE FIGURES	94	85		$18.00
2445	SNOWMAN ON REFLECTOR	OLD MOLD GLASS ORNAMENTS	CLOWNS & MALE FIGURES	93	90	$10.50	$14.95
2464	MINIATURE CLOWN	OLD MOLD GLASS ORNAMENTS	CLOWNS & MALE FIGURES	95	93		$5.90
2467	MONK	OLD MOLD GLASS ORNAMENTS	CLOWNS & MALE FIGURES	94	93	$8.00	$9.90
2470	CLOWN ABOVE BALL	OLD MOLD GLASS ORNAMENTS	CLOWNS & MALE FIGURES	94	93	$42.00	$44.50
2487	CHARLIE CHAPLIN	OLD MOLD GLASS ORNAMENTS	CLOWNS & MALE FIGURES	95	95	$25.00	$62.00
2492	MR. SCI-FI	OLD MOLD GLASS ORNAMENTS	CLOWNS & MALE FIGURES	95	95	$30.00	$30.00
2805	PEAR WITH FACE	OLD MOLD GLASS ORNAMENTS	FRUITS & VEGTABLES	95	85	$7.00	$7.00
2810	ONION	OLD MOLD GLASS ORNAMENTS	FRUITS & VEGTABLES	89	87	$8.25	$79.90
281023	MR. PEAR	OLD MOLD GLASS ORNAMENTS	FRUITS & VEGTABLES	93	84	$6.75	$7.00
281038	GRAPES ON FORM	OLD MOLD GLASS ORNAMENTS	FRUITS & VEGTABLES	87	85	$7.00	$13.95
281053	LG BASKET OF GRAPES	OLD MOLD GLASS ORNAMENTS	FRUITS & VEGTABLES	95	85	$10.35	$11.50
281071	MR. APPLE	OLD MOLD GLASS ORNAMENTS	CLOWNS & MALE FIGURES	88	85	$6.20	$19.90
2812	GREEN PEPPER	OLD MOLD GLASS ORNAMENTS	FRUITS & VEGTABLES	95	87	$8.00	$8.00
2820	CUCUMBER	OLD MOLD GLASS ORNAMENTS	FRUITS & VEGTABLES	89	89	$6.65	$14.50
2825	CHERRIES ON FORM	OLD MOLD GLASS ORNAMENTS	FRUITS & VEGTABLES	93	90	$9.00	$11.90
2831	APRICOT	OLD MOLD GLASS ORNAMENTS	FRUITS & VEGTABLES	95	90	$6.55	$7.00
2385	RASPBERRY	OLD MOLD GLASS ORNAMENTS	FRUITS & VEGTABLES	93	90	$6.20	$8.90
2341432	LARGE STRAWBERRY	OLD MOLD GLASS ORNAMENTS	FRUITS & VEGTABLES	93	85	$4.25	$9.95
2847	VERY LARGE PEAR	OLD MOLD GLASS ORNAMENTS	FRUITS & VEGTABLES	93	90	$10.60	$14.90
2848	VERY LARGE APPLE	OLD MOLD GLASS ORNAMENTS	FRUITS & VEGTABLES	93	90	$10.60	$14.90
2849	LG. FRUIT BASKET	OLD MOLD GLASS ORNAMENTS	FRUITS & VEGTABLES	95	91	$12.50	$12.95
2851	STRAWBERRIES/FLOWER ON FORM	OLD MOLD GLASS ORNAMENTS	FRUITS & VEGTABLES	94	91	$8.50	$10.00
3001	SMALL GOLD HEART WITH STAR	OLD MOLD GLASS ORNAMENTS	HEARTS	93	85	$3.00	$8.75
3004	BURGUNDY HEART WITH GLITTER	OLD MOLD GLASS ORNAMENTS	HEARTS	95	87	$6.90	$7.00
3005	VALENTINE	OLD MOLD GLASS ORNAMENTS	HEARTS	95	87	$5.70	$5.95
3010	HEART WITH FLOWERS	OLD MOLD GLASS ORNAMENTS	HEARTS	93	91	$9.75	$12.95
306767	PINK HEART WITH GLITTER	OLD MOLD GLASS ORNAMENTS	HEARTS	95	85	$6.75	$7.00
3201	RED STOCKING	OLD MOLD GLASS ORNAMENTS	HOUSEHOLD ITEMS	87	85	$9.00	$18.75
3203	BLACK STOCKING	OLD MOLD GLASS ORNAMENTS	HOUSEHOLD ITEMS	93	85	$9.50	$35.50
3204	WINE BARREL	OLD MOLD GLASS ORNAMENTS	HOUSEHOLD ITEMS	90	87	$7.00	$12.95
3206	MONEY BAG	OLD MOLD GLASS ORNAMENTS	HOUSEHOLD ITEMS	94	91	$7.00	$10.00
3209	SMALL CUCKOO CLOCK	OLD MOLD GLASS ORNAMENTS	HOUSEHOLD ITEMS	95	91	$7.00	$6.95
3210	SMALL WINE BARREL	OLD MOLD GLASS ORNAMENTS	HOUSEHOLD ITEMS	93	91	$6.25	$9.95
321060	WALL CLOCK	OLD MOLD GLASS ORNAMENTS	HOUSEHOLD ITEMS	95	85	$11.00	$11.00
321063	CLIP-ON CANDLE	OLD MOLD GLASS ORNAMENTS	HOUSEHOLD ITEMS	95	85	$12.95	$12.95
321091	PASTEL UMBRELLA	OLD MOLD GLASS ORNAMENTS	HOUSEHOLD ITEMS	93	85	$10.95	$14.95
321103	VERY LARGE PINK UMBRELLA	OLD MOLD GLASS ORNAMENTS	HOUSEHOLD ITEMS	86	85	$30.00	$50.00
326729	POCKET WATCH	OLD MOLD GLASS ORNAMENTS	HOUSEHOLD ITEMS	95	85	$5.75	$6.00
3401	LONG CHAMPAGNE ICICLE	OLD MOLD GLASS ORNAMENTS	ICICLES	88	87	$7.25	$14.75
3601	FLOWER BASKET	OLD MOLD GLASS ORNAMENTS	MISCELLANEOUS FORMS	95	85	$10.25	$12.75
3606	SKULL	OLD MOLD GLASS ORNAMENTS	MISCELLANEOUS FORMS	95	89	$7.35	$8.00
3607	RED ROSE ON FORM	OLD MOLD GLASS ORNAMENTS	MISCELLANEOUS FORMS	95	89	$5.85	$6.00
3608	MORNING GLORIES	OLD MOLD GLASS ORNAMENTS	MISCELLANEOUS FORMS	95	89	$8.90	$9.00
3609	FLOWER WITH BUTTERFLY	OLD MOLD GLASS ORNAMENTS	MISCELLANEOUS FORMS	93	89	$9.75	$13.00
3617	SHINY RED CLIP-ON TULIP	OLD MOLD GLASS ORNAMENTS	MISCELLANEOUS FORMS	90	89	$7.45	$8.00
3618	EDELWEISS ON FORM	OLD MOLD GLASS ORNAMENTS	MISCELLANEOUS FORMS	95	90	$8.25	$9.00
3619	POINSETTIAS	OLD MOLD GLASS ORNAMENTS	MISCELLANEOUS FORMS	95	90	$9.90	$10.00
3620	ASSORTED CHRISTMAS STARS	OLD MOLD GLASS ORNAMENTS	MISCELLANEOUS FORMS	95	90	$7.00	$7.00
3624	SUNBURST	OLD MOLD GLASS ORNAMENTS	MISCELLANEOUS FORMS	93	90	$8.00	$7.75
3625	LARGE SEA SHELL	OLD MOLD GLASS ORNAMENTS	MISCELLANEOUS FORMS	95	90	$8.35	$8.75
3626	ASSORTED CHRISTMAS FLOWERS	OLD MOLD GLASS ORNAMENTS	MISCELLANEOUS FORMS	94	90	$8.00	$9.00
3634	CHRISTMAS BALL WITH ROSES	OLD MOLD GLASS ORNAMENTS	MISCELLANEOUS FORMS	95	91	$9.45	$10.00
3636	ASSORTED SPIRALS	OLD MOLD GLASS ORNAMENTS	MISCELLANEOUS FORMS	95	91	$8.25	$9.00
3637164	ICE CREAM CONE	OLD MOLD GLASS ORNAMENTS	MISCELLANEOUS FORMS	88	85	$14.50	$24.00
3640	ASSORTED NORTHERN STARS	OLD MOLD GLASS ORNAMENTS	MISCELLANEOUS FORMS	95	92	$6.20	$6.75
3643	LUCKY SHAMROCK	OLD MOLD GLASS ORNAMENTS	MISCELLANEOUS FORMS	93	93	$7.80	$22.50
3650	ASST. FANTASY FORM WITH WIRE	OLD MOLD GLASS ORNAMENTS	MISCELLANEOUS FORMS	94	93	$20.00	$23.00
3659	VICTORIAN FLORAL DROP	OLD MOLD GLASS ORNAMENTS	MISCELLANEOUS FORMS	95	94		$22.00
3801	CELLO	OLD MOLD GLASS ORNAMENTS	MUSICAL INSTRUMENTS	95	85	$6.65	$7.50
3802	GUITAR	OLD MOLD GLASS ORNAMENTS	MUSICAL INSTRUMENTS	95	85	$6.50	$7.00
3804	LARGE BELL WITH ACORNS	OLD MOLD GLASS ORNAMENTS	MUSICAL INSTRUMENTS	95	87	$9.00	$11.50
3805	BELL WITH FLOWERS	OLD MOLD GLASS ORNAMENTS	MUSICAL INSTRUMENTS	95	87	$5.85	$5.75
3806	CHRISTMAS BELLS ON FORM	OLD MOLD GLASS ORNAMENTS	MUSICAL INSTRUMENTS	95	89	$8.35	$8.75
3809	LYRE	OLD MOLD GLASS ORNAMENTS	MUSICAL INSTRUMENTS	95	90	$8.35	$9.00
3815	SMALL FANCY DRUM	OLD MOLD GLASS ORNAMENTS	MUSICAL INSTRUMENTS	95	90	$7.80	$7.75
383534	CLIP-ON DRUM	OLD MOLD GLASS ORNAMENTS	MUSICAL INSTRUMENTS	95	85	$8.00	$9.00
4002	SANTA ON CONE	OLD MOLD GLASS ORNAMENTS	SANTAS	93	85	$8.00	$16.00
4003	SANTA ON CARRIAGE	OLD MOLD GLASS ORNAMENTS	SANTAS	88	85	$10.00	$28.00
4005	SANTA IN CHIMNEY	OLD MOLD GLASS ORNAMENTS	SANTAS	95	85	$8.50	$16.00
4006	FATHER CHRISTMAS HEAD	OLD MOLD GLASS ORNAMENTS	SANTAS	95	85	$7.80	$8.00
4007	GREEN CLIP-ON SANTA	OLD MOLD GLASS ORNAMENTS	SANTAS	95	85	$7.80	$8.00
4008	ST. NICHOLAS HEAD	OLD MOLD GLASS ORNAMENTS	SANTAS	95	85	$6.50	$7.50
4009	SANTA WITH GLUED ON TREE	OLD MOLD GLASS ORNAMENTS	SANTAS	95	85	$9.00	$9.50
4010	SMALL BLUE SANTA	OLD MOLD GLASS ORNAMENTS	SANTAS	95	85	$5.30	$6.00
401001	LARGE SANTA IN BASKET	OLD MOLD GLASS ORNAMENTS	SANTAS	95	84	$12.95	$14.00
401002	ROLY-POLY SANTA	OLD MOLD GLASS ORNAMENTS	SANTAS	94	84	$7.90	$10.50
401007	OLD FATHER CHRISTMAS HEAD	OLD MOLD GLASS ORNAMENTS	SANTAS	94	84	$7.00	$10.00
401022	SMALL OLD-FASHIONED SANTA	OLD MOLD GLASS ORNAMENTS	SANTAS	94	84	$6.50	$9.00
401026	SANTA AND TREE ON FORM	OLD MOLD GLASS ORNAMENTS	SANTAS	95	85	$9.25	$10.00
401039	FATHER CHRISTMAS WITH TREE	OLD MOLD GLASS ORNAMENTS	SANTAS	95	85	$8.00	$8.00
401043	JOLLY FATHER CHRISTMAS	OLD MOLD GLASS ORNAMENTS	SANTAS	95	85	$7.00	$8.00
401045	GOLD FATHER CHRISTMAS	OLD MOLD GLASS ORNAMENTS	SANTAS	95	85	$7.45	$8.00
4010498	BLUE FATHER CHRISTMAS	OLD MOLD GLASS ORNAMENTS	SANTAS	95	85	$8.00	$9.00
4010499	PINK FATHER CHRISTMAS	OLD MOLD GLASS ORNAMENTS	SANTAS	95	85	$8.00	$9.00

Order No.	Title	Type	Theme	Retired	Intro. Year	Retail Price	Secondary Price
401055	LARGE SANTA WITH TREE	OLD MOLD GLASS ORNAMENTS	SANTAS	94	85	$12.60	$13.00
401065	SMALL SANTA WITH PACK	OLD MOLD GLASS ORNAMENTS	SANTAS	95	85	$5.40	$6.90
4011	PINK CLIP-ON SANTA	OLD MOLD GLASS ORNAMENTS	SANTAS	94	85	$8.25	$9.50
401105	SMALL SANTA IN BASKET	OLD MOLD GLASS ORNAMENTS	SANTAS	95	86	$9.25	$9.50
4012	MATTE RED ROLY-POLY SANTA	OLD MOLD GLASS ORNAMENTS	SANTAS	95	87	$7.90	$7.75
4013	BURGUNDY FATHER CHRISTMAS	OLD MOLD GLASS ORNAMENTS	SANTAS	95	87	$7.80	$16.00
4014	BURGUNDY SANTA CLAUS	OLD MOLD GLASS ORNAMENTS	SANTAS	94	87	$13.95	$14.00
4015	VERY LARGE SANTA HEAD	OLD MOLD GLASS ORNAMENTS	SANTAS	95	87	$13.95	$14.00
4017	SANTA IN AIRPLANE	OLD MOLD GLASS ORNAMENTS	SANTAS	95	87	$13.90	$14.50
4018	SANTA ABOVE BALL	OLD MOLD GLASS ORNAMENTS	SANTAS	95	87	$13.95	$14.00
4019	OLD-FASHIONED SANTA	OLD MOLD GLASS ORNAMENTS	SANTAS	95	87	$5.75	$6.00
4020	ST. NICHOLAS	OLD MOLD GLASS ORNAMENTS	SANTAS	95	89	$10.00	$11.00
4021	VICTORIAN SANTA	OLD MOLD GLASS ORNAMENTS	SANTAS	95	89	$8.45	$8.50
4026	WHITE CLIP-ON SANTA	OLD MOLD GLASS ORNAMENTS	SANTAS	95	90	$7.25	$10.00
4028	BLUE VICTORIAN ST. NICHOLAS	OLD MOLD GLASS ORNAMENTS	SANTAS	93	90	$9.95	$14.00
4029	LT. BLUE ST. NICHOLAS	OLD MOLD GLASS ORNAMENTS	SANTAS	94	90	$6.50	$9.90
4030	CLIP-ON VICTORIAN ST. NICHOLAS	OLD MOLD GLASS ORNAMENTS	SANTAS	95	90	$11.00	$11.00
403223	FATHER CHRISTMAS HEAD	OLD MOLD GLASS ORNAMENTS	SANTAS	94	85	$7.80	$10.00
403224	FATHER CHRISTMAS WITH BASKET	OLD MOLD GLASS ORNAMENTS	SANTAS	94	85	$7.80	$10.00
4034	WEIHNACTSMANN	OLD MOLD GLASS ORNAMENTS	SANTAS	95	90	$9.00	$8.95
4035	ROUND JOLLY SANTA HEAD	OLD MOLD GLASS ORNAMENTS	SANTAS	95	90	$11.00	$12.00
4043	VICTORIAN SCRAP SANTA	OLD MOLD GLASS ORNAMENTS	SANTAS	93	90	$9.50	$15.00
4066	LG. FATHER CHRISTMAS HEAD	OLD MOLD GLASS ORNAMENTS	SANTAS	95	92	$22.50	$24.00
406912	SANTA IN CHIMNEY	OLD MOLD GLASS ORNAMENTS	SANTAS	89	85	$11.00	$17.00
4201	STAR PATTERN REFLECTOR	OLD MOLD GLASS ORNAMENTS	REFLECTORS	94	85	$9.25	$14.00
4202	PINK REFLECTOR	OLD MOLD GLASS ORNAMENTS	REFLECTORS	95	86	$9.50	$9.00
4203	HORSESHOE REFLECTOR	OLD MOLD GLASS ORNAMENTS	REFLECTORS	89	85	$7.80	$14.50
4204	LARGE DROP WITH INDENTS	OLD MOLD GLASS ORNAMENTS	REFLECTORS	95	87	$12.85	$16.50
4206	ASST. REFLECTORS WITH DIAMONDS	OLD MOLD GLASS ORNAMENTS	REFLECTORS	95	90	$9.95	$11.50
4207	ASST. 6CM REFLECTORS	OLD MOLD GLASS ORNAMENTS	REFLECTORS	95	90	$7.00	$7.50
4212	FLOWER IN REFLECTOR	OLD MOLD GLASS ORNAMENTS	REFLECTORS	95	92	$9.25	$10.00
4214	SCRAP SANTA IN REFLECTOR	OLD MOLD GLASS ORNAMENTS	REFLECTORS	93	92	$8.80	$18.00
4215	REFLECTOR WITH TINSEL WIRE	OLD MOLD GLASS ORNAMENTS	REFLECTORS	95	93	$20.00	$19.90
4401	LARGE NUTCRACKER	OLD MOLD GLASS ORNAMENTS	TOYS	95	85	$13.50	$14.00
4402	SMALL NUTCRACKER	OLD MOLD GLASS ORNAMENTS	TOYS	95	85	$10.00	$10.00
4403	DUMB-DUMB	OLD MOLD GLASS ORNAMENTS	TOYS	88	85	$6.45	$23.50
4405	NUTCRACKER GUARD	OLD MOLD GLASS ORNAMENTS	TOYS	95	87	$8.50	$9.00
4409	LARGE DOLL BUGGY WITH DOLL	OLD MOLD GLASS ORNAMENTS	TOYS	95	91	$11.50	$12.00
4413	BOWLING PIN	OLD MOLD GLASS ORNAMENTS	TOYS	95	94	$12.75	$12.75
4437138	DOLL BUGGY WITH DOLL	OLD MOLD GLASS ORNAMENTS	TOYS	94	85	$7.00	$8.50
443793	MATTE DICE	OLD MOLD GLASS ORNAMENTS	TOYS	95	85	$5.75	$6.00
446836	SMALL CAROUSEL	OLD MOLD GLASS ORNAMENTS	TOYS	95	85	$7.00	$7.00
4601	ROLLS ROYCE	OLD MOLD GLASS ORNAMENTS	TRANSPORTATION	89	85	$8.00	$24.00
4602	CABLE CAR	OLD MOLD GLASS ORNAMENTS	TRANSPORTATION	89	87	$8.45	$26.00
4605	LARGE ZEPPELIN	OLD MOLD GLASS ORNAMENTS	TRANSPORTATION	95	90	$8.00	$9.50
4609	RACE CAR	OLD MOLD GLASS ORNAMENTS	TRANSPORTATION	95	91	$7.00	$7.00
461067	CABLE CAR	OLD MOLD GLASS ORNAMENTS	TRANSPORTATION	88	85	$15.00	$24.50
961069	LOCOMOTIVE	OLD MOLD GLASS ORNAMENTS	TRANSPORTATION	93	85	$7.00	$17.00
463747	OLD-FASHIONED CAR	OLD MOLD GLASS ORNAMENTS	TRANSPORTATION	89	85	$6.25	$23.50
4802	LG. MAUVE & CHAMPAGNE CONE	OLD MOLD GLASS ORNAMENTS	TREES & CONES	93	87	$11.85	$17.00
483612	VERY LG. RED & GOLD CONES	OLD MOLD GLASS ORNAMENTS	TREES & CONES	95	85	$7.00	$7.00
486712-5	MED. GOLD CONE WITH GLITTER	OLD MOLD GLASS ORNAMENTS	TREES & CONES	95	85	$3.85	$4.00
5002	BLUE SANTA	OLD MOLD GLASS ORNAMENTS	TREE TOPS	95	85	$37.50	$38.00
5007	ANGEL TREE TOP WITH CROWN	OLD MOLD GLASS ORNAMENTS	TREE TOPS	93	87	$50.00	$70.00
5008	SANTA IN INDENT TREE TOP	OLD MOLD GLASS ORNAMENTS	TREE TOPS	95	87	$25.00	$25.00
5009	ANGEL IN INDENT TREE TOP	OLD MOLD GLASS ORNAMENTS	TREE TOPS	95	87	$27.00	$27.00
5062-66	FANCY GOLD SPIRE WITH BELLS	OLD MOLD GLASS ORNAMENTS	TREE TOPS	93	85	$31.00	$45.00
5062-69	FANCY RED SPIRE WITH BELLS	OLD MOLD GLASS ORNAMENTS	TREE TOPS	93	85	$31.00	$45.00
5202	DOLL HEAD LIGHT COVER	OLD MOLD GLASS ORNAMENTS	LIGHT COVERS	93	93	$5.65	$10.00
5203	PEACOCK	OLD MOLD GLASS ORNAMENTS	LIGHT COVERS	93	93	$5.65	$11.00
5251	SUGAR STRAWBERRY LIGHT COVER	OLD MOLD GLASS ORNAMENTS	LIGHT COVERS	93	93	$5.65	$8.00
5253	SUGAR PLUM LIGHT COVER	OLD MOLD GLASS ORNAMENTS	LIGHT COVERS	93	93	$5.65	$8.00
5256	SUGAR FRUIT BASKET LIGHT COVER	OLD MOLD GLASS ORNAMENTS	LIGHT COVERS	94	93	$5.65	$8.00
5270	FROSTY SNOWMAN LIGHT COVER	OLD MOLD GLASS ORNAMENTS	LIGHT COVERS	93	93	$5.65	$9.00
5271	FROSTY CONE LIGHT COVER	OLD MOLD GLASS ORNAMENTS	LIGHT COVERS	94	93	$5.65	$8.00
5272	FROSTY ICICLE	OLD MOLD GLASS ORNAMENTS	LIGHT COVERS	93	93	$5.65	$8.00
5275	ASSORTED FROSTY BELL LIGHT COVER	OLD MOLD GLASS ORNAMENTS	LIGHT COVERS	93	93	$5.50	$8.00
5276	FROSTY ACORN LIGHT COVER	OLD MOLD GLASS ORNAMENTS	LIGHT COVERS	94	93	$5.65	$8.00
5277	FROSTY RED ROSE LIGHT COVER	OLD MOLD GLASS ORNAMENTS	LIGHT COVERS	93	93	$5.65	$9.50
529001-3	STANDING SANTA LIGHT COVER	OLD MOLD GLASS ORNAMENTS	LIGHT COVERS	87	84	$3.00	$10.00
529001-4	MRS. CLAUS LIGHT COVER	OLD MOLD GLASS ORNAMENTS	LIGHT COVERS	86	84	$1.60	$12.00
529001-1	GNOME LIGHT GOVER	OLD MOLD GLASS ORNAMENTS	LIGHT COVERS	86	84	$1.60	$8.00
529001-5	CLOWN LIGHT COVER	OLD MOLD GLASS ORNAMENTS	LIGHT COVERS	86	84	$1.60	$12.00
529001-3	BEAR LIGHT COVER	OLD MOLD GLASS ORNAMENTS	LIGHT COVERS	87	84	$2.50	$12.00
529001-5	ELEPHANT LIGHT COVER	OLD MOLD GLASS ORNAMENTS	LIGHT COVERS	87	84	$1.60	$10.00
529003	ASSORTED ANIMALS, SET/6	OLD MOLD GLASS ORNAMENTS	LIGHT COVERS	87	84	$10.50	$48.00
529003-2	OWL LIGHT COVER	OLD MOLD GLASS ORNAMENTS	LIGHT COVERS	87	84	$1.60	$10.00
519003-6	PEACOCK LIGHT COVER	OLD MOLD GLASS ORNAMENTS	LIGHT COVERS	87	84	$2.70	$10.00
529003-5	HEDGEHOG LIGHT COVER	OLD MOLD GLASS ORNAMENTS	LIGHT COVERS	87	84	$1.60	$13.00
529003-1	FLOWER BASKET LIGHT COVER	OLD MOLD GLASS ORNAMENTS	LIGHT COVERS	87	84	$1.60	$13.00
529005	ASSORTED FIGURALS SET/5	OLD MOLD GLASS ORNAMENTS	LIGHT COVERS	87	84	$10.25	$54.00
529005-4	SANTA HEAD LIGHT COVER	OLD MOLD GLASS ORNAMENTS	LIGHT COVERS	87	84	$2.70	$12.00
529005-2	HOUSE LIGHT COVER	OLD MOLD GLASS ORNAMENTS	LIGHT COVERS	87	84	$1.60	$12.00
529005-3	CAROUSEL LIGHT COVER	OLD MOLD GLASS ORNAMENTS	LIGHT COVERS	87	84	$2.70	$12.00
529005-5	SANTA ON HEART LIGHT COVER	OLD MOLD GLASS ORNAMENTS	LIGHT COVERS	87	84	$3.00	$10.00
529005-6	CHURCH ON BALL LIGHT COVER	OLD MOLD GLASS ORNAMENTS	LIGHT COVERS	87	84	$2.50	$12.00
529007-1	3 MEN IN A TUB LIGHT COVER	OLD MOLD GLASS ORNAMENTS	LIGHT COVERS	86	84	$1.75	$12.00
529007-3	QUEEN OF HEARTS LIGHT COVER	OLD MOLD GLASS ORNAMENTS	LIGHT COVERS	86	84	$2.70	$12.50
529007-5	L'IL BOY BLUE LIGHT COVER	OLD MOLD GLASS ORNAMENTS	LIGHT COVERS	86	84	$1.60	$13.00
529009-2	RED RIDING HOOD LIGHT COVER	OLD MOLD GLASS ORNAMENTS	LIGHT COVERS	88	85	$1.60	$110.00
529009-1	CLOWN HEAD LIGHT COVER	OLD MOLD GLASS ORNAMENTS	LIGHT COVERS	88	85	$1.60	$10.50
529009	ASSORTED HEADS SET/6	OLD MOLD GLASS ORNAMENTS	LIGHT COVERS	88	85	$10.25	$55.00
529009-3	SANTA HEAD LIGHT COVER	OLD MOLD GLASS ORNAMENTS	LIGHT COVERS	88	85	$3.00	$10.50

Order No.	Title	Type	Theme	Retired	Intro. Year	Retial Price	Secondary Price
529009-4	DOLL HEAD LIGHT COVER	OLD MOLD GLASS ORNAMENTS	LIGHT COVERS	88	85	$1.60	$10.00
529009-5	FATHER CHRISTMAS LIGHT COVER	OLD MOLD GLASS ORNAMENTS	LIGHT COVERS	89	85	$3.00	$8.00
529009-6	L'IL RASCAL HEAD LIGHT COVER	OLD MOLD GLASS ORNAMENTS	LIGHT COVERS	88	85	$1.60	$12.00
529011-1	PEAR LIGHT COVER	OLD MOLD GLASS ORNAMENTS	LIGHT COVERS	89	85	$3.00	$9.00
529011	ASSORTED FRUIT SET/6	OLD MOLD GLASS ORNAMENTS	LIGHT COVERS	89	85	$20.00	$48.00
529011-3	GRAPES LIGHT COVER	OLD MOLD GLASS ORNAMENTS	LIGHT COVERS	89	85	$3.00	$8.00
529011-4	PINEAPPLE LIGHT COVER	OLD MOLD GLASS ORNAMENTS	LIGHT COVERS	89	85	$3.00	$10.00
529011-5	APPLE LIGHT COVER	OLD MOLD GLASS ORNAMENTS	LIGHT COVERS	89	85	$3.00	$10.00
529011-6	ORANGE LIGHT COVER	OLD MOLD GLASS ORNAMENTS	LIGHT COVERS	88	85	$3.00	$7.00
529013-2	SOLDIER WITH GUN LIGHT COVER	OLD MOLD GLASS ORNAMENTS	LIGHT COVERS	88	85	$2.70	$10.00
529013-1	SOLDIER WITH DRUM LIGHT COVER	OLD MOLD GLASS ORNAMENTS	LIGHT COVERS	88	85	$2.70	$10.00
529013	SOLDIER SET/6	OLD MOLD GLASS ORNAMENTS	LIGHT COVERS	88	85	$17.95	$65.00
529013-3	KING LIGHT COVER	OLD MOLD GLASS ORNAMENTS	LIGHT COVERS	88	85	$2.70	$12.00
529015-3	SANTA WITH TREE LIGHT COVER	OLD MOLD GLASS ORNAMENTS	LIGHT COVERS	92	85	$3.00	$10.00
529015	ASSORTED SANTA SET/6	OLD MOLD GLASS ORNAMENTS	LIGHT COVERS	92	85	$20.00	$55.00
529015-6	ROLY-POLY SANTA LIGHT COVER	OLD MOLD GLASS ORNAMENTS	LIGHT COVERS	89	85	$3.00	$12.00
529017-4	NUTCRACKER LIGHT COVER	OLD MOLD GLASS ORNAMENTS	LIGHT COVERS	89	85	$2.70	$10.00
529017-1	CLARA-THE DOLL LIGHT COVER	OLD MOLD GLASS ORNAMENTS	LIGHT COVERS	89	85	$2.70	$10.00
529017	NUTCRACKER SUITE SET/6	OLD MOLD GLASS ORNAMENTS	LIGHT COVERS	89	85	$19.00	$55.00
529017-3	MARIE-THE GIRL LIGHT COVER	OLD MOLD GLASS ORNAMENTS	LIGHT COVERS	89	85	$2.70	$12.00
529017-6	SUGAR PLUM FAIRY LIGHT COVER	OLD MOLD GLASS ORNAMENTS	LIGHT COVERS	89	85	$2.70	$10.00
529019	TRANSPORTATION SET	OLD MOLD GLASS ORNAMENTS	LIGHT COVERS	88	85	$17.90	$58.00
529019-3	AUTOMOBILE LIGHT COVER	OLD MOLD GLASS ORNAMENTS	LIGHT COVERS	88	85	$2.70	$12.00
529019-4	LOCOMOTIVE LIGHT COVER	OLD MOLD GLASS ORNAMENTS	LIGHT COVERS	88	85	$2.70	$12.00
529019-1	TUGBOAT LIGHT COVER	OLD MOLD GLASS ORNAMENTS	LIGHT COVERS	88	85	$2.70	$12.00
529019-2	BALLOON LIGHT COVER	OLD MOLD GLASS ORNAMENTS	LIGHT COVERS	88	85	$2.70	$12.50
529020-6	SCHOOL BUS LIGHT COVER	OLD MOLD GLASS ORNAMENTS	LIGHT COVERS	91	85	$2.70	$13.00
529020-5	CABLE CAR LIGHT COVER	OLD MOLD GLASS ORNAMENTS	LIGHT COVERS	88	85	$2.70	$12.00
529023-3	SANTA ON BELL LIGHT COVER	OLD MOLD GLASS ORNAMENTS	LIGHT COVERS	90	86	$3.95	$12.50
529023-4	ROCKING HORSE ON BELL LIGHT COVER	OLD MOLD GLASS ORNAMENTS	LIGHT COVERS	90	86	$3.95	$9.00
529023-2	TEDDY BEAR LIGHT COVER	OLD MOLD GLASS ORNAMENTS	LIGHT COVERS	90	86	$3.95	$10.00
529023	ASSORTED BELLS SET/6	OLD MOLD GLASS ORNAMENTS	LIGHT COVERS	93	86	$22.50	$48.00
529023-1	TREE ON BELL LIGHT COVER	OLD MOLD GLASS ORNAMENTS	LIGHT COVERS	91	86	$3.95	$9.00
529023-5	ANGEL ON BELL LIGHT COVER	OLD MOLD GLASS ORNAMENTS	LIGHT COVERS	91	86	$4.00	$11.25
529023-6	NUTCRACKER ON BELL LIGHT COVER	OLD MOLD GLASS ORNAMENTS	LIGHT COVERS	93	86	$3.95	$10.00
529031	ASSORTED EASTER EGGS	OLD MOLD GLASS ORNAMENTS	LIGHT COVERS	93	86	$3.00	$8.00
529033-3	CHICK LIGHT COVER	OLD MOLD GLASS ORNAMENTS	LIGHT COVERS	93	86	$3.60	$8.00
529033-2	RABBIT IN EGG LIGHT COVER	OLD MOLD GLASS ORNAMENTS	LIGHT COVERS	93	86	$3.60	$10.00
529033-1	HEN IN BASKET LIGHT COVER	OLD MOLD GLASS ORNAMENTS	LIGHT COVERS	93	86	$3.60	$8.00
529033-6	BUNNY IN BASKET LIGHT COVER	OLD MOLD GLASS ORNAMENTS	LIGHT COVERS	93	86	$3.60	$8.00
529033-5	CHICK IN EGG LIGHT COVER	OLD MOLD GLASS ORNAMENTS	LIGHT COVERS	93	86	$3.60	$8.00
529041-2	TEDDY BEAR WITH RED HEART	OLD MOLD GLASS ORNAMENTS	LIGHT COVERS	92	86	$3.95	$8.00
529041-4	TEDDY BEAR WITH NIGHT SHIRT	OLD MOLD GLASS ORNAMENTS	LIGHT COVERS	94	86	$3.95	$9.00
529041-3	TEDDY BEAR WITH TREE	OLD MOLD GLASS ORNAMENTS	LIGHT COVERS	92	86	$3.95	$10.00
529041	TEDDY BEARS SET/6	OLD MOLD GLASS ORNAMENTS	LIGHT COVERS	91	86	$25.00	$55.00
529041-1	TEDDY BEARS WITH CANDY CANE	OLD MOLD GLASS ORNAMENTS	LIGHT COVERS	92	86	$3.95	$8.00
529043-1	ASSORTED ALPHABET BLOCKS	OLD MOLD GLASS ORNAMENTS	LIGHT COVERS	91	86	$5.00	$12.50
529045-4	ASSORTED PEACH ROSES	OLD MOLD GLASS ORNAMENTS	LIGHT COVERS	90	86	$4.00	$27.00
529045-2	ASSORTED YELLOW ROSES	OLD MOLD GLASS ORNAMENTS	LIGHT COVERS	90	86	$4.00	$9.50
529045	ASSORTED ROSES SET/6	OLD MOLD GLASS ORNAMENTS	LIGHT COVERS	91	86	$23.00	$49.00
529047-3	BLUE FATHER CHRISTMAS	OLD MOLD GLASS ORNAMENTS	LIGHT COVERS	92	86	$3.95	$13.00
529047-1	RED FATHER CHRISTMAS	OLD MOLD GLASS ORNAMENTS	LIGHT COVERS	92	86	$3.95	$12.00
529047-2	GREEN FATHER CHRISTMAS	OLD MOLD GLASS ORNAMENTS	LIGHT COVERS	92	86	$3.95	$13.00
529047	FATHER CHRISTMAS SET	OLD MOLD GLASS ORNAMENTS	LIGHT COVERS	92	86	$25.00	$49.00
529047-4	RED FATHER CHRISTMAS	OLD MOLD GLASS ORNAMENTS	LIGHT COVERS	92	86	$3.95	$12.00
529047-6	PURPLE FATHER CHRISTMAS	OLD MOLD GLASS ORNAMENTS	LIGHT COVERS	92	86	$3.95	$12.00
529047-5	WHITE FATHER CHRISTMAS	OLD MOLD GLASS ORNAMENTS	LIGHT COVERS	92	86	$3.95	$12.00
529049-2	TURKEY LIGHT COVER	OLD MOLD GLASS ORNAMENTS	LIGHT COVERS	92	88	$3.95	$8.00
529049	THANKSGIVING SET/6 LIGHT COVERS	OLD MOLD GLASS ORNAMENTS	LIGHT COVERS	92	88	$25.00	$55.00
529049-3	PILGRIM BOY LIGHT COVER	OLD MOLD GLASS ORNAMENTS	LIGHT COVERS	92	88	$3.95	$12.00
529049-4	PILGRIM GIRL LIGHT COVER	OLD MOLD GLASS ORNAMENTS	LIGHT COVERS	92	88	$3.95	$12.00
529051-1	DRUM LIGHT COVER	OLD MOLD GLASS ORNAMENTS	LIGHT COVERS	92	88	$3.95	$9.00
529051	TOY SET/6 LIGHT COVER	OLD MOLD GLASS ORNAMENTS	LIGHT COVERS	92	88	$25.00	$59.00
529051-2	DOLL LIGHT COVER	OLD MOLD GLASS ORNAMENTS	LIGHT COVERS	93	88	$3.95	$10.00
529051-3	STOCKING LIGHT COVER	OLD MOLD GLASS ORNAMENTS	LIGHT COVERS	92	88	$3.95	$10.00
529051-5	TEDDY BEAR LIGHT COVER	OLD MOLD GLASS ORNAMENTS	LIGHT COVERS	92	88	$3.95	$9.00
529051-6	CLOWN LIGHT COVER	OLD MOLD GLASS ORNAMENTS	LIGHT COVERS	91	88	$3.95	$9.00
529053	CHRISTMAS CAROL LIGHT COVER	OLD MOLD GLASS ORNAMENTS	LIGHT COVERS	91	88	$25.00	$55.00
529055-1	ASSORTED FAST FOOD LIGHT COVER	OLD MOLD GLASS ORNAMENTS	LIGHT COVERS	91	88	$4.00	$12.25
529057-1	ASSORTED BIRD LIGHT COVER	OLD MOLD GLASS ORNAMENTS	LIGHT COVERS	90	88	$4.00	$9.25
529201	SIX RED & WHITE HEARTS	OLD MOLD GLASS ORNAMENTS	LIGHT COVERS	89	85	$15.00	$16.50
529201-3	PINK HEART LIGHT COVER	OLD MOLD GLASS ORNAMENTS	LIGHT COVERS	89	85	$2.85	$10.00
529201-1	RED HEART LIGHT COVER	OLD MOLD GLASS ORNAMENTS	LIGHT COVERS	90	85	$2.85	$9.00
529201-2	WHITE HEART LIGHT COVER	OLD MOLD GLASS ORNAMENTS	LIGHT COVERS	89	85	$2.85	$12.00
529209-1	ASSORTED FIR CONES LIGHT CONES	OLD MOLD GLASS ORNAMENTS	LIGHT COVERS	91	85	$3.00	$8.00
529301-1	ASSORTED SEA SHELL LIGHT COVERS	OLD MOLD GLASS ORNAMENTS	LIGHT COVERS	92	89	$3.50	$12.00
529303-2	SQUIRREL LIGHT COVER	OLD MOLD GLASS ORNAMENTS	LIGHT COVERS	94	89	$6.45	$9.00
529303-1	PANDA LIGHT COVER	OLD MOLD GLASS ORNAMENTS	LIGHT COVERS	94	89	$6.45	$10.00
529303-3	KITTEN LIGHT COVER	OLD MOLD GLASS ORNAMENTS	LIGHT COVERS	93	89	$6.45	$10.00
529303-5	SWAN LIGHT COVER	OLD MOLD GLASS ORNAMENTS	LIGHT COVERS	94	89	$6.45	$12.50
529305	SIX SNOWMAN LIGHT COVERS	OLD MOLD GLASS ORNAMENTS	LIGHT COVERS	93	93	$29.00	$55.00
5283	TEDDY BEAR WITH VEST	OLD MOLD GLASS ORNAMENTS	LIGHT COVERS			$3.95	$7.00
5285	WISE OWL	OLD MOLD GLASS ORNAMENTS	LIGHT COVERS				$150.00
5289	SNOWMAN	OLD MOLD GLASS ORNAMENTS	LIGHT COVERS			$2.50	$10.00
5293	BUNNY	OLD MOLD GLASS ORNAMENTS	LIGHT COVERS			$3.60	$10.50
5296	FROG	OLD MOLD GLASS ORNAMENTS	LIGHT COVERS			$6.45	$10.00
5298	CLEAR ICICLE	OLD MOLD GLASS ORNAMENTS	LIGHT COVERS			$20.00	$48.00
529201	ASSORTED SNOWMEN	OLD MOLD GLASS ORNAMENTS	LIGHT COVERS			$5.60	$10.00
5312	JOLLY SANTA HEAD	OLD MOLD GLASS ORNAMENTS	LIGHT COVERS			$5.50	$16.00
5316	EAR OF CORN	OLD MOLD GLASS ORNAMENTS	LIGHT COVERS			$3.95	$10.50
5321	STRAWBERRY	OLD MOLD GLASS ORNAMENTS	LIGHT COVERS			$3.00	$10.00
5323	PUPPY	OLD MOLD GLASS ORNAMENTS	LIGHT COVERS			$6.45	$10.00
5325	CORNUCOPIA	OLD MOLD GLASS ORNAMENTS	LIGHT COVERS			$3.95	$10.00

Order No.	Title	Type	Theme	Retired	Intro. Year	Retail Price	Secondary Price
5329	INDIAN CHIEF	OLD MOLD GLASS ORNAMENTS	LIGHT COVERS			$3.95	$10.00
5330	CHRISTMAS TREE	OLD MOLD GLASS ORNAMENTS	LIGHT COVERS			$3.95	$9.00
2836	STRAWBERRY CLUSTER	OLD MOLD GLASS ORNAMENTS	FRUITS & VEGTABLES	90	90	$5.25	$6.00
2841	LARGE STRAWBERRY WITH FLOWER	OLD MOLD GLASS ORNAMENTS	FRUITS & VEGTABLES		90	$10.50	$13.00
4047	ALPINE SANTA	OLD MOLD GLASS ORNAMENTS	SANTAS	96		$7.00	$7.00
306925	LARGE MATTE RED HEART	OLD MOLD GLASS ORNAMENTS	HEARTS	85	85	$5.25	$5.95
5206	BLUE MAN IN THE MOON	OLD MOLD GLASS ORNAMENTS	LIGHT COVERS	93	93	$5.50	$5.75
5205	CHRISTMAS HOUSE	OLD MOLD GLASS ORNAMENTS	LIGHT COVERS	93	93	$5.50	$5.75
5204	MAN IN THE MOON	OLD MOLD GLASS ORNAMENTS	LIGHT COVERS	93	93	$5.50	$5.75
5254	SUGAR APPLE	OLD MOLD GLASS ORNAMENTS	LIGHT COVERS	93	93	$5.50	$5.75
5252	SUGAR GRAPES	OLD MOLD GLASS ORNAMENTS	LIGHT COVERS	93	93	$5.50	$5.75
5255	SUGAR PEAR	OLD MOLD GLASS ORNAMENTS	LIGHT COVERS	93	93	$5.50	$5.75
5207	SANTA WITH TREE	OLD MOLD GLASS ORNAMENTS	LIGHT COVERS	93	93	$5.50	$5.75
1491	GLASS CHRISTMAS MAIDENS/SET OF 4	OLD MOLD GLASS ORNAMENTS	COLLECTORS CLUB	93	93	$35.00	$97.00
7258	DRESDENER DRUMMER NUTCRACKER	OLD MOLD GLASS ORNAMENTS	COLLECTORS CLUB	93	93	$110.00	$215.00
1492	SANTA IN MOON	OLD MOLD GLASS ORNAMENTS	COLLECTORS CLUB	94	94		$65.00
7284	THE KONIGSEE NUTCRACKER	OLD MOLD GLASS ORNAMENTS	COLLECTORS CLUB	95	95	$125.00	$250.00
1545	THE BAROQUE ANGEL ABOVE	OLD MOLD GLASS ORNAMENTS	COLLECTORS CLUB	96	96	$40.00	$40.00
7211	THE FLAXON SANTA CLAUS	OLD MOLD GLASS ORNAMENTS	COLLECTORS CLUB	96	96	$135.00	$135.00
1554	THE VICTORIAN CHRISTMAS STOCKING	OLD MOLD GLASS ORNAMENTS	COLLECTORS CLUB	96	96		
4812	MULTI-COLORED TREE	OLD MOLD GLASS ORNAMENTS	TREES & CONES	94	90	$5.55	$9.00
1005	WOODLAND SQUIRREL	OLD MOLD GLASS ORNAMENTS	ANIMALS	95	94	$21.00	$21.00
181079	PINK SNOWBIRD	OLD MOLD GLASS ORNAMENTS	BIRDS WITH CLIP	95	85	$7.25	$80.00

PIPKA'S SANTAS

Order No.	Title	Type	Theme	Retired	Intro. Year	Retail Price	Secondary Price
13916	RUSSIAN SANTA	SANTAS	PS - MEMORIES OF CHRISTMAS		97	$90.00	$103.50
13914	SANTA'S SPOTTED GREY	SANTAS	PS - MEMORIES OF CHRISTMAS		97	$90.00	$103.50
13911	NORWEGIAN JULENISSE	SANTAS	PS - MEMORIES OF CHRISTMAS		97	$90.00	$103.50
13912	ST. NICHOLAS	SANTAS	PS - MEMORIES OF CHRISTMAS		97	$90.00	$103.50
13917	POLISH FATHER CHRISTMAS	SANTAS	PS - MEMORIES OF CHRISTMAS		97	$90.00	$103.50
13915	WHERE'S RUDOLPH?	SANTAS	PS - MEMORIES OF CHRISTMAS		97	$90.00	$103.50
13910	'MEMORIES' DISPLAY SIGN	SANTAS	PS - MEMORIES OF CHRISTMAS		96	$35.00	$40.00
13917	POLISH FATHER CHRISTMAS	SANTAS	PS - MEMORIES OF CHRISTMAS		97	$90.00	$107.00
13900	STARCOAT SANTA/SOLD OUT	SANTAS	PS - MEMORIES OF CHRISTMAS		95	$85.00	$98.00
13901	SANTA'S ARK/SOLD OUT	SANTAS	PS - MEMORIES OF CHRISTMAS		95	$85.00	$98.00
13902	MIDNIGHT VISITOR/SOLD OUT	SANTAS	PS - MEMORIES OF CHRISTMAS		95	$85.00	$98.00
13903	GINGERBREAD SANTA/SOLD OUT	SANTAS	PS - MEMORIES OF CHRISTMAS		95	$85.00	$98.00
13904	STAR CATCHER STAR/SOLD OUT	SANTAS	PS - MEMORIES OF CHRISTMAS		95	$85.00	$98.00
13905	CZECHOSLOVAKIAN SANTA/SOLD OUT	SANTAS	PS - MEMORIES OF CHRISTMAS		95	$85.00	$90.00
13906	AUSSIE SANTA & BOOMER/SOLD OUT	SANTAS	PS - MEMORIES OF CHRISTMAS		95	$85.00	$90.00
13907	UKRANIAN SANTA	SANTAS	PS - MEMORIES OF CHRISTMAS		95	$85.00	$90.00
13908	GOOD NEWS SANTA	SANTAS	PS - MEMORIES OF CHRISTMAS		95	$85.00	$90.00
13909	STORYTIME SANTA	SANTAS	PS - MEMORIES OF CHRISTMAS		95	$85.00	$90.00
11300	MIDNIGHT VISITOR	SANTAS	PS - REFLECTIONS OF CHRISTMAS		97	$39.95	$46.00
11301	CZECHOSLOVAKIAN SANTA	SANTAS	PS - REFLECTIONS OF CHRISTMAS		97	$39.95	$46.00
11302	STARCOAT SANTA	SANTAS	PS - REFLECTIONS OF CHRISTMAS		97	$39.95	$46.00
11303	STAR CATCHER SANTA	SANTAS	PS - REFLECTIONS OF CHRISTMAS		97	$39.95	$46.00
11304	BETTER WATCH OUT SANTA	SANTAS	PS - REFLECTIONS OF CHRISTMAS		97	$39.95	$46.00
11305	AMISH COUNTRY SANTA	SANTAS	PS - REFLECTIONS OF CHRISTMAS		97	$39.95	$46.00
11400	MIDNIGHT VISITOR	SANTAS	PS - COLLECTIBLE ORNAMENTS		97	$17.95	$20.50
11401	CZECHOSLOVAKIAN SANTA	SANTAS	PS - COLLECTIBLE ORNAMENTS		97	$17.95	$20.50
11402	STARCOAT SANTA	SANTAS	PS - COLLECTIBLE ORNAMENTS		97	$17.95	$20.50
11403	STAR CATCHER SANTA	SANTAS	PS - COLLECTIBLE ORNAMENTS		97	$17.95	$20.50
11404	AUSSIE SANTA & BOOMER	SANTAS	PS - COLLECTIBLE ORNAMENTS		97	$17.95	$20.50
11405	UKRANIAN SANTA	SANTAS	PS - COLLECTIBLE ORNAMENTS		97	$17.95	$20.50
13800	COTTAGE ANGEL	ANGELS	PS - EARTH ANGELS		96	$85.00	$98.00
13801	ANGLE OF HEARTS	ANGELS	PS - EARTH ANGELS		96	$85.00	$98.00
13802	GARDENING ANGEL	ANGELS	PS - EARTH ANGELS		96	$85.00	$98.00
13803	MESSENGER ANGEL	ANGELS	PS - EARTH ANGELS		97	$85.00	$98.00
13804	ANGEL OF ROSES	ANGELS	PS - EARTH ANGELS		97	$85.00	$98.00
13805	GUARDIAN ANGEL	ANGELS	PS - EARTH ANGELS		97	$85.00	$98.00
13806	ANGEL GATE SIGN	ANGELS	PS - EARTH ANGELS		96	$35.00	$40.25

POLONAISE

Order No.	Title	Type	Theme	Retired	Intro. Year	Retail Price	Secondary Price
GP301	SMALL CLOWN	POLONAISE	PN - CLOWNS	YES		$13.50	$40.00
GP302	CLOWN ON BALL	POLONAISE	PN - CLOWNS	YES		$22.50	$35.00
GP435	WIZARD OF OZ'S SCARECROW	POLONAISE	PN - WIZARD OF OZ			$22.50	$25.00
GP436	WIZARD OF OZ'S TINMAN	POLONAISE	PN - WIZARD OF OZ			$22.50	$25.00
GP442	SANTA	POLONAISE	PN - SANTAS			$22.50	$25.00
GP443	CATW/BOW 2A	POLONAISE	PN - CAT & MOUSE			$22.50	$23.00
GP447	LOCOMOTIVE	POLONAISE	PN - TRAINS			$27.50	$28.00
GP453	GLASS EAGLE	POLONAISE	PN - FEATHER FRIENDS			$29.95	$28.00
GP454	GLASS SANTA MOON	POLONAISE	PN - NIGHT AND DAY			$27.50	$28.00
GP458	CRECHE	POLONAISE	PN - HOLY FAMILY			$27.50	$28.00
GP460	CLOWN HEAD	POLONAISE	PN - CLOWNS			$22.50	$25.00
GP461	CHRISTMAS TREE	POLONAISE	PN - OTHER			$24.95	$25.00
GP462	COWBOY HEAD	POLONAISE	PN - THE AMERICAN WEST			$29.95	
GP463	INDIAN CHIEF	POLONAISE	PN - THE AMERICAN WEST			$29.95	$30.00
GP464	GLASS ELEPHANT	POLONAISE	PN - HUMPTY DUMPTY & OTHERS			$27.50	$28.00
GP465	HERR DROSSELMEIR	POLONAISE	PN - THE NUTCRACKER SUITE			$29.95	
GP467	PARTRIDGE IN PEAR TREE	POLONAISE	PN - THE 12 DAYS OF CHRISTMAS			$24.95	$34.00
GP469	NOAH'S ARK	POLONAISE	PN - HUMPTY DUMPTY & OTHERS			$27.50	
GP470	GLASS STAR SANTA	POLONAISE	PN - SANTAS			$27.50	$25.00
GP471	TURTLE DOVES	POLONAISE	PN - THE 12 DAYS OF CHRISTMAS			$34.95	
GP473	CARDINAL	POLONAISE	PN - FEATHER FRIENDS			$25.95	$25.00
GP475	GOOSE/WREATH	POLONAISE	PN - FEATHER FRIENDS			$29.95	$30.00
GP476	TUTENKHAMEN	POLONAISE	PN - THE EGYPTIAN COLLECTION			$34.95	
GP477	HUMPTY DUMPTY	POLONAISE	PN - HUMPTY DUMPTY & OTHERS			$29.95	$30.00
GP478	CAT IN BOOT	POLONAISE	PN - CAT & MOUSE			$29.95	$28.00
GP479	SANTA ON GOOSE SLED	POLONAISE	PN - SANTAS			$29.95	$30.00
GP480	GLASS SPHINX	POLONAISE	PN - THE EGYPTIAN COLLECTION			$29.95	

Order No.	Title	Type	Theme	Retired	Intro. Year	Retial Price	Secondary Price
GP482	POL GL EGYPTIAN PRINCESS	POLONAISE	PN - THE EGYPTIAN COLLECTION			$34.95	
GP483	GLASS MUMMY	POLONAISE	PN - THE EGYPTIAN COLLECTION			$34.95	$34.95
GP484	GLASS HORUS	POLONAISE	PN - THE EGYPTIAN COLLECTION			$34.95	$34.95
GP485	GLASS NEFERTITI	POLONAISE	PN - THE EGYPTIAN COLLECTION			$29.95	$33.00
GP487	GLASS CINDERELLA COACH	POLONAISE	PN - CINDERELLA			$34.95	$34.95
GP488	GLASS CINDERELLA	POLONAISE	PN - CINDERELLA			$27.50	$135.00
GP489	PRINCE CHARMING	POLONAISE	PN - CINDERELLA			$27.50	$28.00
GP490	GLASS CINDERELLA SLIPPER	POLONAISE	PN - CINDERELLA			$19.95	
GP492	LITTLE MERMAID	POLONAISE	PN - LITTLE MERMAID			$26.50	
GP494	GLASS SEA HORSE	POLONAISE	PN - LITTLE MERMAID			$24.95	
GP496	KING NEPTUNE	POLONAISE	PN - LITTLE MERMAID			$34.95	$35.00
GP500/4	EGYPT COLLECTION 4P	POLONAISE	PN - THE EGYPTIAN COLLECTION			$100.00	$110.00
GP501	TRAIN SET 5 PCS.	POLONAISE	PN - TRAINS			$125.00	
GP503	4PCS. PETER PAN COLL	POLONAISE	PN - PETER PAN			$125.00	$125.00
GP504	3 PC. HOLY FAMILY	POLONAISE	PN - HOLY FAMILY			$80.00	
GP505	4 PC. WIZARD OF OZ COLLECTION	POLONAISE	PN - WIZARD OF OZ			$125.00	$125.00
GP506	4 PCS. FISH ORNAMENT	POLONAISE	PN - TROPICAL FISH			$110.00	$110.00
GP507	4PC N/C SUITE COLLECTION	POLONAISE	PN - THE NUTCRACKER SUITE			$125.00	$125.00
GP509	BOXED SET OF DICE 2	POLONAISE	PN - OTHER			$55.00	$60.00
GP510	EGYPTIAN COLLECTION 4 PC BOX	POLONAISE	PN - THE EGYPTIAN COLLECTION			$150.00	
GP303	LARGE CLOWN	POLONAISE	PN - CLOWNS	YES		$22.50	$40.00
GP304	KNIGHTS' HELMET W/PLUME	POLONAISE	PN - CHIVALRY	YES		$22.50	
GP312	SNOWMAN W/GLASSES	POLONAISE	PN - LET IT SNOW	YES		$20.00	
GP309	ANGEL	POLONAISE	PN - HOLY FAMILY	YES		$18.00	
GP315	SMALL SANTA'S HEAD	POLONAISE	PN - SANTAS	YES		$13.50	
GP316	ST. NICK	POLONAISE	PN - SANTAS			$28.00	
GP323	PEACOCK ON BALL	POLONAISE	PN - FEATHER FRIENDS	YES		$28.00	
GP324	PEACOCK	POLONAISE	PN - FEATHER FRIENDS	YES		$18.00	
GP326	TURKEY	POLONAISE	PN - FEATHER FRIENDS	YES		$20.00	
GP329	FLYING SPARROW	POLONAISE	PN - FEATHER FRIENDS	YES		$15.50	
GP332	PARROT	POLONAISE	PN - FEATHER FRIENDS	YES		$15.50	
GP333	PUPPY	POLONAISE	PN - OTHER	YES			$16.00
GP338	TEDDY BEAR	POLONAISE	PN - OTHER	YES		$13.50	
GP339	APPLE	POLONAISE	PN - OTHER	YES		$11.00	
GP347	GNOME	POLONAISE	PN - OTHER	YES		$18.00	
GP348	TUTENKHAMEN	POLONAISE	PN - THE EGYPTIAN COLLECTION	YES		$28.00	
GP349	NEFERTITI	POLONAISE	PN - THE EGYPTIAN COLLECTION	YES		$27.50	
GP350	SPHINX	POLONAISE	PN - THE EGYPTIAN COLLECTION	YES		$22.50	
GP355	GOLDEN ROCKING HORSE	POLONAISE	PN - OTHER	YES		$22.50	$75.00
GP359	SPINNER TOP	POLONAISE	PN - OTHER	YES		$9.00	
GP363	WHITE DICE	POLONAISE	PN - OTHER	YES		$18.00	$85.00
GP372	GOLDEN CHERUB HEAD	POLONAISE	PN - OTHER	YES		$18.00	$80.00
GP373	MERLIN	POLONAISE	PN - OTHER	YES		$20.00	$20.00
GP374	LARGE SANTA'S HEAD	POLONAISE	PN - SANTAS			$19.00	
GP377	DOLL	POLONAISE	PN - OTHER	YES		$13.50	$35.00
GP381	ZODIAC SUN	POLONAISE	PN - NIGHT AND DAY	YES		$22.50	$23.00
GP390	CAT W/BALL	POLONAISE	PN - CAT & MOUSE	YES		$18.00	$23.00
GP391	MINNIE MOUSE	POLONAISE	PN - DISNEY	YES		$33.00	$75.00
GP392	MICKEY MOUSE	POLONAISE	PN - DISNEY	95		$33.00	$125.00
GP396	ANGEL WITH/BEAR	POLONAISE	PN - OTHER	YES		$20.00	$37.00
GP397	DINOSAUR/TYRANNOSAURUS	POLONAISE	PN - OTHER	YES		$22.50	$23.00
GP397	DINOSAUR/BRACHIOSAURUS	POLONAISE	PN - OTHER	YES		$22.50	$23.00
GP405	PIERROT CLOWN	POLONAISE	PN - CLOWNS	YES		$18.00	
GP407	SOLDIER	POLONAISE	PN - OTHER	YES			$110.00
GP412	ST. JOSEPH	POLONAISE	PN - HOLY FAMILY			$22.50	
GP413	BLESSED MOTHER	POLONAISE	PN - HOLY FAMILY			$22.50	$23.00
GP414	CHRIST CHILD	POLONAISE	PN - HOLY FAMILY			$20.00	$20.00
GP416	TREASURE CHEST	POLONAISE	PN - OTHER	YES		$20.00	
GP417	SHARK	POLONAISE	PN - HUMPTY DUMPTY & OTHERS	96		$18.00	$18.00
GP419	PETER PAN	POLONAISE	PN - PETER PAN			$22.00	
GP420	CARDINAL	POLONAISE	PN - FEATHER FRIENDS	YES		$18.00	$18.00
GP422	ROMAN CAESAR	POLONAISE	PN - OTHER			$22.00	
GP427	ROMAN CENTURION	POLONAISE	PN - OTHER	YES		$22.00	$22.00
GP446	GRAMOPHONE	POLONAISE	PN - OTHER	YES		$22.50	
GP448	TELEPHONE	POLONAISE	PN - OTHER	YES		$25.00	
GP449	LIGHT BULB	POLONAISE	PN - OTHER	YES		$20.00	
GP450	GLASS CANDLE HOLDER	POLONAISE	PN - OTHER			$20.00	
GP452	ALARM CLOCK	POLONAISE	PN - OTHER	YES		$25.00	$25.00
GP455	HOUSE	POLONAISE	PN - OTHER	YES		$25.00	
GP468	CROCODILE	POLONAISE	PN - PETER PAN	YES		$28.00	$28.00
GP472	DOVE ON BALL	POLONAISE	PN - FEATHER FRIENDS			$25.00	$25.00
GP474	SANTA ICICLE	POLONAISE	PN - SANTAS	YES		$25.00	$42.50
GP495	STINGRAY	POLONAISE	PN - HUMPTY DUMPTY & OTHERS	YES		$28.00	
GP500	EGYPTIAN COLLECTION 14 PCS.	POLONAISE	PN - THE EGYPTIAN COLLECTION	YES		$214.00	$380.00
GP502	ROMAN COLLECTION 7 PCS.	POLONAISE	PN - THE ROMAN EMPIRE COLLECTION	YES		$164.00	$164.00
GP502/4	ROMAN COLLECTION 4 PCS.	POLONAISE	PN - THE ROMAN EMPIRE COLLECTION	YES		$110.00	
GP508	WIZARD OF OZ	POLONAISE	PN - THE ROMAN EMPIRE COLLECTION	YES		$170.00	$275.00
GP511	CINDERELLA COLLECTION 6 PCS.	POLONAISE	PN - CINDERELLA	YES		$190.00	$190.00
GP607	KING BALTHAZAR	POLONAISE	PN - HOLY FAMILY			$31.00	
GP673/SIG	SZLACHCIC	POLONAISE	PN - OTHER	YES	97	$32.50	
GP307	NIGHT & DAY	POLONAISE	PN - NIGHT AND DAY			$19.95	
GP313	SNOWMAN WITH PARCEL	POLONAISE	PN - OTHER			$21.95	
GP317	SANTA	POLONAISE	PN - SANTAS			$21.95	
GP322	GLASS RAGGEDY ANDY	POLONAISE	PN - OTHER		97	$24.95	
GP321	GLASS RAGGEDY ANN	POLONAISE	PN - OTHER			$24.95	$28.00
GP325	GLASS SWAN	POLONAISE	PN - FEATHER FRIENDS			$17.50	$23.00
GP328	GLASS OWL	POLONAISE	PN - FEATHER FRIENDS			$17.50	$20.00
GP351	EGYPTIAN CAT	POLONAISE	PN - THE EGYPTIAN COLLECTION			$27.50	$30.00
GP352	GLASS PYRAMID	POLONAISE	PN - THE EGYPTIAN COLLECTION			$21.95	
GP353	LOCOMOTIVE	POLONAISE	PN - OTHER			$19.95	$20.00
GP354	POLAND TRAIN COACHES/3	POLONAISE	PN - TRAINS			$14.95	
GP356	POLAND GLASS ROCKING HORSE	POLONAISE	PN - TRAINS			$22.50	
GP363/R	GLASS RED DICE	POLONAISE	PN - OTHER			$17.50	

Order No.	Title	Type	Theme	Retired	Intro. Year	Retail Price	Secondary Price
GP365	SANTA GL PILOT	POLONAISE	PN - SANTAS			$34.95	
GP366	BEER GLASS	POLONAISE	PN - SANTAS			$15.95	$18.00
GP367	GLASS SANTA IN CAR	POLONAISE	PN - SANTAS			$34.95	
GP369	GLASS CHURCH	POLONAISE	PN - OTHER			$15.94	$18.00
GP370	POLAND MADONNA W/CHILD	POLONAISE	PN - HOLY FAMILY			$22.50	$23.00
GP371	HOLY FAMILY	POLONAISE	PN - HOLY FAMILY			$27.50	
GP375	BOOT WITH GIFT	POLONAISE	PN - OTHER			$14.95	
GP380	O'FASH AUTO 2/A	POLONAISE	PN - OTHER			$22.50	
GP389A	AFRO AMERICAN SANTA	POLONAISE	PN - SANTAS			$22.50	
GP404	NUTCRACKER	POLONAISE	PN - THE NUTCRACKER SUITE			$19.95	
GP406	MOUSE KING	POLONAISE	PN - THE NUTCRACKER SUITE			$19.95	$20.00
GP408	GLASS CLARA	POLONAISE	PN - THE NUTCRACKER SUITE			$19.95	$20.00
GP409	TROPIC FISH 4/A	POLONAISE	PN - TROPICAL FISH			$22.50	
GP410	TROPICAL FISH 4/A	POLONAISE	PN - TROPICAL FISH			$22.50	
GP429	CARS/ASSORTED	POLONAISE	PN - OTHER			$22.50	
GP415	SAILING SHIP	POLONAISE	PN - PETER PAN			$29.95	$30.00
GP433	WIZARD OF OZ'S LION	POLONAISE	PN - WIZARD OF OZ			$22.50	$23.00
GP434	GLASS DOROTHY	POLONAISE	PN - WIZARD OF OZ			$22.50	
GP512	CINDERELLA COLLECTION 4	POLONAISE	PN - CINDERELLA			$130.00	$134.00
GP513	GLASS LITTLER MERMAID 5P	POLONAISE	PN - LITTLE MERMAID			$165.00	$28.00
GP514	RUSSIAN COLLECTION 5 PC	POLONAISE	PN - RUSSIAN COLLECTION			$180.00	
GP515	EGYPTIAN COLLECTION 4P	POLONAISE	PN - THE EGYPTIAN COLLECTION		97	$150.00	
GP516	GLASS 3 KINGS	POLONAISE	PN - HOLY FAMILY			$120.00	
GP517	COCA COLA BOXED SET 4	POLONAISE	PN - COCA COLA			$135.00	
GP518	WIZARD OF OZ BOXED SET 4 PC	POLONAISE	PN - WIZARD OF OZ			$150.00	
GP519	MEDIEVAL BOXED SET OF 4	BOXED SETS	PN - CHIVALRY			$150.00	
GP520	VATICAN GDN MARY	VATICAN LIBRARY COLLECTION	PN - OTHER			$135.00	
GP521	VATICAN CHERUBIM	VATICAN LIBRARY COLLECTION	PN - OTHER			$150.00	
GP522	ANTIQUE CARS BOX SET 4	POLONAISE	PN - OTHER			$120.00	$124.00
GP534	CHRISTMAS IN POLAND 4 PC.	POLONAISE	PN - OTHER		97	$150.00	
GP538	HANSEL/GRETEL 4 PC.	POLONAISE	PN - HUMPTY DUMPTY & OTHERS		97	$150.00	
GP539	RED RIDING HOOD LIMITED ED.4 PC	POLONAISE	PN - HUMPTY DUMPTY & OTHERS		97	$150.00	
GP543	NAPOLIONIC SOLDIER	POLONAISE	PN - OTHER		97	$150.00	
GP544	LITTLE RED RIDING HOOD 3 PC	POLONAISE	PN - HUMPTY DUMPTY & OTHERS		97	$110.00	
GP545	CIRCUS COLLECTION 5 PC	POLONAISE	PN - OTHER		97	$175.00	$175.00
GP547	ALICE COLLECTION LIMITED ED. 5 PC	POLONAISE	PN - HUMPTY DUMPTY & OTHERS		97	$175.00	
GP548	ALICE COLLECTION 4 PC	POLONAISE	PN - HUMPTY DUMPTY & OTHERS		97	$150.00	
GP550	RAG ANN/ANDY	POLONAISE	PN - HUMPTY DUMPTY & OTHERS		97	$75.00	
GP551	SHERLOCK HOLMES 3 PC. BOX SET	BOXED SETS	PN - HUMPTY DUMPTY & OTHERS		97	$125.00	
GP552	ROYAL SUITE SET 4 PC	POLONAISE	PN - OTHER		97	$110.00	
GP553	NEW COCA COLA SET 3 PC SET	POLONAISE	PN - COCA COLA		97	$130.00	
GP554	TROPICAL FISH 4 PC	POLONAISE	PN - TROPICAL FISH		97	$110.00	
GP555	MGM WIZARD OF OZ 4 PC BOXED SET	BOXED SETS	PN - WIZARD OF OZ		97		
GP555	MGM WIZARD OF OZ 4 PC BOXED SET	BOXED SETS	PN - WIZARD OF OZ		97		
GP556	PEANUTS 3 PC BOX SET	BOXED SETS	PN - PEANUTS		97		
GP557	GONE WITH THE WIND 3 PC BOX SET	BOXED SETS	PN - GONE WITH THE WIND		97		
GP558	SNOW WHITE & 7 DWARFS BOX SET	BOXED SETS	PN - DISNEY				
GP600	GLASS ST. BASIL CATHEDRAL	POLONAISE	PN - OTHER			$34.95	
GP601	GLASS TSAR IVAN	POLONAISE	PN - OTHER			$34.95	
GP602	RUSSIAN WOMAN	POLONAISE	PN - RUSSIAN COLLECTION			$34.95	$35.00
GP603	RUSSIAN BISHOP	POLONAISE	PN - RUSSIAN COLLECTION			$34.95	$35.00
GP604	GLASS COSSACK	POLONAISE	PN - RUSSIAN COLLECTION			$34.95	
GP605	GLASS FIRE ENGINE	POLONAISE	PN - OTHER			$29.95	$30.00
GP606	GLASS WICKED WITCH	POLONAISE	PN - OTHER			$29.95	
GP607	GLASS WICKED WITCH	POLONAISE	PN - OTHER			$29.95	
GP609	3 KINGS ASSORTMENT	POLONAISE	PN - HOLY FAMILY			$29.95	$84.00
GP611	SEVEN DWARFS SET/1 OF 7 PCS.	POLONAISE	PN - DISNEY		97	$29.95	
GP611/23	GLASS 3 ELVES	POLONAISE	PN - OTHER			$29.95	$30.00
GP614	GLASS GIFT BOXES 2	POLONAISE	PN - OTHER			$24.95	
GP615	WINTER BOY OR GIRL	POLONAISE	PN - OTHER			$19.95	$22.50
GP620	GLASS HAT BOXES	POLONAISE	PN - OTHER		97	$27.50	
GP621	GLINDA GOOD WITCH GLASS	POLONAISE	PN - WIZARD OF OZ			$34.95	$32.00
GP622	WIZARD IN BALLOON	POLONAISE	PN - WIZARD OF OZ			$34.95	$35.00
GP623	EMERALD CITY	POLONAISE	PN - WIZARD OF OZ			$29.95	$32.00
GP624	GLASS BETTY BOOP	POLONAISE	PN - HUMPTY DUMPTY & OTHERS			$34.95	
GP625	GLASS STAR SNOWMAN	POLONAISE	PN - OTHER			$29.95	$32.00
GP626	3 FRENCH HENS	POLONAISE	PN - THE 12 DAYS OF CHRISTMAS			$34.95	$33.00
GP630	COCA COLA BEAR	POLONAISE	PN - THE 12 DAYS OF CHRISTMAS			$34.95	$35.00
GP631	COCA COLA BOTTLE	POLONAISE	PN - COCA COLA			$29.95	$30.00
GP632	COCA COLA DISK	POLONAISE	PN - COCA COLA			$24.95	$25.00
GP633	COCA COLA LARGE BOTTLE TOP	POLONAISE	PN - COCA COLA			$24.95	$25.00
GP634	COCA COLA VENDING MACHINE	POLONAISE	PN - COCA COLA			$34.95	$35.00
GP637	JEWELRY BOXES 3/A	POLONAISE	PN - OTHER		97	$15.95	
GP640	MEDIEVAL HORSE	POLONAISE	PN - CHIVALRY			$34.95	
GP641	MEDIEVAL KNIGHT	POLONAISE	PN - CHIVALRY			$34.95	
GP642	MEDIEVAL DRAGON	POLONAISE	PN - CHIVALRY			$34.95	
GP643	MEDIEVAL LADY	POLONAISE	PN - CHIVALRY			$34.95	
GP645	CAVALRY, GUNNER, DRUMMER	POLONAISE	PN - OTHER		97	$29.95	
GP650	VATICAN CHERUB	VATICAN LIBRARY COLLECTION	PN - OTHER			$34.95	
GP651	VATICAN CHERUB BUST	VATICAN LIBRARY COLLECTION	PN - OTHER			$34.95	
GP652	VATICAN DANCE CHERUBS	VATICAN LIBRARY COLLECTION	PN - OTHER			$34.95	
GP653	VATICAN MADONNA/CHILD	VATICAN LIBRARY COLLECTION	PN - OTHER			$34.95	
GP654	VATICAN ROSE RED	VATICAN LIBRARY COLLECTION	PN - OTHER			$34.95	
GP655	VATICAN LILY	VATICAN LIBRARY COLLECTION	PN - OTHER			$34.95	
GP656	VATICAN GLASS EGG	VATICAN LIBRARY COLLECTION	PN - OTHER			$29.95	
GP654/PIV	VATICAN PINK/IV ROSE	VATICAN LIBRARY COLLECTION	PN - OTHER			$34.95	
GP654/R	VATICAN RED ROSE	VATICAN LIBRARY COLLECTION	PN - OTHER			$34.95	
GP657	VATICAN CHERUB EGG PURPLE	VATICAN LIBRARY COLLECTION	PN - OTHER			$29.95	
GP658	VATICAN EGG NOEL	VATICAN LIBRARY COLLECTION	PN - OTHER			$29.95	
GP659	VATICAN PEACE EARTH EGG	VATICAN LIBRARY COLLECTION	PN - OTHER			$29.95	
GP660	GLASS SNOW WHITE	POLONAISE	PN - DISNEY			$29.95	
GP661	GLASS HANDBLOWN WITCH	POLONAISE	PN - OTHER		97	$34.95	
GP662	HANSEL & GRETEL	POLONAISE	PN - HUMPTY DUMPTY & OTHERS		97	$29.95	

Order No.	Title	Type	Theme	Retired	Intro. Year	Retial Price	Secondary Price
GP664	GINGERBREAD HOUSE	POLONAISE	PN - HUMPTY DUMPTY & OTHERS		97	$29.95	
GP665	LITTLE RED RIDING HOOD	POLONAISE	PN - HUMPTY DUMPTY & OTHERS		97	$29.95	
GP666	GLASS THE WOLF	POLONAISE	PN - HUMPTY DUMPTY & OTHERS		97	$34.95	
GP667	GLASS HUNTER	POLONAISE	PN - OTHER		97	$29.95	
GP670	KRAKOW CASTLE	POLONAISE	PN - OTHER		97	$34.95	
GP671	GLASS STAR 3/ASST	POLONAISE	PN - OTHER		97	$19.95	
GP672	GLASS TARTAR PRINCE	POLONAISE	PN - OTHER		97	$34.95	
GP674	GLASS KRAKOW MAN	POLONAISE	PN - OTHER		97	$29.95	
GP675	POLISH MOUNTAIN MAN	POLONAISE	PN - OTHER		97	$29.95	
GP676	GLASS STAR BOY	POLONAISE	PN - OTHER		97	$34.95	
GP677	10MM NY BALL 5/A	POLONAISE	PN - OTHER		97	$24.95	
GP682	GLASS CIOWNS 3A	POLONAISE	PN - OTHER		97	$34.95	
GP688	GLASS CIRCUS SEAL	POLONAISE	PN - OTHER		97	$29.95	
GP689	MAGICIANS HAT	POLONAISE	PN - CIRCUS		97	$34.95	
GP690	CIRCUS STRONGMAN	POLONAISE	PN - CIRCUS		97	$34.95	
GP691	CIRCUS RING MASTER	POLONAISE	PN - CIRCUS		97	$34.95	$35.00
GP692	ALICE IN WONDERLAND	POLONAISE	PN - ALICE IN WONDERLAND		97	$29.95	
GP693	HERALD RABBIT	POLONAISE	PN - ALICE IN WONDERLAND		97	$34.95	
GP695	QUEEN OF HEARTS	POLONAISE	PN - ALICE IN WONDERLAND		97	$34.95	
GP696	GLASS MAD HATTER	POLONAISE	PN - ALICE IN WONDERLAND		97	$34.95	
GP699	GLASS BIG BIRD	POLONAISE	PN - HUMPTY DUMPTY & OTHERS		97	$34.95	
GP800	GOLDEN COCA COLA BOTTLE	POLONAISE	PN - COCA COLA		97	$34.95	
GP801	COLA BEAR SKIING	POLONAISE	PN - COCA COLA		97	$34.95	$35.00
GP802	COLA BEAR SNOWMOBILE	POLONAISE	PN - COCA COLA		97	$34.95	$35.00
GP803	COCA COLA 6 PACK	POLONAISE	PN - COCA COLA		97	$34.95	$35.00
GP805	GONE WITH THE WIND SCARLETT	POLONAISE	PN - GONE WITH THE WIND		97		
GP804	COCA COLA TRUCK	POLONAISE	PN - COCA COLA		97	$37.50	$37.50
GP806	ROYAL SUITE 4/A	POLONAISE	PN - OTHER		97	$29.95	
GP810COL	GRAND FATHER FROST	POLONAISE	PN - OTHER		97	$50.00	
GP811	GLASS SANTA HEAD	POLONAISE	PN - SANTAS		97	$22.50	
GP812	SHERLOCK HOLMES	POLONAISE	PN - HUMPTY DUMPTY & OTHERS		97	$29.95	
GP813	GLASS DR. WATSON	POLONAISE	PN - HUMPTY DUMPTY & OTHERS		97	$29.95	
GP814	ENGLISH BOBBIE	POLONAISE	PN - OTHER		97	$29.95	
GP815	GONE WITH THE WIND RHETT	POLONAISE	PN - GONE WITH THE WIND		97		
GP816	GONE WITH THE WIND TARA	POLONAISE	PN - GONE WITH THE WIND		97		
GP817	BABAR ELEPHANT	POLONAISE	PN - HUMPTY DUMPTY & OTHERS		97		
GP818	MARILYN MONROE	POLONAISE	PN - OTHER		97		
GP819	MGM DOROTHY	POLONAISE	PN - WIZARD OF OZ		97		
GP820	MGM TIN MAN	POLONAISE	PN - WIZARD OF OZ		97		
GP821	MGM COWARDLY LION	POLONAISE	PN - WIZARD OF OZ		97		
GP822	MGM SCARECROW	POLONAISE	PN - WIZARD OF OZ		97		
GP823	SNOOPY PEANUTS	POLONAISE	PN - PEANUTS		97		
GP824	CHARLIE BROWN PEANUTS	POLONAISE	PN - PEANUTS		97		
GP825	LUCY PEANUTS	POLONAISE	PN - PEANUTS		97		
GP826	SMITHSONIAN ASTRONAUT	POLONAISE	PN - OTHER		97		
GP827	GLASS HOLLY BEAR	POLONAISE	PN - OTHER		97		
GP828	FOUR CALLING BIRDS	POLONAISE	PN - THE 12 DAYS OF CHRISTMAS		97		
GP829	JUST MARRIED	POLONAISE	PN - OTHER		97	$22.50	
GP830	MADONNA VATICAN EGG	VATICAN LIBRARY COLLECTION	PN - OTHER		97	$37.50	
			POSSIBLE DREAMS				
713033	CARPENTER SANTA	CLOTHTIQUE SANTAS	SANTAS	92	88	$46.00	
713031	UKKO	CLOTHTIQUE SANTAS	SANTAS	90	87	$40.00	
713030	TRADITIONAL DELUXE SANTA	CLOTHTIQUE SANTAS	SANTAS	90	87	$40.00	
713034	FRONTIER SANTA	CLOTHTIQUE SANTAS	SANTAS	91	88	$44.00	
713036	RUSSIAN ST. NICHOLAS	CLOTHTIQUE SANTAS	SANTAS		88	$45.00	
713035	ST. NICHOLAS	CLOTHTIQUE SANTAS	SANTAS	91	88	$99.00	
713037	WEINACHTSMANN	CLOTHTIQUE SANTAS	SANTAS	91	88	$45.00	
713038	TRADITIONAL SANTA	CLOTHTIQUE SANTAS	SANTAS	92	89	$45.00	$15.00
713042	BABY'S FIRST CHRISTMAS	CLOTHTIQUE SANTAS	SANTAS	92	89	$48.00	$42.00
713039	PELZE NICHOL	CLOTHTIQUE SANTAS	SANTAS	93	89	$49.00	$45.00
713040	SANTA WITH EMBROIDERED COAT	CLOTHTIQUE SANTAS	SANTAS	91	89	$45.00	$40.00
713043	EXHAUSTED SANTA	CLOTHTIQUE SANTAS	SANTAS	92	89	$68.00	$60.00
713041	MRS. CLAUS WITH DOLL	CLOTHTIQUE SANTAS	SANTAS	92	89	$45.00	
713044	WORKBENCH SANTA	CLOTHTIQUE SANTAS	SANTAS	93	90	$75.50	$75.00
713047	SKIING SANTA	CLOTHTIQUE SANTAS	SANTAS	93	90	$68.00	$162.00
713046	HARLEM SANTA	CLOTHTIQUE SANTAS	SANTAS	94	90	$52.50	$50.00
713045	SANTA PLEASE STOP HERE	CLOTHTIQUE SANTAS	SANTAS	92	90	$69.00	$63.00
713048	SANTA WITH BLUE ROBE	CLOTHTIQUE SANTAS	SANTAS	92	90	$52.00	$51.00
713049	1940'S TRADITIONAL SANTA	CLOTHTIQUE SANTAS	SANTAS	94	92	$46.00	$68.00
713054	SANTA ON MOTORBIKE	CLOTHTIQUE SANTAS	SANTAS	94	92	$120.00	$125.00
713050	SANTA ON SLED	CLOTHTIQUE SANTAS	SANTAS	94	92	$79.00	$75.00
713052	NICHOLAS	CLOTHTIQUE SANTAS	SANTAS	95	92	$60.00	$76.00
713058	SANTA ON REINDEER	CLOTHTIQUE SANTAS	SANTAS	95	92	$83.00	$81.00
713056	AFRICAN AMERICAN SANTA	CLOTHTIQUE SANTAS	SANTAS	95	92	$68.00	$65.00
713053	FIREMAN SANTA	CLOTHTIQUE SANTAS	SANTAS		92	$63.00	$60.00
713077	SIBERIAN SANTA	CLOTHTIQUE SANTAS	SANTAS	95	91	$54.00	$50.00
713078	MRS. CLAUS IN WINTER COAT	CLOTHTIQUE SANTAS	SANTAS	95	91	$52.00	$60.00
713075	TRUE SPIRIT OF CHRISTMAS "SILENT NIGHT"	CLOTHTIQUE SANTAS	PD - MUSICAL SANTAS	92	91	$102.00	
713057	ENGINEER SANTA "HERE COMES SANTA CLAUS"	CLOTHTIQUE SANTAS	PD - MUSICAL SANTAS	92	92	$136.00	$130.00
713079	SANTA DECORATING CHRISTMAS TREE	CLOTHTIQUE SANTAS	SANTAS	92	92	$63.00	$60.00
713087	FATHER CHRISTMAS	CLOTHTIQUE SANTAS	SANTAS	95	91	$47.00	$49.00
713091	SANTA ON SLEIGH "HERE COMES SANTA CLAUS"	CLOTHTIQUE SANTAS	PD - MUSICAL SANTAS	95	92	$83.00	$80.00
713095	EUROPEAN SANTA	CLOTHTIQUE SANTAS	SANTAS		93	$48.00	$53.00
713088	KRIS KRINGLE	CLOTHTIQUE SANTAS	SANTAS	93	91	$47.00	$43.00
713076	SANTA IN BED "WHITE CHRISTMAS"	CLOTHTIQUE SANTAS	PD - MUSICAL SANTAS	94	91	$83.00	
713090	SANTA IN ROCKING CHAIR	CLOTHTIQUE SANTAS	SANTAS	95	92	$89.00	
713089	SANTA SHELF SITTER	CLOTHTIQUE SANTAS	SANTAS	95	91	$61.00	$60.00
713097	VICTORIAN SANTA	CLOTHTIQUE SANTAS	SANTAS		93	$58.00	$60.00
713099	SANTA WITH BAG OF GROCERIES	CLOTHTIQUE SANTAS	SANTAS		93	$50.00	$48.00
713096	MAY YOUR WISHES COME TRUE	CLOTHTIQUE SANTAS	STARLIGHT FOUNDATION		93	$53.00	
713102	AFRICAN-AMERICAN SANTA WITH DOLL	CLOTHTIQUE SANTAS	SANTAS		93	$40.00	

Order No.	Title	Type	Theme	Retired	Intro. Year	Retail Price	Secondary Price
713098	HIS FAVORITE COLOR	CLOTHTIQUE SANTAS	SANTAS		93	$48.00	$48.00
713103	THE MODERN SHOPPER	CLOTHTIQUE SANTAS	SANTAS		93	$40.00	$40.00
713110	HOLIDAY FRIEND	CLOTHTIQUE SANTAS	SANTAS		94	$94.00	$55.00
713105	A LONG TRIP	CLOTHTIQUE SANTAS	SANTAS		93	$86.00	
713106	FIREMAN & CHILD	CLOTHTIQUE SANTAS	SANTAS		93	$53.00	$55.00
713111	PLAYMATES	CLOTHTIQUE SANTAS	SANTAS		94	$99.00	$99.00
713108	YULETIDE JOURNEY	CLOTHTIQUE SANTAS	SANTAS		94	$50.00	$56.00
713032	COLONIAL SANTA	CLOTHTIQUE SANTAS	SANTAS	90	87	$40.00	
713026	SANTA WITH PACK	CLOTHTIQUE SANTAS	SANTAS	89	86	$36.50	$60.00
713028	TRADITIONAL SANTA	CLOTHTIQUE SANTAS	SANTAS	89	86	$36.50	$32.00
713109	CHRISTMAS CHEER	CLOTHTIQUE SANTAS	SANTAS		94	$50.00	$59.00
713115	CHRISTMAS IS FOR CHILDREN	CLOTHTIQUE SANTAS	SANTAS		94	$33.00	
713112	A CHRISTMAS GUEST	CLOTHTIQUE SANTAS	PD - MUSICAL SANTAS		94	$71.00	$75.00
713114	A WELCOME VISIT	CLOTHTIQUE SANTAS	SANTAS		94	$54.00	$60.00
713116	OUR HERO	CLOTHTIQUE SANTAS	SANTAS		94	$56.00	$60.00
713118	MRS. CLAUS	CLOTHTIQUE SANTAS	SANTAS		94	$53.00	
713107	GOOD TIDINGS	CLOTHTIQUE SANTAS	SANTAS		94	$47.00	$49.00
713120	BABY'S FIRST NOEL "THE FIRST NOEL"	CLOTHTIQUE SANTAS	PD - MUSICAL SANTAS		94	$60.00	
713117	PUPPY LOVE	CLOTHTIQUE SANTAS	SANTAS		94	$53.00	$50.00
713122	A SPECIAL TREAT	CLOTHTIQUE SANTAS	SANTAS		95	$48.00	$50.00
713121	FINISHING TOUCH	CLOTHTIQUE SANTAS	SANTAS		95	$52.00	$55.00
713127	SOUNDS OF CHRISTMAS	CLOTHTIQUE SANTAS	SANTAS		95	$55.00	$58.00
713123	A MODERN SKIER	CLOTHTIQUE SANTAS	SANTAS		95	$59.50	
713130	FRISKY FRIEND	CLOTHTIQUE SANTAS	SANTAS		95	$44.00	$46.00
713128	HOME SPUN HOLIDAYS	CLOTHTIQUE SANTAS	SANTAS		95	$47.00	$50.00
713124	VICTORIAN PUPPETEER	CLOTHTIQUE SANTAS	SANTAS		95	$49.50	$52.00
713126	THE STOCKINGS WERE HUNG	CLOTHTIQUE SANTAS	SANTAS		95	$60.00	$65.00
713125	VICTORIAN EVERGREEN	CLOTHTIQUE SANTAS	SANTAS		95	$27.00	$49.00
713129	HOOK, LINE AND SANTA	CLOTHTIQUE SANTAS	SANTAS		95	$49.00	$50.00
721002	FATHER CHRISTMAS, ENGLAND	CLOTHTIQUE SANTAS	PD - SIGNATURE SERIES		95	$90.00	$90.00
3003	TRADITIONAL SANTA	CLOTHTIQUE SANTAS	PD - LIMITED EDITION SANTAS	94	89	$250.00	$240.00
3002	KRIS KRINGLE	CLOTHTIQUE SANTAS	PD - LIMITED EDITION SANTAS	92	88	$250.00	$240.00
3000	PATRIOTIC SANTA	CLOTHTIQUE SANTAS	PD - LIMITED EDITION SANTAS	93	88	$250.00	$240.00
3001	FATHER CHRISTMAS	CLOTHTIQUE SANTAS	PD - LIMITED EDITION SANTAS	93	88	$59.50	$240.00
15042	COUNTRY SOUNDS	CLOTHTIQUE SANTAS	PD - AMERICAN ARTIST COLLECTION		95	$72.00	$74.00
15017	FATHER EARTH	CLOTHTIQUE SANTAS	PD - AMERICAN ARTIST COLLECTION		93	$55.00	$77.00
15030	CAPTAIN CLAUS	CLOTHTIQUE SANTAS	PD - AMERICAN ARTIST COLLECTION		94	$69.00	$74.00
15005	A FRIENDLY VISIT	CLOTHTIQUE SANTAS	PD - AMERICAN ARTIST COLLECTION	94	91	$100.00	$103.00
15011	CHRISTMAS COMPANY	CLOTHTIQUE SANTAS	PD - AMERICAN ARTIST COLLECTION	95	92	$77.00	$120.00
15029	THE STORYTELLER	CLOTHTIQUE SANTAS	PD - AMERICAN ARTIST COLLECTION		95	$61.40	$76.00
15028	SPIRIT OF SANTA	CLOTHTIQUE SANTAS	PD - AMERICAN ARTIST COLLECTION		94	$65.00	$65.00
15025	ICE CAPERS	CLOTHTIQUE SANTAS	PD - AMERICAN ARTIST COLLECTION		93	$95.00	$100.00
15010	MUSIC MAKERS	CLOTHTIQUE SANTAS	PD - MUSICAL SANTAS	95	92	$142.00	
15027	A TOUCH OF MAGIC	CLOTHTIQUE SANTAS	PD - AMERICAN ARTIST COLLECTION		94	$64.00	$90.00
15018	EASY PUTT	CLOTHTIQUE SANTAS	PD - AMERICAN ARTIST COLLECTION		93	$110.00	$110.00
15019	THE WORKSHOP	CLOTHTIQUE SANTAS	PD - MUSICAL SANTAS	95	93	$140.00	
15041	A GOOD ROUND	CLOTHTIQUE SANTAS	PD - AMERICAN ARTIST COLLECTION		95	$67.00	$73.00
15006	SANTA'S CUISINE	CLOTHTIQUE SANTAS	PD - AMERICAN ARTIST COLLECTION	94	91	$100.00	$150.00
15038	SANTA AND THE ARK	CLOTHTIQUE SANTAS	PD - AMERICAN ARTIST COLLECTION		95	$69.50	$65.00
15014	HERALDING THE WAY	CLOTHTIQUE SANTAS	PD - AMERICAN ARTIST COLLECTION	95	92	$75.00	$76.00
15020	THE TREE PLANTER	CLOTHTIQUE SANTAS	PD - AMERICAN ARTIST COLLECTION		93	$61.00	$80.00
15044	SUNFLOWER SANTA	CLOTHTIQUE SANTAS	PD - AMERICAN ARTIST COLLECTION		95	$71.00	$75.00
15008	AN ANGEL'S KISS	CLOTHTIQUE SANTAS	PD - AMERICAN ARTIST COLLECTION	95	92	$89.00	$90.00
15032	GIFTS FROM THE GARDEN	CLOTHTIQUE SANTAS	PD - AMERICAN ARTIST COLLECTION		94	$74.00	$74.00
15037	TEDDY LOVE	CLOTHTIQUE SANTAS	PD - AMERICAN ARTIST COLLECTION		94	$75.00	$85.00
15031	THE GENTLE CRAFTSMAN	CLOTHTIQUE SANTAS	PD - AMERICAN ARTIST COLLECTION		94	$70.00	$77.00
15040	RIDING HIGH	CLOTHTIQUE SANTAS	PD - AMERICAN ARTIST COLLECTION		95	$115.00	$115.00
15024	A BRIGHTER DAY	CLOTHTIQUE SANTAS	PD - AMERICAN ARTIST COLLECTION		93	$65.00	$68.00
15003	ALPINE CHRISTMAS	CLOTHTIQUE SANTAS	PD - AMERICAN ARTIST COLLECTION	94	91	$129.00	$133.00
15039	PATCHWORK SANTA	CLOTHTIQUE SANTAS	PD - AMERICAN ARTIST COLLECTION		95	$65.40	$68.00
15026	SANTA AND FEATHERED FRIEND	CLOTHTIQUE SANTAS	PD - AMERICAN ARTIST COLLECTION		94	$74.00	$80.00
15004	TRADITIONS	CLOTHTIQUE SANTAS	PD - AMERICAN ARTIST COLLECTION	94	91	$50.00	$150.00
15007	FATHER CHRISTMAS	CLOTHTIQUE SANTAS	PD - AMERICAN ARTIST COLLECTION	94	91	$250.00	$61.00
15023	JUST SCOOTING ALONG	CLOTHTIQUE SANTAS	PD - AMERICAN ARTIST COLLECTION		93	$71.00	$80.00
15013	OUT OF THE FOREST	CLOTHTIQUE SANTAS	PD - AMERICAN ARTIST COLLECTION	95	92	$63.00	$95.00
15036	SPIRIT OF CHRISTMAS PAST	CLOTHTIQUE SANTAS	PD - AMERICAN ARTIST COLLECTION		94	$56.00	$76.00
15035	CHRISTMAS CALLER	CLOTHTIQUE SANTAS	PD - AMERICAN ARTIST COLLECTION		95	$54.50	$58.00
15009	PEACE ON EARTH	CLOTHTIQUE SANTAS	PD - AMERICAN ARTIST COLLECTION	95	92	$92.00	$103.00
15033	CHRISTMAS SURPRISE	CLOTHTIQUE SANTAS	PD - AMERICAN ARTIST COLLECTION		94	$64.00	$84.00
15016	NATURE'S LOVE	CLOTHTIQUE SANTAS	PD - AMERICAN ARTIST COLLECTION		93	$70.00	$80.00
15015	STRUMMING THE LUTE "O TANNENBAUM"	CLOTHTIQUE SANTAS	PD - MUSICAL SANTAS		93	$60.00	
15034	TEA TIME	CLOTHTIQUE SANTAS	PD - AMERICAN ARTIST COLLECTION		94	$76.00	$86.00
15045	GIVING THANKS	CLOTHTIQUE SANTAS	PD - AMERICAN ARTIST COLLECTION		95	$45.50	$46.00
15002	A PEACEFUL EVE	CLOTHTIQUE SANTAS	PD - AMERICAN ARTIST COLLECTION	94	91	$99.50	$103.00
15000	THE MAGIC OF CHRISTMAS	CLOTHTIQUE SANTAS	PD - AMERICAN ARTIST COLLECTION	94	91	$132.00	$140.00
15012	LIGHTING THE WAY	CLOTHTIQUE SANTAS	PD - AMERICAN ARTIST COLLECTION		92	$89.00	$85.00
15043	SOUTHWEST SANTA	CLOTHTIQUE SANTAS	PD - AMERICAN ARTIST COLLECTION		95	$100.00	$65.00
3602	ROCKWELL PEPSI SANTA	CLOTHTIQUE SANTAS	PD - PEPSI SANTA COLLECTION	94	91	$82.00	
3603	PEPSI SANTA SITTING	CLOTHTIQUE SANTAS	PD - PEPSI SANTA COLLECTION	94	92	$88.00	
3606	JOLLY TRAVELER	CLOTHTIQUE SANTAS	PD - MUSICAL SANTAS	95	95	$90.00	$90.00
3605	HOLIDAY HOST	CLOTHTIQUE SANTAS	PD - PEPSI SANTA COLLECTION		94	$59.00	$62.00
3601	PEPSI COLA SANTA	CLOTHTIQUE SANTAS	PD - PEPSI SANTA COLLECTION		90	$74.00	
3050	CHRISTMAS DEAR SANTA	CLOTHTIQUE SANTAS	PD - SATURDAY EVENING POST COLLECTION	92	89	$189.00	
3051	CHRISTMAS SANTA WITH GLOBE	CLOTHTIQUE SANTAS	PD - SATURDAY EVENING POST COLLECTION	92	89	$105.00	$175.00
3063	SANTA'S HELPERS	CLOTHTIQUE SANTAS	PD - SATURDAY EVENING POST COLLECTION	94	92	$178.00	$179.00
3064	BALANCING THE BUDGET	CLOTHTIQUE SANTAS	PD - SATURDAY EVENING POST COLLECTION		92	$126.00	$125.00
3060	SANTA PLOTTING HIS COURSE	CLOTHTIQUE SANTAS	PD - SATURDAY EVENING POST COLLECTION		91	$168.00	$168.00
3598	SANTA ON THE LADDER	CLOTHTIQUE SANTAS	PD - SATURDAY EVENING POST COLLECTION	95	92	$141.00	$150.00
3599	HUGGING SANTA	CLOTHTIQUE SANTAS	PD - SATURDAY EVENING POST COLLECTION	94	91	$135.00	$150.00
3652	TRADITIONAL SANTA/Smaller	CLOTHTIQUE SANTAS	PD - SATURDAY EVENING POST COLLECTION	92	91	$66.00	$66.00
657136	SANTA WITH LANTERN/SOLD OUT	CRINKLE CLAUS	SANTAS	96	94		
805051	ON A WINTER'S EVE/93-94 CLUB EXCLUSIVE	CLOTHTIQUE SANTAS	PD - SANTA CLAUS NETWORK	94	93	$65.00	$65.00
805052	MARIONETTE SANTA/94-95 CLUB EXCLUSIVE	CLOTHTIQUE SANTAS	PD - SANTA CLAUS NETWORK	95	94	$50.00	$50.00

Order No.	Title	Type	Theme	Retired	Intro. Year	Retial Price	Secondary Price
657137	SLIM LINE SANTA	CRINKLE CLAUS	SANTAS	96	94	$12.00	$12.00
657138	ROLY POLY SANTA	CRINKLE CLAUS	SANTAS	96	94	$12.50	$23.00
657139	SANTA WITH CANDY CANE 5"	CRINKLE CLAUS	SANTAS	96	94	$13.00	$27.00
657140	SANTA WITH STARS	CRINKLE CLAUS	SANTAS	97	94	$14.00	$15.00
657141	SANTA WITH WREATH/SOLD OUT	CRINKLE CLAUS	SANTAS	96	94	$10.00	$17.00
657142	SANTA WITH CANDY CANE 4.5"	CRINKLE CLAUS	SANTAS	97	94	$27.00	$13.00
657224	AMERICAN SANTA 4"	CRINKLE CLAUS	SANTAS			$15.50	$16.00
657225	FOREST SANTA 4 1/4"	CRINKLE CLAUS	SANTAS			$15.50	$15.00
657226	PINE CONE SANTA 4"	CRINKLE CLAUS	SANTAS			$15.50	$16.00
657227	SANTA WITH NOAH'S ARK 4 1/4"	CRINKLE CLAUS	SANTAS			$15.50	$16.00
657229	SANTA WITH LANTERN AND BAG	CRINKLE CLAUS	SANTAS	96	94	$15.50	
657231	SANTA WITH TEDDY BEAR 4"	CRINKLE CLAUS	SANTAS			$16.00	$16.00
657232	SANTA WITH PATCHWORK BAG 6 1/2"	CRINKLE CLAUS	SANTAS			$19.00	$19.00
659001	CRINKLE COUSIN WITH LANTERN 2 3/4"	CRINKLE CLAUS	SANTAS			$15.50	$16.00
659002	CRINKLE COUSIN WITH CLOCK 3"	CRINKLE CLAUS	SANTAS			$15.50	$16.00
659003	CRINKLE COUSIN WITH DOLLS 2 1/2"	CRINKLE CLAUS	SANTAS			$15.50	$16.00
659004	CRINKLE COUSIN WITH CLOWN 2 3/4"	CRINKLE CLAUS	SANTAS			$15.50	$16.00
659005	CRINKLE COUSIN WITH TEDDY 3"	CRINKLE CLAUS	SANTAS			$15.50	$16.00
659006	ROOF TOP SANTA 5"	CRINKLE CLAUS	SANTAS			$28.50	
659007	TIP TOP SANTA	CRINKLE CLAUS	SANTAS	97	95	$23.50	
659008	BELL SHAPE SANTA	CRINKLE CLAUS	SANTAS	97	95	$23.50	
659009	ROLY POLY SANTA	CRINKLE CLAUS	SANTAS	97	95	$23.00	
659010	SANTA WITH BOOK 4"	CRINKLE CLAUS	SANTAS			$13.80	$14.00
659011	SANTA WITH TREE	CRINKLE CLAUS	SANTAS	97	95	$14.20	
659012	JOLLY ST. NICK 3 1/2"	CRINKLE CLAUS	SANTAS			$15.70	$15.00
659016	SANTA PALACE 4"	CRINKLE CLAUS	PD - CRINKLE CLAUS VILLAGE			$15.00	
659017	SANTA CHRISTMAS HOUSE4"	CRINKLE CLAUS	PD - CRINKLE CLAUS VILLAGE			$15.00	$15.00
659018	SANTA FARM HOUSE4"	CRINKLE CLAUS	PD - CRINKLE CLAUS VILLAGE			$15.00	$15.00
659019	SANTA CASTLE 4 1/4"	CRINKLE CLAUS	PD - CRINKLE CLAUS VILLAGE			$15.00	$15.00
659020	SANTA CHURCH 4 1/4"	CRINKLE CLAUS	PD - CRINKLE CLAUS VILLAGE			$15.00	$15.00
659021	SANTA WINDMILL 3 3/4"	CRINKLE CLAUS	PD - CRINKLE CLAUS VILLAGE			$15.00	$15.00
659022	TOP OF THE LIST6 3/4"	CRINKLE CLAUS	SANTAS			$13.20	
659023	HIGH NOTE 6 1/2"	CRINKLE CLAUS	SANTAS			$13.20	
659024	TOP OF THE TREE 6 3/4"	CRINKLE CLAUS	SANTAS			$13.20	
659025	HIGH HO 6 3/4"	CRINKLE CLAUS	SANTAS			$13.20	
659026	HIGHLAND PIPER 2 3/4"	CRINKLE CLAUS	SANTAS			$8.30	
659027	BRITISH JUBILEE 2 3/4"	CRINKLE CLAUS	SANTAS			$8.30	
659029	BAVARIAN CRINKLE 2 3/4"	CRINKLE CLAUS	SANTAS			$8.30	
659028	BRAZILIAN FIESTA 2 3/4"	CRINKLE CLAUS	SANTAS			$10.00	
659030	APALACHIAN LIGHT 2 3/4"	CRINKLE CLAUS	SANTAS			$8.30	
659031	WEST COAST BEAT 2 3/4"	CRINKLE CLAUS	SANTAS			$8.30	
659032	MEDITERRANEAN TREASURE 2 3/4"	CRINKLE CLAUS	SANTAS			$8.30	
659033	LISBON TRAVELER 2 3/4"	CRINKLE CLAUS	SANTAS			$8.30	
659034	HOLIDAY CANE CRINKLE 5 3/4"	CRINKLE CLAUS	SANTAS			$8.30	
659035	FLICKERING CRINKLE 5 1/2"	CRINKLE CLAUS	SANTAS			$14.00	
659036	CHRISTMAS TREE CRINKLE 5 1/4"	CRINKLE CLAUS	SANTAS			$16.30	
659037	TOP SPIN CRINKLE 3 3/4"	CRINKLE CLAUS	SANTAS			$13.70	
659038	STARBURST CRINKLE 5 1/2"	CRINKLE CLAUS	SANTAS			$14.20	
659039	ROCKING CRINKLE 4"	CRINKLE CLAUS	SANTAS				
659100	ENGLISH SANTA 3 3/4"	CRINKLE CLAUS	SANTAS			$15.00	
659101	RUSSIAN SANTA 3 1/2"	CRINKLE CLAUS	SANTAS			$15.70	
659102	NETHERLANDS SANTA 4"	CRINKLE CLAUS	SANTAS			$15.70	
659103	AUSTRIAN SANTA 3 3/4"	CRINKLE CLAUS	SANTAS			$15.80	
805050	SANTA'S SPECIAL FRIEND/CLUB EXCLUSIVE/92-93	CLOTHTIQUE SANTAS	PD - SANTA CLAUS NETWORK	93	92	$59.00	$59.00
805004	CHECKING HIS LIST/MEMBER GIFT/95-96	CLOTHTIQUE SANTAS	PD - SANTA CLAUS NETWORK	96	95	$32.00	$32.00
659104	SCANDINAVIAN SANTA 3 3/4"	CRINKLE CLAUS	SANTAS			$15.80	
659105	GERMAN SANTA 3 3/4"	CRINKLE CLAUS	SANTAS			$18.50	
659106	ITALIAN SANTA 3 1/2"	CRINKLE CLAUS	SANTAS			$15.70	
659107	ARCTIC SANTA 3 1/2"	CRINKLE CLAUS	SANTAS			$15.70	
659108	FRENCH SANTA 3 1/2"	CRINKLE CLAUS	SANTAS			$15.70	$16.00
659109	NORTHLAND SANTA 4 1/2"	CRINKLE CLAUS	SANTAS			$19.90	
659110	CELTIC SANTA 4 1/2"	CRINKLE CLAUS	SANTAS			$19.90	
659111	BISHOP OF MAYA 4 3/4"	CRINKLE CLAUS	SANTAS		96	$19.90	
659112	ICELAND VISITOR 4 1/2"	CRINKLE CLAUS	SANTAS			$19.90	
659113	MERRY OLD ENGLAND 4 1/4"	CRINKLE CLAUS	SANTAS			$19.90	
659114	BLACK FOREST GIFT GIVER 4 3/4"	CRINKLE CLAUS	SANTAS			$19.90	
659115	HARD BOILED SANTA 3 1/4"	CRINKLE CLAUS	SANTAS			$13.70	
659116	SANTA SITTING PRETTY 3 1/4"	CRINKLE CLAUS	SANTAS			$13.70	
659117	CHRISTMAS TREE SANTA 5 3/4"	CRINKLE CLAUS	SANTAS			$19.90	$20.00
659118	HOURGLASS SANTA 5 1/2"	CRINKLE CLAUS	SANTAS			$15.00	$15.00
659119	CRESCENT MOON SANTA 4 3/4"	CRINKLE CLAUS	SANTAS			$19.00	$19.00
659120	TICK TOCK SANTA 4 3/4"	CRINKLE CLAUS	SANTAS			$15.00	$15.00
659121	CANDLESTICK SANTA 5"	CRINKLE CLAUS	SANTAS			$15.80	
659122	PAMPLONA CRINKLE 2 3/4"	CRINKLE CLAUS	SANTAS			$15.80	
659123	CHRISTMAS KING CRINKLE 3 1/4"	CRINKLE CLAUS	SANTAS			$13.40	
659124	FJORD CRINKLE 2 3/4"	CRINKLE CLAUS	SANTAS			$13.40	
659125	BLARNEY STONE CRINKLE 2 3/4"	CRINKLE CLAUS	SANTAS			$13.40	
659126	BUCKINGHAM CRINKLE 2 3/4"	CRINKLE CLAUS	SANTAS			$13.40	
659127	VATICAN CRINKLE 2 3/4"	CRINKLE CLAUS	SANTAS			$13.40	
659128	MOSCOW CRINKLE 4 1/4"	CRINKLE CLAUS	SANTAS			$16.00	
659129	PARIS CRINKLE 4"	CRINKLE CLAUS	SANTAS			$16.00	
659130	MUNICH CRINKLE 4 1/4"	CRINKLE CLAUS	SANTAS			$16.00	
659131	MADRID CRINKLE 4"	CRINKLE CLAUS	SANTAS			$16.00	
659132	KELLY CRINKLE 4 1/4"	CRINKLE CLAUS	SANTAS			$16.00	
659133	SLAVIC CRINKLE 4 1/4"	CRINKLE CLAUS	SANTAS			$16.00	
659301	MERRY OLD ENGLAND PLAQUE 6 1/4"	CRINKLE CLAUS	PD - CRINKLE CRACKER			$15.00	
659302	BLACK FOREST GIFT GIVER PLAQUE 6 1/4"	CRINKLE CLAUS	PD - CRINKLE CRACKER			$15.00	$20.00
659303	ICELAND VISITOR PLAQUE 6 1/4"	CRINKLE CLAUS	PD - CRINKLE CRACKER			$15.00	
659304	NORTHLAND SANTA PLAQUE 6 1/4"	CRINKLE CLAUS	PD - CRINKLE CRACKER			$11.00	
659305	CELTIC SANTA PLAQUE 6"	CRINKLE CLAUS	PD - CRINKLE CRACKER			$11.00	$25.00
659306	BISHOP OF MAYA PLAQUE 6 1/2"	CRINKLE CLAUS	PD - CRINKLE CRACKER			$11.00	$20.00
659400	CRINKLE ANGEL WITH LANTERN 4 1/2"	CRINKLE CLAUS	PD - CRINKLE ANGEL			$19.80	$20.00
659401	CRINKLE ANGEL WITH LAMB 4 3/4"	CRINKLE CLAUS	PD - CRINKLE ANGEL			$19.80	$20.00

Order No.	Title	Type	Theme	Retired	Intro. Year	Retail Price	Secondary Price
659402	CRINKLE ANGEL WITH LYRE 4 1/2"	CRINKLE CLAUS	PD - CRINKLE ANGEL			$19.80	
659403	CRINKLE ANGEL WITH DOVE 4 1/2"	CRINKLE CLAUS	PD - CRINKLE ANGEL			$19.80	$20.00
659404	CRINKLE ANGEL WITH MANDOLIN 4 3/4"	CRINKLE CLAUS	PD - CRINKLE ANGEL			$19.80	$20.00
659405	CRINKLE ANGEL WITH CANDLE 4 3/4"	CRINKLE CLAUS	PD - CRINKLE ANGEL			$19.80	$20.00
659500	CRINKLE DOCTOR 3 1/2"	CRINKLE CLAUS	PD - CRINKLE PROFESSIONAL			$19.50	
659501	CRINKLE POSTMAN 4 1/2"	CRINKLE CLAUS	PD - CRINKLE PROFESSIONAL			$19.50	
659502	CRINKLE POLICEMAN 4 1/2"	CRINKLE CLAUS	PD - CRINKLE PROFESSIONAL			$19.50	$20.00
659503	CRINKLE FIREMAN 4 1/2"	CRINKLE CLAUS	PD - CRINKLE PROFESSIONAL			$19.50	$20.00
659504	CRINKLE FISHERMAN 4 1/2"	CRINKLE CLAUS	PD - CRINKLE PROFESSIONAL			$19.50	$20.00
659505	CRINKLE GOLFER 4 1/4"	CRINKLE CLAUS	PD - CRINKLE PROFESSIONAL			$19.50	$20.00
659506	CRINKLE FOOTBALL PLAYER 4 1/2"	CRINKLE CLAUS	PD - CRINKLE PROFESSIONAL			$19.50	$20.00
659510	CRINKLE TEACHER 4 1/4"	CRINKLE CLAUS	PD - CRINKLE PROFESSIONAL			$19.50	$20.00
659508	CRINKLE HOCKEY PLAYER 4 1/4"	CRINKLE CLAUS	PD - CRINKLE PROFESSIONAL			$19.50	$20.00
659507	CRINKLE BASEBALL PLAYER 4 1/2"	CRINKLE CLAUS	PD - CRINKLE PROFESSIONAL			$19.50	
659509	CRINKLE SOCCER PLAYER 4"	CRINKLE CLAUS	PD - CRINKLE PROFESSIONAL			$19.50	
659511	CRINKLE LAWYER 4 1/4"	CRINKLE CLAUS	PD - CRINKLE PROFESSIONAL			$19.50	
659512	CRINKLE TENNIS PLAYER 4 1/4"	CRINKLE CLAUS	PD - CRINKLE PROFESSIONAL			$19.50	
659600	SANTA IN CHIMNEY WATERDOME 6"	CRINKLE CLAUS	PD - WATERDOME			$45.00	
659601	GERMAN SANTA WATERDOME 6"	CRINKLE CLAUS	PD - WATERDOME			$45.00	
659602	ST. NICHOLAS WATERDOME 6"	CRINKLE CLAUS	PD - WATERDOME			$45.00	
659603	CHRISTMAS WILDERNESS WATERDOME 6"	CRINKLE CLAUS	PD - WATERDOME			$45.00	
659650	LIGHTED CRINKLE WORKSHOP 7"	CRINKLE CLAUS	PD - CRINKLE CLAUS VILLAGE			$70.00	$70.00
659651	LIGHTED CRINKLE CHURCH 7 1/2"	CRINKLE CLAUS	PD - CRINKLE CLAUS VILLAGE			$70.00	$70.00
659652	LIGHTED CRINKLE CASTLE 7 3/4"	CRINKLE CLAUS	PD - CRINKLE CLAUS VILLAGE			$70.00	$70.00
659653	LIGHTED CRINKLE COTTAGE 6 1/2"	CRINKLE CLAUS	PD - CRINKLE CLAUS VILLAGE			$70.00	$70.00
659654	CRINKLE BARN - LIGHTED 6 1/4"	CRINKLE CLAUS	PD - CRINKLE CLAUS VILLAGE			$43.30	
659655	CRINKLE INN - LIGHTED 6 1/4"	CRINKLE CLAUS	PD - CRINKLE CLAUS VILLAGE			$43.30	
659656	CRINKLE GRIST MILL - LIGHTED 6 1/4"	CRINKLE CLAUS	PD - CRINKLE CLAUS VILLAGE			$43.30	
659657	CRINKLE FARMHOUSE - LIGHTED 6 1/4"	CRINKLE CLAUS	PD - CRINKLE CLAUS VILLAGE			$43.30	
659701	GERMAN SANTA ORNAMENT 3"	CRINKLE CLAUS	PD - CRINKLE CLAUS EXPRESS		96	$7.80	
659702	BISHOP OF MAYA ORNAMENT 3"	CRINKLE CLAUS	PD - MINI SANTA ORNAMENTS		96	$7.80	
659703	FATHER CHRISTMAS ORNAMENT 3"	CRINKLE CLAUS	PD - MINI SANTA ORNAMENTS		96	$7.80	
659704	ST. NICHOLAS ORNAMENT 3"	CRINKLE CLAUS	PD - MINI SANTA ORNAMENTS		96	$7.80	
659705	PERE NOEL SANTA ORNAMENT 3 1/4"	CRINKLE CLAUS	PD - MINI SANTA ORNAMENTS		96	$7.80	
659706	BLACK FOREST SANTA ORNAMENT 3 1/4"	CRINKLE CLAUS	PD - MINI SANTA ORNAMENTS		96	$7.80	
659910	BEDTIME STORY/LTD. EDITION 4"	CRINKLE CLAUS	PD - LIMITED EDITION SANTAS			$31.40	
659911	DOWN THE CHIMNEY/LTD. EDITION 5"	CRINKLE CLAUS	PD - LIMITED EDITION SANTAS			$31.00	
965003	CRINKLE CLAUS DISPLAY FIGURINE 4"	CRINKLE CLAUS	PD - DISPLAY FIGURINES			$11.00	
965006	CRINKLE CLAUS VILLAGE DISPLAY FIGURINE 4 1/4"	CRINKLE CLAUS	PD - CRINKLE CLAUS VILLAGE			$10.00	
659708	MADRID CRINKLE ORNAMENT 3 1/4"	CRINKLE CLAUS	PD - MINI SANTA ORNAMENTS			$7.80	
659709	PARIS CRINKLE ORNAMENT 3"	CRINKLE CLAUS	PD - MINI SANTA ORNAMENTS			$7.80	
659710	MUNICH CRINKLE ORNAMENT 3 1/4"	CRINKLE CLAUS	PD - MINI SANTA ORNAMENTS			$7.80	
659712	KELLY CRINKLE ORNAMENT 3"	CRINKLE CLAUS	PD - MINI SANTA ORNAMENTS			$7.80	
659711	MOSCOW CRINKLE ORNAMENT 3 1/4"	CRINKLE CLAUS	PD - MINI SANTA ORNAMENTS			$7.80	
659713	SLAVIC CRINKLE ORNAMENT 3"	CRINKLE CLAUS	PD - MINI SANTA ORNAMENTS			$7.80	
659901	RUNNING DOWN THE LIST/SOLD OUT	CRINKLE CLAUS	SANTAS			$39.00	
659902	DASHING THROUGH THE SNOW/SOLD OUT	CRINKLE CLAUS	SANTAS			$19.50	$45.00
659903	BUCKETS OF FRUIT FOR GOOD BOYS & GIRLS/SOLD OUT	CRINKLE CLAUS	SANTAS			$45.00	$45.00
659904	CHOO-CHOOS FOR THE CHILDREN/SOLD OUT	CRINKLE CLAUS	SANTAS			$10.00	$25.00
659905	FEEDING HIS FOREST FRIENDS/SOLD OUT	CRINKLE CLAUS	SANTAS			$27.50	$28.00
659906	RAG DOLL DELIVERY/SOLD OUT	CRINKLE CLAUS	SANTAS			$34.50	$35.00
659907	NORTH POLE ARTISAN/LTD. EDITION 5 1/2"	CRINKLE CLAUS	PD - LIMITED EDITION SANTAS			$20.00	
659908	SLED FILLED WITH JOY/LTD. EDITION 5"	CRINKLE CLAUS	PD - LIMITED EDITION SANTAS			$31.00	
659909	SOMETHING FOR EVERYONE/LTD. EDITION 4 1/2"	CRINKLE CLAUS	PD - LIMITED EDITION SANTAS			$31.00	
713027	CHRISTMAS MAN	CLOTHTIQUE SANTAS	SANTAS	89	86	$36.50	$60.00
660201	CRINKLE LOCOMOTIVE & COAL CAR (SET OF 2) 4 3/4"	CRINKLE CLAUS	PD - CRINKLE CLAUS EXPRESS			$42.00	
660306	CRINKLE REINDEER 3 1/4"	CRINKLE CLAUS	SANTAS			$13.30	
657134	6 1/4 HIGH HAT SANTA	CRINKLE CLAUS	SANTAS	97	94	$10.00	$14.00
713157	DOCTOR CLAUS 10 1/4"	CLOTHTIQUE SANTAS	SANTAS			$35.00	
3052	HOBO	CLOTHTIQUE SANTAS	PD - SATURDAY EVENING POST COLL.			$95.40	$167.00
3053	LOVE LETTERS	CLOTHTIQUE SANTAS	PD - SATURDAY EVENING POST COLL.			$103.20	$180.00
3058	GRAMPS AT THE REINS	CLOTHTIQUE SANTAS	PD - SATURDAY EVENING POST COLL.			$174.00	$305.00
3059	MAN WITH GEESE IN BASKET	CLOTHTIQUE SANTAS	PD - SATURDAY EVENING POST COLL.			$72.00	$125.00
3101	ROCKWELL SANTA WITH GLOBE	CLOTHTIQUE SANTAS	PD - SATURDAY EVENING POST COLL.		92	$73.00	$175.00
3102	ROCKWELL DEAR SANTA	CLOTHTIQUE SANTAS	PD - SATURDAY EVENING POST COLL.			$70.50	
3103	ROCKWELL SANTA'S HEPERS	CLOTHTIQUE SANTAS	PD - SATURDAY EVENING POST COLL.			$64.90	
3105	ROCKWELL TRIPLE SELF PORTRAIT	CLOTHTIQUE SANTAS	PD - SATURDAY EVENING POST COLL.			$74.50	$250.00
3401	YOSEMITE SAM'S ROOTIN' TOOTIN CHRISTMAS	CLOTHTIQUE	PD - LOONEY TUNES COLLECTION			$59.00	
3402	BUGS BUNNY'S 14 CARROT SANTA	CLOTHTIQUE	PD - LOONEY TUNES COLLECTION			$17.50	
3403	SYLVESTER'S HOLIDAY HIGH JINKS	CLOTHTIQUE	PD - LOONEY TUNES COLLECTION			$65.00	
3404	MERRY MASTER OF CEREMONIES	CLOTHTIQUE	PD - LOONEY TUNES COLLECTION			$55.40	
3405	SELFISH ELFISH DAFFY DUCK	CLOTHTIQUE	PD - LOONEY TUNES COLLECTION			$46.90	
3406	PEPE'S CHRISTMAS SERENADE	CLOTHTIQUE	PD - LOONEY TUNES COLLECTION			$42.80	
3407	TASMANIAN RHAPSODY	CLOTHTIQUE	PD - LOONEY TUNES COLLECTION			$47.30	
3650	LEYENDECKER HUGGING SANTA/smaller	CLOTHTIQUE SANTAS	PD - SATURDAY EVENING POST COLL.			$52.50	$53.00
3651	LEYENDECKER SANTA ON LADDER/smaller	CLOTHTIQUE SANTAS	PD - SATURDAY EVENING POST COLL.		92	$59.00	$59.00
3652	LEYENDECKER TRADITIONAL SANTA	CLOTHTIQUE SANTAS	PD - SATURDAY EVENING POST COLL.		92	$66.00	$125.00
15046	NOT A CREATURE WAS STIRRING	CLOTHTIQUE SANTAS	PD - AMERICAN ARTIST COLLECTION			$44.00	$42.00
15047	REFUGE FROM THE STORM	CLOTHTIQUE SANTAS	PD - AMERICAN ARTIST COLLECTION			$49.00	$49.00
15048	VISIONS OF SUGARPLUMS	CLOTHTIQUE SANTAS	PD - AMERICAN ARTIST COLLECTION			$50.00	$49.00
15049	READY FOR CHRISTMAS	CLOTHTIQUE SANTAS	PD - AMERICAN ARTIST COLLECTION			$99.00	
15050	DRESSED FOR THE HOLIDAYS	CLOTHTIQUE SANTAS	PD - AMERICAN ARTIST COLLECTION			$47.00	$45.00
15051	FRESH FROM THE OVEN	CLOTHTIQUE SANTAS	PD - AMERICAN ARTIST COLLECTION			$49.00	$47.00
15052	TWELVE DAYS OF CHRISTMAS	CLOTHTIQUE SANTAS	PD - AMERICAN ARTIST COLLECTION			$48.00	
15053	A NEW SUIT FOR SANTA SET/2	CLOTHTIQUE SANTAS	PD - AMERICAN ARTIST COLLECTION			$90.00	$90.00
15054	CHRISTMAS STORIES	CLOTHTIQUE SANTAS	PD - AMERICAN ARTIST COLLECTION			$63.50	$62.00
15055	CHRISTMAS LIGHT	CLOTHTIQUE SANTAS	PD - AMERICAN ARTIST COLLECTION			$53.50	$80.00
15056	MORNING BREW	CLOTHTIQUE SANTAS	PD - AMERICAN ARTIST COLLECTION			$44.50	
15057	NORTH COUNTRY WEATHER	CLOTHTIQUE SANTAS	PD - AMERICAN ARTIST COLLECTION			$40.00	
15058	DOWNHILL THRILLS	CLOTHTIQUE SANTAS	PD - AMERICAN ARTIST COLLECTION			$69.00	
15059	YULETIDE GARDENER	CLOTHTIQUE SANTAS	PD - AMERICAN ARTIST COLLECTION			$50.00	
15060	LAST MINUTE PREP	CLOTHTIQUE SANTAS	PD - AMERICAN ARTIST COLLECTION			$52.50	
15061	PEACEABLE KINGDOM SET/2	CLOTHTIQUE SANTAS	PD - AMERICAN ARTIST COLLECTION				

Order No.	Title	Type	Theme	Retired	Intro. Year	Retial Price	Secondary Price
15062	SANTA ON THE GREEN	CLOTHTIQUE SANTAS	PD - AMERICAN ARTIST COLLECTION			$41.00	
15063	COOKIE MAKER	CLOTHTIQUE SANTAS	PD - AMERICAN ARTIST COLLECTION			$55.00	
15064	THE FUN SEEKERS	CLOTHTIQUE SANTAS	PD - AMERICAN ARTIST COLLECTION			$48.00	
15064	THE FUN SEEKERS	CLOTHTIQUE SANTAS	PD - AMERICAN ARTIST COLLECTION			$48.00	
275001	RETURN TO SENDER	CLOTHTIQUE	PD - GARFIELD COLLECTION			$58.00	
275002	LOVE ME, LOVE MY TEDDY BEAR	CLOTHTIQUE	PD - GARFIELD COLLECTION			$51.60	
275003	COUNTDOWN TO CHRISTMAS	CLOTHTIQUE	PD - GARFIELD COLLECTION			$41.60	
275101	WAKE ME WHEN IT'S CHRISTMAS	CLOTHTIQUE	PD - GARFIELD COLLECTION			$20.50	
275102	HERE COMES SANTA PAWS	CLOTHTIQUE	PD - GARFIELD COLLECTION			$20.50	
275103	FROSTBITE FELINE	CLOTHTIQUE	PD - GARFIELD COLLECTION			$20.50	
275200	STOCKING STUFFER	CLOTHTIQUE	PD - GARFIELD COLLECTION			$30.00	
275201	SANTA'S LITTLE HELPERS	CLOTHTIQUE	PD - GARFIELD COLLECTION			$50.00	
275202	DECK THE DOG	CLOTHTIQUE	PD - GARFIELD COLLECTION			$30.00	
625001	SANTA WITH RED COAT ORNAMENT	CLOTHTIQUE	PD - MINI SANTA ORNAMENTS			$15.70	
625102	FATHER CHRISTMAS ORNAMENT	CLOTHTIQUE	PD - MINI SANTA ORNAMENTS			$20.00	
631501	IRISH SANTA ORNAMENT	CLOTHTIQUE	PD - MINI SANTA ORNAMENTS			$19.50	
631502	IRISH SANTA ORNAMENT	CLOTHTIQUE	PD - MINI SANTA ORNAMENTS			$19.50	
713131	HO HO HOLE IN ONE	CLOTHTIQUE SANTAS	SANTAS			$43.00	$43.00
713134	SANTA'S PET PROJECT	CLOTHTIQUE SANTAS	SANTAS			$37.00	$37.00
713135	THE GINGERBREAD BAKER	CLOTHTIQUE SANTAS	SANTAS			$35.00	
713137	THREE ALARM SANTA	CLOTHTIQUE SANTAS	SANTAS			$42.50	$43.00
713138	HEAVENLY SENT	CLOTHTIQUE SANTAS	SANTAS			$50.00	$35.00
713139	JUMPIN' JACK SANTA	CLOTHTIQUE SANTAS	SANTAS			$45.50	$46.00
713140	SHAMROCK SANTA	CLOTHTIQUE SANTAS	SANTAS			$41.50	
713141	MASTER TOYMAKER	CLOTHTIQUE SANTAS	SANTAS			$44.80	$45.00
713142	FOR SOMEONE SPECIAL	CLOTHTIQUE SANTAS	SANTAS			$49.00	
713143	AUTOGRAPH FOR A FAN	CLOTHTIQUE SANTAS	SANTAS			$39.00	
713146	GRAMPA CLAUS	CLOTHTIQUE SANTAS	SANTAS			$41.40	
713147	HOLIDAY GOURMET	CLOTHTIQUE SANTAS	SANTAS			$39.10	
713148	HOLIDAY TRAFFIC	CLOTHTIQUE SANTAS	SANTAS			$47.50	
713150	SANTA WITH NATIVITY	CLOTHTIQUE SANTAS	SANTAS			$36.00	
713151	SANTA ONLINE	CLOTHTIQUE SANTAS	SANTAS			$55.20	
713152	WINTER WANDERER	CLOTHTIQUE SANTAS	SANTAS			$56.40	
713153	LEPRECHAUN	CLOTHTIQUE SANTAS	SANTAS			$18.50	
713154	DOWN THE CHIMNEY HE CAME	CLOTHTIQUE SANTAS	SANTAS			$42.50	
713155	SANTA'S BETTER HALF	CLOTHTIQUE SANTAS	SANTAS			$36.80	
713156	ON CHRISTMAS POND	CLOTHTIQUE SANTAS	SANTAS			$32.30	
713158	SANTA'S GRAB BAG	CLOTHTIQUE SANTAS	SANTAS			$47.50	
713159	EASY RIDIN' SANTA	CLOTHTIQUE SANTAS	SANTAS			$37.50	
713161	DECK THE HALLS	CLOTHTIQUE SANTAS	SANTAS			$39.70	
713162	CELTIC SOUNDS	CLOTHTIQUE SANTAS	SANTAS			$46.00	
713163	NORTH POLE POLKA	CLOTHTIQUE SANTAS	SANTAS			$46.00	
713164	NORTH POLE PRESCRIPTION	CLOTHTIQUE SANTAS	SANTAS			$65.60	
713165	SANTA O'CLAUS	CLOTHTIQUE SANTAS	SANTAS			$41.50	
713677	IRISH LASS	CLOTHTIQUE SANTAS	PD - THE CLOTHTIQUE SANTA COLL.			$26.80	
714001	SANTA WITH STAFF ORNAMENT	MINI SANTA ORNAMENTS	PD - THE CLOTHTIQUE SANTA COLL.			$19.50	
714002	SANTA WITH LIST ORNAMENT	MINI SANTA ORNAMENTS	PD - THE CLOTHTIQUE SANTA COLL.			$19.50	
714003	TRADITIONAL SANTA ORNAMENT	MINI SANTA ORNAMENTS	PD - THE CLOTHTIQUE SANTA COLL.			$19.50	
714004	SKIING SANTA ORNAMENT	MINI SANTA ORNAMENTS	PD - THE CLOTHTIQUE SANTA COLL.			$23.00	
714005	MRS. CLAUS ORNAMENT & TREE TOPPER	MINI SANTA ORNAMENTS	PD - THE CLOTHTIQUE SANTA COLL.			$19.50	
714006	WORKING SANTA ORNAMENT	MINI SANTA ORNAMENTS	PD - THE CLOTHTIQUE SANTA COLL.			$19.50	
714007	SANTA WITH BLUE CAPE ORNAMENT	MINI SANTA ORNAMENTS	PD - THE CLOTHTIQUE SANTA COLL.			$19.50	
714009	BEIGE SANTA ORNAMENT	MINI SANTA ORNAMENTS	PD - THE CLOTHTIQUE SANTA COLL.			$19.50	
714010	BABY'S FIRST CHRISTMAS ORNAMENT	MINI SANTA ORNAMENTS	PD - THE CLOTHTIQUE SANTA COLL.			$19.50	
714012	SANTA IN RED ORNAMENT	MINI SANTA ORNAMENTS	PD - THE CLOTHTIQUE SANTA COLL.			$19.50	
714013	FIREMAN SANTA ORNAMENT	MINI SANTA ORNAMENTS	PD - THE CLOTHTIQUE SANTA COLL.			$19.50	
714014	NICHOLAS ORNAMENT	MINI SANTA ORNAMENTS	PD - THE CLOTHTIQUE SANTA COLL.			$20.00	
714015	1940'S TRADITIONAL SANTA ORNAMENT	MINI SANTA ORNAMENTS	PD - THE CLOTHTIQUE SANTA COLL.			$20.00	
714101	SANTA ORNAMENT	MINI SANTA ORNAMENTS	PD - THE CLOTHTIQUE SANTA COLL.			$16.00	
714016	SANTA IN BED	MINI SANTA ORNAMENTS	PD - THE CLOTHTIQUE SANTA COLL.			$19.50	
714100	TRADITIONAL SANTA ORNAMENT	MINI SANTA ORNAMENTS	PD - THE CLOTHTIQUE SANTA COLL.			$16.00	
714102	MRS. CLAUS ORNAMENT	MINI SANTA ORNAMENTS	PD - THE CLOTHTIQUE SANTA COLL.			$16.00	
714103	1940'S TRADITIONAL SANTA ORNAMENT	MINI SANTA ORNAMENTS	PD - THE CLOTHTIQUE SANTA COLL.			$17.50	
714104	FIREMAN SANTA ORNAMENT	MINI SANTA ORNAMENTS	PD - THE CLOTHTIQUE SANTA COLL.			$15.00	
714105	NICHOLAS ORNAMENT	MINI SANTA ORNAMENTS	PD - THE CLOTHTIQUE SANTA COLL.			$17.50	
714167	IRISH ANGEL	MINI SANTA ORNAMENTS	PD - THE CLOTHTIQUE SANTA COLL.			$19.30	
721001	DEPARTMENT STORE SANTA, USA	MINI SANTA ORNAMENTS	PD - SIGNATURE SERIES		95	$108.00	$108.00
721004	SAINT NICHOLAS	CLOTHTIQUE SANTAS	PD - SIGNATURE SERIES		95	$99.00	$100.00
721005	KRISS KRINGLE	CLOTHTIQUE SANTAS	PD - SIGNATURE SERIES		95	$99.00	$100.00
	YULE POP THE TOP	CLOTHTIQUE	PD - PEPSI SANTA COLL./ORNAMENTS		95	$8.00	$8.00
	CHRISTMAS BELLS & BUBBLES	CLOTHTIQUE	PD - PEPSI SANTA COLL./ORNAMENTS		95	$7.50	$8.00
	HOLIDAY CHEER ON TOP	CLOTHTIQUE	PD - PEPSI SANTA COLL./ORNAMENTS		95	$12.20	$13.00
	GET INTO THE SWING	CLOTHTIQUE	PD - PEPSI SANTA COLL./ORNAMENTS		95	$9.90	$10.00
	UNFURL THE FUN	CLOTHTIQUE	PD - PEPSI SANTA COLL./ORNAMENTS		95	$7.40	$8.00
	WORKING ELVES 6"/SET OF THREE	CLOTHTIQUE	PD - CLOTHTIQUE ELVES			$66.00	$66.00
	GIRL AT MANGER 7"/SET OF THREE	CLOTHTIQUE	PD - CLOTHTIQUE GIRL			$74.00	$74.00
	LI'L DRUMMER BOY 7"/SET OF TWO	CLOTHTIQUE	PD - LIL DRUMMER BOY			$60.00	$60.00
	NIGEL AS SANTA 10"	CLOTHTIQUE	PD - CLOTHTIQUE LONDONSHIRE		93	$54.00	$54.00
	HOLY FAMILY 9-11 3/4"/SET OF TWO	CLOTHTIQUE	PD - CLOTHTIQUE NATIVITIES			$150.00	$150.00
	HOLY FAMILY SET 10 1/2"/SET OF THREE	CLOTHTIQUE	PD - CLOTHTIQUE NATIVITIES			$90.00	$90.00
	HOLY FAMILY SET 12"/SET OF 2	CLOTHTIQUE	PD - CLOTHTIQUE NATIVITIES			$166.00	$166.00
	WISE MEN 7 1/2" - 11 3/4"/SET OF THREE	CLOTHTIQUE	PD - CLOTHTIQUE NATIVITIES			$174.00	$174.00
SANTA'S CRYSTAL VALLEY (FIGI)							
CV-1001	JOURNEY TO CRYSTAL VALLEY	FIGURINES	FG - LIMITED EDITION		96	$700.00	$805.00
CV-401	DREAMS CAN COME TRUE	FIGURINES	FG - LIMITED EDITION		96	$100.00	$115.00
CV-402	ROOM FOR ONE MORE?	FIGURINES	FG - LIMITED EDITION		96	$100.00	$115.00
CV-801	MAGIC IN THE MAKING	FIGURINES	FG - LIMITED EDITION		96	$500.00	$575.00
CV-701	A GIFT FOR SANTA/CLOSED EDITION	FIGURINES	FG - LIMITED EDITION		95	$400.00	$460.00
CV-601	A VERY SPECIAL REQUEST	FIGURINES	FG - LIMITED EDITION			$190.00	$218.50
CV-302	SLEDDING WITH SANTA	FIGURINES	FG - SANTA		95	$100.00	$115.00
CV-301	SMILE, MR. SNOWMAN	FIGURINES	FG - SANTA		95	$100.00	$115.00

Order No.	Title	Type	Theme	Retired	Intro. Year	Retail Price	Secondary Price
CV-303	SANTA'S DILEMMA	FIGURINES	FG - SANTA		95	$100.00	$115.00
CV-101	POLAR BEAR ANGEL	FIGURINES	FG - SANTA		95	$70.00	$80.50

STEINBACH NUTCRACKERS

Order No.	Title	Type	Theme	Retired	Intro. Year	Retail Price	Secondary Price
301	EMPEROR (KAISER)	NUTCRACKER	MINI NUTCRACKER		86		
302	KING (KONIG)	NUTCRACKER	MINI NUTCRACKER	YES	86		
303	PRINCE (KRONPRINZ)	NUTCRACKER	MINI NUTCRACKER		86		
304	AIDE (ADJUTANT)	NUTCRACKER	MINI NUTCRACKER		86		
305	DUKE (KURFURST)	NUTCRACKER	MINI NUTCRACKER	YES	86		
306	COUNT (GRAF)	NUTCRACKER	MINI NUTCRACKER		86		
307	BARON	NUTCRACKER	MINI NUTCRACKER		86		
308	MARSHAL (MARSHALL)	NUTCRACKER	MINI NUTCRACKER	YES	86		
662	DOCTOR (DOKTOR EISENBARTH)	NUTCRACKER	NUTCRACKER	YES	85		
663	CHEF (CHEFKOCH)	NUTCRACKER	NUTCRACKER	YES	85		
664	BLACKSMITH (GLUCKSCHMIED)	NUTCRACKER	NUTCRACKER	YES	85		
665	SHOEMAKER (HOLZSCHUHMACHER)	NUTCRACKER	NUTCRACKER	YES	84		
666	COUNT ZEPPLIN (GRAF ZEPPELIN)	NUTCRACKER	NUTCRACKER	YES	84		
667	BACCHUS	NUTCRACKER	NUTCRACKER	YES	84		
668	MILLER (BACH-MULLER)	NUTCRACKER	NUTCRACKER	YES	88		
669	FARMER (BAUER)	NUTCRACKER	NUTCRACKER	YES	88		
670	UNCLE SAM	NUTCRACKER	NUTCRACKER	YES	84		
671	CHERUSKER (HERMANN DER CHERUSKER)	NUTCRACKER	NUTCRACKER	YES	84		
672	COUNT LUCKNER (GRAF LUCKNER)	NUTCRACKER	NUTCRACKER	YES	83		
673	LIPPE DETMOLD SOLDIER	NUTCRACKER	NUTCRACKER	YES	90		
674	THE WATER CARRIER (WASSERTRAGER)	NUTCRACKER	NUTCRACKER	YES	90		
675	KING AUGUST (AUGUST DER STARKE)	NUTCRACKER	NUTCRACKER	YES	83		
676	KING LUDWIG 2ND	NUTCRACKER	NUTCRACKER	YES	89		
678	TOWN CRIER (BUTTEL)	NUTCRACKER	PICCOLO		90		
679	GRANDMA (OMA) PICCOLO	NUTCRACKER	PICCOLO	YES	83		
680	BARON (BARON MUCHHASEN) PICCOLO	NUTCRACKER	PICCOLO	YES	83		
681	SHERLOCK HOLMES PICCOLO	NUTCRACKER	PICCOLO	YES	83		
680	DR. WATSON PICCOLO	NUTCRACKER	PICCOLO		89		
682	HAMBURG IMMIGRANT (MUSICAL) PICCOLO	NUTCRACKER	PICCOLO	YES	83		
682	BAGPIPER (DUDELSACKPFEIFER)	NUTCRACKER	NUTCRACKER		89		
309	GENERAL	NUTCRACKER	MINI NUTCRACKER		86		
310	ADMIRAL	NUTCRACKER	MINI NUTCRACKER		86		
311	HUNTER (HOFJAGER)	NUTCRACKER	MINI NUTCRACKER		86		
312	GUARD (HOFWACHE)	NUTCRACKER	MINI NUTCRACKER		86		
313	SERVANT (KAMMERDIENER)	NUTCRACKER	MINI NUTCRACKER		8?		
314	GARDNER (SCHOLLSGARTNER)	NUTCRACKER	MINI NUTCRACKER	YES	88		
315	CLOWN (HOFNARR)	NUTCRACKER	MINI NUTCRACKER		88		
316	BLACKSMITH (WAFFENSCHMIED)	NUTCRACKER	MINI NUTCRACKER	YES	88		
317	BUTLER (WAFFENSCHMIED)	NUTCRACKER	MINI NUTCRACKER	YES	88		
318	TAILOR (HOFSCHNEIDER)	NUTCRACKER	MINI NUTCRACKER	YES	88		
319	IMMIGRANT	NUTCRACKER	MINI NUTCRACKER		92		
320	CAPTAIN COOK	NUTCRACKER	MINI NUTCRACKER		92		
321	COLUMBUS	NUTCRACKER	MINI NUTCRACKER		92		
322	DROSSELMEYER IN WOOD BOX	NUTCRACKER	MINI NUTCRACKERS	YES	95	$39.00	$125.00
323	MOUSE KING IN WOOD BOX	NUTCRACKER	MINI NUTCRACKERS		96	$45.00	
324	PRINCE IN WOOD BOX	NUTCRACKER	MINI NUTCRACKERS		96	$45.00	
329	KRIS KRINGLE IN TIN	NUTCRACKER	MINI NUTCRACKERS		96	$45.00	
330	KING LUDWIG IN WOOD BOX	NUTCRACKER	MINI NUTCRACKERS		95	$45.00	
335	MERLIN IN WOOD BOX	LIMITED EDITION	MINI NUTCRACKERS		96	$50.00	$54.00
336	ROBIN HOOD IN WOOD BOX	LIMITED EDITION	MINI NUTCRACKERS		96	$50.00	$55.00
337	KING ARTHUR IN WOOD BOX	NUTCRACKER	MINI NUTCRACKERS			$50.00	
338	ST NICHOLAS IN WOOD BOX	NUTCRACKER	MINI NUTCRACKERS		97	$50.00	
339	NOAH IN WOOD BOX	NUTCRACKER	MINI NUTCRACKERS		97	$50.00	
340	SET OF THREE KINGS IN WOOD BOX	NUTCRACKER	MINI NUTCRACKERS		97	$145.00	
601	HAPPY SANTA	NUTCRACKER	NUTCRACKER COLLECTION	YES	92	$190.00	$212.00
602	EINSTEIN	NUTCRACKER	NUTCRACKER	YES	91		
603	ROSENKAVALIER	NUTCRACKER	NUTCRACKER	YES	91		
604	VIOLINIST	NUTCRACKER	SHORTY, PICCOLO & LG. NUTCRACKERS	YES	91		
605	FRANZ/DIRECTOR PICCOLO	NUTCRACKER	SHORTY, PICCOLO & LG. NUTCRACKERS	YES	91		
605	CHRISTMAS SANTA ON PIANO (MUSICAL)	NUTCRACKER	SHORTY, PICCOLO & LG. NUTCRACKERS		95		
606	TYROLEAN MOUNTAIN CLIMBER	NUTCRACKER	NUTCRACKER		91		
607	COWBOY WITH PIANO (COWBOY AN KLAVIER)	NUTCRACKER	SHORTY, PICCOLO & LG. NUTCRACKERS		92		
608	SMALL COLUMBUS	NUTCRACKER	SHORTY, PICCOLO & LG. NUTCRACKERS		92		
609	SAXAPHONE PLAYER	NUTCRACKER	SHORTY, PICCOLO & LG. NUTCRACKERS	YES	91		
610	MERLIN THE MAGICIAN	NUTCRACKER	CAMELOT SERIES	91	91	$185.00	$4,750.00
611	LINEN WEAVER (LEINEWEBER)	NUTCRACKER	NUTCRACKER	YES	91		
612	LOTTO MAN	NUTCRACKER	NUTCRACKER	YES	91		
613	COBBLER (SCHUSTER)	NUTCRACKER	NUTCRACKER		91		
614	PROPHET	NUTCRACKER	NUTCRACKER	YES	91		
615	NAPOLEON'S GUARD	NUTCRACKER	NUTCRACKER		91		
616	POPOV THE CLOWN	NUTCRACKER	NUTCRACKER	YES	91		
617	BASKET WEAVER (KORBHANDLER)	NUTCRACKER	NUTCRACKER	YES	91		
618	PEARL FISHERMAN (PERLENFISCHER)	NUTCRACKER	NUTCRACKER	YES	91		
619	TCHAIKOVSKY (MUSICAL)	NUTCRACKER	SHORTY, PICCOLO & LG. NUTCRACKERS		92		
620	LUDWIG/FLUTE PICCOLO	NUTCRACKER	SHORTY, PICCOLO & LG. NUTCRACKERS	YES	?		
621	KING ARTHUR	NUTCRACKER	CAMELOT SERIES	93	92	$195.00	$1,750.00
622	ABRAHAM LINCOLN	LIMITED EDITION	PRESIDENTS SERIES	95	92	$195.00	$265.00
623	GEORGE WASHINGTON	NUTCRACKER	PRESIDENTS SERIES	94	92	$195.00	$235.00
624	WIZARD OF OZ	NUTCRACKER	NUTCRACKER		92		
625	DUTCHMAN (HOLLANDER)	NUTCRACKER	NUTCRACKER		92		
626	HISTORIC MAILMAN	NUTCRACKER	NUTCRACKER		92		
627	DENTIST (ZAHNARZT)	NUTCRACKER	NUTCRACKER		92		
628	JAMES COOK	NUTCRACKER	NUTCRACKER		92		
629	NEPTUNE (NEPTUN)	NUTCRACKER	NUTCRACKER		92		
630	GRANDFATHER	NUTCRACKER	NUTCRACKER		93		
631	MASTER FIGARO (MEISTER FIGARO)	NUTCRACKER	NUTCRACKER		92		
632	THANKSGIVING MAN	NUTCRACKER	NUTCRACKER				
633	HERR DROSSELMEYER	NUTCRACKER	NUTCRACKER SUITE SERIES	YES	92	$190.00	$3,000.00

Order No.	Title	Type	Theme	Retired	Intro. Year	Retial Price	Secondary Price
634	PRINCE CHARMING (PRINZ)	NUTCRACKER	SHORTY, PICCOLO & LG. NUTCRACKERS		93		
635	BENJAMIN FRANKLIN	NUTCRACKER	AMERICAN INVENTOR SERIES	96	93	$225.00	$265.00
636	THE MOUSE KING	NUTCRACKER	NUTCRACKER SUITE SERIES		93	$195.00	$800.00
637	SITTING BULL/SOLD OUT	NUTCRACKER	CHIEFTANS SERIES	95	93	$225.00	$500.00
638	SIR LANCELOT	LIMITED EDITION	CAMELOT SERIES		93	$225.00	$265.00
639	CASANOVA	NUTCRACKER	NUTCRACKER		92		
641	SANTA WITH PIANO	NUTCRACKER	NUTCRACKER		91		
642	AVIATOR	NUTCRACKER	NUTCRACKER		92		
643	FISH MONGLE	NUTCRACKER	NUTCRACKER	YES	92		
644	PROFESSOR	NUTCRACKER	NUTCRACKER	YES	91		
645	GOLFER	NUTCRACKER	SHORTY, PICCOLO & LG. NUTCRACKERS	YES	91		
646	GOLFER	NUTCRACKER	NUTCRACKER	YES	91		
644	THEODORE ROOSEVELT	LIMITED EDITION	PRESIDENTS SERIES		93	$225.00	
645	FATHER CHRISTMAS	LIMITED EDITION	CHRISTMAS LEGEND SERIES	96	93	$225.00	$265.00
646	FISHERMAN (ANGLER)	NUTCRACKER	NUTCRACKER	YES	91		
647	BACCHUS	NUTCRACKER	NUTCRACKER	YES	90		
648	BANKER	NUTCRACKER	NUTCRACKER	YES	91		
649	KING (KONIG ERNST AUGUST)	NUTCRACKER	KINGS COAST SERIES	YES	87		
650	GENERAL (GENERAL STEUBEN)	NUTCRACKER	KINGS COAST SERIES	YES	87		
652	HUNTER (HOFJAGER VON DER TANN)	NUTCRACKER	KINGS COAST SERIES	YES	87		
651	GUARD (WACHE AITZEWITZ)	NUTCRACKER	KINGS COAST SERIES	YES	87		
654	PRINCE (KRONPRINZ LUDWIG)	NUTCRACKER	KINGS COAST SERIES	YES	87		
655	DUKE (KURFURST JOHANN)	NUTCRACKER	KINGS COAST SERIES	YES	87		
656	BARON (BARON ROTHCHILD)	NUTCRACKER	KINGS COAST SERIES	YES	87		
657	ADMIRAL (ADMIRAL NELSON)	NUTCRACKER	KINGS COAST SERIES	YES	87		
658	AIDE (ADJUTANT V. TRUTSCHLER)	NUTCRACKER	KINGS COAST SERIES	YES	87		
659	POTTER (TOPFERMIESTER)	NUTCRACKER	NUTCRACKER	YES	85		
660	BUTTRCHURNER (BUTTERMEIR)	NUTCRACKER	NUTCRACKER	YES	85		
661	HENPECKED HUSBAND (PANTOFFELHELD)	NUTCRACKER	NUTCRACKER	YES	85		
683	ST. ANTONIUS (MUSICAL) PICCOLO	NUTCRACKER	PICCOLO	YES	83		
684	WORLD TRAVLER (HAPPY WANDERER)	NUTCRACKER	NUTCRACKER		89		
685	APOTHECARY OR CHEMIST (APOTHEKER)	NUTCRACKER	SHORTY, PICCOLO & LG. NUTCRACKERS		89		
686	SHORTY SONNY BOY	NUTCRACKER	SHORTY	YES	82		
68	PATRICK/GREEN COAT (ST. PATRICK)	NUTCRACKER	PICCOLO		89		
686	PATRICK/GREEN COAT	NUTCRACKER	NUTCRACKER		89		
687	SHORTY DOCTOR	NUTCRACKER	SHORTY	YES	82		
687	UNPAINTED	NUTCRACKER	NUTCRACKER	YES	89		
688	SHORTY CHIMNEYSWEEP	NUTCRACKER	SHORTY	YES	82		
689	SHORTY PASCHA	NUTCRACKER	SHORTY	YES	82		
689	SCRIBE	NUTCRACKER	NUTCRACKER		89		
690	SHORTY KING	NUTCRACKER	SHORTY	YES	82		
690	BRICKLAYER (HAUSLEBAUER)	NUTCRACKER	NUTCRACKER	YES	88		
691	SHORTY BAVARIAN	NUTCRACKER	SHORTY	YES	82		
691	CLOCKMAKER (UHRENMACHER)	NUTCRACKER	NUTCRACKER	YES	88		
692	SHORTY BAKER	NUTCRACKER	SHORTY	YES	82		
692	GOLFER (GOLFSPIELER)	NUTCRACKER	NUTCRACKER	YES	88		
693	SHORTY VIKING	NUTCRACKER	SHORTY	YES	82		
693	TOYMAKER (MUSICAL)	NUTCRACKER	NUTCRACKER		90		
694	SHORTY NIGHTWATCHMAN	NUTCRACKER	SHORTY	YES	82		
694	WOODCUTTER (HOLZHAUER)	NUTCRACKER	NUTCRACKER		88		
695	SHORTY POLICEMAN	NUTCRACKER	SHORTY	YES	82		
695	SANTA (RUPRECHT)	NUTCRACKER	NUTCRACKER	YES	88		
696	NUTCRACKER LATHE	NUTCRACKER	NUTCRACKER	YES	90		
696	REGIMENT NO. 1 PICCOLO	NUTCRACKER	PICCOLO	YES	82		
697	FISHERMAN	NUTCRACKER	PICCOLO	YES	82		
697	COLUMBUS	NUTCRACKER	NUTCRACKER COLLECTION	92	91	$194.00	$215.00
698	POLICE SOLDIER PICCOLO	NUTCRACKER	PICCOLO	YES	82		
698	KING WILHELM (LONIG WILHELM)	NUTCRACKER	NUTCRACKER		91		
699	FIREMAN REDESIGNED	NUTCRACKER	NUTCRACKER	YES	86		
699	FIREMAN (FEUERWEHRMANN)	NUTCRACKER	NUTCRACKER	YES	82		
700	COWBOY	NUTCRACKER	NUTCRACKER	YES	82		$230.00
700	COWBOY REDESIGNED	NUTCRACKER	NUTCRACKER	YES	92		
701	OIL SHEIK	NUTCRACKER	NUTCRACKERCOLLECTION	85	84	$100.00	$450.00
701	FRIEDRICH CHOPIN/PIANO (MUSICAL)	NUTCRACKER	PICCOLO		90		$220.00
702	SANTA (WEIHNACHTSMANN)	NUTCRACKER	NUTCRACKER	YES	NA		
702	SANTA REDESIGNED	NUTCRACKER	NUTCRACKER		86		
703	GARDENER (GARTNER) STRAW HAT, RAKE	NUTCRACKER	NUTCRACKER	YES	75		
703	GARDENER REDESIGNED WOOD HAT, SHOVEL	NUTCRACKER	NUTCRACKER	YES	NA		
704	FISHERMAN (SPORTANGLER)	NUTCRACKER	NUTCRACKER	YES	77		
705	DRUMMER (TROMMLER)	NUTCRACKER	NUTCRACKER	YES	77		
706	HUNTER (JAGER)	NUTCRACKER	NUTCRACKER	YES	75		$225.00
707	CHIMNEYSWEEP (SCHORNSTEINFEGER)	NUTCRACKER	NUTCRACKER	YES	74		$225.00
707	CHIMNEYSWEEP REDESIGNED	NUTCRACKER	NUTCRACKER		86		
708	BAVARIAN (BAYER)	NUTCRACKER	NUTCRACKER	YES	74		
708	BAVARIAN REDESIGNED PICCOLO	NUTCRACKER	NUTCRACKER	YES	86		$220.00
709	MOUNTAIN CLIMBER (BERGSTEIGER)	NUTCRACKER	NUTCRACKER	YES	79		
710	SHEPHERD (SCHAFER) BROWN COAT	NUTCRACKER	NUTCRACKER	YES	83		$220.00
710	BLACK FOREST CLOCKMAKER	NUTCRACKER	NUTCRACKER	YES	77		
710	SHEPHERD/WHITE COAT REDESIGNED	NUTCRACKER	NUTCRACKER	YES	87		
711	GUARD (GARDESOLDAT)	NUTCRACKER	NUTCRACKER	YES	75		
711	GUARD REDESIGNED	NUTCRACKER	NUTCRACKER	YES	87		
712	KING (KONIG)	NUTCRACKER	NUTCRACKER	YES	80		
713	NIGHTWATHMAN (NACHWACHTER)	NUTCRACKER	NUTCRACKER	YES	79		
714	CHUBBY SNOWMAN	NUTCRACKER	CHUBBY		96		
714	CHUBBY TOWN CRIER	NUTCRACKER	CHUBBY	YES	95		
715	KANGAROO	NUTCRACKER	PICCOLO	YES	89		
716	WATCHMAN (NACHTWACHTER)PICCOLO	NUTCRACKER	PICCOLO	YES	80		
716	CHUBBY VIKING (KNILCH WIKINGER)	NUTCRACKER	CHUBBY		95		
717	MRS. GERTRUD (FRAN GERTRUD)	NUTCRACKER	NUTCRACKER		79		
718	CHUBBY SOCKER	NUTCRACKER	CHUBBY		96		
718	SANTA PICCOLO	NUTCRACKER	PICCOLO	YES	79		
718	SKIER PICCOLO	NUTCRACKER	PICCOLO	YES	80		
719	GARDENER (GARTNER) PICCOLO	NUTCRACKER	PICCOLO	YES	80		

Order No.	Title	Type	Theme	Retired	Intro. Year	Retail Price	Secondary Price
719	CHUBBY BOWLER	NUTCRACKER	CHUBBY		96		
720	CHUBBY GOLFER	NUTCRACKER	CHUBBY		95		
720	FALCON KING (JAGDKONIG) PICCOLO	NUTCRACKER	PICCOLO	YES	77		
720	KING (KONIG) PICCOLO	NUTCRACKER	PICCOLO	YES	89		
721	HUNTER (JAGER) PICCOLO	NUTCRACKER	PICCOLO		77		
721	CHUBBY BASEBALL PLAYER	NUTCRACKER	CHUBBY		95		
713	CHUBBY SKIING SANTA	NUTCRACKER	CHUBBY		97		
722	CHIMNEYSWEEP (KAMINFEGER)PICCOLO	NUTCRACKER	PICCOLO	YES	89		
723	DR. EISENBARTH PICCOLO	NUTCRACKER	SHORTY, PICCOLO & LG. NUTCRACKERS	YES	78		
722	ARAMIS/1ST OF 3 MUSKETEERS	LIMITED EDITION	THREE MUSKETEERS		96	$130.00	$135.00
723	CHUBBY MOUNTAIN CLIMBER	NUTCRACKER	CHUBBY		96		
724	BAKER (DER LEBKUCHNER) PICCOLO	NUTCRACKER	PICCOLO	YES	79		
724	BAKER (KOCH) PICCOLO	NUTCRACKER	PICCOLO	YES	89		
724	CHUBBY DENTIST	NUTCRACKER	CHUBBY		96		
725	MOUTAIN CLIMBER (BERGSTIGER)PICCOLO	NUTCRACKER	PICCOLO	YES	80		
725	COSSACK (KOSAK) PICCOLO	NUTCRACKER	PICCOLO	YES	89		
725	CHUBBY PILOT	NUTCRACKER	CHUBBY		96		
726	DRUMMER (TROMMLER)PICCOLO	NUTCRACKER	SHORTY, PICCOLO & LG. NUTCRACKERS	YES	89		
726	CHUBBY JESTER	NUTCRACKER	CHUBBY		96		
727	FORTUNE HUNTER PICCOLO	NUTCRACKER	PICCOLO	YES	80		
727	MAILMAN PICCOLO	NUTCRACKER	PICCOLO	YES	89		
727	CHUBBY CLOWN	NUTCRACKER	CHUBBY		96		
728	CHUBBY AMOR	NUTCRACKER	CHUBBY		96		
728	COWBOY PICCOLO	NUTCRACKER	PICCOLO	YES	89		
729	SHEPHERD (DER SCHAFER) PICCOLO	NUTCRACKER	PICCOLO	YES	84		
729	CHUBBY SKIER	NUTCRACKER	CHUBBY		96		
731	VIKING (WIKINGER)	NUTCRACKER	NUTCRACKER		93		$220.00
731	HAMBURG GUARD (DER HAMBURGER) PICCOLO	NUTCRACKER	PICCOLO	YES	88		
732	BERLIN CITY GUARD (DER BERLINER) PICCOLO	NUTCRACKER	PICCOLO	YES	88		
732	BERLIN ORGAN GRINDER	NUTCRACKER	PICCOLO		93		$245.00
733	PET PASTRY BAKER	NUTCRACKER	NUTCRACKER		93		
733	MUNICH CITY GUARD	NUTCRACKER	PICCOLO	YES	88		
734	CZAR OF RUSSIA (ZAR VON RUBLAND)	NUTCRACKER	NUTCRACKER		93		$245.00
734	FRANKFURT CITY GUARD PICCOLO	NUTCRACKER	PICCOLO	YES	88		$130.00
735	SEA CAPTAIN	NUTCRACKER	NUTCRACKER		93		$220.00
735	NURNBERG CITY GUARD PICCOLO	NUTCRACKER	PICCOLO	YES	88		
736	STUTTGART CITY GUARD PICCOLO	NUTCRACKER	PICCOLO	YES	88		
736	MADAME NUTCRACKER	NUTCRACKER	NUTCRACKER		93		
737	CHARCOAL MAKER (KOHLER)	NUTCRACKER	NUTCRACKER		93		
737	SANTA CLAUS PICCOLO	NUTCRACKER	PICCOLO	YES	88		
738	GUARD (SOLDAT) PICCOLO	NUTCRACKER	PICCOLO	YES	88		
738	MISS CLARA (FRL KLARA) PICCOLO	NUTCRACKER	PICCOLO	YES	NA		
739	VIKING (WIKINGER)PICCOLO	NUTCRACKER	PICCOLO		81		
739N	BAVARIAN (BAYER)	NUTCRACKER	PICCOLO	YES	90		
739	CHUBBY BAVRIAN (KNILCH OBERBAYER)	NUTCRACKER	CHUBBY		93		
740	PRUSSIAN (PREUBE)	NUTCRACKER	PICCOLO	YES	90		
740	MUSICAL IMMIGRANT	NUTCRACKER	NUTCRACKER	YES	86		
740	CHUBBY SNOW-WHITE SANTA (KNILCH SANTA)	NUTCRACKER	CHUBBY		93		
741	CHUBBY KING	NUTCRACKER	CHUBBY		93		
742	CHUBBY WATCHMAN (KNILCH WACHER)	NUTCRACKER	CHUBBY		94		
743	CHUBBY SANTA	NUTCRACKER	CHUBBY		93		
744	CHUBBY YELLOW FARMER	NUTCRACKER	CHUBBY		93		
745	CHUBBY CHIMNEY SWEEP	NUTCRACKER	CHUBBY		93		
746	CHUBBY BROWN HUNTER	NUTCRACKER	CHUBBY		93		
860	CLARA	NUTCRACKER	NUTCRACKER SUITE SERIES		95		
859	SUGAR PLUM FAIRY	NUTCRACKER	NUTCRACKER SUITE SERIES		96	$229.00	
861	NUTCRACKER PRINCE	NUTCRACKER	NUTCRACKER SUITE SERIES		94	$229.00	
862	SIR GALAHAD	LIMITED EDITION	CAMELOT SERIES		94	$229.00	$265.00
863	ROBIN HOOD	LIMITED EDITION	TALES OF SHERWOOD FOREST SERIES	96	92	$225.00	$265.00
864	CHIEF RED CLOUD/SOLD OUT	LIMITED EDITION	CHIEFTANS SERIES	96	94	$225.00	$265.00
865	ST. NICHOLAS	NUTCRACKER	CHRISTMAS LEGEND SERIES	95	94	$225.00	$265.00
866	THOMAS JEFFERSON/4TH	LIMITED EDITION	PRESIDENTS SERIES		96	$195.00	$265.00
868	HERR STUDEBAKER	NUTCRACKER	NUTCRACKER		95		
869	QUEEN GUINEVERE	LIMITED EDITION	CAMELOT SERIES		95	$245.00	$265.00
856	ROYAL GUARDSMAN	NUTCRACKER	NUTCRACKER		97		
857	HUMPTY DUMPTY	NUTCRACKER	NURSERY RHYME		97	$210.00	
870	OLD TIME BASEBALL PLAYER	NUTCRACKER	NUTCRACKER		95		
871	GOLFER	NUTCRACKER	NUTCRACKER		94		
872	FISHERMAN (LUGENDER ANGLER)	NUTCRACKER	NUTCRACKER		94		
873	RANGER - NEW HUNTER (FORSTMEISTER)	NUTCRACKER	NUTCRACKER		94		
874	CEASAR (CASAR)	NUTCRACKER	NUTCRACKER		94		
875	NEW FIREMAN (BRANDMEISTER)	NUTCRACKER	NUTCRACKER		94		
877	WHITE SANTA	NUTCRACKER	NUTCRACKER		94		
878	NEW DOCTOR (PROFESSOR)	NUTCRACKER	NUTCRACKER		94		
879	NUTCRACKER DAD	NUTCRACKER	NUTCRACKER		95		
880	KING OF THE NUTCRACKERS (HERR STEINBACH)	NUTCRACKER	NUTCRACKER		94		
881	CASPAR/THREE WISEMEN	NUTCRACKER	NUTCRACKER		94	$230.00	
885	BEST MOM	NUTCRACKER	NUTCRACKER		95		
886	GENGHIS KHAN	NUTCRACKER	NUTCRACKER		95		
887	BLACK CAT (SOME ARE MUSICAL)	NUTCRACKER	NUTCRACKER		95		
888	LION KING	NUTCRACKER	NUTCRACKER		95		
889	CHIEF BLACK HAWK/SOLD OUT	LIMITED EDITION	CHIEFTANS SERIES	96	95	$225.00	$265.00
890	FRIAR TUCK	LIMITED EDITION	TALES OF SHERWOOD FOREST SERIES		95	$245.00	$265.00
891	1930 SANTA CLAUS	LIMITED EDITION	CHRISTMAS LEGEND SERIES		95	$245.00	$265.00
892	SHERIFF OF NOTTINGHAM/3RD	LIMITED EDITION	TALES OF SHERWOOD FOREST SERIES		96	$260.00	$265.00
893	NOAH AND HIS ARK/1ST	LIMITED EDITION	BIBLICAL SERIES		96	$260.00	
898	KING LUDWIG THE 2ND	NUTCRACKER	NUTCRACKER		96		
1000	STEINBACH JUBILLEE	NUTCRACKER	SHORTY, PICCOLO & LG. NUTCRACKERS	YES	96		
894	MOSES	NUTCRACKER	BIBLICAL SERIES		97		
895	GRANDFATHER FROST	NUTCRACKER	CHRISTMAS LEGEND SERIES		97		
896	EBENEZER SCROOGE	NUTCRACKER	CHRISTMAS CAROL SERIES		97		
897	RICHARD THE LIONHEARTED	NUTCRACKER	TALES OF SHERWOOD FOREST SERIES		97	$265.00	$265.00
973	CHUBBY BAGPIPE	NUTCRACKER	CHUBBY		97		

Order No.	Title	Type	Theme	Retired	Intro. Year	Retial Price	Secondary Price
974	CHUBBY DOCTOR	NUTCRACKER	CHUBBY		97		
975	CHUBBY FIREMAN	NUTCRACKER	CHUBBY		97		
976	CHUBBY PROFESSOR	NUTCRACKER	CHUBBY		97		
977	CHUBBY SHEPHERD	NUTCRACKER	CHUBBY		97		
978	CHUBBY RAILROAD MAN	NUTCRACKER	CHUBBY		97		
979	CHUBBY ST. PATRICK	NUTCRACKER	CHUBBY		97		
980	CHUBBY WOODCUTTER	NUTCRACKER	CHUBBY		97		
703	CHUBBY ARTIC EXPLORER	NUTCRACKER	NUTCRACKER		97		
709	CHIMNEY SWEEP PICCOLO	NUTCRACKER	NUTCRACKER		97		
2001	CHIMNEY SWEEP PIECE IN WOOD BOX	NUTCRACKER	COLLECTORS CLUB		97		
900	GOOD KING WENCESLAUS	LIMITED EDITION	COLLECTORS CLUB	YES	96		
640	SKIER NUTCRACKER	NUTCRACKER	SHORTY, PICCOLO & LG. NUTCRACKERS				
735	THE ADMIRAL	NUTCRACKER	PICCOLO				
884	IRISH SANTA CLAUS	NUTCRACKER	NUTCRACKER				
899	SANTA WITH LIST	NUTCRACKER	NUTCRACKER				
300	KINGS COURT	NUTCRACKER	MINI NUTCRACKER				
996	STEINBACH NUTCRACKER BOOK	NUTCRACKER	SHORTY, PICCOLO & LG. NUTCRACKERS		97		
336	ROBIN HOOD IN WOOD BOX	NUTCRACKER	MINI NUTCRACKERS	96	96	$50.00	
620	WISH LIST SANTA	NUTCRACKER	NUTCRACKER	YES	?		
641	SKIER	NUTCRACKER	NUTCRACKER				
653	EMPEROR (KAISER BARAROSA]	NUTCRACKER	KINGS COAST SERIES	YES	87		
679	MOZART PICCOLO	NUTCRACKER	PICCOLO	YES			
677	RIDER (REITER)	NUTCRACKER	NUTCRACKER	YES			
677	GRANDPA PICCOLO	NUTCRACKER	PICCOLO				
683	WOODCARVER	NUTCRACKER	NUTCRACKER				
688	FATHER & SON	NUTCRACKER	NUTCRACKER	YES			
684	SHORTY SARGEANT	NUTCRACKER	SHORTY	YES			
714	BAVARIAN PICCOLO	NUTCRACKER	PICCOLO	YES			
715	CHUBBY POLICEMAN	NUTCRACKER	CHUBBY				
715	POLICEMAN GUARD PICCOLO	NUTCRACKER	PICCOLO	YES			
717	CHUBBY COOK	NUTCRACKER	CHUBBY				
858	MAD HATTER	LIMITED EDITION	ALICE IN WONDERLAND		95	$230.00	
883	BALTHASAR/THREE WISEMEN	NUTCRACKER	NUTCRACKER		94		
882	MELCHIOR/THREE WISEMEN	NUTCRACKER	NUTCRACKER		94		
328	SNOWMAN IN TIN	NUTCRACKER	MINI NUTCRACKERS				
	MAREK		COLLECTORS CLUB		97		
2000	TOWN CRIER		COLLECTORS CLUB	96	95		

VAILLANCOURT FOLK ART

Order No.	Title	Type	Theme	Retired	Intro. Year	Retial Price	Secondary Price
133	AMERICAN SNOWMAN	FIGURINE	VC - MISC		86	$25.00	
101A	ORIGINAL FATHER CHRISTMAS JR.	FIGURINE	VC - FATHER CHRISTMAS		85	$25.00	
103	SANTA IN SLEIGH	FIGURINE	VC - FATHER CHRISTMAS	87	85	$30.00	$750.00
103BR	SANTA IN SLEIGH/BROWN	FIGURINE	VC - SANTA	87	87	$55.00	$500.00
104B	RUSSIAN FATHER CHRISTMAS/BLUE	FIGURINE	VC - FATHER CHRISTMAS		86	$30.00	
104W	RUSSIAN FATHER CHRISTMAS/WHITE	FIGURINE	VC - FATHER CHRISTMAS		86	$30.00	$350.00
104R	RUSSIAN FATHER CHRISTMAS/RED	FIGURINE	VC - FATHER CHRISTMAS		86	$30.00	
104G	RUSSIAN FATHER CHRISTMAS/GREEN	FIGURINE	VC - FATHER CHRISTMAS		85	$30.00	$550.00
411	ROCKING GNOME	FIGURINE	VC - MISC		90		
412	AMERICAN SANTA	FIGURINE	VC - SANTA		90		
413	LT GREEN WALKING STICK	FIGURINE	VC - MISC		90		
414	BROWN WALKING STICK	FIGURINE	VC - MISC		90		
415	RED BELSNICKEL	FIGURINE	VC - BELSNICKEL		90		
416	SANTA W/GREEN PANTS	FIGURINE	VC - SANTA		90		
417	SANTA IN BLACK PANTS	FIGURINE	VC - SANTA		90		
418	BLACK/BLUE FATHER CHRISTMAS	FIGURINE	VC - FATHER CHRISTMAS		90		
419	RED FATHER CHRISTMAS W/WALKING STICK	FIGURINE	VC - FATHER CHRISTMAS		91		
420	BR FATHER CHRISTMAS ON DONKEY W/SWITCHES	FIGURINE	VC - FATHER CHRISTMAS		91		
421	RED & GOLD ST NICHOLAS W/STAFF	FIGURINE	VC - ST. NICHOLAS		91		
422	WHITE FATHER CHRISTMAS W/TOYS	FIGURINE	VC - FATHER CHRISTMAS		91		
423	BLACK PETER IN BLACK & PURPLE	FIGURINE	VC - BLACK PETER		91		
424	SANTA W/SACK OVER SHOULDER	FIGURINE	VC - SANTA		91		
425	BELSNICKEL	FIGURINE	VC - BELSNICKEL		91		
426	BELSNICKEL	FIGURINE	VC - BELSNICKEL		91		
427	SANTA W/LITTLE GIRL	FIGURINE	VC - SANTA		93		
428	WHITE ST NICHOLAS W/CHECK FLOOR	FIGURINE	VC - ST. NICHOLAS		93		
429	RED ST NICHOLAS W/2 CHILDREN IN TUB	FIGURINE	VC - ST. NICHOLAS		93		
430	RED BELSNICKEL	FIGURINE	VC - BELSNICKEL		93		
431	KRAMPUS	FIGURINE	VC - MISC		93		
433	GLASTONBURY THORN BELSNICKEL	FIGURINE	VC - MISC		93		
435	DARK GREEN BELSNICKEL W/HOLLY	FIGURINE	VC - BELSNICKEL		93		
500G	FATHER CHRISTMAS GREEN COAT W/SANTA ON DAPPLE HORSE	FIGURINE	VC - FATHER CHRISTMAS		88	$60.00	$200.00
500R	RED FATHER CHRISTMAS SANTA ON ROCKING HORSE IN BAG	FIGURINE	VC - FATHER CHRISTMAS		88	$250.00	$700.00
501	AMERICAN SANTA/GROLIER/SOLD OUT	FIGURINE	VC - SANTA		88	$250.00	$700.00
502	FATHER CHRISTMAS/RED W/PUPPY	FIGURINE	VC - FATHER CHRISTMAS		88	$100.00	
502	FATHER CHRISTMAS/RED W/PUPPY	FIGURINE	VC - FATHER CHRISTMAS		88	$80.00	
503	LARGE WINDOW AMERICAN SANTA	FIGURINE	VC - SANTA		88	$100.00	
504	GNOME ON SACK ROCKER	FIGURINE	VC - MISC		88	$60.00	
505	BROWN FATHER CHRISTMAS	FIGURINE	VC - FATHER CHRISTMAS		88	$80.00	
506	FATHER CHRISTMAS W/CAPE/RED	FIGURINE	VC - FATHER CHRISTMAS		88	$60.00	
507	FATHER CHRISTMAS W/WALKING STICK ANGEL HOLDING SACK	FIGURINE	VC - FATHER CHRISTMAS		88	$70.00	
508	FATHER CHRISTMAS/GREEN/14	FIGURINE	VC - FATHER CHRISTMAS		88	$250.00	$350.00
509	BLUE ST NICHOLAS W/LONG BEARD	FIGURINE	VC - ST. NICHOLAS		88	$70.00	
510	FATHER CHRISTMAS RED W/SACK OVER SHOULDER	FIGURINE	VC - FATHER CHRISTMAS		88	$80.00	
511	BELSNICKEL ORANGE/RED/W/SWITCHES	FIGURINE	VC - BELSNICKEL		88	$60.00	
512	BELSNICKEL BLUE W/SWITCHES AND BOY SNACK	FIGURINE	VC - BELSNICKEL		88	$40.00	
513	BELSNICKEL GREEN W/SWITCHES/WHITE SACK	FIGURINE	VC - BELSNICKEL		88	$40.00	
515	SANTA (ST NICK) W/2 CHILDREN IN SACK	FIGURINE	VC - SANTA		88	$50.00	
516	FATHER CHRISTMAS/RED/ON MULE	FIGURINE	VC - FATHER CHRISTMAS		88	$60.00	
517	SANTA W/AIRPLANE UNDER ARM	FIGURINE	VC - SANTA		88	$80.00	
518	BROWN FATHER CHRISTMAS W/CAPE SANTA ON DAPPLE TOY	FIGURINE	VC - FATHER CHRISTMAS		88	$60.00	
519	BELSNICKEL BLUE	FIGURINE	VC - BELSNICKEL		88	$50.00	
520	BELSNICKLE W/HOLLY SACK/6 S BASE	FIGURINE	VC - BELSNICKEL		88	$50.00	

Order No.	Title	Type	Theme	Retired	Intro. Year	Retail Price	Secondary Price
521	THREE GNOMES & ANGEL ON SLED	FIGURINE	VC - MISC		88	$225.00	
527	FATHER CHRISTMAS WINDOW DISPLAY BROWN HOLDING TREE	FIGURINE	VC - FATHER CHRISTMAS		88	$400.00	$800.00
528	FATHER CHRISTMAS WINDOW DISPLAY COAT/GR HOOD TOYS	FIGURINE	VC - FATHER CHRISTMAS		88	$400.00	
529	SANTA ON PIG	FIGURINE	VC - SANTA		88	$50.00	
530	FATHER CHRISTMAS LT GREEN COAT RED CARDINAL & MARIONETTE	FIGURINE	VC - FATHER CHRISTMAS		89	$150.00	
531	FATHER CHRISTMAS RUSSIAN/GREEN	FIGURINE	VC - FATHER CHRISTMAS		89	$60.00	
532	GNOME W/RED HAT/GREEN COAT/BROWN PANTS	FIGURINE	VC - MISC		89	$60.00	
533	SANTA IN CHIMNEY/LARGE	FIGURINE	VC - SANTA	YES	89	$100.00	$250.00
534	FATHER CHRISTMAS LG. PLUM COAT W/SACK OF TOYS & BOOK	FIGURINE	VC - FATHER CHRISTMAS		89	$200.00	$350.00
535	SNOWMAN W/SILLY MAN HOLDING TREE	FIGURINE	VC - MISC		89	$40.00	
536	SANTA W/STRIPED MITTENS	FIGURINE	VC - SANTA		89	$40.00	
537	FATHER CHRISTMAS GERMAN WHITE COAT W/RED HOOD	FIGURINE	VC - FATHER CHRISTMAS		89	$40.00	
538	SNOWMAN W/GREEN SCARF & BROOM	FIGURINE	VC - MISC		89	$40.00	
540	FATHER CHRISTMAS SCANDANAVIAN CUBISTIC	FIGURINE	VC - FATHER CHRISTMAS		90	$200.00	
541	FATHER CHRISTMAS RED W/CARDINAL	FIGURINE	VC - FATHER CHRISTMAS		90	$200.00	
105R	FATHER CHRISTMAS W/POINTED HOOD/RED	FIGURINE	VC - FATHER CHRISTMAS		85	$35.00	
105W	FATHER CHRISTMAS W/POINTED HOOD/WHITE	FIGURINE	VC - FATHER CHRISTMAS		86	$35.00	$650.00
105G	FATHER CHRISTMAS W/POINTED HOOD/GREEN	FIGURINE	VC - FATHER CHRISTMAS		87	$35.00	
105A	FATHER CHRISTMAS W/POINTED HOOD JR.	FIGURINE	VC - FATHER CHRISTMAS		85	$27.40	$400.00
105AW	FATHER CHRISTMAS W/POINTED HOOD/WHITE	FIGURINE	VC - FATHER CHRISTMAS		87	$40.00	
107	FATHER CHRISTMAS HELPER OR RED BELSNICKEL	FIGURINE	VC - FATHER CHRISTMAS		85	$20.00	
108	FATHER CHRISTMAS W/WALKING STICK	FIGURINE	VC - FATHER CHRISTMAS	86	85	$25.00	$825.00
109	FATHER CHRISTMAS W/MARIONETTE	FIGURINE	VC - FATHER CHRISTMAS	86	85	$25.00	$825.00
110	AMERICAN SANTA	FIGURINE	VC - SANTA		85	$30.00	
111	AMERICAN SANTA	FIGURINE	VC - SANTA		85	$25.00	
112	FATHER CHRISTMAS/GREEN COAT	FIGURINE	VC - FATHER CHRISTMAS		85	$25.00	
113	WINTER REINDEER	FIGURINE	VC - SANTA	94	85	$35.00	$350.00
114	LARGE BELSNICKEL	FIGURINE	VC - BELSNICKEL		86	$30.00	
115	MEDIUM BELSNICKEL	FIGURINE	VC - BELSNICKEL		86	$32.50	
116	SMALL BELSNICKEL	FIGURINE	VC - BELSNICKEL		86	$27.50	
117	ST. NICHOLAS/BLUE	FIGURINE	VC - ST. NICHOLAS		86	$25.00	
118	SMALL SAINT NICHOLAS/RED	FIGURINE	VC - ST. NICHOLAS	87	86	$25.00	$300.00
119	FATHER CHRISTMAS ON DONKEY	FIGURINE	VC - FATHER CHRISTMAS		86	$25.00	$200.00
120	TINY FATHER CHRISTMAS ON DONKEY	FIGURINE	VC - FATHER CHRISTMAS	YES	86	$25.00	
121	FATHER ICE CREAM MOULD/RED	FIGURINE	VC - FATHER CHRISTMAS		86	$50.00	$655.00
121W	FATHER ICE CREAM MOULD/WHITE	FIGURINE	VC - FATHER CHRISTMAS		87	$90.00	
122	FATHER CHRISTMAS/REDCOAT	FIGURINE	VC - FATHER CHRISTMAS		86	$20.00	$50.00
123	FATHER CHRISTMAS/PINK COAT	FIGURINE	VC - FATHER CHRISTMAS		85	$20.00	$250.00
123Y	FATHER CHRISTMAS/YELLOW COAT W/WALNUTS BAG	FIGURINE	VC - FATHER CHRISTMAS		86	$35.00	
124	FATHER CHRISTMAS W/BAD BOY PLAQUE	FIGURINE	VC - FATHER CHRISTMAS	YES	86	$50.00	
125	FATHER CHRISTMAS W/GOOD GIRL PLAQUE	FIGURINE	VC - FATHER CHRISTMAS	YES	86	$50.00	
126	DUTCH ST. NICHOLAS ON ROOF/LARGE	FIGURINE	VC - ST. NICHOLAS		86	$65.00	
127	DUTCH ST. NICHOLAS ON ROOF/SMALL	FIGURINE	VC - ST. NICHOLAS	87	86	$75.00	
128	BLACK PETER/HOLLAND	FIGURINE	VC - BLACK PETER		86	$50.00	
129	BELSNICKEL/PURPLE	FIGURINE	VC - BELSNICKEL		86	$30.00	
130	BELSNICKEL/BLUE W/STICKS	FIGURINE	VC - BELSNICKEL		86	$40.00	
131	BELSNICKEL/YELLOW/DRILLED	FIGURINE	VC - BELSNICKEL		86	$40.00	
132	FATHER CHRISTMAS/GREEN W/LANTERN	FIGURINE	VC - FATHER CHRISTMAS		86	$40.00	
134	GNOME HOLDING PUPPET	FIGURINE	VC - MISC	Yes	86	$50.00	$150.00
135	SAINT NICHOLAS W/2 CHILDREN IN TUB	FIGURINE	VC - MISC		86	$85.00	
136	AMERICAN SANTA W/SWITCHES	FIGURINE	VC - SANTA		86	$20.00	
137	CANDLE W/HOLLY HOLDER	FIGURINE	VC - MISC		86	$25.00	
138	ST. NICHOLAS	FIGURINE	VC - ST. NICHOLAS		86	$40.00	
139	FATHER CHRISTMAS ROCKER	FIGURINE	VC - FATHER CHRISTMAS		86	$30.00	$200.00
139SP	FATHER CHRISTMAS ROCKER	FIGURINE	VC - FATHER CHRISTMAS		87		
139BR	FATHER CHRISTMAS ROCKER	FIGURINE	VC - FATHER CHRISTMAS		87	$30.00	
140	SINT NICKLASS W/3 CHILDREN IN TUB(WINDOW)	FIGURINE	VC - ST. NICHOLAS		86	$250.00	
141	AMERICAN SANTA IN CHIMNEY/SMALL	FIGURINE	VC - SANTA	YES	87	$30.00	$80.00
142	FATHER CHRISTMAS/WHITE W/GOLD SASH	FIGURINE	VC - FATHER CHRISTMAS		87	$30.00	
143	AMERICAN SANTA/FLAT	FIGURINE	VC - SANTA		86		
144	BELSNICKEL/TAN COAT	FIGURINE	VC - BELSNICKEL		86	$30.00	
144G	BELSNICKEL/GREEN	FIGURINE	VC - BELSNICKEL		87	$30.00	
146	SANTA, AMERICAN	FIGURINE	VC - SANTA		87	$25.00	
145	SANTA W/CANDY CANE	FIGURINE	VC - SANTA		87	$30.00	
147	SANTA W/DEER	FIGURINE	VC - SANTA		87	$25.00	
148	BELSNICKEL BROWN	FIGURINE	VC - BELSNICKEL		87	$30.00	
149	FATHER CHRISTMAS HOLDING BOY	FIGURINE	VC - FATHER CHRISTMAS	YES	87	$80.00	$450.00
152	VC SANTA ON MOTORCYCLE/SOLD OUT	FIGURINE	VC - SANTA		87	$60.00	$1,200.00
153	FATHER CHRISTMAS WEARING PANTS	FIGURINE	VC - FATHER CHRISTMAS		87	$30.00	
154	TINY ST. NICHOLAS/WHITE	FIGURINE	VC - FATHER CHRISTMAS		87	$30.00	
155	BELSNICKEL/GREEN	FIGURINE	VC - BELSNICKEL		87	$30.00	
156	BELSNICKEL/BLUE	FIGURINE	VC - BELSNICKEL		87	$27.50	
157	BELSNICKEL/PINK	FIGURINE	VC - FATHER CHRISTMAS	YES	87	$25.00	$60.00
159	FATHER CHRISTMAS BLUE COAT W/BOBBY IN SACK	FIGURINE	VC - FATHER CHRISTMAS		87	$50.00	
158	FATHER CHRISTMAS GREEN COAT W/SHOULDER BAG	FIGURINE	VC - BELSNICKEL		87	$35.00	
160	FATHER CHRISTMAS GREEN W/ARK IN SACK	FIGURINE	VC - FATHER CHRISTMAS		87	$60.00	
161	VC NATIVITY	FIGURINE	VC - MISC		87	$200.00	
162	FATHER CHRISTMAS W/WALKING STICK/LARGE	FIGURINE	VC - FATHER CHRISTMAS		87	$60.00	
163	AMERICAN SNOWMAN W/STICK ARMS	FIGURINE	VC - MISC		87	$30.00	
164	VC SANTA ON MOON ROCKER/SOLD OUT	FIGURINE	VC - SANTA		87	$160.00	$1,050.00
165	VC SANTA ON SNOW KING SLED	FIGURINE	VC - SANTA		87	$160.00	
166	SANTA W/ANGEL HOLDING SACK/RED	FIGURINE	VC - SANTA		87	$65.00	$125.00
167	VC FATHER CHRISTMAS IN BROWN COAT W/TEDDY	FIGURINE	VC - FATHER CHRISTMAS		87	$200.00	
170	VC SANTA STUFFING DOLL IN CHIMNEY	FIGURINE	VC - SANTA		87	$200.00	
171	HUNCHED FATHER CHRISTMAS W/BROCADE COAT	FIGURINE	VC - FATHER CHRISTMAS		87	$170.00	
172	SMALL FATHER CHRISTMAS HUNCHED/PINK	FIGURINE	VC - FATHER CHRISTMAS		87	$50.00	
173B	KNECHT RUPPERT BLACK COAT/ICE CREAM MOULD	FIGURINE	VC - KNECHT RUPPERT		87	$150.00	
173R	KNECHT RUPPERT RED COAT/ICE CREAM MOULD	FIGURINE	VC - KNECHT RUPPERT		87	$150.00	
175	BELSNICKEL/PURPLE COAT W/SILVER BROCADE	FIGURINE	VC - BELSNICKEL		87	$60.00	
176	FATHER CHRISTMAS W/GIRL FULL BODY	FIGURINE	VC - FATHER CHRISTMAS		87	$85.00	
177	FATHER CHRISTMAS HOLDING TREE	FIGURINE	VC - FATHER CHRISTMAS		87	$50.00	
178B	RUPPERT JR.	FIGURINE	VC - KNECHT RUPPERT		87	$40.00	
178G	RUPPERT JR.T	FIGURINE	VC - KNECHT RUPPERT		87	$40.00	

Order No.	Title	Type	Theme	Retired	Intro. Year	Retial Price	Secondary Price
179	RED FATHER CHRISTMAS HOLDING LANTERN	FIGURINE	VC - FATHER CHRISTMAS		87	$50.00	
178R	RUPPERT JR.	FIGURINE	VC - KNECHT RUPPERT		87	$40.00	
201	SUMMER REINDEER	FIGURINE	VC - MISC	94	85	$35.00	$350.00
407	FATHER CHRISTMAS/WHITE W/VINES	FIGURINE	VC - FATHER CHRISTMAS		90		
408	BLUE BELSNICKEL	FIGURINE	VC - BELSNICKEL		90		
409	CHRISTMAS TREE W/CANDLES	FIGURINE	VC - MISC		90		
410	PINK BELSNICKEL	FIGURINE	VC - BELSNICKEL		90		
542	FATHER CHRISTMAS WHITE/SOLD OUT	FIGURINE	VC - FATHER CHRISTMAS		90	$200.00	$1,200.00
543	FATHER CHRISTMAS ON CHIMNEY W/TOY BAG	FIGURINE	VC - FATHER CHRISTMAS		90	$80.00	
544	WINDOW DISPLAY FATHER CHRISTMAS WHITE W/MARIONETTE	FIGURINE	VC - FATHER CHRISTMAS		90	$400.00	
545	RED & WHITE FATHER CHRISTMAS W/SANTA ON REINDEER SACK	FIGURINE	VC - FATHER CHRISTMAS		90	$100.00	
546	FATHER CHRISTMAS W/TWO TREES IN SACK	FIGURINE	VC - FATHER CHRISTMAS		90	$100.00	
547	BLUE BELSNICKEL	FIGURINE	VC - BELSNICKEL		90	$50.00	
549	FATHER CHRISTMAS	FIGURINE	VC - FATHER CHRISTMAS				
550	BLUE FATHER CHRISTMAS W/LANTERN	FIGURINE	VC - FATHER CHRISTMAS		90	$100.00	
551	BLUE FATHER CHRISTMAS W/BLUE BIRD	FIGURINE	VC - FATHER CHRISTMAS		90	$150.00	
552	WHITE FATHER CHRISTMAS W/CAPE GREEN STRIPES	FIGURINE	VC - FATHER CHRISTMAS		90	$80.00	
553	PURPLE HUNCHED PERE NOEL	FIGURINE	VC - FATHER CHRISTMAS		91	$80.00	
554	1991 STARLIGHT SANTA	FIGURINE	VC - STARLIGHT SANTA	YES	91	$95.00	$950.00
555	VICTORIAN FATHER CHRISTMAS IN GREEN COAT W/PINK HAT	FIGURINE	VC - FATHER CHRISTMAS		91	$60.00	
556	VICTORIAN FATHER CHRISTMAS W/RED COAT CARRYING DOLL	FIGURINE	VC - FATHER CHRISTMAS		91	$80.00	
557	KRIS KRINGLE W/PINE CONES	FIGURINE	VC - KRIS KRINGLE		91	$80.00	
558	WEINNACHTEN HOLDING RABBIT	FIGURINE	VC - MISC		91	$100.00	
559	SNOWMAN W/EARS	FIGURINE	VC - MISC		91	$40.00	
560	SANTA ON SCOOTER W/SHOOTING STAR COAT	FIGURINE	VC - SANTA		91	$180.00	
561	SCHERENSCHNITTE FATHER CHRISTMAS WHITE COAT	FIGURINE	VC - FATHER CHRISTMAS		91	$100.00	
562	FATHER CHRISTMAS/WHITE/SOLD OUT	FIGURINE	VC - FATHER CHRISTMAS		91	$200.00	$1,200.00
563	LARGE SAINT NICHOLAS IN YELLOW & WHITE	FIGURINE	VC - SANTA		92	$200.00	
564	SANTA W/TREE TEDDY IN POCKET	FIGURINE	VC - ST. NICHOLAS		92	$80.00	
565	SANTA (GIFT GIVER) IN BLUE ROADSTER	FIGURINE	VC - SANTA		92	$80.00	
566	1992 STARLIGHT WISHES	FIGURINE	VC - STARLIGHT SANTA	YES	92	$95.00	$550.00
567	LARGE FATHER CHRISTMAS/RED COAT	FIGURINE	VC - FATHER CHRISTMAS		92	$80.00	
568	MED-LARGE FATHER CHRISTMAS/GREEN COAT	FIGURINE	VC - FATHER CHRISTMAS		92	$60.00	
569	MED FATHER CHRISTMAS/RED COAT	FIGURINE	VC - FATHER CHRISTMAS		92	$50.00	
570	MED SMALL FATHER CHRISTMAS/GREEN COAT	FIGURINE	VC - FATHER CHRISTMAS		92	$40.00	
571	SMALL FATHER CHRISTMAS RED COAT	FIGURINE	VC - FATHER CHRISTMAS		92	$40.00	
573	SANTA IN SLEIGH W/REINDEER, CHECKERED BLANKET	FIGURINE	VC - SANTA		92	$120.00	
574	SNOWMAN W/HOLLY SCARF & BROOM	FIGURINE	VC - MISC		92	$50.00	
575	SNOWMAN W/TREE & BROOM	FIGURINE	VC - MISC		92	$40.00	
577	KRAMPUS W/HORNS AND CHAINS	FIGURINE	VC - MISC		92		
576	SNOWMAN W/RED TREE MITTENS	FIGURINE	VC - MISC		92	$40.00	
578	SNOWMAN W/GREEN SNOWMAN MITTENS	FIGURINE	VC - MISC		92	$40.00	
579	LARGE FATHER CHRISTMAS ON ROOF/BLUE COAT	FIGURINE	VC - FATHER CHRISTMAS		92	$350.00	
580	A WINK OF HIS EYE	FIGURINE	VC - MISC		92	$120.00	
581	A WINK OF HIS EYE/MINI	FIGURINE	VC - MISC		92	$50.00	
582	PERE NOEL (KRIS KRINGLE)	FIGURINE	VC - KRIS KRINGLE		92	$120.00	
583	SANTA AND ANGEL BAKERY	FIGURINE	VC - SANTA		92	$300.00	
584	APRICOT FATHER CHRISTMAS HUNCHED WITH WHITE SACK	FIGURINE	VC - FATHER CHRISTMAS		92	$40.00	
585	ST NICHOLAS W/TWO CHILDREN IN TUB	FIGURINE	VC - ST. NICHOLAS		93	$200.00	
586	FATHER CHRISTMAS ON LOG	FIGURINE	VC - FATHER CHRISTMAS		93	$60.00	
587	CHRISKINDL (ANGEL)	FIGURINE	VC - MISC		93	$80.00	
588	LARGE SANTA IN SLEIGH WINDOW DISPLAY	FIGURINE	VC - SANTA		93	$1,500.00	
589	PERE NOEL W/LARGE TREE	FIGURINE	VC - MISC		93	$80.00	
590	ASHEN CLAUS W/BLUE BAG AND SWITCH	FIGURINE	VC - MISC		93	$100.00	
591	SCANDANAVIAN FATHER CHRISTMAS W/RED COAT & FT	FIGURINE	VC - FATHER CHRISTMAS		93	$200.00	
592	FATHER CHRISTMAS IN GREEN COAT W/CAT & SWITCHES	FIGURINE	VC - FATHER CHRISTMAS		93	$150.00	
593	FATHER CHRISTMAS STUFFING SACK DOWN CHIMNEY SNOWING	FIGURINE	VC - FATHER CHRISTMAS		93	$80.00	
594	1993 STARLIGHT #4 SANTA W/STAR ON SACK	FIGURINE	VC - SANTA	YES	93	$125.00	$450.00
595	FATHER CHRISTMAS PIPE ON WOODEN STAND	FIGURINE	VC - FATHER CHRISTMAS		94	$90.00	
596	SANTA PULLING SLED W/TREE BEAR	FIGURINE	VC - SANTA		94	$300.00	
710	ORNAMENT CHRISTMAS BULB ASSORTED COLORS	ORNAMENT	VC - MISC	YES	NA	$10.00	$10.00
711	ORNAMENT SMALL SANTA	ORNAMENT	VC - SANTA	YES	NA	$10.00	$10.00
712	ORNAMENT SMALL SANTA FACE	ORNAMENT	VC - SANTA	YES	NA	$12.00	$12.00
713	ORNAMENT MEDIUM SANTA	ORNAMENT	VC - SANTA	YES	NA	$15.00	$15.00
714	ORNAMENT LARGE SANTA	ORNAMENT	VC - SANTA	YES	NA	$20.00	$20.00
715	ORNAMENT LARGE SANTA FACE	ORNAMENT	VC - SANTA	YES	NA	$20.00	$20.00
716	ORNAMENT SANTA FACE IN BELL SHAPE	ORNAMENT	VC - SANTA	YES	NA	$12.00	$12.00
718	ORNAMENT SMALL CAT ASSORTED	ORNAMENT	VC - MISC			$25.00	
719	ORNAMENT LARGE HEART ASSORTED	ORNAMENT	VC - MISC				
720	ORNAMENT MEDIUM HEART ASSORTED	ORNAMENT	VC - MISC			$12.00	
721	ORNAMENT SMALL HEART ASSORTED	ORNAMENT	VC - MISC			$15.00	
722	ORNAMENT FLORAL PLAQUE ASSORTED	ORNAMENT	VC - MISC				
723	ORNAMENT SMALL ELEPHANT	ORNAMENT	VC - MISC				
724	ORNAMENT SMALL RABBIT	ORNAMENT	VC - MISC				
726	ORNAMENT SMALL HEN ON NEST	ORNAMENT	VC - MISC				
727	ORNAMENT DRESDEN RABBIT	ORNAMENT	VC - MISC				
728	GOLDEN SOLDIER	FIGURINE	VC - MISC				
728B	GOLD SOLDIER W/BLUE	FIGURINE	VC - MISC				
728R	GOLD SOLDIER W/RED	FIGURINE	VC - MISC				
729	GOLD DRUM	FIGURINE	VC - MISC				
729	GOLD DRUM	FIGURINE	VC - MISC				
729B	GOLD DRUM W/BLUE	FIGURINE	VC - MISC				
729R	GOLD DRUM W/RED	FIGURINE	VC - MISC				
730	ORNAMENT SMALL ROOSTER	FIGURINE	VC - MISC				
731	SANTA FACE PINS	FIGURINE	VC - MISC	YES			
732	PEWTER TREE	FIGURINE	VC - MISC	?	88		
733	PEWTER SANTA FACE	FIGURINE	VC - MISC	?	88		
734	GOLDEN PINE CONE	FIGURINE	VC - MISC	?			
735	ORNAMENT FATHER CHRISTMAS	ORNAMENT	VC - FATHER CHRISTMAS	YES		$20.00	$20.00
736	ORNAMENT ROUND SANTA FACE	ORNAMENT	VC - SANTA	YES		$20.00	$20.00
800	1994 SARLIGHT SANTA SANTA ON STAR	FIGURINE	VC - STARLIGHT SANTA	YES	94	$150.00	$500.00
802	GNOME W/RED SPOTTED MUSHROOM	FIGURINE	VC - MISC		94	$180.00	
803	SIEGEL SANTA IN GREEN COAT	FIGURINE	VC - MISC		94	$100.00	

Order No.	Title	Type	Theme	Retired	Intro. Year	Retail Price	Secondary Price
804	WHITE FATHER CHRISTMAS EMPTYING SACK	FIGURINE	VC - FATHER CHRISTMAS		94	$300.00	
806	FROHE WEINACHTEN IN FUR	FIGURINE	VC - MISC		94	$390.00	
807	SANTA IN RED JAGUAR	FIGURINE	VC - SANTA		94	$350.00	
808	FATHER CHRISTMAS IN RED COAT W/GREEN & WHITE STRIPED BAG	FIGURINE	VC - FATHER CHRISTMAS		94	$100.00	
809	SANTA HOLDING TREE	FIGURINE	VC - SANTA		94	$90.00	
810	10TH ANNIVERSARY SANTA IN SLEIGH W/REINDEER	FIGURINE	VC - SANTA	YES	94	$150.00	
811	FATHER CHRISTMAS IN BLUE COAT CARRYING LANTERN	FIGURINE	VC - FATHER CHRISTMAS		94	$90.00	
813	BELSNICKEL DRILLED W/STICK SWITCHES	FIGURINE	VC - BELSNICKEL		94	$90.00	
814	FATHER CHRISTMAS/RED W/SACK DRILLED TREE	FIGURINE	VC - FATHER CHRISTMAS		94	$160.00	
815	LARGE AMERICAN SANTA	FIGURINE	VC - SANTA		94	$120.00	
1000	CHRISTMAS CHESS SET/SOLD OUT	FIGURINE	VC - MISC		87	$3,000.00	$7,500.00
1003	CHRISTMAS CHESS SET/SOLD OUT	FIGURINE	VC - MISC		88	$3,000.00	$5,500.00
9531	WINDOW DISPLAY ST NICHOLAS W/WALKING STICK	FIGURINE	VC - ST. NICHOLAS		95	$1,900.00	
9532	SANTA W/MOON AND STAR SACK	FIGURINE	VC - SANTA		95	$250.00	
9533	BELSNICKEL W/GREEN COAT & WHITE HOOD	FIGURINE	VC - BELSNICKEL		95	$90.00	
9534	BELSNICKEL W/RED COAT & DRILLED FEATHER TREE	FIGURINE	VC - BELSNICKEL		95	$80.00	
9535	SANTA LEANING ON STICK W/PLAID PANTS	FIGURINE	VC - SANTA		95	$130.00	
9536	CHRISTMAS STOCKING FULL OF TOYS	FIGURINE	VC - MISC		95	$190.00	
9537	BLUE FATHER CHRISTMAS W/SWITCH SNOWMEN ON COAT	FIGURINE	VC - FATHER CHRISTMAS		95	$110.00	
9538	BELSNICKEL W/GREEN COAT	FIGURINE	VC - BELSNICKEL		95	$50.00	
9539	TINY BLUE ANGEL	FIGURINE	VC - MISC		95	$40.00	
9540	SNOW ANGEL	FIGURINE	VC - MISC		95	$70.00	
9541	SANTA ON DONKEY	FIGURINE	VC - SANTA		95	$300.00	
9542	FATHER CHRISTMAS IN WHITE ON DONKEY	FIGURINE	VC - SANTA		95	$250.00	
9543	FATHER CHRISTMAS PULLING SLED W/TREE	FIGURINE	VC - SANTA		95	$300.00	
9570	PINK ANGEL	FIGURINE	VC - MISC		95	$60.00	
9571	VIOLET ANGEL	FIGURINE	VC - MISC		95	$60.00	
9572	BLUE ANGEL	FIGURINE	VC - MISC		NA	$60.00	
9576	ANGEL MATCHED SET OF THREE	FIGURINE	VC - MISC		95	$300.00	
9577	FIRST COLLECTORS BELSNICKEL	FIGURINE	VC - BELSNICKEL		95	$70.00	
95CH1	FATHER CHRISTMAS	FIGURINE	VC - FATHER CHRISTMAS		95	$70.00	
95CH2	FATHER CHRISTMAS W/CHIMNEY	FIGURINE	VC - FATHER CHRISTMAS		95	$70.00	
95CH3	FATHER CHRISTMAS W/STARS	FIGURINE	VC - FATHER CHRISTMAS		95	$70.00	
95CH4	ST NICHOLAS W/STAFF	FIGURINE	VC - ST. NICHOLAS		95	$70.00	
95CH5	FATHER CHRISTMAS W/GOLD COAT	FIGURINE	VC - FATHER CHRISTMAS		95	$70.00	
95CH6	BELSNICKEL RED	FIGURINE	VC - BELSNICKEL		95	$70.00	
95NKD1	FATHER CHRISTMAS/ WHITE COAT/RED HOOD	FIGURINE	VC - FATHER CHRISTMAS		95		
95NKD2	FATHER CHRISTMAS/ WHITE/PEACOCK DESIGN	FIGURINE	VC - FATHER CHRISTMAS		95		
95NKD3	ST NICHOLAS RED	FIGURINE	VC - ST. NICHOLAS		95		
95NKD4	BISHOP W/STAFF	FIGURINE	VC - MISC		95		
95NKD5	SANTA W/REINDEER BELT	FIGURINE	VC - SANTA		95		
95NKD6	FATHER CHRISTMAS RED COAT W/DOTS	FIGURINE	VC - FATHER CHRISTMAS		95		
95NKD7	FATHER CHRISTMAS GREEN FLORAL	FIGURINE	VC - FATHER CHRISTMAS		95		
95NKD8	BELSNICKEL GREEN COAT	FIGURINE	VC - BELSNICKEL		95		
95NKD9	BLACK PETER	FIGURINE	VC - BLACK PETER		95		
95NKD10	ST. NICHOLAS BLUE COAT	FIGURINE	VC - ST. NICHOLAS		95		
95NKD11	FATHER CHRISTMAS VIOLET AND YELLOW	FIGURINE	VC - FATHER CHRISTMAS		94		
95SC1	SNOWMAN W/SNOWBABY	FIGURINE	VC - FATHER CHRISTMAS		95	$70.00	
95SC2	SNOWMAN W/BIRDS	FIGURINE	VC - MISC		95	$70.00	
95SC3	SNOWMAN W/TREE	FIGURINE	VC - MISC		95	$70.00	
95SC4	SNOWMAN W/CANE	FIGURINE	VC - MISC		95	$70.00	
95SC5	SNOWMAN W/STOCKING	FIGURINE	VC - MISC		95	$70.00	
9630	STARLIGHT SANTA #7	FIGURINE	VC - STARLIGHT SANTA		96	$100.00	
9630	STARLIGHT SANTA #7	FIGURINE	VC - MISC		96	$100.00	
9631	SANTA W/BELL	FIGURINE	VC - SANTA		96	$150.00	
9632	SANTA W/SWITCH	FIGURINE	VC - SANTA		96	$90.00	
9633	FATHER CHRISTMA W/BLUE STARS	FIGURINE	VC - FATHER CHRISTMAS		96	$90.00	
9634	FATHER CHRISTMAS WINDOW DISPLAY	FIGURINE	VC - FATHER CHRISTMAS		NA		
9635	BELSNICKEL W/RED COAT	FIGURINE	VC - BELSNICKEL		NA	$350.00	
9636	THREE CHILDREN ON SLED	FIGURINE	VC - MISC		96	$350.00	
9637	STRIDING BELSNICKEL	FIGURINE	VC - BELSNICKEL		96	$70.00	
9638	GERMAN TREE	FIGURINE	VC - MISC		96	$30.00	
9639	TINY SNOWMAN IN VEST	FIGURINE	VC - MISC		96	$50.00	
9640	ARTIST SNOWMAN	FIGURINE	VC - MISC		96	$120.00	
9641	FATHER CHRISTMAS W/JULENISSEN	FIGURINE	VC - FATHER CHRISTMAS		96	$300.00	
9642	FATHER CHRISTMAS ON MOTORCYCLE W/CHERUB	FIGURINE	VC - FATHER CHRISTMAS		96	$130.00	
9643	BELSNICKEL IN BLACK FUR W/BELL	FIGURINE	VC - BELSNICKEL		96	$140.00	
9644	FATHER CHRISTMAS IN GOLD COAT	FIGURINE	VC - FATHER CHRISTMAS		96	$130.00	
9645	ANGEL IN BLUE W/STARS	FIGURINE	VC - MISC		96	$90.00	
9646	SOLDIER SET 4 PIECES W/DRUM	FIGURINE	VC - MISC		96	$150.00	
9647	SOLDIER SET 3 PIECES	FIGURINE	VC - MISC		96	$125.00	
9648	RED DRUM	FIGURINE	VC - MISC		96		
9649	SOLDIER W/RIFLE	FIGURINE	VC - MISC		96		
9650	SOLDIER W/SWORD	FIGURINE	VC - MISC		96		
9651	SOLDIER W/DRUM	FIGURINE	VC - MISC		96		
9652	TREE W/CANDLES & STAR	FIGURINE	VC - MISC		96	$100.00	
9653	TREE W/ROUND BASE	FIGURINE	VC - MISC		96		
9654	TREE W/TOYS	FIGURINE	VC - MISC		96		
9665	COLLECTOR'S WKND PERE NOEL	FIGURINE	VC - MISC		96	$70.00	
9565	COLLECTOR'S WKND PERE NOEL	FIGURINE	VC - MISC		96		
CH1	COUNTRY HOME RED FATHER CHRISTMAS W/SACK OF APPLES	FIGURINE	VC - FATHER CHRISTMAS		93	$90.00	
CH2	COUNTRY HOME WHITE FATHER CHRISTMAS	FIGURINE	VC - FATHER CHRISTMAS		93	$90.00	
CH3	COUNTRY HOME GOLD COAT FATHER CHRISTMAS	FIGURINE	VC - FATHER CHRISTMAS		93	$90.00	
CH4	PINK FATHER CHRISTMAS W/SWITCHES & MOON SACK	FIGURINE	VC - FATHER CHRISTMAS		93	$90.00	
CH5	FATHER CHRISTMAS GREEN COAT AND RED BASE	FIGURINE	VC - FATHER CHRISTMAS		93	$90.00	
CH6	RED FATHER CHRISTMAS W/TOY SACK & DOLL & SWITCHES	FIGURINE	VC - FATHER CHRISTMAS		93	$90.00	
	SANTA HOLDING WOODY	FIGURINE	VC - SANTA		94		
	BLUE BELSNICKEL W/NEEDLEWORK	FIGURINE	VC - BELSNICKEL		94		
	RED & GOLD ST NICHOLAS	FIGURINE	VC - ST. NICHOLAS		94		
	BELSNICKEL BLK	FIGURINE	VC - BELSNICKEL		94		
	GNOME W/SACK	FIGURINE	VC - MISC		94		
	FATHER CHRISTMAS ON DONKEY	FIGURINE	VC - FATHER CHRISTMAS		94		
	GLASTONBURY THORN FATHER CHRISTMAS	FIGURINE	VC - FATHER CHRISTMAS		94		

Order No.	Title	Type	Theme	Retired	Intro. Year	Retial Price	Secondary Price
	ENGLISH SANTA	FIGURINE	VC - SANTA		94		
	RED FATHER CHRISTMAS W/WHITE SILHOUETTE	FIGURINE	VC - FATHER CHRISTMAS		94		
	KRAMPUS RED	FIGURINE	VC - MISC		94		
	FATHER CHRISTMAS WITH LANTERN	FIGURINE	VC - FATHER CHRISTMAS		94		
MD1	ST NICK ON ROOFTOP DUTCH	FIGURINE	VC - ST. NICHOLAS		85	$215.00	
MD2	AMERICAN SANTA	FIGURINE	VC - SANTA		90	$80.00	
MD3	CIVIL WAR STARS & STRIPES SANTA	FIGURINE	VC - SANTA		90	$110.00	
MD4	BLUE FATHER CHRISTMAS W/BOXES	FIGURINE	VC - FATHER CHRISTMAS		90	$130.00	
MD5	FATHER CHRISTMAS BROWN SUIT W/GREEN SACK	FIGURINE	VC - FATHER CHRISTMAS		90	$110.00	
MD6	ST. NICK W/TWO CHILDREN IN TUB	FIGURINE	VC - ST. NICHOLAS		85	$320.00	
MD7	GNOME PULLING SLED OF GIFTS W/FATHER CHRISTMAS	FIGURINE	VC - MISC		90	$400.00	
MD8	BELSNICKEL GREEN COAT AND SACK OF APPLES	FIGURINE	VC - BELSNICKEL		90	$90.00	
MD9	SMALL AMERICAN SANTA W/SACK MARKED TOYS	FIGURINE	VC - SANTA		90	$80.00	
MD10	BELSNICKEL IN BROWN COAT W/SWITCHES AND STICK	FIGURINE	VC - BELSNICKEL		90	$80.00	
MD11	BELSNICKEL W/ DARK GREEN COAT	FIGURINE	VC - BELSNICKEL		90	$70.00	
MD12	BELSNICKEL W/LIGHT GREEN COAT AND BORDERED HOOD	FIGURINE	VC - BELSNICKEL		90	$90.00	
MD13	SANTA IN BROWN SUIT W/LEG IN CHIMNEY	FIGURINE	VC - FATHER CHRISTMAS		90	$110.00	
MD14	FATHER CHRISTMAS IN PURPLE COAT AND BOY AND GIRL	FIGURINE	VC - FATHER CHRISTMAS		90	$275.00	
MD15	BELSNICKEL GREEN BROCADE W/SWITCHES & TEDDY	FIGURINE	VC - BELSNICKEL		90	$225.00	
MD16	FATHER CHRISTMAS HEAD PLAQUE	FIGURINE	VC - FATHER CHRISTMAS		90	$130.00	
MD17	CHRISTMAS TREE PLAQUE W/THREE CHILDREN	FIGURINE	VC - MISC		90	$300.00	
MD18	CHRISTMAS TREE PLAQUE W/THREE CHILDREN	FIGURINE	VC - MISC		90	$300.00	
MD26	FATHER CHRISTMAS IN RED COAT W/WHITE DOTS/SOLDIER IN SACK	FIGURINE	VC - FATHER CHRISTMAS		91	$130.00	
MD27	FAT SANTA W/QUILTED COAT AND 3 CHILDREN IN SACK	FIGURINE	VC - SANTA		91	$130.00	
MD28	FATHER CHRISTMAS PUSHING SHOE SLED W/GIFTS	FIGURINE	VC - FATHER CHRISTMAS		91	$325.00	
MD31	NATIVITY	FIGURINE	VC - MISC		91	$450.00	
MD37	FATHER CHRISTMAS TAN BROCADE W/GOOD/BAD BOOKS	FIGURINE	VC - FATHER CHRISTMAS		93	$300.00	
MD38	JULE NISSEN WITH SACK OF COINS	FIGURINE	VC - MISC		94	$170.00	
MD39	WHITE FATHER CHRISTMAS W/ANGEL HOLDING SACK & SWITCHES	FIGURINE	VC - FATHER CHRISTMAS		94	$170.00	
MD9521	KING & QUEEN	FIGURINE	VC - MISC		95	$270.00	
96NKD1	WHITE VINE FATHER CHRISTMAS	FIGURINE	VC - FATHER CHRISTMAS		96	$400.00	
96NKD2	TRAILING VINE FATHER CHRISTMAS	FIGURINE	VC - FATHER CHRISTMAS		96		
96NKD3	KRIS KRINGLE HOLIDAY FLORAL	FIGURINE	VC - KRIS KRINGLE		96		
96NKD4	FATHER CHRISTMAS WHITE FLORAL	FIGURINE	VC - FATHER CHRISTMAS		96		
96NKD5	MINI FATHER CHRISTMAS W/BOTTLE BRUSH TREE	FIGURINE	VC - FATHER CHRISTMAS		96		
96NKD6	FATHER CHRISTMAS COBALT BLUE COAT	FIGURINE	VC - FATHER CHRISTMAS		96		
96NKD7	BLACK PETER	FIGURINE	VC - BLACK PETER		96		
101	ORIGINAL FATHER CHRISTMAS	FIGURINE	VC - FATHER CHRISTMAS		84	$25.00	
122B	FATHER CHRISTMAS/BLUE COAT	FIGURINE	VC - FATHER CHRISTMAS		87	$50.00	
9530	STARLIGHT #6 BELSNICKEL W/BLACK COAT & STARS	FIGURINE	VC - STARLIGHT SANTA		95	$95.00	
95101	101 SPECIAL SACK	FIGURINE	VC - BELSNICKEL		95	$300.00	$300.00
95SC6	SNOWLADY W/HAT	FIGURINE	VC - MISC		95	$70.00	
	90 STAR STARLIGHT SANTA	FIGURINE	VC - STARLIGHT SANTA		90	$95.00	
95129	BELSNICKEL/PURPLE	FIGURINE	VC - BELSNICKEL		95		
95129	BELSNICKEL/PURPLE	FIGURINE	VC - BELSNICKEL		95		
9730	1997 BELSNICKEL W/PINES	FIGURINE	VC - BELSNICKLE		97	$100.00	
9731	GREEN FR CHRISTMAS TRUDGING THROUGH SNOW	FIGURINE	VC - FATHER CHRISTMAS		97	$60.00	
9732	BUFFALO PLAID TOMTEN	FIGURINE	VC - MISC		97	$110.00	
9733	SANTA ON STUMP	FIGURINE	VC - SANTA		97	$80.00	
9734	FATHER FROST	FIGURINE	VC - FATHER CHRISTMAS		97	$120.00	
9735	FATHER CHRISTMAS IN GRAY COAT	FIGURINE	VC - FATHER CHRISTMAS		97	$90.00	
9736	FATHER CHRISTMAS W/VIOLET EYES	FIGURINE	VC - FATHER CHRISTMAS		97	$120.00	
9737	STAG	FIGURINE	VC - MISC		97	$190.00	
9738	BLUE FR CHRISTMAS BANQUET ICE CREAM MOULD	FIGURINE	VC - FATHER CHRISTMAS		97	$350.00	
9739	RED FR CHRISTMAS BANQUET ICE CREAM MOULD	FIGURINE	VC - FATHER CHRISTMAS		97	$350.00	
9740	ST. NICK RIDING ON AIRPLANE	FIGURINE	VC - ST. NICHOLAS		97	$250.00	
9741	RED FR CHRISTMAS INDIV. ICE CREAM MOULD	FIGURINE	VC - FATHER CHRISTMAS		97	$70.00	
9742	FR CHRISTMAS W/DRILLED TREE	FIGURINE	VC - FATHER CHRISTMAS		97	$60.00	
9743	BLUE FR CHRISTMAS WISHES WINDOW W/DISPLAY	FIGURINE	VC - FATHER CHRISTMAS		97	$1,900.00	
150	LARGE FC (RED) ON DONKEY	FIGURINE	VC - FATHER CHRISTMAS			$60.00	
9574	GIRL ON SWING	FIGURINE	VC - MISC		95	$300.00	

Section 4: Resource Listings

Publications

The Collector's Pocket Planner

Collectors' Publishing Co., Inc.
Pomeroy Avenue
Meriden, CT 06450
(800) 746-3686

Pocket Planners are well-known and respected tools for collectors. Pocket-sized and accordion-style, these collectible line listings are available for more than 50 collectible lines. Great to take on the road.

Display Mania

Dickens' Exchange
5150 Highway 22, Suite C-9,
Mandeville, LA 70471

Display Mania is a 166-page book on how to enhance and build displays for the ceramic and porcelain villages.

The Dickens' Exchange

5150 Hwy 22 Suite C-9,
Mandeville, LA 70471-2515
(504) 845-1954

This a monthly newsletter for collectors of The Original Snow Village Collection, The Dickens' Village Collection, The Christmas in The City Collection, The New England Village Collection, The Alpine Village Collection, The North Pole Collection and Snowbabies.

The Village Press

P.O. Box 556
Rockford, IL 61105-0556
(815) 965-0901
fax. (815) 965-5656

This is the oldest publication for Department 56 collectors.

Glitter Newsletter

1501 Surfbird Court
Raleigh, N.C. 27615
voice and fax. (919) 518-2848
Contact: Brad and Melanie Benham

Glitter is a bi-monthly newsletter for designer ornament enthusiasts with focus on European blown glass ornaments such as Christopher Radko, Old World Christmas, Polonaise and others. Other lines featured include Margaret Furlong and Boyds Bears.

Collector's Mart Magazine

700 East State Street
Iola, WI 54990
(715) 445-2214
fax. (715) 445-4087

The Ornament Collector

Rural Route #1
Canton, IL 61520
(309) 647-3142

Collector Editions Magazine

170 Fifth Avenue
New York, N.Y. 10010
(212) 989-8700

Figurines & Collectibles Magazine

6405 Flank Drive
Harrisburg, PA 17112
(800) 435-9610

Price Guide to Limited Edition Collectibles

Edited by Mary Sieber and the staff of *Collector's mart magazine*
Krause Publications
700 East State Street
Iola, WI 54990-0001
(715) 445-2214
fax. (715) 445-4087

The Collection Connection

26401 Las Alturas Avenue
Laguna Hills, CA 92653-6233
(714) 831-2114
Contact: Ellen Gordon

This is a secondary price guide for Hallmark Keepsake Ornaments and Merry Miniatures.

Rosie's' Secondary Market Price Guide for Hallmark Ornaments

Rosie Well Enterprises, Inc.
22341 E. Wells Road
Canton, IL 61520
(800) 445-8745

Hallmark Keepsake Ornaments—20 Years of Christmas Memories

by Clara Johnson Scroggins

This 11th edition is out-of-print, but copies can be found on the secondary market. The newest edition should be ready by 1998.

Organizations

Unity Marketing

206 E. Church Street,
Stevens, PA 17578
(717) 336-1600

Unity Marketing is a marketing services and research firm serving the collectibles and giftware industries. It publishes the *Collectibles Business* newsletter.

Collectors Society of America

2731 South Adams Road, Suite 112
Rochester Hills, MI 48309
(800) 910-2762

CSA is a non-profit organization founded by collectors to promote the interest of collectors. Membership includes subscription to newsletter, free price guide information on selected manufacturers lines upon request, free classified space for secondary market pieces in newsletter for members

Collectors' Information Bureau

Shoreline Road, Suite 200
Barrington, IL 60010
(847) 842-2200

CIB is a not-for-profit association dedicated to the field of limited edition collectibles. CIB publishes newsletters, directories and secondary market price guides for its members.

Collection Organizer Software Programs

Collectibles Database

MSdataBase Solutions, Inc.
614 Warrenton Terrace NE
Leesburg, VA 20176-2465
orders. (800) 407-4147
(703) 777-5660

This database computer software program enables collectors to keep track of their collections, print reports, and transfer information from actual guides directly into the owner's database.

Treasure Chest--The Collection Organizer

Lyons Computers
346 Cernon St., Suite C
Vacaville, CA 95688
(800) 799-3782

This is a collection organizer computer software program with price guides.

GLOSSARY

allotment – The number, which a manufacturer gives to a dealer or collector, of a particular limited edition.

annual – Describes a limited edition that is introduced, manufactured or available yearly.

backstamp. also called **bottomstamp** – The identification marks directly on the collectible. A backstamp can be hand painted, applied as a decal or imprinted into a piece. A backstamp may include the name of the item, name of the series, year of issue, artist's name or signature, the edition limit and other production details.

cast – The forming of liquid clay, into a particular shape, by pouring into a mold and allowing to dry.

ceramic – A piece made of hard, brittle, heat-resistant and corrosion-resistant materials. Made by shaping and then firing a nonmetallic material, such as clay, at a high temperature.

chasing – The decorating process in sculpting. Small hammers and other tools are used to create detailed cuts, engravings or embossing on ornaments.

closed-end series – A group of collectibles which make up a specific number and are limited in edition. This type is usually announced at the start of the series.

commemorative – A collectible created to honor the memory of a particular event or holiday.

dealer – An individual who is engaged in the buying, selling or distribution of collectibles.

distributor – An individual who distributes, markets or sells collectibles, esp. a wholesaler. The distributor purchases collectibles directly from the manufacturer and sells (distributes) to individual collectors.

edition – The number of a particular item issued or produced. Often made with the same name and decoration.

exclusive – Not always meant in the literal sense and exclusive only for a period of time. Often a certain number of particular collectibles are made available early to a specific group of dealers. At a later date, the collectibles may then become available to all dealers.

first issue – The first collectible in a series.

Hallmark™ – A greeting card and giftware company trademark.

hallmark – A mark indicating quality or excellence.

in stock – Merchandise available for future sale from the retailers' or manufacturers' inventory.

issue – An item or set of items, within a series, made available or introduced at one time.

issue price – The original manufacturer price of a collectible when it first appears on the retail market.

licensed properties – To yield, or give permission to, or for items to which usage rights are held. For example, Santa Claus is not a property, however, the famous image of Santa drinking a Coca-Cola® is a licensed property.

limited edition – An edition, as of a collectible, limited to a specified number of pieces or length of time in production. Typically, an item is limited by number, year or other specific time period.

marks – An inscription, name, stamp, label, or seal placed on a collectible to signify quality, manufacturer, or origin.

mint-condition – Describing a collectible that is in its original, undamaged condition. Also meaning that documents and packaging are available in abundant quantities.

open-ended series – A series of collectibles which are to be produced indefinitely. Although at some point in time a collectible may be closed, or retired, by the artist/ company, it is currently not restrained by definite limits or restrictions.

primary market – Pertaining to the manufacturer, retailer or dealer from which a collectible can be purchased at the issue price.

quote – The current stated price for a collectible.

retired – Refers to a collectible that is no longer in circulation.

second – A collectible of inferior quality. A second should be noted so on the bottomstamp.

second edition – Usually introduced after the first edition has retired. With some modifications, it is often made with the same name and decoration as the first edition.

secondary market – After a collectible has been sold on the retail market, it can then be bought and sold any number of times on what is known as the secondary market. Anyone can buy or sell it on the secondary market. The outstanding stock can be sold through dealers but outside of a stock exchange

secondary market price – The prevailing price for a retired collectible, on the primary market. A collector is willing to sell or buy a collectible for a secondary market price. Factors affecting prices include popularity, time of year or the geographical area.

INDEX

Adler, Kurt S. 83

Amaranth Productions 68

Annalee Doll Society 21

Annalee Doll Museum 20

Annalee Mobilitee Dolls, Inc.

Boyds Collection Ltd.

Browning, Tom

Byers' Choice

Byers, Joyce

Byers, Tom

Christopher Radko

Clothtique

Collector's Society of America

Computer software programs

Crinkle Claus

Department 56

Figi Graphics

Figi, J. Todd

Furlong, Margaret

Hallmark Keepsake Ornaments

Hallmark Keepsake Ornaments Collector's Club

Haney, Lynn

Heritage Village Collection

June McKenna Collectibles

Kehrli, Steve

Kurt S. Adler

Lowenthal, Gary

Lowenthal, Tina

Lynn Haney Collection

Lynn West Designs

Margaret Furlong Designs

Merck, E.M.

MSdataBase Solutions, Inc.

Old World Christmas

Old Word Christmas Collector's Club

Original Snow Village

Pipka Collectibles

Polonaise Collection

Possible Dreams

Prizm Inc.

Radko, Christopher

Santa Claus Network/Possible Dreams

Santa's Crystal Valley

Secondary market

Secondary market dealers

Snowbabies

Starlight Family of Collectors/Christopher Radko

Steinbach Collector's Club

Steinbach, Herr Christian

Steinbach, Karla

Steinbach Nutcrackers

Swap meets

Thorndike, Annalee

Thorndike, Chip

Ulviden, Pipka

Vaillancourt Folk Art

Vaillancourt, Judi

Vaillancourt, Gary

West, Lynn

Author Information

The author, Beth Dees, has been collecting, organizing, polishing and displaying words professionally for sixteen years. Dees has written more than one thousand articles for newspapers and magazines, including: The Los Angeles Times Syndicate, *Woman's' World Magazine*, *Travel South Magazine* and *Southern Magazine*. She credits her mother, who co-owner of a year-round Christmas shop, for teaching her as a child to squint her eyes and peek through her lashes to see the real magic and beauty in a lighted Christmas tree.